The WORLD'S BEST WINES

2010-2011

First published 2010 by Elliott and Thompson Limited
27 John Street, London WC1N 2BX
www.eandtbooks.com

ISBN 978-1-9040-2793-5

With thanks to:
Chris Ashton, James Collins, Richard Hemming, Matthew Johnson,
Ray O'Connor, Andrew Reed, Lee Sharkey, Simon Woods and
everyone associated with the International Wine Challenge

9 8 7 6 5 4 3 2 1

A CIP catalogue record for this book is available
from the British Library.

Printed in China by 1010 Printing

The
WORLD'S
BEST WINES
2010-2011

E&T

VIRTUALLY
TAINT FREE
JUST ISN'T
GOOD ENOUGH

Others claim to have reduced TCA. We have eliminated it. Each DIAM cork is certified to contain releasable TCA below detectable levels; < 0.5 ng.

This means your winemakers can concentrate on what they do best, safe in the knowledge that every time a bottle of their wine is opened, it tastes the way it should.

Find out more at **www.oeneo.co.uk** or contact us at: **info@oeneo.co.uk**

Contents

In the hot seats vii
Rites of passage viii
Grape Guide x
Winemakers of the Year xii
Trophy Winners xvi
Planet Earth Winners xxvi

How to Use This Guide 1

THE MEDAL WINNERS
Argentina 2
Australia 13
Austria 63
Chile 73
France 97
Germany 177
Italy 186
New Zealand 216
Portugal 243
Sake 273
South Africa 285
Spain 303
USA 337
Other Countries 341

The Library Collection 356
Stockists 367

In the hot seats

The experts at the front line of the International Wine Challenge

The IWC has four resident co-chairmen and one guest chairman, who oversee the judging panels and assist the judges with any tough decisions.

Tim Atkin MW

Tim Atkin MW is one of Britain's leading wine writers and an internationally recognised expert. He is the wine correspondent of The Times and wine editor at large of OLN. He also writes for many other publications and appears on the BBC1's Saturday Kitchen.

Atkin has won more than 20 awards for his journalism, including the Glenfiddich Wine Writer Award and the Lanson Wine Writer of the Year Award.

Victor De La Serna

Victor is a Deputy Editor of El Mundo, one of Spain's best national newspapers, and for more than 30 years, he has been writing about wine for Informaciones, El País, Diario 16, Decanter, Sibaritas and El Mundo. De la Serna has twice won Spain's National Gastronomy Award. He is a member of the International Wine Academy, of Spain's Royal Academy of Gastronomy and of the Grand Jury Européen.

Sam Harrop MW

Sam Harrop MW started his career as a trainee winemaker at Villa Maria Wines in his native New Zealand. He spent seven years with Marks & Spencer before beginning his own consultancy.

Charles Metcalfe

Charles Metcalfe co-founded Wine International with Robert Joseph in 1983. They started the International Wine Challenge in 1984 and built it into the world's largest wine competition.

As well as writing books on Spanish and Portuguese wines, and on matching wine with food, Metcalfe has been a television drinks presenter for 17 years.

His latest book is *The Wine & Food Lover's Guide To Portugal* (Inn House Publishing) written with his wife, Kathryn McWhirter.

Derek Smedley MW

Derek Smedley MW joined the wine trade in the great vintage of 1961, working for John Harvey & Sons in Bristol. From there he moved to Gilbeys (IDV), where he worked in buying and sales.

In 1985, he started Smedley Vintners, as well as developing a consultancy string to his bow, helping the likes of Tuscan wine house Antinori. He sold Smedley Vintners in 1999 so he could concentrate full-time on his growing consultancy work.

He joined as co-chairman of the IWC in 2002.

Rites of passage

Just how does the IWC work? Ray O'Connor follows the path of a bottle through the rigorous test of the Challenge

It's not easy being a bottle of wine. As if being at the mercy of local weather conditions wasn't enough, the grapes have to go through a selection of winemaking techniques to make them stand out from the crowd.

Next, the juice is trained and modelled into a style of drink that will stand up and represent its region proudly on the podium of international wines.

Finally, once it's deemed ready to do the locals proud, it's bottled and sent to London to pass the ultimate test – to get past the International Wine Challenge judges.

Five weeks before the main event, delivery trucks loaded with palettes of wine start to roll into London's Barbican Centre.

Sorted by grape variety, the bottles stretch the length of the 200ft floor like a vinous game of dominos. Four samples of each bottle are sent to allow for faulty wine and qualification to the next round and the trophy round, should it make it that far.

This is the last chance the bottles have to show off their labels and individual curves. All identity is concealed as each is bagged and given a unique code to identify it all the way through the competition. Armed with clipboards and trollies, the staff work their way through the hall, collecting the wines according to their number, creating flights of similar styles.

This enables the judges to focus on a single grape from a particular region and vintage in order to assess its relative merits.

Round 1: qualifying heats
With the contenders lined up on tables, the time has come for the judges - five to a table – to sniff, taste and spit their way through each flight, making notes about each

bottle. As this is round one, it's a straightforward matter for the group to decide whether the wine should stay in the competition or be given its marching orders.

A negative result sees the wine sent to the co-chairmen, who grant it a second chance at qualifying for round two by retasting it. This ensures nothing slips through the net and every single bottle is given the fairest chance possible. In this first week a selection of the world's wine experts put around 2,000 wines a day through their paces.

Round 2: medal table

In the second round, wines are scored out of 100 to determine the medal status: 95-100 = gold, 90-94.9 = silver, 85-89.9 = bronze and 80-84.9 = commended. It's in this second week that the competition really comes alive.

With fewer wines as a result of the first round eliminations, more time is spent on each bottle. Judges debate the qualities of each wine and conclude a final score, led by the tables' panel chair. Once

again, to ensure integrity, wines are sent to co-chairs for reassessment, but scores are rarely altered – testifying to the high standard of judging.

By the end of play each day, hordes of three-quarters-full bottles are waiting to be disposed of. In line with the competition's Planet Earth Awards, the IWC holds sustainability in high regard. Instead of filling London's drains with fermented grape juice, the leftover wine is poured into huge containers to be taken away and used for cooking. The glass bottles and cardboard boxes are collected by the council for recycling. Even the corks are reused in pinboards and decorative coffee tables.

Trophies and Champions

In the last leg, wines deemed to be of trophy status are selected from the handful of gold-medal winners, to determine the leaders of their class.

As impressive as this lot are, the five co-chairmen still have the task of choosing the overall champions in the following categories: red, white, sparkling, sweet, fortified and sake. These wines make up the most celebrated selection in the competition.

As you flick through the results on the following pages, spare a thought for the bottles that passed this most rigorous of examinations – they've been through a lot.

Grape Guide

A short introduction to the most common grapes and the wines that they make

WHITE GRAPES

Chardonnay – French in origin but now grown worldwide. Ranges from rich and peachy in warmer regions to tense and appley in cooler regions. Burgundy is the benchmark. Also used for Champagne and other sparklers, often with Pinot Noir.

Chenin Blanc – Sweet or dry, still or sparkling, good Chenins (from the Loire and South Africa) combine rich, occasionally honeyed flavours with tangy apple and citrus freshness.

Gewürztraminer – Exotic lychees and rose-petal aromas are the hallmarks here. Alsace is the main source, but New Zealand also has some crackers.

Grüner Veltliner – Seldom found outside Austria, where it varies from crisp and grapefruity to fuller and peachier, with hints of white pepper in both.

Muscat – At its best making sweet wines, including varying from light and frothy (Asti) to sumptuous and treacly (Australian Liqueur Muscat).

Pinot Gris/Grigio – Varies from pale, crisp and dry in Italian version (Grigio) to plump, musky and off-dry in Alsace (Gris). Whichever version producers elsewhere use indicates the role model.

Riesling – Sweet and delicate in northern parts of Germany, rich and dry in Alsace, Australia and Austria, and usually with stony mineral notes to the floral citrus flavours.

Sauvignon Blanc – Forceful, strident grape with pungent asparagus and gooseberry character, sometimes tinged with herbs. New Zealand, the Loire, Bordeaux, South Africa and Chile make the best versions.

Sémillon – The grape behind great Sauternes and dozens of imitators worldwide also makes pithy, ageworthy dry whites, especially in Bordeaux and Australia.

Viognier – A bit of a tart but tasty one, with voluptuous peach kernel and apricot flavours. Originated in the Rhône (Condrieu is the benchmark), but now grown elsewhere with success, especially in southern France and Australia.

RED GRAPES

Cabernet Franc – Shares the dark fruit flavours of Cabernet Sauvignon, but is lighter and more fragrant. At its best in Bordeaux and the Loire Valley.

Cabernet Sauvignon – Hails from Bordeaux but displays its firm blackcurrant and blackberry charms in many other regions. Often blended with Merlot and/or Cabernet Franc.

Grenache – Soft, spicy and rich in berry flavours, the main grape of Châteauneuf du Pape and other southern Rhône reds, and also a key ingredient in Spain's gutsy Priorat.

Malbec – Responsible for the dense chewy reds of Cahors in France, but at its best making violet-scented, berry-rich wines in Argentina.

Merlot – Shares some of the black fruit flavours of its Bordeaux compatriot Cabernet Sauvignon, but generally softer and plummier.

Chilean and Californian versions can be very good.

Nebbiolo – Seldom strays from its home in North West Italy, where it makes firm but wonderfully aromatic Barolo and Barbaresco.

Pinot Noir – Fickle, even in its home of Burgundy, but at its best, headily perfumed, velvety and packed with supple forest fruit flavours. Oregon, California and New Zealand make classy alternatives, Chile provides the value. Also a main grape in Champagne and other sparklers.

Sangiovese – Another reluctant Italian traveller, but excels in Tuscany, with rich, herby reds such as Brunello di Montalcino and Chianti Classico.

Syrah – Spicy, berry-rich grape making firm, fragrant wines in the northern Rhône and (as Shiraz) richer, beefier reds in Australia.

Tempranillo – Spain's great grape, the power behind Rioja, Ribera del Duero and many more, producing spicy strawberry-scented reds. Known as Tinta Roriz in Portugal.

Zinfandel – Best known for simple off-dry White Zin, but at its finest making chunky, brambly wines tinged with spice. Identical to Italy's Primitivo.

White Winemaker
Callie van Niekerk, Distell

Distell's not a name you'll see on too many bottles of wine, but the company is a giant of the South African wine industry and produces more than a third of the country's still and sparkling wine. It was formed in 2000 when Stellenbosch Farmers Winery merged with Distillers Corporation, and now has under its umbrella several of the Cape's most famous names, such as Alto, Fleur du Cap, Nederburg, Plaisir de Merle, Pongracz, Stellenzicht and Zonnebloem. Some of these function independently, but many are produced in the Distell cellars under the guidance of general manager Callie van Niekerk. Overseeing such a mammoth operation that draws fruit from vineyards throughout the Cape isn't the easiest of tasks, but Callie is helped in his efforts by a group of talented winemakers such as Nederberg's Razvan Macici and Andrea Freeborough of Fleur du Cap. As last year, a Nederberg sweet wine gained a trophy, but the judges were also impressed with both dry and sweet whites from Fleur du Cap. Distell is also a part-owner of the Lomond winery in Cape Agulhas, which gained a gold for its Pincushion Sauvignon Blanc.

Red Winemaker Pierre Vincent, Domaine De La Vougeraie

It's not much more than a decade since Domaine de la Vougeraie came into existence. The 37-hectare estate spreads over 30 different appellations in the Côte d'Or, and includes six grands crus, five red, one white. It was formed by the bringing together of the many vineyards acquired over the course of more than 30 years by the Boisset family, with a large proportion of them coming from the former Pierre Ponnelle domaine. The inaugural vintages were made by the talented Pascal Marchand, formerly of Domaine Comte Armand in Pommard, but in 2006, he was succeeded by Pierre Vincent. Vincent is a less stocky and forceful character than his predecessor, and this comes through in his wines, both reds and whites. As in the past, the characteristics of the different vineyards come through, the legacy of organic and – for the premiers and grands crus – biodynamic farming and low-yielding old vines. But the wines today show a little less extraction and obvious oak, and a little more silkiness and approachability. Or to put it more simply, they're yummy wines from an excellent estate and an exceptional winemaker.

Sweet Winemaker/Len Evans Trophy Hans Tschida

The Angerhof Tschida winery in Burgenland has been one of the stellar performers of the IWC, winning trophies and medals virtually every year since 1996 for its brilliant sweet wines. If you've never heard of the winery, it's largely because owner/winemaker Hans Tschida shuns the limelight, preferring instead to stay at home showering TLC on his 18-hectares of vineyards in Illmitz close to the Neusiedlersee. It's a place that seems to have been created to produce great sweet wines, with foggy autumn mornings giving way to dry sunny afternoons, perfect conditions for the development of botrytis. The range goes from lightly botrytised Spätlese up to the heady delights of Trockenbeerenauslese (TBA).

But the signs are that recognition is finally coming to Hans. One of his wines, a 2006 Beerenauslese, was served at the Nobel Award Winners' banquet in December 2009. Add in the double accolade from this year's IWC of Sweet Winemaker of The Year and the Len Evans trophy for consistent performance over the past five years, and it surely won't be long before he appears on the radar of wine lovers all over the world.

Sparkling Winemaker Régis Camus, P&C Heidsieck

'Blending a wine is not the result of chance or improvisation.' So says Régis Camus, cellar master of P&C Heidsieck since the tragically early death of Daniel Thibault in 2002. The two had been working together since 1994, and together had elevated the fortunes of Charles Heidsieck, and in particular of the non-vintage wines. The last few years have seen Camus effect a similar transformation at Piper-Heidsieck, honing the range, and introducing new wines such as the Demi-Sec Cuvée Sublime. He's also done an excellent job of emulating Thibault in being a regular recipient of this award. And it's not his only accolade for 2010 – at Business Traveller magazine's 'Cellars in the Sky' awards, the Piper-Heidsieck Cuvée Rare was voted the best fizz in First Class, while the Piper-Heidsieck Brut came out top in Business Class. However these awards don't go to his head. True, Piper-Heidsieck has worked with master shoemaker Christian Loboutin to create Le Rituel, an ornate crystal stiletto champagne flute, but Camus is more at home in his cellar, where he feels he's not so much a wizard, more 'the conductor of the large orchestra.'

Fortified Winemaker
Manuel Lozano, Emilio Lustau

This is now the fourth time that a Lustau cellarmaster has been the IWC Fortified Winemaker of the Year, and don't be surprised if Manuel Lozano repeats this success in subsequent years. He's fortunate enough to be able to work with several almacenistas – literally stockholders – who make and mature wines on their premises in the traditional solera systems before delivering them to Manuel and his team. Sometimes these are bottled separately – a designation such as 1/41 indicates that there are 41 barrels in the almacenista's solera system.

At other times, they are used in blends with the extensive stocks in Lustau's three cellars in the three main sherry towns, Jerez de la Frontera, Sanlúcar de Barrameda and El Puerto de Santa María. Having access to a large collection of wines from different sources and of varying stages of maturity makes Manuel's job a rewarding one, and the results are both impressive and diverse, as shown by the difference in the two trophy winning wines. One is a limited edition Manzanilla from a solera of just 21 barrels, the other is a supermarket own-label Oloroso.

Lifetime Achievement Award
Miguel Torres

Has anyone done more to transform the fortunes of Spanish wine than Miguel Torres? Bodegas Torres was already a force on the international stage by the late 1950s, but Miguel's goal was to take the company onto a different plain entirely. Following his studies in France, he introduced concepts such as cool fermentation for white wines and shorter barrel maturation for reds. He upgraded the vineyards, and also planted French varieties alongside the native Catalan grapes. Vindication of his efforts came in 1979, when his 1970 Gran Coronas Black Label (now Mas La Plana) outshone some famous Bordeaux in a Paris tasting. He's led the expansion of the company from Penedès into Priorat, Ribera del Duero, Rioja and other Spanish regions, and is a keen advocate of single-vineyard wines. There are now Torres outposts in Chile, California and, most recently, China. He's published several books on Spanish wine and is a passionate environmentalist, especially on the impact of climate change on the wine world. He's due to retire when he reaches 70, but don't be surprised if you hear of this true wine legend for many years beyond then.

James Rogers Trophy
Haselgrove Bella Vigna Shiraz '08

In the early 1990s, Haselgrove was one of a handful of producers who first made us sit up and take notice of the quietly of McLaren Vale Shiraz. Now in the hands of a quartet of enthusiastic Italian-Australians, the winery is enjoying a new lease of life, and making some terrific value wines such as this honest hearty Shiraz. For the recently introduced Bella Vigna range, the aim of senior winemaker Greg Clack and his team is to produce small batches of wines from special plots in various regions of South Australia that live up to their 'beautiful vineyard' billing.

Currently, the range includes a Coonawarra Cabernet and an Adelaide Hills Sauvignon Blanc, but it's this Shiraz, boosted by fruit from some blocks of 60-year-old vines close to the winery on Sand Road, that caught the attention of the IWC judges. It's been in a mix of new and used French and American oak for 18 months, which has added notes of nuts and spice, but it's the buoyant fruit – mulberries, cassis and plums – that shines through. Add in note soft tobacco and dark chocolate, and a long lively finish, and you have a very impressive debut.

Personality of the Year Award
Gérard Basset

'He's such a nice man.' It's a phrase you often hear about wine maestro Gérard Basset. Maestro is an apt term for Basset, a Frenchman by birth but a UK resident since 1983. He's been a Master Sommelier since 1989, a Master of Wine since 1998, and in 2007 passed the Wine MBA at Bordeaux University. He first rose to prominence as head sommelier at the Michelin-starred Chewton Glen in Hampshire, where he also met his wife Nina. In 1994, the two of them and MD Robin Hutson left Chewton Glen to launch Hotel du Vin in Winchester, a luxury

wine-themed hotel. A decade of expansion followed until in 2004, Hotel du Vin was bought out, leaving Gérard in his mid-forties with a nice wodge of cash in the bank. His latest venture is Hotel Terravina in Hampshire, which since its opening in 2007 has already garnered several awards. But perhaps his proudest achievement came early in 2010 when at the sixth attempt he finally won the World's Best Sommelier competition. Will the success go to his head? No chance. As the hundreds of people whose lives he has influenced will testify, he's such a nice man.

Trophy Winners
White

The Champion White Wine
**International Chardonnay Trophy,
French White Trophy, White Burgundy Trophy,
Puligny Montrachet Trophy**
**Jean Pascal Marks & Spencer Les Chalumeaux Puligny
Montrachet Premier Cru 2007, Burgundy, France**

Intense, full bodied, rich and ripe sweet caramel nose. Lovely weight and
richness on palate. Long flavours.
£38.00 M&S

Alsace Riesling Trophy
Domaine Paul Blanck Riesling
Grand Cru Furstentum 2005,
Alsace, France

Australian Chardonnay Trophy
Step Rd Chardonnay 2007,
South Australia, Australia

Australian White Trophy
McWilliams Mount Pleasant
Elizabeth 2005, South Eastern
Australia, Australia

Austrian Dry White Trophy,
Grüner Veltliner Trophy
Türk Erlesenes Vom
Grünen Veltliner 2008,
Niederösterreich, Austria

Chablis Trophy
Garnier Et Fils Vaudesir Chablis
Grand Cru 2007, Burgundy,
France

Chenin Blanc Trophy,
Vouvray Trophy
Domaine Huet Le Haut Lieu Sec
2007, Loire, France
£17.99 WAIT

Clare Valley Riesling Trophy
Pauletts Aged Release Riesling

2005, Clare Valley, Australia
£11.99 EOR

Dry White Franken Trophy
Divino Nordheim Franconia
Eschendorfer Lump Silvaner
Spätlese Troken 2006, Franken,
Germany

French White Blend Trophy
Domaine Désertaux-Ferrand
Côte De Nuits-Villages Blanc
2008, Burgundy, France
£12.54 3DW

Greek White Trophy
Semeli Mantinia Nassiakos
2009, Mantinia, Greece

International Riesling Trophy,
Germany Dry White Trophy,
Rheingau Riesling Trophy,
Hochheim Riesling Trophy,
Domdechant Werner'sches
Hochheim Riesling Erstes
Gewächs 2008, Rheingau,
Germany
LAI

International Sauvignon Blanc
Trophy, Loire Trophy, Sancerre
Trophy
Pascal Jolivet Sancerre Blanc

Les Caillottes 2009, Loire, France
£20.99

NZ Riesling Trophy
Sandihurst Winery True
And Daring Riesling 2007,
Canterbury, New Zealand

NZ Sauvignon Blanc Trophy
Montana Sauvignon Blanc
2009, Marlborough, New
Zealand
£8.99 SAIN, MRN, TESC, WAIT

**NZ White Trophy, NZ
Chardonnay Trophy, Hawke's
Bay Chardonnay Trophy**
Ngatarawa Alwyn Winemakers
Reserve Chardonnay 2007,
Hawke's Bay, New Zealand

Off Dry Mosel Trophy
Moselland Wine Company
Lieserer Schlossberg Kabinett
2008, Mosel, Germany

**Off Dry White Trophy, Off Dry
Rheingau Trophy**
Schloss Johannisberg Rosalack
Riesling 2007, Rheingau,
Germany
£49.99 HLD

Portuguese White Trophy
Terras De Alter Reserva 2009,
Alentejo, Portugal
DFW

Pouilly Fuisse Trophy
Domaine Pierreclos Terroir de
Vergisson Pouilly-Fuissé 2008,
Burgundy, France
£18.99 DLW, MWW

Rüdesheim Riesling Trophy
Leitz Rüdesheimer Rosengarten
Riesling Kabinett 2009,
Rheingau, Germany
£9.99 WAIT

Savigny-les Beaune Trophy
Domaine Seguin-Manuel
Goudelettes Sauvigny-les-
Beaune 2008, Burgundy, France
£14.99 DLW

Soave Trophy
Pieropan La Rocca Soave
Classico 2007, Veneto, Italy
£21.49 FAW, LAY, LIB, MAJ

South Africa White Trophy
Oak Valley Chardonnay 2009,
Elgin, South Africa

**South Australian White Trophy,
Eden Valley White Trophy**
McGuigan Shortlist Riesling
2004, Eden Valley, Australia

Spanish Sweet Muscat Trophy
Camilo Castilla Capricho De
Goya NV, Navarra, Spain
£10.21

Great Value Champion White

**Great Value White Wine
Under £6**
**Alliance Wine Australia
Moon Bridge Riesling 2009,
South Australia, Australia**
Lovely green olive and
petrol nose. Palate is rich
and balanced. Great.
£5.49 M&S

**Great Value White Wine
between £5 and £10**
Domaine Villargeau Sauvignon
Blanc 2009, Loire, France
£9.99 BTW, ODD, TKW

**Great Value White Wine
between £5 and £10**
Terredora Falanghina Campania
2009, Campania, Italy
£9.99 LAY, MON, ODF, WTA

Trophy Winners
Red

The Champion Red Wine

Italian Red Trophy, Tuscan Trophy
Castello Romitorio Brunello Di Montalcino
Riserva 2004, Tuscany, Italy
Deep, intense and slightly brooding on the nose: leather, hints of tobacco and violets. Red fruits dominate on the palate.

Adelaide Hills Trophy
Longview Red Bucket Shiraz Cabernet 2008, Adelaide Hills, Australia

Alentejo Trophy
Antonio Lobo Silveira E Outro Solar Dos Lobos Grande Escolha 2007, Alentejo, Portugal
£20.99 ICE

Amarone Trophy
Cantine Riondo Trionfo Amarone Della Valpolicella Classico 2006, Veneto, Italy

Argentinean Red Trophy,
International Malbec Trophy
Vistalba Viñalba Malbec Gran Reserva 2008, Mendoza, Argentina

Australian Red Blend Trophy,
Yarra Valley Trophy
Giant Steps Sexton Vineyard Harry's Monster 2008, Yarra Valley, Australia
£16.99 SEL

Barossa Valley Shiraz Trophy
Krondorf Symmetry Bv Shiraz 2007, South Australia, Australia

Beaujolais Trophy,
Henry Fessy Brouilly 2009, Beaujolais, France
£9.99 FNC, FTH, LLA, WAIT

Central Otago Pinot Noir Trophy
Desert Heart Pinot Noir 2007, Central Otago, New Zealand

Chambolle-Musigny Trophy
Domaine De La Vougeraie Chambolle-Musigny 2007, Burgundy, France
BAB, BB&R, FMV

Charmes-Chambertin Trophy
Domaine De La Vougeraie Les Mazoyères Charmes-Chambertin Grand Cru 2007, Burgundy, France
BB&R, HAR

Chilean Pinot Noir Trophy,
Casablanca Valley Trophy
Cono Sur Ocio Pinot Noir 2008, Casablanca Valley, Chile
WAIT

Chilean Red Trophy,
Carmenere Trophy
Terranoble Gran Reserva Carmenère 2007, Maule Valley, Chile
PIM

Chilean Syrah Trophy
Matetic EQ Syrah 2008, San
Antonio Valley, Chile
£18.00 GNS, MAJ, WSO

Coonawarra Trophy
Petaluma Coonawarra Cabernet
Merlot 2007, Coonawarra,
Australia
£19.00 BWL, MWW, ODD

Coteaux Du Languedoc Trophy
Jacques Boscary Château
Rouquette Sur Mer Cuvée
l'Esprit Terroir 2009, Languedoc
- Roussillon, France

Dão Trophy
Antonio Batista Quinta Do
Corujao Reserva 2007, Dão,
Portugal
£9.99 ICE

Echézeaux Trophy
Maison Albert Bichot Domaine
Du Clos Frantin Grands
Echezeaux Grand Cru 2008,
Burgundy, France

Edmund Penning Rowsell
Trophy, Bolgheri Trophy
Grattamacco L'Alberello 2007,
Tuscany, Italy

Elqui Valley Trophy
Falernia Antakari Carmenère
Syrah 2008, Elqui Valley, Chile
£7.49

Gigondas Trophy
Gabriel Meffre Domaine De
Longue Toque Gigondas 2007,
Rhône, France

Gimblett Gravels Syrah Trophy
Forrest Collection Syrah 2006,
Hawke's Bay, New Zealand
£17.99 ADN

Greek Red Trophy
Nemeion Estate Hgemon 2005,
Peloponnese, Greece
£60.00

Hunter Valley Trophy
Tyrrell's Winemaker's Selection
Vat 8 Hunter Valley Shiraz 2007,
New South Wales, Australia
£24.99 VDV

International Merlot Trophy,
Central Valley Trophy
Concha Y Toro Marques De
Casa Concha Merlot 2007,
Central Valley, Chile

Great Value Champion Red

Great Value Red Wine
between £6 and £10
**St Hallett Waitrose Reserve
Shiraz 2008, Barossa Valley,
Australia**
Violet hue. Restrained quality
fruit - cinnamon spicy nose.
Spicy, rich good fruity taste.
Good length.
£8.99 WAIT

Great Value Red Wine
between £10 and £15
Lapostolle Cuvée Alexandre
Cabernet Sauvignon 2008,
Colchagua Valley, Chile
£11.99 TVY, WDR

Great Value Red Wine Under £6
Vindivin La Difference
Carignan 2009, Languedoc
- Roussillon, France
£5.99 TESC

James Rogers Trophy

McLaren Vale Shiraz Trophy
Haselgrove Bella Vigna 2008, South Australia
Huge, with classic style. Loads of black cassis fruit on
the palate with a touch of creamy spice on the finish.

Great Value Champion Rosé

Great Value Rosé Wine between £5 and £10
Viña Leyda Secano Rosé Pinot Noir 2009, Leyda Valley, Chile
Redcurrants and cherries on the nose. Very pleasant palate of ripe
and sweet fruit. Well balanced with a savoury finish.
£7.49 M&S

International Pinot Noir
Trophy, French Red Trophy, Red
Burgundy Trophy
Domaine De La Vougeraie
Bonnes Mares Grand Cru 2008,
Burgundy, France
BAB, BB&R, FMV, HAR

International Shiraz Trophy,
Australian Red Trophy,
Australian Shiraz Trophy, South
Australian Shiraz Trophy
Heartland Directors' Cut 2007,
South Australia, Australia
£17.95 CAM, FFT, GWW, HOF,
MJF, RVL

La Clape Trophy
Gérard Bertrand Château
L'Hospitalet 'La Reserve' 2008,
Languedoc - Roussillon, France
£10.99 WAIT

Languedoc Trophy, Saint-
Chinian Trophy
Cave De Roquebrun La Grange
Des Combes 2008, Languedoc
- Roussillon, France

Marche Red Trophy
Vico Vicari Lacrima Del Pozzo
Buono 2008, Marche, Italy

Martinborough Pinot Noir Trophy
Martinborough Vineyard Pinot
Noir 2008, Martinborough,
New Zealand
£25.00 HAR, HVN

NZ Pinot Noir Trophy,
Wairarapa Pinot Noir Trophy,
Schubert Pinot Noir Block B
2008, Wairarapa, New Zealand
£27.95 NZH

NZ Red Trophy, New Zealand
Syrah Trophy, Waiheke Island
Syrah Trophy
Passage Rock Reserve Syrah
2008, Waiheke Island, New
Zealand

Portuguese Red Trophy, Douro
Trophy
Luis João De Noronha Pizarro
De Castro Quinta De Lubazim
2007, Douro, Portugal

Portuguese Shiraz Trophy
Rui Reguinga Tributo 2008,
Ribatejo, Portugal

Rapel Valley Trophy
Concha Y Toro Terrunyo
Carmenère 2007, Rapel Valley,
Chile

Rhône Trophy, Chateauneuf-du-pape Trophy
Jean-Michel Cazes Domaine Des Sénéchaux 2007, Rhône, France

Ribera del Duero Trophy
Cillar De Silos Torresilo 2006, Ribera Del Duero, Spain
£33.99 AAW, ODF, RSO

South African Red Trophy
Vrede En Lust Boet Erasmus 2007, Simonsberg Paarl,

South Africa
H2F, SAO

Spanish Red Trophy, Tempranillo Trophy, Rioja Alavesa Trophy
Lar De Paula Cepas Viejas 2005, Rioja, Spain

Tupungato Trophy
Domaine Jean Bousquet Grande Reserve Malbec 2008, Mendoza, Argentina
£22.00 VRT

Trophy Winners
Sparkling

The Champion Sparkling Wine
Daniel Thibault Trophy

**Young Vintage Champagne Trophy
P & C Heidsieck Charles Heidsieck Millésime 2000, Champagne, France**

Golden wine, lemon rind, richer style, caramel biscuit, nice length, good finish. Thinkers champagne.
£39.99 BB&R, HAR, SAIN

Great Value Champion Sparkling

Great Value Sparkling Wine between £10 and £15
Medici Lambrusco Reggiano Concerto 2009, Emilia Romagna, Italy
Deep coloured, overly fruity, red with nice tannins and good acidity. Vibrant, bold and joyful.
£12.00 EHB, EVW, HAR, V&C, VIN

Great Value Sparkling Wine between £15 and £20
P & C Heidsieck Waitrose Brut NV, Champagne, France
£19.99 WAIT, WWD, WWW

Great Value Sparkling Wine between Under £10
Villiera Marks & Spencer Brut Natural 2007, Stellenbosch, South Africa
£9.99 M&S

Blanc des Blancs
Champagne Trophy
Paul Goerg Premier Cru
Millésime Brut 2004,
Champagne, France

Mature Vintage
Champagne Trophy
P & C Heidsieck Charles
Heidsieck Charlie 1981,
Champagne, France

Lambrusco Trophy
Cantine Riunite Albinea Canali
Lambrusco Ottocentonero NV,
Emilia Romagna, Italy

Sparkling Rose Trophy,
English Sparkling Trophy
Camel Valley Pinot Noir Rosé
Brut 2008, Cornwall, England
£24.95

Trophy Winners
Sweet

Austrian Chardonnay Trophy
Hans & Christine Nittnaus Essenz
Trockenbeerenauslese 2005,
Neusiedlersee, Austria

International Silvaner Trophy,
German Sweet Trophy
Juliusspital Iphoefer Kronsberg
Silvaner Beerenauslesse 2008,
Franken, Germany

Austrian Ice Wine Trophy
Türk Eiswein Vom
Grünen Veltliner 2008,
Niederösterreich, Austria

International Sweet Muscat
Trophy, Austrian Sweet Muscat
Trophy
Hans Tschida Muskat Ottonel
Schilfwein 2006, Neusiedlersee,
Austria

Canadian Ice Wine Trophy
Strewn Icewine Riesling 2008,
Niagara Peninsula, Canada

International Ice Wine Trophy,
German Ice Wine Trophy
Horst Sauer Escherndorfer
Lump Silvaner Eiswein 2008,
Franken, Germany

Italian Botrytis Trophy
Moncaro Terre Cortesi Tordiruta
Verdicchio Dei Castelli Di Jesi
Passito 2006, Marche, Italy
EUW, EVW

Champion Sweet
Alois Kracher Trophy

Austrian Sweet Trophy
Hans Tschida Sämling Trockenbeerenauslese
2007, Neusiedlersee, Austria
Elegant and nutty with a touch of crunchy apricot
aromas. Almond and marmalade notes on the palate
with lemony fresh citrus notes. Lush and long.

Great Value Champion Sweet

Great Value Sweet Wine between £10 and £15
Tamar Ridge Kayena Vineyard Botrytis Riesling 2007, Tasmania, Australia
Lime and honey fruit, great weight and still very fresh on the finish.
£13.59 ADN, BOF, P&S, TPM, VDV, WAIT

Italian Sweet Trophy
Cavit Aréle Vino Santo Trentino
1998, Trentino, Italy
PBA

Kamptal Botrytis Trophy
Rabl Riesling
Trockenbeerenauslese 2007,
Kamptal, Austria
£37.99 HLD

Sweet German Riesling Trophy
Horst Sauer Escherndorfer
Lump Riesling Auslese 2008,
Franken, Germany

Western Cape Botrytis Trophy
Nederburg Winemasters Reserve
Noble Late Harvest 2009,
Western Cape, South Africa

Trophy Winners
Fortified

Champion Fortified

Amontillado Trophy
Gonzalez Byass Viña Ab NV, Jerez, Spain
Gold, straw style with a developed, rich nose
with caramel hints. Medium bodied, dry,
oxidative (pasada) style. Good length.

Australian Fortified Trophy
De Bortoli Old Boys Tawny Port
NV, New South Wales, Australia

International Fortified
Muscat Trophy
Bacalhôa Moscatel De Setúbal
1999, Península De Setúbal,
Portugal
SAIN, MWW, WAIT

LBV Port Trophy,
Overall Port Trophy
Sogrape Regimental Late Bottled
Vintage NV, Douro, Portugal
BOO

Madeira Trophy
Symington Family Estates
Blandy's Malmsey 1985,
Madeira, Portugal

Manzanilla Trophy
Emilio Lustau Almacenista
Manzanilla Amontillada Cuevas
Jurado 1/21 NV, Andalucía, Spain
£20.00

Oloroso Trophy
Emilio Lustau Sainsbury's Taste
The Difference Oloroso 12 Year
Old NV, Andalucía, Spain
SAIN

Great Value Champion Fortified

Great Value Fortified Wine between Under £10
Hidalgo La Gitana Manzanilla NV, Andalucía, Spain
Glitzy apples, fresh on the palate and elegant style and good length.
£8.39 WI-AV, WAIT

Great Value Fortified Wine between between £10 and £15
Campbells Rutherglen Muscat NV, North East Victoria, Australia
£11.25 ADN, BCR, CPW, ODD

Pedro Ximenez Trophy
Harveys Pedro Ximenez VORS 1980, Jerez, Spain
£20.42 WAIT

Reserve Port Trophy, Great Value Fortified Wine Under £10
Fonseca Bin 27 NV, Duoro, Portugal
£9.99 WI-AV, MRN

Tawny Port Trophy
Sogrape Sandeman 40 Year Old Tawny NV, Douro, Portugal
£50.00 MCT

Vermouth Trophy
Quady Vya Sweet Vermouth NV, California, USA
£16.99 HLD

White Port Trophy
C. Da Silva Dalva Porto Golden White 1963, Douro, Portugal

Trophy Winners
Sake

Regional Nagano Junmai-Daigingo Trophy
Daishinsyu Breweries Teippai 2007, Nagano

Regional Niigata Koshu Trophy
Kaetsu Sake Brewery Kirin Jijyoshu Vintage 2001, Niigata VNO

Regional Shiga Gingo-Daigingo Trophy
Mifuku Shuzo Mifuku Daigin Gokujo 2009, Shiga

Regional Shizuoka Junmai Daigingo Trophy
Isojiman Premium Sake Brewery Daiginjo Junmai 2010, Shizuoka
£45.00 BZI, JP-HAS

Champion Junmai
Regional Fukui Trophy
Katoukichibee Shouten Born: Ginsen 2008, Fukui, Japan
Fresh, touch of petals, floral bouquet. Green fruity, honey, apricot jam. Medium long finish.

Champion Koshu

Regional Hiroshima Trophy
Enoki Shuzo Hanahato Kijoshu Aged For 8 Years 2001, Hiroshima
Toffee, roasted nuts and ripe apple character. Hints of sticky toffee on the palate with good acidity supporting the weight. A raisin, honey finish.
AKE, JPS

Champion Junmai Daigingo

Regional Niigata Trophy
General Partnership Watanabe Sake Brewing Store Nechi 2008, Niigata
Aroma gives promise. Sweetness after palate.

Regional Shizuoka Junmai Trophy
Isojiman Premium Sake Brewery Isojiman Omachi Tokubets Junmai 2010, Shizuoka
£30.00 BZI, JP-HAS

Regional Tottori Koshu Trophy
Fujii Shuzo Hakuyou Koshu 1996, Tottori

Regional Yamagata Gino-Daigingo Trophy
Dewazakura Sake Brewery Daiginjoshu 2009, Yamagata
WSI, WSI

Regional Yamagata Junmai-Daigingo Trophy
Shindo Sake Brewery Gasanryu Gokugetsu 2009, Yamagata
JFI

Regional Yamagata Honjozo Trophy
Shindo Sake Brewery Uragasanryu Koka 2009, Yamagata
JFI

Champion Honjozo

Regional Hiroshima Trophy
Umeda-Shuzoujou Honshu-ichi Muroka Honjozo 2009, Hiroshima, Japan
Sharp apple character with a fresh, citrus ripeness. Warming alcohol with a lingering finish.

Champion Gingo Daigingo

Regional Tochigi Trophy
Inoue Seikichi Sawahime Daiginjo 2009, Tochigi
Powerful green fruit and capsicum aromas. Earthy, mushroom notes lifted by zesty fruitiness. Balanced, long but not elegant.

Planet Earth Awards

Sustainable Trophy

Schubert Pinot Noir Block B 2008, Wairarapa, New Zealand

Mid ruby, dense raspberry and smoke nose with a herb de province overlay. Juicy, jammy palate with good lift. Nice length. Luscious!
£27.95 NZH

Organic Trophy

Domaine De La Vougeraie Bonnes Mares Grand Cru 2008, Burgundy, France

Focused red cherry and raspberry notes with perfect fruit. Supported by cherry oak with a long balanced finish.
BAB, BB&R, FMV, HAR

Biodynamic Trophy

Domaine Huet Le Haut Lieu Sec 2007, Loire Valley, France

Attractive lemon and citrus flavour. Well balanced.
£17.99 WAIT

Fairtrade Award

Stellar Organics Heaven On Earth NV, Olifants River

Burnt orange and caramel flavours with delicate jasmine aromas. Excellent balance and a great finish.
£8.99 EVW, VRT

Get the most out of your guide

This guide lists award-winning wines from the 2010 International Wine Challenge. To make individual wines easy to find, they are organised first by country of origin, then according to the type of medal they won: Gold Medal winners first, then Silver and then Bronze.

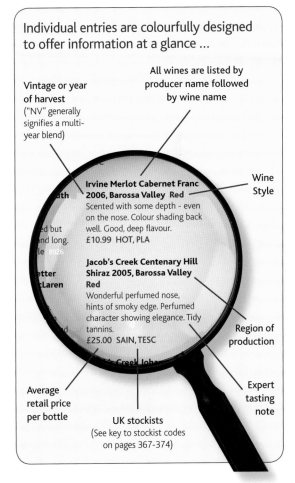

Individual entries are colourfully designed to offer information at a glance ...

Vintage or year of harvest
("NV" generally signifies a multi-year blend)

All wines are listed by producer name followed by wine name

Wine Style

Irvine Merlot Cabernet Franc 2006, Barossa Valley Red
Scented with some depth - even on the nose. Colour shading back well. Good, deep flavour.
£10.99 HOT, PLA

Jacob's Creek Centenary Hill Shiraz 2005, Barossa Valley Red
Wonderful perfumed nose, hints of smoky edge. Perfumed character showing elegance. Tidy tannins.
£25.00 SAIN, TESC

Region of production

Expert tasting note

Average retail price per bottle

UK stockists
(See key to stockist codes on pages 367-374)

Total production
14.68m hectolitres

Total vineyard
225,846ha

Top 10 grapes
1 Malbec
2 Syrah
3 Chardonnay
4 Sauvignon
  Blanc
5 Pinot Gris
6 Cabernet
  Sauvignon
7 Torrontés
8 Bonarda
9 Viognier
10 Pinot Noir

Top 10 regions
1 Mendoza
2 San Juan
3 La Rioja
4 Rio Negro
5 Catamarca
6 Salta
7 Neuquen
8 Cordoba
9 La Pampa
10 Tucuman

Producers
1,322 wineries,
more than 27,000
vineyards

Argentina

Argentina is a country of magnitude: big steaks, big mountains, big reds and big production – it is the fifth biggest wine producer in the world, in fact, ahead of Australia, Chile and South Africa. As an exporter, however, it is smaller, and the UK has only been getting to know these wines in relatively recent history. Malbec is the star offering, a black grape originally from France, that makes reds of rare purity and power in the high vineyards of the Andes. Not for the timid, these wines are potent and powerful and not by chance go extremely well with beef. Also, try checking out the opulent fragrance of Torróntes to experience the liquefied incarnation of talcum powder, rose petals and pot pourri.

2010 IWC PERFORMANCE
Trophies	2
Gold	4
Silver	39
Bronze	70

Cruz De Piedra Blend 2006, Maipú Red

Deep colour with complex aromas. Medicinal, with ripe, red fruit character. Well-structured tannins with highly extracted fruit. Well-balanced with a long creamy finish. A very ambitious wine that will benefit from time.

 TUPUNGATO TROPHY

Domaine Jean Bousquet Grande Reserve Malbec 2008, Mendoza Red

Soft, ripe nose. Lots of new oak. Very toasty nose, black fruits and tar, super ripe fruits. Huge mouthfeel and lots of spice. Big supple tannins hold an enormous weight of fruit.
£22.00 VRT

La Chamiza Martin Alsina 2006, Mendoza Red

Dense, dark colour; complex nose with good integration; oak, plum, mushrooms, spices, black olives; heavy but vibrant. Tannins need time.

 ARGENTINEAN RED TROPHY, INTERNATIONAL MALBEC TROPHY

Vistalba Viñalba Malbec Gran Reserva 2008, Mendoza Red

Very intense, dark ruby, smoky, port like. Dried red fruit nose spice. Juicy, relatively textured dark fruits and acidity. Firm grip to tannins.

Doña Paula Naked Pulp Viogner 2008, Mendoza White

Deep and toasty aromas on the nose. A hint of reductive character working nicely with the rich, ripe fruit. Lemony citrus on the palate with a hint of ripe melon. Lively and juicy on the finish.
£12.99 ODD

Familia Muñoz Territorio 2009, Cafayate White

Tropical fruit nose, ripe fruit palate, slightly honeyed with lovely freshness and good length.

Familia Zuccardi Serie A Torrontes 2009, Salta White

Perfumed, flowery, lemon and lime on the palate. Clean with a good finish.
£7.99

Finca El Origen Torrontés Reserva 2009, Salta White

Good, balanced, fresh, fruity aromas. Fresh and light on the palate.

Michel Torino Don David Reserve Torrontes 2009, Cafayate White

Some light grapefruit and tropical fruit notes with a white pepper finish and some length.
£9.99 HLD

Andean Vineyards Alma Andina Reserve 2008, Mendoza Red

Big, ripe nose of cassis and oak. Well-defined fruit - blackberries, blueberries and vanilla. Good strong finish with mint. Harmonious.
LAI

Argento Reserva Malbec 2009, Mendoza Red

Soft approachable fruits on the nose. Feminine and attractive with some subtle notes of black fruit. Grippy tannins and a great acid balance.

Atamisque Catalpa Pinot Noir 2008, Tupungato Red

Fresh berry fruits on the nose which tickle the palate.

Domaine Jean Bousquet Reserva Malbec 2008, Mendoza Red

Deep colour. Vibrant fruit. Well-balanced. Damson, spicy mid palate following on to the finish.
£10.75 VRT

Domaine Vistalba Corte A 2006, Mendoza Red

Bold, positive aromas of black fruits and cocoa. Rich intensity of fruit on palate - mouthfilling and velvety mocha and toast undertones supporting luscious woodland fruit and cardamom. Lingering finish.
£24.00 FFT GWW

Domaine Vistalba, Viñalba Malbec Reserva 2008, Mendoza Red

Very ripe, dark plums. Juicy and vibrant peach and cherries. Smoke and vanilla. Long finish.
MWW

Domaine Vistalba Viñalba Malbec Touriga Nacional 2008, Mendoza Red

Deep inky colour. Fragrant blackberry and blueberry aromas with chewy tannins and smoky finish. Full and rich.
MWW

Domaine Vistalba Viñalba Patagonia Malbec Syrah 2008, Patagonia Red

Violet hue. Very young fruit, violets on nose. Rich, plummy tannic fruit. Promising.
ASDA

Domaine Vistalba Vinalta Malbec 2009, Mendoza Red

Black fruits and a lovely softness to the palate. Balanced and fresh - an excellent example of Malbec.
M&S

Doña Paula Cabernet Sauvignon 2008, Mendoza Red

Great cassis nose, lovely mouth, sweet blackcurrants and tannins on finish.

Doña Paula Los Cardos Malbec 2009, Mendoza Red

Black cherry and spice with hints of chocolate. Very complex wine with an elegant finish.

Fabre Montmayou Reserva Malbec 2008, Mendoza Red

Lovely blackcurrant spice. Soft, supple tannins. A bit 'spirit' like on the finish.
£9.99 LAI

Familia Schroeder Alpataco Reserve Cabernet Sauvignon 2006, Patagonia Red

Medium intensity of colour, still youthful purple rim. Quite jammy nose. Mature, nice balance with reasonable lifted acidity but a little jammy on the palate.

Familia Schroeder Malbec 2009, Patagonia Red

Slightly burnt on nose - big, meaty, savoury black fruit. Needs time for big, chewy tannins to soften. Rich in black truffle.
LAI

Familia Zuccardi Serie A Malbec 2009, Mendoza Red

Very tropical nose. Lovely intensity and balance.
£8.99

Finca Flichman Expresiones Reserve Shiraz 2008, Mendoza Red

Mulberry and cassis fruit nose. Very ripe fruit palate. Nice tannins.
£9.99 SGL

Kaiken Sainsbury's Taste The Difference Argentinian Mendoza Malbec 2008, Mendoza Red

Beautiful creamy nose
- seductive and sweet on the

palate. Very well-balanced.
£6.99 SAIN

La Celia La Consulta Reserva Malbec 2008, Mendoza Red
Deep crimson colour, smoky bacon aromas and palate, deep red fruit with a lightly juicy clean finish.

La Chamiza Polo Profesional Malbec 2008, Mendoza Red
Blackberries, cherries, ripe fruit, tannic, rich, delicious with a long aftertaste.
£7 WWA

Las Moras Finca Pedernal Malbec 2007, San Juan Red
Bright, juicy fruit. Big, supple wine.

Luigi Bosca Malbec 2007, Lujan De Cuyo - Mendoza Red
Medium deep colour, ripe strawberry and juicy fruit notes on the nose, a soft easy palate and a good firmness of structure. Hard tannins on the finish but well made.
£11.90 BHL, DWS, H&H

Michel Torino Don David Reserve Malbec 2008, Cafayate Red
Mint and raisin, plum fruit on nose. Juicy concentrated richness of plum and fig fruits. Crisp acidity and finely structured palate.
£9.99 HLD

Michel Torino Don David Reserve Tannat 2008, Cafayate Red
Dense, with new oak aromas and flavours on the palate. Ripe with high extraction of fruit, fresh and creamy on the finish.
£9.99 HLD

Pascual Toso Finca Pedregal 2005, Mendoza Red
Complex nose blackcurrant,

slightly herbal/minty with chocolate and mocha hints. Lovely balance.
£35.50

Pascual Toso Malbec Reserva 2008, Mendoza Red
Ripe blackberry aromas. Lovely softness and spice on the tannins.
£12.50

Riglos Gran Malbec 2007, Mendoza Red
Green, herbaceous and minty with coriander finish. Zippy and very quaffable.
£24.99 BDG

RJ Viñedos Joffre E Hijas Grand Bonarda 2007, Mendoza Red
Restrained black fruit with a savoury palate. Fine tannins and good structure with crisp acidity and elegant fresh fruit. A touch of balanced bitterness on the finish.
£11.99 BDG, FAS, LOS

Septima Septimo Dia Cabernet Sauvignon 2008, Mendoza Red
Ripe, mulberry fruit aroma. Developed liquorice with plum notes. Hint of oak, leather and vanilla.
£9.99 COE, SMO, WUO

Sottano Judas Malbec 2007, Lujan De Cuyo Red
Big aroma of lovely ripe summer fruits. A well-made wine with ripe, firm tannins and some complexity.

Trapiche Marks & Spencer Altos del Condo Malbec 2008, Mendoza Red
Leather and meats on nose, also chocolate. Dry and slightly sour berry flavours. Persistent finish.
£6.99 M&S

**Trivento Golden Reserve
Malbec 2007, Mendoza** Red
Gentle mulberry fruit with toasty
oak. Medium to high tannins
and medium acidity support soft
blackberry fruit and ripe (almost
sweet) finish. For drinking now.
£11.99 CYT

**Trivento Gran Pampas 2006,
Mendoza** Red
Bright red with purple edge.
Good balance with hints of spice.
Robust structure with elegance.
£11.99 CYT

**Vistalba Cabernet Merlot
2008, Patagonia** Red
Big ripe fruit nose. Blackberry
and blackcurrant fruit flavours.
Good oak and tannin.

**Las Moras Sparkling Viognier
Shiraz 2009, San Juan**
Sparkling
Exotic aromas of mango &
passionfruit create a crisp zingy
palate with concentrated tropical
fruit, complemented by zippy
citrus notes.

BRONZE

**Alamos Seleccion
Chardonnay 2009, Mendoza**
White
Stone fruit, apricot and sweet
spice on the nose. The palate is
ripe with warm spice and apple
fruit character. Hints of lemon-
lime with a fresh finish.

**Andean Vineyards Alma
Andina Torrontes Sauvignon
Blanc 2009, Salta** White
Lifted, floral aromas; lots of
mineral character without
oiliness; good balance.
LAI

**Argento Pinot Grigio 2009,
Mendoza** White
Good clean style, fresh lemon

fruit, with good balance.
£6.99 WAIT

**Argento Reserva Torrontés
2009, Salta** White
Lovely, perfumed character, good
weight of fruit, fresh and balanced.

**Domaine Jean Bousquet
Chardonnay 2009, Mendoza**
White
Pale gold with green tones. Hint
of honey and peachy-apricot nose.
Butter on the palate with pure
grapefruit finish.
£7.99 VRT

**Domaine Jean Bousquet
Reserva Chardonnay Pinot Gris
2009, Mendoza** White
Grapefruit and liquid honey nose.
Ripe with hints of apple on the
palate. Round with mouthfilling
freshness.
£9.95

**Dominio Del Plata Crios De
Susana Balbo Torrontes 2009,
Cafayate** White
Grapey with big, ripe, tropical fruit,
quite juicy with some length.
£9.99 BDG

**Don Cristobal 1492 Verdelho
2009, Mendoza** White
Expressive green nose, good waxy
lemon fruit, balanced with fresh
acidity.
£7.95 WIDELY AVAILABLE

**Etchart Privado Torrontes
2009, Salta** White
Light, fresh, with some nice fruit.
Easy to drink.
MCT

**La Casa Del Rey Alta Vista
Premium Torrontes 2009, Salta**
White
Floral on the nose. Fresh, floral
palate with tropical fruit notes
and some length.
YOB

NOW AVAILABLE AT TESCO, ASDA, MORRISONS AND WAITROSE

Las Moras Pinot Grigio 2009, San Juan White
Light clean nose, easy lemon palate, waxy character. Zippy.

Pascual Toso Chardonnay 2009, Mendoza White
Pale and golden. Lemon and apple on the nose with rich honey-like aromas. Juicy with apple and grapefruit on the finish.
£7.99

Tamarí Reserva Torrontés 2009, La Rioja White
Herby, floral aromas. Juicy, fresh, grapefruity palate. Nice juicy and firm. Not long but delicious.

Trivento Asda Torrontés 2009, Mendoza White
Leafy geranium quality - fairly subdued aromatics but orangey and nutty. Quite long.
£4.24 CYT

Trivento Amado Sur 2009, Mendoza White
Pineapple and fruit salad notes. Nicely balanced. A good way to calm Torrontes down!
CYT

Alamos Malbec 2009, Mendoza Red
Deep purple in colour. Pure fresh aromas. Finely tuned palate with liquorice and dark chocolate complementing the ripe berry fruits. Fine-grained tannins and clean finish.

Altos Las Hormigas Mendoza Malbec 2009, Mendoza Red
Opaque, minty, ripe. Peppermint notes. Liquorice, long finish.
£9.99 DBY, FAW, HVN, LIB

Andean Vineyards Seleccion Bodegas 2008, Mendoza Red
Bright blackberry on the nose and palate. Chewy tannin and concentrated fruit - lots of promise.

Andean Vineyards Finca La Escondida Malbec Reserva 2008, Mendoza Red
Very dark fruit nose - blackcurrants. Fine tannins and balanced oak.

Antis Cuvée 2007, Mendoza Red
Opaque purple colour. Intense bold black fruit. Dense tannins and good freshness. Long and very spicy.

Argento Reserva Cabernet Sauvignon 2009, Mendoza Red
Fragrant aroma. Ripe, intense, cassis and plum. Soft tannin. Floral and well made.

Argento Bonarda 2009, Mendoza Red
Fruit on the nose with a youthful freshness. Ripe and juicy with a fruit-forward style. Balanced and fresh with a blackcurrant finish.

Argento Malbec 2009, Mendoza Red
Mid purple in colour. Vibrant, lively tannin and bright acidity. Liquorice, black chocolate. Austere, elegant and long.

Caligiore Malbec 2009, Mendoza Red
Deep, dark core with purple rim. Sweeter, more open, blackcurrant nose. Spice and sweet oak notes. Firm, sinewy, chewy tannins.
£7.49 VER

Catena DV Syrah 2007, Mendoza Red
Good colours. Very clean distinct fruits. Soft elegant style. Good structure.

Catena Tesco Finest* Malbec 2008, Mendoza Red
Lively floral nose. Good acid and tannin balance.
TESC

Cobos Bramare Lujan De Cuyo Cabernet Sauvignon 2007, Mendoza Red
Lifted blackcurrant aromas. Smoky spice. Vanilla notes on palate. Good concentration of fruit. Long and elegant.
£22.99 AAW

Cobos Bramare Lujan De Cuyo Malbec 2007, Mendoza Red
Fresh, fruity juice flavours. Well-balanced with good tannins, very soft, very harmonious, good to drink now.
£22.99 AAW

Colome Estate Malbec 2008, Salta Red
Ripe, blackcurrant bramble fruit. Stiff structured tannins. Complex and powerful.
£15.49 WAIT

Domaine Vistalba Cuvée HJ Fabre Malbec 2008, Mendoza Red
Cassis fruitiness, black and blue berries. Ripe fruit flavours with oak balance. Clean and straight with minty character.
£8.99 LAI

Domaine Vistalba Cuvée HJ Fabre Malbec Bonarda 2008, Mendoza Red
Deep crimson. Ripe, red berries and summer pudding on nose. Palate of very ripe sweet fruit. Soft attack, raspberry fruit with fine tannins.
£8.49 LAI

Domaine Vistalba Phebus Cabernet Sauvignon 2009, Mendoza Red
Deep plum, some spice oak,

baked apples, rhubarb and leafy menthol. Soft attack, medium fruit, good vanilla. Simple flavours and good concentration.
WAIT

Domaine Vistalba Phebus Malbec 2009, Mendoza Red
Attractive concentrated cassis, vanilla spice palate. Lovely bitter, cherry fruits with good finish. Young.

Doña Paula Selección De Bodega Malbec 2007, Mendoza Red
Black fruits and Christmas cake. Spiced fruit, long lush flavours with a buttery finish.

El Porvenir De Los Andes Porvenir 2005, Cafayate Red
Toasty, mellow nose. Good, dry, ripe and pleasant aftertaste.

Etchart Arnaldo B 2006, Salta Red
Clean, vibrant damson fruits with plum and violet perfume. Elegant complexity. Fine compact tannins with delicious length.
MCT

Etchart Privado Malbec 2009, Salta Red
Complex mid-palate. Good length. Lovely sweet fruit. Purity.
MCT

Familia Schroeder Saurus Patagonia Select Malbec 2007, Patagonia Red
Smooth, silky, nice blackberry and eucalyptus character. For a Malbec, quite feminine in style. Lively, fresh and attractive.

Familia Zuccardi Santa Julia Magna 2008, Mendoza Red
Creamy fruit, soft and supple with cassis and smoke on the palate.

Familia Zuccardi Santa Julia Magna Malbec 2008, Mendoza Red
Dark ruby. Sweet, heady, oak spice less fruit. Smooth, round, juicy, dark plums and spice. Not big or concentrated but pleasant.

Familia Zuccardi Santa Julia Reserva Malbec 2009, Mendoza Red
Bright and intense. Enticing rich fruit with well-balanced extraction - great with food.

Familia Zuccardi Serie A Bonarda 2009, Mendoza Red
Fresh bramble fruit and savoury flavours on the palate. Fine tannins with elegant complexity. Fresh, long and lingering on the finish.
£8.99

Finca El Origen Cabernet Sauvignon Reserva 2009, Mendoza Red
Deep plum ruby. Some cherry menthol, minty. Soft attack. Vanilla and fruit favour, creamy, silky texture.

Finca El Origen Malbec Reserva 2009, Mendoza Red
Ripe bluberry and mulberry nose with good definition and purity. Smooth earthy tannins. Nice balance on finish.

Finca Eugenio Bustos Altivo Balance Malbec 2006, Mendoza Red
Nice mulberry nose. Sweet fruit on palate, quite juicy.

Finca Flichman Misterio 2009, Mendoza Red
Rich fruitcake nose. Cedar and plum on the palate with well-structured tannins. smoky finish.
£5.49

Finca Flichman Paisaje De Barrancas 2007, Mendoza Red
Sweet, herby nose. Juicy, ripe fruits. Hard tannins.
£11.99 SGL

Finca Flichman Paisaje De Tupungato 2007, Mendoza Red
Complex red fruit compote on the nose with tea leaf characters. Silky elegant tannins.
£11.99 SGL

Gouguenheim Estaciones Malbec 2009, Tupungato Red
Attractive notes on nose. Some lovely, juicy notes on the palate. Feminine with fine grainy tannins. Very attractive.
£6.50 ADN, MWW

La Casa Del Rey Alta Vista Classic Malbec 2008, Mendoza Red
Lovely extraction, careful balancing oak and an interesting cinnamon spice complexity.
YOB

La Celia La Consulta Cellar Selection Pinot Noir 2008, Mendoza Red
Lifted raspberry and cranberry minted nose. Good definition. Strawberry, tomato leaf and red cherry. Lovely balance and freshness.

Lagarde Malbec 2008, Mendoza Red
Ripe, blackcurrant and bramble fruit on the nose. Complex and powerful dark fruit on the palate. Very big, but very pleasing.
£8.99 COE

Las Moras Alma Mora Cabernet Sauvignon 2008, San Juan Red
Cassis nose, pleasant ripe berry fruits, attractive, intense, tasty

oak. Rich, ripe and juicy. Clear structure and good length.

Las Moras Black Label Shiraz 2008, San Juan Red
Great plummy sweet fruit, ripe and clean, great palate, rich and very flavoursome.

Las Moras Gran Shiraz 2006, San Juan Red
Clear fruit-driven commercial nose. Very pleasant wine. Good plum fruit. Nice tannins.

Las Moras Reserve Cabernet Sauvignon Shiraz 2008, San Juan Red
Deep purple, pronounced blackcurrant. Juicy palate with firm tannins and good freshness.

Las Moras Reserve Malbec 2008, San Juan Red
Bright fruits, particularly black berry on the nose and palate. Clean and tangy.

Las Moras Reserve Shiraz 2008, San Juan Red
Lovely soft pepper nose. Great plummy fruit with hints of rubber.

Las Moras Reserve Tannat 2008, San Juan Red
Fresh and lively. Complex structure of fruit. Firm and ripe tannins with pleasant ripe fruit on the palate. Long, with chewy, ripe tannins on the finish. Still youthful, needs time.

Mauricio Lorca Malbrontes 2009, Mendoza Red
Deep raspberry red hue. Violets and appealing fruits on nose. Short, plummy fruit. Moderate length.
£8.99 CBC, DEF, TSC

Nieto Senetiner Don Nicanor Malbec 2008, Mendoza Red
Very purpley colour. Morello cherry jam on the nose with hints of cinnamon. Freshness in the fruit.
£10.49 PBA

Nieto Senetiner Reserva Bonarda 2009, Mendoza Red
Distinct black fruit aromas, balanced with a touch of herbaceousness. Sweet and elegant fruit on the palate with fine tannins and a touch of saltiness on the finish.
£8.00

Riglos Rriglos Gran Corte 2007, Mendoza Red
Whiff of mocha spice and berry fruit lead to a dense palate with tight tannin and subdued fruit. Balanced but needs time to integrate.
£32.99 BDG

Salentein El Portillo Malbec 2008, Mendoza Red
Eucalyptus minty nose. Medium bodied, with good sweet fruit and oak balance. Nice persistent length.
£7.99

Septima The Co-operative Eclectic Range Mendoza Malbec 2008, Mendoza Red
Blueberry/blackcurrant nose and cassis. Blueberry and morello cherry flavour. Good length. Firm tannin structure.
COOP

Sophenia Reserve Malbec 2009, Mendoza Red
Opaque, vanilla and red fruit aroma. Loosely knit ripe fruit. Easy drinking. Long, juicy finish.
£10.99 EOR, RWA, WHD

Sottano Reserve Malbec 2008, Lujan De Cuyo - Mendoza Red
Big aroma. Soft, ripe. Juicy fruit on palate with ripe tannins.

Trivento Pampas Del Sur Reserve 2008, Mendoza Red
Very spicy with high acidity. Exciting wine in a big style.
£6.99 CYT

Trivento Tribu 2009, Mendoza Red
Attractive deep purple colour. Blackcurrant fruit married to up-front ripe tannin. Fresh and invigorating. Slightly chewy finish.
£5.99 CYT

Pascual Toso Brut NV, Mendoza Sparkling
Pale lime, clean mid palate; nuts, pears and pruney fruit. Clean, light, fresh, quite short.
£7.99

Australia

Australia has long been a stalwart of the UK wine scene, but they have had a rough ride in recent years. Overproduction, unfavourable exchange rates and competition from other New World producers have all conspired to pile the pressure on to producers down under. In response, they have upped their game and Australian wines have never been better. From brands to boutiques, Australia has been focusing on emphasising the range of her climates and terroirs, and the difference that makes to her wines. There is no style of wine in the world that Australia can't do well. The wines that follow demonstrate exactly that.

2010 IWC PERFORMANCE

Trophies	12
Gold	65
Silver	238
Bronze	299
Great Value Awards	4

Total production
9.62m hectolitres

Total vineyard
173,794ha

Top 10 grapes
1. Chardonnay
2. Shiraz
3. Cabernet Sauvignon
4. Merlot
5. Semillon
6. Colombard
7. Muscat Gordo Blanco
8. Sauvignon Blanc
9. Riesling
10. Pinot Noir

Top regions
Riverland, Murray Darling Victoria, Riverina, Murray Darling NSW, Barossa, McLaren Vale, Langhorne Creek, Swan Valley Victoria, Padthaway, Limestone Coast, Margaret River, Clare Valley, Hunter Valley, Coonawarra

Producers
2,299

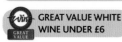

GREAT VALUE WHITE WINE UNDER £6

Alliance Wine Australia Moon Bridge Riesling 2009, South Australia White
Lovely green olive and petrol nose. Palate is rich and balanced. Great.
£5.49 M&S

Angove Family Winemakers Vineyard Select Clare Valley Riesling 2009, South Australia White
Dry, balanced apple with firm and fresh fruit. Lively acidity on the palate, layered with hints of tropical pineapple, ripe red apple and citrus peel. Fragrant with soft fruit character, excellent texture and minerality on the finish.
£9.99 D&D

Cape Mentelle Chardonnay 2008, Margaret River White
Peachy, ripe fruit. Good lifted aromas. Textured palate.

Clairault Semillon Sauvignon Blanc 2009, Margaret River White
A tropical stunner. Medium intensity with a ripe grapefruit nose. Long on the palate with firm grapefruit, lemon and pear nectar. Absolutely delicious.

Eden Springs High Eden Riesling 2008, Barossa Valley White
Richly scented with smoke aromas. Fresh green apples and crisp citrus on the palate with layers of lively pear-drop flavours. Deliciously ripe with good minerality and fresh acidity. Long and very pleasant.

Eden Springs High Eden Riesling 2009, Barossa Valley White
Flowers and citrus on the nose. Fresh and youthful, with an appealing restrained richness. Apple, blossom and lime. Will improve.

Fermoy Estate Reserve Semillon 2008, Western Australia White
Leafy, buttery, oatmeal and nutty grains. Lightly oxidised but beautifully pitched. Lemony fruit. Fabulous fruit sweetness, very long.
EVW

Jeanneret Doozie 2008, Clare Valley White
Fresh squeezed juicy lemon and lime on the nose. Almost limeade-like in character. Lush with ripe citrus fruit, white flower and yellow stone fruit on the palate.

Kellermeister Holdings Trevor Jones Reserve Riesling 2005, Barossa Valley White
Richly perfumed with floral and blossom nose. Sleek and smooth on the palate with subtle lime freshness. Candied peel and orange zest, layers of ripe citrus and red apple fruit. Lively, lush and long.
KHE

Kilikanoon Barrel Femented Semillon 2009, Clare Valley White
Lovely citrus aromas, fresh acidity and nice depth of flavours. Some honey, grassy characters. Lovely long finish.

Knappstein Asda Extra Special Riesling 2008, Clare Valley White
Lemon pale colour with youthful aromatics on the nose. Lemon

and lime freshness cuts the ripe melon palate. Complex with good development, well-balanced with mouth-watering freshness. Lush and delicious.
£7.99 ASDA

McGuigan Bin 9000 Semillon 2003, Hunter Valley White
Ripe, big, flesh guava fruit on the palate with a tangy lemon zest. Honey and hints of ripe citrus and nuttiness on the finish. Very elegant with loads of potential. Will improve over time.

 **SOUTH AUSTRALIAN WHITE TROPHY, EDEN VALLEY WHITE TROPHY**

McGuigan Shortlist Riesling 2004, Eden Valley White
Rich, orange blossom aromas. Silky with supple fruit on the palate. Rich, ripe apple, candied citrus and pear-drop flavour with good complexity and a creamy finish. Long and pleasant.

 **AUSTRALIAN WHITE TROPHY**

McWilliams Mount Pleasant Elizabeth Semillon 2005, South Eastern Australia
White
Pale green-gold in colour. Mineral and citrusy fresh on the nose. The palate is layered with good minerality, guava, lime and zippy passionfruit. On the finish, a touch of honey with long-lingering acidity.

Mount Horrocks Watervale Riesling 2009, Clare Valley
White
Pale lemon colour with a tinge of green. The nose is rich with passionfruit and citrus character.

Lively and lush on the palate with vibrant sweetness and lime flower. Well-balanced and very long.
£17.99 CAM, LIB, SWG, VDV

 **CLARE VALLEY RIESLING TROPHY**

Pauletts Aged Release Riesling 2005, Clare Valley
White
Toasty nose with a touch of oily minerality. Lime and lemon peel on the palate with complex development. Nutty and ripe with racy acidity and a long, elegant finish.
£11.99 EOR

Peter Lehmann Margaret Semillon 2004, South Australia White
Deep straw colour, with an opulent honey and beeswax nose. Firm minerality with a hint of salty character on the palate. Very fresh with a floral and apple finish. Still closed and will improve with time.
£8.49 EHB, WAIT, VDV

Peter Lehmann Wigan Riesling 2004, South Australia
White
Minerally and fresh on the nose with a hint of salty sea breeze. Soft, squished citrus fruit with juicy lime, lemon and yellow stone fruit character on the palate. Supple and soft on the finish.
£30 WSO, WAIT, VDV

Pewsey Vale The Contours Eden Valley Riesling 2004, South Australia White
Spicy with hints of toasty warmth. Fresh with robust citrus and zesty peel. Lush and full on the plate with hints of minerality and a zesty backbone.

Balanced with a long, fresh finish. Delightful.

£12.56 NYW, SEL, SMP, WIE, VDV

Pikes Traditional Riesling 2009, Clare Valley White
Pale lemon with high floral notes, citrus and pineapple on the nose. Minerally palate with approachable acidity, lively lemon peel freshness with good depth of passionfruit richness. Racy and fresh on the finish.

£11.75 FFW, GGR, LEA

AUSTRALIAN CHARDONNAY TROPHY

Step Rd Chardonnay 2007, South Australia White
Scented, herbal, mineral nose. Fine herb freshness on the palate with elegant and classy style. Fruit is ripe and supple on the finish. Terrific.

Tamar Ridge Whirlpool Reach Riesling 2008, Tasmania White
Honeyed and mineral on the nose with very flinty aromas. Light and fruity on the palate with smoky flavours mingling with ripe stone fruits. A touch of residual sugar on the finish. Fresh and clean with lingering acidity.

£9.99 ODD

Tyrrell's Winemaker's Selection Vat 1 Hunter Valley Semillon 1999, New South Wales White
Bright, juicy with youthful nose. Bracing acidity, yet fleshy ripe citrus flavour. Good mineral backbone with honest and balanced character. Very well made.

£29.99 VDV

Wakefield Riesling 2009, Clare Valley White
Lightly floral with a pleasant passionfruit aroma. Delightful balance of elegant citrus fruit with a rich passionfruit tropicality. Lime and mineral on the palate, with ripe apple and flint on the finish.

Woodside Valley Estate Le Bas Chardonnay 2008, Margaret River White
Ripe, peach and passionfruit aromas. Lots of flavour. Great integration and complexity.

Yalumba Eden Valley Viognier 2008, South Australia White
Rich and deep apricot on the nose with hints of almonds and ripe stone fruits. Good textured fruit on the palate with subtle warm spices, juicy stone fruits and lemony freshness. Long and persistent on the finish.

£9.99 EVW, HOU, NYW, TAU, VDV, WAIT

Yalumba The Virgilius Eden Valley Viognier 2008, South Australia White
Deep, rich apricot aromas with attractive nuttiness and hints of spice on the nose. Ripe, lush white stone fruit and apricots with a hint of pear on the palate. Deliciously complex with lingering acidity on the finish.

£22.94 HAR, HDW, NYW, SEL

Bellvale The Quercus Vineyard Pinot Noir 2008, Gippsland Red
Medium ruby red. Red fruits, spicy and stalky but very silky. Elegant finish.

Berton Kelly Country Shiraz 2009, Victoria Red
Deep colour. Minty and smoky. Juicy blackberry fruit, creamy

sweet spice.
£7.99 LAI

Buller Black Dog Creek Shiraz 2008, Victoria Red
Berry fruit, smoky chocolatey nose. Delicious, plump, ripe palate with elegant, silky tannins.

Dorrien Estate Avon Brae Eden Shiraz 2007, Eden Valley Red
Aromatic, spicy, sweet and floral (violets) on the nose. Intense, spicy, raspberry fruit and liquorice on the palate. Very ripe, but fresh and succulent. Long.

Fox Creek Reserve Shiraz 2007, South Australia Red
Bold and serious. A ripe blackberry nose with savoury notes. Spicy, very chocolatey. Rich oaky palate. Very full and ripe but with herbal freshness, grainy tannins and a dark chocolate finish. Long.

AUSTRALIAN RED BLEND TROPHY, YARRA VALLEY TROPHY

Giant Steps Sexton Vineyard Harry's Monster 2008, Yarra Valley Red
Clean pure cassis fruit on nose and palate. Real purity. Great complexity and has some real freshness.
£16.99 SEL

Giant Steps Tarraford Vineyard Pinot Noir 2008, Yarra Valley Red
Medium amber red. Hint of sweet toasted oak. Medium intensity flavours of spicy redcurrant and smoky hues. Good length and pure.
£15.99 WLY

MCLAREN VALE SHIRAZ TROPHY

Haselgrove Bella Vigna 2008, South Australia Red
Huge, with classic style. Loads of black cassis fruit on the palate with a touch of creamy spice on the finish.

Hay Shed Hill Cabernet Sauvignon 2008, Margaret River Red
Opaque core. Ripe, sweet fruit aromas. Damson/black fruit with slightly jammy hints. Very firm tannins on the palate. Youthful. Underlying compact fruit needs time to show, line of acidity adds freshness.

INTERNATIONAL SHIRAZ TROPHY, AUSTRALIAN RED TROPHY, AUSTRALIAN SHIRAZ TROPHY, SOUTH AUSTRALIAN SHIRAZ TROPHY

Heartland Directors' Cut 2007, South Australia Red
Intense, almost black core. Youthful rim. Very stylish, super clean nose. Blackberry and hint of eucalyptus. Ripe, immediate and appealing on nose. Mouthfilling ripe sweet black cherry and cream flavours. Appealing with some creamy vanilla notes on finish. Some grip to tannins but finely textured.
£17.95 CAM, FFT, GWW, HOF, MJF, RVL

Heathcote Winery Mail Coach Shiraz 2008, Victoria Red
Very aromatic, raspberry and eucalypt notes. Sweet ripe fruit on the palate with silky tannins and good length.

Henry's Drive Parson's Flat Shiraz Cabernet Sauvignon 2007, Padthaway Red
Medium garnet. Minty herbaceous clove with rich, ripe and full, spicy fruit. Great structure and length.

Jim Barry The Lodge Hill Shiraz 2008, Clare Valley Red
A toasty, savoury nose. Blackberry, coffee and a touch of earth. Medium bodied firm tannins. Very well-balanced with a lovely mocha fruit.
£9.55 NDJ, TAU, WVM

Kreglinger Norfolk Rise Shiraz 2007, Mount Benson Red
Deep ruby. Intense blackberry and vanilla cream. Juicy, bold, peppery. Good freshness and lively texture. Intriguing, soft finish.
£9.99 PBA

 BAROSSA VALLEY SHIRAZ TROPHY

Krondorf Symmetry Bv Shiraz 2007, South Australia Red
Huge smoky, berry fruits nose. Rich ripe herbal palate. Smoky notes. Very long.

 ADELAIDE HILLS TROPHY

Longview Red Bucket Shiraz Cabernet 2008, Adelaide Hills Red
Super sweet palate with vibrant rich dark fruit.

McGuigan Handmade Shiraz 2008, South Australia Red
Minty fresh damson nose with good definition and purity. Clean, concentrated damson fruit freshness. Excellent.

McPherson Chapter Three Cabernet Sauvignon 2008, Central Victoria Red
Light in the glass, excellent elegant cassis fruit. Well-balanced oak, palate delicious. Luscious, multi-layered, fruit bowl, great tannins and great depth.
£14.49 LNC

Paxton AAA Shiraz Grenache 2008, McLaren Vale Red
Lovely ripe berries on nose. Elegant, smooth with a great finish.
VDV

Penley Estate Gryphon Merlot 2008, South Australia Red
Moderate colour intensity. Soft plum fruit on the nose. Light body with eucalyptus notes on the palate. Juicy with soft tannins. Concentrated despite lightness.
£13.5 MOR

 COONAWARRA TROPHY

Petaluma Coonawarra Cabernet Merlot 2007, Coonawarra Red
Rich, spicy, minty, black fruit aromas with chocolatey oak. Rich and full palate with chocolatey black fruit flavours and touches of spice. Well-integrated. Long and will age.
£19 BWL, MWW, ODD

Pike & Joyce Lenswood Hills Pinot Noir 2009, Adelaide Hills Red

Medium ruby red. Aromas of sour cherry fruit and cranberry undertones. Lovely soft, silky tannins. Well-balanced with great length.
LAI, VDV

Russell Agusta Shiraz Museum Release 2001, Barossa Valley Red

Definite development on the colour and nose but still fresh on the palate. Nicely harmonious. A wine for now!

Schild Estate Ben Schild Reserve Shiraz 2007, South Australia Red

Mint and chocolate on the nose with seductive blackcurrant and bramble fruit. Rich mouthfeel with a long pleasing finish.

Shaw Vineyard Estate Shiraz Cabernet 2008, Canberra Red

Minty, milk chocolate note with briary fruit and coffee notes. Rich but fresh palate with silky texture. Bracing minty fruit with chocolate and great length.

Shingleback The Gate Shiraz 2006, McLaren Vale Red

Tight, bitter tannins underneath fruit. Needs time. Good length.

St Hallett Sainsbury's Taste The Difference Barossa Shiraz 2008, Barossa Valley Red

Very deep dark core. Very sweet, very ripe blackcurrant, blackberry and vanilla on nose. Juicy, powerful flavours and very ripe blackberry.
£7.99 SAIN

GREAT VALUE RED WINE BETWEEN £6 AND £10

St Hallett Waitrose Reserve Shiraz 2008, Barossa Valley Red

Violet hue. Restrained quality

fruit - cinnamon nose. Spicy, good fruity taste. Good length.
£8.99 WAIT

Sticks Yarra Valley No.29 Cabernet Shiraz 2007, Upper Goulburn Red

Bright, rich ruby colour with pink hues. Crushed herb and lavender, berry fruit and fine tannin palate. Good purity of fruit and freshness. Integrated oak and persistence.

Tyrrell's Rufus Stone Heathcote Shiraz 2008, Victoria Red

Sweet, chocolatey nose with coffee bean nuances. Rounded, creamy deep set fruit with ripe supple structure.
£11.99 VDV

 HUNTER VALLEY TROPHY

Tyrrell's Winemaker's Selection Vat 8 Hunter Valley Shiraz 2007, New South Wales Red

Nice coffee and blackcurrant notes. Chocolatey. Sweet taste. Bright fruit. Good length.
£24.99 VDV

Yalumba Hand Picked Shiraz Viognier 2008, South Australia Red

Fragrant red berry and vanilla spice nose. Strawberries, spice, a touch of mint and coffee. Lots of oak, but freshness and definition to the fruit.
£15.59 HOU, NYW, POG, SEL, VDV

Jansz Premium Non Vintage Rosé NV, Tasmania Sparkling Rosé

Pale pink colour with persistent bubbles. Restrained with a

classy, bready, character. Solidly structured, dry with refreshing acidity and good fruit. Long finish. Elegant. Classic.

£11.86 HDW, NDJ, SEL, VDV

GREAT VALUE SWEET WINE BETWEEN £10 AND £15

Tamar Ridge Kayena Vineyard Botrytis Riesling 2007, Tasmania Botrytis

Lime and honey fruit, great weight and still very fresh on the finish.

£13.59 ADN, BOF, P&S, TPM, VDV, WTS

GREAT VALUE FORTIFIED WINE BETWEEN £10 AND £15

Campbells Rutherglen Muscat NV, North East Victoria Fortified

Amber brown. Lifted hessian and spice aroma. Sweet upfront, fruit-cake with hints of raisin and toffee.

£11.25 ADN, BCR, CPW, ODD

AUSTRALIAN FORTIFIED TROPHY

De Bortoli Old Boys Tawny Port NV, New South Wales Fortified

Deep tawny, date and camp coffee nose. Quite fiery on the palate but attractive. Spectrum of dates, coffee and toffee.

Bidgeebong Chip Dry NV, New South Wales Fortified

Attractive golden hue. Dry, salty and nutty nose. Hint of pine nuts, floral notes and baked fruitcake on the palate.

Buller Fine Old Tokay NV, Victoria Fortified

Caramel, toffee, green tea, fig and jasmine nose with a medium brown hue. Chicory, toffee, raisins and green sultanas mid palate. Lovely length and persistence of prunes and coffee creams.

SILVER

Annies Lane Riesling 2006, Clare Valley White

Oily citrus peel and round nuttiness on the nose. Lively and fresh on the palate with mature qualities. Mineral and flinty on the finish. Ripe and round.

£7.99 EVW

Clairault Marks & Spencer Sauvignon Blanc 2009, Margaret River White

Grassy nose, a subtle yet pleasant example of Sauvignon Blanc. Elegant fruit with citrus notes and a long appley finish. Deliciously fresh and well-balanced.

£10.99 M&S

Clairault Sauvignon Blanc 2009, Western Australia White

Lovely complexity of orange with floral aromas. White peach and a touch of nuttiness on the palate with a long and elegant finish.

Coldstream Hills Chardonnay 2008, Yarra Valley White

Clean, ripe peach fruit with subtle nose. Elegant peach fruit on the palate with good structure and lean, green fruit. Fresh and ripe on the finish with a streak of creamy oak.

£13.99 EVW

Cullen Kevin John Chardonnay 2007, Margaret River White

Mature with a touch of

vegetable and rhubarb on the nose. Sweet and sour fruit, tropical and ripe on the plate with plenty of flavour and fresh acidity.
£35.95 LIB, SWG, VLW, WDR, VDV

D'Arenberg The Lucky Lizard 2007, Adelaide Hills White
Elegant and lovely with pure fruit on the nose. Refreshing and ripe on the palate. Drinking well now.
£11.99

D'Arenberg The Lucky Lizard 2008, Adelaide Hills White
Greenish and a touch vegetal on the nose. Fine palate, oaked with good fruit and freshness. Good balance with a very classy finish.

De Bortoli Semillon Chardonnay 2008, South Eastern Australia White
Pale lime-yellow colour with hints of pineapple and lime on the nose. Citrus, melon and guava on the palate. Light attack with a crisp finish.

Dorrien Estate Bin 1a Chardonnay 2008, Mount Benson White
Big, juicy style of wine with fresh acidity. A touch of cashew mixed with guava, passionfruit and tangy citrusy fruit on the palate. Lengthy.

Fonty's Pool Sauvignon Blanc Semillon 2009, Western Australia White
Leafy, herby. Lots of lychee and guava. Good acidity and life. Deliciously balanced.
£9.99 PBA

Geoff Hardy K1 Chardonnay 2008, Adelaide Hills White
Rich and toasty with limey minerality. Lovely depth of flavour, full-bodied with good, rich Chardonnay character. Ready to drink.

Grant Burge Zerk Semillon Viognier 2009, Barossa Valley White
Lime and mineral nose. Well textured with a strong mineral backbone. Clean and well balanced with an elegant finish.
£10.99

Grosset Springvale Watervale Riesling 2009, Clare Valley White
Steely and dry in style. Firm, ripe apple fruit with a mineral backbone. Mouth-watering and fresh with lime juice finish. Delightful.
£17.99 LIB, NYW, P&S

Grossett Hill Smith Mesh Riesling 2009, Eden Valley White
Limes, apple and white flowers on the nose. Delicate fruit on the palate. This wine has a great future.
£13.58 AWO, HGT, P&S, VDV

Hardys Eileen Hardy Chardonnay 2008, Yarra Valley White
Elegant, toasty oak with biscuit tones. Fresh, ripe fruit with lovely balance and a touch of citrus pineapple. Long and tasty finish in classic Australian style.
£19.99 OCO

Hardys HRB Chardonnay 2008, Margaret River White
Tight, classy and refined oak. Elegant style of Chardonnay with a good mineral backbone. Some creaminess on the finish, but still very young.

Hardys Oomoo Chardonnay 2008, Adelaide Hills White
Well defined nose with orange blossom apricot and nectarine

aromas. Medium-bodied, fine thread of acidity and notes of under-ripe lemon and orange zest on the palate. Peachy ripe finish.
£9.99 TESC

Heggies Vineyard Reserve Chardonnay 2008, Eden Valley White

Citrus fresh on the nose, baked lemons and citrus ripeness on the palate. Warm and rich finish with crisp acidity.
£15.07

Heydon Estate The Willow Chardonnay 2005, Margaret River White

Good colour with green hints. Fine, mineral aromas, oak and ripe citrus. Still quite youthful, with glorious flavour and delicious balance of ripe citrus and apple fruit.

Howard Park Chardonnay 2009, Western Australia White

Creamy vanilla aromas with tropical, mineral palate. Almost Burgundian in style with ripe, round and persistent finish. Delicious.

Howard Park Madfish Gold Turtle Flint Rock Chardonnay 2009, Western Australia White

Creamy with a nougat and apricot nose. Intense and tangy on the palate with hints of passionfruit and citrus flavours. Balanced with a clean, fresh finish.

Jeanneret Big Fine Girl 2009, Clare Valley White

Citrus and passionfruit on the nose with a fresh citrus zing. The palate is laden with ripe citrus and tropical melon. Balanced acidity with a floral fresh finish.

Kilikanoon Morts Reserve Riesling 2009, Clare Valley
White

Pale lemon with a tight, citrus nose. Lemon-lime palate with a touch of ripe pear-drop flavour. Balanced fruit with zingy acidity, fresh on the finish.

Knappstein Handpicked Riesling 2009, Clare Valley
White

Pure Riesling aromatics, showing good depth of flavour with ripe apple flavours on the palate. Well-balanced, with racy acidity and a crisp citrus finish.
£8.99 BWL, MAJ

Knappstein Marks & Spencer Ackland Vineyard Riesling 2009, Clare Valley White

Lovely minerality with a pinch of lime flower fruit. Lush with great intensity, well-balanced, ripe and fresh. Lemon-lime citrus, passionfruit and melon on the finish. Delicious.
£11.99 M&S

Leasingham Magnus Riesling 2009, Clare Valley White

Light, with soft and fresh citrus aromatics. Lemon and pear drops on the palate with undertones of green fruit. Firm acidity and attractive minerality. Long and pleasant finish.
£7.99 SAIN, SMF

Leura Park Estate Block 1 Hand Picked Reserve Chardonnay 2008, Geelong White

Open with white stone fruits, peach and apricot on the nose. Juicy and fruity with a nicely formed acid backbone. Fresh fruit on a soft, creamy finish.

McGuigan Bin 9000 Semillon 2004, Hunter Valley White

Ripe and nutty on the nose. Well-balanced with nutty character coming from time spent on the lees. Fine and supple fruit with well-balanced structure.

McGuigan Bin 9000 Semillon 2007, Hunter Valley White
Pale straw colour with green hues. Elegant beeswax and floral aroma with citrus and honeysuckle on the palate. Long and elegant on the finish.

McGuigan Personal Reserve Chardonnay 2007, Hunter Valley White
Warm lemon aromas, ripe and rich palate with a buttery and smoky finish. Well-balanced with good length.

McGuigan Shortlist Chardonnay 2009, Adelaide Hills White
Tropical fruit and oak in a warming style. Full-flavoured, youthful Aussie chardonnay. Drinking well now.

McGuigan Shortlist Riesling 2007, Eden Valley White
Sea breeze fresh with zesty minerality on the nose. The palate is herbaceous with lime and elderflower character. Citrus freshness and lively tropical fruit on the finish.

McWilliams Mount Pleasant Lovedale 2005, South Eastern Australia White
Big, fresh lime cordial style. Youthful with vibrant citrus and nutty character. Very balanced at its core with long and elegant fruit on the finish.

Mitchelton Airstrip Roussanne Marsanne Viognier 2009, Central Victoria White
Clean, elegant but intense. Very fruity. Full body, high alcohol, but very clean and precise. Well done.

To be drunk in small doses.
£13 BWL

Moorooduc McIntyre Vineyard Chardonnay 2008, Mornington Peninsula White
Clean, fresh with some meaty, leesy character on the nose. Good, honest grip with ripe citrus fruit and a pineapple finish.

Moss Wood Semillon 2009, Western Australia White
Pale yellow colour with fresh floral aromas on the nose. Very floral on the palate with youthful characteristics. Will only continue to improve with age.
£14.99 CPW, JOB, LAY, WAIT, WAIT

Nepenthe Ithaca Chardonnay 2006, Adelaide Hills White
Pungent with a touch of reduction. Sweet fruit with plenty of flavour. Very smooth and round with ripe citrus character. Drink now.

Nepenthe Ithaca Chardonnay 2007, Adelaide Hills White
Youthful, classy and quite mineral in character. Sweet fruit, excellent length and balance with zesty freshness to match.

Nepenthe Sauvignon Blanc 2009, Adelaide Hills White
Good, fresh citrus fruit with a rounded lemon fresh palate. Quite stony with nice mineral character. Well-balanced with good acidity on the fresh, lingering finish.
£8.49 TESC, WAIT

Nugan Cookoothama Botrytis Semillon 2007, Riverina White
Lovely layered fruit, with marmalade dominating, still fresh on finish with long flavours.
£11.99 MYL, MRN

One Chain The Googly Chardonnay 2009, South Australia White

Pale lemon in colour with a pear, melon nose. Full and fresh on the palate with hints of ripe apple and creamy citrus. Fruit is fresh and acidity is well-balanced. Refreshing.
£6.49 BRG, CMR, IMB, SEL, TVY

Pemberley Chardonnay 2009, Pemberton White

Fresh sherbet-like character. Very youthful with fresh, vibrant acidity. Terrific length and balance with long and lush fruit on the finish.

Pemberley Sauvignon Blanc 2009, Pemberton White

Gorgeous lemon-lime infused nose. Lively with well-balanced intensity and purity of fruit. Ripe citrus and pear-drop on the finish with zippy acidity and long length.

Penfolds Koonunga Hill Autumn Riesling 76 2008, South Australia White

Oily and lime-like character with mineral notes on the nose. Lime and mineral fruit on the palate with good balance and zesty acidity. Spritzy and fresh on the finish.
£8.99 SAIN, WAIT

Petaluma Hanlin Hill Riesling 2009, Clare Valley White

Ripe lime fruit. Attractive flavours of pure stone fruits with a hint of tropicality. Rich and long with lasting citrus freshness and well-balanced fruit on the finish.
£10.99 BWL, ODD, WAIT, WAIT

Pike & Joyce Adelaide Hills Chardonnay 2008, Adelaide Hills White

Sweet gingery and oaky cream on the nose. Attractive fruit with sweetly balanced acidity. Sweet and fruity, but refreshing.
LEA

Seville Estate Chardonnay 2008, Yarra Valley White

Complex, earthy and ripe. Concentrated mid-palate with ripe citrus flavours. Hints of stone fruit and ripe floral character. Lively on the finish.

Shaw and Smith M3 Chardonnay 2009, Adelaide Hills White

Noticeable oak on the nose with well-defined tropical fruit on the palate. Nice balance with good apple fruit concentration. Long and fresh on the finish.
£20 HAR, LIB, MAJ, P&S

Shaw Vineyard Estate Riesling 2009, Canberra White

Touch of petal, peony notes. Minerality and some weight.

Sirromet Seven Scenes Viognier 2007, Queensland White

Vibrant, fresh nose with green hues. Peachy aromatic character on the nose with hints of bacon, pink pepper and apricots. Apricot and peachy fruit on the palate with a long, lush finish.

Stella Bella Chardonnay 2008, Margaret River White

Peach, melon and pear on the nose with crème bruleé richness. Soft with a zingy citrus finish.
£12.00

Stella Bella Suckfizzle Sauvignon Blanc Semillon 2006, Margaret River White

Medium yellow-lime colour with hints of spice on the nose. Lime and lemon citrus fruits on the palate with a clean, fresh finish.
£19.00

Tempus Two Copper Wilde Chardonnay 2009, South Eastern Australia White
Some nice mineral on the nose with a ripe, round palate. Toasty oak on the finish with warming alcohol. Fresh and forward style of wine.

Tempus Two Copper Zenith Semillon 2004, Hunter Valley White
Ripe lemon and pear-drop flavours mingle with hints of fennel. Very ripe and lush on the palate with ripe pear and lemony citrus on the finish.

Tempus Two Copper Zenith Semillon 2007, Hunter Valley White
Deep straw colour with fresh floral aromas. Muted citrus tones contrasting with lush melon on the palate. Nicely balanced.

Tim Adams Pinot Gris 2009, Clare Valley White
Light apple aromas with hints of sweet spice character. Green citrus balanced with zingy, juicy fruit. Lively with lingering hints of pear-drops and melon on the finish. Very pleasing.
£11.99 AWC, OZW

Tim Adams Semillon 2009, Clare Valley White
Elegant citrus and floral aromas. Mineral overtones and delicate citrus fruit on the palate. Deliciously ripe with good balance and a lingering finish.
£9.99 TESC

Turkey Flat Butchers Block White 2008, South Australia White
Intense, fruit, clean. White fruit and some topical fruit notes. Full body, very grippy.
£9.99 CUM, ODD

Tyrrell's Winemaker's Selection Vat 47 Hunter Valley Chardonnay 2007, New South Wales White
Lees complexity, attractive citrus/grapefruit flavour, long finish, fresh and flavoursome, vibrant acidity, some sweetness.
£24.99

Vasse Felix Chardonnay 2008, Western Australia White
Bright and clean. Delicate lemon, creamy flavours permutate. Well structured and balanced.
£11.06 EGW, EVW, WDI, WIL

Vasse Felix Heytesbury Chardonnay 2008, Western Australia White
Complex nutty characters overlay a tropical citrus base. Well structured.
£19.11 FLA, HGT, NYW, WIE, VDV

Voyager Estate Chardonnay 2007, Western Australia White
Ripe, tropical flavours. Well-integrated and silky smooth.

Wakefield Pinot Gris 2009, Clare Valley White
Fresh pineapple with light floral aromas. Dried fruits, crisp apple and a touch of peachy juiciness on the palate. Long and lingering on the finish.

Wakefield St Andrews Riesling 2005, Clare Valley White
Light with citrus peel aromas. A touch of toasty minerality and ripe apple fruit. On the palate the mineral freshness persists with elegant and lingering fruit. Delicious.

Watershed Awakening Chardonnay 2009, Margaret River White
More simple passionfruit nose.

Good plush fruit on palate. Well-balanced.

Willows Vineyard Semillon 2006, Barossa Valley White
Lovely waxy yet developed style. Complex leafy notes and wax. Very fresh, lemony. Delightful.
£9.99 AWC, OZW, VDV

Yabby Lake Chardonnay 2008, Mornington Peninsula White
Plenty of grip, ripe with a savoury nose. Hints of fresh leesy character. Complex citrus with racy acidity and ripe fruit essence. Elegant style.

Yabby Lake Single Block Release Block 6 Chardonnay 2008, Mornington Peninsula White
Rich, concentrated with a ripe cheese-like nose. Strong citrus and apple fruit with a pleasant pear finish. Long and intense with supple fruit all the way through.

Yalumba Y Series Riesling 2009, South Australia White
Delicate, fine and fresh. Subtle notes of tropical fruit, citrus, flowers and passionfruit with a steely finish. Has a great future.
£7.54 EVW, HOU, MWC, SEL

Aldo's Block Shiraz 2005, McLaren Vale Red
Ripe, luscious, dense chocolate and spicy. Lively but integrated tannins. Balanced.

Angove Family Winemakers Vineyard Select McLaren Vale Shiraz 2008, South Australia Red
Ripe dark fruits, jammy. Very clear. Long, elegant and milky.
£12.99 D&D

Balgownie Esate Black Label Cabernet Merlot 2008, Bendigo Red

Dark, opaque purple. Eucalyptus, cassis, tomato and blackcurrant on nose. Very concentrated fruit on palate. Lots of depth. Mildly angular.
£14.99

Barossa Valley Estate E Minor Shiraz 2008, Barossa Valley Red
Ripe black cherry with a savoury nose and meaty character. Full, juicy black fruit. Textured with a slightly leafy green character and savoury notes. Shows its acid a bit on the finish.
£8.99 POG

Barossa Valley Estate E&E Black Pepper Shiraz 2005, Barossa Valley Red
Opaque, pinkish fruit. Minty blackcurrant, sweetish on palate. Good length.
£49.99 WUO

Barwang Barwang 2008, South Eastern Australia Red
Open cassis, cherry, mulberry nose. Full, blackcurrant fruits of good intensity. Creamy coconut. Tannins still young, nicely balanced acidity and grip.

Bay of Fires Pinot Noir 2009, Tasmania Red
Herbaceous peppery aroma. Structured pomegranate fruit and soft tannins. Medium body. Fascinating fruit finish.

Bethany G R 9 Reserve Shiraz 2004, Barossa Valley Red
Deep, almost blackcurrant-red hue. Good spicy forward fruity nose. Rich spices, good length on palate.
£35 PON

Bird In Hand Shiraz 2008, Adelaide Hills Red
Liquorice and black fruit flavours. A big wine with toast and mint

on the finish.
£14.99 TAN

Blackjack Block 6 Shiraz 2005, Bendigo Red
Eucalyptus and ripe spicy fruit on the nose. Soft and approachable wine with a spicy red fruit finish.

Blackjack Shiraz 2005, Bendigo Red
Plum and sweet cherry aromas. Mint on the palate which is full bodied with chocolate and toffee. Sweet, oaky, smoky finish.

Box Stallion Shiraz 2008, Mornington Peninsula Red
Brambly red fruits, cherries, chocolate and mint. Very well-balanced with fine tannins and a fresh, taut finish.

Brands Laira Blockers 2006, South Eastern Australia Red
Lovely, grainy blackcurrant fruit. Very stylish.

Bremerton Tamblyn 2008, Langthorne Creek Red
Dark ruby core and purple rim. Very ripe fruits. Lots of blackcurrant, vanilla, wood smoke. Concentrated with lots of juicy, sweet, dark plum and cherry notes. Sweet vanilla, creamy juicy finish.
£11.05 WI-AV

Brown Brothers Patricia Shiraz 2006, New South Wales Red
Spice and fudge to nose. Smoky, spicy palate and berry fruit with savoury flavours. Smooth mid-palate. Milky tannins.

Cape Mentelle Cabernet Sauvignon 2005, Margaret River Red
Mid deep garnet colour. Sweet red fruit aromas with plum and spice from oak. Tight black fruit flavour with tannic overlay. Very elegant.

Cape Mentelle Cabernet Sauvignon 2007, Margaret River Red
Intense, vibrant plum, menthol, black cherry, mellow vanilla spice. Well-integrated nose, soft attack, medium intensity. Tight structure, firm acidity. Has potential to age.

Cape Mentelle Shiraz 2007, Margaret River Red
Warm and spicy on the palate with soft forest fruits and a long satisfying finish.

Capel Vale Whispering Hill Mount Barker Shiraz 2008, Great Southern Red
Soft and sweet with ripe, black berry fruits. Leather and spice on the palate with pleasing length. Approachable.

Casella Yellow Tail Limited Release Cabernet Sauvignon 2005, Wrattonbully Red
Eucalyptus nose with strong, minty blackcurrant. Elegant tannins, well-balanced. Great potential.

Casella Yellow Tail Limited Release Shiraz 2005, Wrattonbully Red
Minty and menthol nose with seductive damson fruits. Concentrated damson fruit. Plenty of lush acidity. Fine dense tannins. Complex liquorice and sweet mocha toast. Delicious.

Clairault Marks & Spencer Cabernet Sauvignon 2005, Margaret River Red
Ripe, sweet, berry aromas. Seamlessly integrated fruit, tannin and acid. Long flavoursome savoury finish. Needs time as still very fresh and

youthful. Delicious.
£20 M&S

Cranswick Sarus Shiraz 2008, South Australia Red
Lovely flavour. Acid balance OK. Very good wine.
£10.99 DWS, OZW, STA, WET

Cullen Diana Madelaine 2007, Margaret River Red
Savoury, quite serious, classic style with elegance. Some mintiness. Tannins well managed. Lean fruited and good concentration.

£44.99 FAW, HVN, LIB, WSO

Cumulus Estate Climbing Shiraz 2008, New South Wales Red
Ripe fruit, good oak integration. Soft velvety taste. Well-balanced, delicious with good length.
£12.99 MBW

Cumulus Estate Shiraz 2008, New South Wales Red
Wood smoke - burnt toast nose with some dark fruits. More concentrated and firmly structured.
£18.99 IRV, MBW, SAB, WAD

Dandelion Lion's Tooth Shiraz Riesling 2007, McLaren Vale Red
Dark fruits and black cherry. Well-developed and complex with cigar box and a little spice. Good balance and poise.

De Bortoli Estate Grown Shiraz Viognier 2007, Yarra Valley Red
Lots of lift from the Viognier which gives the wine a floral touch. Cherries and oak on the palate. Intense.
£14.99

Dorrien Estate Avon Brae Shiraz 2008, Eden Valley Red
Fragrant wild strawberry jam aromas. Rich but fresh palate with raspberry, strawberry, chocolate, coffee, pepper, and a creamy smoothness on the palate. Long.

Dorrien Estate BV Cabernet 2008, Barossa Valley Red
Dark fruit and a smoky, minty nose. Big, sweet, juicy fruit flavours on the palate with gentle tannins. Good balance.

Dorrien Estate Mums Block Shiraz 2008, Barossa Valley Red
Penetrating cassis and blueberry aromas with a lot of vanilla. Ripe, sweet blueberry fruit on the palate with lots of vanilla oak and dark chocolate. Full, dry, high alcohol but very long.

Dorrien Estate Tolley Elite Shiraz 2007, Mount Benson Red
Concentrated red black fruits. Spicy warm notes. Great acidity and balance. Elegant and flavoursome.

Ferngrove Stirling Rocks Cabernet Merlot 2008, Western Australia Red
Medium ruby colour, herbal and red cherry aromas, restrained, soft attack, velvety texture, clean fruit, elegant medium concentration in the mid palate with a bitter cherry finish.
£8.99 HLD

Final Cut Wines Final Cut 2006, Barossa Valley Red
Developing savoury and leather nose. Soft, chewy dried and fresh fruit. Very long.
EMP

Forester Estate Cabernet Sauvignon 2007, Margaret River Red
Good, deep, intense fruit with

nice spicy notes and cigar box medium aroma. Rich, good, savoury, nice firm tannins growing on palate. Long.

Forester Estate Cabernet Sauvignon 2008, Margaret River Red

Vibrant plum. Cherry menthol vanilla, red cherry, soft attack, juicy. Medium on palate with a firm finish, nice texture. Real length to cherry flavour.

Four Sisters Shiraz 2008, Central Victoria Red

Plums, black cherries with a slight floral lift. Tannins very firm, good length.
£8.99 EHL

Fox Creek Short Row Shiraz 2008, McLaren Vale Red

Huge, dense aromatics with some floral accents. Malt, toast and cherry oak. Dark, stewed blueberry fruit. Masses of oak on palate too and huge fruit. Brilliant.

Galvanized Wine Group Mr. Riggs The Gaffer Shiraz 2008, McLaren Vale Red

Big cherry, toasty, burnt nose, masses of oak and a baked plum pie. Lots of tight firm tannins and quite high acid. Huge concentration. Lacks a little light and shade.
MOE

Galvanized Wine Group Penny's Hill McLaren Vale Cracking Black Shiraz 2008, McLaren Vale Red

Slightly brighter, juicier fruit on the nose than some from McLaren Vale. Still that coffeeish oak and depth. Thick stripe of tannin and slight drying oak.
£13.50 FSE

Galvanized Wine Group Penny's Hill McLaren Vale The

Specialized Shiraz Cabernet Merlot 2008, McLaren Vale Red

Sweet nose, blackberries on nose. Lovely mouthful, sweet, ripe, perfumed berries. Beautifully balanced.
£13.50 FSE

Gemtree Sainsbury's Taste The Difference Shiraz Grenache 2008, McLaren Vale Red

Ripe berries on nose, smooth, elegant ripe berries. Mouthful of ripe fruit.
£7.99 SAIN

Gemtree Uncut Shiraz 2008, McLaren Vale Red

Quite a fragrant note to this from the oak and ripe fruit. The palate has quite silky tannins.
£15.00 CAM, DBY, NYW, P&S, SCL, VDV

Glaetzer Anaperenna 2007, South Australia Red

Nearly opaque. Spicy, peppery, blackberry fruit. Sweet, firm tannins. Long finish.
£35 FNW, GWW, HVN, SWG, TVK

Glaetzer Bishop Shiraz 2008, South Australia Red

Violet hue. Soft bilberry fruit on nose. Sweetish, good fruit, silky. Peppery edge to taste.
£21 FNW, GWW, HVN, SWG, TVK

Glaetzer Wallace 2008, South Australia Red

Blend of savoury and jammy fruit to the nose. On the palate the fruit is ripe but fresh. Lovely spicy finish.
£14.95 CAM, FFT, FNW, GWW, SMP, WDI

Grant Burge Filsell Shiraz 2008, Barossa Valley Red

Opaque, purplish fruit. Spicy

black fruit nose. Quite soft tannins. Long finish.
£19.99

Hahndorf Hill Shiraz 2007, Adelaide Hills Red

Sweet, creamy, intense. Bright acid. Ripe length.

Hardys Oomoo Cabernet Sauvignon 2006, Coonawarra Red

Soft, ripe fruit. Good red berry fruit. Clean acidity and grippy structure. Medium length.

Harvey River Bridge Estate Buckingham Estate Reserve Shiraz 2007, Western Australia Red

Briary nose: fragrant, sweet and floral. Ripe, sweet fruits with savoury, juicy coffee. Supple tannins. Medium long.
£7.99 MRN

Heartland Shiraz 2008, South Australia Red

Rich and interesting nose. Exquisite. Almost balanced but ripe flavour. Integrated and long.
£10.95 Widely Available

Henry's Drive Dead Letter Office Shiraz 2007, McLaren Vale Red

Sweet, cedary, pipe tobacco. Choc-mint comes through on the palate. Very good flavour and complexity with balanced tannins.

Henry's Drive Pillar Box Reserve Shiraz 2008, Padthaway Red

Oh-so-berry. Deee-licious, black and red berry fruits. Long. Wow!

Hickinbotham Shiraz Cabernet Sauvignon 2008, South Australia Red

Dense purple black. Bold, black fruit and smoky oak. Concentrated Shiraz with massive structure. Powerful and spicy. Full bodied.
£9.99 LAI

Houghton Gladstones Cabernet Sauvignon 2004, Margaret River Red

Lovely Ribena currant nose. Palate complex, scented and deliciously dry.

Howard Park Leston Shiraz 2008, Western Australia Red

Warm and spicy with a hint of eucalypt and firm tannins.
£14.99

Howard Park Madbay Shiraz 2007, Western Australia Red

Eucalypt and spicy fruit on the nose. Round fruit on the palate with a good spicy follow through. Elegant stucture.
TESC

Irvine Merlot Cabernet Franc 2006, Barossa Valley Red

Scented with some depth - even on the nose. Colour shading back well. Good, deep flavour.
£10.99 HOT, PLA

Jacob's Creek Centenary Hill Shiraz 2005, Barossa Valley Red

Wonderful perfumed nose, hints of smoky edge. Perfumed character showing elegance. Tidy tannins.
£25.00 SAIN, TESC

Jacob's Creek Johann Shiraz Cabernet 2002, South Australia Red

Rich and spicy nose with cassis fruit aromas. Round, with a meaty and vegetal palate. Savoury finish with loads of character.
£35.00 SAIN, TESC

Jacob's Creek St Hugo Cabernet Sauvignon 2006,

Coonawarra Red
Ripe cassis blackberries, rich and intense and oily, slightly overwhelming. Tannin grainy and tight. Minty.
£25.00 SAIN, TESC, SAIN

Jim Barry McRae Wood Shiraz 2006, Clare Valley Red
Very deep - opaque dark ruby core. Super clean - dark plums, black cherry and spice. Firm juicy ripe blackberries, cream and vanilla. A textbook Shiraz.
£22.50 LAY, POG, SEL, VDV, WAIT

Katnook Estate Odyssey Cabernet Sauvignon 2005, Coonawarra Red
Clean, juicy, ripe, solid fruit. Dusty chocolate and great length.
£30.00 BWL

Kilikanoon Covenant Shiraz 2007, Clare Valley Red
A little over-extracted on the nose; ripe, zesty, edgy; a touch of raisin and prune; spicy finish.

Kilikanoon M Shiraz 2006, McLaren Vale Red
Warm bramble and custard hint, integrated tannins. Rounded and long.

Killikanoon Spencer Gulf Estate Baroota Shiraz 2008, Southern Flinders Red
Almost black. Smoky, spicy nose; smoky palate with ripe black fruit flavours. Dense, rich, concentrated and flamboyant. Lots of oak, high alcohol, will develop.
£12.99 LAI

Kingston Estate Cabernet Sauvignon 2008, South Australia Red
Intense colours with ruby tints. Black pepper spice on the nose. Spicy herbal edge. Dusty tannins give good structure and will age well.

Kingston Estate Echelon Shiraz 2007, South Australia Red
Zingy blackcurrant nose. Fresh, clean fruit with good weight and structure. Blackcurrant and cherries on the finish.

Kingston Estate Shiraz 2008, South Australia Red
Good tannins and eucalyptus, minty fruit. Fresh blackcurrants with a leafy overtone. Firm tannin finish.

Knappstein Shiraz 2007, Clare Valley Red
Very reserved, bashful on the nose. Blackberry and earthy. Fine tannins, very well-balanced. Smoke and truffle notes, intriguing and cerebral.
£9.99 BWL, MAJ, ODD

Krondorf 30a Shiraz 2008, Barossa Valley Red
Intense black fruit fragrance. Oak well-integrated. Soft with fresh acidity. Good balance and length.

Krondorf Reserve Shiraz 2008, Barossa Valley Red
Good flavour. Quite complex. A lot there and will improve.

Krondorf Growers Shiraz 2008, Barossa Valley Red
Very deep colour. Sweet, briary, slightly baked fruit and sloe nose. Baked black fruit palate, sweet, ripe and full. Spicy, supple and slightly simple but very well-balanced.

Lady Bay Limited Release Shiraz Cabernet Sauvignon 2006, Fleurieu Red
Smooth tobacco oak, hint of honey and spice on the nose, balanced with spicy honey, some red fruit.

Leasingham Bin 61 Shiraz 2008, Clare Valley Red
Intense purple black. Crunchy

black fruit and pepper, really vibrant. Fresh and lively creamy vanilla oak. Lively textured tannins.
£9.99 MCT, OCO

Leasingham Classic Shiraz 2006, Clare Valley Red
Very elegant, lifted nose. Pure, heavenly black plummy fruit. Very tight on the nose. Pinched. Good, but needs 1-2 years.

Leasingham Rider's Row Shiraz 2008, Clare Valley Red
Pure and well defined. Plum and a touch of raisin. Full bodied, good focus; some new oak - needs to be integrated, so 1-2 years.

Lerida Estate Lake George Shiraz Viognier 2008, Canberra Red
Delicate but complex nose with coffee, mint, black fruit and sandalwood. Rich, dense palate. Spicy and very long. Integrated oak, supple tannins. Slightly hot finish.

Long Flat Destinations Cabernet Sauvignon 2008, Coonawarra Red
Deep colour. Intense fresh cassis aromas with very intense and concentrated with blackcurrant fruit and mint leaf notes. Lots of creamy vanilla, good acidity and tannins, very young but has potential.

McGuigan Handmade Shiraz 2007, Langhorne Creek Red
Spicy bright hint. Edgy tannins and great finish.

McGuigan Shortlist Cabernet Sauvignon 2007, Coonawarra Red
Clean, bright, sappy, fruity and fleshy. Balanced and dense with long juicy, minty blackcurrant.

McGuigan Shortlist GSM 2008, Barossa Valley Red
Spicy, hot violety notes and good acidity. Fresh though second class.

McHenry Hohnen Margaret River Shiraz 2008, Western Australia Red
Fresh juicy dark fruits. Delicious and powerful.
£9.99 BAB, CHH, CWA, FAW, SAB

McLeans Farm Farmgate Cabernet Sauvignon 2006, South Australia Red
Opaque, opulent aroma of cassis, chocolate, cigar box and spices. Muted juicy fruit on mid palate. Tightly knit mineral and blackcurrant. Lingering finish.
£14.00 AWC

McLeans Farm Farmgate MSG 2007, Barossa Valley Red
Rich and chewy; some sweet violets balanced by leather and cocoa. Sappy, clean hint and polite tannins.
£12.00 AWC

McPherson Basilisk Shiraz 2007, Central Victoria Red
Intense red fruit with minty notes. Very concentrated black fruits on the palate.
£9.99 LAI

McPherson Basilisk Shiraz Mourvèdre 2008, Central Victoria Red
Lifted blackberry fruit on the nose. Dense meaty fruit on the palate with some pepper spice. Well-integrated tannins and good length.
£9.99 LNC

McWilliams Mount Pleasant Maurice O'Shea 2007, South Eastern Australia Red
Very deep opaque core almost

black. Very squeaky clean and youthful. Sweet blackberry, sweet vanilla spice notes, juicy. Attractive palate, cool, shy, vibrant and youthful.

Mitchelton Crescent Grenache Mourvèdre Shiraz 2006, Central Victoria Red
Big, rich, ripe chocolate and bramble fruit. Smooth and intense on the palate with silky tannins.
£13 BWL

Mitolo G.A.M Shiraz 2005, McLaren Vale Red
Big, black fruit blockbuster with spicy US oak. Good structure. Show wine.
£21.99 HVN, LIB, WDR, VDV

Mitolo Jester Shiraz 2007, McLaren Vale Red
Good classic McLaren Vale Syrah. Big, dark, brooding fruit.
£10.99 FAW, JCC, LIB, RSV, VDV

Mitolo Savitar Shiraz 2006, McLaren Vale Red
Warm baked, riped damson hint. Integrated tannins. Long, good structure.
£30.49 LIB, P&S, WDR, VDV

Murray Street Vineyards The Barossa 2007, Barossa Valley Red
Sweet vanilla laced cedar wood oak, spice, milk chocolate on the nose. Much of the same on the palate with freshness and ripeness of fruit. Chewy, chocolate finish.

Nugan Cabernet Sauvignon 2007, Coonawarra Red
Nice almond character on nose. Floral, mineral, menthol. Lovely texture. Lacks a little length but polished and stylish.
£13.99 MYL

Olssens Second Six 2006, Clare Valley Red
Deep colour. Eucalyptus nose and some herbal notes. Dark cherry flavour. Firm, chewy tannins with lots of juicy acids.

Palmer Cabernet Sauvignon 2007, Margaret River Red
Dark fruits with minty nose. Elegant with good balance.

Paul Conti Medici Ridge Pinot Noir 2009, Western Australia Red
Medium ruby. Medium and intense super sweet vanilla redcurrant. Fresh chalky tannins will settle. Good length.
£12.99 ELV

Pertaringa Undercover Shiraz 2008, South Australia Red
Oak adds vanilla character. Big alcoholic wine but enough supporting fruit.
£11.99 SWS, VDV

Pertaringa Understudy Cabernet Petit Verdot 2008, South Australia Red
Deep colour, plums, spicy complex aroma. Fine-graded tannins support the delicious cassis fruit. Elegant, complex wine with a persistent finish.
£9.99 SWS

Peter Lehmann Mudflat 2008, South Australia Red
Fresh raspberry nose. Intense fresh berry fruit. Some spice and liquorice. Very long.
£5.99 EHB, TESC, VDV

Peter Lehmann Shiraz 2008, South Australia Red
Rich, ripe, spicy, chocolate and blackberry nose. Blackberry fruit on the palate. Sweet and spicy with some bitter chocolate. A little jammy but quite long with

a savoury note.
£8.99 EHB, WAIT

Phi Pinot Noir 2008, Yarra Valley Red

Pale ruby. Sherbety notes on nose. Converts to summer fruit flavours and glazed cherries. Medium length.

Philip Shaw No 5 Cabernet Sauvignon 2006, New South Wales Red

Moderate colour intensity. Savoury aromas. Some tertiary development. Cedar notes. Very elegant on the nose and palate. Fine tannin structure, intense, concentrated tobacco, plum and black fruits. Long length.
£39.67 ABS

Philip Shaw No 89 Shiraz Viognier 2008, New South Wales Red

Interesting nose. Perfumed raspberry and plum, very ripe fruits on the palate. Very drying palate.
£22.11 ABS

Pikes The Red Mullet 2008, Clare Valley Red

A little simple on the nose. Blackberry, bilberry and a touch of menthol. Sappy, juicy palate, nice balance. Fleshy and pure fruits.
£7.99 CVS, FFW, GGR, LEA, VDV

Pirramimma Cabernet Merlot 2004, McLaren Vale Red

Rich brambly nose. Ripe dark forest fruit with a smoky richness.

Pirramimma Katunga Gts 2006, McLaren Vale Red

Lovely berry nose, really ripe, sweet and perfumed berries. Smooth, well-balanced and delicious.

Pirramimma Katunga Shiraz 2008, McLaren Vale Red

Pretty black fruit nose. Pastille, cassis, liquorice flavours. Firm balanced tannins.

Plunkett Fowles Stone Dwellers Shiraz 2007, Victoria Red

Sweet chocolatey, plum, peppery. Concentrated, rich and complex.

Plunkett Fowles The Exception Shiraz 2004, Victoria Red

Very dark opaque core. Very clean. Sweet blackcurrantness, smooth, round and creamy. Vibrant.

Primo Estate Angel Gully Shiraz 2008, McLaren Vale Red

Minty eucalypt with bright red raspberry fruit. High, fresh acid. Elegant chewy tannins with good length.
£20.00 AWC

Primo Estate Joseph Moda 2008, McLaren Vale Red

Smooth, creamy blackberry fruit. Rounded alcohol. Heavy style, long and powerful.
£24.00 AWC

Punt Road Shiraz 2008, Yarra Valley Red

Deep ruby. Sweet red fruits, blackberries. Vanilla - simple and appealing and immediate.
£12.99 TESC

Robertson Of Clare Max V 2007, Clare Valley Red

Blackcurrant and strawberry fruits with fruit tea notes. Full, nutty tannin structure and balanced acidity. Good weight and a savoury finish.
£30.00

Saltram Mamre Brook Shiraz 2005, Barossa Valley Red

Rich rose berries on nose. Rather

flat and lacking grit.
£11.99 MRN

Saltram No1 Shiraz 2002, Barossa Valley Red
Lovely sweet berries on nose. Lovely ripe leathery berries. Smooth and elegant.
£11.99 EVW

Sandhurst Ridge Fringe Shiraz Cabernet Sauvignon 2008, Bendigo Red
Lightly herbal, eucalypt nose. Pleasant dark roasted fruit on the palate with tight, chewy tannins.

Sanguine Estate Shiraz 2006, Victoria Red
Spicy, fresh, mint, concentrated. Bright fruit, long spicy aftertaste.
£19.50 CAM, FFT, FNW, GWW, SMP, WDI

Schild Estate Cabernet Sauvignon 2008, Barossa Valley Red
Stewed fruit on palate. Jammy style. Blueberry, vanilla and cream.

Shaw and Smith Shiraz 2008, Adelaide Hills Red
Dense and ripe with nice berry fruits and a fresh finish.
£21.99 LIB, MAJ, NYW

Shaw Vineyard Estate Cabernet Sauvignon 2008, Canberra Red
Big, tense, juicy, liquorice style. Concentrated cassis/liquorice character. Nice structure, balance and body. Good tender finish.

Shaw Vineyard Estate Winemaker's Selection Shiraz 2008, Canberra Red
Very aromatic, fragrant, briary, spicy sweet. Succulent red cherry fruit. Spice, sandalwood. Notes of dark chocolate. Fine grained tannins.

Shelmerdine Shiraz 2006, Heathcote Red
Bright, attractive pastille quality to the fruit, nice oak. Very juicy palate, grainy tannin and delicious.

Sirromet Night Sky Premium Reserve 2007, Queensland Red
Peppery, stony, savoury nose. Soft, cherry fruit. Medium bodied. Medium concentration. European Syrah style more than Barossa. Ready now.

St Hallett Gamekeeper's Shiraz 2008, Barossa Valley Red
Floral and dark cherry aromas. Red berry fruit and spice on the palate with a soft and lush finish.
£7.99

Stella Bella Skuttlebutt Shiraz Cabernet 2007, Margaret River Red
Intense, minty, milk chocolate with cassis on the nose. Spicy, herbal-green notes on rich, chocolatey fruit. Simple tannins. Long, polished. Will last.
£9.00

Step Rd Cabernet Sauvignon 2006, South Australia Red
Bright ruby tints. Restrained aromas and flavours. Some black fruit character on the palate with nice oily mouthfeel - dusty tannin profile gives structure and length.

Sylvan Springs Hard Yards 2008, South Australia Red
Quite closed with a glimpse of red fruit. Quite long.

Tarrangower Estate 2006, Macedon Ranges Red
Game and spice on the nose. Elegant wine with firm tannins - crushed peppercorn finish and persistent length.

Tempus Two Copper GSM 2008, Barossa Valley Red
Very clear and elegant notes. Black fruits, spice. Hint of smoke/tobacco. Firm, dry, silky fruit. Very good.

The Hundred Of Comaum Vineyard The Tax Collector Reserve Cabernet Sauvignon 2006, Limestone Coast Red
Dark, spicy edge to the black fruits and a chalky edge. Blackcurrant fruits with a gravel edge.

The Standish Wine Company The Standish 2006, South Australia Red
Textured sweet juicy fruit with cedary notes. Long finish.
£75 SFW

Thorn Clarke Shotfire Shiraz 2008, Barossa Valley Red
Lovely, sweet berries on nose. Smooth, elegant, ripe, leathery berries, chocolate and spice. Goes on and on.
£10.99 AAW, GNO, LEA, VDV

Thorn Clarke Terra Barossa Cabernet Sauvigon 2008, Barossa Valley Red
Mint and blackcurrant nose. Lots of oak and vanilla spice on the palate. Ripe fruit underneath, with a soft finish.
£8.25 AAW, GNO, LEA, WOW, VDV

Thorn Clarke Terra Barossa Shiraz 2008, Barossa Valley Red
Sweet red berries on nose. Ripe, smooth, leathery, chocolatey. Ripe tannins on finish.
£8.25 AAW, GNO, LEA, VDV

Tim Adams Shiraz 2007, South Australia Red
Eucalyptus, spicy black fruit. American oak notes. Good depth of bright, spicy, black, slightly jammy fruit. Smooth tannins, a bit of length.
£10.99 TESC

Tintara Cabernet Sauvignon 2007, McLaren Vale Red
Deep, rich, almost violet hue. Restrained damson plums on nose. Good ripe fruity taste, quite tannic.

Tintara Upper Tintara Shiraz 2005, McLaren Vale Red
Rounded smooth cherry pie hint. Dense, integrated and long.

Tintara Wines Clarendon Shiraz 2005, McLaren Vale Red
Lovely rich berries on nose. Sweet, rich perfumed berries. Elegant finish.

Vasse Felix Cabernet Sauvignon 2007, Western Australia Red
Fresh and bright, with cassis nose and leafy notes and berry fruits - a classic Cabernet, lovely.
£14.56 HGT, NYW, P&S, SEL, VDV

Voyager Estate Girt By Sea 2008, Western Australia Red
Lovely berry fruit aromas with a hint of flint and mint leaf. Rich ripe characterful palate displaying cassis and cedarwood.

Wakefield Shiraz 2008, Clare Valley Red
Sweet, ripe, eucalyptus-tinged nose. Good definition; pure, elegant, sappy, black fruit, joyful sorbet-like finish.

Willunga 100 Grenache 2007, McLaren Vale Red
Elegant, ripe fruit nose with strawberries, raspberries and cherries. Floral note. Good tannic grip. Nice ripe fruit, white pepper

and spice with herbs to finish.
£7.99 IMB, SAIN, LIB

**Windows Cabernet
Sauvignon 2008, Margaret
River Red**
Green on the nose with leafy
character. Ripe red fruits on
the palate with ripe, but grainy
tannins. Well rounded wine, with
a long, drying finish.

**Wirra Wirra RSW 2007,
McLaren Vale Red**
Sweet, spicy, brooding Shiraz.
Plenty of flavour with some
pepper notes. Great example of
McLaren Vale Shiraz.
£24.99 VDV

**Wirra Wirra Woodhenge
2007, McLaren Vale Red**
Tight, youthful, leathery aromas.
Excellent density of flavour, bold
gutsy Shiraz. Full bodied and
good length.
£14.99 VDV

**Wolf Blass Grey Label
Cabernet Sauvignon 2005,
South Australia Red**
A nose of cassis with hints of
mint and eucalyptus. Quite
intense palate - black cherries
and plums. Restrained and well-
balanced.
£19.99

**Wolf Blass President's
Selection Shiraz 2008, South
Australia Red**
Warm honeyed tobacco, hint of
chocolate, deep red cherry, good
length.
£12.99 MWW, TESC, WAIT

**Woodstock The Stocks Shiraz
2007, McLaren Vale Red**
Floral red fruit with spice.
Layered, brambly fruit on the
palate. Smoky, soft structured
tannins and good length.
£24.99 RAR

**Woody Nook Gallagher's
Choice Cabernet Sauvignon
2007, Western Australia Red**
Concentrated and balanced
fruits. Almond character. Good
depth, bright bilberry and black
cherry. Still showing youth.
£25 WNW

**Wyndham Estate George
Wyndham Shiraz 2006,
Langhorne Creek Red**
Soft and dense but with liquorice
edges and soft structured
tannins. Bit short.
£13 SAIN, TESC

**Wyndham Estate George
Wyndham Shiraz Grenache
2007, McLaren Vale Red**
Attractive concentrated fruit
nose. Ripe blackberry fruit - tar,
fennel and spice. Good length.
£13 SAIN, TESC

**Yabby Lake Vineyard Pinot
Noir 2008, Mornington
Peninsula Red**
Very pure Pinot aromas, a touch
stewed but quite complex. Sweet
fruit, balanced oak and good
structure. Impressive.

**Yalumba Barossa Bush
Vine Grenache 2008, South
Australia Red**
Minty, strawberry nose. Sweet,
spicy strawberry jam, moderate
concentration. Balanced acidity.
Fine tannins - well-integrated.
Good long length.
£9.55 EVW, TBO, WIE, VDV

**Yalumba The Menzies 2005,
South Australia Red**
Beautifully fresh and quite elegant.
Cabernet style with blackberry
fruits and a chalky edge.
£24.65 AWO, QSS, WDI, VDV

**Yalumba The Octavius 2005,
South Australia Red**
Violet core, tight cherry red rim.

Lovely lively good fruit, spicy.
Leather nose. Good, rich, spicy,
fruity taste.
**£44.28 EVW, HDW, LAY, TAU,
VDV**

Yalumba The Reserve 2002, South Australia Red

Intense dark cassis fruit, leather
and hints of nutmeg. Lots of
weight and character.
£44.28 LAY, QSS, VDV

Yalumba The Scribbler 2008, South Australia Red

Intense black fruits on the nose
with spice and white pepper.
Chocolate, caramel and vanilla
tones on the palate. Lovely full
weight on the palate with a long
finish.
£10.05 FLA, HFW, NYW, TAU

Yalumba The Signature 2005, South Australia Red

Lovely blackcurrant, mocha and
cedar notes with good tannin
structure and excellent balance.
£24.65 FLA, LAY, NYW, TAU, VDV

Jansz Premium Non Vintage Cuvée NV, Tasmania Sparkling

Green hues, mute honeydew
aroma, vibrant fruit and nutty
notes on mid-palate following
through on the finish.
£11.86 HGT, NYW, TAU, VDV

Miceli Michael Brut 2004, Mornington Peninsula

Sparkling

Deep & lively citrus, creamy
aroma crisp floral palate quite
long & fresh.

Barossa Valley Estate E&E Black Pepper Sparkling Shiraz 2004, Barossa Valley

Sparkling Red

Deeply coloured red with
charming up front sweetness
checked by integrated acid and
tannin grip. Drink now to 2012.

Wisdom Creek Prophets Pledge Merlot Cabernet Shiraz NV, Fleurieu

Sparkling Red

Sweet baked red fruit aromas.
Juicy fruit - damson and plum.
Pleasant aftertaste.

Brown Brothers Patricia Noble Rielsing 2006, Victoria

Sweet Oily nose with luscious
candied fruit on the palate,
honey and grapefruit, lots of
body and flavours.

Mount Horrocks Cordon Cut Riesling 2009, Clare Valley

Sweet

Pale straw. Interesting, rich style.
Quite intense, extremely fruity
and very sweet.
**£19.99 LIB, P&S, SEL, SL , VGN,
VDV**

De Bortoli Noble One 2007, Riverina Botrytis

Marmalade fruit on nose and
palate with classic cognac
flavours, very rich and pleasant.
£16.25 WAIT

Tempus Two Pewter Botrytis Semillon 2005, Hunter Valley

Botrytis

Pale lemon, intense and honeyed
nose with ripe pears, caramel and
orange marmalade. Greengage
nuances, very sweet but
balanced with lovely freshness
and elegant spice on the finish.

Buller Fine Old Muscat NV, Victoria Fortified

Dark, marmalade colour. Raisined
nose. Rich, luscious fruit. Smooth.
£11.99 MWW

Pertaringa Full Fronti NV, South Australia Fortified

Intense raisin, toffee and cacao
nose. Slightly burnt, caramelised
treacle. Good length and weight.
£11.99 SWS, VDV

THE MOST AWARDED BOTRYTIS WINE IN HISTORY.

If you could bottle the passion of generations of winemakers, then Noble One would be the essence. This unique Australian wine has won a host of accolades, making it the most awarded botrytis wine in history. **debortoli.com.au**

 DE BORTOLI WINES

Allanmere Durham Chardonnay 2009, Hunter Valley White
Bright melon on the nose with ripe, round tropical fruit on the palate. Biscuits and cream on the finish.
£11.99 ELV

Angove Family Winemakers Australian Reserve Riesling Gewürztraminer 2009, South Australia White
Clean hints of lime on the nose with soft lime zest flavours on the palate. A touch of kerosene and vibrant minerality. Clean and intensely fresh on the finish.
£5.98 D&D, TESC

Angove Family Winemakers Long Row Riesling 2009, South Australia White
Zesty lime aromas on the nose. Lime cordial on the palate with concentrated fresh stone fruit undertones. Clean and zesty on the finish.
£7.99 D&D

Australian Vintage Tesco Finest* Denman Vineyard Semillon 2006, Hunter Valley White
Clean with a tangy and pungent nose. Herbaceous with a touch of lemon curd on the palate. A very honest wine, well-balanced and tasty.
TESC

Barwang 842 2008, South Eastern Australia White
Smoky bacon crisps. Fruity palate with integrated oak.

Bay of Fires Riesling 2008, Tasmania White
Some mineral and floral character on the nose. Fruit-forward with lush flavours of honey and lemon-lime fruit.

Bay of Fires Sauvignon Blanc 2009, Tasmania White
Very pale in colour. Fresh nose of peas and pea-shoots, a touch of asparagus and lashings of citrus. Firm and phenolic on the finish.

Bellvale Athena's Vineyard Chardonnay 2008, Gippsland White
Fresh and elegant with heavy new oak aromas. Beautiful balance with crisp, concentrated citrus fruit and integrated oak. Long and complex finish.

Bird In Hand Two In The Bush Semillon Sauvignon Blanc 2009, Adelaide Hills White
Pungent fruit on the nose with a light hint of fennel. Soft attack of clean, ripe citrus fruit and a touch of nutty roundness. Good depth.
£9.99 TAN

Bremerton Verdhelo 2009, Langhorne Creek White
Very soft and subtle fruit but with a fat, rich ripeness on the palate. Spicy citrus fruit with hints of grapefruit on the long ripe finish.
£10.75 WI-AV, VDV

Brown Brothers Limited Release Banksdale Chardonnay 2008, New South Wales White
Mineral freshness on the nose. A lean style with ripe yet linear fruit on the palate. Crisp, fresh grapefruit finish. Tangy and delicious.

Casella Yellow Tail Reserve Chardonnay 2008, South Eastern Australia White
Honey and stone fruit on the nose with a delicate fruit palate. Ripe apples and smoky citrus on the finish with good freshness.

Chain Of Ponds Black Thursday 2009, Adelaide Hills White
Very supple citrus on the nose and palate. Nicely structured with a lively pear-drop finish.

Chain Of Ponds Corkscrew Road 2008, Adelaide Hills White
Youthful, mineral and very pure. Dry, but quite bold. Lots of well-balanced fruit. Perfect for those who prefer a drier style.

Coolangatta Estate Estate Grown Semillon 2005, Shoalhaven Coast White
Sweet lime and custard on the nose. Elegant green pepper and a leafy floral flavour on the palate. Tangy on the finish with a touch of crème brûlée.

Coolangatta Estate Estate Grown Semillon 2006, Shoalhaven Coast White
Plenty of zip on the lemony fresh nose. Lychee and grapefruit on the palate with a long, pleasing finish.

Dorrien Estate Bin 1a Chardonnay 2007, Tasmania White
Warm toasty oak and fresh acidity on the palate. Ripe, citrus and tropical fruit mingle with minerality. Guava-like on the finish.

Dowie Doole Chenin Blanc 2009, McLaren Vale White
Almost a tinned fruit note on nose. Green apple. Limey. Lovely mineral crisp acidity pulls through the apples and lime on palate.
£11.45

Forester Estate Chardonnay 2008, Margaret River White
Nutty and tropical with ripe, easy-drinking flavours. Good fruit balance with ripe lemon acidity. Attractive style.

Fox Gordon Princess Fiano 2009, Adelaide Hills White
Big and juicy, a very broad style of wine with hints of minerality masked by layers of over-ripe fruit.
M&S, ODF

Giant Steps Sexton Vineyard Chardonnay 2008, Yarra Valley White
Light, toasty, biscuit notes. Elegant fruit with a touch of earthy character. Lovely acid with good balance. Creamy and rich on the finish.
£14.99 GWS

Goulburn Valley Mount Major Chardonnay 2008, Victoria White
Smoke and flint on the nose with elegant, fresh stone fruit. Elegant and balanced palate with a sumptuous texture. Polished with a creamy, fresh peach finish. Complex and long.

Gralyn Estate Chardonnay 2009, Margaret River White
Fleshy, full aroma. Really lively on palate. Great complexity and length.

Hardys HRB Riesling 2008, Clare Valley White
Intense and ripe on the nose with lime zest and lemon freshness on the palate. Crunchy finish with long freshness.

Hay Shed Hill Block 6 Chardonnay 2009, Margaret River White
Distinct lemon and orange peel notes go from start to finish. Good acid on the length.

Heggies Vineyard Chardonnay 2008, Eden Valley White
Ripe banana bread on the nose. Buttery on the palate with a lush tropical finish.
£10.55 CORD, HOU, IMB, WIE

Highland Heritage Mt. Canobolas 2008, New South Wales White

Concentrated nose of floral-lime aromas. Heavy lime character on the palate with full-bodied texture. Smoky and fresh on the finish.

Howard Park Mad Bay Unwooded Chardonnay 2009, Western Australia White

Fresh, clean fruit flavours with a touch of oaky ripeness. Citrus on the palate with a ripe apple finish. Clean and fresh.
BWL, TESC

Howard Park Riesling 2009, Western Australia White

Nice citrus aroma. Fruit-forward with hints of fresh lime on the palate. Juicy and flavourful on the finish.
£12.49

Hunter's Horseshoe Semillon 2008, Hunter Valley White

Clean and bright with a subtle honey nose. Zippy melon and ripe lemon on the palate with a delicate and well-balanced finish.

Jacob's Creek Reserve Riesling 2009, South Australia White

Good, well-balanced fruit with loads of character. Lively citrus and peachy stone fruit with a touch of green herbaceousness on the finish. Firm yet supple.
£8 SAIN, TESC

Jacob's Creek Semillon Chardonnay 2008, South Eastern Australia White

Waxy fruit character with hints of citrus and ripe melon. Fresh and lively on the palate with lingering acidity.
£6.99 TESC, SAIN, MRN, WAIT

Jacob's Creek Steingarten Riesling 2007, Barossa Valley White

Mineral and savoury character on the nose. Again, savoury on the palate with lingering freshness.
£15 SAIN, TESC

Kilikanoon Morts Block Riesling 2009, Clare Valley White

Candied fruit aromas and flavours balanced by firm acidity and sweetly ripe fruit. Pleasant and easy drinking.

Knappstein Ackland Vineyard Riesling 2009, Clare Valley White

Delicate floral, lime and high tropical notes. Mineral with ripe citrus fruit on the palate.
£11 BWL, M&S, MAJ

Leabrook Estate Reserve Chardonnay 2006, Adelaide Hills White

Sweet gingery aromas. Mature, but still very fresh, lovely sweetness of fruit. Enjoyable and drinking now.
£20.99 HLD

Leasingham Bin 7 Riesling 2009, Clare Valley White

Citrus and apple aromatics with hints of floral aromas. Crisp minerality on the palate with a touch of sweetness. Medium-bodied with tropical finish.
£9.99 MCT, OCO

Lindemans Reserve Chardonnay 2008, Padthaway White

Floral grapefruit on nose. Palate sweet with melon, apple and pear showing towards the back.
£6.99

McGuigan Bin 7000 Chardonnay 2008, Hunter Valley White

Bright colour, fresh lime fruit,

lightly oaked, lees character, fresh and appealing but quite simple.

McGuigan Bin 9000 Semillon 2006, Hunter Valley White
Slightly spicy with a tangy, sherbet palate. Well-balanced with a nice citrus finish.

McGuigan Sauvignon Blanc 2009, Adelaide Hills White
Clean, fresh fruit with good balance. Lemony with a touch of lime and passionfruit on the palate. Nice, zippy acidity on the finish.

McGuigan Shortlist Riesling 2009, South Australia White
Lively and youthful, though somewhat closed at this stage. Dry and quite austere at this stage, but will develop well over the next 3 years.

McGuigan Vineyard Select Semillon 2005, Hunter Valley White
A big and powerful wine with lovely, zippy citrus. Lemon, custard and guava on the palate with a long and fresh finish.

Mount Adam Vineyards Tesco Finest* High Eden Valley Chardonnay 2008, Eden Valley White
Light nose of floral aromas. Sweet, tropical fruit palate with round, fat characteristics. Creamy and soft on the finish.
TESC

Murray Street Vineyards Riesling 2009, South Australia White
Limey, vibrant, somewhat closed, youthful, tight and dry. Quite austere now but should 'fill out' and develop well over the next 3 years.

Nepenthe Pinot Gris 2009, South Australia White
Smoky and spicy on the nose with fresh apple and hints of custard on the palate. Long and fresh with zesty finish.

Nugan Coonawarra Chardonnay 2008, South Australia White
Rich, ripe and round on the palate. Balanced citrus-apple fruit with a strong mineral backbone on the finish.
£13.99 MYL

Nugan Chardonnay 2008, King Valley White
Fragrant berry fruit nose. Peach, mandarin and quince. Full bodied with soft acidity. Well made and balanced.

Pauletts Polish Hill River Riesling 2009, Clare Valley White
Fresh, steely lime aromas. Light bodied with lime-lemon freshness on the palate. Easy drinking.
£9.99 EOR, MAJ, RWA, WHD

Penmara Five Families Riesling 2009, Orange Region White
Vibrant and racy on the nose. Lemon-lime with a touch of floral freshness on the palate. Delicate.

Petaluma Asda Extra Special Adelaide Hills Chardonnay 2008, Adelaide Hills White
Bold pear-drop aroma. Warming on the palate with a ripe citrus edge. Lifted finish. Easy to drink.
£7.99 ASDA

Peter Lehmann Back To Back Semillon 2006, South Australia White
Pale colour. Citrusy with a hint of pithy, peach fruit. Still dense and tight but will develop with time.
£6.29 WAIT

Peter Lehmann EV Riesling 2009, South Australia White
Very youthful and restrained on the nose, with juicy fruit tropical flavours balanced by the acidity to give a long finish.
£6.49 CWS, EHB, VDV

Pewsey Vale Eden Valley Riesling 2009, Eden Valley White
Lovely intensity of ripe apple and citrus fruit. Weighty with good depth of flavour and citrus freshness. A touch of herbaceous character on the palate with a mineral backbone.
£9.55 EVW, NDJ, WIE, WIL

Phi Chardonnay 2008, Yarra Valley White
Pale lime, some veg and lime nose. Medium intensity, custard and vanilla. Soft light attack. Fresh, delicate, clean melon and pear flavour. Light with a medium finish.

Plunkett Fowles Ladies Who Shoot Their Lunch Chardonnay 2008, Victoria White
Baked apple and leesy wood on the nose. A touch of oily fruit on the palate with balanced acidity on the finish.

Redbank Sunday Morning Pinot Gris 2009, Victoria White
Citrus nose with bright lime acidity. Fat, but with good structured fruit balanced with fresh acidity and a touch of nuttiness on the finish.
£10.05 AWO, EVW, HDW

Shaw and Smith M3 Chardonnay 2008, Adelaide Hills White
Beautiful, pure fruit with vibrant nose. Generous with floral and white flowers on the palate.

Fresh and well-balanced with crisp, tropical fruit.
£19.99 HAR, LIB, MAJ, P&S

Sidewood Chardonnay 2009, Adelaide Hills White
Fresh and leesy, lime leaf and tropical fruit nose with good lift. Citrus through the palate with a hint of lime flower and nutty sweetness. Finish is fresh.
ADN

Sticks Chardonnay 2008, Yarra Valley White
Light melon and stone fruit with tropical nose leading onto a zesty, lively palate. A persistent and creamy finish.
TESC

Streicker Bridgeland Block Sauvignon Semillon 2009, Margaret River White
Some leafy Sauvignon lift and some nutty background. Passionfruit, very good.

Streicker Ironstone Block Old Vine Chardonnay 2008, Margaret River White
Gentle and lightly oaked with sweet, leesy character. Easy-going and attractive style. Soft and round on the finish.

Tahbilk Marsanne 2008, Central Victoria White
Citrus nose with juicy apple and melon character. Ripe with mineral and spice backbone. Rich and firm on the finish.
£9.99 EHL, SAIN, WSO

Tempus Two Copper Wilde Chardonnay 2008, South Eastern Australia White
Lifted tropical nose, round and ripe on the palate with lots of melon fruit. Ripe and tropical finish with a hint of smoke.

Thorn Clarke Terra Barossa Riesling 2009, Barossa Valley
White
Classic white flower, grapefruit nose with a hint of an oily rag. Full and crisp, with a great texture and lovely finish.
£8.25 AAW, LEA

Tim Adams Riesling 2007, Clare Valley White
Steely and dry with youthful character. Mineral and lime peel on the palate with fresh acidity. Long and lively on the finish.
£8.99 TESC

Tim Adams Riesling 2009, Clare Valley White
Light sherbety freshness with ripe citrus flavours. Lemon peel and zest on the palate with a touch of lively sweetness.
£8.99 TESC

Tyrrell's Marks & Spencer Single Vineyard Hunter Valley Semillon 2006, Hunter Valley
White
Relaxed on the nose. Slightly spicy palate with hints of lemon juice and a touch of herbaceous thyme. Nutty and round on the finish.
£20 M&S

Umamu Estate Chardonnay 2007, Western Australia
White
Bright, sweet fruit with good flavour and mineral balance. Sweet and ripe with fresh acidity, still quite young and will improve in the coming years.
£21 SFW

Verdun Park Lyla Sauvignon Blanc 2009, Adelaide Hills
White
Slight tinge of green on the nose with a subtle creaminess. Very fresh with lively citrus and good weight on the mid palate. Lovely freshness on the finish.

Victory Point Chardonnay 2008, Margaret River White
Pear drops and ripe apple on the nose. Same pear-like character on the palate with fresh acidity. Easy drinking style.
BWE, CHO, MSW, PWS, VCR, VPW

Voyager Estate Chenin Blanc 2009, Western Australia
White
Neutral, oily and sweet nose. Elegant and sweet palate, drinkable.

Wakefield Chardonnay 2008, Clare Valley White
Ripe oak is dominant on the nose. Almond and lemon curd on the palate with a ripe, pure apple fruit finish.

Wakefield Jaraman Chardonnay 2008, Adelaide Hills White
Distinctive green and lime aromas. Creamy, quite smooth, with sweet and green freshness.

Wakefield Jaraman Sauvignon Blanc 2008, Margaret River White
Weighty grassy aromas with much of the same on the palate. Very pleasing with ripe intensity, lush citrus fruit and long-lasting length.

Wakefield Specially Selected Bushland Winemaker's Selection 2008, Clare Valley White
Oily with a nutty nose. Grapefruit peel and yellow stone fruits on the palate with good balance.
£5.99

Willunga 100 Adelaide Hills Pinot Gris 2009, Adelaide Hills White
Rich, with hints of buttery notes.

Ripe mouthfeel with soft, ripe lemon fruit on the palate. Warm and lifting on the finish.
£8.99 LIB

Wirra Wirra Hiding Champion 2009, McLaren Vale White
Fresh and clean with lime flower on the nose. Lime and lemon on the palate with soft and rounded stone fruit on the finish.

Wyndham Estate Bin 222 Chardonnay 2008, South Eastern Australia White
Pear, apple and ripe citrus aromas on the nose. The creamy palate is laden with citrus-pear fruit and a touch of spice. Ripe and lingering.
£7 SAIN, TESC

Yaldara Estate Chardonnay 2008, South Australia White
Nutty aromas with a touch of peach on the nose. Sweet attack with fresh apple and peachy fruit on the palate. Citrus fresh finish.
£10 TESC

Aldo's Block Cabernet Sauvignon 2006, McLaren Vale Red
Cassis on nose. Moderate concentration of black fruit, soft tannins and slightly spicy. Pleasant length. A gentle wine.

Alliance Wine Australia Chalk Spring Cabernet 2009, South Australia Red
Youthful appearance with moderate plus colour intensity. Blackcurrant leaf character on mid palate. Juicy and mouthfilling.
£5.49 MAJ

Angove Family Winemakers Bin Ref Shiraz Carignan 2009, South Australia Red
Deep youthful ruby core. Vibrant with a bubblegum rim. Juicy, vibrant red and black fruits.

Lovely acidity, quite crunchy. Long finish.
£8.99 D&D

Angove Family Winemakers Nine Vines Tempranillo Shiraz 2007, South Australia Red
Slightly reductive on the nose but opens nicely and shows good purity. Very smooth texture, good acidity, with a harmonious plum and liquorice finish.
£6.99 D&D

Balgownie Estate Shiraz 2007, Bendigo Red
Black fruit, plum and berry with hints of smoke and leather. Rich palate with good balance and length.
£24.99

Barossa Valley Estate Ebenezer Shiraz 2005, Barossa Valley Red
Plenty of ripe fresh berries. Chewy tannins. Long.

Barwick The Collectables Blackwood Vallet Cabernet Sauvignon 2007, Western Australia Red
Ripe cassis nose, lovely sweet ripe, intense fruit, spicy, lovely freshness and firm tannin, well-balanced with oak. Long finish.

Bethany Old Vine Grenache 2006, Barossa Valley Red
Dark berry nose. Ripe berries and cherries. Attractive wine.
£8.99 PON

Box Stallion Tempranillo 2007, Mornington Peninsula Red

A complex, refined nose, fresh, vibrant fruits on the palate - raspberry and blackberry - with lovely balance. Cerebral; superb.

Box Stallion The Enclosure Pinot Noir 2008, Victoria Red
Inviting plum nose. Elegant

strawberry palate. Medium body and delicate colour. Woody tannins and a long finish.

Brands Laira The Patron 2006, South Eastern Australia Red
Garnet, ruby, very attractive. Toasty, roasted spice edge to the nose. Nice dense, fresh palate.

Brown Brothers Patricia Cabernet Sauvignon 2005, Victoria Red
A cassis nose with lots of juice fruit and notes of spice and green pepper. Lively acidity, rounded tannins and a long, spicy finish.

Buller Beverford Shiraz 2007, Victoria Red
Leafy herbal notes on a blackcurrant nose. Black fruit on the palate with a firm tannic backbone and powerful finish.

Campbells The Brothers Shiraz 2005, North East Victoria Red
Rich oaky. Complex vanilla aromas, peppery. Bright fruit. Good concentration and length.
£34.99 DWM, SL

Cape Mentelle Cabernet Merlot 2007, Margaret River Red
Overt berry fruit aromas. Plenty of compact fruit checked by firm tannin. Attractive, elegant.

Cape Mentelle Shiraz 2008, Margaret River Red
Fragrant nose with a warm, spicy attack. Structure is solid with layers of lush, ripe fruit.

Capel Vale The Scholar Cabernet Sauvignon 2008, Margaret River Red
Deep garnet colour. Fruit masked by sweet coconut and oak aromas. Blackcurrant and spice

with fruit cake flavours. Good capacity and length.
£50.00 TAU

Cascabel Monastrell 2008, McLaren Vale Red
Ripe, aromatic, luscious nose, ripe berry fruit, firm tannins with a soft finish and decent length.
£15.00 PBA

Casella Black Stump Reserve Shiraz Viognier 2007, South Eastern Australia Red
Quite tannic with sweet blackcurrant fruit on the palate. Some pencil shavings and cedar notes with a fresh and lingering finish.

Casella Yellow Tail Reserve Shiraz 2008, South Eastern Australia Red
Medicinal fruit, jammy with hints of warm spice. Rich and ripe on the finish with a lingering freshness.

Chalk Hill Alpha Crucis Cabernet Sauvignon 2008, McLaren Vale Red
Dark and brooding. Notes of raisins, tar and camp coffee.

Chalk Hill Alpha Crucis Shiraz 2008, McLaren Vale Red
Ripe juicy with hint of creamy toffee. Good structure and clarity. Tough.

Chalk Hill Shiraz 2007, McLaren Vale Red
Sweet rich nose with a hint of chocolate. Savoury creamy character on the palate.

Chapel Hill Bush Vine Grenache 2008, McLaren Vale Red
Quite high, porty. Lots of stewed black fruits. Nice if a little short. Commercial and delicious.
£13.49 BWC

Chapel Hill Cabernet Sauvignon 2008, McLaren Vale Red
A leathery, plum and black fruit nose. Muffled and lacks a little freshness. Sweet, very extracted. Plucky, rounded grippy fruit.
£13.49 BWC

Chapel Hill Shiraz 2008, McLaren Vale Red
Slightly baked fruit, dense and quite chocolatey. Very muscular and dense quality, dry.
£13.49 BWC

Chapel Hill The Vicar 2008, McLaren Vale Red
Some vanilla and solid berry fruit. A touch baked and pruney perhaps. Tight, creamy, muscular tannins. Long and quite spicy.
£29.99 BWC

Château Reynella Cabernet Sauvignon 2006, McLaren Vale Red
Almost violet hue. Heavy, rich, fruity nose. Rich heavy fruit. Promising.

Clairault Cabernet Sauvignon 2007, Margaret River Red
Subtle nose. Palate of ripe fruit, good sweet, juicy fruit and lovely acidity. Attractive wine.

Cumulus Estate Climbing Cabernet Sauvignon 2008, New South Wales Red
Eucalyptus and cassis aroma. Complex, elegant palate. Closed finish.
£12.99 MBW

Cumulus Estate Rolling Cabernet Merlot 2008, New South Wales Red
Coffee, damson, cinnamon aroma. Tightly knit tannins, ripe valuable notes on palate. Lingering finish.
£9.99 IRV, MBW, SAB, WAD

Cumulus Estate Rolling Shiraz 2008, New South Wales Red
Prune and plum nose. Chocolate. Lovely primary fruits on palate. Firm tannins. Good length.
£9.99 IRV, MBW, SAB, WAD

Cumulus Estate Rolling Shiraz Viognier 2008, New South Wales Red
Good colour - mid deep ruby with more delicate violet. Perfumed notes. Smooth creamy initial attack. Attractive and immediately appealing.
£9.99

Dandelion Vineyards Lionheart Of The Barossa Shiraz 2008, Barossa Valley Red
Herbal nose, rich and ripe with a long finish. Spicy.

D'Arenberg The Dead Arm 2006, McLaren Vale Red
Nose genial. Cherry spice. Good tannin.
£26.99 WAIT

D'Arenberg The Galvo Garage 2006, McLaren Vale Red
Sweet blackberry nose. Soft blackcurrant fruit with some smoothness.

De Bortoli Deen Vat 1 Durif 2008, Riverina Red
Ripe, rustic berry fruit with a hint of leather. Soft, with fine tannins and good depth.

De Bortoli Deen Vat 12 Sangiovese 2008, King Valley Red
A mature nose with dried fruits and savoury, meaty notes.
ODD

De Bortoli Deen Vat 9 Cabernet Sauvignon 2008, Limestone Coast Red
Eucalyptus nose with juicy red fruit. Excellent fruit extract, lovely

savoury flavours. Well-balanced wine of good depth.

De Bortoli Windy Peak Pinot Noir 2008, Victoria Red

Vinous violet aromas. A well-balanced and elegant wine with vibrant mineral peony mid palate. A persistent finish.
SAIN

De Bortoli Yarra Valley Estate Grown Pinot Noir 2008, Yarra Valley Red

Pale garnet rim with a ruby core. Nose of red berries. Good length.
£16.99 MAJ, ODD, WAIT

Domaine Terlato & Chapoutier Shiraz Viognier 2007, Victoria Red

Touch of peachy lift, lots of fruit. Palate quite dry - there's a little flatness mid-palate.
£14.99 ODD

Dorrien Estate Bin 1a Shiraz 2008, Padthaway Red

Minty, jammy damson fruit. Fresh fruit excellent. Integrated oak fine. Tannins add structure and balance. Crisp acidity and refreshing style.

Dorrien Estate Tolley Elite Cabernet 2008, Coonawarra Red

Dense colour. Deep, floral, velvet style nose. Some vanilla oak. Perhaps a touch of heat on finish but very rich style.

Dowie Doole California Road Shiraz 2008, McLaren Vale Red

Big, rich, black pepper and deep, velvety black fruit. Big and creamy with gamey tones. Smooth, coffeeish tannins.
£21.99

Eden Springs Shiraz 2007, Barossa Valley Red

Rich and ripe dark fruit. Some spice and very warm mocha oak. Good dark sense of fit on palate.

Eden Springs High Eden Shiraz 2007, Barossa Valley Red

Spicy oak rather dominates the spicy earthy dark forest fruit. Tarry finish.

Ekhidna Grenache 2008, South Australia Red

Ripe cherries on nose. Smooth well-balanced berries and cherries. Body fruity.

Elderton Shiraz 2007, Barossa Valley Red

Ripe and lush with soft, black fruit nose. Warming and supple on the palate with a fresh blackberry flavour. Ripe tannins on the finish.

Elderton Command Single Vineyard Shiraz 2006, Barossa Valley Red

Dark fruit and spice. Full rich palate. Tight and fresh. Syrupy but balanced. High acid.
FMV

Elderton Command Single Vineyard Shiraz 2007, Barossa Valley Red

Spice and cloves on the nose with attractive blackcurrant fruit. Rich spicy finish.
FMV

Eldredge Blue Chip Shiraz 2007, Clare Valley Red

Lovely berry nose. Sweet, ripe berry flavour on the palate. Fresh, approachable and easy to drink.
£15 AWC, OZW

Eldredge Cabernet Sauvignon 2006, Clare Valley Red

Vivid garnet. Elegant, ripe, refined nose with blackcurrants, berries and sultanas. Refreshing acidity, fine grained tannins. Savoury

with a persistent finish.
£14 AWC, OZW

Evans & Tate Redbrook Cabernet Sauvignon 2007, Western Australia Red
Bright deep ruby. Subdued fruit on nose. Medium tannins and fruit on palate. Good length.

Evans & Tate Redbrook Shiraz 2007, Western Australia Red
Intense. Smoky berry and chocolate aromas. Bright, vibrant blackberries. Medium full and well-balanced.

Fermoy Estate Cabernet Sauvignon 2008, Western Australia Red
Deep purple colour, aromas of cassis, pencil shavings and cedar wood. Mid balanced palate with sweet berry fruit, a hint of capsicum complemented by integrated oak and ripe crunchy tannins.
EVW

Fox Creek Duet Cabernet Merlot 2008, McLaren Vale Red
Ripe, savoury, cigar box. Medium bodied, sappy red fruit, juicy and consumer friendly.

Fox Creek Reserve Cabernet Sauvignon 2008, McLaren Vale Red
Lovely ripe blackberry and bilberry nose. Well-integrated oak. Ripe entry, smooth tannins. Harmonious. Touch of blueberry and damson. Lovely.

Fox Creek Shiraz Cabernet Sauvignon Cabernet Franc 2008, McLaren Vale Red
Big blockbuster wine. True to identity and not too much hot alcohol.

Fox Gordon Eight Uncles 2006, Barossa Valley Red
Ruby. Good balance with some

leather and black fruit. Sumptuous dark fruit bomb. Bags of length.
M&S, ODD, VDV

Fuddling Cup Cabernet Sauvignon 2007, Western Australia Red
Good deep colour. Aromas show a little sweetness and greenness along with good varietal profile. Wine is subdued, but shows balance of fruit, oak and tannins.
£18.00

Galvanized Wine Group Mr. Riggs Yacca Paddock Tempranillo 2008, Adelaide Hills Red
An attractive eucalyptus and menthol-scented nose, well defined, very well-balanced, with fine tannins and hints of mocha on the finish. Lovely.
MOE

Gemtree Bloodstone Shiraz Viognier 2008, McLaren Vale Red
Cherry fruit nose with hints of liquorice.
£12.00 ART, BDL, CAM, DBY, IVV, VDV

Gemtree White Lees Shiraz 2007, McLaren Vale Red
Red fruit with a touch of spice and floral notes. Ripe, structured tannins, integrated oak and persistent length.
£21.00 BAP, CAM, NYW, VDV

Giant Steps Sexton Vineyard Pinot Noir 2008, Yarra Valley Red
Pinkish rim with a pale ruby core. Balanced acidity. Dried prune. Average length.
£15.99

Grant Burge Cameron Vale Cabernet Sauvignon 2007, Barossa Valley Red
Cassis and mint on the nose.

Nice juicy dark fruits on the palate that becomes rather savoury with a good tannin/acid balance.
£12.99

Grant Burge Meshach 2005, Barossa Valley Red
Silky fruit. Well-balanced with a good finish. Plenty of fruit.
£65.00

Haan Shiraz Cabernet 2008, Barossa Valley Red
Blackcurrant nose. Intense blackcurrant and blueberry fruit.
£12.99 HLD

Hardys Eileen Hardy Pinot Noir 2008, Derwent/Yarra Valley Red
Lazy pale/mid ruby. Quite firm tannins and acidity. Chalky notes. Red berry fruit. Good length.

Hardys Eileen Hardy Shiraz 2005, McLaren Vale Red
Not obvious but dense chocolate. Good balance and broad.
£39.99 OCO

Hardys HRB Cabernet Sauvignon 2007, Coonawarra Red
Currant and leaf nose. A bit earthy and slightly medicinal. Fine tannins.

Hardys HRB Shiraz 2007, Clare Valley Red
Ripe, red and black fruits with a touch of vanilla spice. Round and soft on the palate with clean and vibrant fruit. Long and lifted finish.

Hay Shed Hill Block 2 Cabernet Sauvignon 2008, Margaret River Red
Dark fruits with minty and herbal notes. Good balance.

Henry's Drive Pillar Box Red 2008, Padthaway Red
Medium ruby. Medium and toasty deep fruit. Spicy cinnamon. Slightly hot and drying at finish.

Henry's Drive The Trial Of John Montford Cabernet Sauvignon 2007, Padthaway Red
Rounded, smooth, creamy cassis hint. Ripe tannins. Good balance. Long.

Heydon Estate WG Grace Cabernet Sauvignon 2004, Margaret River Red
Tertiary fruit character. Lots of bitter chocolate and a touch of green pepper. Elegant finish.

Highland Heritage Estate Mt. Canobolas 2008, New South Wales Red
Some nice fruit on nose. Cassis and red berry. Warming, savoury tapenade character on palate. A little hard on finish but good length.

Hollick Cabernet Sauvignon 2008, Coonawarra Red
Minty, blackcurrant pastille nose. Good fruit on the palate, tight blackcurrant with a leafy edge.
£13.99 Widely Available

Hope Estate Bushland Reserve Shiraz 2008, Hunter Valley Red
Good prunes and spices. Ripe tannins. Good concentration. Fresh taste - a bit jammy.
£3.99

Houghton CW Ferguson Cabernet Malbec 2007, Great Southern Red
Deep ruby. Cassis and violet accent, juicy - jammy blueberry and cream palate, supple tannins and plenty of spice. Good length.

Houghton Jack Mann Cabernet Sauvignon 2004, Western Australia Red
Deep colour. Nice minty aroma. Palate hints to bottle age. Mid palate fruits are slightly overridden by hard tannins.

Houghton The Bandit Shiraz Tempranillo 2008, Western Australia Red
Rhone-style minerally reduction, fresh. Fresh, juicy, firm, dark fruit. Delicious but needs decanting.
£8.99 OCO

Howard Park Abercrombie Cabernet Sauvignon 2007, Western Australia Red
Red fruit with a touch of coffee. Mocha coffee comes through palate with silky tannins and juicy fruit with menthol notes. Subtle finish.
£26.99

Howard Park Scotsdale Shiraz 2008, Western Australia Red
Jammy black fruit and eucalyptus. Vanilla oak on the palate - an easy drinking style.

Hugh Hamilton Jekyll & Hyde Shiraz Viognier 2008, McLaren Vale Red
Fruit forward with a hint of peppery spice and cedar. Good length.
£23.50 LBV

Hugh Hamilton The Rascal Shiraz 2008, McLaren Vale Red
Big, ripe, nutty, super concentrated. Big, ripe and full tannins. Masses of oak notes. Massive length.
£16.95 LBV

Innocent Bystander Pinot Noir 2008, Victoria Red
Classic in style. Lovely raspberry and mocha aromas lead to soft, velvety palate with sweetly spiced red berry and cinnamon flavours. Silky and lingering.
£9.99 GGW, P&S

Irvine The Baroness 2008, Barossa Valley Red
Fragrant, cassis cedar. Concentrated flavour and freshness. Moderate tannins and fresh acidity. Good complexity and richness.
£19.50 HOT, PLA

Jeanneret Denis 2004, Clare Valley Red
A little over-extracted on the nose. Ripe, zesty, edgy, touch of raisin and prune, spicy finish.

Jeanneret Hummer 2006, Clare Valley Red
Ripe berry nose, slightly bitter. Berries and cherries. Long.

John A Sprigg Trevelen Farm The Tunney Cabernet Sauvignon 2008, Great Southern Red
Blackberry, light oak, fresh acidity, intense blackberry and cassis. Juicy palate supported by good acidity, velvet tannins and warm alcohol.

Kalleske Moppa Shiraz 2008, South Australia Red
Lovely ripe fruit. Good tannins - well softened. Plenty of potential.
£20 SFW

Kalleske Pirathon 2008, South Australia Red
Nice texture. Good oak to fruit balance. Medium finish.
£17 SFW

Kangarilla Road Shiraz 2007, McLaren Vale Red
Smoky, leathery ripe berry fruit. Complex and sleekly structured with great balance and finish.
£10.99 MWW

DISCOVER... THE GREAT DIVERSITY OF AUSTRALIA'S WINES AND REGIONS!

australian wines

Katnook Estate Cabernet Sauvignon 2006, Coonawarra Red
Pleasant herbal nose. Moderate fruit ripeness. Clean. Enjoyable if not intense.
£17.99 BWL

Katnook Estate Prodigy Shiraz 2006, Coonawarra Red
Deep and dense but ripe and rounded fruit with integrated oak and soft, plush elegance.
£30.00 BWL

Katnook Estate Shiraz 2007, Coonawarra Red
Lovely berry nose. Ripe berries. Well-balanced with oak.
£17.99 BWL

Kies Family Wines Chaff Mill 2006, Barossa Valley Red
Deep ruby/purple with crunchy berry, brambly fruit. Lithe and smooth with attractive balance.

Kies Family Wines Dedication 2006, Barossa Valley Red
Medium garnet. Medium and spicy, sweet and creamy. Big spicy, toasty vanilla oak, blackcurrant. Cinnamon spice. Great length.

Kies Family Wines Klauber Block 2005, Barossa Valley Red
Ripe fruit and good balance but coarse finish.

Kilikanoon The Duke Grenache 2006, Clare Valley Red
Nice, sweet, spicy fruits on the nose and palate; harmonious and savoury. Good acid structure and breadth of flow.

Lady Bay Cabernet Sauvignon 2004, Fleurieu Red
Warm, ripe fruit. Lush cassis hint. Nice texture and grippy tannins.

Lady Bay Shiraz 2005, Fleurieu Red
Sweet, ripe fruit with good spice and leather character. Fresh acidity and with a ripe bramble finish.

Leura Park Estate Pinot Noir 2008, Geelong Red
Serious and complex on the nose – perfumed and smoky with dark chocolate and raspberry character. Velvety softness and a silky finish.

Longview Nebbiolo 2006, Adelaide Hills Red
Mid garnet core. Very sweet cooked fruits/raspberry jam and tea leaf nose. Sweet, juicy red fruits. Some fresh acidity. Very pleasant.

Magpie Estates Springwater Creek Cabernet Shiraz 2006, Barossa Valley Red
Dark ripe fruit nose. Lovely ripeness is balanced with racy acidity and gentle tannins. Lovely food wine.
ELV

Mantra Cabernet Sauvignon 2007, Margaret River Red
Wow! Quite elegant. Soft managed tannins. Balanced and classy. Lovely.

McGuigan Farms Shiraz 2007, South Australia Red
Ruby. Spice, leather and black fruits. Restrained. Well-integrated black fruit, tannin and vanilla oak.

McGuigan Farms Shiraz 2008, Barossa Valley Red
Deep, dense, ruby. Blackberry, warm oak. Good acidity and freshness. Alcohol warm.

McGuigan Shortlist Cabernet Sauvignon 2006, Coonawarra Red
Deeply coloured. Lots of

blackcurrant and black berries. Some green notes.

McGuigan Shortlist Shiraz 2006, Barossa Valley Red
Harmonious combination of sweet grippy tannins (will soften), food friendly.

McGuigan Shortlist Shiraz 2007, Barossa Valley Red
Deep black fruit. Medium body. Good oak, light pepper.

McGuigan Shortlist Shiraz 2008, Barossa Valley Red
Spice and leather with rich bright blackberry fruit. Rich mouthfeel. Smooth finish.

McLaren Vale Premium Wines III Associates Four Score Grenache 2008, McLaren Vale Red
Strawberries, cranberries and spice. Well structured, ripe tannins, spicy, quite concentrated finish.

McPherson Basilisk Cabernet Merlot 2008, Central Victoria Red
Deep colour, big juicy black fruit on the nose. Very attractive creamy and forward fruit palate. Balanced oak and soft tannins. A very attractive drink.
£9.99 LNC

McPherson Curious Shiraz 2008, South Eastern Australia Red
Tutti frutti nose. Simple commercial palate, sweet well-made finish.
£5.49 LNC

Moppity Shiraz 2008, Hilltops Red
Smoky, earthy nose. Spiced red fruit on the palate - very pleasant.

Moss Wood Amy's 2008, Western Australia Red
Clean lift, varietal nose with greater fruit intensity on the palate, solid tannins, a keeper.
£13.99 JOB, LAY, WAIT

Nazaaray Estate Winery Pinot Noir Reserve 2008, Mornington Peninsula Red
Fine, elegant, gently perfumed. Good juicy fruit, very elegant. Plenty of flavour that lingers well. Very natural balance.

Nepenthe Tempranillo 2008, Adelaide Hills Red
Mid ruby, juicy, vibrant, black cherry fruit with a minty and intense vanilla oak balanced by lively acidity and grainy tannins.

Oxford Landing Grenache Shiraz Mourvèdre 2007, South Australia Red
Mid ruby, sweet fruited. Raspberry jam and vanilla oak. Juicy fruit, nicely balanced with good freshness and gentle tannins, pepper, spice and leathery notes.
£6.25

Palmer 2007, Margaret River Red
Big, rich wine with spice and fruit on the nose and palate. Generous weight and richness with soft acidity and moderate tannins. Good length.

Paper Eagle Linchpin 2007, McLaren Vale Red
Sweet berries on nose, slightly perfumed. Well-balanced.

Paxton Mv Shiraz 2008, McLaren Vale Red
Quite reduced, a bit baked with a certain creaminess. Rich texture and palate too with super sweet mid palate concentration. Touch of green tannins.

Penfolds Bin 2 Shiraz Mourvèdre 2008, South Australia Red
Pure blackberry fruit on nose and palate. Well-integrated tannins and will age. Great length.
£9.99 TESC

Penfolds Thomas Hyland Shiraz 2007, South Australia Red
Dark purple and ruby rim. Herbal, slight menthol, baked fruit. Nose comes through in mouth, long finish, black cherry.
£9.99 NSA, TESC

Penley Estate Hyland Shiraz 2008, South Australia Red
Good rich fruit. Elegant balance. Toasty oaky complexity. Generous fruit/oak balance. Long.
£13.50 MOR

Pertaringa Two Gentlemens Grenache 2008, South Australia Red
Jammy nose. Red fruits and some tannin. Pleasant.
£12.99 SWS

Peter Lehmann Futures 2007, South Australia Red
Chocolate and mocha on the nose with bright ripe blackcurrant fruit. Rich mouthful and a spicy finish.
£7.99 EHB, TESC, WAIT, VDV

Peter Lehmann Layers Red 2008, South Australia Red
Deep damson red. Hot, almost baked fruit nose. Rich, chocolate fruit. Good finish.
£5.99 EHB, TESC

Peter Lehmann Stonewell 2005, South Australia Red
Near opaque. Sweet fruit nose. Minty and slightly leafy. Good length.
£29.99 WAIT, VDV

Philip Shaw No 8 Pinot Noir 2007, New South Wales Red
Pinkish plum core. Judicious nose of oak and lingering strawberry flavour and creaminess. Beach like lushness. Good length and medium alcohol.
£20.90 ABS

Philip Shaw The Idiot Shiraz 2008, New South Wales Red
Plum, pepper, well-balanced, rich and juicy. Good length. Nice roasted coffee notes.
£10.87 ABS

Pike & Joyce Pinot Noir 2008, Adelaide Hills Red
Pale ruby. Hint aromas of crushed red berries and slightly smoky. Medium initial palate of fresh red berries and spicy oak. Well-balanced and drying tannins. Great length.
LEA, VDV

Pirramimma Stock's Hill Cabernet Merlot 2006, McLaren Vale Red
Deep, rich, almost raspberry-red hue. Soft, appealing fruity nose. Good, quite rich balanced fruity taste.

Primo Estate Zamberlan 2007, Clare Valley Red
Cassis fruit with a nutty, developing character. Structured tannins. Rich and long.
£15.99 AWC

Punt Road Cabernet Sauvignon 2008, Yarra Valley Red
Refined, elegant and pleasant. Good varietal character but more restrained. Long finish.
£12.99

Ringbolt Cabernet Sauvignon 2007, Western Australia Red
Massively powerful, minty and leafy on the nose, very rich with great depth.
£9.72 CAM, FLA, VKY, TESC

Rosily Vineyard Shiraz 2005, Margaret River Red

More Rhône in style. Quite classy and complex. Not at all the in-your-face fruit bomb style.

Running With Bulls 2008, Barossa Valley Red

Very pure blackberry and bilberry with good definition and freshness. A well-balanced palate, fresh and defined with a full-on liquorice finish.
£9.99 HAX, HOU, NDJ, NFW

Russell St Vincent Cabernet 2006, Barossa Valley Red

Lovely subdued summer fruits on the nose and a hint of green pepper. The palate is firm with good structure.

Russell The Victor Greenock Farm Shiraz 2006, Barossa Valley Red

Chocolate nose. Dark, lush, blackberry fruit. Good balance.

Rymill Coonawarra Shiraz 2006, Limestone Coast Red

Deep hue. Intense black cherry complex fruit. Lovely fruit and acid balance. Long.

Schild Estate Old Bush Vine Grenache Mourvèdre Shiraz 2009, South Australia Red

Oodles of juicy fruit and punchy pepperiness. Freshness on the palate. Very gentle tannins. Drink young.

Shaw and Smith Pinot Noir 2008, Adelaide Hills Red

Light colour. Sweet and elegant tannins. Pretty, sweet, cherry nose with integrated oak. Pretty and elegant. Lacks some complexity. A medium length.
£21.99 CAM, LIB, SL

Shaw Vineyard Estate Cabernet Merlot 2008, Canberra Red

Intense, slightly floral, oily cassis. Masses of fruit, tangy but angular. Tangy finish.

Sidewood Syrah 2008, Adelaide Hills Red

Sweet, ripe, juicy and simple with fresh berry fruits.
ADN

St Hallett Blackwell Shiraz 2006, Barossa Valley Red

Mouthfilling tannins, just enough acidity and loads of black cherry.
£13 BWL, SAIN

St Hallett Old Block Shiraz 2006, Barossa Valley Red

Closed, sweet ripe fruit to good finish. Youthful. Starts a bit short but pleasant.
£22.99 BWL, WAIT

St John's Road Blood & Courage Shiraz 2008, Barossa Valley Red

A subdued nose. Blackberry juice. Simple and enjoyable.

Starvedog Lane Shiraz Viognier 2008, Adelaide Hills Red

Minty, menthol edge to the nose. Dense, ripe palate.

Stella Bella Cabernet Sauvignon Merlot 2007, Margaret River Red

Ripe berry fruit aromas. Savoury and balanced fruit, tannin and acid though not enough depth. Elegant style and a savoury finish.
£15.00

Stuart Wines Whitebox Heathcote Shiraz 2007, Victoria Red

Creamy, pastille-like black fruit aromas which follow through on the palate. Earthy notes and fine tannin structure.

Tahbilk Cabernet Sauvignon 2006, Central Victoria Red
Light colour, juicy fruits on nose. Fruit bowl of savory flavours. Soft tannins and great length.
£13.99 EHL

Tahbilk Shiraz 2006, Central Victoria Red
Lots of slightly raw oak, some bright red fruit, loads of juicy raspberries. Lip-smacking, well-balanced, fresh finish.
£13.99 EHL

Tatachilla Asda Extra Special Shiraz 2008, McLaren Vale Red
Dry, blue/black fruit, nice source of aromatics with a hint of floral. Palate very dry. Super thick, vinous. A little lacking on charm.
£7.99 ASDA

The Standish Wine Company The Relic 2007, South Australia Red
Ripe pruney nose. Full, chunky chocolate, black cherry. Very long.
£75 SFW

Tidswell Heathfield Ridge 2006, Limestone Coast Red
Juicy fruit on nose, quite tight tannins. Green leafiness, juicy fruit, astringent and fresh.

Tim Adams Cabernet 2005, Clare Valley Red
Good structuring fruit and tannin. Cassis and warm berry fruit. Complex effect.
£11.99 AWC, OZW

Tim Adams Cabernet Malbec 2006, Clare Valley Red
Ripe, stalky hint. Grippy tannins and concentration. Good ripe extraction. Big.
£11.99 AWC, OZW

Tim Adams Shiraz 2006, Barossa Valley Red
Raspberry and mulberry aromas.
Peppery, slightly sooty flavours with raspberry and milk chocolate. Full, supple, fresh, slightly woody.
£10.99 TESC

Tim Adams The Aberfeldy 2006, Barossa Valley Red
Blackcurrant and gooseberry, mint and coffee on the nose. Full, rich, ripe blueberry fruit on the palate with spice and sandalwood. Big, but well-balanced with length and an appealing bitterness.
£27 AWC, TESC

Tim Adams The Fergus 2006, Clare Valley Red
Attractive example of Grenache. Sweet raspberry jam and mint aromas on nose, eucalyptus, raspberry, jam, white pepper. Attractive fruit very huge.
£10.99 TESC

Tintara Shiraz 2007, McLaren Vale Red
Sweet, black fruits - cassis especially. Creamy and richly flavoured.

Tintara Blewitt Springs Shiraz 2005, McLaren Vale Red
Chewy tough tannin core. Chewy spice and vanilla fruit. Tight.

Trevor Jones Wicked Witch Reserve Dry Grown Cabernet 2006, Barossa Valley Red
Very aromatic on the nose with minty eucalypt and stylish blackcurrant notes. Abundant ripe fruits on the palate. Good levels of tannin - characteristically Barossa.

Trevor Jones Wild Witch Shiraz 2006, Barossa Valley Red
Quite strong, oak dominates fruit experience. Quite rich and ripe yet holds taste well. Very tight and youthful. Firm tannins.

Vasse Felix Heytesbury 2007, Western Australia Red
Fresh and bright, a shade green but

with a long, blackcurrant fruit palate.
£31.89 EVW, FLA, WDI, WIE, VDV

Victory Point Cabernet Sauvignon 2007, Margaret River Red

Deep coloured. Complex youthful aromas. Dry tannins but underlying juicy fruit. Long savoury finish. Minty. Needs time.
BWE, CHO, MSW, PWS, VCR, VPW

Voyager Estate Cabernet Sauvignon Merlot 2005, Western Australia Red

Garnet colour, paling rim with medium depth. Blackcurrants, mocha and toasty spice. Toasty coffee aromas with blackcurrant backing. Well layered, smoky, toasty finish with lingering menthol.

Wakefield Eighty Acres Cabernet Shiraz Merlot 2007, Clare Valley Red

Cassis, cherry and plum fruits with liquorice notes. Nutty, savoury tannins. Balanced acidity.

Wakefield Jaraman Cabernet Sauvignon 2008, Clare Valley Red

Blackcurrants with lots of intensity. High tannic integrity. Fine tannins. Needs time but promising.

Wakefield Merlot 2008, Clare Valley Red

Ripe dark fruit, well-balanced with good substantial length.

Wakefield Promised Land Cabernet Sauvignon 2008, South Australia Red

Minty palate with blackcurrant. Gentle tannins and fair complexity.

Wakefield St Andrews Cabernet Sauvignon 2005, Clare Valley Red

Primary fruit and developed notes with a good balance.

Wakefield St Andrews Shiraz 2004, Clare Valley Red

Big, deep, bbq tinged nose. Quite savoury. Ripe entry on the palate. Finely balanced and suprisingly refined on the finish.

Walter Clappis The Hedonist Shiraz 2008, McLaren Vale Red

High acid structure, cooler climer fruit with elegant tannins and medium length.
£10.99 WAIT

Water Wheel Bendigo Cabernet Sauvignon 2008, Bendigo Red

Oak! Crawling all over the nose and palate. Tarry, black, embraced. Very full in style. High alcohol. Dusty with a dry finish.
£13 JWL, OZW, WAD

Water Wheel Memsie Homestead Red 2008, Bendigo Red

Sweet nose with blackberry, blueberry and menthol. Full-bodied and pure.
£10 JWL, OZW, WAD

Watershed Awakening Cabernet 2007, Margaret River Red

Bit of pencil sharpening along with the cassis on the nose. Smooth mouthfeel. Very competent.

Whistler Shiraz 2008, Barossa Valley Red

Sweet perfumed berries on nose. Lovely chocolate, leathery berries. Smooth with an oaky finish.

Whistler The Reserve Shiraz 2008, Barossa Valley Red
Oaky berries on nose. Rich, smooth, chocolate and leather. Nice tannic finish.

Willow Bridge Dragonfly Shiraz 2008, Geographe Red
Eucalyptus nose. Acid is supported by ripe black fruits of good depth. Supple and pleasant.

Willunga 100 Shiraz Viognier 2007, McLaren Vale Red
Clean, weighty fruit with earthy undertones. Dense, dark berries on the palate. Well-balanced.
£8.99 FAW, LIB

Willunga Creek Black Duck Merlot 2006, Fleurieu Red
Soft, open cherries, ripe blackberries and plums. Round tannins, well-balanced with a long fruity finish.

Wine By Brad Cabernet Merlot 2008, Western Australia Red
Menthol nose with hints of black fruits. Slightly firm tannins but integrated with the oak nicely, lacking fruit in the palate.

Wingara Asda Extra Special Coonawarra Cabernet 2006, Coonawarra Red
Plenty of grip and relaxed juicy fruit, tangy and lively. Long, svelte. Really nice, polished wine.
ASDA

Wirra Wirra Catapult 2007, McLaren Vale Red
Big ripe juicy red berry nose with some earthy, coffee notes. Plush berry on the palate with great length.
£10.99

Wisdom Creek Paragon Valley Premium Shiraz 2007, Barossa Valley Red
Herbal nose. Rich fruitcake palate with long green finish.

Wolf Blass Yellow Label Cabernet Sauvignon 2008, South Australia Red
Dark, sweet, red and black fruits - blackberry, some vanilla and spice notes. Smooth, rounded and very good intensity.
£9.29 Widely Available

Wolf Blass Yellow Label Shiraz 2008, South Australia Red
Ripe berries on nose. Pleasant and elegant.
£8.99 ASDA, TESC, MRN

Wonga Estate Heathcote Shiraz 2007, Heathcote Red
Cherry pie and cream nose. Firm tannins and sweet vanilla oak tones on the finish.

Woodside Valley Estate Baudin Cabernet Sauvignon 2007, Margaret River Red
Developed ruby colour; minty and blackcurrant aromas. Firm acidity, a little vegetal. Elegant savoury finish, bit shy.

Woop Woop The Black Chook Shiraz Viognier 2008, South Australia Red
Cigar box and mint on the nose. Ripe, clean black fruit on the palate with a touch of vanilla spice. Long.
FSE

Wyndham Estate Bin 555 Shiraz 2008, South Eastern Australia Red
Soft red fruit, honey & spice, tobacco, oak on the nose, slight jammy flavour with good length and balance.
£9.19 MRN

Yabby Lake Single Block Release Block 2 Pinot Noir 2008, Mornington Peninsula Red
Strawberry jam on nose. Typical Pinot flavour. Medium body. Lively tannins.

Yabby Lake Single Block Release Block 5 2008, Mornington Peninsula Red
Sweet red berry fruit, juicy and earthy. Slightly grainy tannins. Good mouthfeel, refreshing with a good finish.

Yalumba Shiraz Viognier 2008, Barossa Valley Red
Deep ruby. Dense black fruit and mint lift, smoky oak. Very refreshing palate with linen textured tannins. Nice bite.
£10.05 HOU, WDI, WIE, WVM

Zilzie Shiraz Viognier 2009, South Eastern Australia Red
Black cherry, some chocolate on the nose, full bodied, smooth spicy red fruit palate, rich ripe and long.
£7.99 ASDA

Zonte's Footstep Lake Doctor Shiraz Viognier 2008, Langhorne Creek Red
Warm, ripe and spicy fruit. Soft and plush. Integrated and long.
£8.99 CHA

Angove Family Winemakers Nine Vines Grenache Shiraz Rosé 2009, South Australia Rosé
Salmon pink and fresh raspberry jam on the nose. Fresh strawberry, raspberry palate with a fresh citrus finish.
£6.99 D&D

Armidale Estate Hill Grove Petit Verdot Rosé 2009, South Eastern Australia Rosé
Salmon pink and very pretty. Spicy nose with a fresh, zippy and dried spice palate. Full of ripe fruit. Drink now.
£7.08

Brown Brothers Moscato Rosa 2009, Victoria Rosé
Light salmon pink. Roses on the nose. Fruity palate. Delicate flavour. Well-balanced.
£6.49 WAIT

Cumulus Estate Rolling Pink 2009, New South Wales Rosé
Intense pink. Good fruit on the palate. Easy drinking style.
£9.99 IRV

De Bortoli DB Rosé 2009, Riverina Rosé
Salmon coloured with a jammy nose. Fresh and firm fruit on the palate with strawberry and red berry fruit. Hints of spice on the clean finish.

Brown Brothers Patricia Pinot Noir Chardonnay 2005, Victoria Sparkling
Clean, ripe, tropical nose; bready hints. Still youthful, good poise and grip. Lean with good quality and freshness. Well-balanced; quite structured.

Jansz Premium Vintage Cuveé 2005, Tasmania Sparkling
Very green on the nose. Nice balanced mouth. Good acidity and mousse.
£16.39 AWO, FLA, NYW, VDV

Brown Brothers Cienna Rosso NV, Victoria Sparkling Red
Very attractive nose. Distinctive high-toned pastille fruit. Big, deep, fruit packed palate developing chocolatey tones. Delightful sweet red.

Primo Estate Sparkling Red NV, McLaren Vale Sparkling Red
Good mousse. Medium intensity ruby damson and plum. Sweet fruit checked by tannic grip.
£28 AWC

De Bortoli Rococo Rosé NV, Yarra Valley Sparkling Rosé
Attractive nose of rhubarb,

creamy. Lively and fresh, sherberty fruit.

Jacob's Creek Sparkling Rosé NV, South Eastern Australia
Sparkling **Rosé**
Very vibrant, bright colour and nose with cherry and soft strawberry fruit. Nice long finish and simple.
£8.99 SAIN, TESC, MRN, WAIT

Casella Tesco Finest* Dessert Semillon 2005, Hunter Valley
Sweet
Straw colour with liquorice style. Good backbone.
TESC

McGuigan Botrytis Semillon 2005, Hunter Valley Sweet
Golden straw colour, beautiful lanolin nose with delicate perfume. Good acidity nicely balanced with fruit.

De Bortoli Deen Vat 5 Botrytis Semillon 2007, Riverina Botrytis
Deep golden straw colour, it shows some development and alcohol helps balance, with good fruit intensity.

Lerida Estate Lake George Botrytis Pinot Gris 2008,
Canberra Botrytis
Beautiful marmalade, caramel and peach hints. Balancing acidity, lovely mouthfeel without cloying. Elegant.

McWilliams Morning Light 2007, South Eastern Australia
Botrytis
White peach and nectarine on nose, orange and rose petals flavours on palate with good acidity, a big mouthful.

Yalumba Hand Picked Botrytis Viognier 2008, South Australia Botrytis
Bright gold and very pretty. Waxy honey with nutmeg on the nose. Medium sweet, but with good, sharp acidity and fresh citrus finish.
£10.55 FLA, WIE, WIL

All Saints Estate Classic Rutherglen Muscat NV, Victoria Fortified
Orange-amber core. Pungent raisins, cough candy twists and vanilla. Very smooth with a polished finish.
£10.99 IRV

De Bortoli Show Liqueur Muscat NV, Riverina Fortified
Dark Demerara colour. Treacly consistency. Very creamy.

Austria

Austria often seems like one of the wine trade's little secrets – a trove of vinous treasures like Grüner Veltliner, Riesling and Zweigelt that, despite their excellence, remain a niche interest. They may not be cheap, but great wines rarely are, and Austria can compete with the best of them. These wines share something in common with Vienna herself: that fine balance of grandeur and modernity, sophistication and congeniality. Grüner Veltliner deserves special mention as the country's own home-grown variety, with its unique white pepper scent and fresh, bracing citrus fruit. Whether you are tiring of the mainstream styles or not, Austrian wine is eminently worth exploring.

KEY FACTS

Total production
2.5m hectolitres

Total vineyard
51,000ha

Top regions
Niederösterreich, which includes:
Wachau
Kremstal
Kamptal
Wagram
Weinvertel
Burgenland, which includes:
  Neusiedlersee
  Neusiedlersee-Hügelland
  Mittelburgenland
  Südburgenland
Steiermark, which includes:
  Weststeiermark
  Südsteiermark
  Südoststeiermark
Wien

Top 10 grapes
1 Grüner Veltliner
2 Welschriesling
3 Müller-Thurgau
4 Weissburgunder
5 Weisser Riesling
6 Zweigelt
7 Blaufränkisch
8 Blauer Portugieser
9 Blauburger
10 Blauer Wildbacher

2010 IWC PERFORMANCE

Trophies	6
Gold	18
Silver	34
Bronze	46

Rabl Grüner Veltliner Kaeferberg Reserve 2008, Kamptal White

Lots of mineral character on the nose. Fresh, clean apple fruit with a touch of citrus and lemon peel character. Refreshing and clean on the finish. Delicious.
£17.99 HLD

 AUSTRIAN DRY WHITE TROPHY, GRÜNER VELTLINER TROPHY

Türk Erlesenes Vom Grüner Veltliner 2008, Niederösterreich White

Fresh with a lively lemon nose. Honeyed and rich on the palate with a touch of nuttiness and waxy texture. Full and round style with layers of freshness. Nicely complex, delicious.

 **INTERNATIONAL SWEET MUSCAT TROPHY, AUSTRIAN SWEET MUSCAT TROPHY**

Hans Tschida Muskat Ottonel Schilfwein 2006, Neusiedlersee Sweet

Very rich with hazelnuts and caramel flavours. Excellent balance and lovely finish.

Höpler Noble Reserve 2007, Burgenland Sweet

Golden yellow, vanilla, crème brulée nose. Soft attack with clean apricot fruit on the palate.

> **DID YOU KNOW?**
> There are only 281 Masters of Wine in the world. More people have been into outer space!

Fresh with hints of warm spice, medium intensity with good depth and botrytis character.

 **AUSTRIAN ICE WINE TROPHY**

Türk Eiswein Vom Grünen Veltliner 2008, Niederösterreich Sweet

Honey, sweet grapefruit nose. Honest, sweet citrus aromas, enough acid to carry the rich sweetness. Very nice length.

Erwin Beck Sämling 2007, Neusiedlersee Botrytis

Well-balanced with a lusciously sweet aroma. Ripe peach and caramelised orange on the palate. Pure, with good depth and ripe sweetness. Long and fresh on the finish.

 **AUSTRIAN CHARDONNAY TROPHY**

Hans & Christine Nittnaus Essenz Trockenbeerenauslese 2005, Neusiedlersee Botrytis

A very elegant and delicious wine. Complex aromas of vanilla, lime, honeysuckle and citrus. Excellent balance.

Hans Tschida Sämling Trockenbeerenauslese 2004, Neusiedlersee Botrytis

Deep pale gold in colour, explosive and opulent with caramelised orange zest and apricot compote. Delicious and well-balanced with a caramelised finish.

Hans Tschida Sämling Trockenbeerenauslese 2005, Neusiedlersee Botrytis

Golden, very intense with barley sugar and honey nose. Intense concentration with apricot essence and citrus ripeness. Long and fresh on the finish.

Hans Tschida Sämling Trockenbeerenauslese 2006, Neusiedlersee Botrytis
Pale with a prim, elegant nose. Intensely sweet and rich with cream vanilla overtones. Hints of crème brulée, with the perfect amount of acidity on the finish.

 CHAMPION SWEET, AUSTRIAN SWEET TROPHY

Hans Tschida Sämling Trockenbeerenauslese 2007, Neusiedlersee Botrytis
Elegant and nutty with a touch of crunchy apricot aromas. Almond and marmalade notes on the palate with fresh citrus notes. Lush and long.

Hermann Fink Chardonnay Trockenbeerenauslese 2008, Burgenland Botrytis
Lovely fresh apricot and orange peel aromas. Rich, silky layers of fruit integrate with the acidity giving a wine that is sweet and luscious with fantastic freshness and balance.

Kracher No.3 Zwischen Den Seen Trockenbeerenauslese 2007, Burgenland Botrytis
Elegant, fresh and floral on the nose. Intensely sweet with cream and vanilla overtones. Hints of crème brulée, very fresh with a crisp citrus finish. Long and lush with good intensity.
£28.99 NYW

Kracher No.6 Grande Cuvée Trockenbeerenauslese 2007, Burgenland Botrytis
Marmalade and honeyed orange on the nose. Intense, with tightly packed fruit, hints of orange with warming spice character. Deep and rich with long finish.
£34.95

Kracher No.7 Zwischen Den Seen Trockenbeerenauslese 2007, Burgenland Botrytis
Light citrus and lemon peel on the nose. Orange, honey and candied peel on the palate full of vanilla and warm spice. Long and lingering.
£34.95

Kracher No.9 Zwischen Den Seen Trockenbeerenauslese 2007, Burgenland Botrytis
Intense and spicy, very fresh. Apricot and grapefruit with rich and heavy floral tones. Long and very ripe with a clear and bright orange finish. Delicious.
£35.99

Lenz Moser Prestige Beerenauslese 2007, Burgenland Botrytis
Medium yellow gold, with hints of earthy botrytis nose. Sweet, but balanced soft fruits with good acidity and clean, long finish.
£9.79

 KAMPTAL BOTRYTIS TROPHY

Rabl Riesling Trockenbeerenauslese 2007, Kamptal Botrytis
Exotic nose with pear, fig, orange and pineapple following through to the palate. Great acidity and a long honeyed finish.
£37.99 HLD

SILVER

Allram Grauburgunder Hasel 2008, Lower Austria White
Mineral and spice nose. Moderate acid and spicy, feisty fruit. Good

depth of flavours and length.
£13.50 TWK

Allram Riesling Zöbinger Heiligenstein 2008, Lower Austria White
Clean aromas, elegant tropicality with hints of lemon and lime. On the palate, apple and citrus fruit with a touch of floral complexity. Persistent and elegant on the finish.
£13.00

Baumgartner Grüner Veltliner Prestige 2009, Niederösterreich White
Bright, floral nose with a hint of lemon citrus. Lemon custard and cream on the palate with a touch of spice on the finish. Very clean and fresh, most pleasing.

Domäne Wachau Grüner Veltliner Smaragd Achleiten 2009, Wachau White
Flowered, citrus nose with a touch of green. Grapefruit sherbet, good depth supported by ripe green pepper character. Rich and delicious.
£16.49 WAIT

Fred Loimer Riesling Langenlois Terrassen Kamptal Reserve 2008, Niederösterreich White
Clean nose with red apple fruit aromas. Crisp acidity with good depth. Deliciously ripe and long on the palate. Persistent and delicious.
£17.99 WAIT

Johann Donabaum Grüner Veltliner Smaragd Spitzer Point 2008, Wachau White
Expressive pineapple/peachy aroma. A well-balanced spicy fruity wine with a lingering finish.
£20.00 NOV

Johann Donabaum Riesling Smaragd Setzberg 2008,

Wachau White
Rich, warm and spicy apricot with a floral nose. Good weighty palate of stone fruits and spice with a balanced, zippy structure. Lovely crisp finish.
£28.99 NOV

Jurtschitsch Riesling Heiligenstein Alte Reben 2008, Kamptal White
Floral, peach and mineral nose. High acid supported on peachy palate. Nice depth of flavour.
£23.99 EVW, UNC

Kurt Angerer Grüner Veltliner Eichenstaude 2008, Niederösterreich White
Citrus ripeness and white pepper on the nose. Bracing acidity and spicy, ripe apple flavours on the palate. Lemony fresh with a touch of earthy nuttiness on the finish.
£14.00 NYW

Kurt Angerer Grüner Veltliner Loam 2008, Niederösterreich White
Lots of minerality with ripe apple and pear fruits on the palate. Weighty with good structure and fresh, clean, expressive fruit. Long and lingering finish.
NYW

Laurenz V Charming Grüner Veltliner 2008, Kamptal White
Flint and steel on the nose with fresh green apple fruit on the palate. Layers of richness with ripe citrus and lively topicality. Zesty and refreshing with racy acidity on the finish.
£35.00 BWL, WAIT

Laurenz V Silver Bullet Grüner Veltliner 2008, Lower Austria White
Showing good development with a complex mushroom and

undergrowth nose. Rich and ripe with good weight and structure. The palate is fresh with citrus but also has beautiful complexity.
£12.99

Mehofer-Neudeggerhof Grüner Veltliner Wadenthal 2008, Wagram White

Well-balanced and approachable with a tropical, citrus fruit nose. On the palate, creamy lemon and tropical fruit with a touch of peppery spice. Round, fresh and clean.

Pfaffl Haidviertel 2009, Weinviertel White

Bright orange peel nose. Very tropical on the palate with crunchy citrus fruit, white pepper and cream. The finish is long with a touch of lemon custard.
£11.97

Rabl Riesling Schenkenbichl Reserve 2008, Kamptal White

Clean apple aromas with a fresh pear-drop nose. Lush on the palate with pear and floral flavours. Ripe with a full mouthfeel, nicely balanced complexity.
£18.99 HLD, WAIT

Rotes Haus Grüner Veltliner Ried Obere Schos 2008, Vienna White

Delicate floral nose with loads of tropical fruit. Very ripe and round on the palate with well-balanced citrus and tropical fruit. The finish is clean and crisp with long length.

The Dot Austrian Pepper Grüner Veltliner 2009, Niederösterreich White

Bright and crisp with loads of tropical fruit on the mid-palate. Ripe and round with a tropical, white pepper finish. Long and vibrant.

Türk Grüner Veltliner Frechau 2008, Niederösterreich White

Honey and nuttiness on the nose with ripe pear aromas. Lovely and lush with juicy pear fruit on the palate. White pepper and tangy sweetness are layered with zesty citrus fruit. Appetising and delicate on the finish.

Türk Grüner Veltliner Vom Urgestein 2009, Niederösterreich White

Fresh, succulent fruit on the nose. Lots of juicy lemon-lime fruit on the palate with lovely orange blossom character. The fruit is tangy with lively acidity. Long finish.

Walter Skoff Sauvignon Blanc Royal 2007, Südsteiermark White

Quite round with capsicum and green pea on the palate. Ripe apple, pear and spice, balanced with a fresh and lifted finish.

Willi Bründlmayer Riesling Steinmassel 2008, Kamptal White

Pure with good depth of tropical and citrus aromas. Balanced fruit with racy acidity. Long, fresh lime finish.

Josef Sailer Blaufränkisch Wulka 2007, Burgenland Red

Whiff of volatility, with a spicy chewy edge. Palate savoury, drying out slightly. Complex and mature.

Esterházy Cuvée Trockenbeerenauslese 2008, Burgenland Sweet

Fragrant with floral blossom and ripe citrus fruit. Soft, ripe fruit on the palate with jammy marmalade finish.

Hans & Christine Nittnaus Pinorama Trockenbeerenauslese 2001, Neusiedlersee Botrytis

Honeysuckle and citrus aromas. Good acid and a soft, long finish.

Hans & Christine Nittnaus Sämling 88 Trockenbeerenauslese 2006, Neusiedlersee Botrytis
Deep and sweet, opulent with some nutty almond character. Tropical fruit and orange peel on the palate with seductive flavoured. Well-balanced and long.

Hans Tschida Chardonnay Trockenbeerenauslese 2005, Neusiedlersee Botrytis
Complex nose showing strong botrytis and caramel characters. Candied lemon and a hint of melon. Rich and balanced.

Hans Tschida Chardonnay Trockenbeerenauslese 2007, Neusiedlersee Botrytis
Apple and marzipan aromas. Fresh honeyed palate with an intense lingering finish.

Hans Tschida Sämling Beerenauslese 2007, Neusiedlersee Botrytis
Pale to medium gold. Refined fragrance on nose. Ripe melons and peaches. Fresh finish.

Hermann Fink Chardonnay Trockenbeerenauslese 2007, Burgenland Botrytis
Custard, apricots on the nose. Very pure and sweet with fabulous texture and a fresh ripe finish.

Kracher No. 10 Nouvelle Vague Trockenbeerenauslese 2007, Burgenland Botrytis
Complex mineral and quince and marmalade on the nose. Opulent, honeyed palate.
£37.99

Kracher No.2 Nouvelle Vague Trockenbeerenauslese 2007, Burgenland Botrytis
Honeyed and perfumed with lots of lychee aroma. Lovely

waxy texture with buttery, rich opulence.
£28.99

Kracher No.8 Nouvelle Vague Trockenbeerenauslese 2007, Burgenland Botrytis
Rich, honeyed, tropical fruit and vanilla nose. Ginger influence on the palate. Irresistible.
£34.95

Kroiss Chardonnay Trockenbeerenauslese Essenz 2006, Burgenland Botrytis
Candied citrus flavours with pineapple and orange peel. Very good acidity balancing the sweetness.

Lenz Moser Prestige Trockenbeerenauslese 2007, Burgenland Botrytis
Excellent balance of acid and sweetness. Vibrant fresh fruit with a rich honeyed finish.
£14.79

Domäne Wachau Grüner Veltliner Federspiel Weissenkirchen 2009, Wachau White
Bright, shimmering in glass. Focused nose of lithe green apple and pear. Big mouthfeel and soft, bright palate of fruits, and a touch of minerality.

Domäne Wachau Grüner Veltliner Terraces 2009, Wachau White
Aromatic, warm, candied fruit nose. Structured mineral palate. Zippy fresh finish.
£7.99 WAIT

Ferdinand Mayr Grüner Veltliner Na Alsdann 2009, Niederösterreich White
Pale lemon with a gentle white pepper nose. Bright and tropical

notes on the palate with a citrus fresh finish.
£6.99

Fred Loimer Langenlois Käferberg Kamptal Reserve 2008, Niederösterreich
White
Clean and supple citrus aromas on the nose, mineral freshness on the palate. Long and refreshing on the finish.
£31.99 LIB, WDR

Fred Loimer Riesling Kamptal 2009, Niederösterreich
White
Restrained nose with a hint of lime. Piercing acidity with a fresh apple and lime flower finish.
£12.99 LIB, SMP, WDR

Gerhard Wohlmuth Gewürztraminer Steinriegel 2009, Styria White
Bright, floral citrus nose, rose petals and nettle lychee, mineral notes, aromatic, intense and very good balance.
£11.80 HOP

Gerhard Wohlmuth Pinot Gris Gola Privat 2008, Styria
White
Ripe apricot on the nose with hints of white flower. On the palate the fruit is supple, round and quite intense. Very attractive and moreish.
£15.90 HOP

Gerhard Wohlmuth Sauvignion Blanc Kisl 2009, Styria White
Greengage and kiwi fruit on the nose. Mineral on the palate with a juicy attack, excellent fruit and freshness.
£17.55 HOP

Heinrich Hartl Rotgipfler 2008, Thermenregion White
Fine herbal, perfumed spice nose, high acid, good length.
£12.00 CEE, KIT, MWD, WAIT

Johann Donabaum Grüner Veltliner Smaragd Berglage 2008, Wachau White
Deep straw colour and muted floral aroma. One dimensional with a green leaf finish.
£23.00 NOV

Jurtschitsch Grüner Veltliner Dechant Alte Reben 2008, Kamptal White
Clean, spicy nose. Palate is ripe with well-balanced fruit. Ripe lemon and lime on the finish with a touch of sweetness.
£19.99 CSS, HDS, JCC, PUS

Kurt Angerer Riesling Ametzberg 2009, Niederösterreich White
Lemony with a touch of floral character. White fruit with attractive ripe citrus. Lingering and fresh on the finish.

Lenz Moser Prestige Grüner Veltliner 2009, Niederösterreich White
Floral grapefruit and lime on the nose. Lemon-lime with ripe apple and a touch of warm spice on the palate.
£8.99

Mayer Am Pfarrplatz Riesling Nussberg 2008, Vienna White
Hint of minerality on the nose with a ripe citrus palate. Good and weighty with a lingering finish.

Pfaffl Hundsleiten Grüner Veltliner Weinviertel Reserve 2009, Niederösterreich
White
Lemon-lime aromas with a touch of warm spice. Lime-like on the palate with juicy character. Approachable and delicious.
£15.87

Reinmund Reiterer Weisser Burgunder 2009, Südsteiermark White
Fresh blossom nose, pears and kernel notes with ripe melon and white stone fruit. Spicy and warming on the palate with good complexity and nice varietal character. Very fresh, zesty and lingering on the finish.

Roland Horvath Roland One Grüner Veltliner 2008, Kamptal White
Citrus, lime and ripe pepper on the nose. Bright and lifted citrus flavours with good depth of green pepper and peachy fruit.

Roland Horvath Roland One Riesling 2008, Kamptal White
Light and fresh with ripe apple character. Clean and refreshing on the palate. Easy to drink.

Rotes Haus Gemischter Satz Reserve 2008, Vienna White
Aromatic lemon and custard, Turkish delight with racy acidity. Very nicely balanced.

Sepp Moser Breiter Rain 2008, Kremstal White
Fresh with lemon-lime aromas. Palate is fresh with good balance of ripe fruit and acidity. Zippy with a clean finish.
£18.00 PBA

Sepp Moser Grüner Veltliner 2009, Kremstal White
Lightly floral and honeyed nuances. Quite light with a hint of nutty richness. Lively and zesty on the finish.
£7.99 PBA

Türk Grüner Veltliner Thurnerberg 2008, Niederösterreich White
Toffee aromas with ripe pear and melon. The flavours are quite long with delicate layers of crisp citrus and ripe apple. Sweet and fine fruit on the finish. Delicious.

W Baumgartner Gewürztraminer 2009, Burgenland White
Fresh aromatic on the nose and palate. Long finish.

Waldschütz Grüner Veltliner Aturo Kamptal Reserve 2008, Kamptal White
Lightly aromatic with hints of lemon citrus and lime flower. Ripe and racy on the palate. Good length.

Waldschütz Grüner Veltliner Stangl 2008, Kamptal White
Fresh, clean and zesty. Lime acidity, green apple fruit and a zippy, fresh finish.

Walter Skoff Sauvignon Blanc Single Vineyard Hochsulz 2008, Südsteiermark White
Pale lemon green with bright, grassy fruit on the nose. Lovely and fresh on the palate with a hint of apricot and elderflower on the finish.

Willi Bründlmayer Grüner Veltliner Berg Vogelsang 2009, Kamptal White
Apple blossom and flower on the nose. Delicate apple fruit on the palate. Warm and lingering on the finish.
£14.99 WAIT

Esterházy Estoras 2008, Burgenland Red
Mid deep purple colour. Spicy blue fruit aromas. Huge extract of dry fruit. Grippy and dried out on the finish.

Esterházy Tesoro 2007, Burgenland Red
Creamy oak overlay to the fresh berry fruits nose. The palate is

bright and berryish with a plum edge.

Harald Kraft Red Magic 2006, Burgenland Red
Blueberry, plum and blackberry fruits with spice on nose. Good, rich intensity. Savoury hints and developed complexity with integrated firm toasted palate. Very enjoyable.

Heinrich Hartl Pinot Noir Classic 2008, Thermenregion Red
Simple juicy fruits with some meaty secondary aromas. Palate - soft red fruits and soft tannins.
£14.70 CEE, KIT, MWD

Marianne Hahnekamp Sonnensteig 2007, Burgenland Red
Berry fruits. Currant and strawberry palate. Racy but juicy. Better texture than most.

Pfaffl Altenberg St. Laurent 2007, Niederösterreich Red
Opulent aroma. Good depth of dark fruit with supporting acidity. Very nice, long length.
£21.13

Schloss Halbturn Impérial Red 2007, Burgenland Red
Earthy black fruit nose. Long and balanced.

Schloss Halbturn Kœnigsegg Zweigelt Reserve 2008, Burgenland Red
Ripe, vibrant blackberry and black plums. smoky, meaty palate. Dry, austere finish but fresh.

The Dot Austrian Cherry Zweigelt 2009, Niederösterreich Red
Mid pale colour. Strawberry-ish fruit scents with some spice hints. Hollow-ish fruit flavours, mid length finish.

Wellanschitz Hussi 2007, Burgenland Red
Cool, closed fruit aroma. Raspberry-ish characters. Sour and savoury.

Wellanschitz Well 2007, Burgenland Red
Some spicy oak and balanced fruit aromas. High acidity and fresh fruit flavours. Fairly simple.

Lenz Moser Fête Rosé 2009, Niederösterreich Rosé
Very pale pink. Light and fruity, quite subtle with nicely balanced red berry fruit and citrus freshness.

Felberjörgl Strohwein Florian´s Essenz Nr.1 2006, Südsteiermark Sweet
Passionfruit, figs with ripe tropical flavours. Peppery with fresh acidity and heavy sweetness on the finish.

Gritsch Mauritiushof Riesling Vision Wachau Reserve 2007, Wachau Sweet
Good Riesling nose, honey with citrus notes, medium weight at the palate, hint of grapefruit.
SVG

Hans & Christine Nittnaus Rheinriesling Beerenauslese 2008, Neusiedlersee Botrytis
Pale lemon with a touch of mushroom fresh nuttiness on the nose. High floral notes with clean and ripe fruit on the palate.

Josef Umathum Chardonnay Trockenbeerenauslese 2004, Burgenland Botrytis
Juicy fruit aromas. Tangy marmalade and apricot flavours. Ripe and very delicious with good balance and freshness on the finish.
£19.00

Kracher Cuvée Beerenauslese 2007, Burgenland Botrytis
Medium yellow gold with nice

vanilla and earthy aromas. Truffle and toasty cheese flavours with medium intensity, good length.
£13.50 BUT, HVN, NYW, SEL, TAN

Kracher Lenz No.1 Trockenbeerenauslese 2007, Burgenland Botrytis
Mineral nose with hints of

peach and ginger. Nice freshness, good balance.
£27.99 NYW

Kracher No.4 Nouvelle Vague Trockenbeerenauslese 2007, Burgenland Botrytis
Subtle, savoury redcurrant aromas. Very sweet candied fruit is balanced by the savoury character.
£30.99

Chile

Chile suffered a massive 8.8 earthquake in February this year, which seriously damaged some parts of the wine industry, especially in areas closes to the epicentre, such as Bio-Bio, Maule, Curico and Cauquenes. Around 125 million litres of wine were lost, but the industry was able to repair itself remarkably quickly and there is now the same feeling of positivity in Chile as there always was. Certainly, the quality and breadth of wine available is cause for good cheer: Chile is continuing to push the frontiers of viticulture, experimenting with varieties in exciting new terroirs and producing delightfully nuanced wines. Check out their exciting examples of Syrah, Pinot Noir, Riesling and Chardonnay to taste the evidence for yourself.

KEY FACTS

Total production
7.038m hectolitres
(wine with D.O.)

Total vineyard
116,795ha

Top 10 grapes
1 Cabernet Sauvignon
2 Pais
3 Merlot
4 Sauvignon Blanc
5 Chardonnay
6 Carmenère
7 Muscat
8 Syrah
9 Pinot Noir
10 Cabernet Franc

Top regions
1 Maule
2 Colchagua
3 Curicó
4 Cachapoal
5 Maipo
6 Itata
7 Bío Bío
8 Limarí
9 Aconcagua

Producers
Approx 350

2010 IWC PERFORMANCE

Trophies	6
Gold	23
Silver	90
Bronze	165
Great Value Awards	2

Arboleda Chardonnay 2008, Aconcagua Valley White

Nutty, buttery and biscuit characters, mouthfilling and complex with a fat leesy palate - excellent.
£9.99

El Aromo Barrel Selection Chardonnay 2009, Maule Valley White

Buttery colour with lovely, complex nose and palate. A tropical fruit spectrum with well-integrated oak is balanced by steely minerality leading to a long, rewarding finish.
£13.99 TGW

Louis Felipe Edwards Sauvignon Blanc 2009, Leyda Valley White

Green on the nose. Ripe citrus, passionfruit and a tinge of citrusy-pineapple on the palate. Acidity is well-balanced and fruit has good depth and plenty of character. Long and very supple on the finish.
£7.99 CWS

Quintay Q Chardonnay 2008, Casablanca Valley White

Greengage nose. Lovely sunshine fruit with tropical flavours on the palate. Well-balanced and deliciously fresh, with ripe fruit and lovely citrus character on the finish. Long and lush. Drinking well.

Apaltagua Carmenère Reserve 2008, Colchagua Valley Red

Deep ruby. Smoky and leafy fragrance. Tomato leaf and raspberry fruit. Juicy palate, good freshness and nice use of vanilla.
£6.99 ABY

Apaltagua Signature Cabernet Sauvignon 2008,

Colchagua Valley Red

Good colour, lovely fruit acid and tannin balance. Savoury finish. Understated and elegant.
£10.99 ABY

Casas Del Bosque Carmenère Reserva 2009, Casablanca Valley Red

Aromatic nose with damson dominating with balanced acidity and soft tannins. Plum and dark fruit. Long finish.

 INTERNATIONAL MERLOT TROPHY, CENTRAL VALLEY TROPHY

Concha Y Toro Marques De Casa Concha Merlot 2007, Central Valley Red

Super aromas. Elegant, clean, spicy notes. Toffee and coffee notes with cherry. Big body. Very expressive balsamic taste. Great wine with big potential.

 RAPEL VALLEY TROPHY

Concha Y Toro Terrunyo Carmenère 2007, Rapel Valley Red

Black fruits on the nose, lightly oaked with concentrated dark cherry fruits. Fresh with a leafy character. Well-balanced with good tannin structure and generous flavours on the finish.

 CHILEAN PINOT NOIR TROPHY, CASABLANCA VALLEY TROPHY

Cono Sur Ocio Pinot Noir 2008, Casablanca Valley Red

Smoky, earthy beetroot character. Deliciously light and balanced with wonderful tannic

structure caging the fruit.
Well done.
WAIT

Emiliana G 2005, Rapel Valley Red

Ripe, blackcurrant leaf on the nose. Quite savoury with a generous mix of black olive and black forest fruits. Ripe, fresh and clean with lingering tannins and a drying finish.
£33.99 PBA

 ELQUI VALLEY TROPHY

Falernia Antakari Carmenère Syrah 2008, Elqui Valley Red

Opaque, elegant peony, strawberry aroma. Smooth mouthfeel and ripe fruit on mid palate and long finish.
£7.49

Korta Bucarey Barrel Selection Cabernet Sauvignon 2008, Curicó Red

Lovely nose. Good flavour. Masses of fruit. Very long and good tannin structure. Excellent!

 CHILEAN SYRAH TROPHY

Matetic EQ Syrah 2008, San Antonio Valley Red

Rich colours. Spicy, herbal, pepper aromas - balanced palate. Some complexity, cooler climate savoury aromatics and length. Rhone style. Brilliant.
£18.00 GNS, MAJ, WSO

Perez Cruz 2007, Aconcagua Valley Red

Deep red, violets, subtle nose. Spicy fruit palate. Fairly long vanilla finish.
£12.99 NOV

San Pedro Reserva Castillo De Molina Shiraz 2008, Maule Valley Red

Rhubarb and black cherry on the nose. Showing some developed character with hints of vegetal overtones. Lush, ripe black cherry palate laced with vanilla spice. Soft, supple and long.

Santa Rita Medalla Real Cabernet Sauvignon 2007, Maipo Valley Red

A complex bouquet of fruit and perfumed oak. Subtle and elegant palate with a good balance of fruit, oak and acid. A lingering finish yet a touch chalky.
£9.99

Santa Rita Medalla Real Carmenère 2008, Maipo Valley Red

Red fruit present. Good balanced ripe fruit and chocolate. Long finish.
£9.99

Santa Rita Medalla Real Pinot Noir 2008, Maipo Valley Red

Light ruby. Good intensity. Seductive violet and spice nose. Definite oak. Ripe, sweet fruit with balance. A touch hot on finish.
£9.99

Tabalí Reserva Especial Red Blend 2008, Limarí Valley Red

Inky pink. Cassis and sweet oak. Velvety texture and core. Cassis fruit firm but ripe. Long and powerful.
PBA

Tarapaca Gran Reserva Carmenère 2008, Maipo Valley Red

Dark, currants, herbal and lots of grippy tannin. Some sweet fruit. Long and chewy.
£8.99

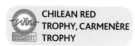

CHILEAN RED TROPHY, CARMENÈRE TROPHY

Terranoble Gran Reserva Carmenère 2007, Maule Valley Red
Lovely, rich, ripe sweet oaky berries on nose, following through on palate with leather and chocolate. PIM

Vistamar Late Harvest Moscatel 2009, Limarí Valley Sweet
Lemon and lime flavours. Very clean and pure with bracing acidity.

Caliterra Tributo Sauvignon Blanc 2009, Leyda Valley White
Ripe and savoury with delicate nettle fruit on the nose. Ripe citrus with good structure and rounded tropical fruit on the finish. Lively and lengthy.
£8.99

Concha Y Toro Amelia Chardonnay 2008, Casablanca Valley White
Good, fresh citrus notes on the nose. A bit more delicate on the palate but acidity is nicely balanced and the finish is long.

Concha Y Toro Casillero Del Diablo Viognier 2009, Casablanca Valley White
Fresh with youthful, zesty fruit aromas. On the palate, citrus and melon with intense white blossoms. Note of spritz, fresh fruit and good lift. Nice and easy drinking.
£7.49 MRN

Concha Y Toro Marques De Casa Concha Chardonnay 2008, Limarí Valley White
Tropical (guava, passionfruit) with bright oak presence. Lemon rind and floral.

Cono Sur Reserva Chardonnay 2008, Casablanca Valley White
Flinty nose with a fresh mineral palate. Easy-going style with ripe fruit, peachy with citrus freshness. Long and fresh on the finish.

Cono Sur Reserva Gewürztraminer 2009, Colchagua Valley White
Tropical fruits on the nose. Attractive peaches and lychees on the palate.

Cono Sur The Loose Goose Sauvignon Blanc 2009, San Antonio Valley White
Pale lemon green in colour. Intensely grassy. Fresh apple and bright with a mineral accent. Well defined.
£6.99 LAI

De Martino Legado Chardonnay 2008, Limarí Valley White
Full, leesy creamy, hazelnut nose, a full ripe texture, flavours of melon and peach supported by good acidity, leading to a long finish.
£8.99 BWC

Errazuriz Max Reserva Chardonnay 2008, Casablanca Valley White
Oak dominates the nose with caramel apples on the palate. Some good acidity with well-balanced fruit and a broad finish.
£9.49

Maycas Del Limarí Reserva Chardonnay 2008, Limarí Valley White
Lovely fresh pineapple and peach

fruits. Bracing lime acidity. Clean fruits with a zingy finish.

Maycas Del Limarí Reserva Especial Chardonnay 2008, Limarí Valley White

Pale lemon colour. Appealing tart Chardonnay fruit. Light, good fruit. Balanced wood finish.
£12.99 WAIT

Quintay Q Sauvignon Blanc 2009, Casablanca Valley White

Nice nettle notes on the nose. Complex with a tinge of passionfruit ripeness. Lightly tropical with a zesty citrus finish. Lively and well-balanced with long length.

Santa Carolina Reserva Sauvignon Blanc 2009, Leyda Valley White

Passionfruit on the nose with a touch of ripe citrus. Gentle ripeness and melon fruit character on the palate. Hints of minerality with lingering complexity on the finish.
£7.99

Valdivieso Reserva Sauvignon Blanc 2009, Leyda Valley White

Fresh nose with strong citrus character. Lime and lemon mingle with ripe melon and fresh apple on the palate. Nice balance and length.
£8.99

Viña Leyda Costero Riesling 2009, Leyda Valley White

Delicate, fresh aromas. Fragrant florals. Lovely acidity and length. Will keep.
£8.99 MWW

Viña Leyda Lot 5 Wild Yeasts Chardonnay 2008, Leyda Valley White

Star-bright, pale lemon. Woody fruit. Rich tasty fruit with good depth.

Viña Leyda Marks & Spencer Secano Estate Sauvignon Blanc 2009, Leyda Valley White

Restrained nose of floral and citrus character. Good citrus acidity on the palate with a long, lingering ripe citrus finish. Well-balanced and clean.
£7.49 M&S

Viña Leyda Marks & Spencer Secano Estate Sauvignon Gris 2009, Leyda Valley White

Lemony fresh, bright fruit with good balance. Very fresh citrus on the palate and hints of tropicality. Zesty finish with well-balanced fruit thoughout.
£7.49 M&S

Viña Leyda Single Vineyard Sauvignon Gris Kadun 2009, Leyda Valley White

Very pale herbal, leafy nose. Soft attack, clean. Mint green with a slightly hard finish and no fruit.
£9.50 GWW, HOT, ODD, WSO

Bisquertt La Joya Syrah Reserve 2008, Colchagua Valley Red

Squishy blackberries and ripe red fruits on the palate. Weighty fruit with good body and balance. Ripe tannins on the finish with long, lingering freshness.

Bisquertt Q Clay Gran Reserve Cabernet Sauvignon 2007, Colchagua Valley Red

Coconut and black fruits on the nose, lovely intensity and extraction, balanced, fresh acidity.

Bisquertt Q Clay Gran Reserve Merlot 2007, Colchagua Valley Red

Green peppers, black cherry and plum. Medium acidity. Integrated tannins.

Bravado Kimbao Cabernet Sauvignon Carmenère 2008, Central Valley Red
Lovely cassis and cedar notes. Tannins body giving, well-balanced.
£8.99 NKW

Canepa Finisimo Cabernet Sauvignon 2007, Colchagua Valley Red
Smooth elegant, violet tinted nose, bit light on acid but comes back in the finish.

Canepa Magnificum Cabernet Sauvignon 2007, Maipo Valley Red
On the nose shows some development with mushroom, chocolate, forest floor and smoky bacon. The palate is juicy, vibrant, rich with ripe tannins and good length.

Canepa Reserva Sangiovese Carmenère 2009, Colchagua Valley Red
Soft strawberry with gentle, leafy fruit. Lots of sweet, soft raspberry fruit on the palate with a juicy, silky finish. Lovely.

Carmen Gran Reserva Carmenère 2008, Colchagua Valley Red
Stylish use of oak. Youthful, still a baby. Slightly grainy finish, but very good potential.

Carmen Winemaker's Reserve Red 2007, Maipo Valley Red
Intense, green pepper/stalky but loads of ripe fruit. Smooth creamy feel with very high tannins, balanced. Sweet mid palate with really juicy edge.
£9.99

Casa Marin Pinot Noir Lo Abarca Hills Vineyard 2006, San Antonio Valley Red
Deep colour. Vinous aroma with violet, cherry notes. Mineral,

morello cherry, spicy flavours. Well-structured. Lingering finish.
£28.49 PBA

Casa Silva Doña Dominga Gran Reserva Cabernet Sauvignon 2008, Colchagua Valley Red
Inky black. Restrained fruit/oak. Balanced tannins. Moderate depth of flavour.
£9.99 WAIT

Casa Silva Doña Dominga Reserva Carmenère 2009, Colchagua Valley Red
Deep ruby, bright red peppery fruit, chocolate and creamy wood palate. Savoury on the finish with lingering length.

Casa Silva Doña Dominga Reserva Shiraz 2009, Colchagua Valley Red
Bright ruby colour. Savoury and animal on the nose. Ripe raisin fruit on the palate with balanced acidity and good structure. Ripe tannins on the finish.

Chocalán Gran Reserva Malbec 2007, Maipo Valley Red
Intense blackberry and damson fruit with toasty oak. Very ripe and rich with a refreshing herbal note. Interesting wine.
LIB

Concha Y Toro Casillero Del Diablo Reserva Privada Cabernet Sauvignon Syrah 2007, Maipo Valley Red
Big meaty and fruity nose with a rich, juicy and chewy palate rounded by ripe tannins. Very good length.
£9.99 SAIN, MRN

Concha Y Toro Terrunyo Syrah 2007, Rapel Valley Red
Intense cigar and floral aroma. Plum and black fruit palate with

The natural choice
Chile – a great place to make wine

The long, thin country running down the west coast of South America - blessed with perfect conditions for winemaking.

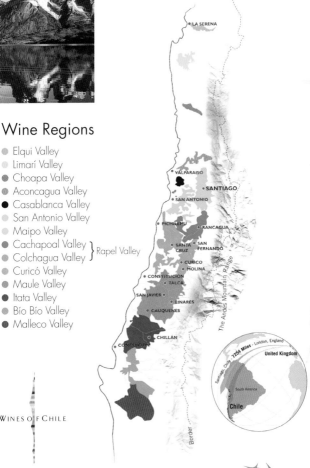

Wine Regions

- Elqui Valley
- Limarí Valley
- Choapa Valley
- Aconcagua Valley
- Casablanca Valley
- San Antonio Valley
- Maipo Valley
- Cachapoal Valley ⎫
- Colchagua Valley ⎬ Rapel Valley
- Curicó Valley
- Maule Valley
- Itata Valley
- Bío Bío Valley
- Malleco Valley

WINES OF CHILE

If you want further information about Chile's wines, please contact Wines of Chile UK: info@winesofchile.org.uk
Tel: 01344 872229   www.winesofchile.org

Chile
All Ways Surprising

ripe tannins and very refreshing acidity. Lovely.

Cono Sur 20 Barrels Limited Edition Cabernet Sauvignon 2007, Colchagua Valley Red
Very well made. Perfumed blackcurrants, plums, spice and cedar. Fresh, full bodied. Ripe tannins. Very silky and refreshing finish.

Echeverria Founders Selection Cabernet Sauvignon 2005, Central Valley Red
Lovely, intense nose, pure blackcurrant fruit. Lovely extraction. Soft, balanced and layered.
£23.99 HLD

Emiliana Coyam 2007, Rapel Valley Red
Nice, ripe berry fruits. Juicy palate with blackberry fruit and cedar overtones. Full-bodied with high acidity and ripe, firm tannins.
£12.99 VGN, PBA

Emiliana Novas Winemaker Selection Syrah 2006, Casablanca Valley Red
Blackcurrants on the nose. Intense fruit. Lovely round tannins. Ripe black fruits. Complex. Spicy oak. Chocolate. Almost porty.
£9.99 PBA

Errazuriz Don Maximiano Founder's Reserve 2007, Aconcagua Valley Red
Ripe black fruit. Floral, spicy, lovely integration. Juicy fruit, structured tannins and balanced oak with long finish.
£40.00

Errazuriz Single Vineyard Carmenère 2008, Aconcagua Valley Red
Deep ruby purple. Crunchy cassis, red capsicum and tobacco. Juicy palate, grippy tannins, fresh and lively. Nice length and balance.
£13.99

Errazuriz The Blend 2007, Aconcagua Valley Red
Ruby fragrant. Mellowed. Morellos. Plums. Big tannins make a big dry and puckering. Well made and elegant. Delicious.
£16.99 WAIT

Errazuriz Wild Ferment Pinot Noir 2008, Casablanca Valley Red
Rich burgundian style nose. Velvety tannins and voluptuous mouthfeel.
£10.99

Errazuriz Winemaker's Selection Cabernet Sauvignon 2008, Aconcagua Valley Red
Blackcurrants on the nose. Ripe and fresh with a green fruity finish.
£6.99

Haras De Pirque Equus Carmenère 2008, Central Valley Red
A generous mix of black olive and black forest gruits. Good acidity. Clean, fresh finish.

Koyle Royale Cabernet Sauvignon 2007, Colchagua Valley Red
Real depth and complexity, lots of cassis fruit. Firm structured and good overall weight.
£14.99

La Rosa La Capitana Carmenère 2008, Rapel Valley Red
Ripe berry fruit on the nose with full, smooth and rich mouthfeel. Warm spice and blackberries on the finish.
£13.00

La Rosa La Palma Carmenère 2009, Rapel Valley Red

Aromas of blueberry, mint, cherry and black liquorice. Supple texture, perfectly integrated polished tannins and lovely, mouthfilling cherry, plum and mint.
£7.00

La Rosa Ossa 2005, Rapel Valley Red

Purpley black colour. Cloves and mahogany. Silky tannins, moderate acidity and ripe fruit, cloves and spice to palate. Tastes expensive. Quite long.
£50.00

GREAT VALUE RED WINE BETWEEN £10 AND £15

Lapostolle Cuvée Alexandre Cabernet Sauvignon 2008, Colchagua Valley Red

Smoky, wild cherry and an excellent buttery finish. Cherry fruits with depth; really delicious.
£11.99 TVY, WDR

Laroche Vina Punto Alto Pinot Noir 2007, Casablanca Valley Red

Delicate wine with strawberry and some oak on the nose. Fresh acidity and ripe fruit on the palate.

Los Boldos Momentos Cabernet Sauvignon 2008, Rapel Valley Red

Deep ruby colour. Rich dark fruits with rich mocha hints. Slightly bitter tannins tasting but mellow finish. Reasonably balanced.
£6.99

Luis Felipe Edwards Reserva Shiraz 2009, Colchagua Valley Red

Ripe with ginger biscuit and orange peel on the nose. Deep plum fruit on the palate with soft, ripe tannins. Delicious and fresh.
£5.99 ASDA, D&D

Maycas Del Limarí Reserva Syrah 2009, Limarí Valley Red

Dense and youthful. Spicy blackberries. Lush velvety fruit but fine tannins. Very firm and persistent.
TESC

Mayu Syrah Reserva 2007, Elqui Valley Red

Ripe, jammy fruit on nose. Clean firm tannins and enough acidity to give the wine a good length.
£9.49 ASDA, MWW

Mayu Syrah Selected Vineyards 2008, Elqui Valley Red

Opaque black. Cassis fruit. Very oaky. Nice fruit but short and finish bitter.
£8.99 WAIT

Miguel Torres Santa Digna Carmenère 2008, Central Valley Red

A smoky oaky wine with a touch of spice and damson aromas. Has a nice spicy finish.

Montgras Quatro 2008, Colchagua Valley Red

Lovely black fruit intensity, smooth and supple with fleshy black fruit flavours, great length.
£9.99 WAIT

Montgras Reserva Carmenère 2009, Colchagua Valley Red

Deep ruby. Bright red fruits with a leafy overlay, smoky tobacco notes. Vibrant fruit, lively acidity, with nice texture. Herbal finish.
£8.19 WAIT

Morandé Edicion Limitada Carignan 2007, Central Valley Red

Spicy, ripe, juicy and ferrous. Aromatic dusty nose and fine grippy tannins. Squid ink, dark plums, hint of coffee and spice. Good length.

Nativa Eco Wines Gran Reserva Cabernet Sauvignon 2007, Maipo Valley Red

Highly scented nose showing some age. Lovely flavour, very smooth. Will improve with age.
£9.99

Nativa Eco Wines Reserva Terra Cabernet Sauvignon 2008, Maipo Valley Red

Intense, savoury, tight, black fruit. Juicy, rounded, acid quite prominent and adds a slightly aggressive touch to a fine, powerful wine.
£6.99

Ochagavía Gran Reserva Cabernet Sauvignon 2008, Maipo Valley Red

Cherries and blackcurrant notes on the nose, lead to a rich, vibrant, intense palate with firm tannins.

Odfjell Orzada Carignan 2006, Maule Valley Red

Big, spicy, eucalyptus, violet aromas. Full and concentrated flavours with black fruit, well-handled oak, ripe tannins and some green, herbal characteristics.
£12.99 AAW

Odjfell Orzada Carmenère 2007, Maule Valley Red

Intense, chocolatey nose showing a juicy palate of fruitcake and spices. Good persistent flavours and velvety soft coating tannins.
£12.99 AAW

Perez Cruz Cabernet Reserva 2008, Maipo Valley Red

Juicy fruit nose, warm with coconut spice on the palate. Spicy and ripe on the palate with warm, soft tannins. Good extraction, fresh and easy drinking.
£8.99 NOV

Santa Alicia Anke Blend 2 2008, Maipo Valley Red

Dense ruby red. Black fruits, light oak and concentrated dark fruits. Well-balanced. Generous flavours and length.
MYL

Santa Alicia Reserva Malbec De Los Andes 2009, Maipo Valley Red

Toasty, smoky oak. Very structured with lovely ripe fruit and good freshness. Long, savoury finish.
MYL

Santa Carolina Specialties Carignan 2008, Cauquenes Red

Plummy, expressive nose, round, smooth, layered; ripe velvety tannins. Medium length. Spicy.
£12.99

Santa Rita Medalla Real Syrah 2007, Maipo Valley Red

Deep, inky, intense in colour and aroma. Powerful aromas of black fruits and black pepper and herbs. Rich, complex structured palate backed with mocha and smoke. Lingering finish.
£9.99

Tabalí Reserva Especial Syrah 2008, Limarí Valley Red

Deep ruby red. Blackberry, spice oak, meaty. Medium tannin and flavour balance. Good concentration and length.
PBA, WSO

Tamaya Syrah Winemaker's Selection 2008, Coquimbo Red

Deep dense crimson. Oak woody - from dry tannin. Concentrated flavours. Spicy with wood notes. Ripe and balanced.

Terraustral Pknt Gold Cabernet Sauvignon 2008, Maule Valley Red

Bright, zingy, blackcurrant on the nose and palate. Blackcurrant fruits. User friendly!

Terraustral Pknt Gold Shiraz 2008, Maule Valley Red

Bright red and black fruit on the nose. Rich, dense damson on the palate with good balance and fresh acidity. Rich and savoury on the finish.

VC Family Estates Agustinos Gran Reserva Cabernet Sauvignon 2007, Acongagua Valley Red

Fresh with well-balanced fruit, acid and oak. Good length with fresh tannins.
£14.99

VC Family Estates Agustinos Gran Reserva Pinot Noir 2008, Bio Bio Valley Red

Vibrant ruby colour. Muted aromas - some savoury fruit on palate. Quite closed on the palate. Fine tannins and an earthy character.
£14.99

VC Family Estates Porta Gran Reserva Cabernet Sauvignon 2008, Aconcagua Valley Red

Deep pine and blackcurrant with herbaceous freshness. Big and concentrated. Excellent.

Viña Leyda Lot 21 Pinot Noir 2008, Leyda Valley Red

Deep colour. Violet and cherry aroma. Vibrant fruit on mid palate, tightly knit. Crisp, long red fruit finish.
£17.50 GWW, HOT, WSO

Viña Leyda Single Vineyard Pinot Noir Las Brisas 2009, Leyda Valley Red

Deep colour. Fruity perfumed aroma. Elegant wine with classy finish. Will age well.
£10.95 GWW, HOT, ODD, WSO

Viña Maipo Gran Devocion Carmenère Syrah 2008, Maule Valley Red

Black fruit nose of medium plus intensity. Blackcurrants, black cherries, herbaceous and sweet spices. Nice acidity and great depth of flavour and body. Long pronounced finish, good mouthfeel.

Viña Maipo Gran Devocion Syrah Petit Syrah 2008, Maule Valley Red

Spicy, black fruits on the nose with a luscious fruit palate. Well-structured and well defined with ripe black cherry and spice on the finish.

Viña Ventisquero Grey Carmenère 2008, Maipo Valley Red

Lovely deep, brooding blackcurrant fruit nose. Lush, smooth, dense palate with really nice grainy texture.
£12.99 CBC, PLB

Viña Ventisquero Pangea 2006, Colchagua Valley Red

Garnet colour with spicy blueberries on the palate. Smooth with ripe fruit compote and balanced, fresh menthol on the palate.
£29.00 CBC, PLB

Vistamar Gran Reserva Cabernet Sauvignon Syrah 2006, Maipo Valley Red

Nice coffee and leathery notes on

the nose with juicy, rich, complex palate, very good length.
£10.99

Vistamar Sepia Reserva Cabernet Sauvignon 2008, Maipo Valley Red
Rich ruby red. Berry aromatics and medicinal character. Lacks hint of depth. Astringent oak on palate.
£6.99

Yali Three Lagoons Syrah 2008, Maipo Valley Red
Lovely mulberry fruit. Ripe yogurty intense fruit. Soft tannic finish.
£8.99 PLB, TESC

Errazuriz Cabernet Sauvignon Rosé 2009, Central Valley Rosé
Vivid pink colour with lovely, vibrant cherry and cranberry fruit. Juicy and rich on the palate with clear purity of fruit. Long and lingering.
£7.99

Santa Helena Solar Rosé 2009, Central Valley Rosé
Lovely cherry nose with a touch of herbaceous aroma. Savoury on the palate with bright cherry, strawberry fruit. Refreshing acidity on the finish.
£6.00 ASDA

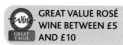
GREAT VALUE ROSÉ WINE BETWEEN £5 AND £10

Viña Leyda Secano Rosé Pinot Noir 2009, Leyda Valley Rosé
Redcurrants and cherries on the nose. Very pleasant palate of ripe and sweet fruit. Well-balanced with a savoury finish.
£7.49 M&S

Valdivieso Eclat Botrytis Semillon 2007, Curicó Valley
Botrytis
Light gold in colour, with

pineapple and lemon-honey nose. Apricots and syrup, tinned peaches with a hint of vanilla on the palate. Good concentration.
£9.99

Altos Vinos Le Chardonnay Grande Reserve Clos Andino 2009, Curicó White
A herbal nose with a palate showing green apple and lees influence with some minerality and nutty notes on the finish.

Bravado Kimbao Sauvignon Blanc 2009, Casablanca Valley White
Restrained nettle nose. Passionfruit and citrus on the palate with balanced acidity and a ripe citrus finish.
£8.99 NKW

Canepa Finisimo Sauvignon Blanc 2009, Casablanca Valley White
Nettles, gooseberries and spice on the nose. Palate is similar to the nose with a balanced and lingering finish.

Carta Vieja Viognier Limited Release 2008, Loncomilla Valley White
Sweet lemon cheesecake with fresh, easy-going fruit. Crisp acidity, with a well-balanced finish.

Casa Marin Sauvignon Blanc Cipreses Vineyard 2009, San Antonio Valley White
A touch of asparagus on the nose with a smoky and peppery palate. Balanced with a refreshingly citrus finish.
£7.99 PBA

Casas Del Bosque Chardonnay Reserva 2009, Casablanca Valley White
Ripe and clean on the nose with

fresh apple and citrus fruit. Well-balanced with a weighty finish.

Concha Y Toro Trio Chardonnay 2008, Casablanca Valley White
Fresh green citrus on the nose. Delicate and ripe on the palate with lush citrus freshness. Ripe and clean on the finish.

Cono Sur Gran Valle De Niebla Riesling 2009, Bio Bio Valley White
Delicate, fruity, fresh acidity. Persistent fruit to balance.
£7.49 LAI

Cono Sur The Loose Goose Chardonnay 2009, San Antonio Valley White
Butter cream on the nose with caramel and tropical fruit. Lovely palate with rich, melon fruits. Quite youthful with spicy ripeness coming through on the finish.
£6.49 LAI

Emiliana Adobe Sauvignon Blanc 2009, Casablanca Valley White
Intense, upfront aromas - gooseberries and grass. Pungent, searing acidity but supported by lively whistle clean fruit with a twist of lime zest.
£7.49 PBA

Errázuriz 1870 Peñuelas Block Sauvignon Blanc 2009, Casablanca Valley White
Delicate, tropical fruit on the nose. Passionfruit and mineral notes, balanced with a zesty finish.
£7.71 MCT

Errazuriz Asda Extra Special Sauvignon Blanc 2009, Casablanca Valley White
Slight tinge of green on the nose with a touch of lemon creaminess. Very fresh with lively citrus and good weight on the mid palate.
£5.99 ASDA

Errazuriz Sainsbury's Taste The Difference Sauvignon Blanc 2009, Casablanca Valley White
Grassy, passionfruit aromas. Delicate flavour of ripe citrus and ripe melon balanced with good acidity. Quite appealing.
£5.99 SAIN

Errazuriz Wild Ferment Chardonnay 2008, Casablanca Valley White
Good melon and grapefruit aromas on the nose. Lovely balance and freshness on the palate. Ripe and lively with a good mineral finish.
£9.99

Falernia Alta Tierra Sauvignon Blanc Reserva 2009, Elqui Valley White
Star-bright, pale green hue. Lovely grassy fruits, stylish nose. Lovely clean blackcurrant fruity taste.
£8.99

Falernia Marks & Spencer PX 2009, Elqui Valley White
Pale, some tropical fruit, neutral.
£4.99 M&S

La Rosa La Palma Chardonnay 2009, Rapel Valley White
Youthful, aromatic and zesty, unoaked with fresh fruit flavours. Crisp and easy drinking.
£7.00

Lapostolle Cuvée Alexandre Chardonnay 2008, Casablanca Valley White
Lime fresh on the nose. Good weight on the fresh palate with good acid structure. Balanced with long length and fresh flavours.
£11.99 PEA, TVY, WDR

Luis Felipe Edwards Claro Chardonnay 2009, Central Valley White
Subtle floral notes - light body with a crisp mineral style. Some citrus notes but quite light and simple.
£4.99 ASDA, D&D

Maycas Del Limari Reserva Especial Sauvignon Blanc 2009, Limarí Valley White
Quite smoky with hints of ripe green citrus fruit, green lemon and a touch of herbaceousness. Dry and minerally but nice generous fruit on the finish.

Mayu Sauvignon Blanc 2009, Elqui Valley White
Pungent with persistent fruit. Zesty and refreshing with lingering gooseberry and lime on the light finish.
£6.87 ASDA

Miguel Torres Chile Cordillera Chardonnay 2008, Curicó Valley White
Well-balanced with a creamy texture and a herbal, stone fruit and apple palate which persists to the finish.

Millaman Limited Reserve Chardonnay 2009, Casablanca Valley White
Fresh crushed vanilla aromas with white peach and nicely integrated oaky finish. Ripe and clean.

Morandé Reserva Sauvignon Blanc 2009, Casablanca Valley White
Lightly floral on the nose with ripe citrus and a touch of minerality on the palate. Easy drinking and easy to like.

Morandé Reserva Pinot Grigio 2009, Casablanca Valley White
Subtle spice. Soft and fruity, easy with a dry finish.

Ochagavía Gran Reserva Chardonnay 2008, Casablanca Valley White
Tropical fruit on the nose with melon and guava notes on the palate. Full bodied with a creamy lees character and crisp acidity.

Quintay Clava Chardonnay 2008, Casablanca Valley White
Mineral smoky nose with a rich palate showing slightly angular mineral notes.

Tabalí Encantado Reserva Especial Chardonnay 2008, Limarí Valley White
Big, rich and ripe with viscous mouthfeel. Ripe lemon and sweet citrus fruit on the palate. Fresh.
£9.99 WAIT

Tabalí Reserva Sauvignon Blanc 2009, Limarí Valley White
Bright colour with a fresh nose of clean lemon fruit. Good length and strong citrus finish.
£6.99 PBA

Tabalí Reserva Viognier 2009, Limarí Valley White
Fresh and peachy with juicy richness on the palate. Plenty of character, good lifting acidity with a long, fresh finish.
PBA

Tarapaca Gran Reserva Sauvignon Blanc 2009, Casablanca Valley White
Light, elegant and grassy. Quite pungent on the palate with an off-dry tinge of ripe fruit. Fruity and ripe on the finish.
£8.99

Undurraga T.H. Sauvignon Blanc Lo Abarca 2009, San Antonio Valley White
Green and pithy on the nose.

Palate is layered with ripe fruit and tinned asparagus. Lively and fresh on the finish.

VC Family Estates Chardonnay 2008, Bio Bio Valley White
Good colour and flavour. A good wine.

VC Family Estates Veranda Oda Chardonnay 2008, Bio Bio Valley White
Star-bright, pale lemon. Light fruit. Some style on nose. Rich, good fruit. Lovely length.
BWL

Viña Leyda Avery's Pioneer Range Leyda Sauvignon Blanc 2009, Leyda Valley White
Grassy and slightly sweet aromas. A touch of tartness on the palate. Green apple acidity with a lingering freshness.
£7.99 AVB

Viña Leyda Secano Sauvignon Blanc 2009, Leyda Valley White
Grassy on the nose with lemon-lime freshness. Angular acidity with ripe citrus fruit and a lashing of tropicality.
£7.49 M&S

Viña Leyda Secano Sauvignon Gris 2009, Leyda Valley White
Pale, simple and restrained. Sweet palate but lacks fruit and depth.
£7.49 M&S

Viña Leyda Single Vineyard Sauvignon Blanc Garuma 2009, Leyda Valley White
A brash and full style of Sauvignon Blanc. Round and supple in the mouth with a light freshness from citrus fruit and a smoky finish.
£9.99 GWW, HOT, ODD, WSO, WAIT

Amayna Syrah 2008, Leyda Valley Red
Intense, inky purple. Wild berry fruit. Chewy tannin. Balanced acid. Very long.

Arboleda Cabernet Sauvignon 2008, Aconcagua Valley Red
Pure fruit and mint on the nose. Dry, big, tannins. Lovely blackcurrant fruit. Vanilla, mint finish.
£12.99

Arboleda Carmenère 2008, Aconcagua Valley Red
Blackcurrant and black cherry nose. Bright ruby colour. Tannin well-integrated. Liquorice finish.
£12.99

Arboleda Syrah 2008, Aconcagua Valley Red
Vibrant colour. Mouthfilling cherry, blackcurrant fruit. Silky tannins, big intense finish. Alcohol slightly hot. Oak gives length.
£12.99

Aresti Limited Release Reserva Cabernet Sauvignon 2008, Curicó Red
Developed, savoury, dark fruit on the nose with fresh acidity and soft tannins on the palate. Delicious.

Benoit Valerie Calvet Tierra Del Sol Merlot 2009, Central Valley Red
Good balance with lively cranberry fruit but warm spice and black pepper on plums.

Bisquertt Q Clay Gran Reserve Carmenère 2007, Colchagua Valley Red
Pleasantly leafy nose with ripe cassis, berry fruit, plums and cocoa, nicely-handled tannin. Gentle, well-balanced with long finish.

CHILE

BRONZE

Botalcura El Delirio Syrah Malbec 2008, Central Valley Red

Blackcurrant red appearance. Young bilberry fruit on nose. Light, supple, jammy fruit. Sweet finish.
£7.89 CLN, GBL, SWM, WAM

Caliterra Anuela Merlot 2009, Colchagua Valley Red

Deep colour. Simple wine, some plum fruit and green pepper. Medium sweetness.
£6.99 SHN

Caliterra Edicion Limitada Carmenère Malbec 2007, Colchagua Valley Red

Very ripe with strong American oak influence. Ripe and minty on the palate with good depth of flavour. Rich with firm tannins and good grip. Long.
£12.99

Caliterra Edicion Limitada Shiraz Cabernet Sauvignon Viognier 2007, Colchagua Valley Red

Earthy, dark red. Ripe fruits, plenty of sun. Vibrant finish.
£12.99

Caliterra Tributo Cabernet Sauvignon 2008, Colchagua Valley Red

Mulled spices on the nose followed by good depth on the back palate.
£8.99

Caliterra Tributo Shiraz 2008, Colchagua Valley Red

Vibrant ruby colour. Menthol and ripe blueberries on the palate. Full-bodied, fruit is well supported by ripe tannins.
£8.99

Carta Vieja Monte Verde Merlot 2009, Central Valley Red

Good blackcurrant fruit aromas.

Soft and supple with fleshy plum fruit flavours.
£5.39 MCT

Carta Vieja Prestige Shiraz 2007, Maule Valley Red

Attractive mineral and berry fruit nose. Full-bodied with chocolate and plum fruit on the palate. Spiced style with fine tannins and ripe fruit providing good balance and length.

Casa Silva Doña Dominga Gran Reserva Carmenère 2008, Colchagua Valley Red

Deep purple. Jammy, juicy and lively fruit with tobacco oak. Attractive, fruity palate with good length. Well-balanced.

Casa Silva Doña Dominga Gran Reserva Shiraz 2008, Colchagua Valley Red

Red fruits and spice on the nose. Smooth and peppery fruity with a generous mouthfeel. Ripe with a liquorice bite on the finish.

Casa Silva Gran Reserva Cabernet Sauvignon Los Lingues 2008, Colchagua Valley Red

Deep violet. Definite substance and richness. Good length.

Casa Silva Gran Reserva Carmenère, Los Lingues 2008, Colchagua Valley Red

Vibrant raspberry and red pepper with smoky bacon and ripe fruit. Fresh and clean.

Casa Silva Gran Reserva Shiraz Lolol 2008, Colchagua Valley Red

Intense, deep colour. Ripe, black fruit with a touch of menthol freshness on the palate. Warm and spicy finish.

Casa Silva Reserva Carmenère 2009, Colchagua Valley Red

Deep purple, metallic with a

touch of tomato leaf
nose. Roasted coffee beans
on the palate with juicy
fruit and nice tannins.
Fresh and leafy.

Casa Tamaya Syrah Reserva 2008, Coquimbo Red

Red and black fruit. Ripe but
juicy. Leafy notes. Good tannin.
Tangy, elegant flavour persists.
£8.99

Casablanca Nimbus Merlot 2008, Colchagua Valley Red

Nice, clean, fruity nose with
hints of cassis. Palate is soft and
balanced. Nice follow up.
£11.99 LOQ, WOW

Casas Del Bosque Cabernet Sauvignon Reserva 2008, Casablanca Valley Red

Touch green, touch menthol.
Tight, a little closed and
ungiving. Savoury, lean and
serious.

Casas Del Bosque Syrah Gran Reserva 2007, Casablanca Valley Red

Blood red. Fruity redcurrants. Big
tannins. Fruity, long with a spicy
finish.

Chocalán Cabernet Franc Reserva 2007, Maipo Valley Red

Some good intense blackberry
fruit aromas, full and extracted
with long flavours. Tannins a bit
dry but has got class.
LIB

Comercial Hugo Casanova Limitada Reserva Carmenère 2008, Maule Valley Red

Deep purple in colour, muted
aromas of liquorice and black
chocolate. A rich christmas
cake-like palate with crunchy
tannins. Very dense with
short finish.

Concha Y Toro Casillero Del Diablo Cabernet Sauvignon 2008, Maipo Valley Red

Elegant, ripe, nose with
blackcurrants, berries and
prunes. Fine-grained tannins
on the palate with a savoury,
persistent finish.
£7.49 TESC, SAIN, MRN, WAIT

Concha Y Toro Casillero Del Diablo Malbec 2009, Rapel Valley Red

Vibrant blackberry fruit and
roasted coffee bean. Jammy, firm
structure, spicy and fresh. Warm
and rich.

Concha Y Toro Terrunyo Cabernet Sauvignon 2007, Maipo Valley Red

Smooth, rounded well-balanced
palate with rich cherry notes
and a long chocolatey aftertaste.
Delicious.

Concha Y Toro Trio Cabernet Sauvignon 2008, Maipo Valley Red

Black fruits on the nose with an
elegant fruity palate balanced by
the tannins and acidity.

Cono Sur 20 Barrels Merlot 2007, Colchagua Valley Red

Intense inky red/crimson. Some
leafy notes on the nose. Good
fruit on palate.

Cono Sur Casa Del Rio Verde Carmenère 2009, Central Valley Red

An attractive simple nose. Light
weight. Some lovely dark plums
and chewy fruit.
£5.99 LAI

Cono Sur Reserva Pinot Noir 2008, Colchagua Valley Red

Light oak and obvious fruit.
Softly spicy red berries. Mid
weight and intensity.
TESC

De Martino 347 Carmenère 2008, Maipo Valley Red
Ripe, black fruit. Lots of sweet ripe character. Palate light and juicy.
£7.49 MAJ

El Aromo Dogma Reserva Cabernet Sauvignon Syrah 2008, Maule Valley Red
Tinned fruits, red cherry notes on the nose. Silky fruit on palate.

El Aromo Private Reserve Cabernet Sauvignon 2009, Maule Valley Red
Good colour, with an attractively fragrant nose. Big and rich on the palate with soft plum fruit and a touch of spice. Lovely.
£8.99 TGW

Emiliana Novas Carmenère Cabernet Sauvignon 2007, Rapel Valley Red
Roasted meats with a savoury aroma. Dry and herbal with savoury, black fruit flavours. Chewy tannins on the fresh finish.
£9.99 VGN, PBA

Emiliana Novas Winemaker Selection Cabernet Sauvignon 2006, Maipo Valley Red
Powerful black fruit, damson and berries. Chewy, firm. Stone fruit on the palate.
£9.99 PBA

Errazuriz Estate Cabernet Sauvignon 2009, Aconcagua Valley Red
Red and black fruits, elegant, big complex nose. Dense fruits, fine tannins. Integrated oak and good persistence.
£8.15 WAIT

Errazuriz Max Reserva Cabernet Sauvignon 2008, Aconcagua Valley Red
Big leafy nose, rich and ripe with a green and smoky finish.
£9.99

Errazuriz Max Reserva Shiraz 2008, Aconcagua Valley Red
Rich, perfumed. Lovely mix of fruit and oak. Sweet, rich red crowd pleaser but with the class and balance to match.
£9.99

Errazuriz Single Vineyard Cabernet Sauvignon 2007, Aconcagua Valley Red
Black fruits, waxy and stalky on the nose. Long on the palate. Lift to the finish.
£12.99

Errazuriz Winemaker's Selection Merlot 2009, Curico Valley Red
Plum nose with tobacco and bay leaf. Very approachable.
£6.99

Estampa Gold Carmenère Cabernet Sauvignon Cabernet Franc Petit Verdot 2007, Colchagua Valley Red
Bright cassis, plum, spicy fruit. Mid depth, nice uniform long finish.

Estampa Reserve Syrah/Viognier 2008, Colchagua Valley Red
Spiced strawberry compote on the palate. Ripe, soft tannins and rich red and black fruit on the palate. Vanilla and cream on the finish.

Falernia Carmenère Reserva 2007, Elqui Valley Red
Opaque damson, spicy aroma, ripe fruit, juicy and well-balanced. Long chocolate and spice finish.
£10.95 CAM, DEF, GWW, HVN, NYW

Indomita Reserva Cabernet Sauvignon 2008, Maipo Valley Red
Rich smoky black fruit, eucalyptus and menthol palate. Firm grippy tannins with very good length.

Intriga Cabernet Sauvignon 2007, Maipo Valley Red
Ruby red with berry aromatics. Tannins slightly firm and palate astringent.
£12.99

Korta Bucarey Barrel Selection Carmenère 2008, Lontue Valley Red
Opulent aroma. Silky mouthfeel, complex, spicy damson palate. Lingering finish with chocolate notes.

Korta Bucarey Barrel Selection Syrah 2008, Curicó Red
Polished, perfumed, very fine. Flavoursome, really good grainy tannins. Chocolate character from oak. Complete, rather good.

Korta Bucarey Varietal Cabernet Sauvignon 2009, Curicó Red
Medium red. Juicy, simple fruit, jammy. Palate soft and juicy. Simple and commercial.

La Rosa La Capitana Cabernet Sauvignon 2008, Cachapoal Valley Red
Slightly herbal, minty with intense blackberry, earth and cinnamon. Full bodied and long.
£13.00

La Rosa La Capitana Merlot 2008, Rapel Valley Red
Deep, dense ruby. Reticent nose but mocha hints coming through. Big alcohol. Structured tannins and well-balanced.
£13.00

La Rosa La Palma Cabernet Merlot 2009, Cachapoal Valley Red
Juicy, round and ripe. Black fruits on the palate with a touch of herbaceous character on the finish.
£7.00

La Rosa La Palma Cabernet Sauvignon 2009, Rapel Valley Red
Juicy, rich, black fruit. Nice acid with a lift on finish.
£7.00

La Rosa La Palma Merlot 2009, Rapel Valley Red
Youthful colour. Muted beetroot and blackberry fruit. Herby, spicy, greenish. Soft tannin. Intensity. Good finish.
£7.00

La Rosa Los Rosales Chapel Vineyard Merlot 2009, Cachapoal Valley Red
Intense pepper, plums and perfume on the nose. Very well constructed. Silky tannins and well-balanced acidity. Long moreish finish.

Lapostolle Cabernet Sauvignon 2008, Rapel Valley Red
Ruby colour. Fresh, blackcurrant nose. Bordeaux-style tannin. Will develop.
£7.99 DBY, MAG

Los Boldos Momentos Merlot 2008, Rapel Valley Red
Light violet appearance. Juicy, forward fruity nose. Good, quite rich, stylish fruit. Mid length.
£6.99

Los Boldos Sensaciones Cabernet Sauvignon 2008, Rapel Valley Red
Moderate ruby hue. Restrained tart fruit, good Cabernet style. Good ripe fruit with mid length.
£8.99

Luis Felipe Edwards Don Cayetano Cabernet Sauvignon 2009, Colchagua Valley Red
Attractive creamy nose, with a lush, ripe palate. Plums and berries on the finish with

soft attack.
£6.49 D&D, LAI

Luis Felipe Edwards Don Cayetano Syrah 2009, Colchagua Valley Red
Meaty, savoury and ripe on the nose. Delicious red fruit with warming spice on the palate. Ripe, round, lush and fresh on the finish.
£4.99 D&D, LAI

Luis Felipe Edwards Paradiso Carmenère 2009, Central Valley Red
Herbaceous and peppery. Juicy palate. Fresh acid with firm dry tannin and warm alcohol. Better with food.
£6.99 D&D, M&S

Luis Felipe Edwards Reserva Carmenère 2009, Colchagua Valley Red
Deep, intense red pepper and herbal, smoky oak. Juicy, jammy fruit, excellent freshness, supple tannins with a long finish.
£5.99 D&D

Luis Felipe Edwards Reserva Malbec 2009, Colchagua Valley Red
Lifted aromatics of red and black fruits. Eucalyptus and a smoky note. Overtly fruity, dense structure and length with a spicy finish.
£5.99 D&D

Luis Felipe Edwards Seleccion De Familia Carmenère 2008, Colchagua Valley Red
Deep ruby with leafy overtones. Tomato leaf and red capsicum, very smoky wood on the palate. Good freshness and grippy tannins. Nice length.
£7.99 ASDA, D&D

Mas O Menos Cabernet Sauvignon 2009, Central Valley Red
Deep ruby colour. Herbaceous cassis and blackcurrant lozenges. Supple tannins. Pleasantly quaffing.
£3.99 MRN

Maycas Del Limarí Reserva Especial Syrah 2007, Limarí Valley Red
Blackberry spice. Oak, vanilla and black fruits. Savoury notes. Concentrated power and balance. Fleshy palate.
£12.99 WAIT

Millaman Limited Reserve Cabernet Sauvignon 2007, Curicó Valley Red
Red forest fruits with chewy tannins and a sweet finish.

Millaman Limited Reserve Zinfandel 2007, Maipo Valley Red
Big ripe, spicy chocolatey nose with plum and raisin flavours. Tannic but ripe. Herbal acidity.

Misiones De Rengo Reserva Carmenère 2009, Rapel Valley Red
Spicy, with oak and black fruit on the nose. The palate is savoury with attractive with moreish flavours.
£6.90

Montes Alpha M 2006, Curicó Valley Red
Lovely and ripe with a blackberry nose. The palate is ripe but has overtones of cedar and cigar box. Smooth tannins with a touch of blueberry and damson on the finish.
£34.99 WAIT

Montgras Reserva Cabernet Sauvignon 2008, Colchagua Valley Red
Savoury, clean, well made wine. Well-balanced with a slight

minty finish.
£7.99

Morandé Mancura Etnia Cabernet Sauvignon 2009, Maipo Valley Red
Nose of dark fruits. Palate leafy, vegetal. Touch green but elegant and fresh.

Morandé Mancura Leyenda Carmenère 2008, Central Valley Red
Slightly savoury, fleshy mid palate of aniseed and liquorice. Generous flavours on the finish.

Morandé Reserva Pinot Noir 2008, Casablanca Valley Red
Supple, delicate Pinot Noir with cherry and red berry flavours.

Ninquén Antu Syrah 2008, Colchagua Valley Red
Blue, inky ruby colour. Spicy plums and menthol on the nose and palate. Biting liquorice and balanced acidity on the finish. Well-balanced and delicious.
£10.99

Ochagavía Gran Reserva Merlot 2008, Maipo Valley Red
Bright red colour with black fruit, mint and eucalyptus aromas. On the palate, nice black and bramble fruit, soft tannins, good balance and length.

Odfjell Armador Carmenère 2008, Maipo Valley Red
Ruby red. Spice, oak and red and black fruit, savoury. Attractive with moreish flavours.
£7.49 AAW

Palo Alto Reserva 2008, Maule Valley Red
Almost violet intensity. Cloves on the nose. Silky, fruity with a nice length.

Perez Cruz Liguai 2007, Maipo Valley Red
Pleasant fruity and herbaceous nose leading to a balanced, rich and complex palate with eucalyptus notes.
£20.69 NOV

San Esteban In Situ Laguna Del Inca 2008, Aconcagua Valley Red
Oak, lightly scented, fine. Fresh, fragrant style, lovely balance on palate. Light, easy drinking but lots of class.
£15.00 DFW

San Esteban In Situ Reserva Carmenère 2008, Aconcagua Valley Red
Mid ruby-garnet. Quite earthy-gamey. Black fruit and spice, eucalyptus. Simple and easy drinking.
£3.99

San Esteban Rio Alto Reserva Cabernet Sauvignon 2008, Aconcagua Valley Red
Dense, minty, cherry fruit. Cool minty finish.
DFW

Santa Alicia Reserva Merlot De Los Andes 2009, Maipo Valley Red
Ripe and oaky on the nose with creamy vanilla aromas. Fresh, ripe fruit on the palate.
MYL

Santa Camila Valle Andino Gran Reserva Cabernet Sauvignon 2007, Colchagua Valley Red
Good lifted aromas, super concentrated, easy style, violet aromas and cassis fruit.

Santa Carolina Reserva Syrah 2008, Rapel Valley Red
Savoury notes with lovely perfumed fruit and spice.

CHILE

BRONZE

Blueberry and spice on the palate, very well-balanced with good acidity and tannin integration. Long finish.
£7.99

Santa Carolina Specialties Malbec 2008, Cachapoal Valley Red

Dark berry fruit and intense, spicy oak. Dense structure, lively freshness with a herbs de provence accent. Pretty.
£12.99

Santa Helena Vernus Cabernet Sauvignon 2008, Colchagua Valley Red

Smooth cassis notes on the nose, lovely balance, supple tannins, fresh acid on the palate. Good length.

Sur Andino Terra Andina Altos Cabernet Franc Merlot 2007, Central Valley Red

Nice lifted fruit, a little bit hot and green but some good concentration mid palate.
£9.99

Sur Andino Terra Andina Varietal Carmenère 2009, Central Valley Red

Smoky, floral oak. Quite oaky but lots of red fruit to match. Firm dry finish.
£5.99

Tabalí Encanto Reserva Syrah 2008, Limarí Valley Red

Dense, dark, ruby red. Black fruit, spice and oak. Green stalks. Good tannin. Dry finish.
£10.99 WAIT

Tabalí Reserva Syrah 2008, Limarí Valley Red

Perfect oak and blackberries. Medium acid. Some concentration. Firm and minty. Medium length.
£6.99 PBA

Terramater Altum Cabernet Sauvignon 2007, Curicó Valley Red

Ripe blackcurrant and plum fruit nose. Medium bodied with pure clean fruit.
£13.99

Terranoble Reserva Carmenère 2008, Maule Valley Red

Smoky chocolaty aroma leads to a more restrained palate with minty, herbal characters. Lovely grainy tannin with excellent overall purity.
PIM

Top Wines La Playa Sol Y Sombra Pinot Noir 2008, Central Valley Red

A good berry fruit. Easy, fleshy structure, tannins then follow.
£8.75 EOR, RWA, WHD

Undurraga Aliwen Reserva Cabernet Sauvignon Carmenère 2008, Rapel Valley Red

Restrained nose. Gentle but well-integrated palate of forest fruits.

Undurraga T.H. Carignan Maule 2008, Maule Valley Red

Roasted, smoky, berry aromas. Dry, with herbal, black fruit flavours. Chewy tannins. Concentrated but austere.

Undurraga T.H. Syrah Limarí 2007, Limarí Valley Red

Opaque, black, ruby. Salmon, game, blackberries and spices. Medium acid. Nice fruit but a bit raw and unresolved. Good length.

Urmeneta Carmenère 2009, Central Valley Red

Friendly and jammy. Four square but honest.

Valdivieso Reserva Merlot 2008, Rapel Valley Red
Indistinct nose. Brambly fruits. Nice tannin. Longish finish.
£8.99

Valdivieso Single Vineyard Cabernet Franc 2008, Colchagua Valley Red
Lots of fruit and spice. Christmas pudding characters with grip. A touch green but okay.
£10.99

Valdivieso Winemaker Reserva Malbec 2009, Rapel Valley Red
Lifted and juicy with a spicy, refreshing finish and firm tannins. Moderate length.
£6.99

Valdivieso Winemaker's Reserva Merlot 2009, Central Valley Red
Pleasant black fruit aromas. Nicely done with some grip to tannins.
£6.99

VC Family Estates Agustinos Gran Reserva Syrah 2008, Aconcagua Valley Red
Forward blackcurrant fruit, pure on nose. Palate juicy profile, well-integrated tannins. Simple but very clean and balanced.
£14.99

VC Family Estates Gracia Syrah Reserva Lo Mejor 2007, Cachapoal Valley Red
Deep red. Some stewed fruit. Fine tannin. Moderate acidity. Big wine.

VC Family Estates Veranda Gran Cuvée Millerandage Pinot Noir 2008, Bio Bio Valley Red
Good hue. Berry style and well made. Clean, full and not complex. Light toast.
BWL

Ventsiquero Yali Wetland Merlot 2008, Colchagua Valley Red
Medium ruby, light cherry nose, sweet cherry flavours, very forward and juicy; hint of herbs on the finish.
£6.49 PLB

Via Oveja Negra Winemakers Selection Cabernet Franc Carmenère 2008, Maule Valley Red
Nice blackberry fruit aromas. Lots of flavour and grip. Juicy tannins with long flavours.
£7.99 HLD

Viña Casablanca Céfiro Syrah Reserva 2008, Rapel Valley Red
Crimson in colour. Ripe fruit on the lifted palate, with good acidity and peppery fruit finish.
£7.99 EAG, HSL, WOW

Viña Casablanca El Bosque Carmenère 2008, Rapel Valley Red
Ripe cassis, berry fruit, plums and cocoa on the nose. Gentle and ripe, with blackcurrant and bramble fruits. Well-balanced with long finish.

Viña Casablanca Neblus 2007, Casablanca Valley Red
Deep colour. Nicely scented. Really good core of flavour, undeveloped at present. Well judged oak.
£34.99

Viña El Rosal Morrisons The Best Chilean Carmenère 2008, Colchagua Valley Red
Leafy, herbaceous but with modest red fruit aromas. Quite intense on the palate with ripe and dry tannins. Lean, but well-balanced, with good length.
£7.37 MRN

Viña Leyda Single Vineyard Pinot Noir Cahuil 2009, Leyda Valley Red

Medium intensity colour. Elegant red fruit aroma. Fine-grained tannins. Vibrant fruit on mid palate. Fresh, long finish.
£14.99 GWW, HOT, WSO, WAIT

Viña Leyda Single Vineyard Syrah Canelo 2008, Leyda Valley Red

Rich colour, clove herbal complexity on the nose. Soft velvety tannins, juicy fruit - very pure, clean herbal complexity. Easy to drink.
£10.95 GWW

Viña Maipo Gran Devocion Cabernet Sauvign on Syrah 2007, Maule Valley Red

Good balance, weight, length. Red fruits on the nose and palate.

Viña Maipo Limited Edition Syrah 2007, Maipo Valley Red

Dark purple, moderately intense, ripe fruit. Lovely luscious fruit on palate. Fresh acidity, plenty of tannins.

Viña Maipo Reserva Carmenère 2008, Rapel Valley Red

Ripe, black fruit on the nose with sweet character. The palate is light and juicy with good freshness.

Viña Maipo Gran Reserva Shiraz 2008, Rapel Valley Red

Earthy with ripe berry nose. Juicy, jammy fruit on the plate with notes of creamy vanilla. Smoky spice finish.

Viña Mar Reserva Especial Pinot Noir 2008, Casablanca Valley Red

Rich weight on the palate with a smooth finish. Rich fruit and superb balance.
£10.99

Visa Nostros Gran Reserva Cabernet Sauvignon 2008, Maipo Valley Red

Mint, red and black cherries on the nose lead to a full blackcurrant palate with firm meaty tannins.
£10.00 AAW

Carta Vieja Monte Verde Merlot Rosé 2009, Central Valley Rosé

Fruit, ripe and fresh. Cherry and berry bright fruit. Jammy with cherry compote on the finish.
£5.39 MCT

Carta Vieja Tierra Carmenère Rosé 2009, Maule Valley Rosé

Vivid pink colour. Soft and fruity on the palate with appealing cherry fruit. Herbaceous and fresh on the finish.
£5.94 MCT

Leyda Single Vineyard Pinot Noir Rosé Loica 2009, Leyda Valley Rosé

Fragrant nose with good cherry-strawberry intensity. Fresh and clean on the finish.
£9.50 GWW, HOT, ODD, WSO

Palo Alto Shiraz Rosé 2009, Maule Valley Rosé

Bright pink colour with a fruit forward nose. Ripe cherry and spice on the palate with a savoury grip. Lively and fresh.

Viña Leyda Costero Pinot Noir Rosé 2009, Leyda Valley Rosé

Fresh redcurrant nose. Ripe, red fruit palate with lush compote flavours. Strawberry fruit finish.
£8.99 MWW

France: Bordeaux

Bordeaux remains at the forefront of wine interest. As relatively new markets like China develop their interest in wine, it is Bordeaux that receives the focus of attention – and for good reason: there is something about the range and complexity of these reds and whites that can not quite be replicated anywhere else in the world. With prices for the fabled 2009 vintage being higher than ever before, it is increasingly tough to find good value bottles from the region. It is even more crucial, therefore, to know which producers and vintages are performing well compared to their peers – read on for a comprehensive snapshot of Bordeaux across all its appellations and styles.

2010 IWC PERFORMANCE

Gold	1
Silver	21
Bronze	60

KEY FACTS

Total production
4.79 Mhl in 2008

Total vineyard
119,000ha

Top 10 grapes
1. Merlot
2. Cabernet Sauvignon
3. Cabernet Franc
4. Semillon
5. Sauvignon Blanc
6. Malbec
7. Muscadelle
8. Petit Verdot
9. Ugni Blanc
10. Colombard

Top 10 production per appellation
1. Bordeaux
2. Premieres Cotes de Blaye
3. Bordeaux Blanc
4. Medoc
5. Bordeaux Superieur
6. Haut Medoc
7. Saint Emilion Grand Cru
8. Red Graves
9. Saint Emilion
10. Entre deux Mers

Producers
9044 winegrowers in 2008, 43 wine co-operatives

**Jean-Christophe Barbe
Château Laville Sauternes
2006** Botrytis

Rich, but balanced. Very
youthful with good tangy
notes. Balanced, pure pineapple,
honey and apricot on the palate
with decent grip and balance.
Complete and complex.
£29.99 LIB, NYW

**Chai Au Quai Le Grand Chai
Bordeaux Blanc 2008** White

Lime zest and vanilla aromas on
the nose, crisp gooseberry fruit
and smooth buttery oak on the
palate. Fresh and clean with racy
acidity on the lingering finish.
£8.99 LAI

**Château Brown Château
Brown 2008** White

Delicate honeyed nose with a
vibrant fruit character. Fresh
lemon and melon on the palate
with a touch of creamy sweetness.
Long and lingering on the finish.
£21.99 EOR, SOH

**Denis Dubourdieu Bordeaux
Blanc 2009** White

Tropical lychee and guava
aromas. On the palate, ripe and
lush with good citrus character.
Well-balanced and fresh on the
finish.

**Barton & Guestier Thomas
Barton Réserve Privée Médoc
2005** Red

Some development, smoke
and flowers. Palate - plum,
stone fruits, dried fruits. Firm
tannins.
£29.99 J&B, PFC

**Castel Frères Château
Montlabert 2008** Red

High roasted coffee bean. Firm,
sinewy, quite muscular. Structured,
good acidity. Quite tight.

**Chai Au Quai Le Grand Chai
Pomerol 2007** Red

Lovely nose of blackcurrant,
cedar and pencil shavings.
A wine of complexity with
juicy blackberry fruit
underpinned by balanced
tannin and oak.
£21.50 LAI

Château Barateau 2007 Red

Simple notes of plum and
chocolate, good tannic
structure and ripe palate. Has
some complexity. Alcohol a
little high.

**Château De Potiron Cuvée
Exceptionnelle 2007** Red

Mid deep ruby garnet. Open
coffee and plum kernel and
berry nose. Mid full, soft juicy
dark fruits. Silky tannins. Lovely
overall balance and length.

Château Guadet 2007 Red

Mid ruby. Open nose - plums,
damsons and spice. Attractive
smoke and plum note but lighter
fruit. Juicy acidity.
£29.99 FAR, ODD

**Château Maurac Les Vignes
De Cabaleyran 2007** Red

Cassis, cinnamon, tabasco,
leather notes. Ripe fruit, good
concentration and length.

Château Perac 2007 Red

Meatiness, smokiness, damson
fruit. Nice, rich palate, tannins
mould well in fruit and acidity.
Nice structure and good length.
£15.99 ODD

**Cordier Mestrezat Grands
Crus Château Tour Massac
2007** Red

Lovely nose, spicy and full.
Excellent balance and length.

Crus Et Domaines De France Château Cantin 2007 Red

Very clean, cedar, modern and stylish on the nose. Quite a stylish length. Cigar box and dark plums.
£19.99 WAIT

Delayat & Fils Château Hourbanon 2007 Red

Juicy, ripe fruit. Youthful brambly. Excellent depth.

Guy Meslin Chäteau Laroze 2007 Red

Deep ruby core. Lots of high toast new oak on nose, roasted coffee - toasty notes. Firm structure, lots of acidity and firm tannins. Smoky, plum notes.

Les Vignobles Andre Lurton Château Bonnet Reserve 2009 Red

Lime and gooseberry on the nose. Very fresh with pear-drops on the palate. Clean and ripe with hints of peach nectar on the finish. Delightful.
£9.99

Pierre Et Herve Lhuillier Château Fleur Haut Gaussens 2007 Red

Deep purple colour, spicy black baked fruit and liquorice on the nose, hints of smoke and cedarwood support plum and bramble on the palate with moderate tannins. Good length.

Thomas Herter Château Segonzac 2008 Red

Cool and juicy red fruits with hints of cigar box. Dry, medium bodied, clean wine with good balance.
£9.49 WAIT

Yvon Mau Jacques Boyd 2007 Red

Wood evident. Fresh. Some fruit. Tannin not obtrusive. Short.
£21.99

Yvon Mau Tesco Finest* Sauternes 2005 Sweet

Ripe with lovely honeycomb and apple on the nose. Plenty of ripe fruit on the palate with tangy orange and honeyed pineapple on the palate.
TESC

Des Eyssards Château Des Eyssards 2006 Botrytis

Lovely orange with layers of sweetened and nutty fruit. Apricot and lemon-peach on the palate. Fresh acidity with a long, lush finish.

Château Carbonnieux Château Tour Leognan 2008 White

Ripe, sweet and tropical on the nose. Fresh acidity and lively, lemon citrus fruit on the palate. Ripe, round and fleshy on the finish.
£12.99 WAIT

Château Toumilon Château Toumilon White 2008 White

Delicate and light on the nose. Fruit on the palate is pungent in contrast. Lime, lemon and ripe passionfruit finish.

Cordier Mestrezat Grands Crus Cordier Prestige 2008 White

Lemon in colour. Soft and rich with honey notes on nose. Round, tropical fruit with soft citrus and lemon on the finish.
£9.97

Didier Laulan Blanc Sec De Château Broustet 2008 White

Tropical and ripe, the fruit is pure and quite full. Lush with a well-balanced citrus finish.

Joel Bonneau Château Haut Grelot 2009 White

Intense petrol and gooseberry

nose, fresh pear and melon palate with broad easy drinking fruit on the finish.
£9.10

Andre Lurton La Bastide Dauzac 2007 Red
Fresh fruit aromas on the nose. The palate has layers of black fruit and slightly green tannins. Nice fruit and good concentration.
£16.99

Bessette Château Rival Bellevue 2008 Red
Big, juicy orange peel and ginger, plush berry fruit. Very well made with a hard finish.
£7.99 WAIT

Bruno, Dominique & Pascal Guignard Château Perron 2009 Red
Ripe, rich and youthful wine. Black fruit flavours and a good length.
THI

Bruno, Dominique & Pascal Guignard Château Roquetaillade La Grange 2008 Red
Black fruit and raspberry flavours. Sour cherry on the palate with firm tannins and a juicy finish.
THI

Bruno, Dominique & Pascal Guignard Château Roquetaillade La Grange 2009 Red
Currants on the nose with cherry and blackcurrant flavours. Good acidity and firm but ripe tannins.
THI

Calvet Prestige De Calvet Red 2009 Red
Crunchy, black cedary fruit on the nose. Attractive herbaceousness. Medium bodied, clean and crisp, crunchy tannins.

Good delineation and typicality on the finish. Very fine.
£10.99 Widely Available

Calvet Reserve Red 2008 Red
Black and redcurrants, creamy oak. Currants come through to palate, chewy tannins. Smoky lingering finish.
£7.99 MRN, WAIT

Castel Frères Château Hourtou 2008 Red
Spicy wood and pungent red fruits on the nose. Roundness and good body on the palate. Well-balanced, attractive wine.

Castel Frères Château Tour Prignac Grande Reserve 2008 Red
Young, soft, red fruits. Quite high in alcohol. Slightly astringent and extracted on palate. Young.
NIC

Castel Frères Famille Castel Bordeaux 2009 Red
Deep ruby with early confectionary aromas. Muted fruit, a little closed. Still, will open in time to be easy drinking.

Chai Au Quai Le Grand Chai Saint-Éstephe 2007 Red
Ruby red. Red fruits, shy nose. Still young with grippy tannins, good acidity, some cedar and blackcurrant notes. Youthful and needs time.
£14.99 LAI

Château Belle Vue 2004 Red
Very attractive nose. Developed, savoury, cedary, dark fruit. Lovely balance. Fresh acidity. Supple tannins. Long profile. Impressive!
ODD

Château Canon Guilhem 2006 Red
Upfront in style, lovely aromas of forest fruits, cigarbox and

It's all in the
delivery

With over 20
years experience
providing supply
chain solutions to the
Beer, Wines and Spirits
industry, we are trusted
to deliver by everyone from
boutique growers to multiple
grocers. Renowned for our
extensive network, market leading
customer service and advanced IT
systems, Geodis represents reliability
on an international scale. And just as
turning grapes into vintage wine demands
skill and attention, we too take care at every
stage of the journey, continually investing and
improving to help our customers reap the benefits.

**To sample our refreshingly innovative service call
0845 676 0016 or Email bws-enquiries.uk@geodis.com**

GEODIS
wine logistics

Image courtesy of ES Group (design and build) and Radisson Zürich (client) Photographer: Benjamin Reusse

chocolate. Palate is fine and structured with silky yet complex tannins supporting vibrant blackcurrant fruit with a elegant lingering finish.
£17.99 ODD

Château De Claribès Vieilles Vignes Malbec 2008 Red

Leafy notes. Black fruit and firm tannins. Perfumed with a dry palate. Savoury and meaty.
£19.90 CLA

Château de Lescours 2007 Red

Leathery, chocolate, mocha and spicy plum. Soft, gentle tannins. Lovely length and persistence.
£24.99 DLW

Château Deyrem Valentin Margaux 2007 Red

Mute nose. Some black fruit and old wood. Good fruit concentration.
£24.99 BTW, CHH

Château Du Gazin 2008 Red

Coconut, raspberry and baked plums nose, stylish mulberry fruity taste, soft tannins and long finish.
£9.99 WAIT

Château Grand Tayac 2006 Red

Ripe and fresh on the nose, with a more developed palate. Soft, black fruits with a touch of grainy tannin. Lush finish.
ODD

Château Guibeau 2004 Red

Ripe berries - blackcurrants and plums. Astringent tannins, high acidity. A little hollow.
£14.99 ODD

Château Laroze Lafleur Laroze 2006 Red

Black cherry and plum fruit. Fresh acidity, sturdy, chewy, savoury tannin structure. Good weight and length. Should develop.

Château Marquis De Terme 2006 Red

Good. Lots of citrus fruit. Fruity and light.

Château Meyre Gallen De Château Meyre 2006 Red

Good, ripe fruit on the nose. Very fresh with high acidity and ripe fruit on the palate. Notes of redcurrants on the finish.

Château Monconseil-Gazin Blaye 2008 Red

Cedar and red fruits and some plum on the nose. Ripe fruit flavours of blackcurrant and berries. Good length.
3DW

Château Mongravey Château Braude Fellonneau Haut-Médoc 2007 Red

Toasty notes on nose. Plum and spice, some ripe sweet fruits on the palate. Acidity pulls the wine through.
£18.57 3DW

Château Mongravey Château De Braude Haut Médoc 2007 Red

Dark, red fruits, slightly jammy. Palate - rich, red fruits and fine tannins which will mellow. Plenty of fruit.
£14.02 3DW

Château Pontoise Cabarrus 2007 Red

Nice gentle crunchy blackcurrant Cabernet fruit with an attractive leafy hint on the fresh finish.
£18.99 ODD

Château Saransot Dupre 2006 Red

Roasted nuts, meaty aspects with intense black fruits. Sturdy style. Quite rich with a savoury finish.
£19.99 DLW

Château Toumilon Château Toumilon 2008 Red
Damson fruits on the nose which follow through on the palate with sour cherry flavours. Firm tannins and a fresh finish.

Cordier Mestrezat Grands Crus Antoine Pouget 2007 Red
Juicy, sweet fruit. Nice and well-balanced. Good commercial. Soft.

Cordier Mestrezat Grands Crus Château Pouget 2007 Red
Vegetal nose. Some black fruit. Good acidity. Quite firm tannin.

Crus Et Domaines De France Château Laroque 2004 Red
Ripe berry and liquorice hints on nose. Drying astringent tannins. Lacking some fruit.
£24.99 WAIT

Denis Dubourdieu Château Haura Graves Rouge 2007 Red
Medium crimson. Nose of smoky baked fruit with spice. Silky initial tannins on palate with lots of oak. Nice balance.

Dourthe Barrel Select Montagne St Emilion 2007 Red
Lovely, soft red berry nose. Light, easy fruit, not complex, but attractive and youthful.
£9.99 WAIT

Dourthe Château Lezin 2008 Red
Fresh and fruity nose. Crunchy fruit. Medium acidity and firm, ripe tannin.
£6.99

Jean Chanfreau Château Lestage 2007 Red
Chewy full-ish bodied. Slightly rustic style of claret, but a good honest drink.

Jean Chanfreau La Tonnelle De Château Fonreaud 2006 Red
Classic cedar, blackcurrant fruit. Perfumed, stylish and well-balanced. Well made.

Jean-Christophe Icard Grand Classique Du Château De L'Orangerie 2007 Red
Medium to deep cherry red. Elegant, fast, fruity nose. Stylish, good supple fruit. Lovely balance.
£11.40

Jean-Michel Cazes Château Villa Bel-Air 2007 Red
Oak and bramble fruit on the nose. Good acidity and fruit on the palate.

Julien De Savignac 2008 Red
Some mocha and lots of mint. Eucalyptus palate. Unusual finish but quite fresh and pleasant.

Lagneaux Blaton Château Petit Bocq 2007 Red
Merry red. Fruity nose. Soft supple fruit taste.
J&B

Lavau Château Tour Peyronneau 2007 Red
Deep, dark ruby. Coffee bean on nose. Smoky cigar box, cedar notes. Smooth initial attack. Textured tannins. A bit drying on finish.

Les Caves De Landiras Cellar Estates Bordeaux Claret Red 2009 Red
Thin, earthy, nice mix of blackcurrant, cedar, sweet cherry. Simple but honest.
£4.99 BES

Marks & Spencer Château de Saÿe 2007 Red
Very structured and quite sinewy in style. Tannins softening slowly. Persistent aromas of black fruit and

eucalyptus. Balanced forest fruit and cedar wood flavours with a well-integrated style.
£8.99 M&S

Mr Gort Château De La Garde 2008 Red
Deep ruby purple. Open mulberry and plum kernel nose. Full, juicy blackcurrants and mulberries with a hint of strawberries and tar concentrated with good integration of creamy oak. Plenty of ripe tannins and a good finish.
SAIN

Nony Borie Château Caronne Ste Gemme 2005 Red
Youthful blackcurrants with cedar. Rich and ripe with firm yet ripe tannin. Well made but needs time.
£12.99 MWW

Patrick Bernard Gerant Château La Fleur Peyrabon 2007 Red
Undergrowth, clean. Mid deep brick, leather, earthy cigar box. Soft attack, medium intensity and concentration. Soft at finish. Elegant, ripe fruits. A little short, good balance.
£15.00 FR-MLL

Verniotte Aux Trois Frères De Verniotte 2008 Red
Decent fruit concentration on the nose. Blackberry and liquorice. Medium bodied, nicely integrated chocolate oak. Fine definition on the palate.
LAI

Vieux Manoir Château Vieux Manoir 2008 Red
Deep ruby colour. Rich cassis plum nose. Beautifully rich, deep cassis flavours. Excellent balance with good tannins. Hints of green.
£6.49 WSO

Villa Des Crus Château Patris 2006 Red
Bordeaux berry style. Savoury leafy, tobacco character. Balanced acidity.
WAV

Denis Dubourdieu Le Rosé De Floridene 2009 Rosé
Clean nose of berry fruits, strawberries and vanilla on the palate. Ripe and round with good freshness.

Château Filhot 2005 Sweet
Big juicy, tangy fruit with fine citrus. Sweet, deep and tangy on the palate with ripe citrus finish.
£24.99 FAR, ODD

Château Guiraud Sainsbury's Taste The Difference Sauternes 2005 Sweet
Deep and ripe with very warming alcohol. Rich apricot and peach flavours on the palate, balanced with lemony freshness.
£11.99 SAIN

Comte De Bosredon Château Belingard Cuvée Blanche De Bosredon Monbazillac 2007 Botrytis
Waxy lemons, pineapple and a touch of fragrant woodiness. Good depth with racy finish.
BWJ, EAR

Denis Dubourdieu Château Cantegril Sauternes 2007 Botrytis
Slight cheese aromas with brilliant spice character. Herbaceous on the palate with fresh stone fruit and a citrus backbone.

Les Vignobles Andre Lurton Divinus 2006 Botrytis
Baked pink grapefruit, brown sugar and pineapple cubes. Medium intensity with a fresh finish.

France: Burgundy

Burgundy can be the most frustrating proposition for wine lovers – a seemingly impenetrable patchwork of *terroirs* and *climats*, and mysterious compound Gallic names. The wines themselves can be just as frustrating, with Pinot Noir's infamous capriciousness and Chardonnay's infinite shapeshifting. With such variety, Burgundy has a wine for every palate, and discovering your favourite is one of wine's most rewarding experiences. However, navigating the labyrinth of options is more than a little daunting! What follows is a signpost to the best of the region, and the following medal winners offer guaranteed selections across all the styles, from austere Chablis to luscious Meursault; from humble Bourgogne Rouge to stately Beaune.

KEY FACTS

Total production
1.5m hectolitres

Total vineyard
120,200ha

Sub-regions
- Chablis
- Grand Auxerrois
- Tonnerre
- Joigny
- Vézelay
- Côte de Nuits
- Hautes Côtes de Nuits
- Châtillonnais
- Côte de Beaune
- Hautes Côtes de Beaune
- Côte Chalonnaise
- Couchois
- Mâconnais

Top grapes
- Pinot Noir
- Chardonnay
- Aligoté
- Gamay

2010 IWC PERFORMANCE

Trophies	6
Gold	24
Silver	95
Bronze	119

FRENCH WHITE BLEND TROPHY

Domaine Désertaux-Ferrand Côte De Nuits-Villages Blanc 2008 White

Herbaceous nose, very full and complex with hits of creamy vanilla. On the palate, ripe, round fruit with hints of melon and peach. Lush, long and juicy finish. Very enjoyable.
£12.54 3DW

Domaine Muzard Champ Claude 2008 White

Mineral and citrus aromas on the nose which follows through intensely on the palate. Good acid gives the wine a lengthy finish.
£15.99 MFW

 POUILLY FUISSÉ TROPHY

Domaine Pierreclos Terroir de Vergisson Pouilly-Fuissé 2008 White

Lovely complexity of fruit delivery. Great structure and a lingering finish.
£18.99 DLW, MWW

 **SAVIGNY-LES BEAUNE TROPHY**

Domaine Seguin-Manuel Goudelettes Sauvigny-les-Beaune 2008 White

Ripe, fresh and tropical aromas on the nose with a citrus edge. Candied peel, ripe red apple and melon on the palate. Very well-balanced with good intensity. Fresh, ripe and delicious.
£14.99 DLW

 CHABLIS TROPHY

Garnier Et Fils Vaudesir Chablis Grand Cru 2007 White

Rich, nutty, evolved nose. Big, powerful, rich but tight citrus peel and mineral flavours. Good acidity. Long and complex.

 CHAMPION WHITE, INTERNATIONAL CHARDONNAY TROPHY, FRENCH WHITE TROPHY, WHITE BURGUNDY TROPHY, PULIGNY MONTRACHET TROPHY

Jean Pascal Marks & Spencer Les Chalumeaux Puligny Montrachet Premier Cru 2007 White

Intense, full bodied, rich and ripe sweet caramel nose. Lovely weight and richness on palate. Long flavours.
£38.00 M&S

Jean-Marc Brocard Domaine De La Boissonneuse Chablis 2008 White

Fresh, nutty, leafy, crème fraiche nose. Nicely intense, creamy lemon palate with a light spicy, peppery finish. Good acidity and a medium length.
£16.99 ADN, BWC, GSL, HTW

Jean-Marc Brocard Vaulorent Chablis Premier Cru 2008 White

Lemon and citrus characters. Orchard fruit on the palate. Clean and pure with good acidity and minerality.

Labouré-Roi Bouches Cheres Meursault Premier Cru 2008 White

Mid-gold fresh ripe stone fruit,

balanced acidity, buttery edge, long lush ripe finish.

Labouré-Roi Clos De La Baronne Meursault 2008
White

Classic style, big, deep, fruity and juicy, tangy, tender, pure.

Laroche Les Clos Chablis Grand Cru 2006   White

Lightly nutty, fresh and lemony nose. Palate is concentrated and structured. Light creamy texture with peppery mineral. Still fresh but not all that complex.

Maison Albert Bichot Domaine Du Pavillon Corton-Charlemagne Grand Cru 2008
White

Pale gold. Integrated tropical flavours dance on the tongue. With a nutty finish.

Patriarche Père Et Fils Puligny-Montrachet 2008   White

Subtly oaked nose. Good, sweet fruit aggressive acidity. Still a little unresolved. Medium length. Requires time but has potential.
£37.22 PAT

Ropiteau Frères Genevrières Meursault Premier Cru 2007
White

Pale lemon, tons of new oaky character, delicate, green fruit notes, balanced oak supported by acidity, long length and elegant.
£50.00

Domaine Chanson Premier Cru Les Caradeux Pernand-Vergelesses 2007 Red

Strong, minerally, perfumed with a smoky nose (suggestions of wild yeast). Peach and spice on the palate with integrated oak, intense yet balanced. Lovely supporting acidity and a long fruit finish. Delicious.
£28.00 FWL

Domaine De La Pousse D'or Clos Du 60 Ouvrees Volnay Premier Cru 2007 Red

Deep mid red. Great strawberry nose. Elegant subtle raspberry flavour. Long and silky tannins.
£59.99 DLW, WAIT, WWC

 INTERNATIONAL PINOT NOIR TROPHY, FRENCH RED TROPHY, RED BURGUNDY TROPHY

Domaine De La Vougeraie Bonnes Mares Grand Cru 2008 Red

Focused red cherry and raspberry notes with perfect fruit. Supported by oak with a long balanced finish.
BAB, BB&R, FMV, HAR

 CHAMBOLLE-MUSIGNY TROPHY

Domaine De La Vougeraie Chambolle-Musigny 2007 Red

Pale ruby. Lovely floral, cream, nutmeg spice and delicate red fruit on the nose. Smooth, creamy. Fine grained tannins. Silky texture. Longish.
BAB, BB&R, FMV

Domaine De La Vougeraie Les Cras Vougeot Premier Cru 2008 Red

Subtle raspberry nose. Soft

approachable strawberry and raspberry fruit. Good depth with a lovely finish.
BB&R, FMV, HAR

CHARMES-CHAMBERTIN TROPHY

Domaine De La Vougeraie Les Mazoyères Charmes-Chambertin Grand Cru 2007
Red
Very intense nose with layers of flavour on the palate and a spicy lingering finish.
BB&R, HAR, HAR

Jean-Claude Boisset Les Jeunes Rois Gevrey-Chambertin 2008
Red
Medium intensity. Red fruits and spice on palate. Balanced. Supple tannins and fresh fruits support lively acid and medium length.

ECHÉZEAUX TROPHY

Maison Albert Bichot Domaine Du Clos Frantin Grands Echézeaux Grand Cru 2008 **Red**
Big, rich and ripe with oaky character. Full in the mouth with ripe fruit and good freshness. Long and lingering.

Pierre André Clos De La Commaraine Pommard Premier Cru 2008 **Red**
Medium colour, restrained morello with mineral notes. Tightly knit. Vibrant red fruit with a lingering finish. Will age gracefully.
RBC

Pierre André Gevrey-Chambertin 2008 **Red**
Medium intensity. Sweet cherry vanilla. Structured fine tannins. Ripe red fruits lifted fresh acidity.

Persistent, elegant finish.
RBC

SILVER

Antonin Rodet La Bressande Rully Premier Cru 2008 White
Woody citrus and mineral nose. Very well rounded with a bright citrus palate. Creamy and fresh with good length.

Auvigue Pouilly-Fuissé Vieilles Vignes 2008 White
Fresh and lively with lovely fruit and a great finish.
£24.25 CSS, FWC, WIL, WSM

Benoit Valarie Calvet Henri De Lorgere Mâcon-Villages 2009 White
Bright, creamy lemon on the nose with nice burnt appley character. Young and refreshing.
£4.99

Blasons De Bourgogne Pouilly-Fuissé Vieilles Vignes 2008 White
Notes of bitter lemon on the nose with smoky fine fruit on the palate. Lovely balance with lemony finish. Ripe, long and complex.
£14.49 MRN

Boisset Chablis 2009 White
Light fruit and strong minerality. Ripe citrus on the palate with apple fruit intensity, hints of peach and lemon ripeness. Long and fresh.
£11.79 BOO

Bouchard Ainé & Fils Bourgogne Chardonnay Réserve 2008 White
Pale straw colour with ripe peachy aromas on the nose. Spicy oak on the palate with a touch of creamy character. Tangy and fresh on the finish with good length.

Bouchard Père & Fils Pouilly-Fuissé 2008 White
Ripe fruit aromas on the nose with a hint of oaky character. Warming on the palate with ripe apple fruit and a touch of bitter lemon. Delicate with nice balance of mineral acidity.

Brocard Chablis 2008 White
Medium intensity of ripe citrus and peach on the nose. Well-balanced with ripe apple and citrus freshness throughout the long and lingering finish.
£8.99 CWS

Cave Des Vignerons De Chablis Petit Chablis 2008 White
Nice, bright wine with good acidity and lemony citrus on the palate. Ripe and round with good freshness and lively acidity. Long.
£8.99 WAIT

Cave Des Vignerons De Chablis Waitrose In Partnership Chablis 2008 White
Green apple fruit on the nose with a hint of vegetal character. Ripe apple palate with a touch of white blossom and citrus-floral flavour. Long.
£9.99 WAIT

Château De La Maltroye Morgeot Vigne Blanche Chassagne-Montrachet Premier Cru 2008 White
Bright and clear. Typical Burgundy nose follows onto the palate with a citrus lift. Silky smooth.
£50.00 WAIT

Château Genot-Boulanger Clos du Cromin Meursault 2008 White
Ripe apple fruit on the nose and palate. A big wine with full mouthfeel. Delicious.
£29.99 DLW

Château Genot-Boulanger Les Bacs Mercurey 2008 White
Integrated oak with an apple citrus nose. Supported by crisp acidity and ripe appley fruit on the palate. Tight minerality with lovely, expressive fruit on the finish.
£14.99 DLW

Domaine Chanson Clos Des Mouches Beaune Premier Cru 2007 White
Plenty of citrus and stone fruit aromas. Complex flavours and firm, fresh acidity.
£56.00 HTG, PAR

Domaine Chapuis Corton-Charlemagne Grand Cru 2007 White
Still closed and tight. Good concentration of flavours, still in primary state. Good acid structure. Long fruit and great potential.
£39.99 DLW

Domaine Chevrot Bourgogne Hautes Côtes De Beaune Blanc 2008 White
Lime cordial and elderflower aromas. Medium bodied with developing mineral character. Melon and pear on the finish.
£11.62 3DW

Domaine De La Pousse d'Or En Callieret Puligny-Montrachet Premier Cru 2007 White
Rich and nutty on the nose. Continues onto the palate with an uplifting citrus nose. Multi-dimensional.
£69.99 BTW, SAIN

Domaine De La Vougeraie Le Clos De Vougeot Monopole Vougeot Premier Cru 2007 White
Ripe and spicy with a gentle, nutty aroma. Fresh and nutty on the palate with good texture. Creamy oak and fresh acidity on

the finish. Delightful.
BB&R, HAR

Domaine De Vauroux Chablis 2008 White

Subtle and creamy nose. Lemon with a leesy character and delicate apple fruits on the palate. Fresh and ripe.

Domaine De Vauroux Montée De Tonnerre Chablis Premier Cru 2008 White

Fine, ripe, youthful and very promising. Excellent core of flavour, salty. Earthy and very long.

Domaine Du Roure De Paulin Pouilly-Fuissé 2008 White

Pale lemon, slight floral aromas with elegant and pungent fruit. Complex and smoky on the palate with a great, lengthy, complex lemon finish.
£17.99 IR-SPQ, JAW

Domaine Feuillat-Juillot Les 761res Montagny Premier Cru 2008 White

Delicate nose of lemon and floral aromas. The palate is ripe with hints of tropical, stony fruit. Ripe complexity with a lingering finish.
£19.99 DLW

Domaine Galopiere Chevalieres Meursault 2008 White

Pale gold, medium intense oak and stone-fruit. Balance. Green fruit acidity, long length, integrated oak supports.
£39.99 DLW, ODD

Domaine Galopiere Ladoix 2008 White

Oak and citrus fruit on the nose. Creamy texture with the citrus nose following through on the palate and a fresh acid backbone.
£24.99 DLW, ODD

Domaine Rochbin Domaine Des Terres Gentilles Macon-Lugny 2009 White

Lime and peachy fruit and good clean acidity and length. Delicately balanced.
£8.99 TKW

Domaine Rochbin Domaine Des Terres Gentilles Mâcon-Villages 2009 White

Positive yeasty nose. Good fruit on palate and long finish.
£8.99 COE

Domaine William Fèvre Chablis 2008 White

Nutty, earthy, mineral and 'sweet' nose. Full, round but intense and fresh palate. Textured and firm. Quite long.

Domaines Brocard Selection Chablis Premier Cru 2008 White

Dark and quite evolved, smoky nose. Buttery richness to palate but mineral too, great balance. Crisp finish, real intensity and flavour.
£12.99 SAIN

J Moreau & Fils Les Clos Chablis Grand Cru 2008 White

Honeyed, nutty nose. Powerful, complex palate. Salty mineral flavours. Intense and long.
FTH, MCT

J Moreau & Fils Montmains Chablis Premier Cru 2008 White

Iodine, white peach, mineral. Good rich style. Very ripe and fleshy with good concentration and underlying minerality. Good acid and length.
MCT

Jean Bourguignon Meursault 2008 White

Rich, creamy, ripe pear, persistent, very good, hint of vanilla oak in good balance.
£17.99 MWW

Jean-Claude Boisset En Remilly St Aubin Premier Cru 2008 White
Very attractive on the nose with a slight nutty aroma, subtle oak and lime.

Jean-Marc Brocard Côte De Léchet Chablis Premier Cru 2008 White
Mineral and citrus nose. Very expressive citrus and mineral palate. A bit of creamy roundness and some good length.

Jean-Marc Brocard Montmains Chablis Premier Cru 2008 White
Good complexity of fine, ripe citrus fruit. The palate is layered with fresh citrus and ripe red apple flavours. Fresh minerality with a long, lush finish.
£18.49 BWC

Jean-Marc Brocard Vau De Vey Chablis Premier Cru 2008 White
Ripe fruit, good flesh. Lemony and appley, mineral and lively. Elegant and persistent with a taut, easy finish. Long and concentrated.
£17.99 BWC

JJ Vincent Et Fils Bourgogne Blanc 2008 White
Fresh and fruity, with a touch of vanilla and spice on the palate. Dense with good length and nice minerality.

La Chablisienne Chablis La Sereine 2008 White
Complex nose with ripeness of fruit. Nutty, rich but dry and mineral palate. Intense but refined. Long, fresh finish.

La Chablisienne Chablis Le Finage 2008 White
Citrus and mineral nose with hints of lemon and celery. Very elegant with a ripe, round character. Green apple and tropical melon on the finish. Long and delicious.

La Chablisienne Côte De Léchet Chablis Premier Cru 2008 White
Pale straw colour. Herby, appley aroma. A well-balanced wine. Grapefruit pith finish.

La Chablisienne La Singulière Chablis Premier Cru 2008 White
Toasty oak influence. Grainy taut minerals, focused and well-integrated. Well-balanced, lively and long.

La Crouze 2008 White
Intense with slightly smoky aromas. Bright fruit on the palate with well-balanced freshness. Round and complete with a long persistent finish.
£11.99

Labouré-Roi Chablis Premier Cru 2008 White
Very clean, fresh, new oak very obvious at the moment, too dominant at present. Will need time to integrate.

Labouré-Roi Chablis Premier Cru 2008 White
Reserved Chablis aromas - tight and a little saline, new oak. Really good intensity on the palate, fresh, mouth-watering, youthful but harmonious.
£11.99 MWW

Labouré-Roi Meursault 2008 White
Deep straw, buttery brioche with a hint of marmalade on the nose. Rich concentrated palate with zesty citrus/lime fruits and mineral acidity. Clean and super fresh.

Lamblin & Fils Chablis 2009
White

Good citrusy acidity with a broad, zesty palate. Mineral tones and hints of ripeness on the palate with peachy overtones. Long and delicate on the finish.

Lamblin & Fils Mont De Milieu Chablis Premier Cru 2009 White

Restrained nose with a hint of perfume floral. Tight mineral core on palate. Has big intensity but very closed.

Laroche Chablis Saint Martin 2008 White

Very nice crisp buttery character. Complex with good acidity and length.

Laroche Reserve de l'Obédience Les Blanchots Chablis Grand Cru 2006
White

Ripe, nutty and fruity palate. Developed but still fresh. Not too complex.

Loron Et Fils Bourgogne Blanc 2008 White

Layers of fruit and oak on nose leading to citrus and peach palate with tart finish but good length.
£7.99

Loron Et Fils Mâcon-Villages Château De Mirande 2008
White

Light yellow. Good intensity on nose. Some butter and leesy structure. Soft but appealing palate. Good for drinking now. Nice roundness.
£10.50

Louis Josse Tesco Finest* Meursault 2008 White

Rich, plum, golden pear, apple, weighty and sweet.
TESC

Maison Louis Jadot Bourgogne Chardonnay 2007
White

Ripe fruit aromas on the nose with a hint of oaky character. Warming on the palate with ripe apple fruit and fresh lemon cream. Delicate with nice balance of mineral acidity.
£11.99 TESC

Maison Louis Jadot Meursault 2007 White

Rich, tropical fruit (peach, tangerine, marmalade) and oak. Beautifully balanced with a persistent, sweet, very long finish.
£25.99 SAIN, WAIT

Patriarche Père Et Fils Chassagne-Montrachet 2008
White

Closed on nose. Palate closed but some zesty fruit comes through on palate. Good length.
£42.64 PAT

Pierre André Saint-Romain 2008 White

Aromas of baked apple and pear drops. Rich and concentrated on the palate with ripe apple fruit, hints of peachy tropicality and good citrus freshness. Mineral balance and good length. Delicious.
RBC

Ropiteau Frères Meursault 2008 White

Clean, bruised apple. Good grippy tannins and Granny Smith acidity. Plenty of fruit. Tense but simple.
£25.00

Simonnet-Febvre Chablis 2008 White

Nice intensity of flinty minerality on the nose. Green apples, lemons on pears on the palate with a good mineral backbone.

Long and lively.
£12.99 BCO, CPB, HFB, QFW

**Union Des Viticulteurs De
Chablis Marks & Spencer
Chablis 2008** White
Minerality, citrus notes with crisp
acidity. Chalky with a long finish.
£9.99 M&S

**Union Des Viticulteurs De
Chablis Marks & Spencer
Côte De Léchet Chablis
Premier Cru 2006** White
Pale straw colour. Expressive
aroma of beeswax and greengage
with a mineral attack. Austere,
mouth puckering finish.
£17.00 M&S

**Union Des Viticulteurs De
Chablis Sainsbury's Taste The
Difference Chablis 2007** White
Slightly honeyed nose. Good
length and well-balanced.
SAIN

**Union Des Viticulteurs De
Chablis Tesco Chablis 2008**
White
Citrus and mineral nose with a
creamy aroma. Green apple and
mineral palate with well-balanced
acidity and good length.
TESC

**Vignerons De Buxy
Bourgogne Aligoté 2009**
White
Steely aromas on the nose with
pungent ripe fruit on the palate.
Lush peach and pear with a
touch of lemony citrus, long
ripeness on the finish.

**Antonin Rodet Clos De
Thorey Nuits-Saint-Georges
Premier Cru 2007** Red
Raspberries and cream on the
nose with a touch of warm spice.
Full mouthfeel with nice, soft
tannins. Very balanced with a
fresh finish.

**Bouchard Aîné & Fils Les
Peuillets Savigny-Lès-Beaune
Premier Cru Cuvée Signature
2008** Red
Easy drinker, dry tannins.
Rounded mouthfeel and
balanced fruit.

**Cave de la Colombe Marks &
Spencer Nuits-Saint-Georges
2007** Red
Black cherry nose with a touch
of strawberry and spice. Slightly
savoury on the palate with good
development of fruit, subtle
tannins and good balance. Fresh
finish.
£25.00 M&S

**Cave Des Hautes Côtes Le
Mont Battois Hautes Côtes
De Beaune 2009** Red
Red fruit and hints of spice.
Fruity Pinot Noir flavours with
round tannin and good balance
- easy to enjoy.

**Château De Melin Chemin De
La Justice Gevrey-Chambertin
2008** Red
Full, earthy, big tannins. Long and
juicy wine with very firm style
but feels like it will age.
£29.99 ODD

**Château St-Michel Rully
2008** Red
Defined cherry and herbal scent
and complexity. Fine tannins.
Texture soft and elegant. Great
balance with fresh acidity.
Excellent, enjoyable wine.
£16.99 DLW

**Domaine Chapuis Aloxe-
Corton Premier Cru 2007** Red
Light pink rim, medium burgundy
middle. Light fruit to nose. Fresh,
strawberry, light and long.
£23.99 DLW

**Domaine Comte De Monspey
Cuvée Du Commandeur 2009**

Red

Rich, crunchy, lovely vibrant cherry and perfumed fruit. Tangy. So lovely, open and refreshing.

Domaine Danjean-Berthoux Givry 2008 Red

Floral nose, fresh light body. Tight tannin lacking complexity but nice freshness and a medium finish.

£12.99 DLW

Domaine De La Pousse d'Or Clos de la Bousse d'or Monopole Volnay Premier Cru 2007 Red

Good red, rich berry aromas. Lots of powerful fruit flavours. Nice long fruity finish.

£59.99 FWL

Domaine De La Pousse d'Or Corton Clos du Roi Grand Cru 2007 Red

Good light red. Delicate raspberry fruits, rich and velvet. Great tannins and delicate finish long.

£89.99 SAIN

Domaine De La Vougeraie Clos Du Roi Corton Grand Cru 2008 Red

Deep red. Light raspberry aromas with earthy notes.

BB&R, FMV

Domaine De La Vougeraie Les Grèves Beaune Premier Cru 2007 Red

Pale ruby. Pronounced intensity with berry cherry aromas integrated with fine oak. A dry finish.

BB&R, HAR

Domaine Gaston Pierre Ravaut Côtes-De-Nuits Villages 2007 Red

Fragrant red fruit nose with hints of pepper. Firm tannins balanced with bright fruit flavours. Very youthful.

£14.99 DLW

Domaine Gavignet Nuits-Saint-Georges 2008 Red

Bright, red fruit on nose with subtle spice. Fresh strawberry fruit on the palate with spicy, white and black pepper. Lively and ripe on the finish.

£28.99 ODD

Domaine Guy Et Yvan Dufouleur Clos Des Perrieres Nuits-Saint-Georges Premier Cru 2006 Red

Black cherry aromas with hints of cherry, caramel, smoke, earth, oak and bacon fat; clean cherry and spicy finish.

Domaine Lucien Jacob En Songe Gevrey-Chambertin 2008 Red

Dark berry aromas and fresh cherry fruit palate, smooth in the mouth, juicy tannins with a chalky feel. Well structured and long.

£18.67 3DW

Domaine Lumpp La Grand Berge Givry Premier Cru 2007 Red

Warm, ripe berry and spice nose. Sour cherry fruit with hints of savoury spice. Refreshing with a long finish.

£19.99 ODD

Domaine Muzard Maladiere Santenay Premier Cru 2008 Red

Light pink rim, medium burgundy mid. Pepper to nose. Very light taste.

£19.99 MFW

Domaine Tortochot Lavaux St Jacques Gevrey-Chambertin Premier Cru 2007 Red

Pretty perfumed nose. Violets and wild strawberries. Gentle,

bright fruit. Very attractive palate. Alcohol on the high side with grippy tannins.
£19.99 DLW, ODD

Dufouleur Frères Le Vaucrain Côte De Nuits Villages 2007 Red

Spicy mocha nose. Coffee, oak and cream flavours. Rich and long.

Dufouleur Frères Les Chaboeufs Nuits-Saint-Seorges Premier Cru 2008 Red

Spicy oak, cedar and tomato leaf aromas. Cassis and faintly meaty, woody, oaky flavours; mouthfilling and very long with lingering, chewy tannins.

Dufouleur Père & Fils Les Chaffots Morey-Saint-Denis Premier Cru 2007 Red

Meaty, complex, savoury nose. Generous fruit and a silky structure.

Jean-Claude Boisset La Dominode Savigny Les Beaune Premier Cru 2008 Red

Savoury soy sauce edge to the nose. The palate shows ripe dark cherry fruit with a spicy savoury finish.
£25.00

Jean-Claude Boisset Les Chardannes Chambolle-Musigny 2008 Red

Good depth of colour. Sweet spice oak and some elements of farmyard. Fresh red fruits with oak and game notes.

Joseph Drouhin Rully 2008 Red

Pine berry fruit nose. Sour cherry palate. Good mineral base. Long finish.
£12.99 BTH, WAIT, WWW

Louis Max Gevrey-Chambertin 2008 Red

Gentle style. Plenty of elegant lithe cherry and raspberry with the fragrance behind.

Maison Albert Bichot Domaine Du Clos Frantin Echezeaux Grand Cru 2008 Red

Fairly muted nose, some Pinot red fruits on palate.

Maison Albert Bichot Les Chabiots Chambolle-Musigny Premier Cru 2008 Red

Strawberries and cream! Fresh Provence herbs on the nose. Quite closed with fruit, lavender and smoky raspberry predominating.

Blasons De Bourgogne Crémant Blanc De Noirs NV Sparkling

Lightly mineral/toasty. Fine mousse. Solid flavour with a definite finish.

Blasons De Bourgogne Crémant Extra Brut NV Sparkling

Developed biscuity aromas, with an excellently creamy palate. Oxidative style but very delicious.

Caves Bailly Lapierre Crémant De Bourgogne Ravizotte NV Sparkling

Simple flavours, quite dulled but good mouthfeel and texture.

Louis Bouillot Rosé Perle D'Aurore Crémant De Bourgogne NV Sparkling Rosé

Pale pink, very frothy. Pure strawberry fruit, very autolytic. Fresh and fruity, easy drinking. Creamy mousse.
LIB

A Roy Montagny Premier Cru 2007 White
Soft nose of pears with floral notes, like acacia. Intense palate with delicious stone fruit and delicate lemon. Long finish.

Auvigue Hors Classe Pouilly-Fuissé 2008 White
Broad, intense, oaky nose. Rich, ripe fruit with good acidity and balance.
£27.99 EVW, HOP

Blasons De Bourgogne Bourgogne Aligoté 2009 White
Pale with a savoury and steely nose. Green leafy character with hints of ripe melon. Lively acidity and integrated fruit on the finish.
£8.99 WAIT

Blasons De Bourgogne Montagny Premier Cru 2008 White
Slightly lifted fruit nose with a complex palate of lemon citrus and stone fruit. Ripe and balanced with good minerality.
TESC

Blasons De Bourgogne Montagny Vieilles Vignes 2008 White
Honey and stone fruit on the nose with a delicate fruit palate. Full with slightly oaky tones and ripe apple freshness on the finish.
SAIN

Blasons De Bourgogne Petit Chablis 2009 White
Lovely, with bright minerality. Crisp green apples with a ripe, peachy character. Long and lush on the finish.

Blasons De Bourgogne Saint Bris 2008 White
Hints of vanilla on the nose with a steely and mineral palate. Lush tropicality balanced with a tinge of citrus. Very pleasing.

Blasons De Bourgogne Saint-Véran Les Pierres Grises 2008 White
Ripe with tropical and nutty aromas on the nose. Hints of citrus on the palate with apple and pear.
£12.99 MRN

Bouchard Ainé & Fils Pouilly-Fuissé 2008 White
Interestingly wild yeasty notes. Very perfumed with pear and citrus fruits. Long.
£15.99 WAIT

Cave De Lugny Macon-Villages Chardonnay 2009 White
Rounded nutty flavour. Really soft good complexity on the the palate. Long finish.
£6.99 ASDA, WAIT

Cave De Lugny White Burgundy Chardonnay 2008 White
Pretty wine with touch of spice and cream. Ripe citrus fruit palate with a savoury finish. Excellent.
£6.98 ASDA

Collovray Et Terrier Chardonnay 2009 White
Attractive pear-like nose. Rich and creamy on the palate with a touch of confected fruit.

Domaine Alain Geoffroy Beauroy Chablis Premier Cru 2008 White
Touch of sulphur, very fresh. Richly flavoured, quite tart but certainly a bold style.

Domaine Alain Geoffroy Chablis 2008 White
Good acidity and fruitiness with

remarkable length. Will improve with time, has good complexity.

Domaine Brelière La Barre Rully Blanc 2008 White
Ripe and delicate with apple and citrus character. Lemon and pear fresh finish.
£12.85 3DW

Domaine Chene Aligoté 2009 White
Light. Gentle balance of fruit and acidity. Clean fruit.
£7.99 DLW, ODD

Domaine Clos Des Roc 2 Monopole 2008 White
Smoke and stewed pears on the nose. Green dry fruit and ripe apples. Fresh and easy to drink.
£15.99 MFW

Domaine Clos des Rocs Monopole 2008 White
Measured elegance. Understated nose. Lovely palate and good finish.
£15.99 MFW

Domaine Clos des Rocs Domaine Clos des Rocs 2008 White
Lovely freshness on nose and palate leads to good fruit delivery and lingering finish. A well made and well-balanced wine.
£13.99 MFW

Domaine Clos des Rocs En Chantone 2008 White
Well-balanced wine with intense stone fruit flavours though oak slightly dominant.
£14.99 MFW

Domaine d'Ardhuy Corton-Charlemagne 2006 White
Some oxidation. Style of wine good but acquired taste.
£89.99 ODD

Domaine De Vauroux Bougros Chablis Grand Cru 2006

White
Bold with ripe fruit and citrus on the nose. Nice citrus characters on palate with a long, fresh finish.

Domaine Des Malandes Chablis 2008 White
Green apple and citrus on the nose. Medium-bodied with fresh fruit and good minerality. Citrus and apple on the palate with nice balance and good freshness.

Domaine Du Château De Marsannay Marsannay White 2007 White
Round and ripe with subtle oak spice and balanced apple notes. A touch medicinal on the palate but works well with the ripe apple fruit.
£9.27 PAT

Domaine Du Château De Meursault Clos Du Château 2008 White
Exotic herb, rhubarb, peaches and cream, fresh tangerine lime, tasty.
£22.76 PAT

Domaine Dupré Mâcon-Villages 2008 White
Green, pear drop aromas. Ripe with gentle, buttery apple finish.

Domaine Gandines Tradicion Viré-Clesse 2008 White
Hints of pineapple on the nose with subtle richness. Fruit is very pleasant with good freshness.
£12.99 ODD

Domaine Guy Et Yvan Dufouleur Les Dames Huguette Bourgogne Hautes-Côtes De Nuits 2008 White
Bright pale yellow and gold in colour. Spicy apples on the nose. Tangy, plenty of oak with a clean, mineral finish.

Domaine Jean Jacques Girard Les Belles Filles Pernand-Vergelesses 2008 White
Soft, peachy, creamy nose with fresh apple and citrus on the palate. A balanced wine with good length and persistence.
£15.99 WAIT

Domaine Jerome Garnier Chablis 2008 White
Some complex aromas. Mineral, ripe fruit on the palate and slightly chalky on the finish.
£13.49 LAI, STC

Domaine Jomain Bourgogne Blanc 2008 White
Clean and light-bodied with a fresh mineral nose. Ripe apple and peach on the palate with a good mineral backbone.
£10.99 MWW

Domaine Louis Moreau Chablis 2008 White
Very green with loads of lemon fruit. Warming on the palate with fresh and ripe citrus fruit coming through. Mineral on the finish.
£9.30 CMR

Domaine Pierreclos Saint-Véran 2008 White
Clean and fresh with a hint of butter on the nose. Lovely fresh acidity with lively fruit flavours.
£16.99 DLW

Domaine Séguinot-Bordet Chablis 2008 White
Creamy vanilla nose and on the palate. Zingy.
3DW

Domaine Séguinot-Bordet Fourchaume Chablis Premier Cru 2008 White
Expressive floral, beeswax aroma. Zingy palate. Citrus notes on mid palate and finish.
£15.75 3DW

Domaine Source de Fees Pouilly-Fuissé 2008 White
Lemon and ripe citrus comes through on the nose. Smoky with ripe nutty fruit on the palate. Ripe and easy drinking.
£19.99 ODD

Domaine Source de Fees Saint-Véran 2008 White
Smoky with hints of tropical aromas. Flower petals and ripe apple blossom on the palate. Ripe and powerful with good depth and length.
£17.99 DLW

Domaine Vessigaud Pouilly-Fuissé 2008 White
Very well-balanced and harmonious with excellent fruit on palate but slightly short finish.
£19.99 BTW, CHH, MFW

Superquinn Petit Chablis 2008 White
Crisp with a hint of voluptuousness on the mid-palate. Lemony and ripe with good intensity. Long and fresh.
£8.99 XXSPQ

FGV Thorin Pouilly-Fuissé 2009 White
Lemon nose with smoky overtones. Ripe and round citrus fruit with hints of citrus blossom. Warming and long on the finish.
£17.09 BOO

J Moreau & Fils Chablis 2009 White
Green apple and juicy lemon on the nose with a touch of flint. Minerally and ripe on the palate with a clean finish.
FTH, MAI, MCT

J Moreau & Fils Fourchaume Chablis Premier Cru 2008 White
Mute aroma. Steely, elegant and

well-balanced.
FTH, MCT

Jaboulet Vercherre Mâcon-Villages 2008 White
Clean bright Chardonnay fruit with a good hint of feisty acidity and some nice stone fruits. Round, creamy.

Jaffelin Saint-Romain 2007 White
Candied citrus fruit on the nose with ripe apple flavours. Good concentration with broad ripeness on the finish.
£14.99

Jean-Claude Boisset Rully 2007 White
Creamy oak and citrus nose. A lot of creamy, textured oak on the palate with citrus fruit freshness. Good depth with long length.
£16.99 JCC, LIB, NYW

Jean-Marc Brocard Bougros Chablis Grand Cru 2008 White
Very youthful with a flinty nose. Long flavour on palate.
£32.99 BWC

Jean-Marc Brocard Chablis From Organically Grown Grapes 2007 White
Crisp and fresh with a nice length.
£12.99 M&S

Joseph Drouhin Rully Premier Cru 2008 White
Integrated oak, citrus and mineral nose. Woody flavours on the citrus laden palate. Strong mineral backbone with a good youthful edge.
£13.99 WWD, WAIT

La Chablisienne Chablis La Pierrelée 2008 White
Lemony with a hint of tinned veg on the nose. Medium intensity with fresh and tart acidity. Ripe and long on the finish.

La Chablisienne Les Vénérables Vieilles Vignes Chablis 2008 White
Fresh fruit and straw nose but a bit evolved with a hint of oxidation. Lemony, crème fraiche palate. Textured.

Labouré-Roi Chablis Le Beaunois 2009 White
Slightly flinty on the nose with juicy ripe fruit. A touch of roundness and warmth on the palate with good length and fresh acidity.

Labouré-Roi Chablis Premier Cru 2009 White
Wonderful minerally apples and roses. Great finesse and balance with a gorgeous toasty edge.

Labouré-Roi Le Beaunois Chablis 2008 White
Flinty, mineral nose with a hint of nice reduction. Balanced acidity and freshness with ripe lemon and melon flavours. Flinty and very long.

Laroche Les Vaillons Vieilles Vignes Chablis Premier Cru 2007 White
Oak gives complexity to the nose, some ripe fruit weight characters with mineral core. Richness and creamy texture, mealy profile.

Les Vignerons Des Terres Secretes Tesco Mâcon-Villages 2008 White
Delicate, clean, lemon, floral nose. Light initially but develops in the mouth. Quite long.
TESC

Loron Et Fils Les Vieux Murs Pouilly-Fuissé 2008 White
Mid bodied. Elegant with ripe

peach, lemon and creamy notes. Medium full bodied red with refreshing acidity. Lovely.
£13.49

Louis Moreau Domaine Jean De Bosmel Chablis 2008 White
Lemony with a Granny Smith like crunch. Full and flavoursome with lifted citrus and good minerality.

Pascal Bouchard Chablis 2008 White
Lemon and lime on the nose. Hint of grapefruit. Light and minerally on the palate.

Pasquier Desvignes Chablis 2009 White
Good acidity with strong mineral character. Very fresh on the palate with citrus and floral flavours. Well-balanced and ripe.

Pasquier Desvignes Viré-Clessé 2009 White
Clean with fresh almondy aromas on the nose. Toasty and nutty on the palate with a rich butter finish.
£7.99 MWW

Pierre André Genevrières Meursault Premier Cru 2008 White
Big, ripe and developed. Bruised apple and pear palate with lush ripeness on the finish.
RBC

Sandrine Loron Louis Loron Et Fils 2006 White
Fresh with ripe apple and lemon citrus aromas. Floral and ripe with a peach blossom palate. Mineral on the finish.

Simonnet-Febvre Montmains Chablis Premier Cru 2008 White

Stony, minerally and citrus nose. Firm acid supports citrus fruit. Nice racy wine. Pleasant intense flavour. A more linear style.
£18.99 CPB, FNC, POG

Simonnet-Febvre Petit Chablis 2008 White
Slightly tropical with hints of floral citrus on the palate. Tart and tangy with lively freshness.
£8.99 FNC, HFB, SWB, TWI, WAIT

Terres Secrètes Saint-Véran 2008 White
Rich, ripe and round on the palate with balanced apple and citrus fruits. Mineral and tropical hints on the finish.

Union Des Viticulteurs De Chablis Sainsbury's Taste The Difference Chablis Premier Cru 2007 White
Pungent, leafy. Highly flavoured, fresh with a good core. Just needs 2 to 3 years to harmonise.
SAIN

Union Des Viticulteurs De Chablis Sainsbury's Taste The Difference Petit Chablis 2008 White
Crisp and dry with good attack. On the palate the fruit is fresh and mineral. Nice, hearty style.
SAIN

Union Des Viticulteurs De Chablis Tesco Finest* Chablis Premier Cru 2007 White
Very subtle, mineral and slightly vegetal. Good concentration. Bone dry with good acidity. Very much a food wine. Long.
TESC

Vignerons De Buxy JS White Burgundy 2008 White
Rounded nutty flavour with good complexity on the palate. Long finish.
SAIN

Vignerons De Buxy Montagny Premier Cru 2008 White
Delicate nose of ripe fruit, zippy and full on the palate with lemon and peach freshness. Pear ripeness on the finish.
£10.99 MRN

Vignerons De Buxy Montcuchot Montagny Premier Cru 2008 White
Citrus and mineral nose. Ripe lemon and oaky cream on the palate. Still quite youthful and will benefit from time.

Vignerons De Buxy Sainsbury's Taste The Difference Bourgogne Aligoté 2009 White
Woody, herbaceous aromas with hints of ripe melon, peach and pear drops. Long with lively freshness.
SAIN

Vignerons Des Terres Secrètes Mâcon-Verzé Croix-Jarrier 2008 White
Lemony palate with fruit fresh ripeness. Complex and well-made.

Vignerons Des Terres Secrètes Pouilly-Fuissé Terra Incognita 2008 White
Fresh citrus and pear. Very elegant on the palate. Good acidity.

Antonin Rodet Château De Rully 2008 Red
Brightly fruity cherryish nose. The palate is fresh and tart with berry fruits and a bit of spice.

Antonin Rodet Domaine de Mercey Hautes-Côtes-de-Beaune Rouge 2008 Red
Fragrant red fruits. Firm and fresh with well-integrated oak. Good balance and weight.

Antonin Rodet Domaine De Mercey Mercurey 2007 Red
Has body, soft tannin and fresh raspberries. Medium acid and long length. Good balance and complexity.

Antonin Rodet Givry 2008 Red
Deep red, jammy nose. Fresh and juicy fruit on palate with a long finish.

Boisset Côte De Beaune Villages 2005 Red
Black cherry and slightly savoury nose. Subtle tannins and good balance.
£13.29 BOO

Bouchard Ainé & Fils Bougogne Pinot Noir Réserve 2008 Red
Bright red cherry/mulberry. Very fresh and youthful. Sweetish fruits at their best.

Château De Melin Le Chainay Santenay 2008 Red
Good red colour. Elegant blackberry nose. Light and easy of nut and broad mouthfeel.
£13.99 DLW

Coudert Fleurie Domaine De La Chapelle Des Bois 2009 Red
Bright purple to ruby. Ripe, fresh fruit on nose. Ripe fruit in palate. A good length.

Des Deux Château Château De La Terriere Brouilly 2009 Red
Deepish ruby. Elegant raspberry nose. Firm style with structure and elegant blueberry finish.

Domaine d'Ardhuy Clos de Vougeot Grand Cru 2006 Red
Dark fruits, quite extracted, spicy.
£89.99 ODD

Domaine De La Madone Fleurie Domaine Du Niagara 2009 Red
Brash, juicy creamy style. Long, fresh bouncy cherry and raspberry. Tangy finish.
£10.68 3DW

Domaine De La Vougeraie Clos De Vougeot Grand Cru 2008 Red
Has some Pinot Noir perfume. Good classic Pinot on palate.
BAB, BB&R, FMV, HAR

Domaine Désertaux-Ferrand Les Perrières Côte-De-Nuits Villages 2007 Red
Berry aromas on the nose with savoury hints. Aniseed, and intense cherry fruit flavours. Well-balanced.
£13.39 3DW

Domaine Du Château De Marsannay Marsannay 2007 Red
Full, red fruit nose with intense red fruits on palate. Ripe, firm tannins. Lingering finish.
£7.92 PAT

Domaine Du Château De Meursault Les Peuillets Savigny Les Beaune Premier Cru 2008 Red
Pale, nice strawberry nose, light and good. Light flavour. Good body and length.
£25.48 PAT

Domaine Guy Et Yvan Dufouleur Fixin Premier Cru Clos Du Chapitre Monopole 2007 Red
Refined nose of red fruits with delicate spice. Full rounded palate of red fruits and some woodland notes.
HOH

Domaine Heresztyn Vieilles Vignes Gevrey-Chambertin 2007 Red
Fragrant, lively, balanced, juicy and fresh. Tannic knit has a velvety core, truffle and forest fruit.
£25.99 WAIT

Domaine Lucien Jacob Les Avaux Beaune Premier Cru 2008 Red
Cherry, jammy spice. Bright and honest.
£18.34 3DW

Domaine Lucien Jacob Savigny-lès-Beaune 2008 Red
Elegant fruit and structure. Well-integrated wine with a touch of spice.
£12.29 3DW

Domaine Michel Gros Aux Brûlées Vosne Romanée Premier Cru 2008 Red
Big bacon fat nose. Smoky flavour and a lovely ripe finish.

Domaine Michel Gros Chambolle-Musigny 2008 Red
Lovely vibrant raspberries and wild strawberries. Some toast and creamy oak notes. Firm, muscular structure but still youthful. Wild red fruits, toast and biscuit. Lively acidity.

Domaine Michel Gros Clos Des Réas Monopole Vosne Romanée Premier Cru 2008 Red
Soft, ripe raspberry. Warm rich flavours with soft, sweet, raspberry fruit.

Domaine Michel Gros Nuits Saint Georges 2008 Red
Pale colour - ruby tints. Lifted tar, rubber aromas. High toast barrels. Moderate weight on palate, silky tannins with some intensity on the finish.

Domaine Noellat Michel et Fils Les Beaux Monts Vosne

Romanée Premier Cru 2007 Red
Bright red fruits. Complex savouriness. Perfumed, tightly focused, soft tannins. Good extraction. Elegant.
£39.99 DLW

Domaine Noellat Michel et Fils Les Suchots Vosne Rommanee Premier Cru 2007 Red
Good colour. Soft easy fruit aroma. Palate boasts of ripeness. Well made with generous tannins.
£39.99 DLW

Domaine Ragot La Grande Berge Givry Premier Cru 2008 Red
Slightly roasted nose. The palate is reduced and spicy with bright berry fruits.
£14.29 3DW

Dufouleur Frères Combe-Dessus Gevrey-Chambertin 2007 Red
Nice smoky coffee style, gentle, juicy but quite alcoholic. Strawberry finish.

Dufouleur Père & Fils Chambolle-Musigny 2007 Red
More held back. Delicate red fruits, cranberries, spice and creamy oak notes (harder and greener notes on palate). More lively redcurrant but slightly lacking mid palate.

FGV Thorin Beaujolais-Villages 2009 Red
Lovely vibrant and sold. Plenty of tang and balance. Earthy notes and red berry finish. Good fun and promising.
£7.49 BOO

Fredric Magnien Marsannay 2005 Red
Intense red cherry and rose petal nose. Refined acidity. Well-balanced and very moreish.
£16.99 DLW

Jean-Claude Boisset Gevrey-Chambertin Le Creot 2007 Red
Medium colour. Earthy morello cherry aroma. Spicy mineral notes on palate. A restrained wine with a very long finish.
£40.00 LIB

Jean-Pierre Teissèdre Beaujolais-Villages Domaine Des Grandes Bruyères 2009 Red
Quite tight, young and simple but honest style. Long and tangy.

Labouré-Roi Red Burgundy 2009 Red
More of a black cherry character but the mulberry of Pinot comes through giving a brightness to the finish.

Loron Et Fils Bourgogne Rouge Pinot Noir 2008 Red
Quite light but has a charming mulberry fragrance. Fresh, firm but sweet.
£8.09

Louis Josse Tesco Finest* Nuits St Georges 2006 Red
Sweet aromas of cherry a nd redcurrant on the nose. Well-balanced, bright red fruits with lifted acidity on the palate. Concentrated red fruits and fine tannins on the lingering finish.
TESC

Louis Latour Pinot Noir Bourgogne 2008 Red
Fresh new fruit. Quite light but lovely and fragrant. Raspberry cherry at the back.
£9.99 Widely Available

Maison Albert Bichot Les Amoureuses Chambolle-Musigny 2008 Red
Bright cherry wine with gentle wood smoke and cherry to nose.

Easy red fruit and refreshing spice. Finishes dry and clean.

Maison Louis Jadot Beaune Premier Cru 2007 Red
Elegant cherryish fruit with a savoury, spicy twist. Attractive and varietally true.
£15.99

Patriarche Père Et Fils Clos De Verger Pommard 2007 Red
Light pink rim. Plum nose. Nice, summer fruit, full and lasting flavour.
£38.53 PAT

Pierre André Bourgogne Pinot Noir Réserve 2008 Red
Bright red fruit on nose. Fresh at the start of the palate. Light and fresh.
RBC

Ropiteau Frères Bourgogne Pinot Noir 2008 Red
Delicious on nose, lovely fresh new fruits. Tower of black cherry fruit flavour from behind.
£9.99

Vignerons De Buxy Bourgogne Côte Chalonnaise Rouge 2009 Red
Ripeness to nose with bramble, refreshed by bilberry. Youthful and long.

Bailly Lapierre Crémant De Bourgogne Pinot Noir NV Sparkling
Light berry nose. Slightly dry. Good length on mid palate. Finishes short.

Bailly Lapierre Crémant De Bourgogne Réserve NV Sparkling
Fresh and fruity. Quite simple but balanced and good structure. Pinot dominated firmness.

Maison Louis Picamelot Cremant De Bourgogne Blanc Brut NV Sparkling
Attractive creamy balanced nose. Good length. Dry, crisp blossom fruit, baked apple, persistent mousse.
£9.95 JAS

France:
Champagne

For the IWC judges, Champagne is always a popular category, funnily enough. Time and again, this region outperforms anywhere else in the world for sparkling wine; there may be many pretenders, but only one true king. Whatever it is, the soil, the cellars, the grapes or the growers, there is something special about these particular bubbles. After a year of dismal sales thanks to the economic downturn, Champagne is back on the agenda in 2010, with financially-smarting producers keen to ensure their Champagnes are better than ever. As ever, the grande marques do well, but there are some small producers worth checking out too.

2010 IWC PERFORMANCE

Trophies	3
Gold	23
Silver	80
Bronze	82
Great Value Awards	1

KEY FACTS

Total production
2.9 m hectolitres,
3.96 million bottles
(2007)

Total vineyard
35,280ha of
which 32,706ha
is productive:
23,722ha in the
Marne Department;
6,681ha in the Aube
and Haute-Marne;
2,303ha in the Aisne
and Seine-et-Marne

Top varieties
- Pinot Noir
- Pinot Meunier
- Chardonnay

Producers
15,000 wine-growers
including 4,733
who produce their
own Champagne
(Récoltants
Expéditeurs), 65
co-operatives and
284 negociants

De Beaumont Des Crayeres Nostalgie 2000 Sparkling
Good levels of fresh apple-cream and citrus nose. Creamy yet lively mousse. Floral aroma adds finesse.

Duval-Leroy Femme De Champagne 1996 Sparkling
Green gold - classic nose. Very richly honeyed, creamy, yeasty nose. Very lively. Fresh citrus, cream and nutty flavours on the palate.

Henriot Vintage 1998 Sparkling
Bright green gold. Bruised apple, nutty aromas, creamy mousse. Fall away is a bit flat.
£39.99 HAR, NIC, SEL

J De Telmont 2000 Sparkling
Delicate, floral, very dainty. Terrific attack, dry. Very fresh, very long. Really elegant, top class champagne.

Lanson Gold Label Brut Vintage 1999 Sparkling
Complex aromatics. Rich and broad full palate, firm structure taste. Persistent length.

P & C Heidsieck Charles Heidsieck Blanc Des Millenaires 1983 Sparkling
Lemon gold hue. Buttered toast and hazelnuts. Lovely ripeness of fruit and great texture on palate. Lively appley acidity (some toastiness) and great length.
£195.00 BB&R, HAR, SAIN

P & C Heidsieck Charles Heidsieck Blanc Des Millenaires 1995 Sparkling
Creamy, warm brioche, freshly baked bread and citrus on nose. Lively, vibrant acidity and quite tight knit. Brisk mousse.
£195.00 BB&R, HAR, SAIN

 MATURE VINTAGE CHAMPAGNE TROPHY

P & C Heidsieck Charles Heidsieck Charlie 1981 Sparkling
Developed showing mushy notes. Complex tertiary, earthy aromas of black truffle mushroom. Palate still alive with middle weight. Sandalwood/gingerbread.

P & C Heidsieck Charles Heidsieck Charlie 1985 Sparkling
Caramelised, mature nutty flavours, baked apples, toasted fruit. Quite long, dry finish, very good.

 CHAMPION SPARKLING, YOUNG VINTAGE CHAMPAGNE TROPHY

P & C Heidsieck Charles Heidsieck Millésime 2000 Sparkling
Lemon rind, richer style, caramel biscuit, nice length, good finish. Thinker's Champagne.
£39.99 BB&R, HAR, SAIN

P & C Heidsieck Co-Operative Les Pionniers 2002 Sparkling
Big, complex and savoury notes. Balanced acidity. Good length. Elegant.
£19.99 CWS

P & C Heidsieck Piper-Heidsieck Rare 2002 Sparkling
Creamy, gentle hints. Light brioche and lovely notes. Elegant balance and long.
£150.00 BB&R, HAR, SAIN

Pannier Egerie De Pannier Extra Brut 2000 Sparkling
Rich and full creamy palate. Lovely

flavours. Oak biscuit, berry nose. Distinctive mineral character. Very good length – definite.
£56.00 COE

Paul Goerg Premier Cru Cuvée Lady Millésime 2000
Sparkling

Lovely lemon cream aromas. Toasty, biscuity nose. Fresh, lively, with a creamy note. Strong finish.

BLANC DES BLANCS CHAMPAGNE TROPHY

Paul Goerg Premier Cru Millésime Brut 2004 Sparkling
Full of bubbles. Lemon. Intense yeasty biscuit, honey pithy notes. Long rounded mouthfeel framed by fresh acidity.

Taittinger Brut Vintage 2004
Sparkling

Intriguing umami nose - soy sauce, celery and lively green fruits. Firm structure and acid, good length with stony minerality.
£45.75

Taittinger Comtes De Champagne Blanc De Blancs 1999 Sparkling
Very tasty nutty nose. Lovely racey citrus characters on palate. Great purity and elegance.
£95.00 WAIT

Union Champagne Marks & Spencer Orpale Grand Cru 1998 Sparkling
Ripe full flavour. Mature developed and round. Well-balanced fruits.
£55.00 M&S

Bollinger Rosé NV Sparkling Rosé
Lovely nose. Vibrant acidity. Cranberry and peach stone fruit.

Very long. A class act.
£49.99 WI-AV, WAIT

Forget-Brimont Brut Rosé Premier Cru NV Sparkling Rosé
Beautiful colour. Saignée. Clean and fresh. Pristine raspberry fruit. Excellent balance with poise. Long.
£22.49 GWI, J&B, JNW, PEA, ROD

Lombard & Médot Philippe Guidon Rosé NV Sparkling Rosé
Subtle savoury notes. Hedgerow fruit, hint of sous bois. Delicate and fine. Persistent.
£22.99 ODD

P & C Heidsieck Charles Heidsieck Rosé 1999
Sparkling Rosé

Biscuity brioche layered aromatics. Lively acidity in bright red fruit and smooth mousse. Persistent and full. Mineral length.
£45.99 BB&R, HAR, SAIN

Pierre Paillard Rosé Grand Cru NV Sparkling Rosé
Attractive bready autolysis and subtle fruit. Elegant palate, fresh, fine, smooth and rounded.

SILVER

Alexandre Bonnet Grande Reserve NV Sparkling
Very slightly yeasty - marmite. Quite an aggressive manner on palate. Fruit balances nicely with acidity and mousse. Nice autolysis on palate.
£26.00

Ayala Brut Majeur NV
Sparkling

Developed, spicy, macaroon note yet also fresh. A sweet, firm fruit, cream texture and good acidity. Some length. Elegant.
£24.00 BB&R

Ayala Perle D'Ayala 2002
Sparkling
Floral, brioche aroma. Grilled toast and citrus notes on palate. Lingering finish.
£57.00 FWL

Besserat De Bellefon Cuvée Des Moines Brut Millésime 2002 Sparkling
Pale youthful straw colour, vegetable aromas. Astringent on the palate and vigorous mousse. Some brioche character on the finish.

Besserat De Bellefon Cuvée Des Moines Extra Brut NV
Sparkling
Fresh nose of apple and savoury bread. Fresh acidity on weight. Zesty, minerally acidity.

Bollinger La Grande Année 2000 Sparkling
Deep and mature. Rich, toasty, almost hot - hollow in the middle.
£38.99 WI-AV, TESC, WAIT

Bollinger Special Cuvée NV
Sparkling
Smooth citrus and brioche notes. Lovely, creamy and complex on the palate with very long flavours. Ripe, toasty and tasty.
£38.99 WI-AV, TESC, MRN, WAIT

Canard Duchene Cuvée Leonie NV Sparkling
Lifted strawberry and apple. Crisp acidity, good mousse. Fresh crisp style, creamy textured length.

Canard Duchene Millésime 2004 Sparkling
Pleasant yeasty nose. Dry citrus, white stone fruit palate. Simple but very likeable.

Ch & A Prieur Grand Prieur Brut Millésime 2000

Sparkling
Fine colour. Lively mousse. Elegant, subtle biscuit - apricot nose. Subtle, almost smoky finish.

Charles Heidsieck Brut NV
Sparkling
Big, ripe, fruity nose, lots of minerality, lovely intensity, long and very fine finish.
£31.99 MRN

De Beaumont Des Crayeres Fleur Blanche 2001 Sparkling
Pale straw colour, rich scented brioche aromas, crisp acidity. Fine mousse with mineral finesse and long length.

Deregard Massing Dubois Caron NV Sparkling
Good yeasty notes. Pinot character. Good acidity. Complex creamy palate.
ASDA

Deutz Cuvée William Deutz 1999 Sparkling
An aromatic nose, with brioche & peach dominant. An excellent palate, with crisp acidity; coming through with black fruits.
£89.49 HVN

Devaux D De Devaux L'Ultra NV Sparkling
Floral and brioche perfume with crème fraiche. Very dry, yeasty palate with citrus fruits. Slightly austere but good length and structure.
£41.99 LIB

Duval-Leroy Brut NV Sparkling
Soft mouthfeel. Crisp acidity. Developed grilled nuts and meaty aromas. Appealing.

Duval-Leroy Duval-Leroy Clos Des Bouveries 2004
Sparkling
Fresh, yeasty nose. Delicate and elegant. Clean finish. Lemon zest

and very well-integrated mousse - short.

Duval-Leroy Fleur De Champagne Brut Premier Cru NV Sparkling
Lively bubbles. Vegetal notes/yeasty. Soft fruit flavour. Biscuits. Firm structure and good mouthfeel. Good length.
£26.99 WAIT

Duval-Leroy Sainsbury's Taste The Difference 2004
Sparkling
Delicious. Good acidity. Well made with bright flavours.
SAIN

Duval-Leroy Vintage 1999
Sparkling
Clean, complex nose showing brioche, biscuity notes. Hints of spices with white pepper nose. Long finish.

Fleury Blanc De Noirs NV
Sparkling
Excellent, fresh, lively Pinot nose. Really elegant, delicate, good depth of flavour, long. Top class.
£29.99 WAIT

Henriot Blanc Souverain NV
Sparkling
Fresh but evolved, creamy, brioche, toast and savoury notes on the nose. Open, ripe apple and citrus fruit. Delicate toasty tones with some mineral on the finish. Balance of acidity. Medium length.
£33.00 HAR, NIC, SEL

J De Telmont Blanc De Blancs Brut 2004 Sparkling
Very dry, solid, ripe, good honest grip and fruit. Some smoky intensity. Floral with a slight dusty chocolate edge.

J De Telmont Grande Reserve Brut NV Sparkling
Pale gold colour. Apples/

autumnal fruit, fresh. Lovely yeasty biscuits at the end.

Janisson Et Fils Blanc De Noirs NV Sparkling
Pale lemon. Delicate, small bubbles. Delicate toasty nose. Great bubbles on the palate. Lemony finish. Delicious mushroom. Youthfully fresh.
£17.99 CWH

Janisson Et Fils Francois De Rozay NV Sparkling
Pale and persistent - yeast, Bovril and hedgerow on nose. Dry, balanced; quite elegant with an excellent length.
£13.99 CWH

JM Gobillard Et Fils Blanc De Blancs NV Sparkling
Good honey nose, lovely development on the palate with nutty ripeness and biscuit flavours. Long and pleasant.

JM Gobillard Et Fils Cuvée Prestige 2005 Sparkling
Lovely and luscious. Richly textured fruit. Long.

Lallement-Dubois François Dubois NV Brut NV Sparkling
Ripe red and black fruit on the palate. Nice evolution and very well-balanced. Delicious and ripe on the finish.
TESC

Lanson Extra Age Brut NV
Sparkling
Lasting mousse. Perfumed with delicate red fruits, cream and brioche. Rich nose. Full, fruity and spicy with biscuity notes. Dry zesty finish.

Le Mesnil Blanc De Blancs Grand Cru 2004 Sparkling
Lush, gentle, creamy and rich flavour. Nice openness. Fruit in good balance with yeast

complexity.
£30.99 WAIT

Maison Lenique Blanc De Blancs NV Sparkling
Delicate floral and straw aromas, lime blossom complexity. Lovely pale gold colour. Kaffir lime on the palate; elegant finish though not awfully long.
£17.60 3DW

Maison Lenique Brut NV 2005 Sparkling
Very fine mousse. Fine rich biscuit, deep brioche. Great length and top class.
£23.83 3DW

Maison Pierrel Black & Gold Limited Edition Vintage Blanc De Blancs 2002 Sparkling
Youthful straw colour. Restrained aromas with fine mineral palate. Some creamy weight and green apple fruit towards the finish.
£29.00 CPE

Maison Pierrel Marquis De La Fayette Brut Sélection NV Sparkling
Lively. Some biscuit/leafy notes. Cream feel. Balanced acid and bruised apple aftertaste.
£20.00 CPE

Maurice Vesselle Brut Cuvée Reserve Grand Cru NV Sparkling
Pale gold. Good mousse, toasty, brioche notes. Fresh and appley. Fresh and dry, powerful, complex and very long finish.

Maurice Vesselle Brut Millésime Grand Cru 2000 Sparkling
Delicate wine with mouth-watering flavours of lively lychee, crisp with lovely lingering structure and finish.

Maurice Vesselle Brut Millésime Grand Cru 2002

Sparkling
Good deep elegant notes. Good, bright toast. Elegant. Good length.

Moet & Chandon Grand Vintage 2003 Sparkling
Deep concentrated. Lovely redcurrant and citrus but precise balanced acidity.
£40.99 WAIT

Moet & Chandon Grand Vintage Collection 1995 Sparkling
Bright green, gold. Citrus. Softly honeyed. The nose has lots of bruised apple but still good acidity. Fresh and clean taste.

Napoléon Blanc De Blancs Brut NV Sparkling
Fresh, biscuity, floral and delicately creamy. Citrus fruit on the palate. Attractively taut, light biscuits. Good length and acidity.

Nicolas Feuillatte Brut Reserve Particuliere NV Sparkling
Straw. Soft and creamy. Blancs and Noirs. Dry. Good solid wine.

Nicolas Feuillatte Cuvée Speciale Millésime 2003 Sparkling
Yeasty biscuit nose, apple fruit, gentle mousse. Good length.

Oudinot Marks & Spencer Vintage 2004 Sparkling
Clean, ripe, pure. Fine smoky style. Good long, solid, tangy, bright and floral. Apple and slight redcurrant.
£26.00 M&S

P & C Heidsieck Charles Heidsieck Brut Reserve NV Sparkling
Gentle autolysis. Nice mix of appley fruit and yeasty feel. Some development. Good

flavour and moderate length.
£30.99 BB&R, HAR, SAIN, MRN, WAIT

P & C Heidsieck Piper-Heidsieck Florens Louis NV
Sparkling
Developed nutty character, a low key nuttiness on mid palate, good concentration, medium to long in length.
£21.00 BB&R, HAR, SAIN

GREAT VALUE SPARKLING WINE BETWEEN £15 AND £20

P & C Heidsieck Waitrose Brut NV NV
Sparkling
Crisp and dry. Good mousse ripe. It is a good drinkable wine.
£19.99 WAIT, WWD, WWW

P & C Heidsieck Waitrose Vintage 2002
Sparkling
Gentle subtle nose, with good fruit at end. Palate delightfully fresh with biscuit and apple flavours. Good acidity and length.
£26.99 WAIT, WWD, WWW

Pannier Brut Blanc De Blancs 2004
Sparkling
Fine bubbles, lemon honey butter. Brioche on nose. Follows through on palate. Creamy mousse. Lovely zesty lemon pith on the finish.
£32.00 COE

Pannier Brut Vintage 2004
Sparkling
Attractive creamy nose with some toast notes. The palate is lively, fresh and toasty. Lovely balance and freshness.
£27.50 COE

Paul Goerg Premier Cru, Absolu Extra Brut NV
Sparkling
French crème fraiche and

minerals with a hint of oxidation on the nose. Dry, steely, mineral, concentrated. Underlying peach fruit.

Perrier-Jouet Grand Brut 1998
Sparkling
Quite pale lemon. Earthy. Some toast, roasted nut. Lively, fresh, crisp mousse, lemon pie and creamy mushroom.
£35.99 HAR, HVN, MAJ

Pierre Gimonnet & Fils Cuvée Gastronome Premier Cru Blanc De Blancs 2005
Sparkling
Maturing honeyed nose, a touch oxidative. Developed, honeyed toasty palate with some fresh citrus fruit. Good acidity. Fairly full. Dry and long.
£30.00

Pierre Gimonnet & Fils Cuvée Premier Cru Chardonnay 2000
Sparkling
Vintage 2000. Creamy, biscuit nutty. Creamy and austere. Nice mineral edge. Quite serious with a good structure.

Pierre Paillard Millésime Grand Cru 2002
Sparkling
Spice, apple, mint. Elegant nose. Nice length.

Pierrel Grande Cuvée Vintage Blanc De Blancs 1998
Sparkling
Bright green gold. Broader palate. Creamy, nutty, delicate. Fresh brioche, hint of honey. Firm bubbles. Brisk and lovely.
£33.00 CPE

Roger Brun Brut Resérve NV
Sparkling
Good froth. Yeasty nose (very definite). Good flavour. Light and balanced.
£29.99 FRW, LIB, VOA

Soc. Champenoise Des Barons Et Associes Barons De Rothschild Brut NV Sparkling
Good mousse. Lovely colour. Vegetal evolved nose. Good balance. Long and complex.

Taittinger Les Folies De La Marquetterie NV NV
Sparkling
Very mineral. Sweet fruit with a nice length.
£47.99

Taittinger Nocturne Sec NV NV Sparkling
Honeyed fruit, citrus and candied almonds. Well-balanced acidity with a racy finish. Quite long and very pleasant.
£40.25

Taittinger Prélude Grands Crus NV Sparkling
Fine bubbles. Good mouthfeel. Crisp apple notes. Soft apple notes/cream. Medium length.
£42.50

Troillard Elexium NV Sparkling
Slightly lactic nose but crisp lemony fruit.

Union Champagne De Saint Gall Blanc De Blancs 2004
Sparkling
Lively lemon. Floral notes. Bready, lemon biscuits. Pithy, zesty acidity supports length.
£28.00 M&S

Union Champagne De Saint Gall Brut Tradition NV
Sparkling
Developed, full concentrated and long. Complex, biscuity and green apple freshness.
£18.00 M&S

Veuve Clicquot Cave Privée 1990 Sparkling
Nutty complex notes. High cutting acidity with rich lush fruit. Still very taut and young. Long mineral finish.

Veuve Clicquot Yellow Label NV
Sparkling
Clean, fresh. Good attack and taut on the palate. Refreshing.
£44.50 TESC, MRN, WAIT

Vincent D'Astrée Empreinte Du Temps 2000 Sparkling
Creamy, nutty, fragrant. Very dry, vegetal style, bit too raw on the palate. Acquired taste.

Vranken-Pommery Monopole Charles Lafitte Grande Cuvée Brut NV Sparkling
Very good balance. Green copper maturity. Pleasant.
£28.99 J&B

Vranken-Pommery Monopole Heidsieck & Co Monopole Gold Top 2004 Sparkling
Pale yellow, good mousse, toasty nose. Ripe & fresh, zingy high acidity.
£32.99 MAJ

Alexandre Bonnet Rosé NV
Sparkling Rosé
Good, fine strawberry fruits on nose. Fleshy fruit on palate. Lovely balance and length.
£25.99 WAIT

Canard Duchene Rosé NV
Sparkling Rosé
Delicate colour. Great intensity and freshness. Long flavours and richness on palate.

Chanoine Frères Tsarine Rosé Brut NV Sparkling Rosé
Pinky orange colour. Fine, elegant, biscuity, berry nose. Lively, fresh fruit and creamy mousse. Excellent finish.
£30.99 WAIT

Claude Baron Cuvée Perle Rosé Brut NV Sparkling Rosé
Fine colour. Nice ripe berry nose.

Good mousse, long finish, creamy and exciting.

Duval-Leroy Sainsbury's Rosé
NV Sparkling Rosé
Pale pink. Elegant floral, currant nose. Solid lovely mousse with a stylish finish.
SAIN

Henriot Rosé NV Sparkling
Rosé
Very pale and attractive hue. Bright raspberry nose. The palate is delicate with some length.
£36.00 HAR, SEL

Jacquart Brut Mosaïque Rosé
NV Sparkling Rosé
Medium salmon. Lovely colour, lasting bubbles. Fresh nose. Fresh, crisp, taste. Nice fruit.

Louis Barthelemy Pink Brut
NV Sparkling Rosé
Light pink. Good nose. Aged character. Balanced, long and elegant.
£32.99 P&S

Maison Pierrel Marquis De La Fayette Brut Rosé NV
Sparkling Rosé
Fine mousse, shows some maturity; autolysis notes, quite rich. Berry fruit and good acid.
£27.00 CPE

Sedi Lavenue Rosé NV
Sparkling Rosé
Lively, youthful fruit. Bright, forward, fruity style. Loads of red fruit with medium length.

Veuve Clicquot Cave Privee
Brut Rosé 1989 Sparkling
Rosé
Jammy pink. Attractive, quite developed aroma, toasty and crab apple jelly. Brioche in the mouth. Soft yet dry. Ready.

BRONZE

Nicolas Feuillatte Brut Rosé Millésime 2004 Rosé
Creamy soda nose with nuances of raspberry and blackberry. The palate is very distinctive with ripe blackberry fruit. Good persistence, ripe and elegant in style.
SAIN, SAIN, LEW

A R Lenoble Grand Cru Blanc De Blancs NV Sparkling
Exotic nose; tropical guava notes. Good acidity and some length but simple and slightly unusual.
£27.00 CMI, EOR

Ariston Aspasie Brut Blanc De Blancs NV Sparkling
Super balance with refreshing, clean green apple fruit. Subtle and restrained but fresh. Very strong.

Arnould-Ralle Grand Cru NV
Sparkling
Fresh, high acid, clean, good length. Fresh zippy fruit, elegant.

Ayala Perle d'Ayala Nature 2002 Sparkling
Pale yellow, white peach almondy aroma. A crisp, fancy wine with a seductive long finish.
£63.00 FWL

Boizel De Vallois Brut NV
Sparkling
Some dusty, papery notes. Broad, dry but awkward.
TESC

Ch & A Prieur Grand Prieur Blanc De Blancs Brut NV
Sparkling
Youthful and yeasty with a hint of brioche. Crisp, full and rounded. Notes of brioche and lemony fruit. Good acidity.

Chanoine Frères Asda Brut NV Sparkling
Yeasty nose, lemony apples.

Flavoured well. Slight yeast.
ASDA

**Chanoine Frères Asda
Extra Special Vintage 2002**
Sparkling
Pale gold colour, restrained
aromas. Very mineral palate with
tight structure, fine mousse.
Some creamy weight on the
finish.
ASDA

**Chanoine Frères Chanoine
Vintage 2005** Sparkling
Rich, malty and substantial.
Creamy, long and well-balanced.

**Chanoine Frères Reynier Brut
NV** Sparkling
Rounded with some yeasty
character and intensity.

**Chanoine Frères Tsarine
Cuvée Premium Brut NV**
Sparkling
Pleasing notes on the nose. Crisp
acidity. Too bubbly in mouth.
Medium flavour apples. Good
length.

**Charles Ellner Charles Ellner
Brut Intégral NV** Sparkling
Lots of briochey autolysis.
Evolved broad apple fruit. Dry
finish.
£24.99 CWH

**Chassenay d'Arce Blanc De
Blancs 2002** Sparkling
Very elegant aromas with rich,
savoury flavours and creamy
texture. Has scented quality and
complexity - very fine.
£23.50

**Chassenay d'Arce Cuvée
Premiere NV** Sparkling
Interesting nose, very lively with
nutty tones. Good development,
nuttiness on mid and end palate.
Gentle acid balance.
£18.50

**Claude Baron Cuvée Topaze
Millésime Brut 2003**
Sparkling
Pale yellow, good mousse. Green
apples with almond notes.

Collet Blanc De Blancs NV
Sparkling
Pale lemon. Delicate, very light
nose. Crisp, clean and light fruit.
WI-AV

Collet Brut NV Sparkling
Soft easy blend. Quite sweet and
ripe fruits.

Collet Millésime 2002
Sparkling
Attractive autolytic character. Cut
apple, crisp, touch austere.

**CRVC De Castelnau Brut
Blanc De Noirs NV** Sparkling
Strawberry, clean simple nose.
Rich, crisp, very cleanly made.
Lots of tangy length.
£24.99 PAT

CRVC De Castelnau Brut NV
Sparkling
Clean straw. Lifted apple with fresh
upfront cinnamon and asparagus
with green bean. Elegant.
£24.99 EVW, PAT

**De Beaumont Des Crayeres
Grand Prestige NV** Sparkling
Some yeasty flavour, juicy, dry
and a touch yeasty. Tart fresh
apples. Good structure at the
end.

Deutz Brut Classic NV
Sparkling
Gentle autolysis. Nice mix of
appley fruit and yeasty feel.
Some development, good flavour,
moderate length.
£32.99 EVW, HUN, SAM

Devaux Blanc De Noirs NV
Sparkling
Restrained aromas with some

complexity from the lees - fine mineral acidity, creamy texture, elegant flavours to finish. Moderate intensity and length.
£29.99 LIB, VOL

Devaux D De Devaux La Cuvée NV Sparkling
Touch of toffee and brioche richness. Lovely mousse, ripe, full palate. Easy drinking style.
£36.99 LIB

Famille Pertois-Moriset Blanc De Blancs Grand Cru NV
Sparkling
Slightly unintegrated wood mass otherwise pleasant. A delicate wine with a sound finish.
£25.95

Forget-Brimont Charmant Brut Premier Cru NV
Sparkling
Apple, light red fruits, great mousse. Fresh acidity on body, fuller style; red fruits, soft palate. Sweet on finish.
£21.99 CWH

Fresne Ducret Brut Origine NV Sparkling
Fresh. A good mousse with yeasty notes and some development.
£17.72 3DW

G H Mumm Brut Millésime 2002 Sparkling
Creamy with lively green zest acidity. Balanced and short.
£37.99 SAIN

G H Mumm Demi-Sec NV
Sparkling
Fresh baked bread with honey. Soft with attractive sweetness and balancing acidity.
£30.99 WAIT

G H Mumm Mumm De Cramant NV Sparkling
Open, floral and creamy with a touch of spice. Rice, creamy, almost buttery palate with citrus, peach and spice. Good acidity.
£44.00 HAR, WAIT

Gobillard Et Fils Grande Reserve Premier Cru NV
Sparkling
Pale lemon gold in colour. Fruit aromas of baked apples and toffee. Strong weight and finish of sherbet.

Henriot Brut Souverain NV
Sparkling
Rounded lighter style. Well made, long finish.
£29.99 HAR, SEL

Jacquart Brut De Nominée NV Sparkling
Biscuit nose. Caramel. Delicate mousse. Soft, fine and elegant.

Janisson Et Fils Carte Blanche NV Sparkling
Toasted apple on nose. Some wet wool notes. Some zippy acidity on palate and green apple notes. Finish fresh with good acidity.
£13.99 CWH

Lallement-Dubois Lucien Dauvignon NV Brut NV
Sparkling
Fresh, yeasty, developed nose. Good length.

Lanson Noble Cuvée Brut 2000 Sparkling
Delicate, fragrant, still undeveloped. Dry, compelling palate, fresh audity. Long, balanced fizz. Built for the long term.

Louis Roederer Brut Premier NV Sparkling
Delicate nutty note. Lively fresh palate, relatively youthful. Approachable now but will

improve.
£32.99 WAIT

Mailly Grand Cru Grand Cru Les Echansons 1999
Sparkling
Nutty, sous bois, raspberry nose, dryish, nutty palate; smooth but dry.
£65.00 BB&R

Maison Bourgeois-Diaz Cuvée Distinguée Brut NV NV
Sparkling
Open, ripe, brioche scented. Rounded, nutty and lightly toasty with some fruit. Soft but fresh acidity. No great complexity.
£21.00 CPE

Maison Burtin Waitrose Blanc De Blancs NV Sparkling
Lively and zingy with fresh lemon and lime fruit. Crisp and refreshing.
£21.99 WAIT, WWD, WWW

Maison Lenique Brut Sélection NV Sparkling
Clean, fresh lifted lemon rind. Some lime and pine. Good blend.
£16.32 3DW

Maison Lenique Grand Cru Blanc De Blancs 2005
Sparkling
Fresh, lemony and floral with light biscuit characters. Very clean. Creamy toasty brioche mineral with sweet citrus fruit. Fine acidity. Long.
£28.95 3DW

Maison Lenique Michel Lenique Cuvée 3 D NV
Sparkling
Pale straw, green hue. Lifted lemon and vegemite. Some cream and green apple.
£19.34 3DW

Maison Pierrel Les Oressences Brut NV NV Sparkling
Hint of caramel, orange blossom

and candid citrus peel. A bit short.
£30.00 CPE

P & C Heidsieck Charles Heidsieck Rosé Reserve NV
Sparkling
Complexity on the nose. Creamy texture with rich nutty flavours. Mineral acidity and good length. Lacks intensity on the finish.
£36.99 BB&R, HAR, SAIN

P & C Heidsieck Co-Operative Les Pionniers NV Sparkling
Pale gold, tiny bubbles, persistent, toasty with some vegetal notes. Fairly dry with some complexity of flavour. Falls down a bit on the finish.
£7.99 CWS

P & C Heidsieck Piper-Heidsieck Cuvée Sublime NV
Sparkling
Full, creamy and ripe with black fruits. Broad and balanced with good acidity and weight on the mid-palate. Long and lingering.
£26.99 BB&R, HAR, SAIN

Pannier Brut Sélection NV
Sparkling
Sweet and yeasty on the nose. Palate is deceptively dry with nuances of celery, pepper; good concentration & lingering length of green apple skin.
£22.00 COE

Paul Goerg Premier Cru Blanc De Blancs Brut NV Sparkling
Coarse mousse but perfumey, flowery with a touch of biscuit. Full, rounded palate. Touch of spice and bitterness. Nicely textured. Balanced acidity. Quite good length.
LAI

Philipponnat Cuvée 1522 Grand Cru 2002 Sparkling
Tight clean nose. Fresh and

wonderfully tight palate. Long and balanced.
£49.00 CAV

Philipponnat Royale Réserve Non Dosé NV Sparkling
Fine mousse. Fresh slightly spicy fruit on the nose with well developed biscuity, toasty notes. Quite developed nose. Full, dry, rounded palate.
£29.50 CAV

Philipponnat Royale Réserve NV Sparkling
Even, yeasty, young nose. Lots of fruit and good acidity. Not much development but some length and a little complexity.
£29.50 CAV

Pierre Gimonnet & Fils Cuvée Fleuron Premier Cru Blanc De Blancs 2004 Sparkling
Very flavoured, very ripe. Fairly laid back. There's loads of ripe rich fruit on offer but it is short.
£35.00

Roger Brun Cuvée des Sires Grand Cru 2005 Sparkling
An attractive, well defined, yeasty nose with a hint of hazelnut. Well defined suave palate, subtle nectarine, citrus flavours. Lovely balance on the first.
£29.99

Roger Brun Grand Cru Brut Reserve NV Sparkling
Very clean with crisp acidity. Green apple fruit and bracing lime acidity. Clean refreshing finish.
£36.99 LIB

Royer Père Et Fils Cuvée De Réserve NV Sparkling
Pale straw with fine mousse. Pear and dry with bovril notes. Balanced and long.
AAW, CAM, KON, MKV, MWO

Royer Père Et Fils Cuvée Prestige NV Sparkling
Evolved nose. Bright, crisp fruit, apple and lemon. Good structure with a crisp refreshing finish.
AAW, CAM, KON, MKV, MWO

Taittinger Brut Reserve NV Sparkling
Pale gold in colour. Ripe but juicy fit. Nice yeasty style. Fresh at the end.
£34.99 MRN, WAIT

Thierry Triolet Cuvée De Réserve NV Sparkling
Toasty richness with good balance and length. Citrus fruit.
£21.49 CWH

Union Champagne De Saint Gall Extra Brut NV Sparkling
Long-lasting fine mousse. Young, yeasty, mineral nose with some toast and macaroon. Full but elegant, dry palate. Good acidity, perhaps lacking a little in the middle.
M&S

Union Champagne Marks & Spencer St Gall Premier Cru Brut NV Sparkling
Good flavour showing some age. Light finish.
£25.00 M&S

Union Champagne Orpale Grand Cru 1998 Sparkling
Very attractive lifted nose & bright in the glass. The palate is clean, fresh and vibrant. Beautifully moreish, very youthful with hints of cashew.
£45.00 M&S

Union Champagne Tesco Finest* Vintage Champagne 2004 Sparkling
Bouncy, bright, melon nose. Ripe orchard fruits.
TESC

Vranken-Pommery Monopole Bisinger Premium Cuvée NV
Sparkling
Golden colour. Some complex reserve wine used, oxidative style. Good length with complex balance.
LDL,

Vranken-Pommery Monopole Heidsieck & Co Monopole Silver Top 2002 Sparkling
Appley nose, toffee/cereal mid palate. Good bubble and mousse. Toasty aroma and good length.
£32.99 SAIN, TESC

A R Lenoble Millésime 2005
Sparkling Rosé
Clean, fresh, light and round. Good citrus freshness and red berry fruit. Approachable.
£28.50 CMI, EOR

Ariston Aspasie Brut Rosé NV
Sparkling Rosé
Great colour. Fresh aromas. Lovely red berry fruit nicely balanced with good length of flavour.

Chassenay d'Arce Cuvée Rosé NV Sparkling Rosé
Rose petals and redcurrant, faintly tainted pink grapefruit rind. Mousse is less present.
£21.00

De Beaumont Des Crayeres Fleur De Rosé 2004 Sparkling Rosé
Cantaloupe nose; palate sits a little forward and the finish is very dry. A contemporary, alive wine.

De Beaumont Des Crayeres Grand Rosé NV Sparkling Rosé
Salmon pink, elegant toast and fruit nose. Some light fruit and complex yeasty notes. Medium length.

Duval-Leroy Brut Rosé NV
Sparkling Rosé
Slightly orange pink. Delicate raspberry nose. Balanced, quite long but simple.
£32.99 WAIT

Duval-Leroy Rosé Sec NV
Sparkling Rosé
Good mousse; mature notes. Good berry fruit. Ripe finish. Mature.

Forget-Brimont Charmant Brut Rosé Premier Cru NV
Sparkling Rosé
Bright red pink, light strawberry fruits and delicate nose. Good fruit and balance. Very elegant with a delicate finish.
£23.99 CWH

Maurice Vesselle Rosé Brut Grand Cru NV Sparkling Rosé
Bright colour. Lifted red fruit aromas. Very round and balanced, generous and rich. Lovely complexity.

Moet & Chandon Grand Vintage Rosé 2003 Sparkling Rosé
Very fine mousse. Gentle raspberry bouquet. Beautifully balanced with elegance. Lovely ripe fruit. Lovely length and dry finish.

Oudinot Marks & Spencer Rosé NV Sparkling Rosé
Pale salmon. Well defined but subtle nose. Rose petal/peach. Good acidity, light and breezy but not complex on the finish.
£24.00 M&S

Paul Goerg Premier Cru Rosé Brut NV Sparkling Rosé
Yeasty, bready with some toasty development. Soft, fruity up front with a firm backbone.
LAI

Péhu-Simonet Grand Cru Brut Rosé NV NV Sparkling **Rosé**
Simple, fresh, pleasant strawberry nose. Balanced fruit and acidity, tobacco. Quite easy.
£29.00 CPE

Roger Brun Cuvée Des Sires La Pelle 2004 Sparkling **Rosé**
Dry and smoky, solid. The fruit feels very mature almost cider like. Too developed for the style.
£29.99

Roger Legros Brut Rosé NV
Sparkling **Rosé**
Crisp, soft nose with nice notes of summer fruits. Clean fruit with some depth.
£21.49

Veuve Clicquot Rosé Brut NV
Sparkling **Rosé**
Round, simple fruit. Round, easy and simple. Balanced.
£40.99 TESC, WAIT

FRANCE

CHAMPAGNE BRONZE

France:
Languedoc-Roussillon

This swathe of vineyards running along the Mediterranean in the south of France remains a contrary wine-producing region. On one hand it churns out a surplus of inferior plonk in such volume it is classified as a lake; on the other hand, it is home to some superlative producers using all sorts of grapes to impressive effect. Full on red wines from varieties such as Carignan are probably amongst the most energising output of the region, which despite their power and intensity can display surprising daintiness and subtlety too. Don't forget the undervalued and fabulous fortifieds like Banyuls and Rivesaltes either.

2010 IWC PERFORMANCE

Trophies	3
Gold	9
Silver	56
Bronze	97
Great Value Awards	1

LANGUEDOC TROPHY, SAINT-CHINIAN TROPHY

Cave De Roquebrun La Grange Des Combes 2008 Red
Ruby, olive, veg, meat (roast beef) nose. Smoky, quite firm finish. Tight.

Chabbert Domaine Du Petit Causse 2008 Red
Dark cherry fruit nose. Dark fruit, black pepper and oak on the palate. Fresh, soft tannins with well-balanced acidity. Ripe and round on the finish. Very attractive and meaty in style.

Château Capion Château 2007 Red
Deep, still youthful appearance. Black cherries on nose and palate. Slight tarry character on mid palate. Hint of bitterness. Quite chewy, meaty, hint of earthiness.

 LA CLAPE TROPHY

Gérard Bertrand Château L'Hospitalet 'La Reserve' 2008 Red
Complex garrigues-like. Provencal character with thyme, olive and delicate tannins. Well made. Refreshing finish. Ripe tannins with good grip.
£10.99 WAIT

Groupe Uccoar Brise De France Cabernet Sauvignon 2009 Red
Impressive depth of red and black fruits with a hint of garrique. Very attractive palate with scented oak. Ripe yet fresh. Supportive tannins. Delicious.
£4.99

 **COTEAUX DU LANGUEDOC TROPHY**

Jacques Boscary Château Rouquette Sur Mer Cuvée l'Esprit Terroir 2009 Red
Ink coloured, prune fruit, some meaty touches. Earthy spicy fruit flavours. Very seductive and creamy bramble jelly flavours.

Jacques Boscary L'Absolu De Château Rouquette Sur Mer 2008 Red
Bags of character on the nose. Spiced black fruit, twist of pepper. Ripe, sweet fruit, treacle but good poise and length.

Les Domaines Paul Mas Les Faisses 2008 Red
Deep colour. Packed tight fruit and oak scents, spice, leather and violets. Could so easily be top Rhone. Fabulous.

Sandrina Hugeux - Christian Cheze La Grange Edition 2008 Red
Dense hawthorn fruit aromas. Creamy oak scents, spice and wood smoke. A cavalcade of fruit flavours with savoury touches, integrated tannins. Great length.

Chai Au Quai La Rousanne Du Baron 2009 White
Medium gold with vanilla custard and apple aromatics. Rich vanilla, spice and apple.
£8.49

Château Capion Château Capion 2008 White
Gentle fruit with floral nuttiness. Interesting lemon zest on the palate with a fresh, floral finish.

Château Capion Fiona 2009
White
Round and soft with smooth apple, pear, hints of peach and white flowers. Lingering finish.

Collovray & Terrier Closerie Des Lys 2009 White
Pale lime yellow, restrained mineral. Pink grapefruuit nose, lychee, quite aromatic. Soft attack, medium depth.
BB&R

Domaine Cazal Viel Viognier Grande Reserve 2008 White
Light, delicate nose with a hint of apricots. Palate is fresh, light and zingy. Tart fruit with balanced acidity on the finish.
£9.99 HLD

Gérard Bertrand Aigle Royal 2008 White
Spicy, fresh, herbal nose with a touch of eucalyptus and orange blossom. Medium full, dry palate with spicy fruit and intensity of citrus flavours. Good acidity and some length.

Gérard Bertrand Viognier Réserve Spéciale 2009 White
Peachy, sherberty nose. Aromatic and peachy on the palate with a creamy richness. Some fresh pepper and lifting acidity balanced with well-integrated oak.

Les Domaines Paul Mas Estate Marsanne 2009 White
Light, apple peel nose. Earthy, spicy, peachy palate with dry textured fruit. Good acidity and a long, balanced finish.

Les Domaines Paul Mas Vignes De Nicole Chardonnay Viognier 2009 White
Attractive tropical nose with over-ripe apple and peach on the palate. Delicate with good

freshness. Clean and pure on the finish. A classy wine.

Les Vignobles Foncalieu Enseduna Muscat Sec 2009
White
Violets, white pepper and salami on the nose. Dry, citrusy fruit with white pepper and spiced notes. Balanced and well-structured with pleasing acidity.

Mont Tauch Les Garrigues Grande Reserve Grenache Blanc 2009 White
Pale lemon gold. Clean mineral nose with some spice and violet. Bit short, mineral finish.

Alain Maurel Château Ventenac Grande Reserve 2007 Red
Very attractive. Gently reductive nose. Herbal in the true sense. Deep and concentration with good grip. Very well made.

Brigitte Chevalier Domaine De Cébène, Les Bancèls 2008
Red
Slightly green, stalky redcurrant nose. Rounded fruit with spice vanilla palate. Long herby finish.

Bunan Marks & Spencer Bandol 2005 Red
Bright, spicy and ripe on the nose. Soft red fruit with a touch of tannic oak. Violet floral finish with good length.
£12.99 M&S

Castel Frères Famille Castel Grande Reserve Cabernet Sauvignon 2008 Red
Deep and inky - needs some decanting. Lovely texture and depth on the palate. Lush fruit and length. 1 to 2 years to age.

Chai Au Quai La Syrah De Folie 2008 Red
Smooth black fruits and hint of coconut. Lovely grip to tannins.

Balanced, long flavours.
£10.99 LAI

Château Camplazens Garrigue 2008 Red
Ripe berry fruit and cassis on the nose with a savoury character. Rich, meaty and savoury with ripe black cherry and toasted almonds on the finish. Deliciously good.

Château Camplazens Premium 2008 Red
Deliciously ripe with hints of floral violets on the nose. Full of expressive character, meaty and savoury flavours balanced with ripe and supple fruit. Long and meaty on the finish.

Château De Flaugergues Les Comtes 2007 Red
Blackberry fruit nose. Chocolate and plum fruit on the palate with spiced flavours. Fine tannins and ripe fruit give good balance and length.
CHW, SGL

Château Des Karantes Diamant 2007 Red
Ripe and lush on the nose with a touch of warm spice. Warm cassis and cherry on the palate with a touch of woody cedar flavour. Well-balanced and quite long.

Domaine De La Baume Les Thermes Cabernet Sauvignon 2009 Red
Dense brambly, black fruit on the nose. Supple, well-balanced, firm tannins. Needs 1 to 2 years in the bottle.
£7.99

Domaine De La Baume Merlot Grand Châtaignier 2009 Red
Spicy, chocolatey, berry, fruits nose. The palate is very sweet and a bit confected. Commercial.
£7.99

Domaine De La Baume Syrah La Jeunesse 2009 Red
Powerful, peppery, meaty Syrah. Youthful complex will age.
£7.99

Domaine De La Pertuisane 2005 Red
Tobacco, chocolate, red fruit nose. Smooth coffee and dark red fruit with hints of spice on the palate with a touch of chocolate. Long finish.
LAS

Domaine De Nizas Domaine 2007 Red
Mid depth. Attractive lifted red fruit on nose. Soft truffly fruit with sappy finish and good length.
GWW

Domaine Du Clos Des Fees 2007 Red
Deep colour. Spicy aromatic, raspberry and blackberry nose. Big, ripe wine with garrigue and mineral and oak flavours. Lots of alcohol and some grainy tannins. Showy. Has potential. Modern style.
£43.00 J&B

Domaine Du Clos Des Fees Vieilles Vignes 2007 Red
Youthful, deep, rich, warm chocolate and vibrant red fruit nose. Spicy palate with ripe tannins, oak and smoke character. Long finish.
£22.00 J&B

Domaine Du Silène 2005 Red
Spicy berry fruit aromas with a whiff of dark chocolate. Tight palate with lots of smoky concentrated cherry fruit. Fine grainy tannin. Excellent length and crisp finish.
£16.99

Domaine Du Silène Esprit Du Silène 2008 Red
Rustic southern France on the

nose. Herbaceous, resplendent perfume and violet on the palate, lovely perfume to fruit ratio. Juicy striking notes on palate and grippy tannins. Yummy!
£9.99

Domaine Paul Mas Ile La Forge Merlot 2008 Red
Dark, blackcurrant fruit and brambles. Good tannins and fruit on palate. Tannin structured.
£4.99

Dourthe Domaine De Serame Syrah Reserve 2008 Red
Deep youthful colour. Spicy, briary, bay leaf and violet aromas. Very pure Syrah nose. Firm peppery, raspberry fruit on the palate with black pepper and bay leaves, oak. Smoothed palate. Dry, quite long and fresh.
£6.99

Famille P & J Allard Château De Lastours "Simone Descamps" 2006 Red
Cherries, slight baked cherries with a touch of smoke and herbs. Cherry.

Gérard Bertrand Domaine De L'Aigle 2008 Red
Ripe, with succulent fruits on the nose. Raspberries and cream on the palate with good expression of varietal style fruit.

Gérard Bertrand Domaine Fontséque 2008 Red
Black purple and fragrant, mahogany, spicy nose. Fragrant, aromatic, sweet fruit on the palate. Balanced tannins. Concentrated.

Gérard Bertrand Domaines des Garennes 2008 Red
Rich. Provence/herbs. Bramble, blackberries, jammy concentration. Black olive. Ample. Lovely palate with fine tannins.

Gerard Bertrand Tesco Finest* Tautavel 2005 Red
Spicy, peppery red fruit nose with a slightly Rhône character. Peppery, mineral palate with crushed elderberries, sweet red fruit and lightly cherry tannins, medium full. Dry. A good length. Robust.
TESC

Jacques Boscary Château Rouquette Sur Mer Cuvée Amarante 2008 Red
Cracking nose, gripp y but ripe. Complex and sweet mid-palate. Firm and grown up.

Julien Seydaux Clos Du Fou Château Des Estanilles 2007 Red
Deep colour and very good intensity, animal. Great concentration and smoothness.

La Jasse Tête De Cuvée 2007 Red
A refined blackberry, green pepper nose. Well defined tannin palate, a little dry. Touches of cocoa inflected with black fruit. Dry finish but a good length.

Laurent Miquel L'Artisan Saint Chinian 2007 Red
Savoury and restrained. Soft, ripe fruit and spice on palate. Mellow vanilla red fruit. Medium core. Fine finish.

Les Domaines Paul Mas Arrogant Frog Lily Pad Red Cabernet Merlot 2009 Red
Rich, ripe fruits. Good and lush, spicy. Well-balanced.

Les Domaines Paul Mas Château Paul Mas Clos Des Mures 2009 Red
A tight hint of oak. Lots of Syrah spice, juicy and attractive.

Les Domaines Paul Mas La Forge Estate Merlot 2009 Red
A yummy wine with lots of

potential. Spicy fruit on the palate and a chewy fruit finish.

Les Domaines Paul Mas La Forge Single Vineyard Collection Malbec 2008 Red
Opaque, youthful, sweet cassis fruit, juicy. Fresh, fruit and quite firm. Good length and lively and young.
TESC

Les Domaines Paul Mas Cabernet De Cabernet 2009 Red
Huge colour. Attractive, earthy concentration. Herbal complexity. Sweet fruit on middle. Well made.

Les Domaines Paul Mas Syrah Viognier 2009 Red
Dark, spicy fruit on the nose. Red fruit with vanilla spice on the palate. Hot, ripe and tannic with good peppery fruit structure. Violets on the finish.

Michel Raynaud Romeo & Julieta Red 2009 Red
Violet hue. Plum, fruity nose. Sweet fruit, plums. Moderate tannic length.

Mont Tauch Single Vineyard Montluzis 2008 Red
Young, purple. Good firm flavours and length.

Skalli F de Skalli 2006 Red
Violet hues. Restrained, appealing, good fruity nose. Good stylised fruit, quite tannic. Promising.
£24.99

Thierry Rodriguez Mas Gabinèle Rarissime 2007 Red
Lovely, spicy herby, blackberry nose. Creamy vanilla, ripe fruit palate. Leading to persistent dry finish.

Venes Domus Maximus 2007 Red
Some ginger, orange peel and Christmas spices, berries and length.
£35.00

GREAT VALUE RED WINE UNDER £6

Vindivin La Difference Carignan 2009 Red
Rich, vibrant, sweet fruits. Very pure fruit. Modern and vibrant style.
£5.99 TESC

Xavier Bruguière La Grenadiere 2007 Red
Confected sweet scents with some coconut oak hints. Juicy fruit. Good tannin structure. Not hugely complex but enjoyable and very well made.

Château De Berne Cuvée Spéciale 2009 Rosé
Pale pink colour. Fresh fruit with apple and lemon aromas. Ripe cherry and strawberry on the palate with a long, fresh finish.
LCB

Domaine De Mas De Madame Bulles De Madame NV Sparkling
Fresh grapey, floral nose. Classic Muscat grapeiness. Very long and more-ish.

Les Vignobles Du Rivesaltais Arnaud De Villeneuve Rivesaltes Ambré Hors D'Age 1982 Sweet
Orange/mahogany, developed. Lovely dried orange and citrussy nose. Gentle yet very concentrated dried oranges and pudding fruit. Lovely acid/ sweetness/fruit concentration and balance.
£12.49 WAIT

Alain Maurel Domaine Ventenac Chardonnay 2009 White
Lightly fragrant nose with pleasant apple notes. Tropical on the palate with long length.

Alain Maurel Domaine Ventenac Chenin Colombard 2009 White
Pale colour, gooseberry nose with soft attack. Firm gooseberry and lime on the palate with medium length.
£6.99 WAIT

Bohler-Peltier Domaine De Cantaussel Vermentino 2008 White
Spicy, waxy and perfumed incense on the nose. Dry on the palate with ripe, succulent fruit. Fresh acidity, supple and very long on the finish.

Bonfils La Maréchale 2008 White
Peach and tropical fruit palate. Good texture with a touch of oiliness. Ripe and lush on the finish. Well made.

Bonfils La Serre 2007 White
Fresh appley nose, baked apple and pear on the palate with delicate flavour.

Castel Frères Famille Castel Grande Reserve Chardonnay 2009 White
Pear drop nose with a very strong candied pear palate. Quite confected, but with nice acidity and balance.

Castel Frères Roche Mazet Chardonnay 2009 White
Classy wine with an attractive oaky character. Good combination of pineapple and citrus fruit on the palate.
STE

Château De Saint Ferreol Viognier 2007 White
Pale colour with a minerally nose. Soft fruit on the palate with ripe apricot and a light fresh finish.
£11.75 Widely Available

Compagnie Rhodanienne Repertoire Gros Manseng Sauvignon 2009 White
Heavy and ripe on the nose with dense, creamy white peach fruit. Layers of stone fruit and creamy spice on the palate.
£5.99 MRN, MYL

Domaine De La Baume Chardonnay Viognier La Grande Olivette 2009 White
Toasty oak with fresh, clean apply flavours. Quite lush, with overtones of lemon and lime citrus. Balanced finish.
£7.99 WAIT

Domaine De La Baume Sauvignon Les Mariés 2009 White
Ripe with hints of green citrus on the nose. Minerality on the palate underpinned by ripe, slightly tropical fruit.
£7.99

Gérard Bertrand Aigle Noir Chardonnay 2009 White
Rich and ripe, succulent fruits. Good varied definition.

Gérard Bertrand Cigalus Blanc 2009 White
Lifted, peachy, floral nose. Peach and tropical fruit palate. Quite full in the mouth. Touch of oiliness and light oak. Well made.

Jan & Caryl Panman Château Rives-Blanques Cuvée De L'Odyssée 2007 White
Sweet and ripe on the nose. Slightly nutty and chalky on the palate with some caramel rich

✳ *Sud de France*

from Languedoc-Roussillon,
where creativity
meets diversity

character.
GWW, TAN

Jan & Caryl Panman Château Rives-Blanques Dédicace 2008 White
Passionfruit nose with a touch of creamy richness. Ripe apricot and vanilla on the palate with a long, fresh, citrus finish.
GWW, TAN

Jan & Caryl Panman Château Rives-Blanques La Trilogie 2008 White
Pear drop nose with a crunchy citrus palate. Intense with a nice ripe apple fruit finish.

Les Domaines Paul Mas La Forge Single Vineyard Collection Marsanne 2009 White
Fresh, but savoury nose with a hint of aniseed. Citrus-peach fruit with clean and ripe character. Well-balanced, dry and long.
TESC

Les Vignobles Foncalieu Enseduna Marsanne 2009 White
Tropical nose with a touch of white pepper spice. Delicious, round fruit with a lemon, peachy character. Fresh and clean finish.

Les Vignobles Foncalieu Le Versant Sauvignon Blanc 2009 White
Clean and straightforward with ripe lemon on the palate. Lingering green notes with a touch of roundness on the finish.

Michel Raynaud Romeo & Julieta 2009 White
Pale in colour with lime flower nose. Citrus and apple-gooseberry palate with soft attack and fresh finish.

Mont Tauch Les Signatures Picpoul De Pinet 2009 White
Very mature nose, but with vibrant, appley fruit on the palate. Crisp, spicy and lemony flavours with a fresh and lengthy finish.

Sieur D'Arques Terroir Vigne Et Truffe 2008 White
A fruity style with gentle peach and pear flavours. Lively fruit on the palate with a touch of ripe apple character.
ODD, ODF

Vineris Chevalier De Fauvert Chardonnay 2008 White
Light, gentle and peachy with a hint of pear and ripe spice. Nice fruit character with a crisp, clean finish.
LDL

Xavier Bruguière Les Muriers 2008 White
Good clean apple fruit nose. Lemon citrus acidity with green grapey flavours. Very fresh and pleasant on the finish.

Aussières Rouge 2008 Red
Pear fruit on the nose. Touch of pepper. Very simple and balanced.

Bagatelle Donnadieu 2009 Red
Medium ruby. Olive nose. Soft attack with fine spices. Some length.

BLB Vignobles Domaine Montlobre La Chapelle 2008 Red
Deep russet colour. Slightly stalky nose with red fruits and grippy tannin but good acidity.

Boisset Bouchard Aine & Fils Pinot Noir 2008 Red
Rustic nose with some earthiness. Stewed and heavy fruits. Hints of oak.
£5.95 ASDA

Bonfils Domaine Aubaret Réserve Merlot 2008 Red
A well made wine with chewy fruit and damson. Elegant, long and fine.
LAI

Bonfils Peilhan 2007 Red
Bit of funk on the nose. Lively grenache character. Dense, very deep flavours - youthful and concentrated. Alcohol just in balance.

Bonfils Reserve Merlot 2009 Red
Really stylish, elegant, pure berry-ish fruit. Very stylish and fruit driven.

Bonfils Reserve Syrah 2009 Red
Big, deep colour. Big full flavour. Good finish. Lots of depth.

Boutinot Les Grands Cailloux Syrah Viognier 2007 Red
Vegetal nose with a touch of tobacco. Ripe brambly fruit leads to a minerally finish.
£7.99 AVB, PBA

Brigitte Chevalier Domaine De Cébène Ex Arena 2008 Red
Plummy, spicy aroma. A well-balanced, elegant wine. Long finish.

Camplazens Grenache Marselan 2008 Red
Ripe hedgerow fruit continues onto the palate. Good balance and length. A great example.

Camplazens Syrah Marselan 2008 Red
Dark youthful purple. Spicy pepper on nose. Powerful. Soft fleshy fruit over a solid backbone of ripe tannin.

Castel Frères Famille Castel Merlot 2009 Red
Aromatic berry fruits nose.

Sweet, ripe, plum, slightly jammy fruit on palate. Ripe and appealing.

Cazes Château De Triniac Côtes-Du-Roussillon Villages Latour De France 2008 Red
Bright ruby red crimson. Redcurrant and raspberry fruits. Firm, dry tannins. Medium length. Liquorice and spice.

Celliers Du Languedoc Origine Vineyard Pinot Noir 2009 Red
Tight, juicy cherry fruit and strawberry. Quite a lot of tight, curranty fruit, juicy and fresh.

Château Cabezac Carinu 2006 Red
Berry nose. Berry and cherry on the palate. Stewed fruits. Well-balanced.
£14.81 JGW

Château De Flaugergues Cuvée Sommelière 2007 Red
Honey and honeysuckle on the nose with a touch of grapefruit and spice. Exotic apricot and peach fruit on the palate. Oily, with good acidity and lively freshness.
£7.99 MWW

Château Saint Roch Chimères Côtes-du-Roussillon Villages 2008 Red
Ripe strawberry fruits. Nice oak and integration.
£11.99 HAR, LIB, NYW

Château Saint Roch Kerbuccio Côtes-du-Roussillon Villages 2008 Red
Spiced raspberry and dry tannins. Savoury plum notes on finish.
£20.00 HAR, LAY, LIB, NYW

Dom Brial Hautes Terrasses Côtes-du-Roussillon Villages 2008 Red
Hint of raspberry on the nose.

Ripe, attractive pure berry fruit. Good concentration and a hint of wild herbs. A good length.
£6.99 DLW

Domaine De Chamans Hegarty Chamans 2007 Red
Berry nose. Mouthful of ripe berries and cherries. Well-balanced and pleasant finish.
ADN

Domaine De Chamans Hegarty Chamans No. 1 2005 Red
Smoky and ripe on the nose. Leathery laced fruit with good acidity and balanced. Hints of spice on the finish.
ADN

Domaine Sainte Rose Le Soleil Du Sud 2008 Red
Attractive nose of red fruits, particularly cherry. Appealing mouthfeel with medium depth of body and good length.
£9.99 MWW

Dourthe Château De Serame Reserve Du Château 2007 Red
Fresh ripe berries on the nose. Firm tannin structure.
£7.99

Dourthe Château De Serame Reserve Du Château Minervois 2007 Red
Ripe plum and prune on the palate with warm spice. Good length and freshness.
£9.49

Dourthe Domaine De Serame Merlot Reserve 2008 Red
Chewy fruit with a touch of menthol on the nose. Damson mid palate with a fruity finish.
£6.99

Foncalieu Asda Corbières 2009 Red
Deep colour. Intense fizzy plum aroma. Medium bodied, liquorice.
£3.22 ASDA

Foncalieu Château Puicheric 2007 Red
Bright redcurrant fruit leads to an attractive balanced palate.
£7.98 ASDA

Gérard Bertrand Cigalus Rouge 2008 Red
Ripe blackcurrant in oaky background. Concentration of rich, ripe fruit - persistent length. Very young, modern style.

Gérard Bertrand Grand Terroir Tautavel 2007 Red
Good freshness and lovely concentrated black fruit. Lots of oak but well-integrated with the fruit.
£7.99 WAIT

Jean-Michel Cazes Domaine L'Ostal Cazes Estibals 2007 Red
Black fruit nose, good acidity. Some liquorice and good black fruit intensity but wood rather drying.

Jean-Pierre Py Domaine Py 2008 Red
Fresh and berryish with a subtle green edge. Some grippy tannins too. Nice fruit.

Julien Seydaux Grande Cuvée Château Des Estanilles 2007 Red
Opaque, chocolate spicy aroma. Silky attack. Well-balanced plummy fruit.

La Jasse Vieilles Vignes 2008 Red
Rich nose of black fruits and vanilla. Lovely black ripe fruits to palate. Well-balanced and acidity. Smooth tannins.

Les Domaines Paul Mas Cabernet Sauvignon 2009 Red
Very deep colour, good, black

fruit nose. More hefty, gripping tannins, good fruit length.
£6.99 WAIT

Les Domaines Paul Mas Chat O Souris Cabernet Merlot 2009 Red
Touch muted and hollow nose. Some herbal/green character on finish. Firm and youthful.

Les Domaines Paul Mas La Forge Estate Cabernet Sauvignon 2009 Red
Toasty, coffee nose. Very good oak integration. Good ripe, intense palate. Sweet and ripe.

LGI Monastier Shiraz 2009 Red
Quite restrained nose, good balanced acidity with crunchy, brambly fruit of good intensity and finish.

Mas Belles Eaux Sainte-Hélène 2005 Red
Rich cassis-led nose. Rather old oak and baked fruit. Very dry on finish but good complexity.
£27.59

Michel Cazevieille Apogee 2008 Red
Intense ruby red colour. Some really nice fruit with some fruited notes. Good minerality. Oaky character. Good tannins.

Mont Tauch Château De Montmal 2008 Red
Herbaceous dark red fruit with deep flavours of red fruit and spice on the palate. Spiced and warm with good structure and a long finish.

Mont Tauch Les Garrigues Grande Reserve Carignan 2009 Red
Pure, fresh, juicy, modern, fruity. Appealing style.

Mont Tauch Les Garrigues Grande Reserve Grenache Noir 2009 Red
Bright, squashy fruit. Lovely balance and great simplicity.

Mont Tauch Les Garrigues Grande Reserve Marselan 2009 Red
Scented raspberry and chocolate nose. Fresh, fruity and lively on the palate with a touch of chocolate and smoke. Good structure and length.

Mont Tauch Les Garrigues Grande Reserve Syrah 2009 Red
Lovely smooth black fruits, great fruit purity. Balanced. Touch of spice.

Mont Tauch Single Vineyard Le Tauch 2008 Red
Dark cherry and herbal aromas. Juicy, fresh. Good purity of youthful fruit with a touch of spice.

Mont Tauch Terroir D'Altitude 2008 Red
Ruby red. Raspberry, damson and cherry fruit.
£7.99 MRN

Mont Tauch Winery Selection Fresh And Fruity 2008 Red
Straightforward. Good fruit. Easy drinking.

Mont Tauch Winery Selection Smooth And Fruity 2008 Red
Pungent with a barnyard nose. Red fruit and spice on the palate with a long, oaky finish and a kick of spice. Delicious.

Moulin De Gassac Classic 2009 Red
Opaque, spicy, liquorice, plummy aroma. A serious wine with many layers of flavours on mid palate. Needs time.

Moulin De Gassac Grande Réserve De Gassac 2009 Red
Huge colour. Very spicy herbal nose of great charm and purity. Very ripe style. Full bodied. Commercial. Well made.
£9.00

Nathalie Estribeau Nathalie & Co 2009 Red
Smooth, balanced fruit. Easy black cherry flavours. Nicely balanced.
£6.99 COOP

P & J Allard Château De Lastours Réserve 2007 Red
Some red/black cherry. Herbal with soft attack. Fine, elegant and nice texture. Clean and simple with some complex potential.

Paul Mas Asda Extra Special Syrah 2009 Red
Youthful jammy fruit. Somewhat Shiraz-like – chippy oak. Good.
£6.98 ASDA

Paul Sapin Domaine Blomac Cabernet Sauvignon 2009 Red
Generous fruits on the nose and palate. Ripe tannins. Intense, juicy and rounded. Good finish and length.

Ph Wine Faugères Domaine Marie 2009 Red
Firm, lovely, vibrant inky nose with lush garrigue undertones. Sweet on finish.
£7.99 WAIT

Pierre-André Ournac Château Cesseras 2007 Red
Meaty, savoury, peppery nose. Quite tight with nice freshness on the palate. Ripe tannins with liquorice and pepper on the finish.
£12.99 BB&R, WAIT

Remparts De Neffies Opulens / Domaine Pech Rome 2005 Red
Ripe scented and creamy with toasty oak aromas. Very fresh with ripe, supple fruit on the palate. Soft, with a warm spice finish.

Skalli Domaine Du Silène 2004 Red
Deep red in colour, aromas of chocolate, spice and cigar box. Full bodied palate, lots of VA, sweet fruit. Balanced with good length.
£16.99

Union Des Producteurs Du Haut Minervois Le Grand Noir GSM 2008 Red
Ripe and fresh on the nose. Soft plum on the palate with ripe tannins and fresh acidity. Approachable and easy to drink.
£6.99

Alain Maurel Domaine Ventenac Rosé 2009 Rosé
Bright, fruity, lively and zesty style. Pretty, floral with rosehip character. Friendly and approachable style.

Bonfils Reserve Rosé 2009 Rosé
Stone fruit and cranberries on the nose and palate. Bright and lively with herbaceous flavours. Some strawberry syrup adds weight to the palate and a touch of complexity.

Coop Val D'Orbieu Mythique Languedoc Rosé 2009 Rosé
Lovely, lifting creamy fruit. Fresh and delicate with rosehip and pomegranate flavours. Twist of lime zest on the finish. Persistent.
£5.00

Domaine Begude Pinot Rosé 2009 Rosé
Red berry fruit on the nose with much of the same on the palate. Confected with a touch of lemony freshness on the finish.
£7.49 MWW

Du Clos Les Arbousiers Côteaux Du Languedoc Cinsault Grenache Rosé 2009 Rosé
Pale pink with a touch of vegetal character. Ripe fruit with a broad attack, zippy acidity with firm fruit on the finish.
£6.99 VGN

Mont Tauch Le Village Du Sud Rosé 2009 Rosé
Light-bodied with strawberry ripeness on the palate. Clean on the finish.

Orosquette Château La Gravette Rosé 2009 Rosé
Pale salmon colour. Light strawberry fruits with a citrusy edge. Delicate and elegant style.
£5.99 MWW

Rimauresq Petit Rimauresq Rosé 2009 Rosé
Baby pink colour. Rosehip and redcurrant flavours on the palate. Clean with a fresh finish.
£8.99 WAIT, PBA

Skalli Couleurs Du Sud Merlot Rosé 2009 Rosé
Strawberry and blackcurrant leaf on the nose. Clean and crisp with pronounced berry fruit character.
£5.99

Mont Tauch Rivesaltes NV Sweet
Smells bubble gummy. Sweet, some acidity but bitter at the end. An intense wine.

Domaine Du Mas De Madame 2006 Fortified
Soft, ripe fruit. Honeyed, peachy, grapey hint nose. Balance and a lingering finish.

Domaine Du Mas De Madame 2007 Fortified
Yellow straw colour. Apple, marmalade, fruity sweet. Light refreshing fruit. Will develop.

Domaine Pouderoux Maury Vendange Mise Tardive 2005 Fortified
Deep colour. Blackberry, fig, raisin aromas. Well-balanced with a nice finish.
£9.50 WAIT

France:Regional

ALSACE, LOIRE VALLEY, RHÔNE VALLEY, SOUTH WEST

Alsace quietly continues to offer up its arrestingly intense whites with aplomb, giving the world of wine definitive examples of Riesling, Gewürztraminer, Muscat and Pinot Gris. The Loire is similarly indispensible, not just for the precious and delightful Sauvignon Blancs of the central vineyards (Sancerre, Pouilly-Fumé et al) but also for some sublime Chenin Blanc from the Anjou district. The Rhône valley is perennially popular with drinkers, from reliable Côtes-du-Rhône to premium Côte-Rôtie, the Rhône is renowned for good reason. The South-West, whilst lesser known, is a great source of good value French country wines that show charming rusticity.

2010 IWC PERFORMANCE

Trophies	6
Gold	34
Silver	96
Bronze	166
Great Value Awards	1

LOIRE VALLEY

GOLD

Domaine De Bel Air Pouilly-Fumé 2009 White
Wonderful fruit. Granite. Perfume and delicate fruit stitched through. Brilliant.
£14.99 CAM, CVS, HIG, LIB

Domaine Gérard Et Hubert Thirot Sancerre Blanc 2009 White
Lime and flint on the nose with a strong mineral quality. On the palate, good ripe fruit with a touch of mineral character, almost like crushed oyster shell. Delicious fruit with well-structured flavours. Elegant and clean on the finish.
£11.99 DHF, DWI

CHENIN BLANC TROPHY, VOUVRAY TROPHY

Domaine Huet Le Haut Lieu Sec 2007 White
Attractive lemon and citrus flavour. Well-balanced.
£17.99 WAIT

Domaine Nicolas Girard Menetou-Salon 2009 White
Brilliantly poised. Mineral charged, powerful fruit and beautifully framed finish. Textbook stuff.
£14.99 WDR

> **DID YOU KNOW?**
> France has now slipped to third place in importance for UK wine imports. California and Australia are in 2nd and 1st, respectively.

Domaine Tabordet Tabordet Pouilly-Fumé 2008 White
Nettles, grass and piercing green fruits. Taut acidity with a mineral finish. A classic example.
£15.49 HLD

INTERNATIONAL SAUVIGNON BLANC TROPHY, LOIRE TROPHY, SANCERRE TROPHY

Pascal Jolivet Sancerre Blanc Les Caillottes 2009 White
Nettle and fresh mint mingle with ripe citrus and melon on the palate. Quite rich with good structure, nicely balanced with lashings of exotic fruits on the supple finish.
£20.99

Château La Variere Anjou-Villages Brissac 2009 Red
A classic. Light yet concentrated berry fruits with floral notes.

SILVER

Caves Des Vins De Sancerre Tesco Sancerre 2008 White
Intensely fruity nose. Lemony with apricot pits and tropical fruits on the palate. Weighty with intense freshness on the finish. Long and lingering.
TESC

Count Henry D'Estutt D'Assay Château De Tracy Pouilly-Fumé 2008 White
Sherbet-lemon nose with hints of ripe melon. Green peppers with hints of gooseberry and lime flower on the palate. Long with a steely finish.
£18.50 HAY, HOH, LAY, LEA, MVC

Domaine FL Savennieres Le Parc 2008 White
Delicate yet complex nose of

sweet apples and citrus leading to a lean, mineral palate with intense fruit flavouring and good length.
£24.99 FAW, LIB, TVK

Domaine Frissant Touraine 2009 White
Green lemon and lime on the nose. Full of mineral freshness on the palate. Lush fruit with fresh acidity on the finish.

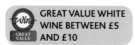

GREAT VALUE WHITE WINE BETWEEN £5 AND £10

Domaine Villargeau Sauvignon Blanc 2009 White
Fresh green, clear and crisp. Subtle sweetness and strong minerality.
£9.99 BTW, ODD, TKW

Eric Louis Les Affaubertis Pouilly-Fumé 2009 White
Lemon and melon ripeness on the nose. Tropical and sweet fruit on the palate but dry in flavour. Delicious and soft.
£13.30

Fournier Père Et Fils Tesco Finest* Pouilly-Fumé 2008 White
Smooth palate enriched with lovely tropical and stone fruit character. Hints of green citrus, nutty sweetness and lime flower, with a long and enjoyable finish.
TESC

Joseph Mellot Asda Extra-Special Pouilly-Fumé 2009 White
Clean. Reductive. Lovely minerality. Beads of grass, lemony fruit and acidity.
ASDA

Laporte Le Rochoy Sancerre 2008 White
Lovely notes of melon and

tamarind on the nose. Ripe with crisp citrusy fruit and lively tropicality. The palate has a good weighty finish.
£16.00 ARL, EOR, JAS, PAT, RWM

Pascal Bellier Cheverny 2009 White
Mineral, Sauvignon-like nose. Character with crisp and some acidity but good palate, weight and length.
Widely Available

Pascal Jolivet Sancerre Blanc 2009 White
The palate is fresh with ripe gooseberry and a touch of warm spice. Good depth and lingering flavours on the finish.
£17.50

Alliance Loire French Connection Saumur Champigny 2009 Red
Bright, cherry nose. Good intensity and balance. Good chalky raspberry palate. Nice, tight, fresh finish.
CWS

Domaine De La Cune Saumur-Champigny Les 3 Jean 2008 Red
Blackcurrants and berries - elegant and perfumed. Ripe fruit, well-structured. Liquorice and blackberries with some persistence.
£10.94 3DW

Domaine De Salvert Anjou Cuvée Les Noëlles 2009 Red
Fresh, crunchy, red fruits. Fresh acidity, chewy earthy tannins but with a nutty ripeness. Good length.
£7.00 3DW

Domaine Paul Thomas Chavignol Sancerre Rouge 2008 Red
Lovely, light raspberry fruit. Lively palate, good acidity. Gentle,

clean, balanced finish.
MWW

**Philippe Raimbault Apud
Sariacum 2009** Rosé
Raspberry fruits with peppery
notes on the nose. Fresh red
cherry on the palate with good
freshness and balance.
£14.99 DLW

**Bouvet Ladubay Taille
Princesse De Gérard
Depardieu 2007** Sparkling
Clean nose, touch of oak. Nice
fruits showing here and good
acidity. Well made.
J&B, MWW

**Château Pierre Bise Beaulieu
Les Rouannières Côteaux de
Layon 2007** Sweet
Generous and mouth-watering.
Intense aromas of honey and
cooked raisins, sweet cinnamon
spice with ripe nectarine fruit.
Palate is voluptuous with a twist
of citrus fruit on the finish.
LEA, SSU

**Château Pierre Bise Rochefort
Les Rayelles Côteaux Du
Layon 2005** Botrytis
Luscious and voluptuous fruit-
forward style. Brimming with
flavours of caramel-dipped baked
apples and raisins on the palate.
Hint of white chocolate on the
finish.
LEA, SSU

**Ackerman Malinge Sauvignon
Blanc 2009** White
Fragrant fruity nose, quite stylish
savoury style. Pleasant, intense
and long finish.
£6.99 MRN

**Barton & Guestier Originel
Sauvignon Blanc 2009** White
Subtle tropical flavours. Delicate

and lovely palate. Satisfying
finish.
£7.99 J&B, PFC

Cellar Estates Sancerre 2009
White
Gooseberry and petrol on the
nose with a steely, mineral
palate. Fresh with ripe citrus and
lively fruit flavour on the finish.

**Château Pierre Bise
Savennières Clos Le Grand
Beaupréau 2008** White
Good aromatic nose. Lovely
lemon and apple flavour with
long finish.
LEA, SSU

**Domaine Bellevue Touraine
Sauvignon 2009** White
Pale lemon with intense grassy
nose. Green apple, kiwi and ripe
tropical fruit on the palate. Well-
balanced with long, pleasing
length.

**Domaine Chervignon
Touraine Sauvignon Blanc
2009** White
A pear nose, over a tropical
palate. Delicious.

Domaine De La Gemière 2009
White
Supple and elegant with a
supple, round mouthfeel. Ripe
gooseberry and citrus round off
the finish.
£12.99 BTW, TKW

**Domaine Des Brosses
Sancerre 2009** White
Lemon and lime character on
the nose. Very ripe and lush
on the palate with a touch of
gooseberry grassiness. Delightful.
£14.99 CKY, JCC, LIB, N&P

**Domaine Du Pré Baron
Touraine Sauvignon 2009**
White
Pale lemon with soft stone fruit

and a hint of minerality. Zesty acidity with lush fruit and long and balanced finish.
£6.99 MWW

Domaine Joël Delaunay Tydy Sauvignon Blanc 2009 White
Hints of nettle and spice, ripe and green fruit on the palate. Long and lean, quite pleasing.
ALE, FFT, QTK, SGL, UPT

Domaine Nicolas Girard Sancerre 2009 White
Fruity and bright with a grassy, mineral palate. Lively and youthful, delicious pungency.
£19.99 LBS, LIB

Domaine Paul Thomas Les Comtesses Sancerre 2008
White
Round, spicy aromas on the nose. Lovely citrus character with a solidly lemony crunch on the palate. Ripe and lush on the tropical fruit finish.
MWW

Edouard Pisani-Ferry Saumur Blanc Les Fresnettes 2007 White
Delicate honeyed nose with some oxidation on palate.

Florian Mollet Taste The Difference Sancerre 2009
White
Pear-drop nose with hints of ripe citrus. Medium weight with good structure and a lemon-citrusy finish.
£11.00 SAIN

Fournier Père Et Fils Tesco Finest* Sancerre 2007 White
Delicate ripeness on the nose with a hint of lemon. Crisp, fresh and crunchy on the palate with a spicy and green fruit finish.
TESC

Gilbert Chon & Fils Domaine Du Bois Maligne 2009 White
Hint of green apple on the nose.

Some depth and character. Slightly bitter finish.
£5.99 MRN

Guy Allion Domaine Du Haut Perron 2009 White
Pale straw colour with hints of green fruit on the nose. Fresh and grassy fruit on the palate. Well-balanced with good length.

Henri Poiron Domaine Des Quatre Routes 2009 White
Grassy aroma with citrus notes. Some fruitiness and fresh citric acidity. Good finish and openness.

Joseph Mellot Pont Du Milieu, Pouilly-Fumé 2009 White
Juicy gooseberry. Overt style. Long fruity finish.
£11.99 WAIT

Joseph Mellot Waitrose In Partnership Sancerre 2009 White
Honey and apple on the nose. Ripe lemon and lime on the palate. Good balance and depth of flavour.
£11.99 WAIT

La Fruitiere Sainsbury's Taste The Difference Muscadet Sèvre-Et-Maine Sur Lie 2009 White
Clean seashore aromas and lovely citrus notes. Balanced palate with complex distinct flavours full of zest and good length.
£5.99 SAIN

Lacheteau Cellars Estates Muscadet 2009 White
Some breadth on the palate and good freshness on the finish.
£6.99 BES

Lacheteau Kiwi Cuvée Sauvignon 2009 White
Lush ripe style, with juicy fruit

and soft creamy melon tones.
£6.49 SAIN, MRN

Lacheteau Muscadet 2009 White
Lifted, clean aromas. Gentle style
with good length.

Lacheteau Pouilly-Fumé 2009
White
Delicious juicy fruit. Intense fruit
on the nose. Just a tiny bit heavy.

**Les Grands Chais De France
Champteloup Touraine
Sauvignon 2009** White
Very pleasing aromatics on the
nose. Green apple and gooseberry
on the palate with a very
refreshing citrus finish.
£6.99 WAIT

**Les Grands Chais De France
Marks & Spencer Sauvignon
2009** White
Nicely perfumed, with a gentle
elegant weight of citrus and kiwi
fruit. Lovely texture.
£5.49 M&S

Maison Domaine Maison 2009
White
Green and herbaceous with a
touch of lime flower on the nose.
Palate is ripe with lingering acidity.

**Malidain Sensation De
Grandlieu 2009** White
Fresh, light and clean pears. Good
yeasty style and acidity balance.

**Matthias & Emile Roblin
Sancerre Ammonites 2008**
White
Lemony sherbet on the nose.
Crisp and fresh with lemon, lime
and melon ripeness on the palate.
Nice balance and length.
HVN, VTL, WUO

**Oscar Brillant Sancerre
2009** White
Light, elegant and fruity. A
straightforward style with hints of

minerality and citrusy freshness.
ASDA

**Paul Buisse Touraine
Sauvignon Blanc 2009** White
Mineral and green fruit nose.
Hint of tinned peas on the palate
with a finish of ripe tropical fruit.
Nicely balanced.

**Philippe Raimbault Mosaique
2008** White
Leafy, very fruity on the palate
with hints of gooseberry and
lime. Long and lush on the finish.
£14.99 DLW

**Pierre Chainier Première
Touraine 2009** White
Pale, green nose with a hint of
tomato leaf. Light bodied with
a fresh palate of citrus and
passionfruit.
£5.99 MRN

**Vignerons De La Vallée
Du Cher Elysis Touraine
Sauvignon Blanc 2009** White
Fresh and green with a hint of
passionfruit on the nose. Quite
vegetal on the palate with long,
lingering freshness.

**Château La Variere La
Chevalerie Anjou-Villages
Brissac 2008** Red
Dusty, green pepper nose. Fresh
fruits on palate with a tart finish.

**Château La Variere Anjou
Rouge 2009** Red
Attractive but slightly confected
note with raspberries and
blackcurrant fruit. Medium length.

**Château La Variere Anjou-
Villages Brissac 2008** Red
Sweet, ripe, fruity and berryish
with nice depth.

**Château Soucherie Champ
Aux Loups 2008** Red
Elegant and defined nose. Fresh

with greenness. Tight palate, very structured acid and long length.

Eric Louis La Côte Blanche Sancerre Rouge 2008 Red
Mid ruby colour, touch of green pepper, grass and herbaceous notes. Good acid, but not too green.
£13.70

Lacheteau Marcel Hubert Merlot NV Red
Hints of herbal character, palate has good balance. Rounded gentle style. Finish is clean with some grip.

Langlois-Château La Bretonnière Rouge Saumur-Champigny 2007 Red
Red fruits with leafy notes. Fresh acidity. Moderate tannins and acidity.
£12.00 MZC

Vins De Rabelais Chinon Rouge Sublime Prestige 2009 Red
A little oxidative on the nose. Barnyardy. A lighter, elegant style but crisp and refined on the finish.

Langlois-Château Crémant De Loire Rosé NV Rosé
Berry nose. Ripe redcurrant flavour. Pleasant and simple wine.
£13.00 ODD

Ackerman 1811 NV
Sparkling
Clean bright nose. Creamy palate. Nice balance.
£6.99

Branchereau Côteaux Du Layon Chaume 2009 Sweet
Honeysuckle and lime zest with fresh citrusy flavours. Pure and light.

Domaine Cady Côteaux Du Layon St. Aubin Harmonie 2002 Sweet
Rich honeyed nose layered with almond ripeness. Luscious with good acidity to balance the fruit. Liquid caramel finish.

RHÔNE VALLEY

Les Vignerons Des 4 Chemins Laudun Blanc Sols Et Sens 2009 White
Rich and pure with lively apple and peachy stone fruit nose. Big mouthfeel but balanced with lively acidity. Lush and round on the finish.
£6.20 LOW

 GIGONDAS TROPHY

Gabriel Meffre Domaine De Longue Toque Gigondas 2007 Red
Spicy red fruit and cherry chocolate. Rich palate. Concentrated and rich.

Gonnet Pere Et Fils Châteaunef-Du-Pape 2006 Red
Developed, broad nose. Herbal and savoury on the palate with fresh, juicy cherry and black fruit flavours. Good acidity and long length.

 RHÔNE TROPHY, CHATEAUNEUF-DU-PAPE TROPHY

Jean-Michel Cazes Domaine Des Sénéchaux 2007 Red
Excellent fruit. Refreshing acidity with well-structured and intense ripe fruits. Still needs time but will develop nicely.

Ogier Oratorio Côtes-Du-Rhône 2007 Red
Lush, ripe and spicy palate of overripe plum, black cherry and raspberries. Vanilla and cream on the lengthy finish.
£10.99

Ogier Oratorio Gigondas 2007 Red
Very powerful meaty, earthy notes, black fruits with savoury aspects. Needs time yet but will evolve beautifully.
£14.99

SILVER

Cyril Marès Mas Des Bressades White Tradition 2009 White
Floral, stone fruit with hints of woody notes. Good concentration of fruit with a full-bodied roundness. Nicely textured with a lingering finish.

Gabriel Meffre La Chasse Reserve Côtes-Du-Rhône White 2009 White
Very fresh fruit. Good structure and nice balance. Harmonious whole.

Les Vignerons Des 4 Chemins Baronnie De Sabran 2009 White
Big and rich with warm, ripe apple and cinnamon spiced fruit. Lush and ripe with layers of flavour and a pleasing, warming finish.
£4.99 LOW

Nathalie Estribeau 2008 White
Good weight and structure, ripe stone fruits with slightly stewed character. Fresh, lively acidity and good oily texture. Pleasant and ripe on the finish.

Cave de Tain Crozes-Hermitage 2008 Red
Earthy and herbal on the palate, backed by lifted red fruit. Dry and spicy, just enough flash in a serious savoury style.
£12.49 PBA

Cave de Tain Saint Joseph 2008 Red
Confected fruit aromas - clove character on the palate, very fine tannins with red fruit concentration. Pepper complexity. Very elegant.
£18.49 PBA

Cave de Tain Tesco Finest* Crozes-Hermitage 2007 Red
Spiced red fruit on the nose. Peppery and meaty on the palate with well integrated fruit and oak. Firm tannins on the finish with good length.
£7.99 TESC, PBA

Cave de Tain Tesco Finest* Hermitage 2005 Red
Dense meaty aromas, fine tannins - gamey complexity on the palate. Ripe fruit on palate. Elegant. Intensity on the finish.

Cellier Des Dauphins Blason Des Papes Châteauneuf-Du-Pape 2009 Red
More muted nose initially but with underlying sweet perfume. Sweet fruit on the palate. Lots of spice. Very supple, moderate backbone. A long spicy finish.
£19.99 WAIT

Cellier Des Dauphins Grande Reserve Côtes-Du-Rhône Villages 2009 Red
Lifted blackberry and cracked pepper. Stunning lush fruit on the palate which is rich and full bodied with dense tannin and refreshing acidity. Exceptional balance.

Chapoutier La Croix Des Grives Côtes-Du-Rhône 2007 Red
Spicy plum on the palate with

soft tannins and fleshy fruit. Dry on the finish.
£10.99 LAI

Chapoutier L'Esquerde Domaine De Bila-Haut Côtes-Du-Roussillon Villages 2008 Red

Bright, red fruits, damson and olives. Refined acidity, good tannins. Cured minerals and veg. Attractive.
£13.99 MZC

Château Beauchene Grande Reserve Châteauneuf-Du-Pape 2007 Red

Clean, restrained and elegant aromas. Red fruit and spice on the palate with nice balance and good acidity. Fresh, supple and delicious.
£22.99 C&B

Château Beauchene Vignobles De La Serriere Châteauneuf-Du-Pape 2007 Red

Delicate fruit aromas. Nicely rounded dark fruits with fresh acidity and good grippy tannins. Complex and well integrated.
£18.08 PVC

Clubs Et Châteaux Terroir Du Rhône Côtes-Du-Rhône 2007 Red

Young still and quite tannic. Ripe strawberry fruit.

Compagnie Rhodanienne Clos Du Bois De Menge Gigondas 2009 Red

Meaty, olive aspects. Some fruit and veg. Firm yet ripe tannins. Needs cellarage to show at its best. Lovely.
£12.49 MYL

Compagnie Rhodanienne Domaine Saint Alimans Côtes-Du-Rhône Villlages Rasteau 2009 Red

Ripe, generous, solid. Slightly oily fruit, good herbs, pepper, orange peel. Long tannins.
£9.99 MYL

Cuvée Du Vatican 2008 Red

Medium deep colour. Spicy from nose with savoury notes. Understated. Big, spicy-peppery. Strong savoury flavours with sweet raspberry fruit. Good backbone.
£20.00

Delas Marquise De La Tourette Hermitage 2007 Red

Nicely herby, peppery nose, with lively cassis fruit. Very well-balanced. Loads of length.
£42.99 HFW, SDC

Domaine Courbis Cornas La Sabarotte 2007 Red

Big, slightly reductive nose, cherry and oak character - lots of toast. Juicy palate. The tannin and oak is a touch dry.
£48.99 HLD

Domaine Du Joncier Lirac Rouge 2008 Red

Herbal spices with elegant oak and lots of black fruits. Round and full on the palate.
£9.99 WAIT

Etienne Gonnet Domaine Font De Michelle 2007 Red

Fragrant, raspberry and minty, earthy spice nose. Full, ripe fruit with lots of spice and a dry, long finish. Ripe tannins. Well-structured and creamy.
£24.99 WAIT

Gabriel Meffre Waitrose Côtes-Du-Rhône Villages 2009 Red

Concentrated damson and raspberry jam characters. Very spicy. On the palate it is juicy, refreshing, lively with good length.
£6.99 WAIT

Grands Vins Sélection Côtes-Du-Rhône Villages La Calade 2008 Red

Rich and ripe with smoke and leather flavours and hints of bramble fruit.

£5.11 MRN

Guigal Côtes-Du-Rhône 2006 Red

Mid ruby-garnet colour, plum and chocolate on the nose. Red berry and soft plum on the palate. Well-balanced and pleasant.

£8.99 MWW, WAIT

La Fagotière Châteauneuf-du-Pape 2007 Red

Primary fruit on the youthful nose. Savoury and ripe on the palate with ripe, firm tannins. Meaty and earthy, long and lingering. Really pure.

£17.87 3DW

Lavau Côtes-Du-Rhône 2009 Red

Fresh black fruits on the nose and palate. Good tannic grip with fresh acidity on the finish. Enjoy now after a good decant.

Lavau Rasteau 2009 Red

Medium colour. Floral cherry with some herbal overtones. Dense, powerful tannin structure. Juicy, chewy black fruit.

Lavau Vacqueyras 2009 Red

Deep raspberry-red appearance. Fruity, spicy, fast fruity nose. Good depth, fruity richness and lovely style.

Les Vignerons De Roaix Seguret Côtes-Du-Rhône Villages Seguret Classic 2009 Red

Big, firm, full and juicy. Lots of bounce, ripe and tangy with earthy herbs.

Louis Bernard Châteauneuf-Du-Pape 2008 Red

Expressive, spicy, strawberry and floral notes to nose. Peppery, spicy, full and mouthfilling. Textured and concentrated. Fine grainy tannins. Long.

Ogier Asda Extra Special Châteauneuf-Du-Pape 2009 Red

Plum and cherry nose. Sweet, juicy fruit, but then a structured firm palate with savoury notes. Milky tannins. Long.

£13.99

Ogier Comte De Raybois 2008 Red

Lovely perfumed black fruits, pepper and spice. Easy going, classic, rustic style of Crozes-Hermitage.

£8.99

Ogier Oratorio Châteauneuf-Du-Pape 2007 Red

Powerful black fruit and spice. Rich and savoury fruit with lashings of oak and firm tannins. Lush and lively finish.

£24.99

Perrin & Fils La Vieille Ferme Rouge 2009 Red

Very perfumed nose with a serious structure, good fruit concentration and length.

£6.39 EHB, MWW, WAIT

Perrin & Fils Reserve 2007 Red

Warm and spicy on the nose. The palate is laden with soft forest fruits and herbaceous, green character. Long and fresh on the finish.

Skalli Caves Saint Pierre Saint-Joseph 2008 Red

Sulphurous nose. Fine, smooth rich black fruit comes through. Lacks a little mid palate charm.

Skalli Caves Saint Pierre Vinsobres 2008 Red
Balanced fruit with damson and plum showing through on the nose and palate. Spicy on the finish.
£12.99

Skalli Caves Saint Pierre Vinsobres 2009 Red
Attractive bramble fruit on the nose. Deep and rich fruit flavours coming through on the palate. Excellent potential.
£11.99

Skalli Grand Vin Du Rhône Roquebrussane Saint Joseph 2007 Red
Nicely restrained, cherry and raspberry fruitiness. Lighter, creamy and juicy. Lovely balance.

Skalli Roc Des Monges Hermitage 2006 Red
Restrained red fruit aromas, some herbal/menthol lift. Light bodied, sweet raspberry fruit in mid palate. Bright fruit to finish.

Vidal-Fleury Côtes-Du-Rhône 2007 Red
Ruby red with fragrant raspberry and spice on the nose. Elegant tannin with ripe black fruit and well-balanced acidity on the palate. Good length.
£9.99 BAB, CHH, P&R

Vignerons De Caractere Collection Du Rhône Vacqueyras 2009 Red
Subtle nose of spice and liquorice, chewy tannins, balanced. Structured and long.

Wine Way 7 Collines Côtes-Du-Rhône Villages 2009 Red
Rich and strong wine. Intense black fruit and white pepper with a slight floral accent. Muscular wine with chocolate and meaty overtones. Very peppery - lovely

oak use.
£6.84 PAT

Jaillance Clairette De Die Tradition Jaillance Lot 1411 NV Sparkling
Watery lemon hue. Clean, appealing fruit on nose. Sweet, clean, lovely.

BRONZE

Chapoutier Condrieu Invitare 2008 White
Floral, honeyed, peachy nose. Intense fruit with apricot and honey. Fades slightly on finish.
£32.99 MWW

Compagnie Rhodanienne Les Combelles Blanc 2009 White
Grapey, tropical fruit with floral overtones. Stone fruit on the palate with soft, round character. Slightly savoury with a light, grapey finish.
£5.99 MYL

M Chapoutier La Ciboise White Luberon 2009 White
Zingy acidity with hints of mineral and herbaceous tones. Pleasant and ripe with a touch of spice on the finish.
£7.99 MZC

Benoit Valerie Calvet Cave De Monterail Châteauneuf-Du-Pape 2009 Red
Aromatic, sweet fruit nose. Very primary. Structured with fine tannins and good acidity. Quite long and very young but promising.
£9.99 ALD

Calvet Vinsobres 2009 Red
Very fruity nose with blueberry dominating. Very easy drinking, elegant wine.

Cave De Cairanne Antique 2007 Red
Deeper colour. Fine French cherry.

Violet nose - quite rich and fun. Very lively.

Cave De Rasteau Ortas Gigondas 2008 Red
Earthiness on nose. Smatterings of white pepper followed by fruit and pepper again. Mineral elements. Keeps you going back for more.
£19.99

Cave de Tain Crozes Hermitage 2007 Red
Attractive, ripe, black fruit nose. Redcurrant and jam on the palate with balanced acidity, firm, juicy black fruit and soft tannins. Meaty with complex finish.
£12.49 PBA

Cave de Tain Crozes Hermitage Les Hauts de Pavières 2007 Red
Restrained, dark fruit nose. Lean in style with good savoury character. Juicy with developed tannins on the finish.
£9.99 WAIT, PBA

Cave de Tain Crozes Hermitage Les Hauts du Fief 2007 Red
Soft, mature, creamy nose. Ripe, sweet red fruit on the palate with loads of vanilla and oak. Fresh, fruity and approachable.
£16.49 PBA

Cave de Tain Hermitage 2006 Red
Quite chocolatey and ripe. There is a density here and a smoothness of fruit and texture - a touch stewed but long and really quite elegant.
£31.49 PBA

Cellier Des Dauphins Côteaux Du Tricastin Cuvée Traditionnelle 2009 Red
Spiced raspberry and plum fruit on the palate with savoury and smoky character. Medium-bodied with a generous finish.
£5.99 ASDA, WAIT

Cellier Des Dauphins Côtes-Du-Rhône Prestige 2009 Red
Young but vibrant with juicy redcurrant fruit. Tight tannin.
£5.49 SAIN, TESC

Cellier Des Dauphins Sainsbury's House Côtes-Du-Rhône 2009 Red
Good structure with ripe tannins, floral and fruity style.
£3.99 SAIN

Celliers Du Languedoc Roche Bastide 2009 Red
Deep peppery red. Black fruit, some spice. Lovely spice and fruit. Good length.

Charmasson Côtes-du-Rhône Villages Plan De Dieu 2008 Red
Strong liquorice and mint on the nose. Sweet black fruit and cracked pepper flavours with a smoky finish.
£7.99 MWW

Chene Bleu Abelard 2006 Red
Meaty, savoury aromas. The sweet fruit shows through on the palate. Very rich.
£60.00 HFB, HFW, HUN

Cristia Collection Vacqueyras 2009 Red
Restrained nose but intense palate. Bursting with spice and liquorice. Lengthy finish. Structured.
£12.99 NKW

Cyril Marès Mas Des Bressades Red Tradition 2009 Red
Bright intense complex nose showing bramble fruit with lots of fruit and length on the palate. Nicely balanced.

Domaine De Cristia Grenache Vin De Pays 2009 Red
Fresh cherry nose with sweet ripe redcurrants and strawberry. Lovely fruity finish.
£8.99 DWS, IR-SPQ, NKW

Domaine De La Brunely Vacqueyras 2009 Red
Smooth, rich, spicy, classic style. Upfront, pronounced peppery, smoky, blackberry jam character overlaid with coffee bean edge and hint of tar. Length good and balanced with sweet contained edge. Serious and classy.
IR-SPQ

Domaine Des Sénéchaux Marks & Spencer Châteauneuf-Du-Pape 2006 Red
Chocolate nose with ripe, juicy, jammy fruit on the palate. Intensely ripe with good balance and fresh acidity.
£24.00 M&S

Domaines Viticoles Renouard Scamandre 2006 Red
Ripe and herbaceous on the nose, lovely aromatics. Black fruit and spice on the palate with chewy tannins on the finish.

Gabriel Meffre Côtes-Du-Rhône Villages Plan De Dieu 2009 Red
Good weight and structure with bright redcurrant fruit. Spice and pepper on the finish.

Gabriel Meffre La Chasse Merlot 2009 Red
Fresh and fruity, plums, with some vanilla. Medium weight with some tannic grip and integrated oak.
£6.49 ASDA

Gabriel Meffre La Chasse Reserve Côtes-Du-Rhône 2009 Red
Some chocolate and liquorice with brambling fruit, smoke and leathers with a clean finish.
£6.99 Widely Available

Gabriel Meffre La Chasse Shiraz Grenache 2009 Red
A young, elegant wine showing ripe, raspberry fruit. Fruity and fresh on the palate.
£8.49 ASDA

Gabriel Meffre La Chasse Winemaker's Selection Côtes-Du-Rhône 2008 Red
Perfumed with spicy, savoury notes. Fresh acidity with grippy tannins, black and red berry fruits on the savoury, dry finish.
£8.99 MRN

Gabriel Meffre Laurus Châteauneuf-Du-Pape 2007 Red
Developed fruits, currants with tobacco-laced spice on the palate. Firm structure with soft acid. Approachable and delicious.

Gabriel Meffre Les Grands Cypres Vacqueyras 2008 Red
Slightly earthy and rustic in style. Some decent liquorice fruit.
£11.99 WAIT

Gabriel Meffre Terres De Galets Côtes-Du-Rhône 2009 Red
Mid raspberry red hues. Young juicy fruity nose. Cherry fruit and sweetened tannins.
£9.99 SAIN

Gabriel Meffre Vacqueyras 2008 Red
Damson red hue. Light spicy fruit on nose. Good length.

GMDF Palais Des Anciens Côtes-Du-Rhônes Villages 2008 Red
Dark, forest fruits on the nose which follows through on the palate with hints of spice

and pepper.
CWS

Jean Luc Colombo Les Gravières Crozes Hermitage 2007 Red
Clean with a sweet, jammy nose. Peppery, black fruit with soft oak and vanilla on the palate. Well-balanced and long.
£13.99 WAIT, WWD, WWW

Lavau Gigondas 2009 Red
Powerful meaty, blackberry fruits. Firm yet ripe tannins. Layered and youthful. Needs time then will be very good.

Le Cellier Des Princes Châteauneuf-Du-Pape 2008 Red
Full, ripe, spicy sweet, very vibrant fruit on palate. Soft, supple tannins. Firm, balanced and straightforward. Ready now.
£13.89 BOO

Les Vignobles Foncalieu Domaine Princemelle 2009 Red
Deep raspberry red. Light herbal fruity nose. Red fruit, soft tannins.

Louis Bernard Chartreuse De Bonpas Réserve 2009 Red
Ripe and round with soft, fleshy fruit on the palate. Warming spice and lush ripeness on the finish with good balance and length.

Louis Bernard Côtes-Du-Rhône Villages 2009 Red
Spicy berry fruit nose with liquorice, tar and pepper. Well-structured with a long finish.

M Chapoutier Les Meysonniers Crozes-Hermitage 2007 Red
Clean, restrained nose. Ripe,

juicy fruit with integrated oak and tannin. White pepper and charred meat on the finish with good tannin structure.
£15.99 ODD

Maison Les Deux Rhônes Côtes-Du-Rhône Reserve De La Tour 2008 Red
Light raspberry red. Light fruity nose, bilberries, tannins.

Marrenon Grand Marrenon 2007 Red
Red fruit and mocha spice. Long lingering finish.
£9.00

Marrenon Vignobles En Luberon Orca Vi 2007 Red
Dark berry and spice aromas. Dark fruit showing through on the finish.
£11.00

Marres Damien Domaine La Grande Bellane 2009 Red
Very bright fruit, sappy with meaty and peppery edge on nose. Solid and balanced. Will come through.

Ogier Boiseraie 2009 Red
Pure sweet berry fruit flavours with good structure.
£7.99

Ogier Oratorio Crozes-Hermitage 2007 Red
Big, oaky, dark fruit nose. Grippy tannins with some black, meaty edges. Vanilla and oak on the finish with a hint of peppery spice.
£14.99

Ogier Reserve Des Argentiers 2009 Red
Very sweet, almost jammy fruit on the nose. Ripe, rich, very full, very sweet and fleshy but with tannin and backbone. Needs time. Long.
£11.79

Perrin & Fils Waitrose In Partnership Châteauneuf-du-Pape 2007 Red
Plenty of ripe blueberry, spice and blackcurrants on the palate. Firm tannins, needs some time.
£19.99 WAIT

Ravoire Et Fils Montrouge Les Côteaux Du Soleil 2008 Red
Spice and red fruit on the nose. The palate has juicy rich fruit and grippy structure with underlying floral notes. Long and spicy finish.

Skalli Asda Extra Special Côtes-Du-Rhône Villages 2009 Red
Vibrant black fruits and spice with a slight herbal accent. Dense, delicious and powerful.
£4.74 ASDA

Skalli Caves Saint Pierre Beaumes De Venise 2009 Red
Ripe, sweet and fruity with lovely balance. Good savouriness coming through on the finish.
£11.99

Skalli Caves Saint Pierre Châteauneuf-Du-Pape 2008 Red
Earthy spicy nose with some cherry fruit. Full on palate. Showing a lot of oak and tannin. Has length.
£18.99

Skalli Caves Saint Pierre Côtes-Du-Rhône Vieilles Vignes 2009 Red
Tinned cherry fruit on the nose, with really enticing black fruit on the palate, well-balanced by refreshing acidity.
£6.99

Skalli Caves Saint Pierre Signargues 2009 Red
Well-rounded blueberry and spice notes. Very quaffable.
£9.99

Skalli Châteauneuf-Du-Pape Dédication 2005 Red
Chocolate and coffee on the nose. Ripe black fruit with a touch of creamy vanilla on the palate. Fresh and bright.

Skalli Côtes-Du-Rhône Cuvée Prestige 2009 Red
Subtle and well presented. Extracted yet balanced. Very well made.
£4.58 SAIN

Skalli Tesco Finest* St Joseph 2008 Red
Sulphurous, struck match character rather dominates. The palate has a lithe juicy fruit with a flat finish.
TESC

Vidal-Fleury Côte-Rôtie La Chatillone 2005 Red
Lovely ripe, bright, juicy fruit - lots of punch and vital energy here. Dry, big tannin but balanced.
£65.00 HFB

Vidal-Fleury Crozes-Hermitage 2008 Red
Slightly muted blackberry and pepper notes, good depth of flavour with grippy tannins, pretty good acidity. Earthy, herbal, a touch dry on the finish.
£16.99 BAB

Vignerons De Beaumes De Venise Tesco Finest* Gigondas 2007 Red
Spicy red fruit, plum. Medium tannin, soft acid and alcohol balance.
TESC

Vignerons De Caractère Eloquence 2007 Red
Medium plum red. Stalky with peppery, spicy fruit. Meaty sausage character with juicy ripe fruit underneath, soft tannins and a very savoury finish.

Vignerons De Caractère Gigondas 2009 Red
Fresh ripe red berry fruits. Good balance of silky tannins. Needs time. Will be sublime.

Vignerons De Caractère Rubis Des Vignes 2009 Red
Plenty of fruit, intense, ripe, balanced acidity, good structure, rather chalky tannins.

Vignerons De Caractere Vacqueyras 2009 Red
Mid raspberry-red hue. Light with a hint of spice on nose. Tart fruit, supple style on palate.

Vignobles La Coterie Côtes-Du-Rhône Villages Séguret Classic 2008 Red
Plenty of earthiness. Balanced and fragrant.

Wine Way 7 Collines Côtes-Du-Rhône 2009 Red
Spicy red fruits on the nose, fine tannins on the palate. Fresh, juicy and well made.
£5.94 PAT

Marrenon Vignobles En Luberon Petula 2009 Rosé
Delicate pink. Cherry fruit with red fruit and spice. Fresh and ripe on the palate.
£9.00

REGIONAL FRANCE

GOLD

 ALSACE RIESLING TROPHY

Domaine Paul Blanck Riesling Grand Cru Furstentum 2005, Alsace White
Pear drops. Intensely aromatic. Well-balanced, great acidity with hints of perfume.

Geiler Gewürztraminer Grand Cru Florimont 2008, Alsace
White
Good balance, with a lovely developed nose. The palate is full of fresh, sweet fruit with undertones of development. Nutty and honeyed on the finish. Very well made. Delicious.
£19.49 CMI, EAR, MAI, WAV

 BEAUJOLAIS TROPHY,

Henry Fessy Brouilly 2009, Beaujolais Red
Dense, taut and intense with lovely vibrant fruit.
£9.99 FNC, FTH, LLA, WAIT

Loron Et Fils Morgon Château De Bellevue 2009, Beaujolais Red
Lovely purity and elegance with vibrant fruit.

SILVER

Alsace Willm Riesling Reserve 2008, Alsace White
Lemon and lime on the nose with a ripe fruity palate. Elegant and forward with an attractively fruity character.

Cave De Saint Laurent D'Oingt Rostre De Bélémnite Beaujolais Blanc Fût De Chêne 2007, Beaujolais
White
Fresh almond-tinged nose with white flowers. Ripe, chalky palate with apple, lime and a touch of white peach. Delicate fruit.

Cave de Turckheim Asda Extra Special Gewürztraminer 2008, Alsace White
Lively orange blossom and lychees. Scented. Full flavoured. Good length.
£6.98 ASDA, PBA

Cave De Turckheim Riesling Vieilles Vignes 2007, Alsace White
Spice. Cinnamon, rounded fruits. Crisp. Roundness and balance, slightly lemony.
£10.49 SAIN, PBA

Chai Au Quai Vent De Folie Vermentino 2009, South West White
Pale yellow, nutty fresh fruit nose. Soft attack. Nice nutty fruit and melon. Clean, fresh and lengthy.
£9.99

Château D'Orschwihr Riesling Bollenberg 2008, Alsace White
A touch of ripe citrus on the nose. The palate is layered with fresh citrus and pear-drop flavours. Quite intense on the finish.
£12.90 ODD, ODF

Clos Poggiale Blanc 2008, Corsica White
Clean, citrus aromas. Ripe apple dominates the palate with a fresh, lemony finish.

Domaine Gruss Gewürztraminer Vieilles Vignes 2008, Alsace White
Exotic and aromatic. Lovely fruit integrity, some slight 'skinny' grip and decent acidity to match.
£12.33 3DW

Domaine Gruss Riesling Cuvée Des Prélats 2008, Alsace White
Delicate aromas with excellent balance and length. Melon and gobs of ripe fruit. Fresh, fragrant and light. Well-balanced acidity on the finish.
£10.68 3DW

Gaec Des Eyssards Château Des Eyssards 2008, South West White
Floral, honeyed, peachy nose.

Intense fruit with apricot and honey on the palate. Ripe and creamy on the finish.

Geiler Gewürztraminer Vendanges Tardives 2007, Alsace White
Vibrant and honeyed with botrytis-like nose. Good depth with warming alcohol and space. Viscous on the finish with ripe, candied pears.
£26.99 CMI, EAR, MAI, WAV

Jacky Passot Domaine De Fontriante Beaujolais-Villages 2008, Beaujolais White
Delicate white peach and almond scented nose. Ripe, leafy palate. Good acidity. Very fine balance on fruit.

Maison Duboeuf Beaujolais Blanc 2007, Beaujolais White
Leafy, appley, pear nose. Juicy and creamy but restrained fruit. Good freshness. Gorgeous!
£6.99

Paul Et Philippe Zinck Gewürztraminer Grand Cru Eichberg 2008, Alsace White
Turkish Delight with savoury undertones. Sweet with plenty of alcohol and just enough acidity to balance. Medium length.
£11.99 MAJ

Paul Et Philippe Zinck Riesling Portrait 2008, Alsace White
Pale lemon in colour with a lovely fruit forward nose. Almonds and lime-flower on the palate with lingering freshness. Well-balanced and delicious.
£7.99 MAJ

Willm Pinot Gris Cuvée Emile Willm 2008, Alsace White
Warm, with a hint of ginger spice. Fresh, ripe and lush on the palate with good citrus character.

Delicious and fresh with a supple, long finish.

Cave Du Château De Chénas Fleurie 2009, Beaujolais Red
Floral tones with raspberries, white currants and sweet fruit with creamy topping. Good acidity. Finishes seductively and lingers with raspberries.

Champier Champier 2009, Beaujolais Red
Ripe juicy bubble gummy nose, mid weight attack. Ripe blueberry fruit character. Nice balance.
£11.99 ODD

Des Deux Châteaux Château De La Terrière Beaujolais-Villages 2009, Beaujolais Red
Candied raspberry nose. Mid full, ripe candied cherry and raspberry fruit. Gentle acidity and ripe tannins on a good long finish.

Domaine Pardon Fleurie 2009, Beaujolais Red
Light depth plus strawberries and cream with violets - a summer afternoon in the garden with sunshine, cream and ripe strawberries in a glass. Aromatic plums. Well-balanced.
£13.00 LAI

Franck Decrenisse Old Vines 2009, Beaujolais Red
Ripe cherries and raspberry creamy summer puddings. Sweet juicy cherries in good acidity. Creamy, juicy, ripe finish lingers of raspberries and cream. Seductive.
£8.99 ODD

Gerard Charvet 2009, Beaujolais Red
Lovely intensity of pure cherry and plum fruit with nice tannic structure. Beautifully ripe. Good earthy fruit with a long finish.
£10.99 DLW

Henry Fessy Morgon 2009, Beaujolais Red
Rich, juicy, earthy and fresh blueberry and blackcurrant. Long, very fragrant and tangy. Lovely finish.
£9.99 ANN, BCO, FAW, FTH

Jean-Luc Baldes Château Labrande 2008, South West Red
Very deep purple, delicate soft fruits. Refreshing but perhaps over strong tannins. Merlot comes through.

Laurent Gauthier 2009, Beaujolais Red
Nicely structured with vibrant berry fruits. Juicy and pure.
£12.99 ODD

Les Vignerons De Buzet Cuvée Z 2008, South West Red
Creamy black fruits. Quite tannic yet good level of spicy black fruits. Chocolaty, liquorice. Creamy finish.

Lucien Lardy Moulin á Vent 2009, Beaujolais Red
Sweet cherry nose. Smooth ripe cherries. Nice mouthfeel of fruit. Well balance.
£11.99 DLW

Maison Louis Jadot Combe Aux Jacques Beaujolais-Villages 2009, Beaujolais Red
Full, fleshy, floral, young, sappy. Comely, fresh, vibrant and fine-boned.
£8.99 TESC, WAIT

Robert Perroud 2009, Beaujolais Red
Vibrant plum, ruby purple. Nice plum/red berries, spicy bread. Soft attack. Medium intensity and concentration. Dry on finish.
£11.99 DLW

Olivier Sumeire Château Coussin 2009, Provence Rosé
Good balance with a palate of

light fruit salad and clean berry notes. Elegant and ripe on the finish.

Skalli Domaine Terra Vecchia 2009, Corsica Rosé
Restrained nose with hint of strawberry cream aromas. Fruity and ripe on the palate with good balance and acidity and length.
£8.99

Schaeffer Pinot Gris Fronholz Vendanges Tardives 2005, Alsace Botrytis
Ripe with medium intense fruit. Lanolin with a ripe citrus freshness on the palate. Clean with good clarity and depth of fruit.

BRONZE

Alsace Willm Pinot Blanc Reserve 2008, Alsace White
Stone fruit aromas with hints of apple and savoury character. Medium to full bodied with good oily texture and fresh fruit flavours.

Bourgeois The Naked Grape Sauvignon Blanc 2009, Charente White
Floral, with green melon on the nose. Ripe melon with strong citrus fruit on the palate. Good purity of fruit on the finish.
£6.99 BTH, PUS, WAIT

Cave de Turckheim Gewürztraminer Preiss Zimmer 2008, Alsace White
Fresh. Tropical fruit on the nose. Lively and spicy.
£7.74 MRN, PBA

Cave de Turckheim Sainsbury's Taste the Difference Gewürztraminer 2008, Alsace White
Ripe melon nose with hints of lemon and lime. Tropical fruit

palate with fresh acidity showing through. Lengthy finish.
£7.64 SAIN, PBA

Cave Du Bois D'Oingt Terrasse Des Pierres Dorées Beaujolais Blanc 2008, Beaujolais White
Pale lemon green. Under-ripe peach and pear with lovely stony overlay. Pretty wine with touch of spice and cream. A savoury finish. Excellent.

Château De Jurque Fantaisie 2008, South West White
Nice, tropical fruit on the nose. Stone fruit and citrusy tropicality on the palate. Very fresh and zingy on the finish.
£9.99

Château D'Orschwihr Pinot Blanc Bollenberg 2008, Alsace White
Lemon curd and custard cream nose, juicy, soft fruit on the palate. Pleasant grip of slate on the finish, with a touch of warming spice.
£13.00 ODD, ODF

Domaine De Rocailles Vin De Savoie Apremont 2009, Savoie White
Fresh, but mature nose. Quite zingy with white floral palate. Lemon citrus freshness and light bodied, clean finish.
£7.99 SGL, WAIT

Domaine De Rocailles Vin De Savoie Apremont Prestige 2009, Savoie White
Light lemony nose, crisp and clean apple-citrus palate. Firm and straightforward.
£10.45 SGL

Domaine Du Tariquet Les 4 Réserve 2008, South West White
Stewed apple fruit on the nose.

Oily texture with hints of tropical citrus on the palate. Well-balanced and smooth with a hint of herbaceousness on the finish.
FRD

Domaine Gruss Pinot Gris Frohnenberg 2008, Alsace
White
Fruity, exotic palate. Fresh, zippy acidity. Off-dry finish.
£11.12 3DW

Dominique Bouillard Domaine De Barvy Beaujolais-Villages Blanc 2008, Beaujolais White
Pale lemon green. Stone fruits and a touch of creamy oak. Chalky accent. A little soft with peachy palate.

Hugel & Fils Gentil 2008, Alsace White
Pale lemon with a lightly fruity nose. Elegant and ripe on the palate. Flinty on the finish.
£9.99 CAM

Jean Pierre Lassalle Perle Blanche 2008, Beaujolais
White
Melony, elegant, herbal and complex with a long aftertaste.

Kuehn Riesling Grand Cru Kaefferkopf 2008, Alsace
White
Ripe apple and smoke on the nose. Red apple and melon on the palate with racy acidity on the finish.
£18.99

Kuehn Tesco Finest* Alsace Gewürztraminer 2008, Alsace
White
Intense, upfront aromas on the nose. Pungent, but with lively, clean fruit flavours and a twist of lime zest on the palate. Fresh finish.
TESC

LGI Vallée Blanche Sauvignon Blanc 2009, South West White
Crisp and lemony on the palate with nicely balanced acidity. Ripe, round and floral on the finish with a touch of sweetness.
MWW

Paul Blanck Riesling Grand Cru Schlossberg 2007, Alsace
White
Fresh lime with lovely citrus balance. Ripe and clean with plenty of good fruit. Grippy finish with fresh acidity.

Paul Et Philippe Zinck Gewürztraminer Portrait 2008, Alsace White
Floral, leafy nose. Honey and lychee, sweet. Decent acidity and a bit of length.
£9.99 MAJ

Producteurs Plaimont Les Vignes Retrouvées Saint-Mont 2008, South West White
Sweet fruit with rich concentration. Light apple character with hints of pleasing lemon, lime citrus fruit on the finish.
£8.99 ENO

Skalli Clos Poggiale Blanc 2007, Corsica White
Sweet banana nose with soft red cherry fruit.
£15.99

Sylvain Rosier Château Du Chatelard Beaujolais Blanc Cuvée Vieilles Vignes 2008, Beaujolais White
Pale lemon colour. Peaches, apricots and citrus element. Lovely freshness. Midweight, creamy, spicy finish. Really beautiful!

Trimbach Riesling Réserve 2007, Alsace White
Mineral and citrus on the nose with floral notes leads to intense

palate with long finish.
£19.95 SAIN

Vignoble De Gascogne Grand Héron 2009, South West
White
Clean and fresh aromatics. Full, with good fruit ripeness on the palate. Finishes with fresh acidity.
£5.99 MAJ

Vivien De Nazelle Cabidos NV, South West White
Delightful, oily fruit - orange peel, straw and flowers with an exceptional sugar balance leading to a long finish.
£15.00 ENO

Bunan Moulin Des Costes 2005, Provence Red
Peppery, black cherry on the nose. White peppery and smooth tannins on the palate with a spicy, chocolaty finish.

Cave Du Bois D'Oingt Beaujolais Terrasse des Pierres Dorees 2009, Beaujolais Red
Candied cherry and raspberry nose. Mid full body, soft tannins and gentle acidity.

Cave Du Château Des Loges Tesco Beaujolais-Villages 2009, Beaujolais Red
Deep plum. Concentrated fruit nose. Full juicy fruit.
TESC

Collin Bourisset Fleurie 2009, Beaujolais Red
Juicy ripe strawberries and aromatic chewy fruit with crisp acidity. Aromatic finish. Summer drinking.

Domaine De La Madone Beaujolais-Villages Tradition 2009, Beaujolais Red
Big, full, tangy and perfumed with plenty of juicy raspberries.

Just tails off.
£5.95

Domaine Pascal Berthier St Amour 2009, Beaujolais Red
Summer pudding fruit and creamy, crisp acidity. Chewy tannins, creamy strawberries with a clean, refreshing finish.
£11.99 DLW

FGV Thorin Fleurie 2009, Beaujolais Red
Sweet juicy ripe currants and creamy cherries. Clean finish lingers with plummy sweetness.
£10.29 BOO

Gaec Des Eyssards Domaine Des Eyssards 2009, South West Red
Cherry fruit with some toasty oak, bramble fruit and grippy tannins. Good intensity and length.
£6.49 WAIT

Georges Duboeuf Sainsbury's Taste The Difference Beaujolais-Villages NV, Beaujolais Red
Light ruby. Slight perfume on nose. Light raspberry fruit.
£5.99 SAIN

Henry Fessy Beaujolais-Villages 2009, Beaujolais Red
Deep ruby, cheerful berry nose. Lovely structured style with good concentration mid palate. Elegant finish.
£9.99 ANN, FTH, GHL, HFB, WEA, WAIT

Jean-Luc Baldes The New Black Wine 2008, South West Red
Saturated, inky black purple to rim. Dark fruit. Firm but fine-grained with good length and a hot finish.

Labouré-Roi Beaujolais-Villages 2009, Beaujolais Red
Young, fleshy, earthy. Has

attractive, crunchy fruit. Young, lively cherry, red berry - vibrant and earthy.

Les Grands Chais De France Calvet Fleurie 2009, Beaujolais Red
Rich, youthful colour and moderate intensity. Soft berry character on the nose. Silky tannins. Light body with concentrated cherry fruit. Very polished. Perfumed finish.

Les Vignerons De Buzet Merlot Cabernet 2008, South West Red
Youthful, subdued, slightly meaty. Firm, mineral, accented acidity and ripe but firm tannins. Needs a little time.

Loron Et Fils Xavier Et Nicolas Barbet Moulin Á Vent 2009, Beaujolais Red
Ripe, sweet, nice structure. Cherry and berry fruit with lovely intensity.
£12.99

Maison Louis Jadot Beaujolais Lantignie 2008, Beaujolais Red
Mid light ruby. Delicate strawberry and raspberry nose. Medium full but a little short.
£8.99

Skalli Corse Rouge 2008, Corsica Red
Broad with smoky tobacco aromas. Savoury and ripe with dark red fruits on the palate. Firm tannins with good focus. Interesting and delicious.

Château D'Esclans Garrus 2008, Provence Rosé
Pale pink. Clean banana nose with a touch of oak. Soft and clean on the palate with a ripe, red fruit finish.

Château Pigoudet Cuvée La Chapelle 2009, Provence Rosé
Pungent cherry fruit with a touch of grenadine on the nose. Cherry and warm spice on the palate with a touch of strawberry fruit. Nice.
£7.99 MWW

Domaine De L'Amaurigue Fleur De L'Amaurigue 2009, Provence Rosé
Pale pink, salmon colour. Nice intensity of fruit, like summer in a glass. Ripe, fresh fruit on the finish.

Orenga De Gaffory Patrimonio Rosé 2008, Corsica Rosé
A refreshing wine. Hints of red fruits on the palate with a good finish.
£13.00 CPE

Skalli Clos Poggiale Rosé 2009, Corsica Rosé
Fresh red berry nose. Lifted red berry fruit on the palate in a very easy drinking style. Fresh finish.
£15.99

Domaine les Rocailles Brut Vin de Savoie NV, Savoie Sparkling
Beautiful tropical nose. Well-balanced acidity. Good mousse. Some development.
£12.45 SGL

Kuehn Tesco Finest* Cremant d'Alsace Riesling 2005, Alsace Sparkling
Pale lemon. Oily characteristics coming through - petrol minerals. Very lively on the palate. Fresh finish. Well made wine with some complexity.
TESC

Les Grands Chais De France Phillipe Michel Cremant De Jura 2007, Jura Sparkling
Very light, peach notes some cream on nose. Lively, crisp mousse, crunchy green apples on

finish. Fresh and live.
£6.99

Château Belingard Monbazillac 2007, South West Sweet
Nice, open marmalade fruit with some good fruit character. Fresh on the finish.
£11.99 BWJ, COE, EVW, LFW

Schaeffer Cuvée Cecile Klevener De Heiligenstein 2007, Alsace Sweet
Very pale gold. Orange marmalade and toffee, with creamy hints and juicy fruit. Late harvest style with balanced acidity and a hint of minerality. Lovely with creamy goats cheese.

Germany

Germany remains staunchly unfashionable, much to the consternation of wine lovers everywhere. Here, Riesling achieves greatness that nowhere else on earth can match. Not just sweet wines either, there is a vanguard of 'trocken' dry Rieslings to enjoy. These wines need our support – not just because of their intrinsic quality, but also to prevent the go-ahead of a new bridge that will cut straight through some of the best vineyard sites in the Mosel valley. Horrified wine professionals are rallying to prevent its construction, and every bottle of German Riesling sold will lend weight to their campaign. Also, the country is making leaps and bounds with the quality of its reds – try any of the Spätburgunders (aka Pinot Noir) featured here to believe the hype.

KEY FACTS

Total production
10m hectolitres

Total vineyard
102,340 ha

Top 10 grapes
1 Riesling
2 Müller-Thurgau (Rivaner)
3 Spätburgunder (Pinot Noir)
4 Dornfelder
5 Silvaner
6 Grauburgunder (Pinot Gris)
7 Portugieser
8 Weissburgunder
9 Kerner
10 Trollinger

Top 10 regions
1 Rheinhessen
2 Pfalz
3 Baden
4 Württemberg
5 Mosel
6 Franken
7 Nahe
8 Rheingau
9 Saale-Unstrut
10 Ahr

**Producers
(Qualitätswein &
Prädikatswein)**
11, 000 (estimated)

2010 IWC PERFORMANCE

Trophies	8
Gold	19
Silver	40
Bronze	28

Balthasar Ress Rüdesheim Berg Rottland Riesling Erstes Gewächs 2008, Rheingau
White

Rich mineral and honeyed grapefruit on the nose. Almost a touch of fudge. Mineral with a hint of bruised peach on the palate. Long and fresh with lively acidity running through to the finish.
£20.00

 DRY WHITE FRANKEN TROPHY

Divino Nordheim Franconia Eschendorfer Lump Silvaner Spätlese Trocken 2006, Franken White

Deep colour of green gold. Honeyed and sweetly green notes. Grapefruit and pithy flavours. Luscious full character.

 INTERNATIONAL RIESLING TROPHY, GERMANY DRY WHITE TROPHY, RHEINGAU RIESLING TROPHY, HOCHHEIM RIESLING TROPHY

Domdechant Werner'sches Hochheim Riesling Erstes Gewächs 2008, Rheingau
White

Exuberant and fragrant honey-flower nose. The fruit is ripe with floral accents, with tight green apple accents. The acidity is fresh and lively with a mineral edge. Dry and long.
LAI

Domdechant Werner'sches Hochheimer Domdechaney Riesling Spätlese 2008, Rheingau White

White flower, lemon and honey on the nose. Vibrant acidity with lovely, fresh fruit salad character. Chalky and light on the finish. Fabulous.
LAI

Dr Loosen Urziger Würzgarten Riesling Kabinett 2009, Mosel White

Chalk and apple nose with hints of rose petal and tangerine on the palate. Vibrant, lively and deliciously long.
£12.99 BTH, JNW, WAIT, WAIT

Friedrich Altenkirch Lorcher Krone 2008, Rheingau White

Mineral and peach like aromas on the nose. Gentle with a touch of residual sugar on the palate. Spicy peachy fruit with lively acidity and zesty character. Intense and fresh on the finish.

Güterverwaltung Stiftungsweingüter Trabener Würzgarten Riesling Kabinett 2008, Mosel White

Apple and petrol. Nice friendly nose. Well-balanced fruit with a bit of complexity. Long finish. Well-balanced and clean. Will be very nice in 5 years.

Horst Sauer Escherndorfer Lump Riesling Trocken Grosses Gewächs 2008, Franken White

Pure and crisp with bright citrus aromas on the nose. Lemon peel fruit on the palate. Fresh acidity with lemon-lime character. Refreshing and zingy on the finish.

Josef Leitz Marks & Spencer Leitz Rudesheimer Berg Roseneck Riesling 2008, Rheingau White

Very pale lemon green. Apple, flower and cream on the nose with mineral overtones. Incredibly complex with gorgeous fruit and racy acidity.

Long and plush. Phenomenal.
£19.00 M&S

Leitz Rüdesheimer Magdalenenkreuz Riesling Spätlese 2009, Rheingau White
Pale lemon green. Beautiful, honeyed apple aromas. Absolutely beautiful sweetness with well-balanced acidity. Lingering finish.
£14.25 BTH, JCC, LBS, SWG

 RÜDESHEIM RIESLING TROPHY

Leitz Rüdesheimer Rosengarten Riesling Kabinett 2009, Rheingau White
Bright mineral and honeyed nose. Apple, honey and white flower flavours with racy acidity and a weighty palate. Dry fruit finish.
£9.99 WAIT

 OFF DRY MOSEL TROPHY

Moselland Wine Company Lieserer Schlossberg Kabinett 2008, Mosel White
Deep pale green yellow. Good balanced fruit freshness and acidity, with super potential.

 OFF DRY WHITE TROPHY, OFF DRY RHEINGAU TROPHY

Schloss Johannisberg Rosalack Riesling 2007, Rheingau White
Pale lemon green. Orange marmalade and toffees. Delicate but concentrated. Great balance between high sweetness and very crisp acidity. Appley finish.
£49.99 HLD

Schmitt Söhne Eiswein 2008, Rheinhessen White
Mouth tingling, vibrant and utterly delicious. Brimming with candied orange peel, honeysuckle and leather supported by a lively twist of fresh lime. Balanced, well made and very silky.

Winzergemeinschaft Franken Zeiler Eulengrund Riesling Spätlese Trocken 2008, Franken White
Rich and sumptuously aromatic. Firm and ripe with a rich mouthfeel. Full of tightly packed fruit, lemon citrus, ripe apple, grapefruit and lime essence. Racy acidity with good balance and a long, lingering finish.

 SWEET GERMAN RIESLING TROPHY

Horst Sauer Escherndorfer Lump Riesling Auslese 2008, Franken Sweet
Great fruit concentration, apricot, pineapple, floral notes. Still very youthful and fresh with great integration. Delicious.

 INTERNATIONAL ICE WINE TROPHY, GERMAN ICE WINE TROPHY

Horst Sauer Escherndorfer Lump Silvaner Eiswein 2008, Franken Sweet
Sweet stewed apple aromas. Very pure. Pronounced stewed apple fruit on palate too. Intensely sweet and delicious.

Horst Sauer Escherndorfer Lump Silvaner Trockenbeerenauslese 2008, Franken Botrytis
Deep golden with intense nose of apricot, sweet spice, honey

and maramalade. Lingering spicy aftertaste.

Juliusspital Iphoefer Kronsberg Silvaner Beerenauslesse 2008, Franken
Botrytis

Mineral, honey and ripe citrus on the nose. Juicy, rich honey and apple supported by lovely acidity, mineral complexity and layers of lush, ripe fruit. Long and lingering on the finish.

Divino Nordheim Franconia Muller-Thürgau Spätlese 2008, Franken White
Very aromatic nose with ripe, floral accents. Fresh citrus and lush tropical fruit. Pungent and lengthy on the finish.

Divino Nordheim Franconia Silvaner Spätlese Trocken 2008, Franken White
Good depth of colour. Honey, lemon, some mineral notes. Tangy with bitter lemon flavours, good mid weight, soft with a minerally finish.

Dr Loosen Graacher Himmelreich Riesling Kabinett 2009, Mosel White
Lime leaf green hue with floral and stone fruit aromas. Peach, pear fruit with racy acidity, gorgeous fruit and a long finish.
£11.45 SAIN

Dr Loosen Satyricus 2008, Mosel White
Textbook nose, very fresh and clean with green apple fruit. The palate is crisp but light with intense citrus and spritzy character. Sweet fruit with lime and mineral edge.
£11.99 EVW

Dr Loosen Urziger Wurzgarten Riesling Trockenbeerenauslese 2007, Mosel White
Deep golden, ripe pineapple and mango on the nose, soft palate with lifted fruit, caramel and toffee. Well-balanced.
BRI, FAR

Friedrich Altenkirch Lorcher Schlossberg 2008, Rheingau
White

Fresh apple and lime on the nose with a touch of pineapple. Steely, lime and green apple fruit. Lots of minerality and intensity of flavour on the finish. Fine, linear and long.

Fritz Allendorf Rüdesheimer Berg Roseneck Riesling 2008, Rheingau White
Clean with lime jelly aromas. Spicy and peachy on the palate with zesty lime-flower flavours. A touch of minerality with good balance and long length.

Güterverwaltung Stiftungsweingüter Trabener Würzgarten Riesling Spätlese Feinherb 2008, Mosel White
Delicate floral apple with fresh acidity. Apple and light passionfruit. Lovely balance.

H Sichel Blue Nun Winemaker's Passion Riesling 2008, Mosel White
Pale lemon green very fine Riesling. Stony apple and pear. Crisp, medium style.

Horst Sauer Escherndorfer Lump Riesling Spätlese Trocken 2008, Franken White
Bright and fresh with crisp green apple on the palate layered with

vibrant mineral flavours. Lemony and fresh on the finish.
J&B

Horst Sauer Escherndorfer Lump Silvaner Trocken Grosses Gewächs 2008, Franken White
Clear and bright with medium intensity. More mineral notes with a touch of floral on the palate. Peach and melon on the finish. Long length. Good complexity.

Juliusspital Bt Trocken 2008, Franken White
Star-bright, mid straw hue. Invitingly good fruity nose. Rich, supple fruit. Styled and lengthy.

Juliusspital Randersackerer Pfuelben Riesling Trocken Grosses Gewächs 2008, Franken White
Pleasantly fresh pear and peach fruit on the nose and palate. Crisp, citrus acidity with lively candied peel flavour. Pure expression, with long length.

Juliusspital Wuerzburger Stein Silvaner Trocken Grosses Gewächs 2008, Franken White
Medium intensity, lemon straw in colour. Slightly spritzy. Pink grapefruit and bitter almond characters. Medium in length, melon notes on the finish.

Loosen Dr L Riesling 2009, Mosel White
Pure green apple and mineral-floral aromas. Lovely acacia honey, good acidity with fruit-forward character. Balanced and delicious.
£7.99 Widely Available

Peter Mertes Bernkasteler Johannisbrünnchen Feinherb 2008, Mosel White
Delicate floral apple with tropical notes. Zingy acidity, delicate balance, weight and mineraly. Elegant and balanced.

Prinz Von Hessen Johannisberger Klaus Riesling Erstes Gewächs 2008, Rheingau White
Green, floral aromas. Honeyed, rich and steely with zesty acidity. The fruit is fresh and intense at the core with orange and pepper on the palate. Long and spritzy with a lime flower finish.
BWL

Prinz Von Hessen Riesling Dachsfilet 2008, Rheingau White
Juicy and ripe with long expressive fruit character. Lemon and apple with a mineral edge to the flavours. Long and refreshing on the finish. Delightful.
BWL

Prinz Von Hessen Riesling Kabinett Trocken 2008, Rheingau White
Lively, lovely, juicy fruit. Lemon and lime with ripe red apple sweetness. Delicate floral and mineral layers, with racy acidity and a long, pleasing finish.
BWL

Prinz Von Hessen Winkeler Jesuitengarten Riesling Erstes Gewächs 2008, Rheingau White
Fresh with fragrant, spicy and mineral nose. Spritzy with fine grapefruit, pear and spice on the palate. Elegant and well-structured, long and delicious.
BWL

Reichsrat Von Buhl Pechstein Forst Grosses Gewächs 2008, Pfalz White
Fragrant nose with well-balanced and vibrant banana and mineral notes on the palate. A lovely Pfalz style wine.

Reiss Würzburger Pfaffenberg Pinot Blanc & Pinot Gris Cuvée Holzfass Spätlese Trocken 2008, Franken White
Deep gold colour. Beautifully complex nose. Clean, citrus, vague petrol. Super clean acidity overlaying rich palate. Delicious.

Salwey Riesling Eichberg Grosses Gewächs 2008, Baden White
Greengage and lime leaf aromatics. Attractive fruit and pineapple with melon ripeness on the palate. Beautiful freshness and a lovely floral finish.

Schales Dalsheimer Hubacker Weisser Burgunder Selection 2008, Rheinhessen White
Pure nose of rose petal and lemon. Juicy and fresh, delicious with a lovely floral finish. Pear and white peaches with an earthy nuance.

Schmitt Söhne Thomas Schmitt Private Collection 2008, Mosel White
Attractive honeyed and citrus forward nose. Lively on the palate with more honeyed fruit and ripe apple character. Lime freshness on the finish with good balance and length.

St. Urbans-Hof Riesling 2009, Mosel White
Pale and green with expressive grapefruit character. Light and fresh with delicate mineral notes. Young but lively and very drinkable.

Winzergemeinschaft Franken Frankenpraedikatswein Müller-Thurgau Kabinett Trocken 2009, Franken White
Floral and almost honeyed on the nose with citrus, ripe fruit on the palate. Nice mouthfeel with a long, lingering finish.

Winzergemeinschaft Franken Frankenpraedikatswein Silvaner Kabinett Trocken 2008, Franken White
Pale lemon, fresh nose with lightly spritzy character on the palate. Mineral, flinty overtones with ripe citrus and spice. Apricot on the finish with good balance.

Winzergenossenschaft Bocksbeutel-hof Escherndorfer Lump Riesling Kabinett Trocken 2008, Franken White
Commendable expression of Riesling fruit quality. Layered with citrus and exotic fruits. Fine minerality with a zingy, tropical finish.

Bischöfliche Weingüter Trier Kanzemer Altenberg Riesling Spätlese 2008, Mosel Sweet
Pure lemon. Elegant, floral, perfumed nose, peach and lime. Nicely structured. Lime, apple, peach - persistent and balanced.

Bischöfliche Weingüter Trier Kaseler Kehrnagel Riesling Kabinett 2008, Mosel Sweet
Ripe peach, lemon and apple blossom fruit. Fresh, lively acidity and balanced sweetness. Subtle stone fruits and mineral length. Good weight and texture.

Darting Marks & Spencer Darting Estate Scheurebe Beerenaulese 2007, Pfalz Sweet
Apricot, glycerine, honey and orange on the nose. The palate shows dried apricot, fig and leather. Lusciously sweet but enough acidity.
£14.99 M&S

Divino Nordheim Franconia Silvaner Beernauslese 2007, Franken Sweet
Pears, raspberries, orange zest

and floral notes on the palate, complex fruits and caramel on the palate.

Divino Nordheim Franconia Spatburgunder Eiswein 2008, Franken Sweet
Deep yellow colour with an earthy honey aroma. Bittersweet notes on palate. Long, clean and precise on palate.

Schales Riesling Eiswein 2007, Rheinhessen Sweet
Lively aromas of heather and stone fruit. Good, bright acidity. Lovely finish, elegant.

Horst Sauer Escherndorfer Lump Riesling Trockenbeerenauslese 2008, Franken Botrytis
Complex rich aromas of quince, honey, mushrooms, lime and lemon, very fresh and persistent taste with good length.
J&B

Winzer Sommerach Sommeracher Katzenkopf Silvaner Trockenbeerenauslese 2007, Franken Botrytis
Caramel orange and exotic ripe fruit on the nose. The palate is rich and layered with stone fruits. Ripe and round with very sweet yet balanced flavours. Long.

Winzer Sommerach Sommeracher Katzenkopf Weißburgunder Eiswein 2008, Franken Botrytis
Elegant honey with a white peach aroma. A beautifully crafted wine. Superb balance and elegant. Luscious apricots and quince marmalade on finish. Vibrant yet luscious.

Winzergemeinschaft Franken Grosslangheimer Kiliansberg Silvaner Eiswein Edelsuess 2008, Franken Botrytis
Intense lemon and orange blossom aromas. Marmalade icing in the mouth with balancing acidity.

Winzergemeinschaft Franken Stettener Stein Bacchus Edelsuess Beerenauslese 2008, Franken Botrytis
Honeyed, floral and lightly scented nose. Rich, ripe fruit with lashings of honey on the palate. Well-rounded with firm acidity and a nice long finish.

BRONZE

Bischöfliche Weingüter Trier Ayler Kupp Riesling Spätlese Feinherb 2008, Mosel White
Hint of blackcurrant and lemon. Palate of lemon and lime zest and green apple. Good length.

Divino Nordheim Divino Weisser Burgunder Trocken 2008, Franken White
Elegant spritz with a touch of spice on the palate. Some ripe pear fruit with a nice length.

Domdechant Werner'sches Hochheim Riesling 2007, Rheingau White
Spicy sweet, peach and mineral nose. Rich with spicy peach and melon fruit on the palate. Supple and delicate.
LAI

Domdechant Werner'sches Hochheimer Domdechaney Riesling Auslese 2007, Rheingau White
Elegant, light apricot, fruity nose. White sweet with tart acidity. Restrained style, but very lovely.
LAI

Friedrich Altenkirch Grauschiefer 2008, Rheingau White
Muted apple nose with bruised

apple fruit on the palate. Crisp lime acidity, dry with a brightness of intensity.

Fritz Allendorf Riesling Charta 2008, Rheingau White
Pale lemon. Concentrated lime and lemon fruit. Medium dry style. Elegant, crisp and youthful.

Gebruder Loosen Naked Grape Riesling 2009, Mosel White
Rose petals and lime cordial aromas. Mineral and fruity on the palate with gorgeous freshness, light-bodied with an off-dry finish.
£7.99 BTH, CBW, FFT, WAIT

Güterverwaltung Stiftungsweingüter Riesling Hochgewächs Trocken 2008, Mosel White
Mineral and citrus on the nose, the palate is ripe with peach and ripe pears. Lime fruit with a long, fresh, mineral-citrus finish.

Horst Sauer Weisser Burgunder Spätlese Trocken 2008, Franken White
A quaffable wine with some floral notes.

Kaiserstühler Weinhaus Dyade 52 Connoisseur's Choice Baden Riesling 2008, Baden White
Floral with a touch of green apples. Mineral and ripe with racy acidity and a long lively finish.

Karl Pfaffmann Hawesko Riesling 2009, Pfalz White
Clean, fresh, delicate with lime and orange blossoms on the palate.

Matthias Gaul Riesling Kallstadter Saumagen 2008,

Pfalz White
Stone fruit nose, citrus ripeness and apple character on the palate. Floral and fresh with mineral finish. Lively and delicious.

Matthias Gaul Riesling Steinrassel Trocken 2008, Pfalz White
Deep lime aromas. Palate is fresh with zesty citrus fruit and ripe, tropical, apricot flavours. Full-bodied with vibrant intensity.

Moselland Wine Company Bernkastel Kueser Kardinalsberg Spätlese 2008, Mosel White
Light floral apple, passionfruit. Zesty acidity and balanced sweetness. Slight minerality on nose. Palate flavour concentrated and persistent.

Moselland Wine Company D: vine Pinot Grigio 2009, Pfalz White
Ripe and fruity nose with a pleasant aroma. Sweet fruit, melon and apple on the palate with a very long finish.
ASDA

Prinz Von Hessen Winkeler Hasensprung Riesling Erstes Gewächs 2008, Rheingau White
Toasty with a hint of nuttiness. Citrusy fruit with a touch of ripe tropicality. Lime and lemon on the finish.
BWL

Reh Kendermann Black Tower Riesling 2009, Rheinhessen White
Fresh, vibrant and youthful. Grapefruit and tangy citrus on the palate. A touch of ripe apple fruit on the finish with a fresh zing of acidity.
£5.49

Reiss Hannah-Sophia Cuvée Spätlese Trocken 2008, Franken White
Soft but pure fruit. Ripe on the palate with clean and fresh acidity. Fruit-forward and easy to drink.

Schloss Johannisberg Riesling Gelback 2008, Rheingau White
Plenty of fleshy, juicy guava fruit with long and tangy flavours. Like sweet and sour with fresh, vibrant acidity.
£17.49 HLD

Sonnenhof Gündelbacher Wachtkopf Riesling Selection 2007, Württemberg White
Lovely and floral on the nose with rose petal aromas. Gorgeous juicy palate, racing acidity with a savoury finish.
£12.00

Theodorus Riesling Gutswein 2008, Pfalz White
A rich style with sweetly ripe fruit on the nose. Floral and stone fruit palate, full-bodied and well-balanced.

Winzer Sommerach Katzenkopf Silvaner Spätlese Trocken 2008, Franken White
Fresh, clean nose. Gentle floral in fragrance. Honeyed palate.

F W Langguth Erben Erben Dornfelder Trocken 2009, Pfalz Red
Forest fruits on the nose. Juicy palate with redcurrant fruit – well-balanced.

Fritz Allendorf Quercus Pinot Noir 2007, Rheingau Red
Pale red with orange hues. Good cherry red fruits with a herby finish.

Reh Kendermann Dornfelder 2009, Pfalz Red
A fairly light, pleasant wine with juicy fruit flavours and creamy redcurrants on the palate. Well-balanced.

Reh Kendermann Kendermanns Dornfelder Rosé 2009, Pfalz Rosé
Very delicate. Smooth and silky. Good structure. Long sweet strawberry aftertaste.

Divino Nordheim Franconia Silvaner Extra Trocken 2007, Franken Sparkling
Crisp and apple-scented with some quite subtle floral notes. Only a hint of yeast. Crisp, quite lean. Sugar adding a touch of weight but slightly cloying.

Peter Mertes Cellar Estates Piesporter Michelsberg 2008, Ahr Sweet
Light green apple and mineral accent. Very fresh, medium dry style. Soft finish.

Italy

You could spend a lifetime investigating Italian wines and never get to the bottom of them, although you'd be buried with a smile on your face. Italy continues to offer a baffling array of every type of wine you can think of (and plenty more that you can't) made the length and breadth of the country from the alpine chill of the northern Alto Adige region to the African heat of Sicily in the south. To most drinkers, though, Pinot Grigio is the Italian wine of choice, and is gaining hugely in popularity, now ranking just a whisper behind Sauvignon Blanc according to the latest consumer surveys.

GOLD

Araldica Sainsbury's Taste the Difference Gavi 2009, Piedmonte White
Intense, orange-zest bouquet. Crisp acidity on the palate. A good length.
£6.99 SAIN, PBA

Genagricola Friulano Poggiobello 2008, Friuli Venezia Giulia White
Super herbal notes with light zest and spice. Long and harmonious.

Lunae Bosoni Etichetta Grigia 2009, Liguria White
Nettle and herbaceous aromas with rich blossom and spice. Vibrant, zesty and incredibly long.
£9.99 JAW

 SOAVE TROPHY

Pieropan La Rocca Soave Classico 2007, Veneto White
Spicy and ripe aromas on the nose. Lemon and cream on the palate with spicy overtones. Rich, but fresh on the finish. Interesting long length.
£21.49 FAW, LAY, LIB, MAJ

Alpha Zeta Amarone Della Valpolicella 2007, Veneto Red
Fruit nose. Concentrated fruit flavour. Good balance of oak and fruit with a lovely long length.
£26.99 FAW, HVN, LIB, MAJ, SMP

Argentiera 2006, Tuscany Red
Very deep ruby. Intense blackcurrant fruit and smoky oak on nose. Crunchy fruit palate. Lovely freshness and linen textured tannins. Long but needs time.
EUW, EVW

Ascheri Sainsbury's Taste The Difference Barolo 2006, Piedmonte Red
Smoky, herbaceous, savoury character. Soft mid palate. Needs time to integrate more fully and mature.
£14.99 SAIN

Bonelli Chianti Classico Riserva 2006, Tuscany Red
Cherry, plum, wood, liquorice and mocha notes on the palate. A good length.
£20.00 LEA

Caldora Yume Montepulciano D'Abruzzo 2007, Abruzzo Red
Juicy and fruity upfront. Modern style. Needs time to develop to its full potential, a serious wine.
£5.00

Canicatti Aquilae Nero D'Avola 2008, Sicily Red
Herbal and rubbery nose. Good black fruit and tar. Good concentration, complexity and length.
£9.00 EVW, VIN

Cantina Di Soave Cadis Amarone Della Valpolicella 2007, Veneto Red
Aromas of cherry, raspberry. Fresh and pure with a nice rich colour. Juicy fruits, cherries and prunes with a good finish.
£20.00 CTL, VSO

 AMARONE TROPHY

Cantine Riondo Trionfo Amarone Della Valpolicella Classico 2006, Veneto Red
Fine black fruits and slightly floral nose. Full bodied, jammy and well-balanced on the palate. Great long finish. Not a shy wine!

CHAMPION RED, ITALIAN RED TROPHY, TUSCAN TROPHY

Castello Romitorio Brunello Di Montalcino Riserva 2004, Tuscany Red

Deep, intense and slightly brooding on the nose: leather, hints of tobacco and violets. Red fruits dominate on the palate.

Felsina Fontalloro 2006, Tuscany Red

Lovely Tuscan nose. Very well-balanced acidity with juicy plum fruits. Wonderful!
£41.99 HVN, LIB

EDMUND PENNING ROWSELL TROPHY, BOLGHERI TROPHY

Grattamacco L'Alberello 2007, Tuscany Red

Very ripe, voluptuous nose, very oaky. Well-balanced red fruit, lush. Succinct balance. Fine tannins, sensual finish.

La Casa Di Bricciano Sangiovese 2006, Tuscany Red

Good concentration of flavour with black cherry fruit. Integrated oak with supporting acidity. A complex and interesting wine with great length.

Michele Chiarlo Cerequio Barolo 2005, Piedmonte Red

Lovely, smoky fruit. Elegant and well-balanced. Firm and full bodied. Juicy on the finish.
£53.99 HLD

Pinino Brunello Di Montalcino 2004, Tuscany Red

Dark plum and violet nose. Clean and bright with lots of minerality. Silky texture with fine tannins. Crisp and crunchy dark

fruits. Elegant.
£36.00 EVW, HAR, V&C, VIN

Tenuta Sant'Antonio Selezione Antonio Castagnedi 2006, Veneto Red

Rich almond and cherry nose. Full concentrated palate with spice and peppers. Mouthfilling with good structure.

MARCHE RED TROPHY

Vico Vicari Lacrima Del Pozzo Buono 2008, Marche Red

Very perfumed, almost lychee with some lead pencil too. A love it or hate it wine.

LAMBRUSCO TROPHY

Cantine Riunite Albinea Canali Lambrusco Ottocentonero NV, Emilia Romagna Sparkling Red

Good colour. Nice mousse. Nice fruits, very clean. Delicious, sweet with lovely flavours.

ITALIAN SWEET TROPHY

Cavit Aréle Vino Santo Trentino 1998, Trentino Sweet

Good candied peel character layered with ripe citrus and honeyed fruit. Crisp with orange blossom sweetness but very refreshing. Delicious.
PBA

ITALIAN BOTRYTIS TROPHY

Moncaro Terre Cortesi Tordiruta Verdicchio Dei Castelli Di Jesi Passito 2006,

Marche Botrytis
Caramel and nutty-honey on the palate. Very sweet with layers of marzipan and pineapple. Long and ripe with good depth on the finish.
EUW, EVW

Araldica Gavi del Commune di Gavi 2009, Piedmonte
White
Pear, citrus and a touch of lime on the nose. Fresh and vibrant on the palate. Well-balanced with good acidity. A hazelnut finish.
£8.99 M&S, PBA

Bove Safari Percorino 2009, Abruzzo White
Peachy nose, soft peach fruit on the palate. Fresh citrus fruit and warming alcohol dominate the finish.
£9.99 HLD

Cantina Di Monteforte Terre Di Monteforte Soave Classico 2009, Soave White
Mineral and bright with a honey-tinged nose. Good depth of citrus and pear fruit flavours. Fresh and pleasant on the finish with long length.
£5.99 LIB

Cantina Di Monteforte Vigneti Di Montegrande Soave Superiore Classico 2008, Veneto White
Lifted citrus aromas with elegant, delicate fruit on the palate. Pear and melon with a touch of lemon freshness. Long and lingering.
£7.99 LIB

Cantine Del Notaio La Raccolta 2008, Basilicata
White
Sunshine yellow in colour, bright lucid fruit, good style, long flavours.

Cavit Bottega Vinai Gewürztraminer Trentino 2009, Trentino White
Lovely tropical fruit on the nose. Rich ripe peaches and pineapple on the nose. Smooth feeling fruit, delicious.

Fontana Candida Luna Mater Frascati Superiore 2008, Lazio
White
Nice fruit salad with apple, pear and peach on the nose. Silky yet minerally texture. Spice and peachy fruit on the palate. Complex and stylish.
£12.99 MCT

Genagricola Gavi Di Gavi Bricco Dei Guazzi 2009, Piedmonte White
Attractive light elegant. Complex herbaceous. Rich.

Genagricola Sauvignon Torre Rosazza 2008, Friuli Venezia Giulia White
Waxy citrus on the nose with clean and bright fruit on the palate. Surprisingly rich, long and ripe. Very classy with a lingering and enjoyable flavour.

La Scolca Gavi Del Comune Di Gavi White Label 2009, Piedmonte White
Minerally, lemon, lime. Good varietal definition. Good balance and purity. A good length.
EUW, EVW

Marramiero Anima Trebbiano D'Abruzzo 2009, Abruzzo
White
Clean and bright, medium intensity lemon. Youthful, green apple. White pepper. Green apple character continues to palate. Medium weight, with nice minerality and length.

Michele Wassler Inama Vigneti Di Foscarino Soave Classico 2008, Veneto White
Pear drops and honey with ripe lemon-lime aromas. Complex balance of fruit and acidity with fresh overtones of pear and juicy stone fruit. Delicious.
£18.00 BLV, CAV, HFB, UNC, WAIT

Monte Schiavo Le Giuncare Verdicchio 2006, Marche White
Complex nose, biscuit, honey and toasty almonds on the nose. Crisp acidity.
£14.49 PBA

Orion Triade Della Campania 2009, Campania White
Interesting spice on the nose. Serious character with complexity of apples, pears and summer fruits. Well-balanced.

Piersanti Bachero 2008, Marche White
Slightly rubbery on the nose. Palate has fruit with integrated oak. Firm acidity cuts through the fruit and wood to give a well-balanced wine.

San Paolo Greco Di Tufo 2008, Campania White
Some good lemon fruit, lacks acidity but nice enough.

Santa Barbara Verdicchio Dei Castelli Di Jesi Le Vaglie 2008, Marche White
Bright colour. Slight perfumed aromas. Palate shows soft fruits.
£13.00 EHB, EVW, HAR, V&C, VIN

Terre Di Sava Masseria Pietrosa Verdeca Puglia 2009, Puglia White
A Sauvignon note on nose, a little acid on mid palate but good on the finish.
LIB

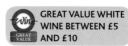

GREAT VALUE WHITE WINE BETWEEN £5 AND £10

Terredora Falanghina Campania 2009, Campania White
Fresh lime fruit aroma, lovely, easy style.
£9.99 LAY, MON, ODF, WTA

Vesevo Greco Di Tufo 2009, Campania White
Some fresh lemon fruit on nose, a little watery and dilute but nice enough.
£12.99

Agriva Refosco Dal Peduncolo Rosso 2008, Friuli Venezia Giulia Red
Mild green pepper character. Fairly restrained but with good structure.

Allegrini La Poja 2006, Veneto Red
Rich, ripe and fruity. Good bright colour. Well-balanced with a lingering fruity finish.
£54.99 LIB, P&S

Allegrini Palazzo della Torre 2007, Veneto Red
Perfumed nose. Layered and balanced. Integrated fruit. Firm structure with spice, dark chocolate and cherries.
£14.99 HAW, LIB, RWM

Araldica Barolo Flori 2005, Piedmonte Red
Toasted vanilla notes. A touch of raisin on the palate.
£7.99 VGN, PBA

Araldica Castelvero Barbera 2007, Piedmonte Red
Vibrant. Attractive berry and floral nose. Mouthful of ripe berries and cherries. Packs a fruity punch.
£6.99 SAIN, PBA

Argentiera Villa Donoratico 2007, Tuscany Red

A savoury, meaty nose that needs more freshness. Very tight, reserved, a 'cool' Bordeaux blend with the Cabernet Franc dominating the finish. Classy.
EUW, EVW

Ascheri Barolo Rocca Ripalta 2006, Piedmonte Red

Tea leaves, bitter cherry and savoury notes on the nose and palate. Some spicy notes.
£15.99 TESC

Baroncini Vino Nobile di Montepulciano San Colombaio 2007, Tuscany Red

A plummy wine with layers of ripe fruit, savoury black cherry flavours with good structure and long length.
£10.99 SAIN

Basilica Cafaggio Chianti Classico Riserva 2006, Tuscany Red

Tight structure with good tannins. Damson and bramble fruits with spice and leather.
£16.99 HTW, SAB

Batasiolo Barolo Bricolina 2006, Piedmonte Red

Good concentration of black fruit. Long length, Tightly wound, will relax with time for optimal drinking.
£51.10 MON

Bidoli Merlot 2007, Friuli Venezia Giulia Red

Deep ruby with a rich brambly nose. Rich and enveloping blackcurrant fruit. Great length.
£9.99 M&S

Bolla Le Origini Amarone Della Valpolicella 2006, Veneto Red

Sweet, subtle flavours. Red berries and well-integrated fruit.
£30.00 MCT

Canicatti Nero D'Avola Aynat 2007, Sicily Red

Caramel wood. Lovely structure. Fresh acidity. A very serious wine.
£21.00 EVW, VIN

Cantina di Montalcino Palazzo Comunale Brunello di Montalcino 2005, Tuscany Red

Deep and intense nose. Damson and black plums and liquorice. Great minerality underpins full ripe tannins. Very moreish.
£35.99 LIB, WMN

Cantina Di Soave Rocca Alata Amarone Della Valpolicella 2007, Veneto Red

Light violet aromas. Cranberry fruit flavours. Slight liquorice notes to the finish.
£20.00 TESC

Cantina Di Soave Rocca Sveva Ripasso Valpolicella Superiore 2007, Veneto Red

Fragrant, sweet cherry nose. Sweet cherry palate with spice and savoury notes. Soft tannins, well-balanced.
£30.00 ANA, CTL, VSO

Cantina Sociale Della Valpantena Amarone Della Valpolicella 2007, Veneto Red

Raisins, cakey aromas. Beautiful concentration. Excellent balance. Good length of fruit with an attractive finish.
£40.00 ENO

Cantina Sociale Della Valpantena Amarone Pagus Bisano 2006, Veneto Red

Spicy ripe black fruit. Concentrated mid palate with sweet blackcurrant and

blackberry. Intense, vibrant with a long finish.
£45.00 ENO

Cantina Sociale Della Valpantena Terre Di Verona Amarone Della Valpolicella 2007, Veneto Red
Smoky, brooding nose. Intense. Lush, sour cherry fruit with a long smoky finish. Very fine.
£40.00 ENO

Cantina Valpolicella Negrar Domini Veneti Amarone Della Valpolicella Classico 2007, Veneto Red
Fresh, light with lovely ripe fruit. A well-balanced wine, oozing quality.

Cantina Valpolicella Negrar Rosso Veronese Appassionata 2007, Veneto Red
Intense raisins, rum, spice and roast coffee. Silky powerful palate. Needs time.

Cantina Valpolicella Negrar Verjago Valpolicella Classico Superiore 2006, Veneto Red
Ripe cherries on the nose with a hint of almonds. Lovely and smooth with a fruity finish.

Cantine Del Notaio Il Sigillo 2006, Basilicata Red
Modern style, ripe but not over-ripe cherry flavours. Succulent, dry. Will develop.

Cantine Del Notaio La Firma 2007, Basilicata Red
Young and vibrant. Smoky, spicy concentration of strawberry tarts and vanilla extract. Good length.

Cantine Gemma Barolo 2004, Piedmonte Red
Lovely secondary aromas of leather, and spice. Dry on the finish.
£13.99 MRN, MRN

Cantine Leonardo Chianti 2009, Tuscany Red
Juicy cherry fruit. Good concentration on the finish.
£10.00 LIB

Carpineta Dofana 2006, Tuscany Red
Bright with upfront blueberries. Savoury tastes and filled with complex fruit on the palate.

Castellani Asda Extra Special Chianti Riserva 2005, Tuscany Red
Ripe cherry fruit on the nose following through on the palate. Well-balanced.
£7.08 ASDA

Castello Di Querceto I Colombi Chianti Classico Riserva 2007, Tuscany Red
Smoky on the nose, lots of mocha and black cherry fruit. Long length.

Castello Monaci Piluna Primitivo Salento 2008, Puglia Red
Cigar box and leather on the nose. Full of fruit and currants.
£8.49 REV

Cavit Maso Toresella Rosso Superiore 2005, Trentino Red
Ripe hedgerow fruit. Fresh and crisp in the mouth. Well-balanced.

Cecchi Campo Al Moro Chianti Classico 2007, Tuscany Red
Primary and concentrated dark fruit, tight, pure and focused.
£9.99 SAIN

Corte Giara Ripasso Valpolicella Superiore 2008, Veneto Red
Sweet spicy nose. Cherry fruit with elegant vanilla oak on the palate. Ripe tannins and delicate

acidity. Mouthfilling. Long finish.
£10.99 HAX, LIB, NYW

Cummo Casa Vinicola Sicania 1908 Nero Cappuccio 2006, Sicily Red
Aniseed, fennel and raisined fruits. Fiery.

Da Vinci Brunello di Montalcino 2005, Tuscany Red
Inky rich nose of forest floor. Blackcurrant, roasted nuts on the palate. Delicate, balanced. Blackberry, coffee and a splash of dark chocolate.
£40.00 DBY, LIB

Emera Anima Di Niuru Maru 2008, Puglia Red
Clean, black fruit nose. Very tannic, bitter dark fruit, concentrated and long.

Enrico Serafino Pasiunà Roero 2007, Piedmonte Red
Tar and smoke with good tannins. Bramble and blackberry fruit to taste. Smoky, earthy finish.

Erste + Neue Puntay Lagrein Riserva 2007, Abruzzo Red
Ripe red berries on the nose, leather on the palate, concentrated finish.

Fattoria Il Lago Pian De Guardi 2004, Tuscany Red
Savoury, spicy leather. Good depth of cherry fruit flavour. Nicely balanced, and a very long length.
£18.05 GRO, LOQ, NOS

Fattoria Nittardi Chianti Classico Riserva 2005, Tuscany Red
Lots of attractive bright, ripe cherry fruit. Fleshy palate with great length.
£32.99 RIW

Fattoria Petrolo Galatrona 2007, Tuscany Red
A little farmyardy, leather on the nose. Black truffle. Harmonious palate, very fine balance, insistent grip.
£91.99 LIB

Fattoria Petrolo Torrione 2007, Tuscany Red
Round, ripe and juicy with a touch of savouriness. Fresh cherries and hints of orange blossom.
£29.99 LIB, P&S

Fazi Battaglia-Fassati Pasiteo Vino Nobile Di Montepulciano 2007, Tuscany Red
Spicy, ripe, oaky fruit on nose. Ripe and structured fruit on the palate, with firm tannins and a lush blackcurrant finish.
£15.00 MON

Felsina Vigneto Rancia Chianti Classico Riserva 2007, Tuscany Red
Sangiovese savoury nose. Lovely, lively lifted aromas. Fruity and spicy notes, elegant with a long finish.
£39.99 LIB, P&S

Fontodi Vigna del Sorbo Chianti Classico Riserva 2006, Tuscany Red
Concentrated black morello cherry fruit. Nice and ripe, rich bramble fruit with a hint of pepper. Long chocolatey finish.
£33.99 HVN, JOB, LIB, SMP

Genagricola Cesanese - Solonio 2009, Lazio Red
Deep colour, ripe and juicy. Light but attractive. Clean and fresh.

Genagricola La Presidenta - Bricco Dei Guazzi 2006, Piedmonte Red
Floral and spicy on the nose.

Pleasant berry and cherry flavours. Light and appealing with good persistence.

Gianni Brunelli Brunello Di Montalcino 2005, Tuscany Red

Rich, concentrated sweet plums and hints of prune sweetness. Palate is smooth with integrated plums, firm tannins, oak spice and length.
£29.00 WSO

Giordano Primitivo Manduria Alberello 50 2007, Puglia Red

Dark rich blackberry fruit. Deep, rich and long.

Grattamacco Bolgheri Rosso 2008, Tuscany Red

Soft, luscious and complex. Plums, custard and forest floor nose. Elegant, rounded palate, savoury, long and fine tannins.

Grattamacco Bolgheri Superiore 2007, Tuscany Red

Very elegant red-berry, tobacco aromas. Hints of seaweed. Beautifully silky tannins, precise sensual finish. Sophisticated and blue-bloodied.

Il Borro Pian Di Nova 2007, Tuscany Red

Ruby red. Attractive oak spice. Savoury. Red fruit. Dry with a core of cherry. Savoury finish.
EUW, EVW

Isole e Olena Chianti Classico 2007, Tuscany Red

Earthy, rustic nose, dark fruit and spice, lovely tannins and balance.
£11.99 FAW, LIB, P&S

John Matta Castello Vicchiomaggio 2006, Tuscany Red

Well defined on the nose. Blackberry, redcurrant, well-integrated oak. Silky smooth, very

sensuous and feminine. Fine tannins, quite tense but oozes panache.

Lo Zoccolaio Barolo Cru Ravera 2005, Piedmonte Red

Lifted, scented nose. Well-balanced. Juicy on the palate and with a very long finish.
£60.00

Lo Zoccolaio Suculè Barbera D'Alba 2006, Piedmonte Red

Ripe fruits on the nose. Lovely sweet ripe berries, leather and chocolate on the palate. A lovely smooth lingering finish.
£9.99

Manfredi Barolo Patrizi 2006, Piedmonte Red

Dried fruits. Spicy, balsamic notes. Good fruit intensity. Will mature nicely.
£14.99 PBA

Masottina Montesco Colli Di Conegliano Rosso 2004, Veneto Red

Elegant, fine, fragrant with some ripe tannins and fresh acidity. A real lift of sweet fruit on finish.
TTC

Massolino Barolo Parafada 2006, Piedmonte Red

Tar on the nose. Cherry fruit to taste. Long length, needs time to age to its potential.
£55.00 LIB, P&S

Moncaro Terre Cortesi Nerone Conero Riserva 2006, Marche Red

Sweetly perfumed fruit, very spicy on the nose. Palate is fresh and bright with firm tannins that hold the ripe fruit.
EUW, EVW

Moncaro Terre Cortesi Terrazzano Rosso Piceno 2007, Marche Red

Soft, easy, ripe aroma. Juicy

and fruity with ripe tannins. Characteristic.
EUW

Morassino Barbaresco 2006, Piedmonte **Red**

Tarry nose gives way to spicy plummy fruit. Good depth supported with ripe tannins and good acidity.
£25.00 M&S

Morgante Don Antonio 2008, Sicily **Red**

Lifted, very rich powerful fruit. Dried fruits and figs. Hot and long.

Morini Campo Leon Amarone Della Valpolicella 2005, Veneto **Red**

Plums and dark cherries. Ripe aromas and chocolate. Rich spice cake. A well-balanced wine with a long finish.
£30.49 AAW

Morini Campo Prognai Valpolicella Superiore 2006, Veneto **Red**

Sweet ripe cherry nose. Pleasant cherry flavours on the palate. Savoury and mouthfilling.
£14.99 AAW

Nino Negri Vigneto Fracia Valtellina Superiore 2005, Lombardia **Red**

Dried fruits, leather and bacon aromas. Fruitcake flavour on the palate with good texture and balanced acidity.
ENO

Orion Passitivo 2008, Puglia **Red**

Violet nose. Fiery fruit on the palate. Raspberry jam, blackberries and rosemary. Lingering.

Ormanni Borro Del Diavolo Chianti Classico Riserva

2006, Tuscany **Red**

Oak, red fruit aromas. Cherry flavours on the palate. Chocolate and mocha notes. Firm tannins. Spiced hickory on the finish.
£23.00 BOF, BUT, CVS, DMR, DWS, SOM

Piantate Lunghe Rosso Conero 2006, Marche **Red**

Fresh, dark fruits with a spicy and savoury palate. Layers of flavour with long length.
£12.00

Piccini Villa Al Cortile Brunello Di Montalcino 2005, Tuscany **Red**

Ripe, rich on the nose. Damsons and cherries on the palate. Clean and vibrant, ready to enjoy now.

Pinino Brunello Di Montalcino Riserva 2004, Tuscany **Red**

Very punchy; blackberry, dark plum and blueberries. Still young with great length and finish.
£45.00 VIN

Podere Sapaio 2007, Tuscany **Red**

Plum and tar, black fruit and cherry. Firm tannins and solid structure.

Podere Sapaio Volpolo 2007, Tuscany **Red**

Youthful floral aroma. Ripe fruit, plum and leather notes with smoky tannin.

Poderi Colla Barolo Bussia 2005, Piedmonte **Red**

Hints of orange peel and plum on the nose. A touch of blackcurrant on the palate.
£29.99 PBA

Poggio al Tesoro Sondraia 2007, Tuscany **Red**

Black cherry and blackcurrant fruit. Supple tannins and great balance.
£24.99 GGW, HDS, LIB

ITALY

SILVER

Poggio al Tesoro W Dedicato a Walter Cabernet Franc 2007, Tuscany Red
Great varietal character on the nose. Red bell pepper, touch of tar and cocoa. Very distinctive palate. Well defined tannins, a hint of chocolate and a beautifully svelte finish.
£44.99 CVS, HAR, LIB

Poggio Bonelli Chianti Classico 2007, Tuscany Red
Spicy, earthy, warm nose, a touch of brett, typical classico-style, quite firm with a lot of tight fine tannin.
£12.00 LEA

Poggio San Polo Brunello di Montalcino 2005, Tuscany Red
Rounded. Seamlessly integrated. Black cherry, bramble and leather. Excellent balance.
£44.99 LIB

Poggiotondo Chianti Superiore 2007, Tuscany Red
Clean, fruity, berry and tobacco nose. Deliciously crunchy berry fruit. Dry but savoury with a good spicy finish.
£11.99 FAW, LIB

Proprietà Sperino Coste della Sesia Uvaggio 2006, Piedmonte Red
Nose beautifully perfumed. Lush with bright firm structured frame.
£19.99 FAW, HIG, LIB, SEL

Proprietà Sperino Lessona 2006, Piedmonte Red
Elegant notes of furniture polish, liquorice, tar and violets. Refreshing balance of acidity, nicely structured with cherries, liquorice, spice. Complex and well-balanced.
£42.99 HAR, LIB

San Felice Chianti Classico Riserva Poggio Rosso 2004, Tuscany Red
Very elegant wine which is refined and complex.
£24.49 PBA

San Felice Perolla Maremma Toscana 2008, Tuscany Red
Smoky, tangy accents over rich plum fruit on nose. Mature, gamey palate with herbal accent. Moderate length.
£8.99 PBA

Scrimaglio Nizza Acse Barbera D'Asti Superiore 2005, Piedmonte Red
Chocolate, plums, vanilla rich and smooth with a lovely oak and cherry palate. Soft, dry tannins and fresh acidity to balance. A good finish.

Sella & Mosca Cannonau Di Sardegna Riserva 2006, Sardinia Red
Sweet, appetising red fruit and meaty aromas. Well-integrated tannins with a touch of pithiness. Very dry and smoky.

Tenuta Di Biserno Il Pino Di Biserno 2006, Tuscany Red
Medium intense nose with meaty and earthy notes. Nice balanced mouth with good oaky notes. Nice finish.
£43.00

Tenuta Di Capraia Chianti Classico 2007, Tuscany Red
Lovely ripe nose, bright sweet fruit with orange peel flavours, clean fresh finish.
EUW, EVW

Tenuta Moraia Il Pacchia Maremma Toscana 2008, Tuscany Red
Deep red. Classic fruit. Sweet. Elegant. Mid palate ripe and interesting.

Tenuta Moraia Monteregio Di Massa Marittima 2008,

Tuscany Red
Attractive, leafy redcurrant on the nose with hints of pepper. Palate is very well-balanced.

Terre Di Sava Masseria Pietrosa Malvasia Nera Salento 2008, Puglia Red
Rich bramble nose with good complexity. A rich, full bodied, balanced wine. Lovely savoury edge with sweet fruit. Vanilla notes throughout.
LIB

Terredavino Barolo Essenze 2005, Piedmonte Red
Herbaceous on the nose. Good layered blackcurrant and spice flavours. A vigorous wine.
£30.00 EVW, HAR, VIN

Terredavino Bricco Garelli Barbera D'Asti Superiore 2007, Piedmonte Red
Spicy oak on the nose. Juicy palate. Good depth of flavour. Black cherry fruits. Integrated oak, long length. Great ageing potential.
£6.98 MRN

Terredora Taurasi Campore Riserva 2003, Campania Red
Spicy, smooth, beefy wine. Developed, sweet dried fruit on the palate. Savoury nose. Big cherry mouthfuls and gamey flavours. Layered and complex with a long finish. Will last.

Terredora Taurasi Pago Dei Fusi 2003, Campania Red
Gamey fruit and truffles on the nose and palate. Big cherry flavours in the mouth. Full bodied and well-structured. Silky mid palate. Quite muscular, good ageing potential.

Tollo Cagiòlo Montepulciano 2007, Abruzzo Red
Fruity cherries. Bitter chocolate.

Oak notes. Good flavour with lots of depth. Long finish.
£13.25 ALI

Vallone Giardinelli Rosso Salice Salentino 2006, Puglia Red
Raisin and sweet plum character, raspberry in the mouth, well-balanced tannin.
£7.99 PBA

Valpanera Rosso Di Valpanera 2008, Friuli Venezia Giulia Red
A complex wine. Pure ripe fruit, almost creamy character, great concentration and length.

Vicchiomaggio Ripa Delle Mandorle 2008, Tuscany Red
Sour cherry with perfumed aromas. Wonderful savoury fruits on the palate. Chalky and firm, with a long finish.

Vicchiomaggio Riserva Gustavo Petri 2007, Tuscany Red
Dark fruit aromas, savoury middle palate. A tight, focused wine with good balance.

Vicchiomaggio Riserva La Prima 2007, Tuscany Red
Scented and lifted aromas of cherry and vanilla. Smooth and supple on the palate. Leathery. Great balance and length.

Villa Sandi Marinali Rosso 2007, Veneto Red
Perfumed, fragrant, a note of tobacco. Quite cool but seems to be good fruit here, savoury tannins, chocolatey oak. Complex and very long.
D&D, HOT

Vini Giribaldi Barbera 2006, Piedmonte Red
Some savoury notes with bramble and dark forest fruits.

Lovely rich black fruit on the palate.
£16.99 MFW

Vini Giribaldi Barolo 2005, Piedmonte Red
Gamey fruit on the nose and palate. Full bodied and well-structured.
£23.99 MFW

Zenato Amarone Della Valpolicella Classico 2006, Veneto Red
Floral nose with well-developed fruit and lavender.
EUW, EVW

Zeni Costalago 2007, Veneto Red
Cherry red berry fruits. Dry finish. Good concentration of flavour. Balanced with an attractive good length.

Bortolomiol Senior Valdobbiadene Superiore Prosecco 2009, Veneto Sparkling
Ice cream soda and pear drops on the nose. Fresh and lively on the palate.
£7.00 LPW, V&C, VIV

Cantina Colli Del Soligo Spumante Prosecco Cuvèe Extra Dry NV, Veneto Sparkling
Apple aromas on the nose. Rich, dry fruit on the palate. Persistent finish.
EUW, EVW

Cantine Riondo Oro Cuvée Excelsa NV, Veneto Sparkling
Sweet Muscat style. Fruity, bright, quite sweet with appealing grapey fruit and nice balance.

Carpene Malvolti Conegliano Valdobbiadene Prosecco Superiore Cuvée Extra Dry

NV, Veneto Sparkling
Restrained nose. Dense rich mid palate, great balance of acidity and concentration. Lingering finish.
£11.99 HLD

La Gioiosa Prosecco Treviso Spumante NV, Veneto Sparkling
Lush lemony confected. Good balance. Elegant light and delicious.
£8.99 TESC, SAIN

Martini & Rossi Prosecco NV, Veneto Sparkling
Good clear colour. Nice nose - citrus fresh. Fresh taste. Good fruit and long length.
£12.99 Widely Available

Villa Sandi Il Fresco Brut NV, Veneto Sparkling
Floral with pear drop nose. Refreshing, zesty, mouthfilling flavour and mousse. Good concentration and balance. Good length.
£11.99 D&D, HOT

Albinea Canali Vivante Lambrusco NV, Emilia Romagna Sparkling Red
Very clean with apple and redcurrant fruit. Strong finish with clean, vibrant notes.

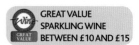
GREAT VALUE SPARKLING WINE BETWEEN £10 AND £15

Medici Lambrusco Reggiano Concerto 2009, Emilia Romagna Sparkling Red
Deep coloured, overly fruity, red with nice tannins and good acidity. Vibrant, bold and joyful.
£12.00 EHB, EVW, HAR, V&C, VIN

Vicari Vico Amaranto Del Pozzo Buono 2008, Marche Sweet
Chocolate and spice on the nose.

Very smooth on the palate. Lush fruit with fresh acidity. A great oddball.

Carlo Pellegrino Passito di Pantelleria Liquoroso 2008, Sicily Fortified

Fresh, pure, grapey. Lovely aroma. Very fine and pure. Lively, with marmalade and great freshness on the palate. Really uplifting!
£9.49 HLD

BRONZE

Adria Vini Casa Lella Catarrato 2009, Sicily White

Salad fruits, fresh acidity. Green peppers and lemon peel on the palate.
£4.98 ASDA, PBA

Anna Maria Cruciata Auramaris 2009, Tuscany White

Lively. Fragrant. Greengages on the nose and palate.
£11.50 BBL, HFB, P&S

Araldica Gavi Battistina 2009, Piedmonte White

Minerally, lemon, lime a pretty wine. A good length.
£7.99 PBA

Araldica La Monetta Gavi della Commune di Gavi 2009, Piedmonte White

Very subtle, slightly biscuity nose. Excellent balance and smoothness on the finish.
£9.49 WAIT, PBA

Araldica Marks & Spencer Chardonnay Piedmont 2008, Piedmonte White

Intense confected, pineapple and citrus nose. Fresh and deep on the palate with lively ripeness on the finish.
£4.99 M&S, PBA

Azienda Marramiero Altare Trebbiano D'Abruzzo 2007, Abruzzo White

Rich, toasty nose, backed up by impressive minerality. A flinty wine with hints of lemon acidity.

Batasiolo Gavi Di Gavi 2009, Piedmonte White

Pretty floral aroma with a smoky lift. Lovely nectarine, rose petal and jasmine bouquet. Really attractive with lively acidity and a hint of ginger and spice.
£15.00 MON

Bidoli Pinot Grigio 2009, Friuli Venezia Giulia White

Pale lemon. Lively and attractive pear flavours.
£7.99 M&S

Bidoli Sauvignon Blanc 2009, Friuli Venezia Giulia White

Fresh lemon juice and grapefruit on the nose; palate has good texture underpinned by good acidity. Silky length.
£6.99 M&S

Caldora Colle Dei Venti Pecorino Terre Di Chieti 2009, Abruzzo White

Good intensity of fruit on the nose. Ripe peachy citrus and white blossom fruit on the palate. Long, firm and fresh.

Cantina Di Monteforte Clivus Pinot Grigio Del Veneto 2009, Veneto White

Pale lemon. Some pear, pea flavours with a good length.
£6.20 LIB

Cantina Novelli Trebbiano Spoletino 2009, Umbria White

Liquorice, menthol, herbal, waxy nose. Strong eucalyptus notes. Round palate. Expressive. Weighty wine. Quite mature fruit on the palate.

Casale Del Giglio Antinoo 2008, Lazio White

Apricot, vanilla on the nose. Hints of honeysuckle and peach.
EUW, EVW

Casale Del Giglio Petit Manseng 2009, Lazio White

Fresh, clean, tangy, apple blossom. Lemon aromas. Nice balance and length.
EUW, EVW

Cavit Maso Toresella Chardonnay Trentino 2007, Trentino White

Subdued ripeness with a fresh lemon aroma on the nose. Good expressive fruit with some lifted citrus and lime. Good balance and nice weight.

Cavit Maso Toresella Cuvèe Vigneti Dolomiti 2008, Trentino White

Gentle, some tropical nose. Grassy palate. Very light but zesty. Refreshing acidity with a long and elegant finish.

Cavit Zeveri Müller Thurgau Trentino Superiore 2008, Trentino White

Subtle citrus and floral notes. Green apple dominant. Racy on the palate with lemon and ginger notes. Elegant with a good finish.

Cevico Group Galassi Albana Di Romagna Secco 2009, Emilia Romagna White

Creamy, crushed almonds on the nose and palate. Sweetness and weight. Balanced.
£6.99 D&D

Citari Selezione La Torre Lugana 2008, Lombardia White

Leesy nose with almond and biscuits. Fresh lime fruit. Ripe apple fruit and nutmeg notes. Ripe, sweet and weighty. Drink now.

Concilio Pinot Grigio Trentino 2009, Trentino White

Juicy fruit with apricot and peach aromas. Peaches on the palate with a soft, pithy texture. Fresh and lingering on the finish.

Concilio Sauvignon Blanc Trentino 2009, Trentino White

Crisp and grassy with a delicate nose. Gooseberry and citrus fruit on the palate with clean and fresh acidity. Dry and agreeable on the finish.

Erste + Neue Puntay Sauvignon 2008, Alto Adige White

Passionfruit and white flowers on the palate with layers of light tropical fruit. Good concentration and ripeness on the finish.

Erste + Neue Stern Sauvignon 2008, Alto Adige White

Firm and textured fruit on the palate with nice freshness. Melon and tropical fruit on the finish. Needs time to develop.

Farnese Casale Vecchio Pecorino 2009, Umbria White

Peach and stone fruit nose, with a lively peachy, citrus palate. Good intensity and structure with a zingy, fresh finish.
£11.99

Farnese Gran Sasso Pecorino Terre Di Chieti 2009, Abruzzo White

Delicate, ripe fruit aromas. Fresh and zesty with lime juice overtones, ripe peachy fruit and a touch of honey. Lingering freshness on the finish.
£11.99

Farnese Vesuvium Greco Di Tufo 2009, Campania White

Lovely crushed lemon fruit on

nose, spritzy palate (with a bit of astringency). Ripe melon on nose.
£11.49

Farnese Villa Farnia Pecorino Terre Di Chieti 2008, Abruzzo White
Good depth with fresh tropical fruit aromas and flavours. Light with a touch of herbaceousness on the finish.
£7.99

Fazi Battaglia-Fassati Massaccio Verdicchio Dei Castelli Di Jesi Classico Superiore 2006, Marche White
Aromas quite honeyed on this wine. Palate shows discreet fruits and is well-balanced.
£12.00 MON

Fazi Battaglia-Fassati Titulus Verdicchio Dei Castelli Di Jesi Classico 2009, Marche White
Nose minerally and a little pithy. Delicate wine, balanced and long on the finish.
£8.20 MON

Fazio Catarratto 2009, Sicily White
Ripe, juicy lemon fruits. Crisp, fresh acidity with subtle weight. Well-balanced and clean aroma.
£5.99 D&D

Fondo Antico Grillo Parlante 2009, Sicily White
Subtle pear drops on the nose. Ripe citrus and apple. Minerality balanced. Zesty and persistent.

Fontana Candida Vigneto Santa Teresa Frascati Superiore 2008, Lazio White
Honey and almond aromas. Almondy on the palate. A well made wine.
£8.99 MCT

Gian Piero Marrone Tre Fie Langhe Arneis 2009, Piedmonte White
Fresh with honeydew and melon on the nose. Light spicy flavours and a harmonious finish.

Livio Felluga Illivio Bianco 2007, Colli Orientali del Friuli White
Cedar and peach notes on the nose. Classy clean fruit with integrated oak. Sweet and long.
£28.99 LIB

Marco Cecchini Tove 2008, Friuli Venezia Giulia White
Ripe nose with apple and pear. Light, refreshing on the palate with a hint of celery.

Mesa Giunco Vermentino di Sardegna 2009, Sardinia White
Fresh, juicy ripe lemon fruits with a herbal character. Capsicum on the palate. A hint of minerality and nice finish.
£14.99 LIB

Moncaro Terre Cortesi Anfora Leopardi Verdicchio Classico Conti 2009, Marche White
Clean refreshing light with a lemon twist. Very appealing, elegant. Well-balanced.
LAI, LAI

Moncaro Terre Cortesi Le Vele Verdicchio Dei Castelli Di Jesi Classico 2009, Marche White
Medium intensity. Herbs and green vegetal nose. Soft and easy on the palate.
EUW, EVW

Mondo Del Vino Piazza Liberta Catarratto Viognier 2009, Sicily White
Ripe, peach and apricot with citrus zest. Crisp, lively acidity with subtle weight. Well-balanced with clean finish.
£6.49 LAI

Piersanti Previata Verdicchio Del Castelli 2009, Marche
White
Nice aromas with a hint of tea leaf. Good firm fruits on the palate with good flavour. Attractive balanced acidity.
BOO

Pighin Pinot Grigio Collio 2009, Friuli White
Balanced. Pears and creaminess on the palate with a nice length.
£16.00 MON

Planeta Cometa 2008, Sicily
White
Light pineapple aromas. Rounded. Leafy nose, smooth and buttery on the palate. Nice crisp finish.
£24.99 WAIT

Provinco Asda Soave Classico 2009, Soave White
Mineral, honey and pear drop nose. Ripe citrus on the palate, zesty and racy with good freshness.
Very pleasant.
ASDA

Sartarelli Verdicchio Dei Castelli Di Jesi Classico 2009, Marche White
Orchard fruits. Rich, round, intense, appley on the palate.
ODD

Scolaris Traminer Aromatico 2009, Friuli Venezia Giulia
White
Pale gold. Lifted stone fruit aromas. Honeysuckle, soft, light, gently spiced. Very drinkable.

Settesoli Inycon Grower's Selection Fiano 2009, Sicily
White
Clean, fresh nose. Minerally on the palate, zesty with good intensity. A long floral finish.

Surani Pietrariccia Fiano Del Salento 2009, Puglia White

Clean and fresh. Light fruit aromas. Some sweet floral characteristics.
£10.99 EHB, EVW, HAR, V&C, VIN

Tenuta Ulisse Unico Cococciola Terre Di Chieti 2009, Abruzzo White
White blossom, grassy green and capsicum nose. Ripe, fruity flavours. Balanced.

Tenuta Ulisse Unico Pecorino Terre Di Chieti 2009, Abruzzo
White
Buttery, honeyed nose with green fruit on the palate. Refreshing citrus bite with a long, fresh finish.

Tenuta Ulisse Unico Trebbiano D'Abruzzo 2009, Abruzzo White
Grassy, green pea nose with a dusting of white pepper. Zesty and expressive with ripe pear and white peach notes. Elegant, quite long.

Tollo Pinot Grigio 2009, Abruzzo White
Pale lemon. Intense aromas of white blossom and sweet pears on the palate. Off-dry in style.
£7.49 ALI, WAIT

Tramin Pinot Grigio Alto Adige 2009, Alto Adige White
Medium fruit. Pears and tropical fruit. Fresh.
£10.99 HLD

Valle Di Cembra Cantina Di Montagna Dicembra Sauvignon Trentino 2009, Trentino White
Pale lemon with a pungent asparagus green nose.
Passionfruit and ripe melon with a slightly oily texture. Fresh and clean finish.
£8.49 UWI

Vallerosa Bonci San Michele Verdicchio Dei Castelli Di Jesi Classico Superiore 2008, Marche White
Gold colour. Tropical fruit aromas. Palate showing a hint of lime and citrus peel.
£16.00 TRW

Villa Sobrano Donna Sabina Grechetto di Todi 2007, Umbria White
Honeyed and almondy on the nose and palate. Big full, fleshy, peachy aromas. Ripe with a long pineapple flesh finish.

Vinci Vini Bramato Grillo 2009, Sicily White
Subtle perfumed nose, blossom and pear/peach. Refreshing acidity, minerally and persistent.

Zenato Lugana Riserva Sergio Zenato 2007, Veneto White
Hints of cooked apple and banana with some nutmeg. A gentle finish. Good for drinking now.
EUW, EVW

Zeni Costalago Bianco Delle Venezie 2009, Veneto White
Honey-pear nose. Bright, racy acidity with citrus, pear topicality on the palate. Fresh, ripe and clean on the finish.

Adria Vini Casa Lella Nero d'Avola 2009, Sicily Red
Lovely colour and flavour with a hint of vanilla. Good palate with lots of fruit.
£4.98 ASDA, PBA

Adria Vini Italia Primitivo 2008, Puglia Red
Red berry nose with currants, Christmas pudding. Long finish.
£6.49 MRN, PBA, WAIT

Agricole Vallone Vigna Castello 2007, Puglia Red
Lightly floral, violets and bright red fruits. Smooth tannins, raspberry to finish.
L&W

Agricoltori Del Chianti Geografico Contessa Di Radda Chianti Classico 2007, Tuscany Red
Light berry fruit, good character, a bit fuzzy but user friendly.

Agricoltori Del Chianti Geografico Montegiachi Chianti Classico Riserva 2006, Tuscany Red
Intense cherry fruit with firm dry tannins. Medium concentration of cherry and liquorice on the palate. Good finish.

Allegrini La Grola 2007, Veneto Red
Spicy black fruits, new oak. Savoury finish with a nice length.
£19.99 CVS, FAW, LIB, NYW

Allegrini Valpolicella 2009, Veneto Red
Light and bubble-gummy. Hints of cranberry.
£9.99 BEN, HVN, LIB, NYW

Alpha Zeta Valpolicella Superiore Ripasso 2008, Veneto Red
Vibrant cherry and plum, spice and vanilla. Mouthfilling and layered. Dry, but supple tannins. Good length.
£10.99 CVS, JAK, LIB, NGR

Anna Maria Cruciata Reviresco 2007, Tuscany Red
Slightly leathery restrained nose. Well defined, subtle. Medium bodied. Touch of tomato vine, tart cherry.
£6.10 BBL, BEC, HFB, P&S, VDI

Antonio Apollonio Terragnolo Negramaro Salento Rosso 2004, Puglia Red
Soft black jam nose, deep

refreshing dark plum fruits,
big oak.

**Antonio Apollonio Terragnolo
Primitivo Salento Rosso 2004,
Puglia** Red
Plums, ripe notes, rich black fruit.
Flavours well-balanced. Fruit and
soft acidity. Will last long.
£9.00

**Antonio Apollonio Valle Cupa
Salento Rosso 2004, Puglia**
Red
Black fruits and vanilla in
abundance. Lovely balanced
fruit. Oak and acidity with ripe
tannins.
£9.00

**Araldica Asda Extra Special
Barolo 2005, Piedmonte** Red
Aged colour. Fruity with hints of
wood on the nose.
£14.98 ASDA, PBA

**Araldica Barolo Castiglione
2005, Piedmonte** Red
Forest floor and warm red fruits.
Very cherry on the palate. Good
length.
£9.99 MRN, PBA

**Araldica Il Cascinone Rive
Barbera 2007, Piedmonte** Red
Oak on the nose and subtle fruit
on the palate. A good food wine.
£12.49 PBA

**Ascheri Glacomo Tesco
Finest* Barolo 2005,
Piedmonte** Red
Tea leafy. Bitter cherry fruit.
Attractive nose. Very firm
tannins. Fruit to balance.
TESC

**Azienda Marramiero Incanto
Montepulciano D'Abruzzo
2007, Abruzzo** Red
Dry fruit on the nose. Stewed
fruits with some violet character.
Good with food.

**Batasiolo Barbaresco 2007,
Piedmonte** Red
Cherry nose. Well-balanced with
a good finish. Needs time to
reach its potential.
£28.19 MON

**Batasiolo Barbera Sabri 2007,
Piedmonte** Red
Berry nose, scented fruits. Spicy
notes with a pleasant finish.
£12.70 MON

**Batasiolo Barolo Cerequio
2006, Piedmonte** Red
Fresh nose. Ripe fruit. Smooth
with a long length and great
structure.
£46.32 MON

**Batasiolo Bofani Barolo 2006,
Piedmonte** Red
Broad brooding nose. Very
well-structured. Long finish.
Will age well.
£46.32 MON

**Bonacchi Chianti Classico
2008, Tuscany** Red
Cherry, red berry fruits. Dry and
fresh on the palate with good
depth of flavours. Racy acidity
and ripe, but firm tannins.
£9.99 HLD

**Bonacchi Chianti Riserva
2005, Tuscany** Red
Lovely varietal nose with hints of
sweet cherry fruit. Firm tannins
and well-balanced.
£8.49 HLD

**Ca del Matt Barbera d'Asti
2008, Piedmonte** Red
Herbaceous and refreshing.
Well-balanced fruit and acidity.
Vegetal notes with a burst of ripe
black cherry. Round and smooth.
£6.99 LIB

**Cà Di Rajo Marinò 2006,
Veneto** Red
Cedary nose. Fresh structure,

grippy dry tannins. Long, complex finish. Builds gradually on the palate.
£12.00

Canicatti Scialo 2007, Sicily Red

Attractive berry nose. Berries and well-integrated oak on the palate. Smooth flavours and rich finish.
£16.00 EVW, VIN

Cantina Di Soave Ripasso Valpolicella Cadis 2008, Veneto Red

Perfumed sweet fruits with dried cherries on the nose and palate. Well-integrated oak. Supple, dry and long.
£20.00 CTL, PLB, VSO

Cantina Di Soave Spar Valpolicella NV, Veneto Red

Blackcurrant fruits on the nose and palate. Light and juicy.
£5.49 SPR

Cantina Sociale Della Valpantena Torre Del Falasco Amarone Della Valpolicella 2005, Veneto Red

Bramble fruits. Very nicely integrated with spice and chocolate. Long flavours.
£45.00 ENO

Cantina Sociale Della Valpantena Torre Del Falasco Amarone Della Valpolicella 2006, Veneto Red

Coffee and spice and all things nice. Lovely perfumed nose with a full richness and texture on the palate.
£45.00 ENO

Cantina Sociale Della Valpantena Valpolicella Ripasso Superiore Torre Del Falasco 2008, Veneto Red

Intense, vanishing dried fruit. Full bodied, chocolate, raisins on the palate and finish.
£30.00 ENO

Cantina Valpolicella Negrar Valpolicella Classico Maskalzoni 2008, Veneto Red

An elegant wine, albeit fairly restrained and youthful. Blackberry notes on the nose and palate.

Cantina Valpolicella Negrar Vigneti Di Jago Amarone Della Valpolicella Classico 2004, Veneto Red

Earth black cherry fruit. Complex with some sweetness. Rich and concentrated, lovely tobacco with big cherry fruit flavours coming through. A long finish.

Capezzana Ghiaie Della Furba 2006, Tuscany Red

Lot of high tone nose. Chocolate and tough tannins, still time to go.
£32.99 LIB

Casa Girelli Marks & Spencer Puglia Rosso 2009, Puglia Red

Light red fruit at the nose. Lifted, delicate red, black fruit, juicy and acidic. Very tannic mouthful.
£4.79 M&S

Casale Del Giglio Mater Matuta 2006, Lazio Red

Oak berries on nose, lovely sweet ripe berries. Hints of leather and spice.
EUW, EVW

Castellani Campomaggio Chianti Classico 2007, Tuscany Red

Tar and spice on the nose. Black-cherry fruit, sweet vanilla and dark chocolate with a dry finish.
BWL

Castellani Campomaggio Toscana 2006, Tuscany Red

Spice and pepper. Soft bramble

fruit on the palate.
BWL

Castellani Poggio Al Casone Chianti Riserva 2007, Tuscany Red
Black cherry aromas. Fleshy palate with good balance and supple tannins.
£8.15 ASDA

Castellani Villa Lucia Chianti Riserva 2006, Tuscany Red
Medium ruby. Light cherry and plum flavours on the palate.
£4.96 ASDA

Castello Monaci Medos Malvasia Nera Del Salento 2008, Puglia Red
Aromas of red fruit and smooth tannins. A touch of savoury character.
£9.99 REV

Caviro Dino Sangiovese Di Romagna 2009, Emilia Romagna Red
Floral nose. Red fruits on the palate. Drying finish. Good with food.
£8.99 TESC

Cavit Bottega Vinai Lagrein Dunkel Trentino 2007, Trentino Red
Opaque. Complex berry fruits and opulent with a pleasant finish.
PBA

Cavit Bottega Vinai Teroldego Rotaliano 2008, Trentino Red
Earthy aromas. Vibrant fruits with an eerily long finish.
PBA

Cavit Maso Cervara Teroldego Rotaliano 2007, Trentino Red
Opaque. Morello cherry, almond aromas. Good acidity. Crying out for food!
PBA

Ceretto Barolo Bricco Rocche Brunate 2005, Piedmonte Red
Good concentration. A well-balanced wine with a nice length.
£48.57 BWL, MWW

Ceretto Bricco Asili Bernardot Barbaresco 2006, Piedmonte Red
Concentrated pure berry fruit on the nose and palate. Nice complexity. Fairly dry. A good food wine.
£43.00 BWL

Cerulli Spinozzi Torre Migliori 2005, Abruzzo Red
Medium ruby. Spicy notes. Cedar nose and palate.

Cevico Group Galassi Sangiovese Merlot Rubicone 2009, Emilia Romagna Red
Fruity, rich and complex. Concentrated, silky structure. Good length.
£4.99 D&D

Cevico Group Masselina 158 Sangiovese Cabernet Sauvignon 2008, Emilia Romagna Red
Bright blackcurrant fruits and prunes on the palate. Mid weight and grippy tannins with a good length.
£10.99 D&D

Concilio Teroldego Rotaliano Braide 2008, Trentino Red
Opaque. Opulent. Austere on the palate. Will age well.

Conti Di San Bonifacio Docet 2007, Tuscany Red
Bright, red berry, cherry fruit on the nose. Touch of saddle leather. Good definition. Ripe entry, firm tannins with a touch of white pepper. Gripping finish.
£20.00

Conti Di San Bonifacio Monteregio Di Massa Marittima

2007, Tuscany Red

Black fruits and redcurrants on the nose. Blackcurrant leaf palate with a touch of spice. Interesting and complex.

£16.00

Da Vinci Chianti 2008, Tuscany Red

Ripe fruit on the nose. Sweet cherry, raspberry on the palate. Firm tannins with a balance of fruit all the way through. Young but elegant wine.

£8.99 FAW, LIB

Da Vinci Chianti Reserva 2006, Tuscany Red

Cherry, leather, rustic, earthy notes. Black and bramble fruits. Good flavour concentration and a good length.

£13.99 LIB

Dallevigne Collezione Speciale Chianti 2007, Tuscany Red

Lifted cherry on the nose. Savoury cherry fruit on the palate. Elegant fruit with concentration and good length. Integrated fresh finish with some chocolate notes.

Desmonta Nero D'Arcole 2007, Veneto Red

Smoky bacon, cheesy, sweet aroma. Dry, mature, fresh, zippy - lovely balance.

Due Palme Pillastro 2008, Puglia Red

Ripe fruit and plum aromas. Very rich plum flavours. Very big wine.

Due Palme Tenuta Albrizzi 2008, Puglia Red

Clean nose of dark cherry. Dry cherry flavours with a punchy finish.

Due Palme Trezanti Salento Negroamaro 2008, Puglia Red

Clean, red fruits, elegant nose. Balanced, ripe cooked fruits. Soft oak and integrated tannins.

Persistent finish.

£8.99 EHB, MRN

Due Palme Villa Quinziana 2008, Puglia Red

Attractive, ripe, dark bramble nose. Sweeter, jammy palate, red black fruit concentrate. Good tannin and oak.

Farnese Gran Sasso Montepulciano D'Abruzzo Colline Teramane 2006, Abruzzo Red

Spice, oak and cedar. Fruit and spice on the palate.

Farnese Gran Sasso Sangiovese 2009, Tuscany Red

Well made quaffable wine with a likeable fresh finish.

£7.99

Farnese Montepulciano D'Abruzzo Colline Teramane 2006, Abruzzo Red

Rich oaky nose. Lovely spiced notes with blackberry and fruit. Nice concentration, good length and smooth texture.

£15.00

Farnese Opi Montepulciano D'Abruzzo Colline Teramane Riserva 2006, Abruzzo Red

Vibrant ruby in colour. Subdued earthy nose with a hint of chocolate. Red fruits and dried fruits on the palate.

£16.00

Farnese Sangiovese Terre Di Chieti 2009, Abruzzo Red

Spicy cherry brandy and herbs on the nose and palate. Quaffable and refreshingly satisfying bitter finish.

£7.99

Farnese Villa Farnia Montepulciano D'Abruzzo 2009, Abruzzo Red

Deep black colour. Sweet

blackberry and blackcurrant, vanilla and creamy notes. Rich and full bodied.
£6.99

Farnese Villa Farnia Sangiovese Daunia 2008, Tuscany Red
Spicy morello cherry fruits. Vanilla. Soft and very easy drinking.
£6.99

Fattoria Di Valiano Chianti Classico 2007, Tuscany Red
Bright primary fruit, quite lifted and pretty, quite savoury, good balance.

Fattoria Di Valiano Poggio Teo Chianti Classico 2006, Tuscany Red
Sour berries and cherries, cranberry character with some herbaceous notes. Balanced finish.
£9.00 TESC

Fattoria Varramista Chianti Monsonaccio 2007, Tuscany Red
Lots of coffee and rich toasty notes. Sweet, nose and palate. Tangy, pure with good length and harmony.

Fazi Battaglia-Fassati Gersemi Vino Nobile Di Montepulciano 2006, Tuscany Red
Savoury, leather nose with structured black cherry fruit. Good spice and depth of flavour.
£18.60 MON

Felsina Chianti Classico Berardenga 2008, Tuscany Red
Stalky, green aromas with a touch of ripe cherry. On the palate, sweet cherry fruit with racy acidity. Good, persistent length.
£18.99 CAM, CPW, LIB, P&S

Firriato Wild Cat Nero D'Avola 2008, Sicily Red
Ripe nose with a touch of floral aroma. Ripe cherries on the palate. Fresh and friendly quaffer.
£6.49 WAIT

Fondo Antico Il Canto Di Fondo Antico 2006, Sicily Red
Light fruit and well managed oak. Lovely juicy finish and bags of spice.

Genagricola Solonio Merlot 2009, Lazio Red
Herbal, fresh, fragrant, perfumed nose. Fresh, crunchy, red fruit. Elegant, fresh, baked with good depth. Youthful and attractive.

Giordano Salento Rosso Ricarico 2007, Puglia Red
Red and black fruits. Ripe, juicy flavours. Warming with a pleasant finish.

Giordano Tarantino Rosso Piu' Uve Unico 2007, Puglia Red
Medium intensity of colour. Aromas of black fruit. Jammy.

Gulfi Nerojbleo 2006, Sicily Red
Good colour with some fruit lift. Black fruit on the palate.
£14.99 ODD

Il Borro Il Borro 2007, Tuscany Red
Very fruit driven nose, juicy blackcurrant and bilberry, pastille character. Sweet entry, rounded tannins.
EUW, EVW

John Matta Tenuta Vicchiomaggio Ripa Delle More 2007, Tuscany Red
Rich, ripe, bramble and blackberry fruit, firm tannin and a long persistent finish.

John Matta Villa Vallemaggiore Colle Alto 2007, Tuscany Red
Deep ruby. Black fruit and plenty

of smoky oak. Vibrant fruit with excellent acidity. Lingering spicy finish.

La Sansonina Sansonina 2006, Veneto Red
Deep. Very expressive and earthy, sweet aromas. Good fragrance and freshness. Very lifted.
EUW, EVW

Le Chiantigiane Chianti Loggia Del Conte 2008, Tuscany Red
Cherry red fruit and light oak on the nose. Dryish on the palate and finish.
MWW

Li veli Orion Salento Primitivo 2008, Puglia Red
Rosemary and tobacco on the nose. Pepper and black cherry on the palate.
£10.99 CKY, LIB

Lo Sardo Marsello Ruggero li 2008, Sicily Red
Herbal notes and fresh cherry fruit on the palate. Good concentration and complexity. Fairly youthful, will improve.
£19.00

Marchesi Antinori Villa Antinori 2006, Tuscany Red
Black fruit and smoky oak. Vibrant fruit with excellent acidity and firm tannins. Liquorice, with a lingering spicy finish.
£12.99 GPS, HAC, TAN, WAIT

Marchesi de Frescobaldi Luce della Vite Lucente 2007, Tuscany Red
Smooth black fruit with smoke and leather. Good strong finish.
£25.99 HLD

Marchesi de Frescobaldi Nipozzano Riserva Chianti Rufina 2006, Tuscany Red
Elegant, cedar, floral and cherry nose. Balanced tannin, nicely balanced oak and cherry. Fresh finish.
£17.49 HLD

Marchesi di Gresy Martinenga Barbaresco 2006, Piedmonte Red
Leather and cherry fruit nose. Elegant balance with a good finish.
£45.99 PBA

Marramiero Montepulciano D'Abruzzo 2008, Abruzzo Red
Spicy oak, cherry and black fruit on the nose and palate. A good length.

Masi Fojaneghe Bossi Fedrigotti 2006, Trentino Red
Lovely soft fruit. Good tannin. Long length, great blueberry fruit. Excellent.

Masottina Cabernet Sauvignon Piave 2008, Veneto Red
Very fresh, primary, red fruits. Juicy, dry with plenty of flavour. Crunchy fruit.
TTC

Melini Borghi D'Elsa Chianti 2009, Tuscany Red
Juicy red fruit. Juicy on the palate with some floral violet character. Young but powerful.
£7.49 WAIT

Mesa Buio Carignano del Sulcis 2008, Sardinia Red
Typical savoury nose with a splash of cherry. Palate of juicy fruits, blended light tannins. A hint of wood.
£14.99 LIB

Moncaro Terre Cortesi Cimerio Conero Riserva 2007, Marche Red
Ripely pronounced fruit, quite lush with very open bouquet and

palate.
EUW, EVW

Moncaro Terre Cortesi Le Silve Rosso Conero 2008, Marche Red
Fresh and open fruit with ripe cherry and plum notes on the palate.
EUW

Moncaro Terre Cortesi Rosso Piceno Superiore Conti Leopardi 2007, Marche Red
Nicely balanced with dense, sweet fruit. Earthy and spicy on the finish.
LAI

Moncaro Terre Cortesi Vigneti Del Parco Conero Riserva 2006, Marche Red
Fresh, dark fruits with a spicy and savoury palate. Layers of flavour with long length.
EUW, EVW

Mondo Del Vino Asda Extra Special Montepulciano 2008, Abruzzo Red
Cherry fruit nose. A pleasant sweetness on the palate contrasted with sour cherries.
ASDA

Mondo Del Vino Co-Operative Montepulciano D'Abruzzo 2008, Abruzzo Red
Seductive, rich, juicy, chocolatey, plummy with a very long chocolatey finish.
£7.99 CWS

Mondo Del Vino Itynera Montepulciano 2008, Abruzzo Red
Nice fruity flavour. Good balance. Quaffable.
CBG

Mondo Del Vino Luigi Bersano Bric Di Bersan Dolcetto 2007, Piedmonte Red
Light cherry fruit character. A refreshing drop!
£6.99 LAI

Mondo Del Vino Nespolino Sangiovese 2008, Emilia Romagna Red
Cherries on the nose. Silky, soft, smooth, plum rich and juicy.
£5.99

Monte Schiavo Adeodato 2006, Marche Red
Dense, firm, spicy and jammy. Drying tannins with tangy, earth fruit on the finish.
£20.00 PBA

Monte Schiavo Panse 2009, Marche Red
Simple but pleasant. Soft berry fruit characters. Refreshing acidity.
£7.99 PBA

Montresor Capitel della Crosara Valpolicella Ripasso 2008, Veneto Red
Spicy cherry fruits on the nose and palate. Quite savoury.
£11.99 PBA

Nino Negri Sfursat Tradizionale Valtellina 2006, Lombardia Red
Fragrant nose of dried fruits. Rich palate and a long finish.
£24.99 ENO

Olivi Cantine Le Buche 2007, Tuscany Red
Cherry on the nose. Juicy and quaffable.

Olivi Cantine Memento 2007, Tuscany Red
Lifted with polished complexity. Luscious, generous palate with sweet chocolate finish.

Piccini Gran Prugnello Toscana 2008, Tuscany Red
Soft and gentle. Plum fruit. Youthful with a long finish.

Piccini MHV Chianti Classico 2008, Tuscany Red
Roasted and savoury on the palate with layers of raspberry and sour cherry fruits. Juicy with good depth of flavour. Long.
£8.89 BOO

Piccini Tenuta Moraia Chianti Classico Riserva 2006, Tuscany Red
Ruby red. Red tart cherry fruit. Zesty.

Piccini Toscana 2008, Tuscany Red
Plum and sage nose. Complex with sweet floral aromatics. Excellent balanced palate. Complex with red fruit and soft fine tannins.

Planeta Cerasuolo Di Vittoria 2008, Sicily Red
Bright, cherry fruit. Smooth accents, really juicy with fresh acidity and fine tannins. Spicy finish.
£14.99 WAIT

Podere Castorani Montepulciano D'Abruzzo 2004, Abruzzo Red
Deep garnet colour. Dried fig, stewed plum nose, spicy oak. Good depth and length. Nice, rich, style.
HOH

Poggiotondo Cerro del Masso Chianti 2008, Tuscany Red
Creamy, moderate, nicely rounded palate. Lots of black fruit sweetness. Very complex, harmonious with good length.
£7.99 HAX, LIB, RSV, WAIT, WWN

Provinco Revero Valpolicella Ripasso Superiore 2008, Veneto Red
Vanilla and plums on the nose. Rounded cherry palate. Pure and quite concentrated. Well made, with some chocolate notes. Long.

Provinco Via Vecchio Valpolicella Ripasso 2009, Veneto Red
Spicy, sweet ripe fruit and savoury nose and palate. Unripe cherries. Still fairly young, but with potential.

Racemi I Monili Primitivo Del Tarantino 2009, Puglia Red
Complex and interesting. Quite elegant. Well-balanced.
£7.49 MWW

Rosalba Vitanza Volare Toscana 2007, Tuscany Red
Big complex fruity nose. Velvet cherries and smooth vanilla on the palate.
£8.00 BHL, HAX, MVC

San Silvestro Brumo Nebbiolo 2007, Piedmonte Red
Elegant perfumed nose. Cherries, liquorice, tar and violets. Well-structured with racy acidity, velvety tannins, cherries and concentrated finish.
£9.49 HLD

San Silvestro Domina Barbera D'Alba 2008, Piedmonte Red
Bright. Forest berry nose. Red cherries and spice on the palate. Crisp and refreshing.

San Silvestro Ottone Barbera 2008, Piedmonte Red
Young and refreshing. Berry and cherry pie nose. Spicy notes.
£6.99 HLD

Santa Barbara Rosso Piceno Il Maschio Da Monte 2007, Marche Red
Deep purple colour, very concentrated with juicy redcurrant flavours. Warm and soft on the finish.
£22.00 EVW, VIN

Santa Tresa Avulisi 2007, Sicily Red
Herbal nose with good black fruit on the palate. Good structure and length.

Sartori Regolo 2006, Veronese Red
Lovely pure sweet berry fruit. Concentrated but fresh and not too heavy. Good length.

Sartori Sainsbury's House Valpolicella NV, Veneto Red
Ripe cherries and a hint of herbs on the nose. Light, soft, fleshy wine.
£3.66 SAIN

Schenk Italia Boccantino Nero D'Avola Sicilia 2009, Sicily Red
Juicy, simple, fresh and full of character. A lunchtime quaffer.

Scrimaglio Croutin Barbera D'Asti Superiore 2005, Piedmonte Red
Gently wooded. Spicy fruit and moderate concentration on the palate. Oak and spice on the finish.

Selvanova Vigna Del Sasso 2007, Campania Red
Ripe cherry nose. Mineral palate with cherry. Dry, long.
£11.99 ODD

Selvapiana Vigneto Bucerchiale Chianti Rufina Riserva 2006, Tuscany Red
Big smoky cherry wood notes. Intense red and black fruits. Good flavour, with a good length.
£18.99 CKY, LAY, LIB, POG

Settesoli Connubio Nero D'Avola Shiraz 2008, Sicily Red
Black fruits, very ripe, tobacco overlay. Jammy, rich and very full bodied. Lively acidity and smooth textured.
£6.12 SAIN

Settesoli Inycon President Selection Nero D'Avola 2008, Sicily Red
Good colour with some wood evident. Good flavour.

Settesoli Sicilian Red NV, Sicily Red
Raspberry, cherry and red fruits. Light and fruity, soft and generous.

Surani Costarossa Primitivo 2008, Puglia Red
Medium plum aromas. Good fruit. Pleasant, easy drinking finish.
£10.99

Talamonti Tre Saggi Montepulciano D'Abruzzo 2007, Abruzzo Red
Basil, cherry on the nose. Light oak, hints of blackcurrant and cherry fruits on the palate and finish.
£15.00 EVW, V&C, VIN

Tenuta Carretta Cascina Ferrero 2005, Piedmonte Red
Floral and red cranberry fruit with a truffle nuance. Lovely, juicy fruit. Firm structure, already developing. Lingering finish.
£18.80 FAL

Tenuta Di Biserno Insoglio Del Cinghiale 2008, Tuscany Red
Spicy black red berries and savoury. Ripe fleshy tannins, dusty softness and very long.
£22.15

Tenuta Ulisse Amaranta Montepulciano D'Abruzzo 2008, Abruzzo Red
Jammy, concentrated cooked fruit. Dark cherry and blackberry. Creamy vanilla hints with a smoothness on the palate.

Tenute Neirano Neirano Barolo 2006, Piedmonte Red
Discreet nose. Soft fruit attack. Youthful, will improve over time.

Terre Del Barolo Via Collina Dolcetto Di Diano D'Alba 2009, Piedmonte Red
Sweet ripe cherry nose. Pleasant cherry flavours on the palate.
£7.99 WAIT

Terredavino Barolo 2006, Piedmonte Red
Whiff of red fruits on the nose and palate. Integrated oak and red fruits. Needs time to reach its potential.

Terredavino Bric Corderi Barbera D'Asti Superiore 2007, Piedmonte Red
Savoury, black cherry flavours. A long cedary finish.

Teruzzi & Puthod Peperino Toscana Rosso 2007, Tuscany Red
Complex. Great scented fruit. Scent of blueberry fruit. Lush, dry and long.

Tollo Aldiano Montepulciano 2008, Abruzzo Red
Briary, blackberry, quite lifted nose. Some sweet fruit on the palate. Blackberries, violets with a fine persistence.
£8.90 ALI

Tollo Kult 2008, Abruzzo Red
Roast tomato, blackberry on the nose. Cherries, juicy and delicious. Smoky with a long finish.
£5.00 ALI

Umberto Cesari Tauleto Sangiovese 2004, Emilia Romagna Red
Coffee and leather nose. Blackcurrant, tobacco notes. Rich and complex.
£36.99 HLD

Valentino Cirulli Ginepreta 2007, Umbria Red
Nose is dominated by vanilla oak. Very full bodied, powerful style. Liquid blackcurrants, figs and cherries.

Valle Di Cembra Cantina Di Montagna Dicembra Pinot Nero Trentino 2008, Trentino Red
Elegant perfumed nose. Well-structured. A long finish of rose petal.
£8.49 UWI

Vesevo Beneventano Aglianico 2008, Campania Red
Full. Aromatic cherry and violet on the nose. Juicy notes and cherry fruit tart.
£10.99 LIB

Zenato Cormi Corvina Merlot Del Veneto 2006, Veneto Red
Good bouquet and flavours of red fruit. Will be great when has time to age.
EUW, EVW

Bidoli Cabernet Franc Rosé 2009, Friuli Venezia Giulia Rosé
Lifted strawberry fruit and rose petal nose. Intense and very well-balanced. Fresh with good acidity. Pretty and elegant.
£6.29 M&S

La Prendina Rondinella Pinot Grigio Rosé 2009, Lombardia Rosé
Subtle, earthy nose. Good definition with light strawberry and cherry fruit. Fresh and clean.
£7.49 M&S

Adria Vini Prosecco Dolci Colline NV, Venezie Sparkling
Fresh appley aromas, mouthfilling mousse, floral. Balanced fruit and

persistent finish.
£7.99 VGN, PBA

Araldica Asda Asti NV,
Piedmont Sparkling
Clean lithe fruit. Good balance
of acidity, sugar and fruit. Good
length.
£4.36 ASDA, PBA

Bisol Tesco Finest* Prosecco
Di Valdobbiadene NV,
Valdobbiadene Sparkling
Aromatic and fruity with lemony
freshness Crisp and attractive.
TESC

Bisol valdobbiadene Prosecco
Jeio Colmei NV, valdobbiadene
Sparkling
Crisp, taut and fruity with nice
lemon and pear fruit. Appealing
and full.

Cà Di Rajo Prosecco
Millesimato Treviso 2009,
Veneto Sparkling
Pear drops and lemon sweets on the
nose. Off-dry, soft and gentle on the
palate with a creamy mousse.
£9.00

Canevel Valdobbiadene
Prosecco Extra Dry 2009,
Veneto Sparkling
Fine, light mousse with citrus
and apples on the nose. On the
palate flavours of lychee, apples
and peach blossom show through.
Smooth finish.
£16.50 EVW, HAR, VIN

Castel Frères Villa Veroni Asti
NV, Piedmont Sparkling
Grapey, aromatic, Golden
Delicious with medium bubbles.
Foam comes through to palate
with light acidity.

Cesarini Sforza Spumanti
Cuvée Brut Riserva NV,
Trentino Sparkling
Citrus and apple. No obvious

autolytic character. Refreshing
and zesty, bubbles quite
aggressive. Good balance and
length.
£12.00 TESC

Dezzani Moscato D'Asti
Morelli 2009, Piedmont
Sparkling
Lovely floral Tropicana tinged
nose. Pure and well defined.
Well-balanced, slightly honeyed
palate and a long finish.
EUW, EVW

Dogarina Ca'di Pietra
Prosecco Brut NV, Veneto
Sparkling
Crisp, green, balanced fruit,
Granny Smith apples with a
good finish.
£9.89 CRE, FMC

Genagricola Borgo Magredo
Prosecco Spumante NV,
Veneto Sparkling
Lifted floral aromas. Mouthfilling
and palate with dry fruit and a
pleasing, persistent finish.

La Gioiosa Prosecco
Spumante Treviso NV,
Veneto Sparkling
Pale straw. Citrus aroma.
Confected notes on mid palate.
Fresh finish.
£8.99 SAIN

La Marca Prosecco Spumante
Conegliano-Valdobbiadene
NV, Veneto Sparkling
Appley aroma, green notes on
palate. Citrus flushing. Light and
creamy.
£11.99 MWW

La Marca Prosecco Spumante
Conegliano-Valdobbiadene
NV, Veneto Sparkling
Floral nose. Concentrated mid
palate, ripe dense dry fruit
character. Persistent finish.
£14.99 MWW

Le Contesse Prosecco Spumante NV, Veneto
Sparkling
Quince, citrus aroma. Well-balanced. Floral notes on palate following through to the finish.
£8.99 M&S

Marco Pederiva Valdobbiadene Prosecco Sparkling Brut Treser 2009, Veneto
Lightly honeyed, lemon sweets on the nose which follow through to the palate. Citrus and lemon flavours persist on the finish.
£11.00

Martini & Rossi Asti NV, Piedmonte Sparkling
Fresh oranges, grapey nose. Sweet but fresh and not cloying with delightful orange candied peel character.
£6.99 Widely Available

Schenk Italia La Gondola Prosecco Frizzante NV, Veneto Sparkling
Somewhat lacking in sparkle. Dense fruit on the palate. Light and elegant.

Terre Di San Venanzio Fortunato Valdobbiadene Brut 2009, Veneto Sparkling
Perfumed, pear drop with hints of pineapple. Quite refreshing

acidity - citrus and stone fruit. Not much autolytic character.
£11.00 VSO

Terre Di San Venanzio Fortunato Valdobbiadene Extra Dry Prosecco 2009, Veneto Sparkling
Crisp, bright and very fresh with citrusy fruit and nice precision.
£11.00 VSO

Contero Brachetto d'Acqui 2009, Piedmonte Sparkling Rosé
Faint sherry nose. Lovely, sweet, ripe berries and cherries. Fresh and mouthfilling.
£15.99 CAM, FAW, GGW, HAR, LIB

Schenk Italia Marks & Spencer Pinot Grigio Frizzante NV, Veneto Sparkling Rosé
Clean firm aroma. Palate good, agreeable flavour, perhaps a little neutral. Has sweetness. Good.
£6.99 M&S, M&S

Fratelli Martini Cellar Estate Lambrusco Rosso NV, Lazio Fortified
Grippy, baked cherries, fruity intense to nose. Sweet Morello cherries with a hint of vanilla pod. Simple and uncomplex. Long length.
£2.99

New Zealand

New Zealand's stellar success as a
wine producer has been the envy
of every country with vineyards.
The ripeness and purity of fruit
in their wines – as exemplified by
the now ubiquitous Marlborough
Sauvignon Blanc – was a revelation
in the wine aisles. There are no
signs that the world is tiring of
the style, with exports increasing
healthily each year – most recently,
up by 34% in 2009. There is wine
beyond Sauvignon here, though,
and the Pinot Noirs from Central
Otago continue to plough their
own furrow, again impressing
palates with their concentration
and vivacity.

2010 IWC PERFORMANCE	
Trophies	8
Gold	21
Silver	88
Bronze	191

GOLD

Matariki Chardonnay 2007, Hawke's Bay White

Lemon and citrus with toasty oak aromas on the nose. Sweet lemon and baked apples on the palate with hints of ripe figs. Pure fruit expression with lovely character and a long, lingering finish.

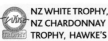 **NZ SAUVIGNON BLANC TROPHY**

Montana Sauvignon Blanc 2009, Marlborough White

Very pale in colour. Ripe nose with tropical and citrus notes. Guava and ripe cantaloupe on the palate with a nice, elegant attack. Lovely, round guava finish with long, lingering fruit. Delicious.

£8.99 SAIN, MRN, TESC, WAIT

 **NZ WHITE TROPHY, NZ CHARDONNAY TROPHY, HAWKE'S BAY CHARDONNAY TROPHY**

Ngatarawa Alwyn Winemakers Reserve Chardonnay 2007, Hawke's Bay White

Full, bold but stylish wine. Silky pineapple and passionfruit overlaid with a hint of spice and a shortbready, creamy finish. Well made and harmonious.

Saint Clair Family Estate Wairau Reserve Sauvignon Blanc 2009, Marlborough White

Nettle and gooseberry nose. Nettley herbal palate. Dry and quite concentrated. Quite long.

£18.99 HLD

 NZ RIESLING TROPHY

Sandihurst Winery True And Daring Riesling 2007, Canterbury White

Wonderful, slightly evolved Riesling nose with kiwi fruit and lime marmalade scents. Crystalline purity with beautifully balanced fruit, acidity and sweetness. Long.

The Crossings Awatere Sauvignon Blanc 2009, Awatere White

Great intensity on the nose with cool, green apple and kiwi fruit on the palate. Lovely poise with subtle green fruit and hints of lemongrass on the finish. A stunning wine.

£9.99 F&M, SEL

Vavasour Clifford Bay Awatere Valley Sauvignon Blanc 2009, Marlborough White

Pungent with sweetly perfumed fruit. Gooseberry and citrus with understated melon on the plate. Ripe and well-structured with good floral character and a nicely balanced finish. Very pleasing.

£9.99 BWJ, COE, EVW, HAR, LFW

Villa Maria Reserve Clifford Bay Sauvignon Blanc 2009, Marlborough White

Grassy sugar-snap aromas and flavours. Mineral intensity on the palate. Green fruit with some complexity, and quite long.

£12.99 SAIN

Amisfield Pinot Noir 2008, Central Otago Red

Fragrant sweet raspberry aromas. Ripe but fresh and elegant fruit on the palate. Textured. A hint of gaminess but

fresh finish. Has potential.
£22.00 EVW, SEL, WHF

 CENTRAL OTAGO PINOT NOIR TROPHY

Desert Heart Pinot Noir 2007, Central Otago Red
Fragrant, rose petals and spice with a hint of game on the nose. Sweet and juicy on the palate. Textured, with well handled oak and fresh but no acerbic acidity. Quite complex and long.

Domain Road Pinot Noir 2008, Central Otago Red
Strawberry and vanilla fruit aromas with a touch of herbaceousness. Great depth of flavour with a long, lingering, creamy finish.
GMP, MAN, POR, PWA, SHJ

 GIMBLETT GRAVELS SYRAH TROPHY

Forrest Collection Syrah 2006, Hawke's Bay Red
Gorgeous creamy white pepper and light cracked black pepper. Great structure. Powerful but elegant. Good lengthy finish.
£17.99 ADN

Gladstone Pinot Noir 2008, Wairarapa Red
Lovely, smoky bacon and vegetal character. Soft mid palate. Lots of fruit delivery and lovely tannins. Excellent expression of Pinot.
£13.95 CAM, FFT, GWC, GWW, HVN, LEA

Grasshopper Rock Central Otago Pinot Noir 2008, Central Otago Red
Red plummy fruit with a touch of vanilla gives way to spicy herbaceousness, plum and berry flavours. An elegant wine, with a lingering smoky finish.

Man O'War Vineyards Dreadnought 2008, Waiheke Island Red
Dense and chunky with ripe, spicy dark fruits. Quite firm with a savoury, peppery dimension. Very nice.
£24.00 SFW

 MARTINBOROUGH PINOT NOIR TROPHY

Martinborough Vineyard Pinot Noir 2008, Martinborough Red
Quite earthy and vegetal. Lovely beetroot. Smooth and refined. More fruit on finish, spicy, oaky, ripe and juicy. Elegant and so fine.
£25.00 HAR, HAR, HVN

 NZ RED TROPHY, NEW ZEALAND SYRAH TROPHY, WAIHEKE ISLAND SYRAH TROPHY

Passage Rock Reserve Syrah 2008, Waiheke Island Red
Very dense, ripe brooding meaty, light fruits. The palate is bold with menthol and spice and medicine notes. Distinctive.

 NZ PINOT NOIR TROPHY, WAIRARAPA PINOT NOIR TROPHY

Schubert Pinot Noir Block B 2008, Wairarapa Red
Mid ruby, dense raspberry and smoke nose with a herb de province overlay. Juicy, jammy palate with good lift. Nice length. Luscious!
£27.95 NZH

Schubert Pinot Noir Marion's Vineyard 2008, Wairarapa Red
Creamy, rich, undergrowth quality. Dense, sweet fruit. Has real intensity with fleshy mid-palate. Lovely!
£24.95 SOM, TSC

Spy Valley Pinot Noir 2008, Marlborough Red
Elegant aroma. Well-balanced wine. Delicious ripe fruit under lined by vibrant acidity. Lingering finish.

Waipara Hills Southern Cross Selection Central Otago Pinot Noir 2008, Central Otago Red
Soft red fruit and spice on the nose. An explosion of raspberry, cherry and cinnamon. Rich, full and creamy in the mouth.
£12.99 SAIN

Mazurans Gold Medal Port 1957, West Auckland Fortified
Deep chocolate brown hue. Lifted caramel and chocolate sauce, fresh molasses on the palate with a rich finish.

SILVER

Artisan Kauri Ridge Chardonnay 2008, Auckland White
Deep and lemony with a clean, toasty nose. Oak and vanilla layered palate with lemon curd and melon fruit ripeness. Ripe and round with an apple custard finish.

Astrolabe Discovery Awatere Valley Sauvignon Blanc 2009, Marlborough White
Very pungent on the nose with bell-pepper and grassy ripeness on the palate. Leafy and green with a youthful appeal.
£14.99 EOR, RWA, WHD, WAIT

Babich Individual Vineyard Cowslip Valley Sauvignon Blanc 2009, Marlborough White
Grassy and mineral on the nose. Vibrant citrus with ripe lemon-lime character. Zippy with a strong mineral finish.

Blackenbrook Sauvignon Blanc 2009, Nelson White
Mineral freshness on the nose. Crisp lemony citrus with a touch of cat pee and green gooseberry on the palate. Refreshing passionfruit finish.

Blind River Blind River 2009, Marlborough White
Ripe and grassy with a passionfruit nose. Lovely grapefruit on the palate with a zesty finish. Well defined with fantastic structure and length.
£11.99 ODD

Drylands Riesling 2007, Marlborough White
Apricots and orange blossom on the nose. Bright Riesling fruit, lively acidity with a wonderfully structured, savoury finish.
MCT

Esk Valley Vineyard Selection Chenin Blanc 2009, Marlborough White
Lemon, pear drop and mineral notes on the nose. Lean palate, focused white fruits with minerality throughout. Good acidity to finish.
£8.99

Forrest The Doctors Riesling 2009, Marlborough White
Ripe mineral and slate aromas. Clean citrus and green leafy character with lovely balance and a fine, lengthy finish.
£9.99 ADN

Giesen The Brothers Marlborough Sauvignon Blanc 2008, Marlborough White
Clean with a green and herbaceous nose. A touch of mint and gooseberry on the palate with a dry, herbaceous, fruity-bell pepper finish. Long and zesty.
£15.99 C&B, WAV

Grove Mill Grand Reserve Riesling 2009, Marlborough White
Touch of toffee sweetness, candied apple and lemon on the palate. Sweetly ripe fruit with candied peel and zesty acidity. Long and lush.

Grove Mill Grove Mill Riesling 2009, Marlborough White
Nice hints of waxy character with mineral overtones. Ripe and intense with mineral rich palate. Lovely with lots of apple fruit intensity. Complex and long.
£8.49

Hatch Esk Valley Sauvignon Blanc 2009, Marlborough White
Tropical aromas on the nose with passionfruit ripeness on the palate. Mouth-watering freshness and crisp lemon acidity. Light spritzy character is nicely refreshing on the finish.
£8.99 LAI

Kim Crawford Marlborough Sauvignon Blanc 2009, Marlborough White
Gooseberry aromas on the nose. Fresh acidity on the palate. Nicely complex with a pungent finish.
£10.99 ABY, FAW, HAX, LIB

Kim Crawford SP Spitfire Sauvignon Blanc 2009, Marlborough White
Tropical on the nose with richly mouth-watering passionfruit on the palate. Clean and weighty with fresh fruit purity and lingering freshness on the finish.
£13.49 LIB, SL , WDR

Lawson's Dry Hills Gewürztraminer 2009, Marlborough White
Tropical fruit on the nose and palate. Well-balanced with a good finish.
£10.99

Marisco The Ned Marlborough Pinot Grigio 2009, Marlborough White
Pear and peach fruit with hints of subdued gooseberry on the nose. Lively lemon citrus and ripe melon with a touch of warm spice on the palate. Good texture and balance with sustaining length.
£9.99 MWW

Matariki Sauvignon Blanc 2009, Hawke's Bay White
Fresh grassy, floral pea-shoot aromas. Intense, with spicy-grassy flavours and a hint of salty minerality on the palate. Long and elegant.

Mission Estate Jewelstone Chardonnay 2008, Hawke's Bay White
A crisp dry and refreshing wine with elegance. Passionfruit, citrus aromas.
£19.00 WDR

Montana Ormond Gisborne Chardonnay 2007, Gisborne White
Rich, mature creamy character. Bold tropical fruit and butterscotch flavours. Good balance and lingering finish.
£11.99

Mud House Swan Marlborough Sauvignon Blanc 2009, Marlborough White
Pungent, rich, complex, with rich

TŶ NANT
NATURAL MINERAL WATER

Proud sponsors of International Wine Challenge

☎: +44 (0) 1974 272111
🖷: +44 (0) 1974 272123
www.tynant.com

green fruit and stone fruit. Full bodied with length and depth.
£13.99 POG, SSU

Nautilus Marlborough Pinot Gris 2009, Marlborough White
Subtle and fine aromatics, ripe citrus, tight and focussed.
£14.08 F&W, SL , WDI

Ngatarawa Glazebrook New Zealand Chardonnay 2007, Hawke's Bay White
Balanced, elegant and stylish. Creamy exotic fruit with soft, toasty supporting oak.

Oyster Bay Marlborough Sauvignon Blanc 2009, Marlborough White
Steely flinty, mineral nose. Intense lychee and guava palate with good concentration and acidity.
£8.99 Widely Available

Ra Nui Marlborough Wairau Valley Sauvignon Blanc 2009, Marlborough White
Ripe, aromatic nose of lime and mango. Good fruit attack with rich mid-palate and a lovely transition to a long finish.
£9.99

Saint Clair Family Estate Pioneer Block 1 Sauvignon Blanc 2009, Marlborough White
Smoky notes and tropical fruit on the nose. Full, ripe, tropical fruit palate with a touch of green pepper. A touch of sweetness.
£15.99 HLD

Saint Clair Family Estate Pioneer Block 3 Sauvignon Blanc 2009, Marlborough White
Smoky, grassy, pea pod mineral palate with gooseberry, lime and a slightly sweet finish.

Medium length.
£15.99 HLD

Spy Valley Chardonnay 2008, Marlborough White
Ripe lemon cream on the nose. Full, juicy and ripe on the palate. Lively acidity and well-balanced fruit character.

The New Zealand Wine Company Mobius Sauvignon Blanc 2009, Marlborough White
Tinned peas on the nose with a hint of tropicality. Good complexity of flavours with ripe melon and tropical citrus on the palate. Long and lingering with fresh acidity on the finish.
£8.99

Tiki Single Vineyard 2009, Marlborough White
Melon aromas with soft floral accents. Round and ripe on the palate with lime-flower, ripe lemon, hints of herbaceousness and lush melon. Well-structured.

Tohu Sauvignon Blanc 2009, Marlborough White
Candied ginger aromas with intensely ripe fruit on the nose. Ginger again on the palate with lashings of ripe melon and attractive citrus. Long and lingering on the finish.

Tupari Sauvignon Blanc 2009, Marlborough White
Interesting aromas with floral accents. Quite tropical with pineapple and citrus flavours. Good fruit character with vibrant intensity. Long with lingering freshness.
£14.99 ODD

Vavasour Awatere Valley Sauvignon Blanc 2009, Marlborough White
Floral and pungent. Very ripe fruit

with a strong mineral backbone. Lush melon and ripe citrus are perfectly balanced on the palate with a long and lingering finish.
£9.99 BWJ, COE, EVW, HAR, LFW

Vavasour Dashwood Marlborough Sauvignon Blanc 2009, Marlborough White
Grassy green nose with a rounded palate of rich and tropical fruit. Firm and citrus and crunchy gooseberries with a nicely rounded finish. Excellent.
£7.99 ODD

Vavasour Redwood Pass Marlborough Sauvignon Blanc 2009, Marlborough White
Pungent aromas. Very crisp and clean on the nose. The palate is laden with gooseberry and ripe citrus fruit. A touch of lychee on the finish.
£7.99 BWJ, COE, EVW, HAR, LFW

Wairau River Pinot Gris 2009, Marlborough White
Firm, sappy, vibrant nose. Intense apricot fruit. Off-dry. Fresh and balanced.
£12.95 DVY, EOR, WHD

Wither Hills Chardonnay 2008, Marlborough White
Loads of cream vanilla oak with a touch of goats cheese and butter. Delicate with ripe citrus flavours. Long and lengthy finish.
£8.99 BWL, MWW, WAIT

Akarua Cadence Pinot Noir 2007, Central Otago Red
Lots of fresh, cherry pepper with quite a lot of oak. Palate of fresh, crunchy fruit. Mouthfilling and savoury.
£19.80 OWL

Ant Moore Wineworks Pinot Noir 2008, Central Otago Red
Fresh, ripe plum and cherry fruit

with quite an overlay of oak to nose. Fresh, sweet, cherry palate with a touch of spice. A marked acidity with oak enriched texture.
£8.99 PBA

Ata Rangi Crimson Pinot Noir 2009, Martinborough Red
Very young tight, briary aromas. Lots of rich, sweet, concentrated fruit. Long with complex fruit and retired tannins.
£15.00 F&M, FAW, HIG, LIB, NYW

Bald Hills Central Otago Single Vineyard Pinot Noir 2008, Central Otago Red
Herbaceous blueberry fruit with a clean fresh palate with notes of plum and aromatic violets. Good length lingers with red fruit and spice.

Bald Hills Three Acres Pinot Noir 2008, Central Otago Red
Red fruit aromas with a touch of creamy vanilla. Fresh raspberry and blueberry fruit with a touch of cinnamon smoke. Good length.

Carrick Pinot Noir 2007, Central Otago Red
Earthy truffle, gamey and floral nose. Rich and slightly gamey with sweet plum fruit, oak smoothed texture. Quite a lot of oak and some gentle tannin.
£19.95 CAM, FNW, GWW

CJ Pask Winery Declaration Syrah 2007, Hawke's Bay Red
Blackberry on the nose. Improves and opens with aeration, becoming more floral. Superb balance, refined.

Coopers Creek Select Vineyards Hawkes Bay Syrah Chalk Ridge 2008, Hawke's Bay Red
Fresh, nice red fruit character

with a hint of pepper and a firm finish.

Craggy Range Merlot Gimblett Gravels Vineyard Hawkes Bay 2007, Hawke's Bay Red

Quite extracted oaky style but they have done it well. Big chocolate and coffee, long berry and blackcurrant.
£12.99 OCO, WAIT

Craggy Range Merlot Gimblett Gravels Vineyard Hawkes Bay 2008, Hawke's Bay Red

Rather obvious oak, nice earthy, leafy style, not too intense. Berries and spice.
£12.99 OCO, WAIT

Crossroads Talisman 2008, Hawke's Bay Red

Round, slightly vegetal aroma. Dry, raspberry, zingy fresh. Creamy fruit underneath.
£19.99 MZC

Delta Hatter's Hill Pinot Noir 2008, Marlborough Red

Good deep colour. Strawberry fruit and some tannin on finish.
£19.99 EVW, LIB, LKB, VLW

Elephant Hill Estate Reserve Syrah 2008, Hawke's Bay Red

Gaminess falls exactly where it should on the palate to finish nicely with sweet fruit.

Esk Valley Reserve Merlot Malbec Cabernet Sauvignon 2006, Hawke's Bay Red

Mature, mellow, spicy aroma. Dry, full bodied, nice acid. Clean fresh, nice liquorice.
£16.99

Esk Valley Syrah 2007, Hawke's Bay Red

Pepper hints and blackberry on the nose. Northern Rhône style, quite lean, but lovely structure. Pepper and fig, nice balance and decent length.
£11.99

Folding Hill Pinot Noir 2008, Central Otago Red

Ripe, aromatic nose with strawberries and cherries with a touch of spice, savoury with mineral notes. Silky texture. Well-integrated oak. Long.
£17.50 RSV

Forrest Newton Forrest Cornerstone 2007, Hawke's Bay Red

Good depth of colour. Ripe plum cocoa nose - harmonious. Sweet, soft, long, succulent, ripe, juicy fruits and a good lift on finish.
£17.50 ADN

Kingsmill Tippet's Dam Pinot Noir 2007, Central Otago Red

Lifted, floral, orange-blossom nose with spice. Sweet, spicy, sandalwood favours on the palate with rich plum and cherry fruit. A substantial length. Plenty of oak but well-integrated and complex.

Man O'War Vineyards Ironclad 2008, Waiheke Island Red

Sweet coffee, smooth texture. Concentrated black peppery fresh fruit. Long sweet liquorice finish.
£24.00 SFW

Matariki Aspire Merlot Cabernet 2007, Hawke's Bay Red

Pronounced ripe nose with some minerality. Juicy fruit on palate. Fresh and slightly savoury on finish. Elegant.

Matariki Pinot Noir 2007, Hawke's Bay Red

Restrained, elegant and lovely. Full bodied with plenty of ripe,

well-balanced fruit. Long and
fresh on the finish.

**Mission Estate Pinot Noir
2007, Central Otago** Red
Elegantly perfumed, cherry nose.
Delicate. Fragrant red fruits
with a touch of orange and
spice. Shows its oak but good
backbone and structure.
£10.99 C&C, WAIT

**Mission Estate Syrah 2009,
Hawke's Bay** Red
Pure elegant fruit and white
pepper. Good palate, plum,
cherry and black pepper finish.
£10.99 C&C

**Mt Aspiring 36 Bottles 2008,
Central Otago** Red
Lots of toasty oak giving
spiciness to the nose overlaying
ripe red fruit. Oaky, full and
ripe palate but maintains its
freshness. Showy.

**Mt Difficulty Pinot Noir 2008,
Central Otago** Red
Aromatic, violet notes with spice
and red fruit on the nose. Plummy
fruit with a long, elegant finish.
£21.99 WAIT

**Mt Difficulty Roaring Meg
Pinot Noir 2008, Central
Otago** Red
Aromatic nose - fresh, sweet
cherry fruit, quite a lot of oak
but finely balanced acidity. Hint
of tannin.
£13.99 MWW

**Nautilus Marlborough Pinot
Noir 2008, Marlborough** Red
Lifted mushroom aroma
combined with red fruit. Grainy
tannins, concentrated fruit and a
persistent finish. Exquisite!
£15.08 EVW, NYW, SL

**Ngatarawa Alwyn Winemakers
Reserve Merlot Cabernet 2008,**

Hawke's Bay Red
Cool, fragrant aromas with a
note of caramel. Creamy, fresh,
good middle palate. Certainly
builds in intensity.

**Oyster Bay Marlborough
Pinot Noir 2008, Marlborough**
Red
Elegant cherry brandy, creamy.
Consumer friendly wine packed
with ripe red fruit. Lingering
aftertaste. A classy wine.
£9.99 Widely Available

**Paritua 21.12 2007, Hawke's
Bay** Red
Muted cassis nose. Nicely
concentrated cassis flavours.
Well-balanced; fresh, very
nice long length tinged with
wood.
£32.50 CHH

**Passage Rock Reserve
Cabernet Sauvignon Merlot
2008, Waiheke Island** Red
Opaque, milky aroma. Elegant
and restrained on palate. Lightly
fruited. Long, mineral, earthy
finish.

**Peregrine Pinot Noir 2008,
Central Otago** Red
Strong black cherry aromas on
nose. Palate is rich yet fresh.
Elegant with good length.
£18.00 BB&R, CHH, NZH, ODD

**Quartz Reef Pinot Noir 2008,
Central Otago** Red
Mouthfilling, red and black
cherry flavours, some plummy
fruit, medium length with a long,
smoky finish.
£17.00 ENO, MWW

**Sacred Hill Hawkes Bay Syrah
2008, Hawke's Bay** Red
Butterscotch and toffee nose,
sweet ripe fruit with spicy toffee
finish.
£8.99 SAIN

Saint Clair Family Estate Pioneer Block 16 Awatere Pinot Noir 2008, Marlborough Red
Dark cherries. Crisp and juicy. Quite elegant with light tannin and long finish.
£17.99 HLD

Tarras Vineyards Pinot Noir 2008, Central Otago Red
Intense red berry aromas - summer pudding. Cherry and raspberries - still young with marked acidity. Just a touch of tannins but balanced.
£20.00 SPV

Te Kairanga Runholder Pinot Noir 2007, Martinborough Red
Ripe, red berry fruits with leathery notes. Good ripeness with a savoury character. Well-integrated tannin structure and fresh acidity. Good length with complexity.

Vavasour Awatere Valley Pinot Noir 2008, Marlborough Red
Good cherry colour. Fresh nose. Acidity and tannic here with balance. Will improve.
£10.99 BWJ, COE, EVW, HAR, LFW

Villa Maria Single Vineyard Taylor Pass Pinot Noir 2007, Marlborough Red
Attractive strawberry, soft, delicate and well-integrated. Good length, very soft and primary.
£19.99

Waipara Springs Pinot Noir 2009, Canterbury Red
Touch of bright, cherry fruit, lovely fruit sweetness. Tight, focused, lovely fruit - long and elegant. Finishes with delightful precision.

Whitehaven Marlborough Pinot Noir 2008, Marlborough Red
Mild strawberry and red berries

fruits. Nice balance. Clean fresh and simple.
£13.95 Widely Available

Wild Rock Cupids Arrow Central Otago Pinot Noir 2008, Central Otago Red
Redcurrants and cranberries with lots of liquorice and violets. Refreshing acidity, light tannins. Balanced and quite persistent.
£12.99 AMP, BCR, GWI, NZH, POG, WAIT

Wild Rock Gravel Pit Red Hawkes Bay Merlot Malbec 2008, Hawke's Bay Red
Cedar and red fruit to nose. Ripe, fresh fruit intensity. Oodles of gravelly tannins. Persistent full length.
£9.99 WAIT

Wither Hills Asda New Zealand Pinot Noir 2008, Marlborough Red
Pale colour, mute earthy aroma. Vibrant raspberry fruit - well-balanced. Elegant lingering finish.
£9.99 ASDA

Bluff Hill Brut NV, Hawke's Bay Sparkling
Crisp apple and citrus lemon nose. Very fine definition. Tensile, nicely poised and very Champagnoise!
£8.99 M&S

Hunter's Mirumiru NV, Marlborough Sparkling
Pale lemon. Very frothy! Toast and digestive biscuits, redcurrant and golden apple. Juicy palate, creamy texture, really long. Tropical and peachy.
£12.95 Widely Available

Johanneshof Cellars Noble Late Harvest Riesling 2007, Marlborough Sweet
Dark smoky marmalade and burnt orange notes. Lots of

> **DID YOU KNOW?**
> Last year, the UK imported 1.7 billion bottles of wine, which generated 600,000 tonnes of waste. Reducing this wastage is one of the trade's current top priorities.

sweet, rum, luxurious toffee flavours. Delicious.

Ngatarawa Glazebrook Noble Harvest Riesling 2009, Hawke's Bay Sweet

Fairly subdued aromatics. Nutty, honey, some barley sugar and quince roundness. Quite punchy and sweet with a very nice zesty lift.

Forrest John Forrest Collection Riesling 2006, Marlborough Botrytis

Petrolly, parrafin wax development, sweet, thick and rich. Simple but impressive.
£19.99 ADN

Mazurans Old Tawny Port 1967, West Auckland Fortified

Amber brown. Lifted spirit and toffee nose. Sweet malt and iced coffee. Hints of chocolate wafer and butterscotch on the palate and finish.

Mazurans Royal Reserve Port 1947, West Auckland Fortified

Deep chocolate with a green hue. Lifted mudcake and molasses. Sweet rich chocolate cake and fruit on the palate. Cake hints with a fresh malt finish.

Mazurans Vintage 1977, West Auckland Fortified

Mahogany brown, raisin and treacle on the nose and palate, with coffee chocolate to finish.

Astrolabe Durvillea Marlborough Pinot Grigio 2009, Marlborough White

Concentrated red and green apple flavours with a spicy finish.
£12.95 EOR, RWA, WHD

Astrolabe Voyage Marlborough Pinot Gris 2008, Marlborough White

Fragrant tropical fruit with lime blossom and white flowers. Light and lively with good varietal character. Zingy finish.
£15.99 EOR, RWA, WHD

Astrolabe Voyage Marlborough Sauvignon Blanc 2009, Marlborough White

Grassy, gooseberry nose. Crisp and round on the palate with ripe citrus, green gooseberry and a touch of melon.
£13.99 EOR, HAR, NZH, WHD

Bascand Riesling 2009, Wairarapa White

Toasty and nutty on the nose. Citrusy fruit with a touch of ripe tropicality. Lime and lemon on the finish. Very fresh.

Bellbird Spring The Pruner's Reward 2009, Wairarapa White

Fresh, grapefruit nose. Pungent, grassy, apple fruit on the palate with a tough of pepper. Quite linear.

Brown Family Vineayrds Cape Campbell Marlborough Pinot Gris 2009, Marlborough White

Soft white peach, stone fruit and vibrant zesty character. Ripe and clean with citrus fresh finish.
£10.99 D&D

Brown Family Vineyards Cape Campbell Marlborough Reserve Chardonnay 2008, Marlborough White
Subdued coconut edged bouquet. Youthful citrus note with a touch of apple ripeness. Lush with good complexity.
£12.99 D&D

Coopers Creek Swamp Reserve Chardonnay 2008, Hawke's Bay White
Mineral and pineapple on the nose. Mouthfilling on the palate with creamy, balanced oak and good length.
BWC

Craggy Range Old Renwick Vineyard Sauvignon Blanc 2009, Hawke's Bay White
Delicate grassy notes on the nose. Mineral and grassy-green fruit on the palate. The fruit and acidity are perfectly balanced.
£11.99 OCO, WAIT

Crossroads Hawkes Bay Chardonnay 2008, Hawke's Bay White
Medium lemon colour. Ripe pears on nose. Pear and green apples. Sweet.
£9.99 MZC

Domain Road Riesling 2009, Central Otago White
Honeyed and ripe on the nose with a clean minerally, floral palate. Vibrant and dry on the finish.
GMP, MAN, POR, PWA, SHJ

Edition Wines Freeman's Bay Sauvignon Blanc 2009, Marlborough White
Fresh, peachy nose with a touch of pea-pod flavour. Ripe and crisp on the palate with pineapple and sweet fruit finish.
£5.99

Elephant Hill Estate Elephant Hill Viognier 2009, Hawke's Bay White
Bright with fresh fruit aromas. Honey on the palate, good balance with long juicy length.

Esk Valley Vineyard Selection Marlborough Sauvignon Blanc 2009, Marlborough White
Fragrant with flowers and pea shoots. Fine, spicy palate, sweet fruit and minerals. Long and persistent.
£7.99

Esk Valley Vineyard Selection Pinot Gris 2008, Hawke's Bay White
Fine and delicate with ripe melon undertones. Warming spice, ripe citrus and a touch of bitter melon on the finish.
£8.99

Essenze Pinot Gris 2009, Wairarapa White
Tight and zesty with lifted tropical fruit on the palate, zesty acidity on the finish.

Essenze Sauvignon Blanc 2009, Marlborough White
Guava and intense pungent fruit on the nose. Approachable palate with nice balance of fresh melon and gooseberry. Long, elegant finish.

Framingham Classic Riesling 2009, Marlborough White
A bit of nettle aroma and under-ripe apple. The palate has sweetness with a touch of honey and ripe apple fruit.
£10.99 CAV

Framingham Sauvignon Blanc 2009, Marlborough White
Elderflower, grapefruit, white flowers and gooseberries on the nose. Good acidity. A little bit of mineral on the back palate.

Medium length.
£10.99 CAV

Gibbston Highgate Estate Dreammaker Pinot Gris 2008, Central Otago White
Lychee nose with hints of perfumed citrus. Lively and ripe stone fruit on the palate. Good length.

Glover Family Vineyards Zephyr Sauvignon Blanc 2009, Marlborough White
Grassy nose with a clean floral palate. Long and fresh on the finish with refreshing acidity.
£9.99

Goldridge Estate Pinot Grigio 2008, Matakana White
Fresh with hints of vegetal flavours, slightly smoky with fresh minerality on the finish.

Goldwater Chardonnay Marlborough 2008, Marlborough White
Intense nose of green plums and concentrated pear. Nice wood integration with lean and vibrant fruit on the palate. Fresh finish.
£9.99 HLD

Grove Mill Grand Reserve Sauvignon Blanc 2009, Marlborough White
Tinned asparagus and sweet pea on the nose. Ripe and complex on the palate with confected fruit on the palate. Racy acidity and a lively finish.

Grove Mill High Ground Riesling 2009, Marlborough White
Lime cordial aromas. Pure Riesling character in a very chalky and lean style. Full and elegant.
£11.99

Highfield Estates Tesco Finest* Marlborough Riesling 2008, Marlborough White
Lovely mineral notes, floral accents and citrus fruit. Vibrant stone fruit with great structure. Beautifully balanced.
TESC

Highfield Estates Tesco Finest* Marlborough Sauvignon Blanc 2009, Marlborough White
Pungent, grassy nose. Intensely ripe fruit on the palate with some attractive spice. Crisp on the finish.
TESC

Hunter's Sauvignon Blanc 2009, Marlborough White
Gentle hints of lemon on the nose. Mouth-watering freshness with ripe gooseberry and minerality on the palate. Lingering finish.
£10.95 Widely Available

Invivo Sauvignon Blanc 2009, Marlborough White
Intense and ripe. Spicy, gooseberry nose and palate. Lemony, good length, persistent.
£9.99

Johnson Estate Satellite Sauvignon Blanc 2009, Marlborough White
Fresh yeasty note on the nose. Broad, nutty palate. Rich with good weight and balance.

Kaituna Hiils Sauvignon Blanc 2009, Marlborough White
A fruit forward style. Fresh citrus-tropical aromas with a fleshy palate. Long and lingering on the finish.
£7.99 M&S

Kaituna Hills 40 Knots Sauvignon Blanc 2009, Marlborough White
Intensely aromatic. Ripe and round with hints of tropical

melon and lime. Quite weighty on the palate with a lush finish.
£12.99 M&S

Kaituna Hills Pinot Grigio 2009, Marlborough White
Poached pear nose, toasted fennel and warm spice on the palate. Full and round with lovely pear character. Long, fresh and clean.
£7.99 M&S

Kim Crawford Pinot Gris 2009, Marlborough White
Ripe citrus fine and focussed with fine acidity.
£14.99 LIB, SL , SMP, VLW

Kingsmill Tippet's Race Riesling 2009, Central Otago White
Lean, minerally and clean. Peachy white fruits on the nose. Refreshing and full on the finish.

Lawson's Dry Hills Pinot Gris 2009, Marlborough White
Lightly spicy and tropical aromatics. Fresh and zesty until finish.
£10.99

Mission Estate Reserve Hawkes Bay Sauvignon Blanc 2009, Hawke's Bay White
Smoky and flinty on the nose with hints of green grass flavours on the palate. Long with good minerality and a spicy, warm finish.

Moncellier Marlborough Pinot Gris 2009, Marlborough White
Lemon on the nose with lively ripe fruit on the palate. Well-balanced with good texture and length.
£9.99 DLW, MFW

Moncellier Sauvignon Blanc 2009, Marlborough White
Ripe with a touch of bitter

melon and green pepper flavours. Nicely balanced with a fresh and zippy finish.
£8.99 DLW, MFW

Montana Reserve Sauvignon Blanc 2009, Marlborough White
Pungent lime and mineral nose. Green melon and elegant citrus on the palate. Long and floral on the finish.
£9.28 MRN

Morton Estate Black Label Awatere Sauvignon Blanc 2009, Marlborough White
Aniseed and fennel on the nose. Soft attack, with a mellow flavour and rounded character. Nicely textured with elegant fruit on the finish.
£11.00 Widely Available

Morton Estate Coniglio 2004, Hawke's Bay White
Lovely grapefruit nose showing age and development. Complex finish.
£28.00 Widely Available

Mount Riley Sauvignon Blanc 2009, Marlborough White
Lemony with nice, ripe citrus fruit. Lively fruit and a long refreshing finish.
£8.99 Widely Available

Mud House Marlborough Sauvignon Blanc 2009, Marlborough White
Floral blossom, snow pea, fresh, flinty nose. Zippy palate - tight, mouthwateringly good green hints with lush, mineral, nutty complexity and length.
£10.99 POG, SSU

Mud House South Island Pinot Gris 2009, South Island White
Perfumed nose, pure core of white stone fruit. Very elegant

with an understated finish.
£10.99 POG, SSU

Mud House Waipara Riesling 2009, Wairarapa White
Lifted lime nose. Crisp aromatic and zingy. Tight youthful and vibrant.
£10.99 POG, SSU

Ngatarawa Glazebrook New Zealand Sauvignon Blanc 2009, Marlborough White
Pure, grassy notes on the nose. Dry, fruity and herbaceous flavour. Fresh with good length, a very nice wine.

Ngatarawa Glazebrook Viognier 2008, Hawke's Bay White
Well-balanced fruit and acidity with layers of honey and a grapefruit-peachy finish.

O:tu Single Vineyard 2009, Marlborough White
Clean and crisp, zesty, minerally, slatey notes. Good balance.
£12.99 COL, TPF

O:tu Sauvignon Blanc 2009, Marlborough White
Lime flower and floral nose. Light-bodied with mineral freshness and zingy citrus on the palate.
£9.99 Widely Available

Osawa Prestige Collection Chardonnay 2009, Hawke's Bay White
Creamy lemon curd nose. Clean, refreshing citrus on the palate with a soft butterscotch edge.

Oyster Bay Marlborough Chardonnay 2008, Marlborough White
Ripe citrus with lemon and apple flavours, slightly confected with a fresh finish.
£8.99 Widely Available

Sacred Hill Wild South Marlborough Sauvignon Blanc 2009, Marlborough White
White peach and gooseberry nose with floral overtones. Intense lychee, grapefruit and apple palate with a persistance of flavour and length. Some good mineral, nutty complexity.
£10.50 H&H

Saint Clair Family Estate Omaka Reserve Chardonnay 2008, Marlborough White
Upfront nose. Lots of wood and lime juice on the palate with a touch of nutty pineapple. Broad and suggestive.
£13.99 HLD

Saint Clair Family Estate Pioneer Block 12 Gewürztraminer 2008, Marlborough White
Lovely fresh tropical fruit on the nose. Attractive sweet tropical fruit on the palate.
£14.99 HLD

Saint Clair Family Estate Selection Sauvignon Blanc 2009, Marlborough White
Herbal, grassy, smoky nose. A concentrated, crisp, herbaceous fruit with a little ripe fruit sweetness. Medium length.
£10.99 HLD

Sandihurst Winery Sauvignon Blanc 2008, Marlborough White
Sweet pepper nose and lightly pungent. Ripe tropical fruits with a hint of green undergrowth. Light and refreshing.

Scott Berry Bascand Riesling 2009, Canterbury White
Fresh, lime and green apple with good balance and length.

Sileni Cellar Selection Sauvignon Blanc 2009,

Marlborough White
Melon, stone and a touch of vegetable on the nose. Asparagus on the palate with a soft attack of ripe fruit. Apple and pear with hints of nettle. Lovely and lush.
£7.99 NYW, SOM, VLW, WRK

Sileni The Straits Sauvignon Blanc 2009, Marlborough
White
Scented, mineral, ripe, with a sweet fruit entry and good weight mid-palate. Good balance. Long but soft.
£9.99 NYW, TESC

Southbank Estate Marlborough Sauvignon Blanc 2009, Marlborough White
Tropical fruits on the nose. Some grapefruit zest and well-balanced lime lemon fruit on the palate. Lemon-drop finish.
£7.99 MWW

Sowman Family Estate 2009, Marlborough White
Sweetly confected floral nose with complex mineral and mango notes on the palate. Lovely balance. Long but austere.
£9.49 LAI

Spy Valley Pinot Gris 2009, Marlborough White
Pear and vanilla spice on the nose. Soft attack with fresh apple, melon and ripe citrus freshness on the finish.

Spy Valley Riesling 2009, Marlborough White
Crisp, mineral palate with a touch of smokiness. Palate has fine, sweet fruit and complex intensity. Lush and ripe on the finish.

Spy Valley Sauvignon Blanc 2009, Marlborough White
Clean pineapple nose; soft and sweet; subtle and elegant. Structure with persistence.

Stoneleigh Rapaura Series Sauvignon Blanc 2009, Marlborough White
Smoky notes with lime and lemon fruit on the nose. Melon and peaches on the palate with a soft attack and lingering sweetness on the finish.

Stoneleigh Sauvignon Blanc 2009, Marlborough White
Subtle and elegant with beautiful balance and character. Ripe citrusy fruit on the palate and a lemon-lime finish.
£9.99 WAIT

Teece Family Vineyards Mt Beautiful Cheviot Hills Sauvignon Blanc 2009, North Canterbury White
Smoky, green bean aromas. Concentrated, intense and grassy on the palate with a touch of spice. Good mineral finish.
£8.95 GNS

Terrace Heights Estate T H E 2009, Marlborough White
Classical nose with tropical fruit notes and flinty aromas. Fruity palate with some length.

The New Zealand Wine Company Sainsbury's Taste The Difference Sauvignon Blanc 2009, Marlborough White
Tropical and citrus fruits dominate the palate. Long-lasting ripeness balanced with zippy acidity. Full and fresh.
£7.99 SAIN

The New Zealand Wine Company Sanctuary Sauvignon Blanc 2009, Marlborough White
Citrus ripe nose with mouth-watering acidity and elegant tropical fruit on the palate. Long and refreshing finish full of zesty acidity.
£6.99 SAIN

Tinpot Hut Marlborough Sauvignon Blanc 2009, Marlborough White
Gooseberry and lime on the nose with fresh floral and passionfruit flavours on the palate. Very clean style with ripe melon and citrus fruits on the finish.
£9.99 JCC, LIB, NYW, RSV, SMP, VLW

Tohu 2009, Nelson White
Hints of tinned veggies, green peas and ripe citrus on the palate. Soft and round on the finish.

Toi Toi Marlborough Brookdale Vineyard Reserve Pinot Gris 2009 2009, Marlborough White
Delicate nectarine notes on the nose with soft lemony lift. Ripe and round on the palate with soft citrus freshness.

Toi Toi Marlborough Riesling 2009, Marlborough White
Clean honey minerality, green apples with hints of zippy lime. Clean mineral finish. Good length.

Vavasour Awatere Pass Marlborough Sauvignon Blanc 2009, Marlborough White
Intense aromas, quite tropical. Mouth-watering citrus with grapefruit intensity. Long, lush and lingering on the palate.
THP

Vavasour Awatere Valley Pinot Gris 2009, Marlborough White
Good minerality, with nice textured fruit. Ripe tropicality with peachy freshness. Nicely balanced with lingering acidity.
£9.99 BWJ, COE, EVW, HAR, LFW

Vavasour The Pass Marlborough Sauvignon Blanc 2009, Marlborough White
Pleasant with ripe fruit concentration. Well rounded with good freshness and subtle citrus melon character.

Vidal Marlborough Riesling 2009, Marlborough White
Aromatic with pear, green apple and floral blossoms. Juicy, lively and fresh with an attractive finish.
£7.99

Vidal Marlborough Sauvignon Blanc 2009, Marlborough White
Very ripe on the nose. Sweet fruit, quite spicy and fresh. Easy drinking.
£7.99

Villa Maria Cellar Selection Chardonnay 2008, Marlborough White
Gentle and elegant in style. Herbaceous with lots of ripe fruit on the palate. Tangy on the finish with good complexity and weight.
£10.99

Villa Maria Cellar Selection Sauvignon Blanc 2009, Marlborough White
Asparagus and white flowers on the nose. Intense, spicy green fruit on the palate with crunchy herbaceousness. Balanced acidity. Long and quite elegant.
£10.99 TESC

Villa Maria Private Bin Gewürztraminer 2009, East Coast White
Subtle hint of spice and lychee on the nose and palate. Long finish.
£9.99 SAIN, WAIT

Villa Maria Private Bin Riesling 2009, Marlborough White
Lime juice, aromatic apricot and

lemon blossom on the palate with good acidity and nice length.
£7.99 WAIT

Villa Maria Private Bin Sauvignon Blanc 2009, Marlborough White
Muted nose, spritzy elderflower palate, simple gooseberry fruit; ripe with piercing acidity and a touch of sweetness on the finish.
£8.99 TESC, SAIN

Villa Maria Reserve Wairau Valley Sauvignon Blanc 2009, Marlborough White
Lightly grassy, lemony nose, sweet lemon fruit on the palate, with nicely integrated acidity and grassy, mineral notes on the finish.
£12.99

Villa Maria Single Vineyard Omahu Gravels Viognier 2007, Hawke's Bay White
Lovely clean and fresh fruity nose. Almonds and honey on the palate with a long, well-balanced finish.
£14.99

Vynfields Classic Riesling 2009, Martinborough White
Complex aromas of honey and melon mingle with ripe apple. Racy acidity balanced with sweet fruit. Delicious and firm on the finish.

Waimea Estates Nelson Gewürztraminer 2009, Nelson White
Tropical fruits on the nose and palate. An easy-drinking style.
£10.99 MWW

Waimea Estates Nelson Sauvignon Blanc 2009, Nelson White
Classic nose. Ripe, with clean gooseberry freshness on the palate. Zingy and fresh on the finish.
£8.99 MWW

Waimea Estates Spinyback Nelson Pinot Gris 2009, Nelson White
White peach and perfumed fruit with hints of lemon and lime flower. Lush and round on the palate with balanced finish.
£8.99 CHN

Waimea Estates Spinyback Nelson Sauvignon Blanc 2009, Nelson White
Fresh asparagus nose. Ripe, yet with sharply refreshing acidity. Easy drinking style with lingering freshness.
£7.99 CHN

Waimea Nelson Pinot Gris 2009, Nelson White
Very heady, exotic, lychees and Nivea cream nose. Medium sweet and very scented. Soft and full, lacks a bit of acidity. Slightly hot finish.
£10.99 MWW

Waipara Springs Premo Dry Riesling 2009, Canterbury White
Lightly, gingery, spicy nose. Sweetish. A little disjointed. Decent but abrupt tangy finish.

Waipara Springs Sauvignon Blanc 2009, Canterbury White
Supple and weighty on the nose with vibrant citrus fruits and melon on the palate with a hint of mineral flavour. Fresh and long.

Wairau River Sauvignon Blanc 2009, Marlborough White
Aromatic with a candied fruit nose. The palate is full of mineral character with hints of candied orange and ginger. Lively and delicious.
£12.95 DVY, EOR, NZH, WHD

Whitehaven Mansion House Bay Single Vineyard Marlborough Pinot Grigio 2009, Marlborough White
Ripe citrus and white fruit aromatics. Some apricot, tropical flavour and finish.
£9.95 ENO

Whitehaven Mansion House Bay Single Vineyard Marlborough Sauvignon Blanc 2009, Marlborough White
Clean and elegant with ripe citrus fruit palate. The finish is clean and fresh with lingering sweetness.
£9.95 ENO

Whitehaven Marlborough Sauvignon Blanc 2009, Marlborough White
Pleasant and subtle with a tinge of ripe melon and citrus on the palate. The finish is ripe with a touch of minerality.
£9.95 Widely Available

Wither Hills Asda New Zealand Sauvignon Blanc 2008, Marlborough White
Vibrant, grassy and zesty tropical fruit on the nose. Tropical citrus palate with zingy and supple finish.
£7.99 ASDA

Wither Hills Fairleigh Estate Marlborough Riesling 2009, Marlborough White
Lovely mineral and flinty lemon on the nose. Pure and ripe on the palate with lovely round fruit. Dense and intense on the finish.
£7.99 MWW

Wither Hills Rarangi Sauvignon Blanc 2009, Marlborough White
Fresh elderflower and nettle nose. Zesty citrus peel plate with a touch of ripe apricot fruit. Lively and pleasing.
£9.99 BWL, WSO

Wither Hills Sauvignon Blanc 2009, Marlborough White
Grapefruit nose with lively floral aromas. Crisp citrus, grapefruit and lime on the palate. Pleasingly refreshing with lingering acidity on the finish.
£8.99 BWL, MWW, TESC

Woollaston Nelson Riesling 2009, Nelson White
Very typical. Fresh and ripe on the palate with hints of white stone fruits. Slightly tropical on the finish.

Yealands Estate Co-Operative Pinot Grigio 2009, Marlborough White
Fresh apple and pear fruits, a little hard on the palate.
£7.99 CWS

Yealands Estate Flaxbourne Sauvignon Blanc 2009, Marlborough White
Green fruit nose with crisp acidity and lemon-lime fruit on the palate. Very fresh with a weighty finish.
£7.99 M&S

Yealands Estate Sauvignon Blanc 2008 2008, Marlborough White
Sweet, fresh-cut grass and citrus aromas on the nose. Very green on the palate with a touch of ripe melon and minerality. Lingering finish.
£9.99 LIB, OZW, VLW

Yealands Estate Tawhiri Sauvignon Blanc 2008, Marlborough White
Mineral and green on the nose. Hints of herbaceous flowers and ripe melon on the palate. Ripe crisp and dry on the finish.
£7.99 CWS

Astrolabe Voyage Marlborough Pinot Noir 2008, Marlborough Red
Cherry red with a vibrant nose. Fresh

and fruity, with a lifted finish.
Approachable and easy to drink.
£15.99 EOR, RWA, WHD

Babich Winemaker's Reserve Pinot Noir 2008, Marlborough Red
Light crimson, ruby. Ripe red fruits, berry and tarry flavour concentration. Softness and good length and persistence.

Brookfields Vineyards Cabernet Merlot 2007, Hawke's Bay Red
Opaque. Cassis, clove aroma. Silky mouthfeel - fruity, spicy notes on finish.

Capricorn Lone Range Gimblett Gravels Red 2008, Hawke's Bay Red
Rich, full strawberry aroma. Soft, plum rich palate. Slightly herbal taste. Good length and depth. Nice herby finish.
£9.99 M&S

Delegat's Hawkes Bay Cabernet Merlot 2008, Hawke's Bay Red
Smoky, spicy with red fruit. Tight, firm structure. Fine long tannins.

Delegat's Reserve Hawkes Bay Cabernet Sauvignon Merlot 2007, Hawke's Bay Red
Juicy berry, cherry and plum. Ripe vanilla and cherry. Fairly straightforward.

Delegat's Reserve Hawkes Bay Merlot 2007, Hawke's Bay Red
Good grippy tannins. A bold wine for Merlot with rich plums and a good structure.

Drumsara Central Otago Pinot Noir 2008, Central Otago Red
Light, red fruit aromas with

elegant blueberries flavours, raspberry, coffee and pepper on the finish.
£20.00 LAI

Escarpment Escarpment Pinot Noir 2008, Martinborough Red
Smoky and earthy. A touch vegetal. Nice Pinot. Nice beetroot and veggie fruit on palate. Nice fruit sweetness.
£17.99 WI-AV

Esk Valley Black Label Merlot Cabernet Sauvignon Malbec 2008, Hawke's Bay Red
Tight, ripe, dark berries, earthy and smoky. Ripe and well-balanced fruit on palate. Has personality. Elegant weight with a savoury finish.
£10.99

Framingham Pinot Noir 2008, Marlborough Red
Good oak integration. Nice strawberries concentrated. A good balance.
£12.99 CAV

Giesen The Brothers Marlborough Pinot Noir 2008, Marlborough Red
Medium ruby. With wild strawberries, good intense fruit on nose. Soft attack. Some oak spice and vanilla on palate mid concentration. Long spicy vanilla and red fruit flavour.
WAV

Hinton Estate Pinot Noir 2008, Central Otago Red
Leather, smoke and blackcurrant aromas, chewy and spicy plums with a lingering smoky finish.

Invivo Pinot Noir 2008, Central Otago Red
Show some oak on nose which slightly masks the fruit. Fresh, savoury with slightly herbaceous but attractively crunchy fruit.

Shows its oak and a bit of alcohol on finish.
£19.99

Kim Crawford Rise And Shine Pinot Noir 2007, Central Otago Red
Deep colour. Earthy, spicy nose. A bit minted. Spicy and slightly earthy with just ripe curranty fruit. Good acidity. Gentle tannin. Savoury.
£19.99 LIB, NZH, SL

Kingsmill Tippet's Dam Pinot Noir 2008, Central Otago Red
Leather, spice, raspberries and cassis on the nose. Red fruit with creamy overtones, peppery. Balanced on the palate with a long lingering finish.

Marisco The Ned Marlborough Pinot Noir 2008, Marlborough Red
Good colour. Attractive juicy style. Fairly light and pleasant. Good length.
MWW, WAIT

Matariki Cabernet Sauvignon Merlot 2007, Hawke's Bay Red
Meaty focused cassis flavours. Lifted acidity. Good depth of flavour with pleasantly lingering flavours.

Matariki Quintology 2007, Hawke's Bay Red
Big, soft, ripe, rounded blueberry. Very nicely balanced if a bit light.

Matua Marlborough Pinot Noir 2008, Marlborough Red
Plum, violets and strawberry on the nose. Elegant palate with red fruits, a nice spiciness and toast. Fresh, acid, well-balanced.
£7.99 EVW

Michelle Richardson Pinot Noir 2007, Central Otago Red
Bright and lively sweet black fruits on the nose but a touch of greenness. Sweet, fragrant fruit on the palate.
£23.00

Mission Estate Hawke's Bay Syrah 2008, Hawke's Bay Red
Peppery, spicy, meaty nose. Some clove. Fresh, peppery with nice bright fruit.
£10.99 LBV, MGM

Mission Estate Jewelstone Cabernet Sauvignon 2008, Hawke's Bay Red
Ruby. Smoky, dried, concentrated black fruits - silky texture. Well-balanced acidity. Fruit and fine structured tannins. Smooth finish.
£19.00 LAI

Mission Estate Jewelstone Syrah 2008, Hawke's Bay Red
Ruby colour, chocolate and spice with ripe fruit. Fresh finish with chocolate spice.
£19.00 LAI

Mission Estate Merlot 2009, Hawke's Bay Red
Big, spicy, almost soapy, intense, juicy, good but slightly processed.
£10.99 YOB

Mission Estate Reserve Syrah 2009, Hawke's Bay Red
Deep cherry coloured wine, easy soft red fruit. Ripe cherries and clean dry finish.
£13.99 LBV

Moncellier Central Otago Pinot Noir 2008, Central Otago Red
Fresh cranberry nose with some slightly herbal notes. Fresh, leafy red fruits palate, spicy and light.
£13.99 DLW, MFW

Montana Marks & Spencer Kaituna Hills Reserve Pinot Noir 2008, Wairau Valley Red
Big coffee and cream nose, a

touch too charry in terms of oak. Creamy and big. Acidity jars slightly with tannins but still stylish.
£10.99 M&S

Montana Terraces Marlborough Pinot Noir 2008, Marlborough Red
Medium colour. Raspberry and vanilla aroma. Elegant. Sweet fruit on mid palate. Medium finish. A delicious core.
£13.99

Morton Estate Black Label Syrah 2007, Hawke's Bay Red
Brickish colour with some fruit and a touch of drying spice. Hot finish.
£12.00 Widely Available

Mount Riley Pinot Noir 2009, Marlborough Red
Pale cherry. Raspberry and strawberry fruits. Fresh raspberry and strawberry flavours. Hints of cedar and spice.
£10.99 EUW, PAT

Mud House Central Otago Pinot Noir 2008, Central Otago Red
Sweet ripe, fragrant nose. Very fresh fruit. Silky texture and a good length.
£13.99 POG, SSU

Mud House Hawkes Bay Merlot 2008, Hawke's Bay Red
Very pure, bright, black fruits. Juicy attack, plenty of flavour. Really attractive style, soft tannins. Delicious.
£10.99 POG, SSU

Ngatarawa Alwyn Winemakers Reserve Merlot Cabernet 2007, Hawke's Bay Red
Fragrant nose with mineral complexity. Savoury complex

fruit. Fresh, elegant, simple structure. Stylish. Long savoury finish. Simple.

Ngatarawa Glazebrook New Zealand Merlot Cabernet 2007, Hawke's Bay Red
Intense, liquorice, reserved. Very bright fruit, crunchy and fresh. Refreshing and easy drinking.

Ocean's Edge Pinot Noir 2008, Marlborough Red
Earthy aromas. Redcurrant on the palate. Fine tannins and a good middle. Dry finish.
£9.19 TESC

Oyster Bay Hawkes Bay Merlot 2009, Hawke's Bay Red
Modern, scented, very attractive bright red plum fruit and scent. Fair tannins but gently warm finish. Long finish. Will age.
£8.99 SAIN, MWW, SMF, TESC, WAIT

Peregrine Marks & Spencer Saddleback Pinot Noir 2008, Central Otago Red
Aromatic, perfumey, red fruits nose. Ripe, almost exotic, raspberry fruit. Silky texture. Good concentrative and mineral. Long and nicely developed.
£14.99 M&S

Peregrine Saddleback Pinot Noir 2008, Central Otago Red
Pale colour. Floral and slightly nutty - gamey, savoury nose. Sweet but delicate on the plate with a hint of gameiness, spicy elegant fruit. Soft tannins. Fresh but just a touch alcoholic.
£15.00 M&S

Richardson Michelle Richardson 2008, Central Otago Red
Green limes with juicy citrus aromas. Full of lime juice flavours

and a touch of vanilla nuttiness. Easy to drink.
£23.00

Rockburn Pinot Noir 2008, Central Otago Red
The nose shows a lot of oak but some sweet fruit. Quite oaky on the palate but ripe, sweet fruit. Good acidity.
NOV

Saint Clair Family Estate Marlborough Pinot Noir 2008, Marlborough Red
Veg, spicy, fruit and forest fresh. Attractive fruit with a slight tannic grip. Fair length.
£10.99 HLD

Saint Clair Family Estate Merlot 2008, Marlborough Red
Fruity cherry nose. Lovely cherry fruit style with a moderate length.
£10.99 HLD

Saint Clair Family Estate Pioneer Block 14 Doctors Creek Pinot Noir 2008, Marlborough Red
Rich red berry fruits, plum, meaty savoury notes. Moderate tannin but rich and flavoursome palate and length.
£17.99 HLD

Saint Clair Family Estate Pioneer Block 4 Sawcut Pinot Noir 2008, Marlborough Red
Some strawberry jamminess on nose. Good concentration. Light and savoury.
£17.99 HLD

Sileni Cellar Selection Syrah 2008, Hawke's Bay Red
Bright ruby wine with dusty floral fruity nose. Juicy ripe red fruit. Easy approachable finish.
£8.99

Sileni Estate Selection The Triangle Merlot 2008,

Hawke's Bay Red
Ripe fruit with a luscious texture. Fine tannins and moderate acidity. Some oak spice interest. Long.
£10.99 BOQ

Stoneleigh Pinot Noir 2008, Marlborough Red
Sweet aroma of earth and redcurrants. Exquisite balance of fine grained tannins, lifted acidity. Concentrated red fruits and fine lingering finish.
£10.99 WAIT

Stoneleigh Rapaura Series Pinot Noir 2008, Marlborough Red
Opulent aroma, lacing of raspberry, vanilla and minerality on mid palate. Long finish.

Tarras The Steppes Pinot Noir 2008, Central Otago Red
Redcurrants and rose petals to nose. Crunchy red fruits with a savoury mineral character. Pure but a little young.
£25.00 SPV

Te Kairanga Pinot Noir 2008, Martinborough Red
Ripe cherries and liquorice, toast on the nose and cranberries. Some boldness on palate - soft tannin.

The Aurora Vineyard The Legacy Syrah 2008, Central Otago Red
Very fresh and bright on the palate with nice juicy, meaty fruit and a hint of olive. Nice finish.

The Aurora Vineyard The Partners Pinot 2008, Central Otago Red
Vibrant cherry nose; warm, soft, peppery, red fruit with hints of tobacco and juniper. Creamy finish.

Tohu Pinot Noir 2008, Marlborough Red
Nice raspberry nose. Restrained soft light attack. Fresh, light, balanced. Clean with an oak spice finish.

Vidal Hawkes Bay Pinot Noir 2008, Hawke's Bay Red
Clean fruit on the nose. Palate is ripe with layers of ripe cassis. Fresh and fruit forward. Very pleasing.
£10.99

Villa Maria Cellar Selection Hawkes Bay Syrah 2008, Hawke's Bay Red
Sublime blackberry, cranberry and loganberry nose. Very Côte Rôtie style. Savoury palate, faultless balance and long finish. Heavenly.
£12.99

Villa Maria Cellar Selection Pinot Noir 2008, Marlborough Red
Lifted cherry and earth aromas with damson on the nose. Firm balance of fruit and gentle tannins. Long finish.
£12.99

Villa Maria Private Bin Pinot Noir 2008, Marlborough Red
Earthy, red fruit aroma. Medium bodied tannins still have some grip. Persistent fruit character and a good finish.
£9.99 TESC, SAIN

Villa Maria Reserve Hawkes Bay Merlot 2008, Hawke's Bay Red
Bright bramble fruit on nose. Sweet, red and black fruit, fresh and ripe. Structured tannins and good length.
£16.99

Villa Maria Reserve Pinot Noir 2007, Marlborough Red
Strawberries, raspberries and beetroot notes. Fleshy palate with attractive balance and length.
£16.99 TESC

Vynfields Pinot Noir 2008, Martinborough Red
Pleasantly mineral, juicy cherry and some herbal lift. Lovely juicy sweetness of the fruit. Long and very focused.
£10.99 WAIT

Wairau River Home Block Pinot Noir 2008, Marlborough Red
Some mild strawberry - restrained, soft, light attack. Fresh and clean. Easy to drink.
£14.99 EOR, NZH, WHD

Walnut Block Collectables Sauvignon Blanc 2009, Marlborough Red
Crisp citrus on the nose. Well-balanced fruit with round citrus and ripe tropical fruit. Lengthy with a fresh, round finish.

Wild Earth Central Otago Pinot Noir 2008, Central Otago Red
Delicate, floral red fruit fragrance. Red fruit concentration on the palate with spicy sandalwood notes and a touch of bitterness. Slightly hot and tannic finish.
£19.99 FAW, LIB, M&S, NYW, SMP, VOA

Wither Hills Fairleigh Estate Marlborough Pinot Noir 2008, Marlborough Red
Berry and grassy aromas. Fine balance of fruit, grainy tannins, acidity and concentration in a light wine. Long finish.
£9.99 MWW

Wooing Tree Pinot Noir 2008, Central Otago Red
Sweet raspberry, attractive oak and vanilla flavours, grippy

tannins, broad and long finish.
£23.00 Widely Available

**Woollaston Nelson Pinot
Noir 2008, Nelson** Red
Good raspberry fruit aromas.
Raspberry and cream on the
palate with serious intensity.
Good balance of fruit and
tannins. Long.

**Woollaston Wingspan Nelson
Pinot Noir 2008, Nelson** Red
Light colour with nice aroma.
Palate expresses good Pinot Noir
fruit with flint and damson spice.
Good tannins and length.

**Yealands Estate Pete's Shed
Pinot Noir 2009, Marlborough**
Red
Pretty floral and fresh with
raspberry nose. Simple fruit.
Clean fresh acidity.
£9.99 LIB

**Bascand Estate Rosé 2009,
Wairarapa** Rosé
Floral nose. Light spritz. Refreshing.
Floral fruity palate.

**Domain Road Pinot Noir Rosé
2009, Central Otago** Rosé
Blackcurrant leaf on the nose.
Soft strawberry palate with a hint
of cream. Clean and crisp with
pronounced berry fruit character.
GMP, MAN, POR, PWA, SHJ

**Saint Clair Family Estate
Pinot Noir Rosé 2008,
Marlborough** Rosé
Meaty, salami nose. Red berry
fruit on the palate with a ripe
and slightly dried fruit flavour
on the palate. Textured and well-
balanced.
£9.99 HLD

**Deutz Marlborough Cuvée Brut
NV, Marlborough** Sparkling
Gently toasty. Lots of herbs
and nettle. Very fresh, not huge

complexity and slightly brittle
texture.

**Lindauer Special Reserve
Brut Cuvée NV, Hawke's Bay**
Sparkling
Hint of spice on finish. Very pale
pink. Crunchy red fruits and
pretty yeast overlay. Delicate
fruit, good freshness, creamy
texture and mousse. Long.
£10.99 WAIT

**Morton Estate Black Label
Methode 2002, Hawke's Bay**
Sparkling
Biscuity, toasty, nice creamy
fruits - lemony with plenty of
good acidity.
£13.00 Widely Available

**Morton Estate Blanc De
Blancs 2000, Marlborough**
Sparkling
Pale lemon, yeasty, biscuity,
green apple and pear, creamy
mousse. Lovely acidity, good
length. Sparky!
£12.00 Widely Available

**Morton Estate NV Brut
Methode NV, Hawke's Bay**
Sparkling
Aperitif style. Very appley with
toasty overlay. Creamy texture,
lively and fresh. Lovely brisk
finish.
£9.50 Widely Available

**No 1 Family Estate Cuvée No
1 NV, Marlborough** Sparkling
Understated, brioche nose. Nice
definition. Touch of sulphur
saddling the lift. Soft and creamy,
very approachable but needs
more tension up front.
£19.49 H2F

**Montana Chardonnay Pinot
Noir Rosé NV, Marlborough**
Sparkling Rosé
Pale pink, vivid, delightful colour.
Sweetish nose, soft red fruits.

Pure, juicy fruit. Really gorgeous fizz. Well-balanced. Good.
£9.99 WAIT

Haythornthwaite Gewürztraminer Susan 2009, Wellington Sweet
Luscious and grapey aromas. Fresh citrus with a touch of lychee on the palate. Very pure and very refreshing.

Oyster Bay Marlborough Botrytised Riesling 2004, Marlborough Sweet
Brilliant amber colour with lifted orange marmalade character, slightly fades on the finish but with great length.

Mazurans Cream Sherry NV, West Auckland Fortified
Light amber brown. Fresh acidity, citrusy flavours, orange peel and marmalade.

Mazurans Vintage 1987, West Auckland Fortified
Dark amber brown. Malt and soy, lifted lemon candy. Spiced oranges and figs on the palate with a hint of pepper. Raisins to finish.

Portugal

The buzz around Portuguese wines is getting louder and louder. Long known for its fortified reds, now innovative producers are increasingly focussing on table wines made from native grapes such as the violet-scented Touriga Nacional. From the baked slopes of the Douro to the cooler climes of Vinho Verde, Portugal has variety to ensnare the most seasoned wine aficionado. Special mention should be made of Madeira this year too. Earlier this year, landslides devastated much of the island – although much of the vineyards were spared, infrastructure was seriously damaged. Madeira wine is hugely undervalued in today's marketplace, so what better excuse is there than supporting a community in need whilst rediscovering some of the world's most exciting wine styles?

2010 IWC PERFORMANCE

Trophies	11
Gold	35
Silver	145
Bronze	198
Great Value Awards	1

KEY FACTS

Total production
7.3m hectolitres

Total vineyard
239,951ha

Top 10 grapes

Whites:
1 Fernão Pires
2 Arinto
3 Alvarinho
4 Loureiro
5 Encruzado

Reds:
1 Touriga Nacional
2 Castelão
3 Trincadeira
4 Aragonês
5 Baga

Top regions
1 Trás-os-Montes (includes Douro and Porto)
2 Beiras (includes Dão, Bairrada, Beira Interior)
3 Minho (includes Vinho Verde)
4 Estremadura
5 Alentejo
6 Ribatejo
7 T Sado (includes Palmela, Setúbal and Moscatel)
8 Algarve

Producers
7,000

Casa Ermelinde Freitas Dona Ermelinde 2009, Setúbal
White

Lime accented minerality on the nose with hints of pineapple and coconut. Very good balance of the ripe, elegant fruit and the citrus freshness. Complex palate, very weighty with overtones of mineral, pear and lime flower. Long and delicate on the finish.

Casa Santos Lima Varas 2009, Lisboa White

Citrus, melon and spice on the nose with similar ripeness on the plate. Fresh with lively acidity, very well-balanced with delicate floral overtones. Ripe and lush on the finish with warming spice.

 PORTUGUESE WHITE TROPHY

Terras De Alter Reserva 2009, Alentejo White

Sweet floral perfume, passionfruit flowers, apricot and peachy flavours on the palate. Aromatic with good varietal character, balanced with mineral and citrusy finish. Long and complex.
DFW

 DÃO TROPHY

Antonio Batista Quinta Do Corujao Reserva 2007, Dão
Red

Ripe, dry and earthy on the palate with richly flavoured chocolate notes. Firm tannins with great freshness on the finish. Lengthy and lingering.
£9.99 ICE

 ALENTEJO TROPHY

Antonio Lobo Silveira E Outro Solar Dos Lobos Grande Escolha 2007, Alentejo Red

Deep colour. A lot of chocolate and slightly dusty oak on nose. Very ripe, extracted black fruit palate with tannin and acidity. A big wine, high alcohol - muscular.
£20.99 ICE

Casca Monte Cascas Reserva Alentejo 2008, Alentejo Red

Big powerful nose of blackberry fruit. Lovely intensity on the palate. Some spice. Excellent texture and structure. Great finish.

Domingos Alves De Sousa Vale Da Raposa Touriga National 2007, Douro Red

Ripe and round on the nose with notes of plum and bramble. On the palate, tight damson fruit with layers of cherry and ripe blackcurrant. Delicious smoky character with a grippy texture. Long and lingering on the finish.
£25.00 ATC, TOP

Esporão Private Selection Red 2007, Alentejo Red

Good berry fruit aromas with hints of cedar oak. Youthful ripeness on the palate with complex richness and hints of creamy vanilla. Nice balance and structure.

 PORTUGUESE RED TROPHY, DOURO TROPHY

Luis João De Noronha Pizarro De Castro Quinta De Lubazim 2007, Douro Red

Complex, earthy fruits on the nose. Nicely balanced, supple, juicy palate. Complex, tasty style. Long and savoury to finish.

Manuel Joaquim Pinto Quinta Vila Maior 2007, Douro Red

The mix of black cherry and bramble gives liveliness. Lovely mix of flavours on the palate. Peppery with underlying sweetness. Powerful yet elegant.

Maria Adelaide Melo E Trigo Quinta Do Couquinho Grande Reserva Tinto 2007, Douro Red

Inky, opulent aromas of sweet cherry, cinnamon, coffee, this wine explodes on the palate with notes of liquorice, ripe blackberry and leather. Silky tannins and a long finish.

Quatro Ancoras Vale D'Algares D 2007, Ribatejo Red

Lovely fruit and depth on nose, bilberries. Rich, stylish, good spicy fruit. Long length.

Quatro Ancoras Vale D'Algares Selection Red 2008, Ribatejo Red

Deep, spicy warm red fruit and tobacco. Jammy on the nose, perfectly balanced tannins, fascinating notes of minerality.

Quinta Da Rosa Waitrose Quinta De La Rosa Douro Valley Reserva 2008, Douro Red

Aromatic and floral, with rich, ripe berry fruits, firm tannins and a crunchy berry fruit finish.
£9.99 WWD, WWW, WAIT

Quinta Do Crasto Douro Red 2008, Douro Red

Attractive red berry fruit with some brambly tones. Delicious bright fruit on the palate with some coconut in the background. Full bodied and rich.
£9.99 EHB, MAJ, WSO

 **PORTUGUESE SHIRAZ TROPHY**

Rui Reguinga Tributo 2008, Ribatejo Red

Black purple. Very spicy leathery nose. Slightly reduced juicy and jammy. Very rich. Good classic style.

Sogrape Callabriga Douro 2007, Douro Red

Rich nose with black fruits. Lush, structured and with a bit of muscle. Mix of flavours.
£8.99

Sogrape Quinta dos Carvalhais Alfrocheiro 2003, Dão Red

Fresh wooded aromas with warmth and a touch of fruitcake on the nose. Vivid and ripe on the palate with great length and depth of flavour.

Unicer Mazouco Reserva 2007, Douro Red

Lovely, sweet and oaky notes. Well-balanced, smooth and elegant. Lush, ripe blackberry. Good structure and integration.

 **INTERNATIONAL FORTIFIED MUSCAT TROPHY**

Bacalhôa Moscatel De Setúbal 1999, Península De Setúbal Fortified

Sultanas, nuts and crushed aromatic seeds. Green plums, ginger and cedar palate. Persistent and flavoursome. Fresh and lifted acidity.
JSM, MWW, WAIT

Bacalhôa Moscatel Roxo 1999, Península De Setúbal Fortified

Dusty on the nose, lots of

character - moss, nuts - really interesting. Palate also full of character, slightly sweet. Great with cheese. Quite special.
JSM, MWW, WAIT

 WHITE PORT TROPHY

C. Da Silva Dalva Porto Golden White 1963, Douro Fortified
Rich and supple with great depth. Sumptuous and big with rich honeycomb. Fantastic length. Fabulous.

 RESERVE PORT TROPHY

 GREAT VALUE FORTIFIED WINE UNDER £10

Fonseca Bin 27 NV, Duoro Fortified
Sweet nose - lavender and violets. Chocolate minty middle with black cherries. Smooth and juicy.
£9.99 WI-AV, MRN

Henriques & Henriques 10 Year Old Malmsey NV, Madeira Fortified
Mahogany brown. Fig and wood polish nose. Intense raisin. Concentrated and long.
£13.99 WSO

Henriques & Henriques Single Harvest 1998, Madeira Fortified
Amber brown. Lifted cloves and

hessian. Sweet with some fruit, nuts and ginger. A concentrated spicy finish.
£16.99 WAIT

Justino's Boal 1978, Madeira Fortified
Awesome, complex, nutty flavours. Dry on the finish. Really delicious.

Quinta Do Noval Colheita 1995, Douro Fortified
Ruddy amber. Soft apricot with candied citrus peel notes. Rich, intense, full, concentrated spice and dried fig and apricot. Persistent length.
TAN

 LBV PORT TROPHY, OVERALL PORT TROPHY

Sogrape Regimental Late Bottled Vintage NV, Douro Fortified
Plummy nose with nutmeg and marzipan undertones. Very rich and sweet with grippy tannins and a tight structure.
BOO

Sogrape Sandeman 10 Year Old Tawny NV, Douro Fortified
Very fruity nose, plums with good intensity, delicate, peppery tanginess, plums, raisins, dried fruit, very well-balanced.
£14.99 MCT

 TAWNY PORT TROPHY

Sogrape Sandeman 40 Year Old Tawny NV, Douro Fortified
Ruby amber with green inflection. Very spicy, clove, cinnamon and dates on nose. Very rich, full, complex -

marmalade, fig, dates and quince on finish.
£50.00 MCT

MADEIRA TROPHY

Symington Family Estates Blandy's Malmsey 1985, Madeira Fortified
Varnish, chemical notes. Very rich aromas - complex, exotic. Orange peel and lime. Beautiful bitter, long finish.

Symington Family Estates Blandy's Terrantez Vintage 1976, Madeira Fortified
Very intense and powerful nose. Varnish, butterscotch with clove hints. Marmalade and roasted coffee beans. Dried figs, dates and cinnamon on the palate with a great length.

Symington Family Estates Smith Woodhouse Late Bottled Vintage 1999, Douro Fortified
Complex nose of cherry, eucalyptus, choc mint and violets. Rich palate with a long juicy finish and good balance.

Taylor's Marks & Spencer Vintage Port 1994, Douro Fortified
Lifted liquorice and lavender, sweet plums and brandy sauce with hints of cola and peppercorn.
£24.99 M&S

Vallegre Late Bottled Vintage Unfiltered 2004, Porto Fortified
Lifted fruit concentrate. Fresh mulberry and chocolate with hints of lavender. Chalky tannins.

Adega Cooperativa De Borba Montes Claros Reserva 2008, Alentejo White
Mineral with petrol-like development on the nose. Weighty ripe fruit and citrus fresh on the finish.

Adega Cooperativa De Redondo Anta Da Serra Branco 2009, Alentejo White
Highly floral on the nose. Peaches and apricots with a lemony finish. Fresh, lively preserved lemon flavour.

Anselmo Mendes Muros Antigos Alvarinho 2009, Vinho Verde White
Pale straw colour, smoky, mineral aromas, an oily mouthfeel. Some citrus fruit flavours; acidity supports fruit weight.

Casa Agrícola Das Mimosas Chocapalha Reserva White 2008, Lisboa White
Lifted and youthful fruit on the nose with some nutty character. Lemon fruit with good acidity on the palate. Great mineral balance with firm acidity. Long.
£20.00

Caves Transmontanas Vertice Grande Reserva Branco 2008, Douro White
Oaky, toasty. Good fruit, juicy, textured and well handled oak. Nice and simple. Well made.

Companhia Das Quintas Morgado Santa Catarina 2008, Bucelas White
Fresh, bright, herbal and lemony with a mineral edge. Lively and precise. High acidity.

Encosta Da Murta Myrtus Reserva 2008, Estremadura White
Fresh, lemony, tangy and toasty

with good weight. Smooth and deep with very balanced fruit. Complex and refreshing.

Ermelinde Freitas Casa Ermelinde Freitas 2008, Setúbal White
Melon and peachy aromatics on the nose. Light, crisp and fresh fruit on the palate with deep concentration. Very ripe and supple with long elegant fruit flavours and persistent length.

Esporão Private Selection 2008, Alentejo White
Ripe, savoury, toasty (oak), complex nose, rich dynamic. Lovely fleshy, spice, good fruitiness and length. Complex and ripe finish.
CHN

Esporão Verdelho 2009, Alentejo White
Vibrant with mineral notes on the nose. Flinty and oily with a weighty palate. Fresh and well-structured fruit with good intensity and a balanced finish.
CHN

Henrique Uva / Herdade Da Mingorra Alfaraz Reserva Branco 2008, Alentejo White
Pungent coconut nose. Lovely fruity palate. Very long.

Herdade Da Malhadinha Nova Malhadinha 2008, Alentejo White
Lifted intense tropical fruit - pineapple and guava. Compact texture and broad supporting structure and toast. Excellent. Delicious burgandian feel.
REY

Moncao Muralhas De Moncao 2009, Vinho Verde White
Lemon, lime fruit with herbal notes on the nose. Fresh, mineral character on the palate with ripe tropical fruit. Herbaceous and complex finish.
£8.99 EVW, MAP

Quinta Do Minho Agr. E Turismo, S.a. Quinta Do Minho 2008, Vinho Verde White
Some nutty complexity on the nose with waxy lanolin flavours. Good flavour concentration, balance and intensity with zesty acidity.

Quinta Dos Roques Encruzado 2008, Dão White
Smoky, oaky, savoury nose with some fruit. Crisp on palate. Long and firm with a good finish.
£14.99 Widely Available

Quintas De Melgaço Alvarinho Qm 2009, Vinho Verde White
Nice appley fruit, clean and crisp, quite simple and abrupt on the finish. Well put together.

Adega Cooperativa De Redondo Latitude Tinto 2009, Alentejo Red
Lovely and juicy raspberry character. Perfumed, pure and elegant. Good depth and intensity of fruit with a seductively long finish.

Adega Cooperativa De Redondo Reserva 2008, Alentejo Red
Black cherry with herbaceous notes. Juicy black cherry on the palate with grippy tannins and fresh acidity. Ripe and sweet with a weighty and lengthy finish.

Alexandre Relvas Eira De São Miguel 2008, Alentejo Red
Nicely perfumed and floral with meaty and cherry fruit nose. The palate has supple cherry fruit with a clean finish and hint of juniper.

LOST YOUR BOTTLE?

WHERE CAN I BUY

vini portugal.co.uk

PORTUGUESE WINE

Alexandre Relvas Herdade São Miguel Reserva 2007, Alentejo Red

Blackcurrant fruit with a ripe cherry and meaty, savoury-like aroma. Very ripe with loads of juicy fruit and a touch of leather. Fresh red fruits on the palate with a black pepper finish.

Alianca Quinta dos Quatro Ventos 2007, Douro Red

A complex and rich wine with red cherry and sultana flavours. Crisp, fresh palate with juicy fruits.
£14.49 PBA

Alianca Vista 2008, Beiras Red

Juicy redcurrant fruit with hints of banana and coconut on the nose. The palate is lush with red berry fruit, smooth vanilla and a touch of warm spice. Elegant and ripe on the finish.
£5.99 PBA

Barão De Vilar Zom Douro 2008, Douro Red

Aromatic nose with floral notes. Brilliant, brambly fruit. Well-balanced with tannins to last.

Boas Quintas Quinta Da Fonte Reserva 2008, Dão Red

Intense and vibrant plum. Ripe berry, floral violets, mellow soft attack. Vanilla and raspberry flavours. Well-balanced.

Boas Quintas Quinta Da Fonte Touriga Nacional 2008, Dão Red

Vanilla spice. Soft attack of cooked apple and cinnamon, clove flavour. Slightly dry finish, fresh.

Casa Santos Lima Amoras 2008, Lisboa Red

Attractive, yet discreet aromas. Cherry fruit in the mouth with layers of ripe tannins and spice. Grippy and round on the finish.
£6.99 LAI

Casca Cape Roca Fisherman Red 2009, Tejo Red

Blackcurrant nose with light cherry and berry on the palate. Elegant richness is balanced with lashings of toasty ripeness. Long on the finish. Delicious.

Castro De Pena Alba Picos Do Couto Reserva 2007, Dão Red

Intense violet nose with some orange flower. Elegant, earthy and smooth. Nice concentration and spicy finish.

Caves Transmontanas Vertice Grande Reserva 2007, Douro Red

Bouquet of some fruit but highlighting oak. Lots of extracted fruit.

Celso Pereira Foral Da Vila Red 2008, Douro Red

Leather and red fruit nose. Elegant balance with chocolate overtones on the finish.

Centro Agricola De Tramagal Casal Da Coelheira Reserva 2008, Tejo Red

A panoply of hedgerow fruit, smoky oak dominates. Fruity, chewy tannins follow.

Churchill Graham Churchill Estates Reserva 2007, Northern Red

Powerful black cherry structure. Hints of oak and spice without being over-dominant.
£12.00 SFW

Cortes De Cima Homenagem A Hans Christian Andersen 2008, Alentejo Red

Attractive and well-balanced with lots of ripe, juicy blackberry and raspberry fruit. Nice structure.

Cortes De Cima Petit Verdot 2008, Alentejo Red
Weighty but fresh on the nose with ripe, oaky fruit. On the palate, ripe cherries and black fruits with layers of warming spice.

Cortes De Cima Syrah 2007, Alentejo Red
Sweet and ripe and well balanced with nice plummy cherry fruit and a spicy twist. Quite pure.
£10.99 WAIT

Cortes De Cima Touriga Nacional 2007, Alentejo Red
Deep crimson red. Juicy fruit. Nice length with a good structure.

Domingos Alves De Sousa Quinta Da Gaivosa Vinha De Lordelo 2007, Douro Red
Perfumed nose. Flowery and elegant. Mineral and intensity present. Good personality.
ATC, TOP

Douro Family Estate Premium 2007, Douro Red
Nice roasted coffee aromas, bright fruit with damson and vanilla on the palate. Good concentration and length.

Duorum Colheita 2008, Douro Red
Smoky, floral nose, deep, dense fruit with a hint of chocolate. A serious, interesting wine.
£10.99 OWA, TAN

Enoport Quinta De S. João Batista Syrah 2007, Ribatejo Red
Grapey nose. Blockbuster with excellent balance. Delicious tannins and bountiful fruit liquorice. Intriguing. Will age.

Enoport Quinta De San João Batista Touriga Nacional 2007, Ribatejo Red
Spicy youthful oaky nose.

Intense ripe peppery on the palate. Lovely concentration and length. Very good potential.

Esporão Alicante 2007, Alentejo Red
Ripe, sweet nose. Lots of oak. Dense, cherry. Very young. Ripe tannins, marked acidity.
ATC

Esporão Quatro Castas 2008, Alentejo Red
Floral, violet-like nose. Red peony and sweet briar character. Floral, elegant and perfumed. Well integrated and elegant.

Falua Conde De Vimioso Reserva 2007, Tejo Red
Deep and rich, with red fruit aromas. Good, crunchy fruit with hints of blackcurrant and vanilla jamminess. Full on the palate with good structure and a long finish.
£15.00 OWA

Fracastel Lua Nova Em Vinhas Velhas 2008, Douro Red
Dark red with rich fruit palate and a soft tannin finish. A well-balanced wine.

Gr Consultores Rhea Reserva 2006, Douro Red
Floral and wild berry nose. Juicy ripe berries, spicy. Warming on the finish.

Herdade Dos Grous Herdade Dos Grous 2008, Alentejo Red
Ripe, spicy and quite oaky with a touch of a roasted coffee edge. The fruit is fine but firm.

Herdade Dos Grous Reserve 2007, Alentejo Red
Medium bodied with blackcurrant aromas and fresh herbal character. Ripe and round on the palate with a nutty edge

to the red fruit. Juicy and fresh on the finish.

Ilex Pausa NV, Alentejo Red
Spiced plums on the nose with intense fruit character on the palate. Good concentration of ripe berry, plum and cherry with well-integrated tannins on the finish.
£6.00

Ilex Pausa Reserva NV, Alentejo Red
Cedar and earthy notes on the nose with hints of spicy cassis. Beautifully integrated with very classy fruit on the palate. Almost like Portugal meets Bordeaux with ripe freshness and great complexity.
£9.00

Jean-Hugues Gros Odisseia Reserva 2006, Douro Red
Good cherry fruit on the nose. Forward good fruity nose. Rich, good silky finish. Good length.

José Manuel Cabrita 2008, Algarve Red
Damson ripeness on the nose. Fruit-forward intensity with ripe jammy character on the palate. Rich, lovely and round with fruity taste and good length.

Lemos & Van Zeller Quinta Vale D. Maria Douro 2007, Douro Red
Baked berries on the nose with a touch of oak. Elevated fruit. Good balance and length.
£18.00 C&B, D&F, LAI, TAN, WAIT

Lemos & Van Zeller Rufo 2008, Douro Red
Fresh, aromatic nose with sweet-tasting ripe berry fruit. Tannic, but well-balanced.
£9.50 C&B, D&F, LAI, TAN, WAIT

Manuel Joaquim Pinto Casa Da Palmeira 2007, Douro Red
Smoky black cherry on the nose. Rich mix of flavours on the palate. Lovely complexity with blackberry and some cherry.

Manuel Pinto Hespanhol Zimbro 2006, Douro Red
Developed nose with good cherry fruit. Well-balanced. Good acidity and length.
£8.99 ICE

Margens Antigas Elipse 2007, Douro Red
Deep colour and opulent aromas of red fruit, cherries and vanilla. Tightly knit with well-integrated oak, and good length.

Michael Brian Mollet Herdade Da Maroteira Cem Reis Reserve 2008, Alentejo Red
Very ripe meats and spicy nose, sweet fruited palate. Bold, ripe and meaty.
£16.00

Patrick Agostini Quinta Do Francês Odelouca River Valley 2007, Algarve Red
Juicy notes on the nose. Nicely balanced with good fruit ripeness and oaky richness. Delicious and long on the finish.

Quinta Da Alorna Reserva 2007, Tejo Red
Black cherry, liquorice and angelica notes on the nose. Fresh acidity with ripe, grippy tannins. Weighty and lengthy on the finish.

Quinta Da Plansel Colheita Seleccionada 2007, Alentejo Red
Deep ruby and crimson red. Rich, porty, spicy with cinamon notes. Good fruit, structure and length.

Quinta Da Romaneira 2007, Douro Red
Good colour. Bouquet shows dryness with emerging fruits on the palate, true to the nose. Soft, ripe tannins.
£34.99 LIB

Quinta Das Apegadas Velha Red Great Reserve 2007, Douro Red
A lifted violet and blackcurrant nose. Ripe essence and fruity on the palate with soft tannins. A big wine but with charm.

Quinta Do Noval Douro 2007, Douro Red
Sweet, ripe and full of blackcurrant character. Damson and blackberry fruits on the palate with integrated oak and spice. Peppery with a rich finish. Delicious.
£35.00 MWW

Quinta Do Pôpa Vieilles Vignes 2007, Douro Red
Fresh, juicy fruit on the nose. Elegant weight. Refreshing, balanced with juicy fruit. Some tannic grip leading to a pleasant finish.

Quinta Do Portal Auru 2007, Douro Red
Bouquet stewed fruits. Some stone fruit character. Hints of oak. A good finish of fruit and nice length.
£49.00 GWW

Quinta Do Soque Vinhas Velhas 2007, Douro Red
Lovely ripe fruit on the nose. Light tannins and fruit on the palate. Well-balanced with oak ageing and good length.

Quinta Do Tedo Grande Reserva 2007, Douro Red
Prunes, chocolate, cherries and fresh oak on the nose. Juicy, bright fruit on the palate, with good concentration and length.
£25.00 MKV

Quinta Do Tedo 2008, Douro Red
Fruity nose with plums, blackberry and a hint of coffee. Concentrated fruit on the palate supported by tight tannins. A well made wine.
£9.99 MKV

Quinta Nova Nª Srª Carmo Grainha 2007, Douro Red
Lovely ripe oaky nose. Intense. Good balance and length. Mouthfilling raspberry berries.

Quinta Nova Nª Srª Carmo 2008, Douro Red
Big, smoke and leather on the nose with a spicy and confected flavour. Mixed berry fruits with a ripe tinge of vanilla. Spicy and smoky on the finish with good length.

Quinta Nova Nª Srª Carmo Quinta Nova Reserva 2007, Douro Red
Deep ruby red with nice red and black fruit on the palate. Tannins are well evident. This wine will last and improve.

Quinta Nova Nª Srª Carmo Touriga Nacional 2007, Douro Red
Rich, chocolatey aromas. Bright fruit. Very juicy and concentrated. Great ageing potential.

QVE T-Nac By Falorca 2007, Dao Red
Deep plum. Savoury, quince on the nose. Some floral notes of jasmine. Soft attack, clean with medium intensity. Elegant fine tannins.
£13.40 JAW

Samuel Magalhaes E Silva Quinta Da Prelada Grande Reserva 2007, Douro Red
Deep colour, vinous, brambly,

coffee aromas. Sinewy tannins balance the vibrant red berries. A lingering finish.

Santos Lima Eximius 2009, Lisboa Red
Pale and bright, melon and peach with a hint of apricot on the nose. Palate rich with fruit and layers of herbaceousness, fresh apricot and citrus with pepper and warm spice lingering on the finish. AVB

Serrano Mira Herdade Das Servas Touriga Nacional 2006, Alentejo Red
Dark fruits and floral character on the nose, and palate. Cherry, liqourice with medium tannins. Good concentration and flavour.

Sivipa Ameias Syrah 2009, Terras Do Sado Red
Almost caricature on nose. Very rich depth, coffee almost. Good finish.

Sogrape Casa Ferreirinha Vinha Grande 2007, Douro Red
Medium intensity. Earthy notes with a touch of fruit. Well-balanced with a nice length. £9.99 BWC

Sogrape Herdade do Peso Colheita 2007, Alentejo Red
Excellent palate. Subdued fruit. Great structure. Will last. £15.99

Sogrape Herdade do Peso Reserva 2007, Alentejo Red
Sweet stewed finish with chocolate. True to nose, plus spice on the palate. Long finish. £29.90

Sogrape Herdade do Peso Vinha do Monte 2008, Alentejo Red
Nice, bright berryish fruit with some spice and vanilla on the finish. Clean and balanced. £6.99

Sogrape Quinta dos Carvalhais Único 2005, Dão Red
Sweet, red fruit on the nose. Elegant firm tannins.

Symington Family Estates Pombal Do Vesuvio Douro 2008, Douro Red
Fresh blackberry and blueberry nose good concentration of fruit with some chocolate notes culminating in a smooth finish.

Symington Family Estates Prazo De Roriz 2008, Douro Red
Nice and fresh with ripe berry fruit on the nose, some spice and vanilla on the finish. Clean and balanced.

Vale De Joana Grou Grey 2006, Alentejo Red
Plum, prune and coffee notes. Easy drinking.

Veredas Do Douro Quinta Da Revolta 2007, Douro Red
Spice leather and bramble on the nose. Creamy vanilla finish.

Vinha De Reis Wine Note 2008, Dão Red
Vibrant with cinnamon spice. Spice, apple strudel and cassis flavours. Needs time to develop and finish to reach its full potential.

Wine & Soul Pintas Character Douro Red 2007, Douro Red
Damson and bramble with light smoky aromas. Rich and round with a ripe fruit finish. Lovely. £27.00

Caves Da Raposeira Rosé Bruto 2006, Lamego Sparkling Rosé
Lovely crisp nose, wild strawberry.

Creamy middle with racy mineral finish.

Enoport Fragas 2004, Douro Sweet
Spirity nose, tangerine and stewed citrus fruit. Not cloying. Fresh.

Andresen 40 Year Old NV, Douro Fortified
Lifted brazil nut, quince, butterscotch and cinnamon. Smooth and polished finish of chocolate figs.
£60.00 LAI

Bacalhôa Moscatel De Setúbal 2003, Península De Setúbal Fortified
Apricot hue, nose is tight. Dried on finish, dried apricot, nutty notes on finish. Long.
JSM, MWW, WAIT

Barbeito Boal Casks 48 & 84 NV, Madeira Fortified
Nutty beeswax aromas. Sweet honeycomb, fruit, sultana, nuts, figs, coffee liqueur and a fabulous length.
£22.00 REY

Barbeito Madeira Sercial Frasqueira 1988, Madeira Fortified
Nose has lifted cantalope and white peach. Flavours of sweet green apple, cedar and honey suckle.
£22.00 REY

Barbeito VB Reserva Lote 2 Medium Dry Cascos 12d & 46a NV, Madeira Fortified
Golden brown. Lifted pine and almonds. Sweet upfront cloves with hints of cinnamon, nutmeg and pepper on the finish.
£22.00 REY

Croft Quinta Da Roeda 1997, Duoro Fortified
Inky garnet colour. Cherry fruit

flavours with mint nuances.
£19.99 MWW

D Matilde Feueerheerd's Vintage 2007, Cima Corgo Fortified
Lifted raspberry and currants. Sweet ripe fruit concentrate and chalky tannins with strong strawberry jam finish.

Dourocaves Moscatel Do Douro 2003, Douro Fortified
Alcohol rather than fruit/sweetness on nose. Ripe concentrated candied fruit and tangerine.

Dow's Trademark Finest Reserve Port NV, Douro Fortified
Lifted cherry and dusty cedar. Clean and fresh with some currants and hints of mulberry and plums.
EOR, RWA, WHD

Gran Cruz Porto Late Bottled Vintage 2001, Douro Fortified
Fresh, youthful cassis and cherry on the nose. Well-integrated with grippy tannin, poise and balance.

Henriques & Henriques 10 Year Old Sercial NV, Madeira Fortified
Lemon marmalade and blanched almond nose. Fine, racy acidity and long refreshing finish. Excellent balance.
£13.99 WAIT

Henriques & Henriques 15 Year Old Bual NV, Madeira Fortified
Liquorice, cinder toffee on the nose. Nuts and dry orange peel. Great intensity of flavours, quite complex with cigar boxes and lovely length.
£19.99 WAIT

Henriques & Henriques 20 Year Old Malmsey NV, Madeira Fortified
Amber brown. Lifted pine and ginger nose. Sweet malt and coffee bean. Hints of orange peel and cinnamon on the palate and finish.
£30.00 MZC

Henriques & Henriques Marks & Spencer Malmsey Madeira 2001, Madeira Fortified
Medium amber. Spicy lifted nose. Clean, precise fruit - fresh long finish with excellent balance.
£16.99 M&S

Oscar Quevedo Vintage 2007, Douro Fortified
Deep crimson, steely, cassis nose. Raw concentration with grippy tannin. Great concentration.
£45.00

Quinta & Vineyard Bottlers Marks & Spencer 10 Year Old Tawny NV, Douro Fortified
Amber, bright clean date and fig nose, very sweet, fresh acidity, good length, persistent.
£12.99

Quinta Do Portal Late Bottled Vintage 2005, Douro Fortified
Deep, dark and nutty. Rich sweet nose. Soft, full and well-balanced.
£16.50 Widely Available

Quinta Do Portal Vintage 2007, Douro Fortified
Violets, Pontefract cakes, liquorice, plums and fresh coffee. Rich, concentrated and long with elegant tannins.
£34.25 CFN, ESL, GWW, N&P

Quinta Seara D'ordens Late Bottled Vintage 2005, Douro Fortified
Very rich, round, intense fruit, blackcurrant and cassis. Round, fruity and pleasant.

Ramos Pinto 30 Year Old Tawny NV, Douro Fortified
Bright amber. Ripe raisin, clove and quince jelly – very sweet, marmalad-y and intense.
MMD

Ramos Pinto Vintage 2007, Douro Fortified
Lifted blackberry and fruit concentrate. Sweet ripe currants, full and chunky tannins. Good finish.
MML

Sogrape Ferreira 10 Year Old Tawny NV, Douro Fortified
Nice berry nose, with plum, anise, good natural fruit taste, finish persistent finish, very well-balanced.
£16.99 BWC

Sogrape Ferreira 20 Year Old Tawny NV, Douro Fortified
Reddish amber - youthful nose. Fresh long finish. Good spice and length.
£49.00 BWC

Sogrape Ferreira Late Bottled Vintage 2005, Douro Fortified
Nice, dry finish. Good and persistent. Rock on the palate.
£15.99 BWC

Sogrape Ferreira Vintage Porto 2007, Douro Fortified
Very deep opaque - concentrated violet/cassis aromas. Very solid, firm structure. Powerful, intense and long.
£50.00 BWC

Sogrape Offley 10 Year Old Tawny NV, Douro Fortified
Amber brown colour. Sweet cedar and cola. Fresh hints of mint and lavender.
£14.99 SGL

Sogrape Offley 30 Year Old Tawny NV, Douro Fortified
Medium amber. Nutty pot pouri

on nose. Soft and very sweet. Long and complex. Excellent balance.
£50.00 SGL

Sogrape Offley Late Bottled Vintage 2005, Douro Fortified
Spicy and rich. Juicy, long, excellent fruit, fresh and peppery.
£11.99 SGL

Sogrape Offley Vintage 2007, Douro Fortified
Perfumed, spicy notes of blackcurrant leaf, cinnamon, liquorice and patchouli. Rounded tannins and long, spicy finish. Very well-balanced.
£50.00 SGL

Sogrape Sandeman Vintage 2007, Douro Fortified
Big, inky colour. Sweet juicy fruit nose with violet tones.
£50.00 MCT

Symington Family Estates Blandy's Bual Vintage 1968, Madeira Fortified
Vanilla, buttery. Rich, full and smooth. Intense concentration. Very, very long. Complex flavour throughout.

Symington Family Estates Dow's 30 Year Old Tawny NV, Douro Fortified
Tawny brown core, richly spiced aromas of fig, black toffee, cinnamon, black pepper. Long spicy finish. Very smooth. Delicious.

Symington Family Estates Dow's Crusted Bottled 2003 2003, Douro Fortified
Vibrant cherry red with lifted cloves and lavender. Sweet cherry on nose. Strong currants and mulberries.

Symington Family Estates Dow's Late Bottled Vintage

2005, Douro Fortified
Black pepper, spicy nose. Blackberries. Good balance of fruit/intensity. Nice jammy finish.

Symington Family Estates Dow's Quinta Do Bomfim 1998, Douro Fortified
Rich, spicy nose of liquorice root, white pepper, coriander seed, brambles and lavender with hints of citrus. Good grip and balance with a long, dryish, finish.
TESC

Symington Family Estates Graham's 20 Year Old Tawny NV, Douro Fortified
Nutty spice on palate. Long and firm. Dry finish. Complex with an excellent balance.

Symington Family Estates Graham's 30 Year Old Tawny NV, Douro Fortified
Lifted plums and cola, sweet cedar cloves, dates and a hint of fruit cake and marmalade.

Symington Family Estates Graham's 40 Year Old Tawny NV, Douro Fortified
Sweet plum and brandy sauce. Fresh cloves, dried fruits, strong spice, cinnamon and mandarin.

Symington Family Estates Graham's Late Bottled Vintage 2005, Douro Fortified
Very deep opaque. Tight, concentrated blackberry fruit. Powerful, full and long.
£13.29 MRN, WAIT

Symington Family Estates Graham's Quinta Dos Malvedos 1999, Douro Fortified
Deep cherry red colour. Flavours of sweet plum sauce, cherry and berries. Firm tannins.

Symington Family Estates Graham's Six Grapes NV, Douro Fortified

Rich and spicy on nose. Good length and concentration of fruit.

Symington Family Estates Graham's Vintage 1980, Douro Fortified

Lifted cloves and anise. Sweet cloves with hints of liquorice. Earthy peppercorn finish.

Symington Family Estates Graham's Vintage 1994, Douro Fortified

Deep ruby. Soft ripe spicy damson fruit. Good balance. Long and complex.

Symington Family Estates Morrisons Late Bottled Vintage 2004, Douro Fortified

Deep ruby. Lifted fresh cloves and lavender. Fresh cherry berry, hint of mulberry and juicy blackcurrant to finish.
£8.99 MRN

Symington Family Estates Quinta Do Vesuvio Vintage 1994, Douro Fortified

Lifted plums and blackberries. Fresh ripe mulberries. Strong with white chocolate.

Symington Family Estates Tesco Finest* 10 Year Old Tawny 1999, Douro Fortified

Delicate, young, medium amber. Soft nutty nose. Good spicy balance and a long finish.
TESC

Symington Family Estates Warre's Bottle Matured Late Bottle Vintage 2000, Douro Fortified

Choc mint and spicy plums on the nose. Silky palate with a refreshing finish.
£20.99 WAIT

Symington Family Estates Warre's Vintage 1985, Douro Fortified

Spicy plum and damson nose with hints of liquorice. Dry tannic structure and length.

Symington Family Estates Warre's Vintage 2000, Douro Fortified

Spice and cinnamon on nose. Good fruit and concentration in palate.

Taylor's 20 Year Old Tawny NV, Duoro Fortified

Amber orange. Lifted cola and hessian. Fresh dried apricots with dates and hints of marmalade.
£34.00 JSM, WAIT

Taylor's Late Bottled Vintage 2004, Duoro Fortified

Crimson ruby. Full fruit, well-integrated alcohol. Firm medium grained tannin with a long finish.
£12.99 WI-AV, MRN

Taylor's Quinta De Terra Feita 1999, Duoro Fortified

Deep cherry red colour. Hints of plum, cherry and cedar.
£23.00 ODD

Vranken-Pommery Monopole Rozes Late Bottled Vintage 2000, Douro Fortified

Deep black cherry core with savoury rounded aromas of liquorice, clove and allspice. Long chocolatey finish.
£15.99 J&B

Wiese & Krohn Ambassador Ruby Port NV, Douro Fortified

Lifted blackberries with hints of lavender on the nose. Fresh, up-front wine with flavours of currants and Ribena.
£9.99 PBA

Wiese & Krohn Rio Torto Reserva Port NV, Douro
Fortified
Very deep purple colour, opaque. Black cherries/berries with slight bitter chocolate to finish.
£11.99 PBA

Adega Cooperativa De Ponte De Lima Adamado 2009, Vinho Verde White
Fresh, light and citrusy with lots of refreshing spritz.

Adega Cooperativa De Portalegre Conventual Reserva 2008, Alentejo White
Very floral on the nose. Peachy stone fruit and a touch of white flower on the palate, quite juicy and ripe on the finish.
£4.79

Adega Cooperativa De Redondo Albarrada Azul 2009, Alentejo White
Lifted with white floral aromas. Some delicate floral flavours with a ripe peachy palate. Light body with zesty, citrus acidity. Fresh, elderflower finish.

Bacalhôa Catarina 2008, Península De Setúbal White
Softer, richer honey notes on nose. Round, smooth, soft. Quite rich flavourings with a salty tang.
JSM, MWW, WAIT

Bacalhôa Quinta Dos Loridos Alvarinho 2008, Estremadura White
Floral, citrus, mineral nose. Lifted citrus fruits. Moderate depth of flavour and a nice long length.
JSM, MAJ, WAIT

Carlos Alonso Quintela Reserva 2008, Douro White
Clean and fresh. Lovely fruit character of Muscat and grapey flavours. Dry on the palate with soft, clean fruit on the finish.

Casa Santos Lima Espiga 2009, Lisboa White
Honey notes, barley sugar. Dry, interesting flavour contrast. Quite long.
ENO

Casa Santos Lima Fernão Pires 2009, Lisboa White
Aromatic, citrus on the nose. A hint of sweetness.
ODD

Celso Pereira Foral Da Vila White 2008, Douro White
Fragrant, floral nose of lychee and flower petals leading onto a lively, austere palate bursting with zingy citrus fruit.

Companhia Das Quintas Quinta Do Cardo Siria 2009, Beira Interior White
Fresh peach and apricot on the nose and palate. Light, with off-dry character. Clean apricot and flinty mineral finish.

Cortes De Cima Chaminé White 2009, Alentejo White
Pear and pineapple freshness with fruity minerality on the palate. Quite persistent with a pear-drop finish.

Diniz Monte Da Ravasqueira White 2009, Alentejo White
Wet stone and mineral aromas. Grapefruit and zesty citrus flavours on the palate. Fine mineral core with good weight and long length.

Douro Family Estate Classic 2008, Douro White
Pale lemon in colour. Clean, floral and mineral nose with light and fresh citrus fruit on the palate. Soft and elegant.

Enoport Bucellas 2009, Bucelas White
Stony peach fruit on the nose with a touch of toasty oak. Hints of pleasing citrus with slightly gripping tannins.

Enoport Catedral Branco 2009, Dão White
Fresh, clean and fruity nose. Mineral and tropical fruit flavours on the palate with a touch of peach on the finish.

Enoport Quinta Do Boição Reserva Branco 2009, Bucelas White
Big, tangy and juicy fruit with rich and creamy texture. Nice complexity with good balance.

Enoport Quinta Do Boição Special Selection Branco 2008, Bucelas White
Big, sweet and floral pineapple with clean and tangy fruit. Solid pear flavours with nutty overtones. Rich, long and full, almost like white Rioja meets Burgundy, with a hint of salt on the finish.

Enoport Serradayres Branco 2009, Ribatejo White
Peach melba palate with gentle and juicy fruit. Lush and ripe on the finish.

Esporão Duas Castas 2009, Alentejo White
Restrained aromas with a white floral character. Delicate stone fruit with ripe, zesty citrus freshness on the palate. Earthy and herbaceous on the finish.
CHN

Esporão Reserva 2008, Alentejo White
Ripe with fresh, chunky fruit on the palate. White pepper and peach with warm spice and citrus on the palate. Fresh and attractive.
CHN

Fita Preta Palpite 2008, Alentejo White
Peach and pear fruits bound together with lovely aromatic structure.

Herdade Dos Grous Reserve 2008, Alentejo White
Lemon, citrus nose. Dominant oak with a buttery, round palate. Long, with a peachy, floral fruit character. Supple and soft on the finish.

Isidro Pegoes Adega De Pegoes Select Harvest White 2009, Peninsula De Setúbal White
Fresh lime nose. Lovely freshness with creamy texture. Good balance and finish.

Isidro Pegoes Stella Blanco White 2009, Peninsula De Setúbal White
Honey, nectarine and apricot aromatics. Palate is full of fresh fruit, white flowers, finishing with a hint of nuttiness.

Jean-Hugues Gros Odisseia Reserva 2008, Douro White
Intense white chocolate and dried apricot on the palate. Super clean with moderate acidity and warm finish.

Matilde Dona Matilde White 2009, Douro White
Ripe and fruity with a touch of pear drop on the nose. Dry on the palate with peachy ripeness on the finish.

Pinheiro Adoraz 2009, Vinho Verde White
Green hues and mineral, fresh, floral aromas. Banana and citrus notes on the mid-palate. A

refreshing wine which is also quite long.

Quanta Terra Grande Reserva Branco 2008, Douro White
Moderate gold in colour and some hints of citrus on nose, leading to steely, minerally palate of lively fruit and persistent finish.

Quanta Terra Terra A Terra Reserva Branco 2009, Douro White
Pear and lemon drop nose with supple, fresh peach on the palate. Citrus lemon and lime freshness with a light, lifting finish.

Quinta Do Judeu Quinta Do Judeu 2008, Douro White
Ripe stone fruit nose. Fresh and clean with zingy citrus fruits on the palate. Well-balanced and long.

Quinta Do Pinto Vinhas Do Lasso 2008, Lisboa White
Soft, solid juicy fruit with a strong and weighty palate. Good fruit intensity and pleasing length.

Quinta Dos Vales Marques Dos Vales Grace Vineyard Branco 2009, Algarve White
Bright, fruity with peach and pear melba aromas. Good weight with clean citrus finish lifted with guava fruit freshness.

Quinta Nova Nª Srª Carmo Grainha 2008, Douro White
Full ripe fruit palate though oak rather dominant on finish.

Reguengo de Melgaco Alvarinho Minho 2009, Vinho Verde White
Estery peardrop nose, more generous on the palate with poached pear with a spicy edge and long length. A creamy, rich appealing texture.
£14.49 HLD

Sogrape Quinta de Azevedo 2009, Vinho Verde White
Peach and floral notes on the nose, white peach on the palate; very fresh and zesty, yet delicate. Some austere character but quite floral on the finish.
£6.49

Sogrape Quinta dos Carvalhais Encruzado 2008, Dão White
Good balance between fruit and oak and a reasonably good length.
£14.99

Vasco Faria Encosta Do Xisto 2009, Minho White
Pale lemon yellow, grapefruity on the palate. Fresh, cleansing and simple.

Abilio Fernandes Monte Amarelo 2007, Alentejo Red
Spicy and herbaceous nose. Rich, ripe, soft fruit. Big mouthfeel. Rich palate.

Adega Vila Real Adega Vila Real 2008, Douro Red
The nose is firm with red cherry underpinning the black fruit. Spicy cedar aromas. Needs time to reach its full potential.

Adega Vila Real Reserva Red 2007, Douro Red
Oak dominant on the nose and palate. Vanilla flavours.

Alexandre Relvas Atlântico 2008, Alentejo Red
Attractive cherry spice and plum notes on the nose. Ripe and forward fruit on the palate with warm spice and savoury notes.

Alexandre Relvas Cicónia 2008, Alentejo Red
Soft perfumed red berry fruit and pencil lead on the nose. Fresh and fruity on the palate. Good length.

Alexandre Relvas Cicónia Reserva 2008, Alentejo Red
Crunchy black fruit on the nose. Racy acidity with citrus hints on the palate.

Alexandre Relvas Merino 2008, Alentejo Red
Bright, clean and fruit driven. Ripe cherry and vanilla on the palate with a cherry-raspberry finish.

Alexandre Relvas Montinho São Miguel 2008, Alentejo Red
Raspberries and floral characters. Sweet, slightly jammy fruit on the palate.

Alexandre Relvas Montinho São Miguel Reserva 2008, Alentejo Red
Vibrant, crunchy red fruit. Perfumed with purity. Great elegance and long fruity finish.

Alexandre Relvas São Miguel Das Missões Reserva 2008, Alentejo Red
Clean, fresh, perfumed nose. Pure berry fruit on the palate. Intense yet well-balanced. Good length.

Alexandre Relvas São Miguel Dos Descobridores Reserva 2007, Alentejo Red
Very ripe, black fruit with spicy oak. Very young.

Alianca Quinta da Garrida Reserva 2007, Dão Red
Lacks depth, coconut and American oak nose with cedar. Soft attack, rich and balanced, long warming finish.
£13.99 PBA

Alianca Quinta dos Quatro Ventos Reserva 2007, Douro Red
Lovely ripe fruit on the nose. Good balance on the palate.
Tannins with fruit coming through. Good length.
£14.49 PBA

Alianca Reserva 2007, Dão Red
Clean aromatic nose. Sweet fruit entry. Pleasant juicy balance.
£6.99 PBA

Bacalhôa JP Azeitão Red NV, Península De Setúbal Red
Vibrant black fruit palate with a good balance of savoury, smoky fruit and fresh berry ripeness. Lush and ripe on the finish.
JSM, MWW, WAIT

Bacalhôa JP Private Selection 2006, Setúbal Red
Deep purple, juicy, jammy, supple fruit with some used wood. Good freshness, spicy mid palate and grainy tannins. Good length.
JSM, MWW, WAIT

Bacalhôa Quinta Dos Loridos Tinto 2008, Estremadura Red
Firm structure that supports the ripe fruit on the palate. Easy drinking with ripe cherry flavours. Round on the finish.
JSM, MAJ, WAIT

Bacalhôa Tinto Da Ânfora 2007, Alentejo Red
Slightly dusty, spicy nose. Earthy palate with pruney red berry fruit. Medium bodied, slightly earthy. Soft, dry tannins.
£7.29 JSM, MAJ, WAIT

Barão De Vilar Zom Touriga Nacional Douro 2008, Douro Red
Deep, dense blackberry fruit supported by firm acidity. Slightly drying tannins, but a long finish.

Borges Lello Tinto 2008, Douro Red
Floral, grainy aromas. Balanced tannins. Black fruit. Mineral.

Brites Aguiar Brites Aguiar 2007, Douro Red
Bright, deep ripe fruit on the nose. Cherry and ripe fruit and a good balance on the palate. Good length.

Cade Pousio Red 2008, Alentejo Red
Aromatic cherry and berry fruit nose. Fresh, light and berry-ish. Simple.
£7.00 CAL

Carm Reserva 2007, Douro Red
Intense black cherry and liquorice on the nose. Mocha and toast on the palate with firm spicy and savoury tannins.

Casa Ermelinde Freitas Valoroso Cabernet Sauvignon Castelão 2008, Setúbal Red
Floral cherry, violet aroma. Fruity spicy flavour with fine tannins and freshness with a hint of herbs.

Casa Santos Lima Csl Castelão 2007, Lisboa Red
Spicy, peppery, firm attack. Juicy palate and spicy oak with lovely acidity and a grippy finish.
ODD

Casa Santos Lima Lx 2008, Lisboa Red
Deep, primary black fruit aromas with good, juicy damson fruit on the palate. Relatively earthy with a smoky finish. Delicious.

Casa Santos Lima Quinta Do Espírito Santo 2008, Lisboa Red
Deep, dark and lively fruit with spicy oak and full rich attractive fruits on the palate. Good freshness and lively texture with a lingering finish.
LAI

Casal Branco Falcoaria Reserva 2007, Tejo Red
Red plums and ripe cherry flavours. Quite grippy with round and almost sappy tannic character. Fresh with a nice, round finish.
£19.99

Casal Branco Quinta Do Casal Branco 2008, Tejo Red
Elegant. Ripe fruit aromas with a spicy attack, gives way to a relatively long finish.
£12.99

Casca Cape Roca Boat Red 2007, Douro Red
Vibrant. Slightly bitter fruit. Good finish.

Casca Monte Cascas Reserva 2008, Douro Red
Lifted, primary notes. Cassis and pepper. Fresh, rich, primary fruit. Lovely purity of flavour. Gently tannins. Rather delicious!

Castelinho Premium 2007, Douro Red
Bright, very deep ruby. Delicate ripe fruit on the nose. Tannins with fruit coming through. A good length.

Caves Do Solar De São Domingos São Domingos 2007, Bairrada Red
Tangy, smoky nose. Good tannins. Smoky red berry fruit.

Caves Do Solar De São Domingos São Domingos Reserva 2007, Bairrada Red
Lovely floral fruit nose. Rich and elegant, nicely balanced.

Churchill Graham Churchill Estates Grande Reserva 2007, Northern Red
Intense, smoky dark berry nose. Leathery and earthy on the palate. Spicy, long concentrated

complex finish with savoury notes.
£23.00 SFW

Companhia Das Quintas Fronteira Selecção Enólogo 2007, Douro Red
Nice clean aroma. Palate shows good fruit. Integrated oak with summer fruits. A good finish.

Companhia Das Quintas Herdade Da Farizoa Reserva 2008, Alentejo Red
Meaty, oaky, ripe and spicy. The palate is round with lots of ripe, dense cherry fruit. Spicy and rich on the finish.

Companhia Das Quintas Quinta De Pancas Touriga Nacional Reserva 2007, Lisboa Red
Opaque, opulent. Spicy, silky. Chewy fruits on mid palate. Medium finish with a red fruit and spicy notes.

Cortes De Cima Aragonez 2007, Alentejo Red
Black cherry with a young and ripe aroma. Straightforward fruit with lively acidity and fresh cherry ripeness on the palate. Grippy with a long finish.

Cortes De Cima Chaminé 2009, Alentejo Red
Smooth, sweet, pure ripe berry fruits. Open, fresh, fruity palate. Simple and appealing.

Cortes De Cima Syrah 2008, Alentejo Red
Slight roasted reductive nose. Palate is fruity, a bit meaty, with ripe fruit. Lovely rich finish.
£10.99 WAIT

D Diniz M R Premium Red 2007, Alentejo Red
Dense, vegetal, liquorice nose. Inky, very extracted palate but enough fruit for the future. Concentrated with acidity and ripe but strong tannins.

D Diniz Monte Da Ravasqueira Red 2008, Alentejo Red
Ripe, angular wine with ripe cherry and oak on the palate. Gripping tannins and ripe fruit on the finish.

D Matilde Dona Matilde Red 2008, Douro Red
Aromatic, full fruit palate (plums, black fruits) with spicy notes of pepper and cloves. Very tight tannins and a rich finish.

De Borba Montes Claros Garrafeira 2006, Alentejo Red
Red fruits. Cedar, cassis. Some dryness. Quaffable.

De Borba Sense Touriga Nacional 2008, Alentejo Red
Fresh, bright, plum and cherryish on the palate with nice fruit and good acidity.

De Redondo Porta Da Ravessa Tinto 2009, Alentejo Red
Red berry fruit on the nose with a touch of confected sweetness. High notes of cherry and a touch of oak on the finish.

DFJ Caladoc & Alicante Bouschet 2008, Lisboa Red
Black fruit and bramble aromas. Violets and bruised apples on the palate with a youthful, drying finish. Impressive fruit with unique appeal.
£8.99

DFJ Fonte Do Beco 2008, Lisboa Red
Juicy, jammy red fruit, hint of bramble character, very fresh acidity, crunchy tannin texture with good length.
£6.99

DFJ Grand'arte Alfrocheiro 2008, Lisboa Red
Deep and perfumed with cassis and wine gums on the nose. Juicy, crisp, elegant and appetising. Very fresh and pungent in an easy-drinking style.
£8.99

DFJ Grand'arte Special Selection 2007, Lisboa Red
Nice upfront fruit, deep plum, spicy brambly aroma, sublime finish.
£9.99

DFJ Ramada Reserva 2007, Tejo Red
Bright, with good concentration and ripe forest fruits on the palate. Spicy notes with a ripe finish.

Diniz Monte Da Ravasqueira Vinha Das Romãs Red 2008, Alentejo Red
Vibrant, spicy, meaty, oak fruits. The palate is fresh, structured and fruity.

Douro Family Estate Signature 2007, Douro Red
Spicy, black fruit aromas together with cherries on the palate. Medium bodied, balanced with resolved tannins and a nice finish.

Edite Maria Alves Joao Clara 2008, Algarve Red
Almost violet, good nose of jammy, ripe fruit. Lovely and fresh with sweet stewed fruit on the palate. Bramble and spiced finish.

Encostas De Estremoz Reserva 2007, Alentejo Red
Intense, ripe black fruit matched to sweet oak. Ripe tannins.

Ermelinde Freitas Dona Ermelinde 2008, Setúbal Red
Juicy, red fruit with confected and soft cherry on the palate. Grainy tannins and lovely acidity with a ripe spicy finish.

Ermelinde Freitas Touriga Nacional 2008, Setúbal Red
Light red fruits. Redcurrant. Nice follow through.

Ermelinde Freitas Valoroso Syrah Aragonés Alicante 2008, Setúbal Red
Spicy, vibrant red fruit with well-balanced oak and ripe jamminess. Youthful but elegant.
LAI

Esporão Aragones 2007, Alentejo Red
Toasty, charry oak. Concentrated red berry fruit. Quite high acidity and tannin. Liquorice. Rather dry.

Esporão Arco 2008, Alentejo Red
Tart, fresh plum and cherry fruit with straightforward, yet nicely balanced fruit.
£7.11 WAIT

Esporão Arco Do Esporão 2008, Alentejo Red
Well crafted wine. Vegetal notes on the nose and palate.
£9.99 WAIT

Esporão Monte Velho Red 2008, Alentejo Red
Black cherry fruit with a meaty character. Juicy and fresh on the palate with a cherry-strawberry like flavour. Grippy with balanced acidity.
CHN

Esporão Touriga 2007, Alentejo Red
Deep plum. Ripe plum nose. A real bitter chocolate and plum mouthful.

Esporão Vinha Da Defesa 2008, Alentejo Red
Tannic and chunky with bold

flavours. Ripe cherry fruit and bold spicy character. Nicely balanced and very pretty.

Falua Conde De Vimioso 2008, Tejo Red
Dark, red fruit with hints of spice, honey and tobacco. Chewy tannins give way to spicy red fruits.
£5.99 HAX, OWA

Falua Touriga Nacional 2007, Tejo Red
Ripe, clean and berryish. Juicy and vibrant. Medium bodied with good balance.
£6.99 M&S

Fita Preta Fita Preta 2007, Alentejo Red
Sweet, briary, raspberry and blackberry aromas. Concentrated yet fresh. Well-balanced oak, crisp finish.

Fundação Abreu Callado Dom Cosme Reserva 2007, Alentejo Red
Sweet, creamy raspberry nose and palate. Vanilla oak. Sweetness, tannins and fruit come through the oak and last.

Herdade Da Malhadinha Nova Aragonês Da Peceguina 2007, Alentejo Red
Slightly gamey nose with sweet, earthy, raspberry fruit, spicy, chocolatey notes. Dry tannins, good acidity, slightly dry wood.
REY

Herdade Da Malhadinha Nova Malhadinha 2007, Alentejo Red
Oaky, spicy, chocolatey, oak dominated nose. Dense cherry, concentrated palate with high alcohol, high acid and high tannin. Needs time.
REY

Herdade Da Malhadinha Nova Monte Da Peceguina 2008 2008, Alentejo Red
Elegant nose. Floral, pleasant on the palate.
REY

Herdade Do Rocim Grande Rocim Reserva 2007, Alentejo Red
Black fruit with hints of cedar on the nose. Oak and vanilla flavoured fruits on the palate with an aggressive finish.

Herdade Do Rocim Olho De Mocho Reserva Tinto 2007, Alentejo Red
Nice meaty edge to the dark fruit nose. Plate is rich, meaty, spicy with nice intensity.

Ilex Margalha NV, Alentejo Red
Dark, perfumed berry fruits, with nice structure. A very pretty wine with layers of ripe cherry fruit and spice on the finish.
£4.00

Ilex Pausa NV, Alentejo Red
Herbaceous black fruit on the nose, sweet berry and cherry on the palate with a touch of drying tannin on the finish.
£6.00

Isidro Pegoes Adega De Pegoes Aragonez 2008, Palmela Red
Very deeply coloured with strong, warming, toasty aromas. Rich and intense with big, ripe and heavily oaked fruit. Bold and rich.

Isidro Pegoes Adega Pegoes Select Harvest Red 2007, Península De Setúbal Red
Red and ripe fruit on the nose with much of the same on the palate. Crunchy tannins give way to a lean but pleasing finish.

José Mesquita Guimarães Quinta Dos Poços Grande Reserva 2005, Douro Red
Nose shows black fruits and liquorice. Palate is well-balanced with fine spicy tannins, cherry fruit and liquorice. Good acidity and structure - very enjoyable wine.

Júlio Bastos Dona Maria Reserva 2006, Alentejo Red
Dark fruits with and spice. Liquorice and cherry. A nice finish.

Lemos & Van Zeller Van Zellers 2007 Douro Red 2007, Douro Red
Elegant. Intense and juicy. Vibrant, good personality. Minerality. Wild herbs and spices for oak. Will age.
£16.00 C&B, D&F, LAI, TAN, WAIT

Manuel Pinto Hespanhol Calcos Do Tanha Reserva 2006, Douro Red
Deep cherry red. Fruity on the nose. Rich, silky and fruity taste. A nice length.
£11.99 ICE

Margens Antigas Reserva 2007, Douro Red
Black cherry and sweet violet perfume on the nose. Attractive, lively plum and cherry fruits on the palate. Concentrated fleshy structure, crisp acidity with well managed toast and oak.

Parras Evidencia 2007, Dão Red
Pleasant easy drinking. Soft fruit flavours. Some herbaceous notes. Resin and fresh attack. Elegant with smooth entry. Tannic structure. Spicy, fruity concentration.

Quanta Terra, Terra A Terra Reserva 2007, Douro Red
Light fruit, simple but elegant. Quaffable.

Quinta Da Alorna 2008, Tejo Red
Lifted plum with a hint of jam. Black cherry fruits and finely textured tannins.
£7.00

Quinta Da Veiga Azul Douro Reserva 2007, Douro Red
Inky, pronounced aromas of strawberry compote, redcurrants and spices. Multi-layered flavours on the palate with a long finish. Needs time to develop.

Quinta Das Bajancas 2006, Douro Red
Jammy red berries with a touch of spice. Juicy, soft tannins with a lift of smoke on the finish.

Quinta De Chocapalha Chocapalha Reserva Red 2007, Lisboa Red
Bramble fruit and smoky-wood aroma, excellent drying tannins.
£24.00

Quinta Do Conde 2 Uvas 2008, Lisboa Red
Bright primary fruit with a touch of pear-drop aroma. Sweet and ripe with high notes of thick jammy character. Delightful and easy to drink.

Quinta Do Couquinho Colheita Tinto 2007, Douro Red
Smoky, peppery, tannic, full bodied with rich, brambly palate and complex coffee and tobacco notes. Acidity and tannins are balanced. A good finish.

Quinta Do Crasto Sainsbury's Taste The Difference Douro 2008, Douro Red
Very youthful, peppery, fresh.

Really juicy and appetising. Good easy drinking wine.
JSM

Quinta Do Noval Cedro Do Noval 2007, Douro Red
Barnyardy, smoky, red cherry, full body, balanced, jammy with some spice. Medium length.
£14.99 TAN

Quinta Do Passadouro Passadouro Douro Red 2007, Douro Red
Brambly blackberry with ripe fruit character. Rich mouthfeel with smoky and leathery overtones. Good integration and lovely freshness on the finish.
£19.00

Quinta Do Passadouro Reserva Red 2007, Douro Red
Lovely violet flower. Concentration and good fruit, along with chocolate hints.
£32.00

Quinta Do Soque Reserva 2005, Douro Red
Good ripe fruit on the nose. Redcurrants, good acidity and integrated wood. Smooth tannins.

Quinta Dos Termos Reserva 2006, Beira Interior Red
Light and juicy on the palate with some jammy fruits. Easy to drink.
QDT

Quinta Dos Vales Marques Dos Vales Grace Vineyard 2007, Algarve Red
Ripe cranberry fruit with a touch of floral aromas on the nose. Fresh acidity, grippy tannins, savoury and long on the finish.

Quinta Nova Nª Srª Carmo Pomares 2008, Douro Red
Aromatic and earthy. Quite complex fruit. Cherry structure. A good balance. Spicy. A good tasty mouthful.

Quinta Nova Nª Srª Carmo Quinta Nova Grande Reserva 2007, Douro Red
Lifted violet aromas. Restrained oak and beautiful, delicate red fruit. Acidity and tannins are in balance. A poised wine – very fine and elegant.

Ramos Pinto Collection 2007, Douro Red
Bright, deep ruby. Ripe fruit nose. Lovely soft fruit on the palate. Oak and tannin. Well-balanced with a good length.
MMD

Ramos Pinto Duas Quintas Reserva 2007, Douro Red
Bright, deep ruby. Delicate ripe fruit on the nose. Well-balanced fruit and tannins. Some oak coming through. Good length.
MMD

Ramos Pinto Marques De Borba 2008, Alentejo Red
Lead pencil and light fruit on the nose. A sound wine.
£9.00

Samuel Magalhaes E Silva Poyares 2005, Douro Red
Jammy, slight touch of vanilla. Moderate length.

Samuel Magalhaes E Silva Quinta Da Prelda Porto 20 Years Old NV, Douro Red
Medium amber colour with firm, spicy, nutty nose. Dryish long finish.

Santos Lima 4uvas 2008, Lisboa Red
Light, fresh nose gives way to ripe fruits and spicy undertones on the palate. Finish is long and dry.

Silvestre Ferreira Herdade Do Pinheiro Reserva 2004, Alentejo Red
Fragrant. Plum, prune and floral notes. Soft, fruity and savoury notes. Fresh and pleasant.

Sogrape Callabriga Alentejo 2007, Alentejo Red
Good intensity. Red fruits, juicy, tannic. Dry. Heavy fruit.
£8.99

Sogrape Callabriga Reserva 2005, Alentejo Red
Red and black fruits, oak and a splash of savoury.
£15.99

Sogrape Callabriga Reserva 2005, Dão Red
Deep plum. Celery and nuts. Mellow spice. Soft attack. Hints of oak and dryness.
£15.99

Sogrape Callabriga Reserva 2007, Douro Red
Oaky berry nose. Woody, vanilla, berries on the palate. Dry.
£15.99

Sogrape Casa Ferreirinha Quinta da Leda 2007, Douro Red
Lightish with a hint of earthiness. Firm structure.
£39.00

Sogrape Herdade do Peso Reserva 2005, Alentejo Red
Soft juicy red fruits on the palate. Easy drinking style with good length.
£15.99

Sogrape Quinta dos Carvalhais Reserva 2002, Dão Red
Deep with sweet spice and cacao on the nose. Chocolatey, chunky tannins with a touch of oak on the finish.

Sogrape Quinta dos Carvalhais Tinta Roriz 2003, Dão Red
Chestnut and red fruit on the nose. Good weight and true to style.
£15.99

Touquinheiras Clemen Reserva 2009, Vinho Verde Red
White flower notes on the nose, a mineral core with a refreshing citrus palate. Mouthwatering acidity and a hard finish.

Unicer Planura 2008, Alentejo Red
Leaded and lightly fruited on the nose. Shows distinctive variatel character.

Unicer Planura Syrah 2007, Alentejo Red
Sweet, pure liqueur-like berry and chewy fruits. Supple, ripe, nicely fruited plate with hints of meat.

Casa Santos Lima Quinta Da Espiga 2009, Lisboa Rosé
Spice, intense fruit flavours with a nice length.

DFJ Pink Elephant 2009, Estremadura Rosé
Bright colour with a nice strawberry fruit nose. Nicely balanced.
£5.99 BTH, MRN, TESC

Quinta Da Falorca Rosé Touriga Nacional 2009, Dao Rosé
Bright strawberry in colour. Serious character. Savoury finish.
£11.20 JAW

Consultores Crooked Vines 2008, Douro Sweet
Honeyed nose and palate with acidity balanced by fruit delivery.

Enoport Thasos 2008, Setúbal
Sweet
Lavender and coriander seed
on the nose. Some mandarin,
tight on the palate. Good length,
vibrant with orange citrus notes
- akin to a Napoleon liqueur.

**Barbeito Boal Old Reserve
10 Year Old NV, Madeira
Fortified**
Smoky notes with a delicious
flavour of toffee. Developed
nutty flavours. Ageing well with a
long finish.
£28.00 REY

**Barbeito Malvasia Old
Reserve 10 Year Old NV,
Madeira Fortified**
Very delicate nose and acidity.
Lifted pine and ginger. Fresh
citrus peel.
£28.00 REY

**Barbeito Sercial Old Reserve
10 Year Old NV, Madeira
Fortified**
Medium amber, gold core with
toasted almond flavour. Good
acidity.
£28.00 REY

**C. Da Silva Dalva Vintage
2007, Douro Fortified**
Dusky with rich Dundee cake,
black pepper, cumin and Victoria
plum. Fine young tannins, good
structure and long violet flavour
finish.

**D Matilde Quinta Dona
Matilde Vintage 2007, Douro
Fortified**
Deep vibrant red. Lifted stewed
currants, fresh full chocolate and
fruit concentrate. Longish.

**Fonseca Guimaraens 1996,
Duoro Fortified**
Good colour - deep garnet.
Cherry fruit flavours and aromas.
£24.99 F&M, WAIT

**Fonseca Terra Prima Organic
Reserve NV, Duoro Fortified**
Ruby red. Lifted blackberry cedar.
Fresh cloves and spice. Some
cedar, cloves, spice and nutmeg.
£14.99 MWW

**Gran Cruz Porto Vintage 2007,
Douro Fortified**
Crimson colour. Good grip tannin.
Fresh, ripe aromatic fruit.

**Henriques & Henriques 15
Year Old Verdelho NV,
Madeira Fortified**
Pot pourri on the nose with
aromas of pine and ginger. Fig
toffee and coffee on the palate
with hints of mint and soy.
Assertively crisp.
£19.99 WAIT

**J H Andresen Late Bottled
Vintage 2005, Douro Fortified**
Very deep ruby. Great grip
and tannin.
£13.99 LAI

**Miguel Ferreira Adega De
Favaios Moscatel Do Douro
1980, Douro Fortified**
Intense, lush, Seville orange palate.
Cinnamon and mixed spice.

**Miguel Ferreira Moscatel Do
Douro Adega De Favaios 10
Years Old NV, Douro Fortified**
Floral, spicy cinnamon and clove
nose. Ripe, sweet. Lots of red fruit,
currants. Luscious and spicy, tangy
and fresh. Very good length.

**Miguel Ferreira Moscatel Do
Douro Adega De Favaios NV,
Douro Fortified**
Very sweet, alcohol poking through
and tangerines. Long finish.

**Quinta & Vineyard Bottlers
Marks & Spencer Late Bottled
Vintage Port 2004, Douro
Fortified**
Powdery tannins, red and black

fruit. Some nice freshness, balance and length.
£10.99

Quinta And Vineyard Bottlers Sainsbury's Ruby Port NV, Douro Fortified
Fresh plum and damson nose with peppery spice. Full, sweet, well defined fruit with nutmeg on the finish.
£5.22 JSM

Quinta Do Crasto Late Bottled Vintage 2005, Douro Fortified
Ruby red. Lifted dust, fruit concentrate, sweet plum, some cloves and nutmeg.

Quinta Do Infantado Reserva NV, Douro Fortified
Deep ruby red. Fresh plums and currants, fine chalky tannins and a hint of aniseed.
LIB

Quinta Do Noval 10 Year Old Tawny NV, Douro Fortified
Good garnet hue. Tight nose of orange peel and nuttiness.
£17.25 WAIT

Quinta Do Noval Unfiltered Late Bottled Vintage 2003, Douro Fortified
Black toffee and plum cake nose. Stewed fruit palate.
£12.99 OCO, TESC

Quinta Do Passadouro Late Bottled Vintage 2005, Douro Fortified
Lifted blackberries. Sweet cherry, mulberries, blackcurrant and peppercorn.
£25.00

Quinta Do Portal Quinta Do Portal Cellar Reserve NV, Douro Fortified
Fresh, ripe, clean berry fruit. Firm tannic structure, integrated and

good length.
£14.00 CAR, ESL, GWW, MJF

Ramos Pinto Late Bottled Vintage 2004, Douro Fortified
Deep ruby. Lifted blackberry and lavender, sweet cherry and mulberry. Firm tannins.
MMD

Sivipa Sivipa 1996, Setúbal Fortified
Cheesy and smoky on the nose. Nutty on the palate. Good length. Sweet 'edges' with finish a little forward.

Sogrape Ferreira 10 Year Old White NV, Douro Fortified
Golden honey. Toffee floral nose. Syrup, apricot, toffee and honey - sweet and persistent.

Sogrape Sandeman 20 Year Old Tawny NV, Douro Fortified
Amber orange. Lifted spice and hessian. Sweet upfront, cola, hints of apricot and pomegranate.
£35.00 MCT

Sogrape Sandeman 30 Year Old Tawny NV, Douro Fortified
Orange amber core. Nutmeg, cantaloupe, raisin, brazil nut. Hint of bitter chocolate on finish.
£50.00 MCT

Sogrape Sandeman Late Bottled Vintage 2005, Douro Fortified
Spice and pepper on nose. Big, rich and grippy. Long finish.
£11.99 MCT

Symington Family Estates Blandy's 15 Year Old Malmsey NV, Madeira Fortified
Dark amber. Toffee and cake flavours. Very long finish.
£24.99 WAIT

Symington Family Estates Blandy's Malmsey 1992 Colheita 1992, Madeira Fortified

Delicate with a soft Demerara sugared nose. Long and spicy with nice lift on the palate. Honeyed and ripe on the finish.

Symington Family Estates Dow's Quinta Do Bomfim 1999, Douro Fortified

Deep crimson colour. Spicy black cherry fruit flavours. Good balance, length and grip.

Symington Family Estates Graham's Crusted Bottled 2002, Douro Fortified

Red berry and plum jam with menthol notes. Nice balance in a friendly style.

Symington Family Estates Sainsbury's 10 Year Old Tawny Port NV, Douro Fortified

Amber brown, herbal nose, cedar fresh lavender, currants, dried cedar, rose petal.
£11.49 JSM

Symington Family Estates Warre's Otima 10 Year Old Tawny NV, Douro Fortified

Very good nose, plums, cloves, well maturated and complex

fruit, mouth full of apricots, raisins, long finish, good balance.
£12.29 TESC, MRN, WAIT

Symington Family Estates Warre's Quinta Da Cavadinha 1996, Douro Fortified

Spicy, citrus nose. Rich and long on the palate with a long firm finish.
£29.99 WAIT

Taylor's 10 Year Old Tawny NV, Douro Fortified

Very clean, plenty of character, well-balanced and concentrated finish.
£19.99 WI-AV, TESC, WAIT

Vinoquel Quevedo Colheita 1996, Douro Fortified

Pale tawny garnet. Light strawberry and cherry nose. Very light and slightly hot.

Vranken-Pommery Monopole Terras Do Grifo 2007, Douro Fortified

Smoky, peppery fruit nose. Ripe, with black and red fruits, a hint of pencil shaving and warm spice on the palate. Fresh and lively with a long finish.
J&B

Wine & Soul Pintas Vintage 2007, Douro Fortified

Sweet baked fruit. Pleasant herbal quality. Relatively accessible style.
£50.00

Sake

Sake is to the Japanese what wine is to the French or Italians. It is rich in their culture and enjoyed with national cuisine. Dating back as far as the third century, the art of sake-making has withstood the test of time and popularity has begun to grow overseas for this fascinating drink. Like grapes, the end product depends on the quality of rice grown and the type of water used for brewing plays a vital role also. The 'Kuramotos' (sake brewers) define the style of sake produced by determining how much of a 'polish' to give the grains of rice and whether to add alcohol or not. Sake enjoyed its most successful year to date with an impressive fourteen Golds. Try these sakes straight from the fridge or gently heat at your leisure and prepare to be astounded.

2010 IWC PERFORMANCE

Trophies	14
Gold	14
Silver	40
Bronze	74

KNOW YOUR SAKE SPEAK

Futsu-shu: "normal sake", the equivalent of table wine

Tokutei meishoshu: special designation sake, which is divided into four further categories:

Honjozo-shu: fortified with some distilled alcohol

Junmai-shu: "pure sake" made from rice only

Ginjo-shu: produced from rice with a weight polished to 40 per cent or less

Daiginjo-shu: produced from rice with weight polished to 50 per cent or less (the term junmai can be added to ginjo or daiginjo if no alcohol is added)

Kuroshu: sake from brown rice

Koshu: aged sake

Taruzake: sake aged in cedar barrels

Shizuku-dori: sake that is separated from lees.

GINGO-SHU, DAIGINJO-SHU

REGIONAL YAMAGATA GINO-DAIGINGO TROPHY

Dewazakura Sake Brewery Daiginjoshu 2009, Yamagata
Soft and melony aroma with a hint of white flower. Refreshingly sweet at the same time. Palate contains lovely mouthfeel of ripe melon. Good acidity to balance. Long finish.
WSI

CHAMPION GINGO DAIGINGO, REGIONAL TOCHIGI TROPHY

Inoue Seikichi Sawahime Daiginjo 2009, Tochigi
Powerful green fruit and capsicum aromas. Earthy, mushroom notes lifted by zesty fruitiness. Balanced, long but not elegant.

REGIONAL SHIGA GINGO-DAIGINGO TROPHY

Mifuku Shuzo Mifuku Daigin Gokujo 2009, Shiga
Rich texture with flavours of apricot and canned peach on the palate. Flavoursome.

Daishinsyu Kozuki Hiden Daiginjo 2008, Nagano
Crisp, green nose. Fruity characters of passionfruit and young persimmon. Medium finish.

Harashuzou Koshinohomare Daiginjo 2009, Niigata

White pepper and green pear aromas. Rich but subtle flavours of wet stones, green pears and plums. Long, smooth finish. Harmonious.
JP-OKA

Kikuhime Ginjyou 2009, Ishikawa
Clean and mineral on the palate with a hint of melon and pear. Soft textured finish.
JP-OKA

Matsui Daiginjo Muroka Kagura 2010, Kyoto
Gentle aromas of steamed rice, jasmine and ripe melon. Clean, crisp apple on the under note, spicy palate. Clean finish.

Miyashita Sake Brewery Masumi Yumedono 2007, Nagano
Soft, elegant nose with apple and pear flavours on the palate. Warming and ripe on the finish.
£65.00 WSI

Morishima Shuzo Taikan Daiginjyo 2009, Ibaraki
Pear, white peach and sweet fruits on the palate. Very fresh and clean on the finish.

Murashige Kinkan Kuromatsu Daiginjo Nishiki 2009, Yamaguchi
Pungent, floral jasmine. Very aromatic on the palate but slightly sugary. Simple finish.

Okuizumo Syuzou Senju No Izumi Ginjo 2009, Shimane
Koji on the nose with a ripe, passionfruit palate. Warming alcohol but well-balanced.

Saito Shuzo Eikun Iwai 35 Daiginjo-shu 2009, Kyoto
Muted, elegant honeysuckle and jasmine on nose. Mouthfilling with excellent minerality and good balance of acidity and

sweetness. Long, dry, floral finish. Very elegant.

Sakuramasamune Daiginjyo Ohkaichirin 2009, Hyogo

Typical Gingo style with fresh citrus aromas. Ripe and fruit forward on the finish.

Shimizu Jozo Zaku Daiginjo 2009, Mie

Clean nose of strawberry and peach, powdery but melon on the palate. Medium acidity and dry finish.
JP-HAS

Tsuka Shuzo Otafuku Daiginjo 2009, Hiroshima

Earthy, vegetal nose. Maturity round medium to full body with nutty characters. Hot finish.

Watanabe Shuzo Kyokko Daiginjo 2009, Tochigi

Refined and subtle on the nose. Mouthfilling pineapple, kumquat, candied citrus peel with underpinning earthiness. Excellent structure and minerality.

BRONZE

Dewazakura Sake Brewery Dewazakura Oka Ginjoshu 2009, Yamagata

Floral petal and perfume nose, fresh pineapple on the palate with green undertones. Gentle spice on the finish.
WSI

Fukuda Shuzo Nagasaki Bijin 2009, Nagasaki

Clean and straightforward on the nose. Subtle cashew nuttiness on the palate. Smooth texture, melon fruit and a light, dry finish.

Heiwa Shuzou Maniounowakatsuru 2009, Wakayama

Green and citrus aromas on the nose. Bamboo and citrus on the palate with a hint of toasted almonds on the finish.
£60.00 JP-HAS, NSH

Ishiokashuzo Tsukuba Daiginjo Murasakinomine 2009, Ibaraki

Savoury, fruity aromas. Silky mouthfeel with smoky, ripe pear and buttery notes. Subtle and long.

Kikuisami Kikuisami Daiginjo Hiden 2008, Yamagata

Gently perfumed, elegant duck pear, water apple and kaffi lime. Subtle, well-integrated with crisp acidity. Mineral fresh.

Kitaya Daiginjo Gokujo Kitaya 2009, Fukuoka

Round, compact aromas of water melon and yellow peach pops out from the glass. A hint of herbs, minty, sense of cool. Palate is succulent, refreshing juicy melon and peach.

Koshinohana Shuzo Daiginjo Koshinaha Chotokusen 2009, Niigata

Restrained aromas on the nose. Vibrant green fruit and smooth on the palate. Attractive but less aromatic than some.

National Trading Inc Kimura Brewery Daiginjo Fukukomachi 2010, Akita

Soft aromas of white peach and nectarine. Crisp minerality with mouth-watering finish.

Obata Shuzo Manotsuru Maho 2009, Niigata

Lychee fruit nose with herbaceous notes. Fresh and ripe on the palate with a green citrus finish.
JFI

Okuizumo Syuzou Nitamai Daiginjo Kairyo-hattan-

nagare 2009, Shimane
Roasted, spiced pineapple, muscovado sugar and allspice. Crisp and refreshing.

Saiyashuzoten Honjyouzou Yukinobosha 2009, Akita
Nutty and ripe style with fresh banana and over-ripe fruit on the palate. Warm, fresh and balanced.

Saura Daiginjo / Urakasumi 2008, Miyagi
Restrained, perfumed camomile and black pepper.

Tonoike Shuzouten Sanran Daiginjyou 2009, Tochigi
Calvados and over-ripe apple on the palate with warming alcohol and fresh spice. Long and lingering on the finish.

Toyokuni Shuzo Ginjo Sinjitu 2010, Fukushima
Ripe apple and bitter melon on the palate with a smooth, fresh finish.

Umeda-Shuzoujou Honshu-ichi Daiginjo 50% Seihaku 2007, Hiroshima
Gentle aromas of cream, jasmine and white pepper leaf. Well-structured.

HONJOZO-SHU

GOLD

 REGIONAL YAMAGATA HONJOZO TROPHY

Shindo Sake Brewery Ura-gasanryu Koka 2009, Yamagata
Nutty with a savoury appeal. Palate is ripe and round with tropical fruits and refreshing citrus flavours.
JFI

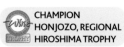 CHAMPION HONJOZO, REGIONAL HIROSHIMA TROPHY

Umeda-Shuzoujou Honshu-ichi Muroka Honjozo 2009, Hiroshima
Sharp apple character with a fresh, citrus ripeness. Warming alcohol with a lingering finish.

BRONZE

Kamotsuru Chotokusen Tokutousyu 2009, Hiroshima
Well-balanced with banana and melon fruit on the palate. Fresh citrus finish.

Miyashita Sake Brewery Honjozo Kiwamihijiri 2009, Okayama
Mature aromas with a nutty-ripe palate. Banana and white blossoms on the finish.

Oishi Sake Brewery Okinazuru Tengori 2009, Kyoto
Light-bodied style with a touch of cheesy aroma on the nose. Fresh acidity with a long finish.

Saura Genshu Urakasumi 2008, Miyagi
Flower blossoms and fresh pineapple on the palate with a clean, fresh finish.

Shimizu Jozo Zaku Wa-no-tomo 2009, Mie
Pear sweetness on the palate with a touch of bitter melon. Well-balanced, ripe and soft on the finish.

JUNMAI GINJO-SHU, JUNMAI DAIGINJO-SHU

GOLD

REGIONAL NAGANO JUNMAI-DAIGINGO TROPHY

Daishinsyu Breweries Teippai 2007, Nagano
Clean and clear. Acid is agreeable. Smooth alcohol. Crispy.

CHAMPION JUNMAI DAIGINGO, REGIONAL NIIGATA TROPHY

General Partnership Watanabe Sake Brewing Store Nechi 2008, Niigata
Aroma gives promise. Sweetness after palate.

REGIONAL SHIZUOKA JUNMAI DAIGINGO TROPHY

Isojiman Premium Sake Brewery Daiginjo Junmai 2010, Shizuoka
Herby melon. Sweetness pronounced. Well-balanced acidity.
£45.00 BZI, JP-HAS

REGIONAL YAMAGATA JUNMAI-DAIGINGO TROPHY

Shindo Sake Brewery Gasanryu Gokugetsu 2009, Yamagata
Herbaceous and clean on the nose with a fresh lemon aroma. Ripe and well-balanced with apple freshness on the palate. Almost grassy on the finish. Delicious.
JFI

SILVER

Akita Seishu Yamatoshizuku Junmaiginjo 2010, Akita
Melon and green apple. Quite rich flavour with long length.

Bunraku Junmai Daiginjo 2009, Saitama
Bubble gum, metallic nose hint. Melony, slippery tongue feel. Refreshing.

Chiyokotobuki Toraya Chiyotobuki Toranoko 2009, Yamagata
Smoky, ripe fruit nose. Fresh fruit, smoked fish, tarry, nectarine. Finishes dry, smoky, long, soft and harmonious.

Harada Brewer Sansya Junmai Ginjyo Hanakoubo 2009, Gifu
Lively citrus and bay leaf nose. Fruity, ripe nectarines, bay leaf, mineral. Silky feel. Fresh and harmonious. Long.

Ishikawashuzo Tamajiman Junmai Daiginjo Haruno Yorokobi 2010, Tokyo
Passionfruits. Palate quite light with a light body.
£23.00

Komachi-Shuzo Nagaragawa Junmaiginjo Tenkawa 2009, Gifu
Confected/boiled sweets, orange peel nose. Chestnuts, melon, anise on the palate. Juicy and creamy with a long mineral finish. Some warmth.

Otani Shuzo Junmai Daiginjyo 2003, Tottori
Restrained white pepper leaf, lime and shitake tea. Subtle palate, gently perfumed. Good structure with refreshing, toasted rice character. Mineral finish.

S Imanishiki Harushika Junmai Ginji Sake 2009, Nara
Elegant, perfumed notes of jasmine,

apple blossom, green apple and nutmeg. Very subtle, elegant and well-structured.

Saito Shuzo Eikun Ichigin Junmai Daiginjo-shu 2009, Kyoto

Clean nose of peach and jasmine. Aromatic on the palate with subtle flavour of melon with a spicy finish.

Shata Shuzo Tengumai Yamahai Junmai Ginjo 2007, Ishikawa

Pale colour. Good acidity. Smooth with a clean aftertaste.

Shimizu Jozo Zaku Miyabi-no-tomo Nakadori 2009, Mie

Light mandarin. Semi-sweet. Good palate with finesse.
JP-HAS

Tenju Shuzo Junmai Daiginjo Tenju 2009, Akita

Earthy, ripe with a touch of mineral character. Banana and citrus on the palate with well-balanced acidity. Fresh and delightful.

Toshimori Sake Brewery Sakehitosuji Akaiwaomachi 2008, Okayama

Soft, grassy nose. Ripe, stone fruit, fresh mown grass. Zesty, soft and juicy.

Umeda-Shuzoujou Honshu-ichi Muroka Junmai Ginjo Shu 2009, Hiroshima

Melony, fruity nose. Fruity round palate. Well-balanced.

Watanabe Shuzo Tamaka Kimoto Junmai-Ginjo 2009, Tochigi

Fresh, creamy, caramel nose. Caramel, toffee, salt, creamy and refreshing on the palate. Big and juicy but a little alcoholic. Dry.

BRONZE

Aiyu Shuzo Tomoju Junmai Ginjo 2009, Ibaraki

Pear, yellow apple and minty hint. Banana, pear, savoury, rice undertone. Well balanced acidity. Medium long finish.

Akita Seishu Dewatsuru Hihaku 2010, Akita

Fresh nose with a hint of greenness. Apple and candied. Sweet with a low acidity.
BOW

Aoki Shuzo Kakurei Junmaiginjo 2009, Niigata

Candied nose and a little musty. Vegetal. Traditional pine tree with sea breeze, ricey.
WTS, WWD, WWW

Haginishiki Shuzo Haginishiki Junmai Ginjo 2009, Shizuoka

Mandarin oranges and cream on the nose. Ripe stone fruit. Long.
JAL

Hanaharu Shuzo Hanaharu Junmai Daiginjyo-syu 2009, Fukushima

Baked apple to the nose. Ripe, sweet fruit, very harmonious. Soft, mineral finish.
£26.11

Hinomaru Jozo Kimoto Junmai Ginjo Manabito 2009, Akita-ken

Green apple, herbal palate. Green apple with roundness at the end on the palate. Good balance, refreshing.

Kato Kahachiro Shuzo Junmai Daiginjo-shu Gingarinshou 2009, Yamagata

Savoury, hint of nut, vegetal on the nose. Vegetal, savoury palate with a hint of nut.

Kato Kahachiro Shuzo Junmai Ginjo-shu Ginsuika 2008, Yamagata

Mature with hints of savoury character. Ripe stone fruit with layers of savoury, smoky flavours. Herbaceous and long.

Katoukichibee Shouten Tokusen Junmai Daiginjo 2008, Fukui

Ripe, tropical fruit with fresh aromas. Citrus, apple and tea leaf on the palate. Well-balanced.

Kitaya Junmai Daiginjo Kitaya 2009, Fukuoka

Citrus, yellow flowers; apples on the nose. Round, a hint of peach and melon on the palate. Ricy character. Long finish.

Kusumi Sake Product Nanadaime 2010, Niigata

Lightly aromatic with fresh citrus and floral aromas. Ripe and fresh, lemon-lime flower palate with a lingering finish.

Masuda Sake Company Masuizumi Junmai Daiginjo 2009, Toyama

Intense melon on the nose. Melon, caramel, mineral palate with a creamy texture. Fresh and clean. Long.
TZK

Matsuse Shuzo Fifa World Cup Matsunotsukasa 2009, Shiga

Creamy nose with light nuttiness. Smooth hint of cheddar and chocolate, good balance.
JP-HAS

Midorikawa Sake Company Snow Aged Rice Wine 2008, Niigata

Well-balanced with fresh acidity and ripe fruit on the palate. A delicious style.

Momokawa Brewing Inc Junmai Ginjo-shu Sugidama 2009, Aomori

Floral nose with pineapple but also mineral. Aromatic on the palate.

Omuraya Shuzojo Junmai Daiginjo Onnanakase 2009, Shizuoka

Ripe bananas on the nose. Soft texture with continued banana flavours. Clean, dry finish.

Sakuramasamune Junmai Daiginjyo Kazahana 2009, Hyogo

Rose and floral aromas on the nose. Fresh, floral palate with a touch of white pepper spice. Long and delicious.

Sasaki Shuzo Jurakudai Junmai Daiginjo-shu Shizukusake 2009, Kyoto

Supple, round aromas on the nose. Citrus ripeness on the palate with hints of lime flower. Ripe and clean on the finish.

Saura Yamadanishiki Junmai Daiginjo / Urakasumi 2008, Miyagi

Alcohol is quite pronounced. Good after palate. Simple and clean.
JPS, STE

Saura Yamahai Junmai Daiginjo Hirano / Urakasumi 2008, Miyagi

Pineapple well pronounced. Nice style. Simple.

Tajima Shuzo Fukuchitose Fuku 2008, Fukui

Ripe and mature, hints of tea leaf and over ripe banana. Nutty and round on the finish.

Tamanohikari Sake Brewing Tamanohikari

Junmai Daiginjo Chouzen Yamadanishiki 2009, Kyoto

Warm and floral on the nose. White pepper spice on the palate with well-structured flavours. Long and fresh on the finish.

Tanakaya Brewing Mizuo Junmai-ginjyo 2009, Nagano

Warm with ripe banana character. Banana and citrus on the palate with a very clean, very fresh finish.

Tenju Shuzo Junmai Ginjo Chokaisan 2009, Akita

Well-balanced and very elegant. Warm and ripe on the palate with a delicate finish.

Tsuji Zenbei Shoten Jyunmai Ginjyo Tsuji Zenbei 2009, Tochigi

Refreshing, soothing aroma, cedar, pine and cold melon punch.

Umenishiki Yamakawa Umenishiki Junmai Daiginjo Sake 2007, Ehime

Mature and ripe with a touch of savoury character. Lingering banana fruit on the finish with a good citrus kick.

Umenoyado Brewery Katsuragi Junmai-daiginjyo 2010, Nara

Mint, elegant and clean. Very attractive and dynamic.

Yukawa Shuzoten Kisoji Junmai Daiginjo 2009, Nagano

Nose - strawberry, wild strawberry. Palate - melony, creamy, rich and smooth with tangy and astringent finish.

JUNMAI-SHU

 REGIONAL SHIZUOKA JUNMAI TROPHY

Isojiman Premium Sake Brewery Isojiman Omachi Tokubets Junmai 2010, Shizuoka

Youthful and fresh with a smooth, banana fresh palate. Warm and ripe on the finish.
£30.00 BZI, JP-HAS

 CHAMPION JUNMAI, REGIONAL FUKUI TROPHY

Katoukichibee Shouten Born: Ginsen 2008, Fukui

Fresh, touch of petals, floral bouquet. Green fruity, honey, apricot jam. Medium long finish.

Akashi Sake Brewery Akashitai Junmai 2008, Hyogo

Fresh aromas of white flowers followed by crisp minerality. Long and balanced with a delicious savoury quality.
EDV

Chiyokotobuki Toraya Dewanosato Chiyokotobuki 2009, Yamagata

Beautiful flavour of white flower and also sugar syrup. Quite spicy. Would go well with any food.

Kamikokoro Shuzo Kamikokoro Amakuchi Junmai Haktou Koubo 2009, Okayama

Cheese and koji nose with a ripe, toasty palate. Smoky and creamy on the finish.
JP-OKA

Kobori Shuzoten Manzairaku Tsurugi Yamahai Junmai 2009, Ishikawa

Warm alcohol on the palate with fresh flavours of banana and tropical melon fruits.

Komachi-Shuzo Nagaragawa Junmaishu 2009, Gifu

Fresh and bright with ripe citrus fruit and a hint of banana on the palate. Fresh with high acidity.

Saito Shuzo Eikun Otaka Tokubetu Junmai-shu 2009, Kyoto

Full bodied with ripe citrus on the nose. Banana and citrus lime on the palate. Fresh.

Shata Shuzo Gorin Junmai-shu 2008, Ishikawa

Shiitake mushroom, soft sauce sweetness. Soft, light texture with a clean finish.

BRONZE

Bizen Shuzo-honten Specially Junmai-shu Dainagawa 2009, Akita

Pronounced nose of ripe fruit. Soft koji, with a semi-dry finish.

Bunraku Houjun Junmai-shu 2009, Saitama

Spicy and minerally on the nose. Quince and banana flavours with a touch of nuttiness on the finish.

Hiraizumi Honpo Hiraizumi Yamahai Junmai Maruhi No. 12 2009, Akita

Banana ripeness with a fresh pear palate. Warming alcohol with fresh acidity on the finish.
JP-OKA, TZK

Ichishima Sake Brewery Silk Deluxe 2009, Niigata

Ripe with a smooth, round mouthfeel. Fresh citrus fruit and lime flower on the palate. Hints of floral on the finish with long, lingering length.

Kikuhime Tsurunosato 2008, Ishikawa

Minerals and gently earthy. Boiled white asparagus. Alcohol high with a very dry finish.
JP-OKA

Kikuhime Mazuippai 2008, Ishikawa

Touch mature. Clean chestnut, cashew with peach coming through. Light and smooth.
JP-OKA

Kobori Shuzoten Manzairaku Jin Junmai 2009, Ishikawa

Ripe and sweet on the palate with a fresh finish.

Machida Shuzoten Machidashuzo 55 Gohyakumangoku 2009, Gunma

Peppery and warm on the palate with a fresh clean finish.
VER

Mitsutake Shuzojyo Tezukuri Junmaishu Mitsutake 2009, Saga

Mature and ripe with a nutty nose and warming palate. Fresh and clean on the finish.

Miyashita Sake Brewery Kiwamihijiri Sunshine Country Okayama Junmai-shu 2009, Okayama

Ripe and nutty with a mature character. Fresh with over-ripe banana on the finish.

Niida Honke Kinpou Shizenshu 2009, Fukushima

Full-bodied with a mouthfilling ripeness. Banana and melon on the warm, tropical finish.

Omuraya Shuzojo Junmai Wakatake Onikoroshi 2009, Shizuoka

Fresh, clean and zesty with a long, tropical finish.

Shata Shuzo Tengumai Yamahai-jikomi Junmai-shu 2007, Ishikawa

Rich perfumed white flowers and truffles. Good structure. Long savoury finish.
TZK

Shindo Sake Brewery Ura-gasanryu Fuka 2009, Yamagata

Melon and peach on the nose. Clean, ripe and fresh on the palate with good length.
JFI

Tenju Shuzo Tenju Komekarasodateta Junmaishu 2009, Akita

Melon and sweet banana on the palate. Clean and fresh on the finish.

Umeda-Shuzoujou Honshu-ichi Muroka Junmai Shu 2009, Hiroshima

Muscat aromas with a melon-banana palate. Fresh and peppery on the finish.

KOSHU

 CHAMPION KOSHU, REGIONAL HIROSHIMA TROPHY

Enoki Shuzo Hanahato Kijoshu Aged For 8 Years 2001, Hiroshima

Toffee, roasted nuts and ripe apple character. Hints of sticky toffee on the palate with good acidity supporting the weight. A raisin, honey finish.
AKE, JPS

 **REGIONAL TOTTORI KOSHU TROPHY**

Fujii Shuzo Hakuyou Koshu 1996, Tottori

Hay, chicken broth and clove on the nose with a touch of curry powder. Woody and savoury on the palate with a creamy, spicy finish.

 REGIONAL NIIGATA KOSHU TROPHY

Kaetsu Sake Brewery Kirin Jijyoshu Vintage 2001, Niigata

Coffee, black pepper and cinnamon on the nose with baked apple and brown sugar on the palate. Long, lingering flavours of burnt toffee with a fresh finish.
VNO

Daiichi Sake Brewery Kaika Kanpyoukaisyuppinshu 15 Nen Jukusei 1994, Tochigi

Clean and mature with pure umami. Elegant fruit undertones with pure, clean fruit. Apricots on the finish.

Goto Shuzoten Limited Partnership Benten Junmai Daiginjo Genshu Koshu Yamadanishiki 1993, Yamagata

Dried fish with nutty, toffee ripeness. Palate is coffee, candied fig and dried mango. Dried and lingering finish.

Kiuchi Brewery Kikusakari Junmai Ginjyo 2009, Ibaraki

Aroma is very pronounced with notes of pineapple candy. Palate is fresh with well-balanced fruit.

Sake is brewed with rice, water, and sophisticated and delicate techniques. Sake is born and grows in the changing four seasons of Japan. Surely, it is the fruit of blessing from rich Japanese nature and Japanese wisdom, and is a cultural asset and the pride of Japanese people.

The Sake Samurai Association was established in 2005 as an officially recognized organization of the Japan Sake Brewers Association, and carries out many projects to send messages on sake and sake culture both inside and outside Japan. In particular,

we confer the title of "Sake Samurai" on several people who love sake and sake culture and have a prominent influence in proliferating its splendor, showing our respect for them.

Moreover, since 2007, we have been cooperating with the International Wine Challenge (IWC) as an official coordinator for the sake category at IWC, and dealing with various tasks on preparing for the sake category, for example, to invite participants to enter

in the competition and recommend some judges from Japan.

In addition, we do various activities to inform of wonderful and tasty sake to the world through various opportunities at sake seminars, Kuramoto Dinner, and so on.

✉ For further information and inquiry, please contact:
Sake Samurai Secretariat c/o
The Japan Sake Brewers Association Junior Council
1-1-21 West Shimbashi, Minato Ward, Tokyo, JAPAN 105-0003
TEL 03-3501-0101 FAX 03-3501-6018
E-mail info@sakesamurai.jp

Matsuse Shuzo Matsunotsulcasa Special Seizaburo Seto 2005, Shiga
Warming spice on the nose with ripe pear and banana aromas. Soft, clean fruit with a touch of grassy herbaceousness. Lush. JP-HAS

Suehiro Sake Brewery Ruten Honjyouzou 1988, Fukushima
Nutty, toffee richness with sweet peach fruit on the palate. Fresh and clean.

BRONZE

Bunraku Daikoshu 1999, Saitama
Nutty with pickled vegetable character. Almost like oxtail soup. Mellow and soft on the palate with caramel and nougat finish.

General Partnership Watanabe Sake Brewing Store Nechi 2005, Niigata
Clean minerals on the nose, a touch of burdock. Rich flavours of melon and peach on the palate. Powder light finish.

Goto Shuzojo Seiun Koshu Kojijyunrei 2005, Mie
Fresh apple and asparagus on the nose, clean flavours of apple and pear on the palate. Pleasant acidity.

Ichishima Sake Brewery Hizou Koshu Aumont Ginjo Genshu 1997, Niigata
Roasted caramel and nuts on the nose. Caramelised pear with warm Christmas spice on the palate. Well-balanced.

Ishikawashuzo Tamajiman French Oak 1997, Tokyo
Yellow candied flower nose. Mango chutney on the palate with a fresh, warming finish.
£45.00

Kaetsu Kaganotuki Kohakutsuki 2007, Ishikawa
Nutty and ripe with a hint of pickled vegetable flavour. Sweet, but with balanced acidity. Ripe, lush and long.

Kinmon Akita Shuzo Yamabuki Gold 2000, Akita-ken
Coffee and caramel nose. Warming spice and vegetal character on the palate.

Kinmon Akita Shuzo Yamabuki Premium 1995, Akita-ken
Intense mixture of roasted nuts, coffee, cold English breakfast tea and vegetables on the nose. Palate is strong and savoury with caramel and toffee finish.

Nanbu Bijin Nanbubijin All Koji 2004, Iwate
Toffee with a fermented vegetable edge. Nougat with baked apple and nutty aromas. Lovely with an astringent taste, balanced, perfect for the style.

Ono Shuzo Oigame Gonenjukusei Junmaishu Hizouoigame 2003, Hiroshima
Pickled vegetable with a touch of toffee on the nose. Warming and sweet on the palate with good acidity and freshness.

South Africa

With the eyes of the sporting world on South Africa for the World Cup this year, there is an inevitable surge of activity around the wines. The Cape winelands are some of the most beautifully situated vineyards in the world, and can make some smashing wines to boot. From verdant and zippy Sauvignon Blanc to dense and thick Pinotage, there really is something for every palate in South Africa. As a country, it has also championed the Fairtrade movement, so look out for wines displaying that logo – as well as the IWC medal stickers, of course!

KEY FACTS

Total production
The annual harvest in 2006 amounted to 1.3 million tonnes of which 70 per cent was used for wine.

Total vineyard
102,146ha

Top 10 varieties
1. Chenin Blanc
2. Sauvignon Blanc
3. Colombard
4. Chardonnay
5. Shiraz
6. Cabernet Sauvignon
7. Viognier
8. Pinotage
9. Pinot Noir
10. Merlot

Producers
- Worcester
- Paarl
- Stellenbosch
- Malmesbury
- Robertson
- Olifants River
- Orange River
- Little Karoo

Producers
4,185

2010 IWC PERFORMANCE

Trophies	4
Gold	10
Silver	74
Bronze	137
Great Value Awards	1

Fleur Du Cap Unfiltered Semillon 2009, Coastal Region White

Pale lemon colour. Rich, creamy, oaky nose with citrus guava fruit. Lovely oaky attack with creamy tropical depth and lovely vanillary length.

Lomond Pincushion Single Vineyard Sauvignon Blanc 2009, Cape Agulhas White

Fresh, bright mineral nose. Good tropicality, very lemony with fresh acidity and mineral balance. Long.
SAO

 SOUTH AFRICA WHITE TROPHY

Oak Valley Chardonnay 2009, Elgin White

Elegant citrus aromas. Lovely balance on palate. Zippy acidity, great purity of fruit.

Dunstone Shiraz 2008, Western Cape Red

Peppery, medicinal palate. Has something extra to offer. Good length. Balanced tannin.

 SOUTH AFRICAN RED TROPHY

Vrede En Lust Boet Erasmus 2007, Simonsberg Paarl Red

Full on, upfront style yet packs a punch with vibrant freshness. Rich, blackberry, mint and dark chocolate flavours, tannins, softening slowly. Needs time but powerful, complex with bags of style. Intense and gloriously lengthy finish.
H2F, SAO

Klein Constantia Vin De Constance 2005, Constantia Sweet

Intense and floral with apricot and sugary notes. Very concentrated, rich but firm with apricot and peach prettiness. Balanced acidity.
£30.00 BB&R, HVN, MWW

Stellar Organics Heaven On Earth NV, Olifants River Sweet

Burnt orange and caramel flavours with delicate jasmine aromas. Excellent balance and a great finish.
£8.99 EVW, VRT

Fleur Du Cap Noble Late Harvest 2008, Coastal Region Botrytis

Burnt caramel, with a hint of toast on the nose. Apricot and lemon with soft honeyed palate. Good acidity with a touch of oxidative character. Very attractive.
£10.99

Fleur Du Cap Noble Late Harvest 2009, Coastal Region Botrytis

Apple and toffee spice on the nose. Crisp acidity with a rich apple, toffee spiced palate. Juicy and harmonious. Clean and ripe on the finish.
£10.99

 WESTERN CAPE BOTRYTIS TROPHY

Nederburg Winemasters Reserve Noble Late Harvest 2009, Western Cape Botrytis

Rich, ripe, red apple fruit. Spicy marmalade with candied orange and lemon peel on the palate. Round and warming with lush apple and nutmeg spice. Lingering on the finish.

Backsberg John Martin Reserve Sauvignon Blanc 2009, Paarl White
Lifted pungent fruit on the nose. Lychee and tropical fruits on the palate with a floral overtone. Complex and balanced with a long finish of lush fruit.
£13.00 IRV, SBB, WHD

Bouchard Finlayson Crocodiles Lair Chardonnay 2009, Overberg White
Tropical passionfruit on the nose with pawpaw and lime aromas. A fresh and lifted palate with mineral, citrus backbone. Zingy and fresh on the finish.
£12.25 WI-AV

Buitenverwachting Husseys Vlei Sauvignon Blanc 2009, Constantia White
Delicate elderflower, fine with a touch of vegetal character. Bright, dry and flavoursome. Long, fresh and mouth-watering finish with a good mineral edge.
£15.00

Cederberg Private Cellar Waitrose Foundation Chenin Blanc 2009, Cederberg White
Lemon, flinty and limey. Ripe, mouthfilling flavours. Acidity balanced lingering finish.
£7.99 WAIT

De Grendel Winifred 2009, Western Cape White
Lively, lifted fruit. Grapefruit and citrus with hints of herbaceous character on palate. Punch of acidity on the long finish.
ODD, SWS

De Grendel Koetshuis Sauvignon Blanc 2009, Coastal Region White
Sugar snap nose with fresh minerality. The palate has a flinty edge with ripe citrus fruit and a touch of creaminess. Well-balanced and fresh.
£16.99 ODD, SWS

Delaire Graff Delaire Sauvignon Blanc 2009, Western Cape White
Green apple and lychee fruit on the nose. Green apple with a touch of Welch's Grape juice on the palate. Fresh and pleasing.

Delaire Graff Estate Chardonnay 2008, Western Cape White
Ripe lime, orange blossom and apricot on the nose. Good acidity on the palate with lively peach fruit. Attractive and fresh with a very lively finish.

Diemersdal Mm Louw Sauvignon Blanc 2009, Durbanville White
Natural with a very fresh citrus palate cut grass and a bit of smoky character with a ripe, stoney fruit finish. Juicy and pithy.

Elgin Vintners Viognier 2009, Elgin White
Apricot and warm spice aromas. Almonds and chewy fruit with a touch of peachy sweetness on the palate. Marzipan and stone fruit finish.
£14.99 HAR, JAS, SAO

Fleur Du Cap Unfiltered Semillon 2008, Coastal Region White
Waxy, lanolin and lemon pie aromas on the nose. Pure and clean flavours on the palate with juicy, lively fruit and flavours of green apple.

Groot Constantia Grand Constance Muscat 2007, Constantia White
Delicate wine with orange and tangerine flavours. Complex

and concentrated.
£19.99 HLD

Groot Constantia Sauvignon Blanc 2009, Constantia
White
Intriguing aromas - floral, with soft red fruits. Spritzy and lifted on the palate with good grip. Dry and appetising.
£10.99 HLD

Jordan Nine Yards Chardonnay 2008, Stellenbosch White
Ripe, oaky nose. Vanilla and a touch of cream. Very well-balanced, good acidity, fresh and vibrant with nice minerality on the finish. Excellent.
£20.45 CBC, CPW, PCC

KWV Sauvignon Blanc 2009, Stellenbosch White
Elegant and complex aromas of floral and blackcurrant leaf. Silky and textured on the palate with vibrant acidity and minerality. Long with pleasing Sauvignon character.

KWV The Mentors Sauvignon Blanc Semillon 2009, Stellenbosch White
Very grassy and herbaceous on the nose. Good, pungent fruit with gooseberry flavour and zippy acidity. Fresh and cleansing finish.

La Motte Chardonnay 2008, Western Cape White
Chunky charm. Lots of flavour, not shy on oak but well-integrated.
£13.99

Lomond Sauvignon Blanc 2009, Cape Agulhas White
Fresh, lemony nose with a lemon-lime palate. Very zingy with fresh, ripe fruit. A touch of herbaceousness on the finish.

Lomond Snowbush 2009, Cape Agulhas White
Nice, clean gooseberry fruit. Grapefruit and ripe citrus on the palate. Well-balanced with long length and good depth of flavour.
CWS

Plaisir De Merle Chardonnay 2008, Paarl White
Rich oaky nose leads to a tropical palate. Good length and balance.

Rustenberg Chardonnay 2008, Stellenbosch White
A pleasing aroma of toastiness. Ripe and full bodied on the palate with concentrated tropical fruits, and balanced acidity. Excellent structure.
£11.49 WI-AV, WAIT

Rustenberg Five Soldiers 2008, Stellenbosch White
Good, complex nose leading to a palate of generous fruit. Ripe apple and a touch of minerality on the creamy finish. Very complex and very enjoyable.
£25.99 WI-AV

Swartland Winery Eagles Crest Chenin Blanc Chardonnay Viognier 2009, Western Cape White
Stewed apple fruit on the nose with hints of ripe citrus. On the palate, fresh and clean fruit, zesty citrus and roundness on the finish. Very pleasing and easy to drink.
£5.81 TESC

Vergelegen Chardonnay Reserve 2008, Stellenbosch White
Crisp, fresh, green apple, pear and grass clippings on the nose. Very good definition. Crisp and well defined on the palate, zesty and racy. Great length. Excellent.
£13.99 JOB

Villiera Marks & Spencer Barrel Fermented Chenin Blanc 2009, Stellenbosch White
Very complex mineral/honey. Great oily viscous length. Fantastic.
£7.99 M&S

Waterkloof False Bay Chenin Blanc 2009, Coastal Region White
Flint and mineral nose. Some nice spice, apple, nettle and sweet apple. Lovely complexity and lingering finish.
£6.99 PBA

Zonnenbloem Sauvignon Blanc Ltd Edition 2009, Western Cape White
Ripe, sweet fruit on the nose with a vegetal, asparagus aroma. Ripe fruit on the palate with a peppery finish.
£8.99

Bellevue Morkel Pinotage 2008, Stellenbosch Red
Lifted soy animal aromas. Moderate body oak slightly dominates fruit weight but tannins well-integrated.
£8.99

Bellingham Merlot With A Dash Of Malbec 2007, Coastal Region Red
Clean nose with brambly fruit, plum and spice. Velvety tannins and good length.
£7.99 CWS, TESC

Bellingham The Bernard Series Bush Vine Pinotage 2007, Stellenbosch Red
Blackcurrant leafy cedar notes. Core fruit good weight. Firm acid maintained. Good length.
£10.99 DGB

Bernheim JH Pacas 2004, Paarl Red
Lifted, scented, cedary - fine.

Sweet fruit, nicely balanced acidity and soft tannins. Rather tasty.

Bouchard Finlayson Galpin Peak Pinot Noir 2009, Walker Bay Red
Earthy, cherry aromatic nose. Well-balanced fruit on the palate with sleek tannins and a long savoury finish.
£20.95 WI-AV

Bruwer Raats MR De Compostella 2007, Stellenbosch Red
Leafy, slightly smoky, earthy nose. Bags of flavour, tannic grip with good freshness and balance.
£38.00 AAW

Citrusdal Cellars Sainsbury's Fairtrade Pinotage 2008, Western Cape Red
Fresh, juicy, raspberry fruit on the nose with a touch of green leaves. Clean, fresh raspberry fruit on the palate with a seductive, nicely textured finish.
SAIN

Darling Cellars Dc Six Tonner Merlot 2008, Western Cape Red
Spicy forest floor aromas. Oak dominated palate. Ripe, grainy tannin overpowers the coffee/mocha fruit profile.
£6.00

Drostdy-Hof Merlot 2009, Western Cape Red
Smoky chocolate aroma. Savoury structured palate with integrated tannin, ripe with a long persistent finish.

Ernie Els Big Easy 2008, Stellenbosch Red
Primary, bright fruit on the nose. Subtle chocolate flavours and delightful sweet fruit on the palate. Big tannins with vibrant

and tangy acidity.
£15.75 WI-AV

Fairview Cyril Back Shiraz 2007, Coastal Region Red
Dense black fruit, pepper and fruit concentrate. Lovely spice, fine tannins. Long finish.
£25.99

Fairview Shiraz 2008, Coastal Region Red
Rich medium brick/crimson, very well developed, aged. Palate is firm and complex.

Flagstone Writer's Block Pinotage 2008, Western Cape Red
Quite reduced on the nose but lots of red berry fruit on the palate. Good concentration with fresh, green flavours and toasty oak on the finish.
£14.99 POG

Julien Schaal Syrah 2008, Hermanus Red
Good bacon/chocolate, spicy. Generous, clean and soft. Good palate, pure fruit.
£11.00 HDW, HRC

Kanonkop Estate Paul Sauer 2006, Stellenbosch Red
Pure blackcurrant aroma. Fresh and aromatic on palate with blueberry, black cherry. Smooth tannins. Fresh acidity.
TESC

Klein Constantia Cabernet Merlot 2007, Constantia Red
Ripe berry jam aromas. Fairly rich mineral cedar currant flavours. Supple but chewy tannin. Good acidity. Mineral finish and balanced.
£9.99 WSO

KWV The Mentors Petit Verdot 2008, Stellenbosch Red
Spicy nose showing vanilla oak aromas over creamy black fruit. The palate is smooth with very elegant tannins and excellent depth of flavour.

KWV The Mentors Shiraz 2007, Stellenbosch Red
White pepper and some new oak vanilla nose. Gentle pine fruit, a bit herbal. Nice texture and length, supple tannin and obvious style. Well done!

La Vigne Estate Single Vineyard Shiraz 2007, Western Cape Red
Deep ruby. Pronounced blackberry notes. Some leather with full black fruit flavours. Good length.

Lanzerac Pinotage 2008, Stellenbosch Red
Spicy red fruit, intense attractive aromatics with fruit acid and bright red fruit. Well handled, persistent length.
£12.50 H2F

Louis Wines Louis 2007, Stellenbosch Red
Stylish good fruity nose. Good style fruit with a promising taste.

Manley Private Cellar Manley 2005, Coastal Region Red
Some spice, plum and prune fruit. Good tannic structure. Full bodied and high account. Medium length.
WBW

Manley Private Cellar Pinotage 2006, Coastal Region Red
Smoky with a floral, earthy aroma. Soft, smooth and sweet with ripe vanilla flavour. Round and elegant with a nice finish.
WBW

Môreson Pinotage 2008, Paarl Red
Earthy and ripe with dense fruit and good tannins on the palate. Sweet and well-balanced with fresh acidity.

Nederburg Private Bin R181 Merlot 2006, Western Cape Red
Some red cherry/leafy character, some herbal, savoury. Soft attack, medium concentration. Soft tannins, some depth. Medium and smoky finish.

Obikwa Cabernet Sauvignon 2009, Western Cape Red
Fresh and juicy, with an attractive fruitiness. Delicious.

Pierre Wahl Rijk's Estate Syrah 2007, Tulbagh Red
Opulent aromas, chocolate and well-balanced with juicy fruit.

Pierre Wahl Rijk's Estate The Master 2007, Tulbagh Red
Dusky, damson, earthy aromas. Chewy tannin, ripe berries, lingering finish.

Plaisir De Merle Cabernet Sauvignon 2007, Paarl Red
Quite pure Cabernet aromas, mature. Fruity and nicely balanced. Excellent acidity.

Rust En Vrede Cabernet Sauvignon 2007, Stellenbosch Red
Fresh blackcurrants, figs, plums, liquorice on the nose. Full bodied with silky tannins and vibrant acidity. Will evolve well.
£16.75 WI-AV

Rust En Vrede Single Vineyard Syrah 2007, Stellenbosch Red
Very juicy. Good length. Nice finish.
£37.50 WI-AV

Spice Route Malabar 2006, Swartland Red
Substantial coffee and spice aromas. Bread and black fruit on the palate. Poised and elegant.
£25.99 SWG

Spice Route Shiraz 2007, Swartland Red
Liquorice nose and oak fruits. Black fruit, spicy. Feel of sweet, black, jammy fruit. Good length.
£11.99

Spier Creative Block 3 2007, Stellenbosch Red
Good concentration with resolved tannin. Good concentration of fruit and length.

Spier Creative Block 5 2007, Stellenbosch Red
Rich, ripe, well made style. Black pepper, all spice and stewed forest fruits dusted with coca flavours dominate. Edge of liquorice. Sinewy but structured with a persistent finish.

Stellenzicht Golden Triangle Pinotage 2007, Stellenbosch Red
Stylish, restrained, quite dense, dark fruit, some pepper and quite giving with backbone. Ambitious.
SAO

Sumaridge Epitome 2007, Western Cape Red
Nice cherries, complex, delicious, light and elegant.

Swartland Winery Indalo Cabernet Sauvignon 2007, Western Cape Red
Deep ruby. Dense dark berry fruits, tobacco and coffee. Lovely freshness. Attractive texture.

Swartland Winery Indalo Pinotage 2007, Western Cape Red
Bright, fruity plums with a touch

of vanilla. Medium weight with ripe and dry tannins. Sweet, ripe fruit on the palate with a plum fruit finish.

Waterford Estate Cabernet Sauvignon 2006, Western Cape Red

Leaf, cedar and blackcurrant fruit - lovely and intense. Concentrated black fruits with complex cigar box. Fine, brisk acid and compact, fresh tannins.
£16.20 BB&R, FMV

Bon Courage Jacques Brueré Brut Reserve 2006, Western Cape Sparkling

Creamy melon and baked pears on nose and palate. Well-integrated and balanced. Lovely ripe, smooth finish. Vibrant and lively.
£13.99 GRP, TSS

 GREAT VALUE SPARKLING WINE UNDER £10

Villiera Marks & Spencer Brut Natural 2007, Stellenbosch Sparkling

Strong, yeasty, autolytic character. Very rich and strongly flavoured. Clearly warm climate; soft acidity.
£9.99 M&S

Nederburg Edelkeur 2007, Paarl Sweet

Honeyed orange marmalade on the nose and palate. Buttery finish with good complexity.

Nederburg Edelkeur 2008, Paarl Sweet

Warm and ripe on the palate with crisp acidity and sweet marmalade character. Nutmeg spice on the clean, orange blossom finish.

Nederburg Eminence 2007, Paarl Sweet

Well developed, with ripe and heady aromas. Apricots, honey and rose petal flavours on the palate with a zingy citrus streak. Very well-balanced and long.

Nederburg Eminence 2008, Paarl Sweet

Marmalade and sweet peas on the nose. Canned peaches on the palate with lush sweetness. Honeyed with a long, fresh acid finish.

Meerendal Chenin Blanc Natural Sweet 2009, Durbanville Botrytis

Juicy apple and sultana spiced buns. Good acidity, spicy, fresh apple fruit with tangy and tart flavours. Long with an apple juice box finish.
£18.00 K&L

BRONZE

Bellingham Chardonnay With A Splash Of Viognier 2008, Coastal Region White

Good pure fruit. Lovely intensity. Balanced with long flavours.
£8.16 Widely Available

Bellingham The Bernard Series Hand-Picked Viognier 2009, Coastal Region White

Apricot nose with hints of creamy richness. Juicy stone fruit palate with lingering apricot on the finish.
£9.99 MWW, SAO

Bizoe Henrietta 2009, Franschhoek White

Clean, fresh nose with grassy, green fruit on the palate.

Black Oystercatcher Sauvignon Blanc 2008, Elim White

Big, lush, tropical nose. A touch

of savoury, smoky fruit balanced with ripe, citrus acidity. A big wine with good length.

Bouchard Finlayson Walker Bay Sauvignon Blanc 2009, Walker Bay White

Lovely floral and peachy fruit on the nose. Spritz on the palate with ripe apricots and green apple. Fresh and clean on the finish.
£10.50 WI-AV

Buitenverwachting Chardonnay 2009, Constantia White

Attractive floral aromas, some oak character coming through. Quite long, clean, attractive finish.
£16.00

Buitenverwachting Sauvignon Blanc 2009, Constantia White

Very fine, pure and grassy notes. Dry, fruity and very natural flavour. Fresh with good length.
£10.00

Cederberg Private Cellar Sauvignon Blanc 2009, Cederberg White

Pungent, tropical fruit. Guava and lychee with soft sherbet like flavours. Florally and juicy on the green tinged finish.
£11.50

Delaire Graff Estate Sauvignon Blanc Coastal Cuvée 2009, Western Cape White

Supple lychee and a bit of lime with a backbone of tropicality. Lush and fresh on the finish.

Douglas Green Chardonnay 2009, Wellington White

Clean fruit with good intensity. A touch of residual sugar with melon and juicy apple flavours. A

touch of toffee on the finish.
£5.75 BTH

Durbanville Hills Biesjies Craal Sauvignon Blanc 2009, Durbanville White

Sweet blackcurrant leaf, fine aromas with a hint of stone fruit. Interesting style with restrained spritz. Almost sweet and sour in style with a juicy, ripe finish.
£11.89 SAO

Escapade Sauvignon Blanc 2009, Stellenbosch White

Tropical fruits on the nose. Some grapefruit zest and well-balanced lime-lemon fruit on the palate. Lush and fresh on the finish.

Flagstone Flagstone Word of Mouth Viognier 2008, Western Cape White

Apricots and spicy almond aromas with well-balanced juicy fruit. Crisp acidity and heady almond tones on the palate with stone fruit finish.
£9.99 MCT

Flagstone Marks & Spencer Knockon Wood Sauvignon Semillon 2008, Western Cape White

Delicate style of wine with tropical fruit notes and a good dash of acidity on the finish.
£8.99 M&S

Fleur Du Cap Unfiltered Limited Release Sauvignon Blanc 2009, Western Cape White

Quite ripe with fresh citrus on the nose. A touch of herbaceousness and pepper on the palate with long, citrus freshness on the finish.

Fleur Du Cap Unfiltered Viognier 2008, Stellenbosch White

Fresh honeyed nose, lovely ripe

fruit on the palate with good length.

Fleur Du Cap Unfiltered Viognier 2009, Stellenbosch White

Melon and pineapple notes, full lush ripe pear flavours with good acidity and length.

Glen Carlou Chardonnay 2008, Paarl White

Very fragrant peach and apricot tinged nose. Good definition of fruit with well-balanced acidity. Fresh and clean on the finish.
£11.95

Graham Beck Bowed Head Chenin Blanc 2008, Coastal Region White

Bold and quite nutty on the nose. Rich, sweet, bold fruit on palate with a touch of oak and some sweetness.

Grande Provence Chardonnay 2008, Coastal Region White

Smooth, integrated nose. Great tropical flavours with real grape fruit edge. Long and fresh on finish.
£18.00

Hermanuspietersfontein Die Bartho 2009, Western Cape White

Oily and lean on the nose. A very crisp palate of nettle and ripe citrus. Clean and lingering finish.

Hidden Valley Land's End Sauvignon Blanc 2009, Elim White

Succulent tropical fruit on the nose with more of the same on the palate. Lush and ripe on the finish.
£8.99 ODD

Jordan Chardonnay 2009, Stellenbosch White
Understated but developing

nicely. Ripe with cohesive fruit. A touch of oak on the palate with a ripe, vanilla like finish.
£12.45 BTH, GHL, GWI

Jordan The Outlier Sauvignon Blanc 2009, Stellenbosch White

Green, asparagus notes with hints of gooseberry. Fresh and fruity on the palate.
£10.99 BCW, EVW

Ken Forrester Sainsbury's Taste The Difference Chenin Blanc 2009, Western Cape White

Flint nose and palate of warm fruits and minerality. Perhaps a little short.
£6.99 SAIN

Ken Forrester Workhorse 2009, Stellenbosch White
Light, elegant, soft and smooth with a good structure and length. Oily and attractive.
£6.99 M&S

Klein Constantia Sauvignon Blanc 2009, Constantia White

Stewed and overripe fruit on the nose with lush apricot and melon on the palate. Long, lush and pleasing.
£11.99 MWW

KWV Spar South African Chenin Reserve 2009, Western Cape White
Light, nutty with a hint of peppermint. Soft, fruity, slightly sweet palate.
£4.99 SPR

KWV The Mentors Semillon 2008, Western Cape White
Good, clean, fresh fruit with balanced and zippy acidity. Good fruit character with long, fruity finish.

Lomond Sugarbush Single Vineyard Sauvignon Blanc 2009, Cape Agulhas White
Dried herbs and peppercorn on the nose. Spicy and warm on the palate with ripe citrus fruits. Lifting acidity on the finish.
ODF

Lutzville Cool Climate Chardonnay 2009, Lutzville Valley White
Melon and apple on the nose. Light, fine and fresh fruit on the palate with a medley of fresh fruit salad. Well-balanced minerality with a soft finish.

Môreson Premium Chardonnay 2008, Franschhoek White
Bright tropical notes lead to a rich and easy palate. A great example.

Nederberg Manor House Sauvignon Blanc 2009, Coastal Region White
Ripe, tropical fruit on the nose. Hints of asparagus and tinned vegetable on the palate. Refreshing and clean.
£8.99

Nederberg Private Bin D252 Sauvignon Blanc Semillon 2009, Coastal Region White
Very forward style, ripe fruit with lean acidity. Good balance with long and lingering ripeness.

Nederburg Fnd Chardonnay Viognier 2009, Western Cape White
Light lime and green apple on the nose. Hints of vanilla on the palate with a touch of ripe fruit on the finish.
£5.49 MRN, WAIT

Nederburg Private Bin D234 Sauvignon Blanc 2009, Groenekloof White
Crisp and lively with soft creamy fruit on the palate. Concentrated grapefruit and balanced acidity on the finish.

Oak Valley Sauvignon Blanc 2009, Elgin White
Quite austere with good steely fruit on the palate. Fresh and citrusy on the finish. Long with a strong acid finish.

Riebeek Cellars Reserve 2009, Western Cape White
Citric lemon flavours, lozenge. Good length and flavours.

Robertson Wide Winery Cullinan View Chenin Blanc 2009, Robertson White
Flint and mineral nose. Apple, honey and acidity all balanced.
£5.21

Rustenberg Roussane 2009, Stellenbosch White
Herbaceous and grassy on the nose. Hints of fresh floral and ripe fruit flavours. Very oily texture, nicely balanced.
£14.99 WI-AV

Saam Mountain Middelburg Chenin Blanc 2007, Paarl White
Big, oily aroma, flint. Good weight in glass. Big mouthfeel of peach and oils. Racy acidity, good balance with some nuttiness.
£7.99 BWL

Spier Creative Block 2 2009, Stellenbosch White
Lush and pungent on the nose. Overripe melon balanced with ripe citrus. Light and fresh on the finish.

Spier Private Collection Chardonnay 2007, Stellenbosch White
Touch of Tropicana on the nose. A little mango with ripe rounded entry. Good purity, orange peel,

mango and concentrated citrus on the palate.

Spier Private Collection Chardonnay 2008, Stellenbosch White
Fragrant and well-defined on the nose. Lemon, mineral and green apple fruit on the palate. Ripe and well-balanced, quite dry but delineated on the finish.

Spier Private Collection Chenin Blanc 2008, Stellenbosch White
Very stylish, rich and home-grown. Lean yet with great elegance. Very good.

Stellenzicht Semillon Reserve 2008, Stellenbosch White
Honey and beeswax on the nose. Rich flavours with lots of mouthfeel.

Sumaridge Chardonnay 2009, Western Cape White
Fresh, clean nose that eschews oak to great effect, but the palate is determined, long and fresh with nicely creamy character.

Uitkyk Estate Sauvignon Blanc 2009, Stellenbosch White
Pale lemon green. Pungent grassy and gooseberry, elderflower. Juicy fruit with pear and passionfruit, good grip, moderate length.

Villiera Marks & Spencer Crows Fountain Sauvignon Blanc 2009, Stellenbosch White
Full, minerally and peppery aromas. Confected citrus fruit on the palate with a ripe, long finish.
£7.99 M&S

Waterford Estate Chardonnay 2008, Western Cape White
Late ripened fruit on the nose. Apple and a touch of dried mango on the palate. Oaky with a creamy, lush finish.
£18.90 BB&R, FMV

Waterford Estate Sauvignon Blanc 2008, Western Cape White
Dried herbs and fresh cut grass on the nose. The palate is ripe with fresh citrus and melon fruits. Long and lush on the finish.
£12.80

Allesverloren Shiraz 2008, Swartland Red
Some leather and black fruit. Pure concentrated dark fruit.
SAO

Arabella Arabella 2009, Western Cape Red
Nice full aromas of juicy red fruits on the nose. Smooth, elegant flavours of sweet spices and red cherries. Lovely balance of acidity, soft tannins and alcohol. Long vibrant finish.
£7.99

Baarsma Lyngrove Platinum Latitude 2007, Stellenbosch Red
Nicely blended, balanced, red fruit and slightly but pleasantly leafy.

Baarsma Lyngrove Platinum Pinotage 2007, Stellenbosch Red
Nose quite restrained. Well-balanced wine with ripe berry concentration, ripe tannins and hot alcohol finish.

Baarsma Lyngrove Platinum Shiraz 2007, Stellenbosch Red
Black fruits, oak coffee spice. Juicy with good extraction.

Barton & Guestier Shiraz Cabernet Sauvignon 2007, Walker Bay Red
Spicy, chocolatey, rich and

complex. Tannic and full bodied.
£6.99 BTN

Bellevue Morkel Tumara 2005, Stellenbosch Red
Medium intense cherry and cassis fruit. A touch of savoury character as well. Solid tannin.
£8.99

Bizoe Estalet Syrah 2008, Western Cape Red
Sweet red fruit aromas, very ripe with a stewed fruit nose. Fresh and ripe on the palate.

Boekenhoutskloof Porcupine Ridge Syrah 2009, Western Cape Red
Rich, ripe and balanced. Sweet and ripe with complex spice and fruit on the palate.
£7.49 CAM, P&S, WAIT

Boekenhoutskloof The Wolftrap 2009, Western Cape Red
Spice and herbs with red fruit character. Acidity and tannins in good balance.
£6.99 KIN, ODD, PWC, SAO

Boschendal Reserve Collection Grande Reserve 2007, Coastal Region Red
Blackberries, black cherries with oak dominant. Chocolate notes. Lovely complexity. Cigars. Great spicy finish. Ripe with great character.

Bosman Family Vineyards Pinotage 2008, Paarl Red
Ripe plum, cherry and strawberry aromas. Loads of ripe oak with stewed fruit on the palate. Fresh and long with balanced tannins.
£30.00

Brahms Shiraz 2005, Paarl Red
Meat and red fruit aromas. Ripe and very savoury on the palate. Well made with a long finish.

Citrusdal Cellars Hope's Garden Cabernet Sauvignon 2008, Western Cape Red
Vibrant wild berry fruit and smoky oak nose. Bright and fresh, juicy, dense and long with a slight animal finish.
ASDA

Constantia Glen Constantia Glen 2007, Constantia Red
Mocha, rich, black fruits with juicy ripeness.

Dieu Donné Vineyards Merlot 2007, Franschhoek Red
Full, scented nose. Fruity flavour with long farewell. An attractive wine.
£9.83 PAT

Doolhof The Minotaur 2007, Western Cape Red
Lively red luscious damson plum fruits with exceptional intensity and sweet floral edge to nose. Plush, juicy palate. Silky rich tannins with freshness.

Douglas Green Cabernet Sauvignon 2009, Western Cape Red
Restrained mossy nose. Mocha infused palate.
£5.49 BTH, MRN

Elgin Vintners Agama 2007, Elgin Red
Medium red/orange hues. Lifted rich complex fruit. Oak age. Great, soft tannin and good depth.
£14.99 HAR, JAS, SAO

Ernie Els Bordeaux Blend 2006, Stellenbosch Red
Lush, slightly ripe red berry fruit. Good wine, balanced and long.
£41.75 WI-AV

Ernie Els Cirrus Syrah 2007, Stellenbosch Red
Pepper and spice with brambly fruit and some orange peel.

Slightly short.
£25.75 WI-AV

Ernie Els Engelbrecht Els 2007, Stellenbosch Red
Very attractive nose - minty blackcurrant. Plenty of sweet ripe fruit, tannin and fresh acidity. Appetising.
£21.50 WI-AV

Escapade Merlot 2006, Stellenbosch Red
Black fruits, well-balanced with tannins, flavours, integrated oak leading to a great finish. Elegant and great finesse.

Fairview Primo Pinotage 2008, Coastal Region Red
Meaty with some spice on the nose. Smoky, rich and sweet on the palate with spicy flavours. Ripe, red fruit balanced with soft oak and grainy tannins.
£12.99 SAO

Firstcape Blue Range Shiraz 2009, Western Cape Red
Bright colour, very fruity and ripe with good balance. Fresh berry fruits on the finish.
ASDA

Firstcape Millstone Shiraz 2009, Western Cape Red
Lush and ripe with black forest fruits. Fresh and clean on the finish.
ASDA

Flagstone Dragon Tree Cabernet Sauvignong Shiraz Pinotage 2007, Western Cape Red
Restrained cedar and black cherry to nose. Rich, luscious black fruit and plum. Softly textured tannins and soft acidity.
£9.99 MCT, TESC

Flagstone Music Room Cabernet Sauvignon 2007,

Western Cape Red
Intense smoky accents overlying very ripe Cabernet fruit. Full bodied and rich. Good freshness. Grippy tannins.
£14.99 POG

Fleur du Cap Unfiltered Merlot 2008, Stellenbosch Red
Touch leafy, with a attractive note of toasty oak.
£10.49

Glen Carlou Cabernet Sauvignon 2007, Paarl Red
Leafy, savoury style with hints of tobacco and berry fruit on the finish.

Grande Provence The Grande Provence 2005, Coastal Region Red
Bright nose with light fruit and peppery aromas. Sweet and rich on the palate.
£30.00

Guardian Peak Lapa Cabernet Sauvignon 2008, Stellenbosch Red
Ripe, black fruit nose. Rich flavours, liqueur like texture with fresh tannin and good length. Nice energy with a bit of a short finish.
£16.99 WI-AV, WAIT

Hidden Valley Land's End Syrah 2007, Elim Red
Some spice on nose. Balance of acidity. Concentrated fruit - blackberries. Some soft tannin. Medium length.
£14.99 ODD

Home Of Origin The Siren Stormhoek Red Blend 2008, Stellenbosch Red
Nice ripe fruits. Medium bodied, spicy and herby. Some grippy tannins on the finish.

Iona The Gunnar 2005, Elgin Red
Slightly lifted nose. Rounded fruit

on the palate with good, juicy character. Tannins will soften with age.
£11.99 EHB, VLW

Jordan Cobblers Hill 2006, Stellenbosch Red
Fragrant, herbaceous, pea pod, fresh, crunchy fruit. Lively with dryish but smooth tannins.
£20.45 CPW, HDS, WWT

Kaapzicht Cabernet Sauvignon 2007, Stellenbosch Red
Oak, chocolate, cherry and vanilla on the nose. Concentrated flavours and a rich palate. Great balance of acid, tannin and alcohol.
£10.75 WI-AV

Kanu Shiraz 2005, Stellenbosch Red
Nice bottle age on nose. Good fine fruits on palate. Juicy but dries towards finish. Tannins generous.

Kleine Zalze Shiraz Mourvèdre Viognier 2009, Western Cape Red
Savoury with juicy, ripe fruit on the palate. Good length with a firm, pleasing finish.
£6.49 WAIT

KWV Cathedral Cellar Pinotage 2006, Paarl Red
Meaty and savoury on the nose. Soft, black fruit on the palate with a good, long, savoury finish.

KWV The Mentors Canvas 2008, Stellenbosch Red
Concentrated coffee and leather. Good balance.

La Motte Cabernet Sauvignon 2007, Western Cape Red
Good fruit notes on the nose. Juicy, tight, with some minerality.

Dusty chocolate and mocha. Moreish.
£10.99 MAJ

La Motte Pierneef Shiraz Viognier 2007, Western Cape Red
Oaky cherries, complex, rich with nice acidity. Excellent balance, good length.
£22.99 HAR

La Motte Shiraz 2008, Franschhoek Red
Deep red, tight cherry rim, jammy fruit with a touch of vanilla.
TESC

La Vigne Estate Owner's Selection 2006, Western Cape Red
Ripe blue fruit nose. Palate is well-balanced, some drying tannins.

Lanzerac Pioneer Pinotage 2007, Stellenbosch Red
Spicy (cloves etc), floral, black pepper, black fruit, balsamic, spice, firm, elegant, generous and fresh. Very good.
£30.00 H2F

L'Avenir Grand Vin de Pinotage 2007, Stellenbosch Red
Deeply scented with some animal notes. Drying with juicy ripe fruit character. Lush and lovely on the finish.

L'Avenir Pinotage 2009, Swartland Red
Jammy, raspberry bonbon nose. Quite spicy with juicy, beetroot, raspberry fruit and fine grainy tannins. Succulent with a dry finish.

Lomond Conebush Single Vineyard Syrah 2007, Cape Agulhas Red
Ripe spicy nose. Cherry oak, ripe cherry and spice.

Lutzville Diamond Collection Shiraz 2007, Olifants River Red
Balanced acid and well integrated tannins. Elegant black fruit. Good length.

Meerendal Bin 159 Shiraz 2005, Durbanville Red
Prune, concentrated cooked black fruit, custard pie. Quite tannic grip. Nice mouthfeel. Some length.
£25.00 K&L

Meerendal Heritage Block Pinotage 2006, Durbanville Red
Rich, spicy, well-balanced, sweet fruit. Well natured, good dense wine. Fresh acid.
£35.00 K&L

Nederburg Manor House Shiraz 2008, Coastal Region Red
Bright red fruit aromas and flavours. Nice backbone of acidity, savoury finish.
£9.49

Nederburg Private Bin R109 Cabernet Sauvignon Merlot 2007, Western Cape Red
Ripe blackcurrant aromas, dry tannins with a good structure. A touch of cassis with a dry finish.

Nederburg Private Bin R121 Shiraz 2006, Western Cape Red
Savoury, quite subtle oak, well-integrated, tannin firm on finish.

Nederburg Winemasters Reserve Shiraz 2008, Western Cape Red
Attractive red fruit, sweet and vibrant with balanced, firm tannins. Nice fruit on the finish.
£7.29

Oak Valley Pinot Noir 2008, Elgin Red
Toasty oak and cherry jam on the nose. Fresh cherry palate and ripe tannins.

Oldenburg Vineyards Cabernet Sauvignon 2008, Stellenbosch Red
Ripe berry fruit with savoury notes. Quite tannic. Good depth and balance - round.

Oldenburg Vineyards Syrah 2008, Stellenbosch Red
Ripe and round on the nose with light, ripe cherry. Zingy intensity on the palate. Good length.

Rietvallei Estate Esteanna 2007, Robertson Red
Mocha nose. Juicy, sweet fruit, soft oak.
£9.99 HIC

Rust En Vrede Shiraz 2007, Stellenbosch Red
Ripe berries, dark fruits. Tight structure, fine tight peppery tannins.
£17.05 WI-AV

Spice Route Chakalaka 2008, Swartland Red
Opaque, elegant red fruit. Pleasant aroma with velvet fruit on the palate and fresh dry finish.
£11.99 SAO

Spier Lesebo Pinotage 2007, Stellenbosch Red
Deep with sweet, chocolate nose. Very classy with lovely, juicy, ripe fruit character. Plenty of flavour with an oak dominated finish.

Spier Private Collection Pinotage 2007, Stellenbosch Red
Deeply scented liquorice and gingery oak on the nose. High-toned with an edgy, drying palate. Chewy, ripe tannins on the finish.

Spier Vintage Selection Pinotage 2007, Stellenbosch Red

Sweet, American oak on the nose with ripe, lush fruit on the palate. Refreshing acidity balanced with heavy oak on the finish.

Stellenrust Jj Handmade Picalot 2007, Stellenbosch Red

Note of chocolate and caramel character. Drying, fresh and warm on the palate. Well-balanced acidity with a long, lingering finish.

Stellenzicht Syrah 2003, Stellenbosch Red

Good, deep colour. Big almost dirty aroma. Palate shows generous amounts of fruit, hardish tannins. Juicy. Some bottle age.

Stumble Vineyard Merlot Malbec 2009, Western Cape Red

Ripe, red berry fruit, juicy and concentrated. Vibrant and structured.
£6.49 LAI

Swartland Winery Indalo Shiraz 2007, Western Cape Red

Medium colour. Fresh bright berry. Light commercial style but good length.

Swartland Winery Tesco Pinotage 2009, Western Cape Red

Ripe, jammy and spicy with fresh plum fruit palate with hints of chocolate and spice on the finish.
TESC

Table Mountain Merlot 2008, Western Cape Red

Evolving nose, clean and tight fruit. Smooth and elegant, not great depth but nice balance between tannin, alcohol, oak and fruit.
£4.99 MRN

Tukulu Vineyards Fairtrade Unwooded Syrah 2009, Darling Red

Brambles, stalky, open feel. High-toned tannin. White pepper and fruit. Lively wine.

Two Oceans Merlot 2009, Western Cape Red

Smoky nose, firm tannins on the palate. Nice acidity and reasonable length.

Uniwines Cape Promise Pinotage NV, Western Cape Red

Sweet, jammy fruit on the nose. Ripe red fruit on the palate with some spice and warmth. Smooth and oaky on the finish.

Uniwines Palesa Pinotage 2008, Breedekloof Red

Bright red berry fruit. Okay depth. Some fruit length. Quite eloquent.

Vineris Cimarosa Pinotage 2009, Western Cape Red

Ripe, jammy and floral on the nose. Full-bodied and deep with ripe, dark fruits and vanilla oak on the palate. Warming with soft tannin finish.
LDL

Vondeling Averys Pioneer Range Pinotage 2009, Paarl Red

Jammy with youthful, ripe fruit aromas. Ripe plum flavours with a touch of strawberry freshness. Easy drinking.
£7.49 AVB

Graham Beck Blanc De Blancs 2006, Robertson Sparkling

Inviting gentle creamy aroma. Lovely yeasty palate. Balanced acidity. Good length with shortbread notes.

Graham Beck Brut NV, Western Cape Sparkling
Youthful, ripe, lemon aromas. Fruity, soft rounded. Very easy drinking. Lovely lift on finish.
£12.99 WAIT

KWV Laborie Blanc De Blancs 2006, Stellenbosch Sparkling
Exotic guava fruit on nose. Luscious, mouth-watering creamy fruit. Fresh acidity.

Villiera Monro Brut 2004, Stellenbosch Sparkling
Fine, lightly yeasty, classy. Dry, fresh, lingering, wine. Mouth-watering and harmonious.

Du Toitskloof Co-Operative Fairtrade Cape Sparkling Rosé 2009, Western Cape Sparkling **Rosé**
Pale salmon colour with small bubbles. Light confected red fruits. Rose hips and some bready yeast. Red fruits with lemon zip on finish.
£7.99 CWS

Darling Cellars Onyx Noble Late Harvest 2009, Western Cape Botrytis
White and pink grapefruit with a touch of stewed fruit. Marmalade with orange spice, ripe and soft with fresh grapefruit acidity.
£13.50

Monis Muscadel 2004, Breede River Valley **Fortified**
Tamarind, tangerine rind and clove spice. Ripe, pungent and sweet with a luscious, tangy, spicy-sweet finish. Very good length.

Orange River Red Muscadel 2008, Northern Cape **Fortified**
Light musk and rose petal. Sweet delicate sherbet hint. Strawberries, pawpaw and passionfruit.

Orange River White Muscadel 2008, Northern Cape **Fortified**
Lifted caramel and grapey nose. Thick, viscous texture with barley sugar flavours and spiced cake fruits with a touch of vanilla. A luscious finish.

Spain

There is irrefutable flair about Spanish wine, and Rioja remains a mainstay of any self-respecting wine list. Excited murmurings are emerging from nearby red wine areas such as Priorat, Ribera del Duero and Toro. The wines here are often fiercely potent, but also display wonderful complexity and balance. Sherry always performs well at the IWC too, demonstrating great versatility from racy Fino to incredible nutty Oloroso as well as the luscious lure of Pédro Ximinez. Where Sherry really excels is as an accompaniment to food, and with a surge of interest in tapas and pintxos restaurants, Sherry might finally be poised to receive the attention it deserves.

KEY FACTS

Total production
45m hectolitres

Total vineyard
1.154m hectares

Top 10 regions
1 Castilla-La-Mancha
2 Extramadura
3 Valencia
4 Castilla-Leon
5 Catalonia
6 Murcia
7 Rioja
8 Aragon
9 Andalusia
10 Galicia

Top 10 grapes
1 Airén
2 Tempranillo
3 Bobal
4 Garnacha Tinta
5 Monastrell
6 Pardina
7 Macabeo
8 Palomino
9 Albariño
10 Viura

2010 IWC PERFORMANCE

Trophies	7
Gold	20
Silver	145
Bronze	234
Great Value Awards	1

SPANISH SWEET MUSCAT TROPHY

Camilo Castilla Capricho De Goya NV, Navarra White

Fantastic array of aromas - bread baking, autumn leaves and burnt toffee. Great complexity and balance.

£10.21

Carlos Serres Onomastica Blanco Reserva 2006, Rioja White

Huge, oxidised, heavily oaky style. Buttery, rich palate, the lemony freshness of the acidity powering through.

£19.99 CDL, D2H, LBV

Cien Y Pico Doble Pasta 2007, Castilla La Mancha Red

Sweet blackberry, some vanilla spice - herbal. North Rhone quality. A powerful intense blockbuster style. Long, concentrated and firm.

£10.00

Cien Y Pico Knights Errant 2007, Castilla La Mancha Red

Inky deep colour – Syrah-like, narrow and intensely powerful bite with compact firm tannins. Lots of blackberry, shiny new oak and vanilla. Intense refined oak.

£20.00

 RIBERA DEL DUERO TROPHY

Cillar De Silos Torresilo 2006, Ribera Del Duero Red

Chocolaty and ripe, with a little hint of floral life. Juicy, beautifully delicate palate. Fabulous length and balance.

£33.99 AAW, ODF, RSO

CVNE Vina Real Gran Reserva 2001, Rioja Red

Good intensity and depth of colour. Nice aromas of clean, ripe and well-balanced dark fruits. Firm gripping tannins on the palate with lashings of ripe cherry, lush bramble and soft vanilla. Soft and lingering on the finish.

£19.99

Javier Santamaria Diaz Marques De Murillo Crianza 2006, Rioja Red

Meaty, savoury quality. Aromas of sweet cardamom spice with a touch of vanilla. Structured, rich and dense with blackberry fruit, cocoa and a hint of liquorice. Great complexity and a gloriously lengthy finish.

 SPANISH RED TROPHY, TEMPRANILLO TROPHY, RIOJA ALAVESA TROPHY

Lar De Paula Cepas Viejas 2005, Rioja Red

Cedar and leather with red cherries and ripe jammy fruit underneath. Fine but expressive tannins on the palate with fresh acidity. Big, ripe and lush on the finish with a lot of potential.

Luis Cañas Amaren Reserva 2001, Rioja Red

Dark fruits and creamy hints of vanilla on the nose. Herbaceous and savoury on the palate with a rich and savoury dark fruit finish. Nicely complex with firm tannins. Still young and need a few years to improve.

£23.00 LAI

Matarromera Matarromera Crianza 2007, Toro Red

A traditional style. Sweet, creamy richness of black and dried fruit held together by firm tannins.

Lovely depth of flavour, good acidity, complex and compelling.

Ramon Bilbao Viña Turzaballa 2001, Rioja Red

Complex and elegant with a black cherry nose. Ripe and subtle with hints of spice and savoury character. Wooded notes and creamy hints of vanilla are layered on the jammy ripe palate. Delicious and fresh.
£15.99 MWW

Tábula 2005, Ribera Del Duero Red

Rich, plum aromas with underlying minerality. Good complex fruit and oak balance with an elegant finish. Will age well.
£21.99

Murviedro Marks & Spencer Moscatel Rosado 2009, Valencia Sweet

Luscious grapey character on the nose with delicate floral aromas. Rose and raspberry fruits on the palate with balanced acidity and a hint of warm spice. Light, delicate and beautiful.
£5.99 M&S

Toro Albala PX Gran Reserva 1982, Montilla Moriles Sweet

Rich: fig, toffee, raisin and treacle nose. Sticky lusciousness.
£17.87

 MANZANILLA TROPHY

Emilio Lustau Almacenista Manzanilla Amontillada Cuevas Jurado 1/21 NV, Andalucía Fortified

Deep gold colour, toffee and iodine nose, sultanas and caramel favouring. Bone dry and a long savoury finish.
£20.00

Emilio Lustau Almacenista Oloroso Pata De Gallina 1/38 NV, Andalucía Fortified

Rich spiced figs, dates and candied lemon. Fresh and smooth on the palate. Long, fresh finish.
£20.00

 OLOROSO TROPHY

Emilio Lustau Sainsbury's Taste The Difference Oloroso 12 Year Old NV, Andalucía Fortified

Delicate, medium amber. Spicy, rich and figgy nose. Great balance with a long, nutty finish. Delicious and fresh.
SAIN

 CHAMPION FORTIFIED, AMONTILLADO TROPHY

Gonzalez Byass Viña Ab NV, Jerez Fortified

Gold, straw style with a developed, rich nose with caramel hints. Medium bodied, dry, oxidative (pasada) style. Good length.

 PEDRO XIMENEZ TROPHY

Harveys Pedro Ximenez VORS 1980, Jerez Fortified

Opaque and luxurious, dark chocolate and chocolate covered raisins. Creamy texture and finish of pecan pie with nice acidity. Smooth finish.
£20.42 WAIT

 GREAT VALUE FORTIFIED WINE UNDER £10

Hidalgo La Gitana Manzanilla NV, Andalucía Fortified

Glitzy apples, fresh on the palate,

elegant style and good length.
£8.39 WI-AV, WAIT

Adega Castrocelta Castrocelta 2009, Galicia White
Fresh lively citrus nose, good clean crisp fruit palate.
IDO

Adega Maior De Mendoza 3 Crianzas 2007, Galicia White
Floral citrus note with bright racy citrus body, good depth and flavour.
D&M

Baigorri Blanco Fermentado En Barrica 2007, Rioja White
Banana custard nose with a touch of almond. Fresh lightly creamy palate with melon, banana and sherbert acidity.
MOR

Domecq Terra D'Ouro 2009, Galicia White
Classic varietal peach and pear fruit character. Refreshing, fruity palate with subtle weight and good acidity. Quite persistent.
£8.99

Hijos De Antonio Barcelo Cosme 1894 Blanco 2007, Rioja White
Appley with some vegetable, raisin, spicy oak. Soft attack. Fresh palate and firm finish, long, lush and spicy.
£49.99 HAR, WSO

Hijos De Antonio Barcelo Triptico White Verdejo Sauvignon Blanc 2008, Castilla Y León White
Savoury nose with ripe fruit character. Crisp on palate with lemon-lime freshness and a touch of nutty cream. Long and firm with a good finish.
£19.99

Hijos De Antonio Barcelo Viña Mayor Fermentado En Barrica 2008, Ribera Del Duero White
Beautifully scented with honeysuckle and tart apple fruit nose. Full, round and rich mouth, good acidity, complex and well-balanced. Very delicious.

La Val Orballo Albariño 2008, Galicia White
Spice rich nose. Nice ripe grapefruit palace, well-balanced.
£9.99 PBA 1690

Luis Cañas Blanco Fermentado En Barrica 2008, Rioja White
Fresh, lemony style. Touch of leafy green herbs. Lean, savoury, lemony palate but fine balance and orangey vitality.
AAW

Mar De Frades Finca Valiñas 2008, Rias Baixas White
Fresh lime nose, soft citrus palate with good acidity.
£18.99 MWW

María Victoria Dovalo Méndez Veiga Naúm 2009, Rias Baixas White
Lovely fragrant floral note, good definition with touch of peach, great balance, fresh good acidity, hazelnut tinged finished, excellent.

Martin Codax Salterio 2009, Galicia White
Apricot and vanilla pod on the nose, good definition, well-balanced with fresh acidity and orange zest.
£8.99

Miguel Torres Viña Esmerelda 2009, Catalunya White
Very pale and delicate. Honeyed

Spain. As many wineries as landscapes.

In Spain there are almost as many wineries as there are landscapes. The diversity of viticulture in the country is reflected in more than 90 grape varieties from 69 denominations of origin.

Our wines mirror our country's infinite beauty. Soil and climatic conditions ensure variety, personality and richness of style to please all discerning palates.

and grapey with hints of lychee on the nose. Off-dry on the palate with loads of fresh acidity.
£7.49 WAIT

Naia Naia 2007, Rueda White
Savoury and toasty nose with dynamic fruit character. Lovely fleshy, spice, good fruitiness and length. Delicious and lush on the finish.
£10.99 PBA

Palacio De Bornos Sauvignon Blanc 2009, Rueda White
A grassy, green fruit nose and a clean, youthful, crisp palate with apple, zesty citrus and some herbal notes.
£10.70 CPW

Pazo De Señorans Selección De Añada 2004, Rias Baixas White
Deep colour with mature, waxy, oily nose. Toasty palate with lime and lemon with fresh acidity and good length. Well-balanced.
VTS

Terna CORD Class Sauvignon Blanc 2009, Rueda White
Good intensity and ripeness on the nose. Tropical and sweet fruit on the palate but dry in flavour. Delicious and soft.
£9.19

Terna V3 2008, Rueda White
Floral on the nose with ripe fruit overtones. Peaches and apricots with a lemony, ripe flavour. Preserved lemons on the finish with delicate sweetness.
£22.43

Txomin Etxaniz Txomin Etxaniz 2008, Txacoli De Guetaria White
Lightly aromatic with apple notes and fresh citrus character. On the palate, good appley flavours with crisp citrus and

refreshing acidity. Long and juicy on the finish.
£14.49

Valdespino Tio Diego NV, Jerez White
Cream, caramel nose. Bone dry, medium full, persistent Amontillado style length.
£18.99

Viñas Del Vero La Miranda De Secastilla Garnacha Blanca 2009, Somontano White
Ripe nose, lemony, leesy quality. Dry, crisp, zesty, mouthwatering, finishing with an edge.
£9.99 OCO

Abadia Retuerta Pago Garduña 2006, Valladolid Red
Medium to dark colour. Fine developed aroma. Juicy wine, well-balanced, firm and ripe. Quite hard tannins on finish.
£70.00 LIB

Abadia Retuerta Selección Especial 2007, Valladolid Red
Youthful, modern style. Plenty of ripe fruit and spice on the nose. Firm and well-balanced tannins on the palate with good acidity and freshness. Needs time to develop its full potential.
£19.99 HVN, JOB, LIB, NYW, RSV

Amaren Ángeles De Amaren 2006, Rioja Red
Perfumed red fruit aromas. Concentrated and very youthful flavours. Ripe fruit with grippy tannins and fresh acidity on the palate. Well-balanced and long.
AAW

Aragonesas Tesco Finest* Old Vines Garnacha 2008, Campo de Borja Red
Clear with savoury raspberry fruit. Juicy ripe attack, given depth by generous finish.
TESC

Astrales Astrales 2006, Ribera Del Duero Red

Smoky aromas, a tight core of tannins on the palate with savoury fruits; very young with hints of new wood flavours. Will develop and become more elegant with age.
£30.99

Baigorri Crianza 2006, Rioja Red

Pure and intense fruit character on the nose. Lovely ripe plum and vanilla on the palate with fine yet well-integrated tannins. Ripe strawberry and cherry on the finish.

Baigorri De Garage 2005, Rioja Red

Vanilla pods, fruity balanced nose. Super concentrated fruit, well-integrated oak.
£37.99

Baigorri Reserva 2004, Rioja Red

Red and damson fruit on the palate with elegant cedar oak flavours. Lightly smoky with soft texture. Well-balanced, long and supple.
£21.99

Baron De Ley 7 Viñas 2004, Rioja Red

Dried fruit and fruit cake, restrained, dense and well-balanced with a delicious finish. Effortless.
TESC

Baron De Ley Corte Mayor Reserva 2005, Rioja Red

Ripe and jammy fruit on the nose with very intense red fruit on the palate. Well-integrated vanilla oak with lingering tannins on the finish.

Baron De Ley Finca Monasterio 2007, Rioja Red

Big and polished style. Ripe and solid red fruit with good grip and creamy vanilla spice. Oaky wood finish with solid balance and length.

Baron De Ley Gran Reserva 2001, Rioja Red

Firm, ripe aromas of red cherry fruit. Palate is smooth and ripe with softly rounded, yet gripping tannins. Very nicely balanced with fresh acidity.

Baron De Ley Reserva 2005, Rioja Red

Cherry-strawberry aromas on the nose. Toasty vanilla character with softly gripping tannins. Soft fruit on the finish with long and lingering ripeness.

Berberana Carta De Oro Rioja Crianza 2007, Rioja Red

Ruby red fruits and black forest bramble aromas. A hint of herbaceousness with ripe jammy fruit and spicy oak. Grippy tannins on the finish.

Bodega La Viña El Prado Tinto 2009, Valencia Red

Dark fruits nose with lovely sweetness. Ripe and round on the palate with good fruit structure. The tannins are well-integrated with the ripe fruit. A fresh, lingering finish.
£5.99

Borsao Mitico 2009, Zaragoza Red

Perfumed nose of plums and black fruits; good fruit on the palate with medium length.
£5.99 PBA

Buil & Giné, Giné Giné 2008, Priorat Red

Bright ruby, attractive red fruit. Fresh, refreshing cherry/berry flavours. Well-balanced but lacks fruit concentration.

**Campillo Gran Reserva 1995,
Rioja** Red

Dark colour, dusty American
oak, blackcurrant on the nose.
Supple black cherry fruit, smooth
elegant fruit, nice length.
£25.99 DBY, PWI, SAB, WAD

**Ca'n Vidalet Cabernet
Sauvignon 2005, Mallorca
Red**

Attractive cassis nose. Slightly
green blackcurrant flavours but
good. Not overly complex.

**Carchelo Vedré 2007, Murcia
Red**

Anchovy/olive nose. Oily and
intense chocolatey palate. Long
and exciting finish.
IDO, ODD

**Carlos San Pedro Perez De
Viñaspre Colección Familiar
2004, Rioja** Red

Plum and oak aromas with
hints of fig and spice on the
palate. Ripe, rich and round. Very
pleasing with good length.

**Casar De Burbia Casar De
Burbia 2007, Bierzo** Red

Nicely balanced with berry fruit
and clove on the nose. Very
earthy, with smoke and leather
character. Ripe and lush on the
finish.

**Castell D'Or Francoli Tinto
2008, Catalunya** Red

Medium plum colour. Mellow
spice and liquorice with ripeness
on the palate. Long and smooth
on the finish.

**Cavinas Decana Reserva
2006, Valencia** Red

Fresh and lively black fruits on
the nose. Fresh and crunchy on
the palate with vanilla overtones.
Soft and supple. A very easy
drinking style.
£4.99

**Celler El Masroig Etnic 2006,
Montsant** Red

Spicy, mineral, warm, baked
cherry and vanilla nose, full, dry,
mineral palate with sweet, cherry
fruit and mineral flavours. Chewy
but ripe tannins. Clean finish.
£17.50

**Cillar De Silos El Quintanal
Tempranillo 2009, Ribera Del
Duero** Red

Blueberry and cherry fruit
aromas. Firm fruit and ripe
tannins with cherry and
raspberry flavours on the palate.
Soft and well-structured.
£8.99 ODD

**Cillar De Silos Joven De Silos
2009, Ribera Del Duero** Red

Sweet cherry aromas, with
redcurrant on the palate. Ripe
red fruits, with spicy vanilla and
chewy tannins. Chalky on the
finish.

**Cooperativa Nuestra Senora
De La Paz Castillo La Paz
Tempranillo Syrah 2009,
Castilla La Mancha** Red

Baked cherry and cherry pie
nose. Full, ripe and cherry fruit
palate. Muscular with lots of oak
and vanilla. Ripe chewy tannins
with a very dry finish.
£6.49 WAIT

**Corral Marques De Morano
Rioja Crianza Tinto 2006,
Rioja** Red

Big, meaty and savoury in style.
Orange peels and lovely lactic,
smoky balance. Deliciously ripe
with soft tannins and lingering
acidity. Savoury on the finish.
£7.53 MCT

**Cuna De Reyes Edición
Limitada 2007, Rioja** Red

Ripe and warm with strawberry-
cherry aromas on the nose. Deep
concentration of fruit with ripe,

jammy character. Vanilla and warm spice are balanced with chewy tannins. Nicely balanced.
£25.53 COW

Cuna De Reyes Reserva 2004, Rioja Red

Bright and juicy. A vibrant and youthful style with fresh acidity balanced with warm, ripe fruit. Raspberry and cherry on the finish.
£15.67 COW

CVNE Contino Reserva 2005, Rioja Red

Soft and creamy on the palate with ripe strawberry character. Fresh acidity and green tannins are underpinned by juicy ripe fruit. Fresh and long on the finish.
£27.49 WAIT

Domecq Marques De Arienzo 2001, Rioja Red

Sweet cherry aroma on the nose, with sour cherry and redcurrant on the palate. Spicy vanilla and chewy tannins on the finish.
£13.99

Domecq Tarsus Reserva 2004, Ribera Del Duero Red

Light berry nose. Elegant fruit on the palate with silky tannins and a long finish.
£19.99

El Coto De Rioja Coto Vintage Crianza 2006, Rioja Red

Meaty on the nose. Smoky and spicy on the palate with fresh cherry fruit. Lush and rich on the finish but with well-balanced acidity.
ACG, BSE, C&C, DHF, EHB, WMA

El Coto De Rioja Real Reserva 2005, Rioja Red

Strawberry fruit on the nose. Soft palate that has layers of red and black fruit, spicy vanilla and

good, gripping tannins. Long and lush but will continue to develop with time.
YOB

El Coto De Rioja Vintage Gran Reserva 2000, Rioja Red

Well coloured with a youthful tinge. Nice, clean, soft aromas on the nose. Well-structured tannins with smooth vanilla spiciness. Ripe and balanced with long and lingering finish.
YOB

El Coto De Rioja Vintage Reserva 2005, Rioja Red

A developed style with a complex nose. Hints of cedar and leather with ripe jammy fruit underneath. Ripe and lush on the finish with excellent character and potential to improve with time.
Widely Available

El Escoces Volante Papa Luna 2007, Catalunya Red

Spicy, tar and leather on the nose. Deeply flavoured with bramble fruit and vanilla spice. Rich, smoky, savoury and leathery on the finish with good length and intensity.
£7.99 MWW

El Villar Señorio Don Pedro De La Vega 2001, Valencia Red

Coffee and leather on the nose. Lovely and smooth but with developed fruit character. Very nicely balanced with well-integrated green tannins. Plum ripeness on the finish. Really very impressive.
£7.49 MWW

Faustino 9 Mil 2004, Rioja Red

Youthful and full-bodied wine with sold tannins and spicy wood. Ripe plum, coffee-chocolate flavours, lingering finish.

Felix Solis Castillo De Albai Reserva 2005, Rioja Red

A very youthful style. Full of ripe fruit and gripping tannins. This wine is drinking well now with layers of ripe, jammy fruit. But it will only improve with time.
ASDA

Finca Museum Museum 2006, Cigales Red

Complex red fruit on the nose. Balanced tannins with ripe yet compact fruit. Still very youthful and will only benefit with time.
£9.99 YOB

Finca Museum Museum Real 2005, Cigales Red

Savoury with hints of warming spice. Good concentration of black fruit, warm spice and hints of vanilla. Lovely with a lengthy finish.
£15.00 YOB

Francisco Gomez Fruto Noble 2006, Alicante Red

Red fruits, green and meaty notes. Green pepper on the palate.

Franco Espanolas Rioja Bordon Crianza 2006, Rioja Red

Very fragrant aromas, velvety, fresh, youthful - highly flavoured and savoury with allspice notes. Very easy drinking.

Franco Espanolas Rioja Bordon Gran Reserva 2001, Rioja Red

Constrained, but firm aromas of black and red fruits. On the palate the fruit is well-structured with hints of violets, sausage and a touch of crackling on the mid palate. Very nice indeed.

Golf Global Handicap Zero 2006, Rioja Red

Meaty and savoury on the nose. Smoky and spicy on the palate with good depth of flavour and well-integrated tannins. Nicely fresh with good length.

Grandes Vinos Y Viñedos Corona De Aragon 2009, Cariñena Red

Medium bright ruby, nice fruit nose, spicy pepper. Soft attack, light and juicy. Fresh red fruit flavour. Simple.

Hijos De Antonio Barcelo El Portico Crianza 2007, Rioja Red

Ripe, rich with hints of coffee aromas. Weighty, black fruit with hints of soft vanilla. Ripe and complex with chewy and gripping tannins. Delicious.
£9.99 WSO

Hijos De Antonio Barcelo Finca Anzil 2005, Castilla Y León Red

Very approachable. Deep spicy red with a scented, minty nose ripe blackcurrant flavours and soft mature tannins. Complex and balanced with a lovely spicy finish.

Hijos De Antonio Barcelo Hachon Gran Reserva 2001, Ribera Del Duero Red

Light berries and a slight mineral nose. Rich plum fruit on the palate and excellent length.

Hijos De Antonio Barcelo Viña Mayor Reserva 2004, Ribera Del Duero Red

Ripe raspberry nose. Elegant on the palate with blackberry flavours and silky tannins. Smooth, light and balanced with a lovely finish.

Huerta de Albala Taberner 2007, Cadiz Red

Deep spicy wine with impressive savoury overtures, lovely soft

gentle finish despite the alcohol.
£19.99 PBA

Iñaki Núñez Pago De Cirsus Cuvée Especial 2006, Navarra Red

Mineral elegance on the palate with well-balanced fruit. Delicious layers of spice and black fruit on the finish. Long and lingering.

Iñaki Núñez Pago De Cirsus Selección De Familia 2005, Navarra Red

Fresh and spicy nose, good layers of fruit with warming spice and a hint of savoury character. Still very youthful and will develop further.

Iñaki Núñez Senda De Los Olivos Edición Especial 2006, Ribera Del Douro Red

Huge vanilla nose, massive chewy fruit and tannin. Ultra dense and fabulous example of this style.
LAI

La Mejorada Las Cercas 2006, Castilla Y León Red

Savoury, wooded nose with hints of warming spice. Good concentration of black fruit, warm spice, ripe tannins and hints of vanilla. Lovely representation of fruit with a lengthy finish.

Labastida Manuel Quintano 2004, Rioja Red

Damson fruit on the nose with a touch of warm spice. Palate is laden with fresh cherry fruit and balanced tannins. Delicious, rich, dense and long.

Labastida Montebuena Tempranillo 2008, Rioja Red

Bright, black cherry, vanilla and spice on the nose. Blueberry ripeness on the palate with a

refreshing zing of acidity. Leafy and green on the finish with grainy tannin structure.
£5.99 WAV

Lar De Paula Madurado 2009, Rioja Red

A rich and generous style. Ripe fruit, vanilla and liquorice spice on the palate. Warm and jammy with chewy tannins and a zing of fresh acidity on the finish.

Legaris Reserva 2005, Ribera Del Duero Red

Violets, plums and tar on the nose. A balanced, silky smooth wine with fine tannins and good length. Very typical of the region.
£19.99 ODD, SCL, TVY

Luis Cañas Amaren Reserva 2002, Rioja Red

An earthy nose with subtle red fruit aromas. Earthy on the palate with big, chewy tannins and lashings of dark brambles and vanilla. Long and savoury on the finish.
£23.00 LAI

Luis Cañas Crianza 2007, Rioja Red

Vanilla and oak with red fruit flavours. Concentrated and long with plum jam richness. Ripe raspberries and soft tannins on the finish.
AAW

Luis Cañas Hiru 3 Racimos 2005, Rioja Red

Vanilla and red fruit on the nose. Concentrated with plum jam and warm spice richness. Soft tannins.
AAW

Manzanos Reserva 2005, Rioja Red

Good fruit character on the nose, with ripe redcurrant and black bramble fruits. Warm vanilla

spice and clean, fresh acidity on the finish.
AAW

Marques De Caceres Gran Reserva 2001, Rioja Red

Ripe and round with warm spice and juicy red fruit. Deliciously balanced with good structure of wood and fruit. Long and lush on the finish.
£20.00

Miguel Torres Grans Muralles 2006, Conca De Barbera Red

Coffee, savoury nose. mouthfilling ripe fruit. Waxy finish.

Miguel Torres Mas La Plana 2006, Penedès Red

Deep colour with spice. Lots of extract. Very oaky notes of stewed blackcurrant. Spicy oak. A show wine but tannins are smooth, slightly too international.

Miguel Torres Salmos 2007, Priorat Red

Some plum/raspberry fruits. Soft attack red fruit and vanilla flavour. Nice texture, soft, clean finish. Bitter cherry flavour. Medium length.
£16.25 WAIT

Muga Selección Especial 2005, Rioja Red

Restrained but deeply scented nose. Ripe red fruit and dark bramble berries combine with a creamy streak of vanilla. Deliciously ripe with soft tannins and good length.
£20.99 CPW, IRV, MAJ, RWM, WAIT

Muñoz Artero Crianza 2007, Castilla La Mancha Red

Elegant, peppered nose with touches of strawberry fruit. Medium bodied with good

intensity of red, juicy fruit and spice. A mineral edge with lively, chewy tannins. Good length and freshness.
PHA

Muriel JME 2007, Rioja Red

Cherry fruit on the nose. Hints of soft plum and vanilla on the palate. Jammy and ripe with soft tannins and a touch of spice on the lengthy finish.
D&D

Navalon Anciano Aged 5 Years Reserva 2004, Valdepeñas Red

Elegant violet and floral nose. Chocolate and toffee spice on the palate with rounded fruit. Perfectly balanced on the finish with lingering freshness.

Ondarre Ursa Maior Crianza 2008, Rioja Red

Good depth of concentration with smoky, plum fruit on the palate. Tobacco and chocolate on the finish. Well-balanced with ripe tannins.
SPR

Pagos Del Rey Altos De Tamaron Roble 2009, Ribera Del Duero Red

Fresh red fruit with good intensity. Sweet and ripe in the palate with ripe tannins and a drying but fresh finish.

Pirineos Montesierra Tempranillo Cabernet 2009, Aragón Red

Pure and intense fruit character on the nose. Lovely ripe plum and vanilla on the palate with fine yet well-integrated tannins. Ripe cherry on the finish.

Pradorey Reserva 2005, Castilla Y León Red

Rich, ripe plum and damson fruit which follow through on the palate. Balanced tannins, rich, dense and long.

Principe De Viana Albret Crianza 2006, Navarra Red
Cassis and cedar notes on the nose. Hints of warm, jammy fruit under the cedar overtones. Damson and savoury black fruit on the finish.

Ramon Bilbao Edicion Limitada 2007, Rioja Red
Sturdy, ripe fruit with red jammy aromas. Well-balanced with strong red fruit character. Ripe and fresh with lingering vanilla spice and lively acidity.
£10.99 MWW

Ramon Bilbao Mirto 2006, Rioja Red
Blackberry, leather that blossoms with aeration. Plump, strong tannins but good backbone. Excellent. Needs 3-5 years or serious decanting.
£28.99 MWW

Regalia De Ollauri Teran Versum 2008, Rioja Red
Plum and cigar box on the nose. Smoky and jammy with a touch of pepper and cherry fruit on the palate. Chewy and dusty tannins with cigar box overtones. Earthy on the finish.

Roda Reserva 2006, Rioja Red
Clean, spicy blackcurrant fruit with tobacco and leather on mid palate.
£25.00 ODD

Rodrigo Letras 2006, Rioja Red
Fresh, ripe red fruit on the nose. Grippy, young red crunchy fruit on the palate with a hint of warm spice. Tannins and juicy fruit on the long, supple finish.

Santo Cristo Marquesa De La Cruz Tempranillo 2008,

Campo De Borja Red
Lovely and sweet on the nose with pure berry fruits on the palate. Mellow spice with warm sun-ripened fruits. Long and lingering with good structure and fine tannins.
£7.15 WAIT

Sobreño Finca Sobreño Reserva 2005, Castilla Y León Red
Blood red. Plummy, rich, ripe berries and big tannins, with notes of chocolate and cigars. Oak derived complexity with a long, spicy finish.
PLB

Solar Viejo Vaza Crianza 2006, Rioja Red
Fragrant red fruit with hints of spice on the nose. Ripe with good acidity and balance with hints of vanilla on the palate. Warming and soft on the finish.

Sonsierra Reserva 2005, Rioja Red
Heady nose of dark berry fruits. Ripe and lush on the palate with blackberry jam and dark cherry compote. Vanilla and warm spice with soft tannins give the wine a lovely finish.
£12.99 BOD

TBA Heredad Torresano Crianza 2006, Madrid Red
High-toned raisin aromas with hints of warm spice. On the palate, fresh with almost stewed berry fruits. Complex with well-balanced tannins and lingering acidity on the finish.

Valdemar Inspiracion 2007, Rioja Red
Clean with warm spice aromas, red and black fruits and hints of spice. The palate is rich and jammy with lovely firm and gripping tannins. Well-structured with long length.

Valdemar Inspiracion Coleccion Varietales 2005, Rioja Red

Lifted, scented on the nose. Modern in style with black fruit, grainy tannins, integrated oak – fabulous balance.

Viñas Del Jaro Sembro 2008, Ribera Del Duero Red

Earthy, redcurrant aromas with a touch of savoury character. Ripe fruit, earthy and savoury on the palate as well with ripe cherry tannins. Good structure and intensity.

Viñedos De La Aragona Zabrin Joven 2008, Jumilla Red

Plum red colour and plum to note. Dry, ripe and tannic.

Winery Exchange Castillo El Destaca Crianza 2005, Ribera Del Douro Red

Cherry aromas with a hint of rosemary. Tannins are well-balanced with subtle fruit flavours and a long finish.
£8.99 MWW

Conuisa Sainsbury's Taste The Difference Vintage Cava 2008, Cava Sparkling

Quite light and fresh with elegant balance of fruit and acidity. Good length. Has good balance and a degree of complexity.
£11.99 SAIN

Grupo Yllera Cantosan Brut NV, Rueda Sparkling

Apple on nose. Attractive palate with fruit and depth. Lovely acids.

Heretat Mas Tinell Carpe Diem 2004, Cava Sparkling

Good depth, well-balanced. Slightly bitter acidity but nicely evolved and good length. Attractive yeast character, complexity and depth.

Juve & Camps Reserva De La Familia Gran Reserva Brut Nature 2006, Catalunya Sparkling

Clean, fresh, lively, slightly toasty, not huge fruit, but pleasing fresh lemony finish.
£14.99 EHL, HAC, LAY, TAN

Pere Ventura I Família Cupatge D'Honor Brut Nature NV, Cava Sparkling

Fresh, elegant style. Good bead, stone fruit, and pear hints.

Raimat Gran Brut NV, Costers Del Segre Sparkling

Autolytic character, brioche and apples on nose. Fresh, clean and moreish.

Segura Viudas Brut Reserva NV, Cava Sparkling

Some melon/peaches. Soft attack. Clean fresh, slightly bitter finish. Some length. Fresh apple flavour.
£9.99 EVW, ODD

Castelldor Cava Brut Rosé Marques De La Sardana NV, Cava Sparkling Rosé

Soft berries. Persistent bubbles. Balanced. Soft honey, yeasty and peppery with good length.

Alliance Wine Spain Los Pecadillos Glotonia Gluttony PX NV, Montilla Moriles Sweet

Hazelnuts and caramel, balance on palate. Good freshness.
£9.99 ANN, BHL, TVK, WAIT

Camilo Castilla Moscatel Goya NV, Navarra Sweet

Apple, caramel and treacle flavours.
£5.99

Iñaki Núñez Pago De Cirsus Moscatel Vendimia Tardía 2006, Navarra Sweet

Fine melon, pineapple and honey flavours. Good mouthfeel and length.

Murviedro Estrella Moscatel De Valencia 2009, Valencia
Sweet
Heady gardenia aroma. Very delicate and light on the palate with excellent balance, great acid and fruit.
£3.69 MRN

Principe De Viana Vendimia Tardia De Chardonnay 2008, Navarra Sweet
Luscious fruit with waxy and layered fruit aromas. Bright lemon with hints of apricot and lanolin. Good depth and length with fresh finish.

Castaño Monastrell Dulce 2006, Murcia Fortified
Rich, raisined, summer pudding. Sweet primary layer of fruit and fresh site of acidity. Delicious.
£14.49 LIB, WMN

Emilio Lustau Almacenista Palo Cortado Vides 1/50 NV, Andalucía Fortified
Fresh nutmeg and spice on nose. very good balance. Long complex finish.
£20.00

Emilio Lustau Añada 1990, Andalucía Fortified
Lifted malt nutmeg. Sweet up-front. Iced coffee hints of honey suckle caramel.
£19.49 WAIT

Emilio Lustau East India Solera NV, Andalucía Fortified
Toffee, fig rolls, cold tea. Sweet and sour, toffee and tar. Quite light but reined in by mineral salty tang. Yum.
£9.19 WAIT

Emilio Lustau Sainsbury's Taste The Difference Amontillado 12 Year Old NV, Andalucía Fortified
Mahogany amber. Delicate

hazelnut and dried apricot nose. Caramel and spice character on palate.
SAIN

Emilio Lustau Solera Reserva Amontillado Los Arcos NV, Andalucía Fortified
Honeyed amber core with beguiling fresh almonds, cinnamon, toast and spiced orange fruit. Sustained savoury finish.
£11.00

Emilio Lustau Solera Reserva Moscatel Emilín NV, Andalucía Fortified
Fresh and fizzy, floral, brown sugar, spicy cake bouquet. Rich, a bit fresh yet the fruit luscious and fresh. Lovely caramel on finish.
£14.00

Emilio Lustau Solera Reserva Pedro Ximénez San Emilio NV, Andalucía Fortified
Christmas cake, caramel, rich and quite complex tasting. More integrity.
£14.00

Emilio Lustau Solera Reserva Puerto Fino NV, Andalucía Fortified
Distinct flor character. Clean, bruised apple notes and lingering finish.
£11.00

Emilio Lustau Waitrose Solera Jerezana Manzanilla Pasada NV, Andalucía Fortified
Lifted asparagus hint of lychees. Sweet cashew pear and rock melon, Granny Smith apple.
£8.19 WAIT

Gonzalez Byass Apostoles Palo Cortado VORS NV, Jerez Fortified
Lifted honey and coffee bean.

Sweet cedar hints.
£16.29 WAIT

Gonzalez Byass Del Duque Amontillado VORS NV, Jerez Fortified
Yellow-amber core with sweet lemon and tropical fruit flavours. Full bodied with tangy lemon finish.

Gonzalez Byass Noé Pedro Ximenez VORS NV, Jerez Fortified
Raisins and candid walnuts. Brown sugar. Pleasant note of orange peel and orange spice.

Osborne Fino Quinta NV, Jerez Fortified
Pale, bright bready floral aromas. Fresh, elegant clean finish.

Valdespino Oloroso Solera 1842 NV, Jerez Fortified
Muscovado sugar nose with a rich and complex palate. Slightly bitter with a touch of iodine and almond on the palate. Ripe finish.
£30.42

Williams & Humbert Marks & Spencer Dry Fino NV, Jerez Fortified
Lifted lanolin and bacon rind. Sweet cashew, asparagus, green bean.
£5.99 M&S

Williams & Humbert Sainsbury's Taste The Difference 12 Years Old Pedro Ximenez NV, Jerez Fortified
Dark coffee. Candid walnuts and quite hot finish.
SAIN

BRONZE

Agricola Castellana Cuatro Rayas Viñedos Centenarios 2009, Valladolid White
Spritzy with fresh green fruits on

the palate. Nicely balanced with a fruit-forward finish.
BWL

Agricola Castellana Tesco Finest* Rueda Verdejo 2008, Rueda White
Mineral edge to the palate with floral character, crisp and elegant fruit. Delicate and supple at the same time.
TESC

Altos De Rioja Altos R Blanco 2009, Rioja White
Fresh apple and pear nose. Light tropical and citrus fruit. Some delicate richness to the mid palate.
£9.99 LAI

Chai Au Quai V.O. NV, Rioja White
Honeyed, stone fruit nose. Very ripe and honeyed on the palate with a lingering, fresh finish.
£8.99 LAI

Chozas Carrascal Las Tres 2009, Utiel Requena White
Citrus freshness with cream oak on the nose. Much of the same on the palate with a touch of racy acidity.
CHN

Covitoro Marques de la Villa Malvasia 2009, Zamora White
Creamy apricot and peach nose. White peach notes on the palate with a creamy and oily texture and good acidity.
£6.49 PBA

Felix Sanz Viña Cimbron Rueda 2009, Rueda White
Spritz on the palate with pleasing lemon flavours. Light-bodied and easy drinking.
£8.00

Francisco Gomez Fruto Noble Sauvignon Blanc 2009, Alicante White
Ripe, sweet and tropical on the

nose. Clean fruit on the palate with fresh lift and acidity.

Frutos Villar María De Molina Verdejo 2009, Valladolid
White

Ripe and well-balanced with citrus freshness on the palate. Lengthy peach and pear flavours persist on the finish.
£8.99 NKW

Gonzalez Byass Altozano Verdejo Sauvignon Blanc 2009, Castilla White

Lovely lime fruit with lemon character too. Lovely length, this wine shows nice varietal character.
£6.99 OCO

Gran Baron Blanco Suave 2008, Penedès White

Pale lemon colour, with light floral aromas. Zesty and fresh citrus with a touch of an off-dry finish.

Hijos De Antonio Barcelo Viña Mayor Verdejo 2009, Ribera Del Duero White

Grassy green aromas with clean, crisp acidity on the palate. Well-balanced with persistent length.
£8.99

Maior De Mendoza Maior De Mendoza 2009, Galicia White

Aromatic nose, ripe palate of soft, juicy and spicy fruit. Nutty finish with good weight.
£14.00 D&M

Marques De Riscal Finca Montico 2008, Castilla Y León
White

Citric nose, honeyed with long lemon-lime citrusy length. Very refreshing and pleasing.

Marques De Riscal Rueda Verdejo 2009, Castilla Y León
White

Very fresh with lovely, lifted lime flower and citrus flavours. Long and zippy on the finish.
£7.49 EHB, SAIN, MAJ

Martin Codax Albariño 2009, Galicia White

Chalky, floral nose, lemony, lacey palate, nice length.
£8.99

Martin Codax Burgans 2009, Galicia White

Spicy rich note, nice ripe grapefruit palate, well-balanced.

Martin Codax Mara Martin 2009, Galicia White

Fresh fragrant and floral, white stone fruit, good weight and good length, concentrated fruit.
£8.99

Miguel Torres Milmanda 2008, Conca De Barbera White

Integrated oak and citrus-pear nose. Creamy and rich on the palate with pear and citrus character. Nice creamy length.

Muriel Barón De Barbón Blanco 2009, Rioja White

Fresh, herbaceous, herbal and pear nose. Bit of spritz then crisp, herby, pear palate. Some creaminess mid-palate with good acidity and some length.
£7.99 LAI

Naia Pazo de Monterrey 2008, Monterrei White

Muted mineral nose, bright lemon lime flavours, moderate concentration, a bit of length tinged with mineral flavours.
£9.99 PBA

Navajas Blanco Crianza 2007, Rioja White

Citrus nose with a creamy oaky attack. Clean, fresh and modern style with a lovely structured finish.
£9.99

Palacio De Bornos Verdejo 2009, Rueda White
Bright and freshly aromatic. Crisp acidity with lush stone fruit and pithy melon flavours. Well-balanced and refreshing.
£8.29 WAIT

Pazo De Señorans Albariño 2009, Rias Baixas White
Honeydew melon with a fresh fruit salad aroma. Ripe cut grass on the palate. Fresh with good mineral length and a peppery capsicum finish.
VTS

Pazo De Señorans Sol De Señorans 2006, Rias Baixas White
Ripe lime fruits with apricot notes. Soft acidity with smoky but well-integrated oak character.
VTS

Pradorey Verdejo 2009, Castilla Y León White
Pronounced melon and citrus fruit on the palate. Layers of ripeness underpinned with vibrant acidity on the finish.

Raimat Viña 27 Chardonnay 2009, Costers Del Segre White
Pear, apple and ripe citrus aromas. Fresh acidity supports the creamy, citrus-pear fruit palate. Ripe and lingering.
£7.99 L&C, MCT, TVY

Segura Viudas Creu De Lavit 2008, Penedès White
Highly aromatic, boiled sweets on the nose, dry and lively lemon zest on the finish.

Val De Vid Condesa Eylo 2009, Rueda White
Sweetly perfumed nose, very ripe fruit on the palate. Well-balanced with lingering acidity.
BWC

Val De Vid Eylo 2009, Rueda White
Green, lime-fresh fruit aromas, waxy character with good balance and weightiness.
BWC

Val De Vid Verdejo 2009, Rueda White
Clean, fresh aromas, good lemon and lime citrus character. Lifted with a touch of spritz on the palate.
BWC

Valsanzo Viña Sanzo Verdejo 2009, Rueda White
Balanced acidity rounded with lemon drops and ripe, round melon fruit. Lovely and fresh on the finish.
£6.00 WAV

Vega De La Reina Marques De La Concordia Vega De La Reina Verdejo 2008, Rioja White
Fresh and floral on the palate with good candied fruit flavours. Pleasant and easy to drink.

Vinos Sanz Finca La Colina Sauvignon Blanc 2009, Castilla Y León White
Quite intense asparagus and tropical fruit aromas on the nose. Pink grapefruit with grassy vegetal notes - an unusual style.

Virgen Del Aguila Agoston Viura Chardonnay 2009, Aragón White
Light, fresh and clean wine.

1898 Ramon Roqueta Tempranillo 2009, Catalunya Red
The palate is layered with red fruit, vanilla and lingering spice. All underpinned by fresh acidity on the finish.

Abadia Retuerta Pago Valdebellon 2005, Valladolid Red
Mint and cassis on nose. Intense,

deep and rich. Gritty, hot juicy fruit with oak balance and length.

Abadia Retuerta Petit Verdot 2006, Valladolid Red
Spicy, bricky, roasted meat nose. Big bruising inky black fruit. Full bodied, chewy, rich, with lots of cherry oak.

Alliance Wine Spain El Primero Graciano 2009, Castilla La Mancha Red
Very spicy, fresh and vibrant. A fresh drinking, firm red. Good commercial wine.
£6.99 AAW

Alliance Wine Spain Los Pecadillos Lujuria Lust Graciano Garnacha Navarra 2008, Navarra Red
Rich, fresh violet nose. Good fruity base. Tannins need longer.
£6.99 ANN, HIG

Amaren Reserva Tempranillo 2004, Rioja Red
Earthy with savoury, dark fruit on the nose. Loads of coconut and vanilla on the palate with a strong finish of lively dark fruit and jam.
AAW

Aragonesas Campaneo Arbusto Tempranillo 2009, Campo De Borja Red
Sweet and jammy style with rich nose. On the palate the fruit is well-structured with a jammy richness. Plum and berry finish with lingering tannins and freshness.

Aragonesas Campaneo Old Vines Garnacha 2009, Campo De Borja Red
Bright cherry red, light cherry aromas on the nose with fresh berry fruits on the palate. Creamy vanilla on the finish.
SAIN

Aragonesas La Copa Garnacha 2007, Campo De Borja Red
Rich and ripe fruit with very firm tannins. A slightly confected style, but well-balanced with fresh acidity.
£6.99

Aragonesas La Copa Tempranillo 2007, Campo De Borja Red
Very pure and aromatic berry fruit nose. Sweet plum and berry palate with attractive fruit finish.
£6.99

Artiga-Fustel Monasterio De Santa Cruz 2008, Tarragona Red
Rustic-earthy. Easy drinking, good with food.
£6.99 LAI, STC

Axial Globalizacion De Vinos Penelope Sanchez 2009, Campo De Borja Red
Elegant cherry nose. Smoke, leather and tar on the palate with ripe, supple fruit. Lush and clean on the finish.

Baigorri De Garage 2005, Rioja Red
Spicy and savoury on the nose. Sausage character on the palate, ripe fruit and vanilla mingle with fine tannins.
MOR

Baigorri Reserva 2005, Rioja Red
Ripe, sweet, red cherry fruit aromas on the nose. Jammy with soft vanilla overtones on the palate. Delicate and ripe on the finish.
MOR

Berberana Clasico 1877 Reserva 2005, Rioja Red
Sweet red fruits, iodine, meaty. Powerful cherry dark fruits, juicy, acidity, tangy, meaty and savoury.

**Beronia Graciano 2007,
Rioja Red**
Very fresh and vibrant. Good
ripe nose. Fruity and chocolatey.
Pronounced acidity but in
balance.

**Beronia Tempranillo
Elaboración Especial 2008,
Rioja Red**
Warm and ripe on the nose.
Dark fruits and toasty oak are
balanced with lashings of soft
vanilla and attractive green oak
tannins.
£9.99 OCO, WAIT

**Borsao Tres Picos 2008,
Campo De Borja Red**
Rich and full-bodied with ripe
banana and pear fruits mingled
with dark berries. Smoke and
leather on the finish.
£12.99 PBA

**Buil & Giné Baboix 2006,
Montsant Red**
Perfumed, fresh, lovely, not
overly serious.

**Campo Viejo Dominio De
Campo Viejo 2006, Rioja Red**
Ripe red fruit on the nose with
hints of vanilla spice on the
palate. Chewy tannins and ripe
fruit on the finish.

**Carchelo Altico 2008, Murcia
Red**
Light and soft nose. Palate is soft
cranberry with nice grippy tannins.
£10.45 IDO, ODD

**Carchelo Carchelo 2009,
Murcia Red**
Light purple. Rich, full and
intense chocolate and fruit with
a long finish.
£9.49 IDO, ODD

**Carlos Serres Crianza 2005,
Rioja Red**
Red fruit and white pepper nose.

Oak and firmly structured fruit
on the palate, soft attack and
ripe but pleasant mid-palate.
Firm tannins with cream and
vanilla on the finish.
£8.99 CDL, D2H, LBV

**Casa Primicia Bodegas
Primicia Tinto 2009, Rioja Red**
Soft, juicy and round. A touch of
grass with bright cherry fruit on
the palate. Fruit forward for easy
drinking.
£8.00

**Chivite Gran Feudo Edicion
Seleccion Especial 2007,
Navarra Red**
Earthy and minerally on the
palate with firm, gripping
tannins. Fresh with hints of green
on the finish.
£10.99 FUL

**Classica Hacienda López De
Haro 2006, Rioja Red**
Sweet spicy nose, fresh, with a
good sweet attack. Excellent fruit
- juicy, fresh and pure supported
by subtle oak. Very fine.
TRW

**Cooperativa Nuestra Senora
De La Paz Castillo La Paz Old
Vines Tempranillo 2009,
Castilla La Mancha Red**
Exuberant bubble-gum, cherry
and pepper nose. Young and juicy
with ripe fruit extract. Vanilla
and oak on the palate with a ripe
cherry finish.

**Corral Don Jacobo Crianza
Rioja 2005, Rioja Red**
Sweet, allspice aromas with
caramelised fruit on the nose and
blackberry and plum on the palate.
Light body and gentle tannins.
£9.01 MCT

**Corral Don Jacobo Red
Crianza 2006, Rioja Red**
Fresh, bright and lively with a

gamey, smoky nose. Plums on the palate, medium bodied, with a very ripe fruit finish.

Cosecheros Y Criadores Sierra Almirón Malbec Syrah 2008, Castilla La Mancha Red
Rich cassis nose. hints of new leather. Tannins in background but there. Pleasing wine, simple example.
£6.99 LAI

Covinas Toro Loco 2008, Valencia Red
Complex notes of spicy fruit and leather. On the palate the fruit is elegant, underpinned by green tannins. Good structure.
£3.49

Covitoro Bos 2008, Toro Red
Attractive red fruit aromas. nice overall tannins, firm fruits on the palate, very dry savoury finish. Food wine.

Criadores De Rioja Altivo Reserva 2005, Rioja Red
Tight fruit on the nose with hints of woody character. Ripe fruit with balanced intensity. Creamy hints of vanilla on the finish.
£12.99 SAIN

Criadores De Rioja Cepa Alegro 2004, Rioja Red
Soft, juicy, lively style with a touch of grass with bright cherry fruit. Simple and easy drinking.
£9.19 SAIN

Criadores Tesco Viña Mara Rioja Crianza 2006, Rioja Red
Slightly vegetal on the nose, dry plum, long finish.
TESC

Cruz De Alba 2007, Ribera Del Douro Red
Fruit fresh nose with cranberry and red fruit aromas. Vanilla ripeness with lush red fruit and

a touch of drying tannin. Fresh acidity and good spice on the finish.
£11.99 MWW

CVNE Imperial Reserva 2004, Rioja Red
Mellow with complex earthy aromas. Liquorice and spice on the palate with red berry fruit and good freshness. Well-balanced with medium length.
£9.99

CVNE Viña Real Crianza 2007, Rioja Red
Ruby red fruit and pungent richness on the nose. Light red cherry concentration with a touch of vanilla cream on the finish.
£9.99

De Cal Grau Les Ones 2006, Catalunya Red
Some good intense black fruits. Very jammy on palate and porty.

De Castilla Castillo De Calatrava Reserva 2004, Castilla La Mancha Red
Ripe, plums, violets and spice on the nose with a touch of horseradish. Plum and cherry fruit on the palate with spicy flavours. Cherry finish, quite attractive.
£6.49 R&B

De La Marquesa Valserrano Gran Reserva 2003, Rioja Red
Sweet cherry fruit and vanilla on the nose. Ripe tannins and a touch of white pepper. Medium bodied with a concentrated, well-balanced finish.
WIL

Del Jaro Chafandín 2007, Ribera Del Duero Red
Spicy cranberry and redcurrant fruit on the palate with drying tannins. Good length and freshness.

Domecq Marques De Arienzo 2001, Rioja Red

Sweet spicy nose, fresh, with a good cherry and strawberry fruit. Excellent ripeness and juicy fruit character. Fresh and pure in style.
£9.99

El Coto De Rioja Coto De Imaz Reserva 2005, Rioja Red

Vibrant cranberry and redcurrant fruit on the palate with fine, but chewy tannins. Good length and freshness.
Widely Available

Eliseo Perez Bodegas El Durazno 2009, Canary Islands Red

Very ripe fruit, direct and very commercial wine. Good length and acidity.

Emilio Lustau Marks & Spencer Palo Cortado NV, Andalucía Red

Lifted cedar and nutmeg. Fresh hint of lime peel and some slight paraffin tones on finish.
£7.49

Enguera Megala 2007, Valencia Red

Nice, fresh, fruit nose. Full bodied. Good finish but short.

Ernesto Martín García Viña Valdemazón 2006, Castilla Y León Red

Currants and a date-like nose. A core of very nice fruit, creamy, dense, smooth and simple.

Felix Solis Albali Arium Reserva 2004, Valdepeñas Red

Clean, fresh, black cherry nose. A touch of spice and clove on the mid palate with good length and balance.

Felix Solis Castillo De Albai Crianza 2007, Rioja Red

Spicy and fragrant. Dark berry fruit and warm vanilla spice on the palate. Well-balanced and lush on the finish.
£6.99 ASDA

Finca Constancia 2008, Castilla Red

Clear ruby wine, soft approachable fruit underpinned by dark chocolate. Spicy dry finish with gentle persistence.

Finca Constancia Tempranillo 2009, Castilla Red

Raspberry and cherry aromas on the intensely fruity nose. Very supple with hints of violet and raspberry fruit on the palate. Rather pleasing to drink.

Frutos Villar Muruve Crianza 2007, Toro Red

Delicate, summer fruit aromas, fresh, pleasing with soft, quite rich tannins with a creamy coating.

Fuentespina Crianza 2006, Ribera Del Duero Red

Some raspberry fruits on the nose, simple red fruit on the palate. Moderate weight with firm tannins and structure. Elegant finish.
£11.99

Gonzalez Byass Altozano Tempranillo Shiraz 2009, Castilla Red

Bright and youthful - upfront and lively. Aromas of fresh red fruits and candied peel. Cardamom on the palate with ripe, sweet, blackberry fruit. Very approachable.
£6.99 OCO

Grandes Vinos Y Viñedos Valdemadera Gran Reserva 2004, Cariñena Red

Intense coffee and black fruit aromas with very pleasing grip on the palate. Full-bodied with ripe fruit and developed animal-like character.

Groupo De Vinartis Pata Negra Gran Reserva 2002, Valdepeñas Red
Easy and ripe on the nose. Clean black cherry flavours with a hint of clove on the palate. Jammy and lush on the finish.

Guelbenzu Evo 2006, Ribera Del Queiles Red
Dark chocolate, cedar, mint palate. Tannic balance.
£17.99 HAR, HVN

Guelbenzu Lautus 2004, Ribera Del Queiles Red
Subtle fruit on the nose. Silky tannins and good complexity on the palate.
£49.99

Hacienda De Susar Marques De La Concordia Rioja 2005, Rioja Red
Dried fruits but still very fresh and fragrant; strongly oaked, firm tannins, a highly structured wine. A bit over-extracted but exciting.

Herminia Crianza 2006, Rioja Red
Jammy, fresh and ripe. A nicely youthful style with black pepper and cherry fruit on the finish.
WAIT

Herminia Excelsus 2007, Rioja Red
Clean and bright. Fresh cherry and raspberry fruit, soft tannins - light and easy to drink.
ODD

Herminia Reserva 2004, Rioja Red
Vanilla and plum on the palate with good weight and mouthfeel. Slightly dried with powdery textured finish.

Hijos De Antonio Barcelo Cosme 1894 Tinto 2007, Rioja Red
Lovely ripe fruits, intense

strawberry, raspberry, vanilla and sweet spice. Palate reflects nose, lovely complexity, elegant tannins, fresh black cherries.
£49.99 HAR, WSO

Hijos De Antonio Barcelo Cosme Palacio Reserva 2005, Rioja Red
Black fruits and woody character on the nose. Ripe and smooth on the palate with drying tannins and good oaky grip. A jammy mouthful.
£19.99 SAIN, TESC

Hijos De Antonio Barcelo Cuesta Del Aire Red Tempranillo Shiraz 2007, Castilla Y León Red
Light, elegant nose gives way to a burst of ripe forest fruit on the palate. Ripe red fruit is overlaid with hints of apple and warm spice. Delicious.
£7.99

Hijos De Antonio Barcelo Glorioso Crianza 2006, Rioja Red
Ripe and warm with juicy plum aromas. Spicy red fruit with a touch of fragrant vanilla pod on the palate.
£8.99 ODD

Hijos De Antonio Barcelo Glorioso Crianza 2007, Rioja Red
Meaty nose with ripe black fruit on the palate. Creamy and rich with hints of warm spice. Full-bodied with good balance.
£8.99 ODD

Hijos De Antonio Barcelo Hachon Crianza 2006, Ribera Del Duero Red
New wood on the nose, green sappy characters on the palate. Loads of fruit on the palate.

Hijos De Antonio Barcelo Secreto Roble Francés 2007, Ribera Del Duero Red
Spicy and earthy aromas. Red cherry fruit with fresh acidity and chalky tannins on the palate. Fresh finish with lingering flavours.

Hijos De Antonio Barcelo Viña Mayor Crianza 2006, Ribera Del Duero Red
Savoury aromas, moderate weight with some oak complexity. Firm tannin structure, vanilla softens and gives good length.
£9.99 BTH

Hijos De Antonio Barcelo Viña Mayor Roble 2008, Ribera Del Duero Red
Sweet cherry and redcurrant flavours. Ripe cranberry and raspberry on the palate with light, earthy, savoury character. Fresh and chalky on the finish.
£8.99

Iñaki Núñez Pago De Cirsus Vendimia Seleccionada 2007, Navarra Red
Mineral, earth notes on the palate with hints of spicy white pepper on the finish.

Juan Gil Silver Label 2007, Murcia Red
Spicy, dark berry fruits on nose. Full, soft, juicy dark fruits with a hint of gorse herbs and chocolate.
£12.49 PBA

La Catedral Epulum Gran Reserva 2004, Rioja Red
Very modern oak nose, good intensity, firm tannins, hints of mocha and spice on the finish.

La Catedral Gran Epulum 2009, Rioja Red
Creamy and ripe with red fruit aromas. Creamy, yet subtle vanilla with ripe black fruit on the palate. Lush with nicely formed tannin.

La Mejorada Las Cercas 2004, Castilla Y León Red
Savoury and meaty on the nose. Ripe with hints of savoury black fruits on the palate. Firm and ripe tannins with pleasing length.

Lar De Paula Reserva 2005, Rioja Red
Dark bramble fruit and warm vanilla spice on the nose. Rich and ripe with lingering sweetness on the finish.

Las Rocas Garnacha Viñas Viejas 2007, Aragón Red
Smoky red fruit, intense black raspberry, liquorice aromas. Excellent balance with ripe, black fruit palate. Will age well.
£14.49 CAM, LIB, NYW

Legaris Crianza 2007, Ribera Del Duero Red
Crushed raspberries with intense spicy flavours. Redcurrant with a touch of savoury, meatiness on the palate. Chalky finish.
£14.99 LWC, MAG, MGM, ODD, WUO

Les Grands Chais De France Fuego Supremo 2009, Castilla La Mancha Red
Ripe cherry and vanilla on the nose. Fresh cherry bite on the palate with a touch of reduction. Well-balanced and weighty.

Les Grands Chais De France Fuego Tempranillo Red 2009, Regional Spain Red
Plump, ripe and juicy, little bit jammy. Dry pure tannins.

Long Wines Conde Galiana 2004, Catalunya Red
Warm spicy cherry. Slightly commercial with attractive oak. Blend works well.

Luis Alegre Parcela Nº 5 2006, Rioja Red
Sweet spicy nose. Fresh red fruit with good cherry character. Pure and ripe, supported by subtle oak on the finish. Delicious.

Luis Alegre Pontac 2005, Rioja Red
Ripe on the nose with lively spiced aromas. Dark fruit and chocolate on the palate with hints of savoury character. Full bodied and quite weighty.

Luis Cañas Juan Luis Cañas Reserva 2001, Rioja Red
Dark fruits on the nose with ripe red fruit and spice on the palate. Mouth-filling with ripe tannins. Quite chewy but delicious.
£13.49 LAI

Luis Cañas Reserva 2004, Rioja Red
Deep, black fruit on the nose. Cherry and ripe bramble with hints of light but grippy tannin on the palate. Good balance and length.
AAW

Luis Cañas Reserva De La Familia 2003, Rioja Red
Subtle dark fruits, with a touch of herbaceous complexity. Lovely structure and good balance.
£15.49 AAW, WAIT

Macia Batle Crianza 2007, Mallorca Red
Warm, dense fruit. Good concentration. Good tannin with hard acidity and a good finish.

Macia Batle Reserva Privada 2006, Mallorca Red
Warm, sunny fruit, easy style. Clean, balanced and juicy, simple fruit.

Manzanos Joven 2009, Rioja Red
Delicate with ripe red fruits on the nose and palate. Grippy and coarse tannins with lively acidity on the finish.
£6.04 AAW

Marques De Grinon Rioja Tempranillo 2008, Rioja Red
Red plum colour. Perfumed nose of rich, ripe, black and red fruits on the palate. Balanced acidity. Drinking well now.

Martin Codax Cuatro Pasos 2008, Castilla Y León Red
Medium ripe cassis and black cherry. Very rustic but has some charm.
£8.90

Martin Codax El Camino 2007, Rioja Red
Rich, plum fruit on the nose. Spicy red fruit on the palate with a touch of cream and smoky character. Spicy and smoky on the finish.

Matarromera Emina Verdejo 2009, Castilla Y León Red
Lemony notes on the nose with well-structured and firm melon-like fruit on the palate. Lifting and fresh on the finish.

Mauro Y Maurodos San Roman 2006, Castilla Y León Red
A delicate aroma of ripe blackberries. Fresh, oaky, with a rather dry spicy finish.
£32.69

Medievo Gran Espital Rioja 2008, Rioja Red
Rich and jammy nose, ripe and dark fruit on the palate. Juicy and jammy with tight and grippy tannins. Long and dry on the finish.

Miguel Torres Gran Sangre De Toro 2007, Catalunya Red
Enchanted colour, deep ruby. Complex spice and dark ripe fruit

aromas. Nice backbone of firm tannin and acidity through to savoury finish.

Miguel Torres Ibericos 2007, Rioja Red
Cherry and smoky oak on the nose with spicy red fruit on the palate. Well-balanced with ripe, gripping tannins.
£8.99 WAIT

Montecillo Gran Reserva 2003, Rioja Red
Ripe, sweet red cherry fruit on the nose. Jammy with soft vanilla overtones on the palate. Delicate and ripe on the finish.

Muñoz Y Mazón Azuel Roble 2008, Ribera Del Duero Red
Confected cherry aromas with light, elegant cherry fruit on the palate. Bright, with soft tannins and a savoury finish.

Muriel Barón De Barbón 2008, Rioja Red
Oaky with nicely formed dark fruit aromas. Spicy with good fruit concentration. Lively acidity and gripping tannins round off the finish.
LAI

Muriel Gran Reserva 2001, Rioja Red
Clean and fresh aromas with a touch of woodiness. Nice palate of red, ripe fruit. Touch of development.
D&D

Muriel Marques D Elciego Selección 2008, Rioja Red
Red and black fruit nose. Ripe and warm with jammy vanilla spice on the palate. Long and fresh with soft, ripe tannic finish.

Muriel Reserva 2005, Rioja Red
Sweet, oaky and cream laden nose. The palate is balanced with ripe, red fruit, subtle oak and soft tannin. Long, and easy drinking.
D&D

Murviedro Crianza 2007, Valencia Red
Clean, easy drinking style. Fresh and ripe red fruits on the palate with a touch of warming spice on the finish.
SAIN

Mustiguillo Finca Terrerazo 2007, VT el Terrerazo Red
Good, rounded chunky fruit with spice and chocolate. Structured.
£24.99 G&B, HAR, LIB

Navajas Tinto Crianza 2007, Rioja Red
Slightly closed on the nose, rich plummy ripe fruit on the palate. Good structure and balanced. Drinking well now.
£9.99

Olarra Clasico Crianza 2008, Rioja Red
Plum red fruit on the nose. Ripe and jammy on the palate with zesty acidity and ripe, soft tannins.
SAIN

Olarra Clasico Reserva 2005, Rioja Red
Red cherry and coconut nose with mellow and restrained fruit. Soft on the palate with ripe fruit and creamy vanilla flavours. Long and well-integrated finish.
SAIN

Ondarre Reserva 2004, Rioja Red
Red berries on the nose with hints of warm spice. Good development with ripe plum flavours. Well-balanced with ripe tannins and good length.
HLD

Ondarre Ursa Maior Reserva 2005, Rioja Red
Spicy and warm on the nose.

ppreciation through perfection.

:HOTT ZWIESEL is the global market leader among the best hotels, restau-
ints and bars. Our patented **Tritan® crystal glass** has set the benchmarks for
rilliance, break and dishwasher resistance. The Pure collection offers cutting
ige design, informed with sommelier skill. For more information visit our web
te or call +44 (0)1629-56190.

e glass of the professional.
ppreciation through perfection.

Tritan®
International
patent

SCHOTT
ZWIESEL

Sausage character on the palate, ripe fruit and vanilla with a touch of leather. Fine tannins on the finish. **SPR**

Osborne Artista 2008, Castilla La Mancha Red
Ripe, well-rounded with supple fruit and light tannins. Warming finish with hints of vanilla spice.

Osborne Solaz 2007, Tierra De Castilla Red
Light, fresh and well-balanced. Attractive red fruits, blackberry and cherry, with well-integrated tannins. Quite a modern style.
£4.99

Pago De Montal Monastrell 2008, Tierra De Castilla Red
Spicy pepper nose. Ripe, crunchy raspberries on palate. Nice and sweet, balanced and concentrated.

Parxet Tionio Crianza 2005, Ribera Del Duero Red
Deep, red rich plum nose with subtle violet aromas.

Paternina Banda Azul 2006, Rioja Red
Restrained style, cherry fruit supported by high acidity and balanced tannins.

Paternina Clisos 2008, Rioja Red
Plums and vanilla on the palate with a finish of dusty and smoky tannins.
£6.99

Pedro Luis Martinez Alceño Roble Monastrell Syrah 2008, Murcia Red
Light style. Fruitiness in mid palate.

Piedemonte Crianza 2006, Navarra Red
Green stalky nose. Round red berry fruit palate. Balanced, clean and fresh tasting.
£8.95 ROD, WLY, WSM

Principe De Viana Albret French Oak 2007, Navarra Red
Extracted berry fruit. Some elegance and mineral but dry and short.

Principe De Viana Albret La Viña De Mi Madre 2005, Navarra Red
Primary blackcurrant leaf with intensity, crunchy. Slightly porty although finish is good.

Principe De Viana Reserva 2004, Navarra Red
Intense complex aromas. Very savoury, firm long finish. Vanilla and spice and long lingering acidity.

Real Compañía De Vinos Cabernet Sauvignon 2009, Tierra De Castilla Red
Very primary red cherry fruit. Palate is bright but simple and firm.
£5.99 D&D

Real Compañía De Vinos Colección Privada 2009, Rioja Red
Lifted, jammy fruit on nose. Some good blackcurrant fruit on palate but tannins very grippy.
D&D

Real Compañia De Vinos Finca Libertad Coleccion Privada 2009, Tierra De Castilla Red
Ripe fruit on the nose with a good showing of wood and spice. Savoury plum on the palate with hints of raspberry jam. Firm tannins with good structure. Long length.

Real Compañía De Vinos Shiraz 2009, Tierra De Castilla Red
Hot, sweaty nose. Palate is rich with plummy dark fruits. Very big tannins.
£5.99 D&D

Real Compañía De Vinos Tempranillo 2009, Tierra De Castilla Red

Plums and damsons on the nose give way to ripe fruits of the forest on the palate. Warming, with lively acidity and good length.
£5.99 D&D

Remelluri 2005, Rioja Red

Pure dark fruit on the nose. Layers of sweet, jammy red and black fruit on the palate. Ripe and full-bodied with good length.
£19.49 AAW, WAIT

Rioja Vega Castillo Rojo Crianza 2007, Rioja Red

Ruby colour, juicy, cherry and plum notes. Integrated oak, balanced and ripe.
ASDA

Rioja Vega Crianza 2007, Rioja Red

Youthful red fruit aromas, some complexity, lovely fruit. Finishes long, lean, dry and savoury.

Rodrigo Tierra 2006, Rioja Red

Creamy and ripe on the nose. Red fruit and grippy tannins on the palate. Very soft finish with hints of spicy oak.

Ruconia Tubal 2005, Rioja Red

Fine colour. Good aged aroma, juicy and chewy. Good structure, ripe tannins. Well made.

San Gregorio Vina Fuerte Garnacha 2008, Calatayud Red

A little spritzy with soft ripe fruit on the palate. Black cherry, coffee and spice with a touch of smoke on the finish.
£5.99 ASDA, CWS, SAIN, TESC

Señorio De Barahonda Casa Del Canto Roble 2007, Yecla Red

Slightly mushroomy on the nose. Fresh entry, hay, tobacco and cedar. Austere finish. Demands respect.

Sierra Norte Fuentseca Organic Red 2009, Utiel Requena Red

Nice red fruit flavours, intense. Good finish.
£6.99 PBA

Sobreño Crianza 2007, Toro Red

Blood red, aromatic bouquet of ripe plums and black cherries with leather notes. Lovely, rounded tannins with a minty, pepper finish.
PLB

Solar Viejo Vaza Cosecha 2009, Rioja Red

A very pretty wine with loads of jammy fruit and redcurrant flavours. Delicious and well-balanced.

Sonsierra Tempranillo 2009, Rioja Red

Concentrated dark fruits on the nose. Warm and jammy on the palate with intense vanilla spice with lingering sweetness on the finish.
£6.99 BOD, HKN

Sonsierra Vendimia Seleccionada 2007, Rioja Red

Pungent nose of ripe aromatic fruit. Full of warm spice and a touch of savoury character, the fruit is well-balanced with grippy tannins.
£10.99 BOD

Taron Crianza 2006, Rioja Red

Stewed and ripe on the nose. Dark fruit and chocolate on the palate with hints of green. Quite weighty.
£6.15 VDR

Toresanas Amant Roble 2008, Toro Red

An earthy nose. Refreshing and fruity, with notes of smoke, tea and bubblegum. Dry-ish tannins

and a fruit gum finish.
£8.30 ULT

Val De Vid Rueda 2009, Rueda Red

Nice, fresh lemon fruit balanced with good ripe fruit flavours on the mid palate. Light and fresh on the finish.
BWC

Valcarlos Fortius Gran Reserva 1999, Navarra Red

Fruitcake nose with light earthiness. Clean, fresh plums on the palate with good balance and weight. Mineral tones on the finish.
£20.00 EVW, MCT, PWI

Valdemar Conde De Valdemar Reserva 2004, Rioja Red

Earthy nose with hints of ripe fruit on the nose. Soft attack with ripe plum fruit on the mid palate. Lush with grippy tannins.

Valtravieso Tinta Fina 2006, Ribera Del Douro Red

Some elegant aromas and violet notes. Moderate red fruit with dry but balance structure.

Valtravieso Vt Vendimia Seleccionada 2006, Ribera Del Douro Red

Complex aromas with a herbal edge on the palate. Firm tannic structure, alcohol well-balanced. Tobacco and cedar notes on the finish.

Vega Real Crianza 2006, Ribera Del Duero Red

Meaty, dense and quite reductive. Big dry tannins in the mouth, very juicy.

Vega Tolosa Vega Tolosa Bobal Old Vines Barrique 2008, Castilla La Mancha Red

Deep black fruit aromas. Lush and ripe black fruit palate with very grippy tannins. Delicious.

Viñas Del Vero Secastilla 2007, Somontano Red

Black cherry fruit and some spicy, vanilla notes. Firm tannins balanced by acidity and medium length.
£19.99 OCO

Vinedo Solarena Vega del Rayo Reserva 2005, Rioja Red

Well-structured red berry fruit. On the palate there are hints of vanilla and spice. Fresh and easy drinking style.
£9.99 PBA

Vinedo Solarena Vega del Rayo Seleccionada 2007, Rioja Red

Creamy and fresh on the nose with a hint of nuttiness. Creamy fruit on the palate with coffee and vanilla flavours. Well-balanced.
£7.49 PBA

Vinicola De Castilla Castillo De Calatrava Gran Reserva 2002, Castilla La Mancha Red

Mature, earthy, spicy and plum nose. Spicy red fruit on the palate, dry with gentle and soft tannins. Well-structured.
£9.99 SAIN

Vinicola De Castilla Marques De Calatrava Organic Tempranillo Seleccion Reservada 2008, Castilla La Mancha Red

Cherry fruit on the palate with ripe tannins and a touch of white pepper. Medium bodied with a concentrated, well-balanced finish.
£7.19 WAIT

Vinos De Arganza La Mano Mencia Roble 2008, Bierzo Red

Dark red and black fruits with a floral note. Lavender and cherry blossom, fairly jammy red berries with a vegetal note. Long finish.

Virgen Del Aguila Agoston Garnacha Syrah 2009, Cariñena Red

Really nice clean fruity everyday

wine. Palate is also nice and clean. An excellent BBQ wine.

Virgen Del Aguila Agoston Tempranillo Cabernet 2009, Cariñena Red

Lovely, intensely perfumed. Rich black fruit and spice with hints of creamy vanilla on the palate. Long length.

Virgen Del Aguila Señorio Del Aguila Gran Reserva 2001, Cariñena Red

Deep cherry fruit aromas, ripe and round on the palate with a very modern appearance. Cedar on the finish balanced with lashings of vanilla and black fruit.

Zgm Los Vividores Tempranillo La Mancha 2008, Castilla La Mancha Red

Ripe cherry nose and palate with fresh acidity and good balance. Ripe and lingering on the finish.
£5.99 MRN

Bodega La Viña El Prado Rosado 2009, Valencia Rosé

Dry and elegant with juicy ripe fruit. Summer pudding fruits on the palate with very good balance.
£5.99

D Rafeal Arevalo Rodriguez Mayor De Castello Rosado 2009, Burgos Rosé

Fresh and tangy, nettle and wild raspberry on the nose. Palate is ripe with good balance and length.
£4.99

Muga Rosado 2009, Rioja Rosé

Medium baby pink, melon and strawberry palate with broad attack. Fresh lemon and citrus finish.
£8.15 BCW, MAJ, WNS, WAIT

Murviedro Las Falleras Rosé 2009, Utiel Requena Rosé

Fresh on the nose with ripe strawberry and citrus fruit. Good,

pure fruit and fresh acidity.
M&S

Santo Cristo Marquesa De La Cruz Garnacha Rosé 2009, Campo De Borja Rosé

Ripe cherry and some vanilla on the nose. The palate is cherry ripe with firm fruit. Clean and fresh.
£7.15 WAIT

Valdemar Conde De Valdemar Rosado 2009, Rioja Rosé

Pear drop nose. Round, with rose petal and apple sweetness on the palate. Clean and fresh on the finish.

Verde Marte Naranjal 2009, Utiel Requena Rosé

Intense and concentrated fruit. Sweet on the palate with vibrant freshness from well-balanced acidity. Firm fruit finish.

Vilarnau Pinot Noir 2009, Penedés Rosé

Juicy fruit aromas. Supple and honest with peppery ripe fruit on the palate. Clean and fresh.

Ca N'Estella Cava Rabetllat I Vidal Brut Nature 2008, Penedès Sparkling

Lovely complexity on nose. Ripe, round, autolytic notes. Fresh.

Castellblanch Waitrose Cava Brut NV NV, Cava Sparkling

Delicate nose and elegant attack. Good creamy development & subtle layered fruits. Clean brioche/toast finish.
£6.49 WAIT

Codorníu Anna De Codorníu Brut NV, Cava Sparkling

Lovely balanced body, great freshness and good length.
£9.99

Codorníu Gran Plus Ultra Brut NV, Cava Sparkling

Fine mousse and pale gold. Appley

attack leads to a bright crisp palate.

Codorníu Jaume Codorníu Brut NV, Cava Sparkling
No great complexity or character but nicely balanced and moderate length. Clean, fresh easy drink.
£21.99 DBW, FEN, INX, VWS

Codorníu Reina Maria Cristina Reserva Vintage Brut 2007, Cava Sparkling
Pale gold with a fine mousse. Appley nose leading to a crisp bright finish.
£18.99 LWC, MAJ, MCT

Codorníu Selección Raventós Brut NV, Cava Sparkling
Good fruit nose. Well-balanced. Good length.
£9.99 MAJ, MCT, ODD, VWS

Freixenet Brut Vintage Reserva 2007, Cava Sparkling
Pale colour. Lime fruit nose. Soft attack. Clean, fresh, simple, short. Fresh flavour.
£12.99

Freixenet Cordon Negro Reserva Brut NV, Cava Sparkling
Fresh, creamy, sherbet lemons, elegant almond finish.
£8.99 BWL, TESC, WAIT

Freixenet Elyssia Gran Cuvée NV, Cava Sparkling
Clean and fresh on the nose with hints of ocean & oyster. Lean on the palate with some minerality & dash of lime. Bead very delicate.
£14.99 SOH, WAIT

Freixenet Excelencia Vintage Brut 2008, Cava Sparkling
Light mousse. Slight pear and apricot floral notes. Good richness, but slightly short finish.
£11.99 WAIT

Marques De Monistrol Clos Monistrol Vintage Brut Cava 2007, Cava Sparkling
Grapefruit creamy, fresh up-front flowers. Short length.
SAIN

Marques De Monistrol Gran Tradicion Vintage Brut Cava 2007, Cava Sparkling
Clean elegant nose with a soft orchard fruit palate. Simple finish.

Marques De Monistrol Tesco Reserva Cava NV, Cava Sparkling
Lemony nose. Balanced and crisp with bright lemony fruit. Nice.
TESC

Torre Oria Torre Oria Brut NV, Valencia Sparkling
Crisp focused with attractive citrus fruit and a hint of chalkiness.

Vilarnau Brut Nature 2007, Penedès Sparkling
Pale yellow with a minerally, steely nose. Lovely elegant fizz with apple and pear fruit. Richness on finish and good length.
£9.99 OCO

Codorníu Pinot Noir Rosé Brut NV, Cava Sparkling Rosé
Frothy head and good small beaded bubbles, autolysis. Creamy strawberry fruit with a touch of yeasty fruit finish with strawberry length.
£10.99 MAJ, MCT, ODD, VWS

Marques De Monistrol Premium Cuvée Vintage Rosé Cava 2007, Cava Sparkling Rosé
Medium bead bubbles, strawberry. Bright acidity balanced with fresh fruit and yeasty notes. Citric clean finish.
£11.99 MRN

ANNA
DE CODORNIU

the best selling Cava in Spain
is now available at Sainsbury's and
www.tauruswines.co.uk

Marques De Monistrol Vintage Rosé Cava 2007, Penedés Sparkling Rosé
Strawberry raspberry nose. Bright fruit. Crisp acidity and grip. Full bodied and long.

René Barbier Rosado NV, Cava Sparkling Rosé
Warm herbaceous. Medium acidity, soft currants and a medium length.
BWC

Macia Batle Blanc Dolc 2008, Mallorca Sweet
Honey, with delicate balance of acidity and ripe fruit. Tangy and fresh on the palate with good fruit expression.

Emilio Lustau Marks & Spencer Amontillado NV, Andalucía Fortified
Lifted cashew and nutmeg. Sweet green apples and hints of melon and cantaloupe.
£5.99

Emilio Lustau Marks & Spencer Oloroso NV, Andalucía Fortified
Lifted cedar and toffee. Fresh coffee bean. White chocolate and pepper finish.
£7.49

Emilio Lustau Sainsbury's Manzanilla NV, Andalucía Fortified
Pale, straw green hue. Salty/tangy. Sweet pear. Strong cantaloupe finish.
£5.49

Emilio Lustau Solera Reserva Manzanilla Papirusa NV, Andalucía Fortified
Very clean, light nose with fresh bread undertones. Zingy palate, almonds and hazelnuts.
£11.00

Emilio Lustau Solera Reserva Oloroso Don Nuño NV, Andalucía Fortified
Aromas of cracked caramel and toasted almonds. Smooth, crisp palate. Good finish.
£14.00

Gonzalez Byass Matusalem Oloroso Dulce Vors NV, Jerez Fortified
Deep amber with a heavy nose. Sweet fruit with a nutty almond character, the palate is fresh and ripe with a lingering finish.
£16.29 WAIT

Gonzalez Byass Nectar PX NV, Jerez Fortified
Lovely burnt toffee character. Lots of layered spice and orange fruit.

Hidalgo Palo Cortado Wellington Vors 30 Years Old NV, Andalucía Fortified
Light restrained nose, delicate spicy palate with a citrus peel character on finish.
£23.00 MZC

Luis Caballero Morrisons Fino Sherry NV, Jerez Fortified
Fresh lifted green bean. Prawn cracker, asparagus.
£4.85 MRN

Rey Fernando de Castill Antique Palo Cortado NV, Andalucía Fortified
Lifted ginger and cinnamon, upfront cedar with hints of varnish.
£27.49 PBA

Rey Fernando de Castill Classic Manzanilla NV, Andalucía Fortified
Good intensity on the nose with bruised apple and salty ting. Some sweetness and a little style.
£10.99 PBA

USA

California, like Australia, has suffered from massive overproduction in recent years, following the gold rush of plantings through the 1990s. It is a polarised category: on the one hand it is home to the UK's best-selling brand, Blossom Hill; on the other it offers ultra premium, highly sought after Cabernet Sauvignons like Harlan or Screaming Eagle. It has the best of wines and the worst of wines, and in-between, a great many very good ones. Finding the latter, however, is not always so easy – often they are simply not exported. The chase is worth it, especially if you like their generous, fruity but serious style.

KEY FACTS

Total production
20m hectolitres

Total vineyard
208,000ha

Top 10 grapes
1 Cabernet Sauvignon
2 Merlot
3 Zinfandel
4 Pinot Noir
5 Syrah
6 Chardonnay
7 Sauvignon Blanc
8 Chenin Blanc
9 Pinot Gris/Grigio
10 Viognier

Top 10 regions
1 San Joaquin Valley
2 Lodi
3 Sonoma
4 Sierra Foothills
5 Napa Valley
6 Monterey
7 Santa Barbara
8 Paso Robles
9 Mendocino
10 Santa Cruz Mountains

Producers
Producers 1,605;
Growers 4,500

2010 IWC PERFORMANCE

Trophies	1
Gold	3
Silver	15
Bronze	24

Paul Hobbs Crossbarn Cabernet Sauvignon 2006, Monterey Red
Touch of leafy sophisticated quality. Cool climate. Slightly green vegetal. Nice dryness.

Robert Mondavi Napa Valley Pinot Noir 2008, California Red
Black cherry, raspberry and mulberry aromas with a hint of smokiness. Good tannin structure. A svelte and stylish wine.
£14.99

 VERMOUTH TROPHY

Quady Vya Sweet Vermouth NV, California Fortified
Botanical and delicate with layers of complex aromas, mulled wine and holiday spices. Ripe and rich on the palate with sweet, sour and spicy flavours, nutmeg and orange rind. Long and very distinctive.
£16.99 HLD

SILVER

Sonoma-Cutrer Sonoma Coast Chardonnay 2008, California White
Quite heavy fruit with apricots on the nose. Ripe apricot and fresh citrus on the palate. Good length and balance. Very drinkable.
£14.99 BTH, MWW, OCO, WAIT

Anne Amie Pinot Noir 2007, Oregon Red
Fresh, restrained cherry nose. Palate is welcoming and juicy with a long, well-balanced finish.
£10.99 NWD, WAIT

Blackstone Merlot 2007, California Red
Herbal and mixed fruit bouquet with subtle palate. A little simple yet a continual mid palate and dry flavoursome finish.
MCT

Eos Reserve Petite Sirah 2007, California Red
Spiced raisins. Easy drinking, fleshy, with soft but dry tannins.

M By Michael Mondavi Cabernet Sauvignon 2006, Monterey Red
Silky, soft violet nose. Rich in cassis notes. Palate very balanced, excellent fruit. Very soft tannins.
£250.00 HAR

Ravenswood Napa Valley Zinfandel 2007, California Red
Deep raspberry red. Soft nose. Good flavour. Big rich finish.
£11.99

Ravenswood Sonoma Zinfandel 2007, California Red
Deep, red, subtle fruity nose. Rich, ripe fruitcake palate with a delicate green finish.
£11.99

Robert Mondavi Napa Valley Cabernet Sauvignon 2007, California Red
Fairly discreet and subdued but a pure black fruit quality. The palate is a touch lean but nice balance. Supple tannins. Stylish.
£14.99

Robert Mondavi Private Selection Cabernet Sauvignon 2007, California Red
A touch under-ripe but then a nice blackcurrant sweetness comes through. Very succulent fruit. Nice length and clarity, very sophisticated.
£9.99 TESC

Robert Mondavi Reserve Cabernet Sauvignon 2006, California Red
Big, deep, eucalyptus nose with

menthol and abundance of ripe cassis fruit. Intense on palate with massive concentration but supple tannins and good length.
£49.99 POG

Rosénthal The Malibu Estate 2005, California Red

Ripe blackcurrant and ripe cherry - juicy, rich, graphite, spicy flavours. Fine tannin. Very elegant finish with a hint of muted floral on finish.

Sonoma-Cutrer Russian River Valley Pinot Noir 2007, California Red

Ripe cherry on the nose with some minerality. Cherry and raspberry jam flavours on the palate with smoky oak nuances showing through. Stylish and complex.
£20.00 MWW, OCO, WAIT, WUO

Trinchero Family Estates Napa Cellars Zinfandel 2007, Monterey Red

Big and bold but well-balanced. Quite oaky but with ripe sweet fruit to match. Mouthfeel warm and rich.

Trinchero Family Estates Terra D'Oro Barbera 2007, California Red

Floral spice, vanilla. Ripe dark fruits. Soft yet robust.

Trinchero Family Estates Terra D'Oro Zinfandel 2007, California Red

Cigar box and cedar on the nose. Full of fruit with a long, good mouthfeel. Warm, rich and fulfilling.

BRONZE

Château Lafayette Reneau Dry Riesling 2008, New York State White

Flinty and floral with a mellow softness. Melon and pineapple on the palate with a lime fresh finish. Delicate and drinkable.

Eberle Estate Bottled Chardonnay 2008, California White

Star bright with pale straw hue. Fresh and ripe on the nose and palate with a slightly waxy finish. AAW

Firesteed Riesling 2008, Oregon White

Delicate citrus nose, fresh and crisp on the palate with layers of pineapple and grapefruit. Light and refreshing.

First Press Napa Valley Chardonnay 2008, Monterey White

Ripe apple fruit on the nose with citrus, pineapple and ripe apple on the palate.
£13.99

Five Rivers Chardonnay 2008, California White

Tropical fruit palate with lots of warmth and roundness. Good body.
£8.99 MWW

Les Grands Chais De France River Wild Californian White NV, California White

Light and nutty nose. Ripe yellow peach and melon on the palate. Lingering freshness on the finish.

Marimar Don Miguel Vineyard Chardonnay 2005, California White

Citrus and mineral nose with good acidity.

Trinchero Family Estates Folie A Deux Chardonnay 2008, Monterey White

Ripe tropical fruit palate that is round and full bodied. Big buttery finish.

Beringer Founders Estate Old Vine Zinfandel 2007, California Red

Smoke and leather on the nose.

Rich blackberry and bramble character.
£8.99 EVW

Bogle Vineyards Phantom 2006, California Red
Big, ripe, meaty palate. Lingering finish.
£16.95 DEF, GWW

Bonterra Merlot 2007, California Red
Subtle fruit. Quite dry and serious style. Savoury and grippy. Fine.
£11.99 BKT, OCO, VER, WAIT

Domaine Carneros Avant-Garde Pinot Noir 2008, California Red
Cherry sweets and stony mineral nose. Complexity on the flavour with savoury minerality and a long finish.
£16.99

Eos Blackburn & James Merlot 2008, California Red
Wow! Varied fruit core, juicy, Morello cherries. Good weight and big tannins. Some mineral on finish.
£7.49 CWS

Evergreen Pinot Noir 2006, Oregon Red
Oak and dried plum on the nose. Lush, soft savoury fruit on the palate and supple structure.

Gallo Redwood Creek Merlot 2008, California Red
Jammy, floral, subtle toast and vanilla. Soft, ripe, sweet fruit. Medium weight with a dry finish.
£7.49 TESC, MRN

Hahn Family Wines Hahn Estates Cabernet Sauvignon 2008, California Red
Cinnamon and cloves on the nose. Spicy red fruit on the palate with clover showing through strongly. Good tannin stucture.
£11.24 PAT

Langetwins Green Hills Cabernet Sauvignon 2007, California Red
Earthy, mineral cassis. Good flavour and richness. Slightly light on finish.
£7.99 D&D

Ravenswood Lodi Zinfandel 2007, California Red
Raspberry nose. Powerful, ripe and fruity with a herbal finish.
£8.99 SAIN, MWW, OST

Ravenswood Teldeschi Zinfandel 2007, California Red
Sweet tinned fruit aromas. Sweet, good fruit on the palate.
£24.99 POG

Scotto Zinfandel Barbera 2007, California Red
Hot scent on the nose. Light and supple fruit on the palate.
£7.15 WI-AV

Seghesio Old Vine Zinfandel 2007, California Red
Spicy and juicy on the nose. Good rich fruit. Good length.
£27.99 Widely Available

Story Ridge Vineyards Panamera Cuvée Napa 2007, Monterey Red
Dark, clean with blackcurrant fruit taste. Lovely fruit mid palate and herbal fruit finish.
£26.00 HOH

Trinchero Family Estates Folie A Deux Cabernet Sauvignon 2007, Monterey Red
Delicate nose but bright and fruity. Jammy palate (raspberry).

Niederrhein Gold California Zinfandel Rosé 2009, California Rosé
A quaffable wine. Easy drinking style with redcurrant fruits upfront and soft feel.
LDL

Other Countries

2010 IWC PERFORMANCE

Trophies	4
Gold	10
Silver	50
Bronze	102

Brazil, England, Bulgaria, Holland, Turkey, Uruguay … it might sound more like a football tournament than a wine competition, but these countries – and all the others in this section – take their wine very seriously. Each offers something unique to the ever-expanding vinous world, and while there are inevitably some less auspicious examples around, quality can be as good as anywhere. Furthermore there are some really charismatic discoveries to be made here: English sparkling is becoming more and more celebrated, Bulgaria has fabulous value reds, Brazil does fantastic things with Merlot – the list goes on. For something that will really surprise and delight you, look no further than the medal winners that follow.

BRAZIL

SILVER

Geisse Vinho Branco Espumante Moscatel 2009, Serra Gaúcha Sparkling
Pale. Nice fresh grapey nose as would expect from the Muscatels. Sweet and lots of fizz in the mouth.

BRONZE

Salton Talento 2005, Rio Grande do Sul Red
Fine, fresh fruits of the forest. Rhubarb, ripe tannins. Chocolate.

Cooperitiva Aurora Espumante Prosecco Brut NV, Rio Grande do Sul Sparkling
Creamy mousse on the palate, delicate fruit apple blossom and peach. Raspberry finish.

Wine Park Gran Legado Moscatel NV, Serra Gaúcha Sparkling
Floral, biscuit nose. High acid. Yeasty notes. Moderate depth of flavour. Appley with pleasant length.

BULGARIA

SILVER

Domaine Boyar International Solitaire Grands Cepages 2008, Thracian Valley Red
Deep, dense, ruby, crimson. Cassis, cedar, red grapes. A rich wine with powerful flavours.

Katarzyna Encore 2008, Thracian Valley Red
Slightly meaty nose. Fleshy, dark fruits and smooth oak flavours. Long and fresh. Needs time.
£8.50

BRONZE

Katarzyna Mezzek 2009, Thracian Valley White
Apple, pear and slight toast on nose. Moderate acid supports apple and pear fruit with integrated oak flavours. Simple, pleasant wine with nice length.
£2.30

Domaine Boyar Silver Rock Cabernet Sauvignon 2009, Trakia Valley Red
Ripe cassis on nose. Pleasant ripe blackcurrants, well-balanced.
£3.79 EHL, MRN

Edoardo Miroglio Pinot Nero 2007, Thracian Valley Red
Good juicy fruit, brambly. Some silkiness. Good finish.
£9.90 BVL

Katarzyna Contemplations Red 2008, Thracian Valley Red
Ripe berry nose. Berries and cherries. Well-balanced but a bit short.
£3.28

CANADA

GOLD

Magnotta Riesling Icewine Limited Edition 2007, Ontario Sweet
High, zesty nose - orange and lime/ginger. Ripe burnt orange and cinnamon body. Good acidity and long cleansing finish.

 CANADIAN ICE WINE TROPHY

Strewn Icewine Riesling 2008, Niagara Peninsula Sweet
Beautiful nose of honey and tangerines. Marmalade too very inviting. Honeysuckle, lychee, satsuma and lime. Good

balance and intensity. Rapier like finish.

SILVER

Ganton & Larsen Prospect Winery Birch Canoe Pinot Blanc 2008, Okanagan Valley
White
Fresh, clean, honeyed fruit on nose. Soft peachy fruit, low to medium acidity. Honeyed finish.

Mission Hill Family Estate Select Lot Collection Syrah 2006, Okanagan Valley Red
Very attractive good varietal depth. Dark berry fruit and smoky oak on the palate. Bold, rich and full-bodied with good freshness.

Mission Hill Family Estate Select Lot Collection Syrah 2007, Okanagan Valley Red
Very minerally with tar and spice on the nose. Dark, firm fruit with a leather and smoke finish.

Pelee Island Winery Cabernet Franc 2008, Ontario Red
Quite complex with pepper spice and bramble fruit nose. Nice long, red and tight - has reached ripeness. Well made with good definition and also durable.
£11.99 HLD

Inniskillin Cabernet Franc Icewine 2007, Niagara Peninsula Sweet
Very pretty floral, red berry compote nose. Concentrated raw jelly intensity. Great acidity and freshness. Long length and very impressive.
£60.00

Inniskillin Sparkling Vidal Icewine 2007, Niagara Peninsula Sweet
Ripe honeyed apricot nose. Clean sweet attack, honey and citrus

flavour. Good acidity, clean nice length. Long dried apricot flavour.
£50.00 OCO, WAIT

Jackson-Triggs Vidal Icewine 2007, Niagara Peninsula
Sweet
Lovely flowery honey nose. Rich sweet berry and tropical fruit.
£12.99 LAI, OST

Magnotta Cabernet Franc Icewine Limited Edition 2007, Ontario Sweet
Redcurrant jelly nose with more savoury rosehip note. Mouth-watering acidity. Clean, delicious.

Pelee Island Winery Vidal Icewine 2007, Pelee Island
Sweet
Lovely sweet flowery nose. Lovely summer fruits, honey and marmalade. Delicious.
£34.99 HLD

Peller Private Reserve Vidal Icewine 2008, Niagara Peninsula Sweet
Rich flowery nose. Sweet, flowery, herbal flavour on the palate with a long, fresh finish.

Peller Riesling Ice Wine 2007, Ontario Sweet
Gorgeous deep, rich, floral notes. Rich complexity and length. Harmonious acacia honey.
£43.50 WAIT

Pillitteri Icewine Riesling 2007, Ontario Sweet
Wonderful bouquet of apple/peach blossom, banana and raisins. Noble in the mouth, very fine lime acidity. Honeysuckle, marmalade notes. Good.

Pillitteri Vidal Icewine 2008, Ontario Sweet
Sweet, herbal nose. Ripe, summery fruit with a floral edge. Sweet herbs follow on the finish.

Beaufort Siegerrebe 2009, British Columbia White
Sweet potato nose with hints of ripe apple underneath. Almost vegetal like character with a touch of lemony citrus. Intriguing.

Magnotta Riesling Medium Dry 2007, Ontario White
Fine floral lime. Intense nose. Medium and chalky flowers. A dry and spicy finish with honey notes.

Thirty Bench Small Lot Chardonnay 2007, Niagara Peninsula White
Fresh lemon aroma on the nose . Good, expressive fruit with some lifted citrus and lime. Balanced with a good mouthfeel and fresh finish.

Magnotta Enotrium Gran Reserva 2005, Ontario Red
Pot pourri, spicy nose. Spicy, cloves, oak and wild berries with a dry finish.

Magnotta Meritage Limited Editon 2007, Ontario Red
Big, sweet, almost Chilean style. Bright blackcurrants and also some mint but slight reduction.

Mission Hill Family Estate Reserve Merlot 2007, Okanagan Valley Red
Chewy yet ripe tannins. Luscious brambly fruit. Good oak, balance and length.

Magnotta Sparkling Vidal Icewine Limited Edition 2008, Ontario Sparkling
Treacly sweetness. Hints of marmalade. Light fizz on the palate. Hint of toffee.

Garton & Larsen Prospect Winery Lost Bars Icewine
2007, Okanagan Valley
Sweet
Lychee and slightly sweet. Syrupy and herbal.

Mission Hill Family Estate Family Estate Reserve Riesling Icewine 2008, Okanagan Valley Sweet
Fresh orange peel and blossom nose. Rich, still has zesty acidity behind sweetness. Long and round.

Peller Oak Aged Icewine 2007, Niagara Peninsula
Sweet
Rich, sweet, herbal nose. Slightly bitter sweetness.

Peller Riesling Ice Wine 2007, Ontario Sweet
Light caramel nose. Rounded crème brulée note. Light caramel palate. Strong finish.
£43.50 WAIT

Peller Vidal Icewine 2008, Niagara Peninsula Sweet
Sweet, flowery nose. Lovely honey and marmalade with attractive sweet finish.

Strewn Icewine Cabernet Franc 2008, Niagara Peninsula
Sweet
Uncomplex nose. Red cherry and almond jam and spice. Lovely palate. Clean and quite crunchy and very well made.

CHINA

Helan Mountain Premium Cabernet Sauvignon 2008, Guangxia Helan Mountain Red
Sweet, open nose with liqueur like berry fruits. The palate is sweetly fruited with nice flavours. Berry-ish finish.

CZECH REPUBLIC

Baloun Pálava Batch Nr. 45/09 2009, Moravia
White

Lemon nose with tropical notes; red grapefruit and lemon on the palate; quite complex with good depth and finish.

Baloun Ryzlink Rýnský Batch Nr.11/09 2009, Moravia
White

Hint of aromatic grassy character on the nose. Floral with sweet nectarine palate. Lush with apricots and a clean, fresh lime finish.

Baloun Sylvánské Zelené Batch Nr.17/09 2009, Moravia
White

Vanilla, guava nose and light pepper. Lovely acidity, green apples and ripe pears with a mineral edge. Single dimensional and light bodied.

Baloun Veltlínské Zelené Batch Nr.3/09 2009, Moravia
White

Green and tight on the nose, but lovely ripe lime-cordial fruit on the palate. Lemony and zesty with good length.

ENGLAND

Nyetimber Blanc De Blancs 2001, West Sussex Sparkling

Frothy mousse, pale youthful colour. Toasted hazelnut and baked pear aromas, some tertiary yeast. Mouthfilling creamy tarte tatin flavours. Good acidity and balance. Long.
£28.99 BB&R, BRI, CHH, FAR, LIB, WAIT

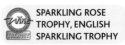 **SPARKLING ROSE TROPHY, ENGLISH SPARKLING TROPHY**

Camel Valley Pinot Noir Rosé Brut 2008, Cornwall
Sparkling Rosé

Very light pink hue. Light, clean fruity nose. Delicate Pinot Noir. Crisp and clean with an austere edge. Good length.
£24.95

Bolney Autumn Spice 2009, Sussex White

Fresh, zesty and ripe. Good acidity with lemon citrus, candied lemon and apple peel on the palate. Nicely balanced with a long finish.
£7.59 BOV, WAIT

Camel Valley Bacchus 2009, Cornwall White

Clear and pale lemon green. Grassy, lively lemon peel aromas, green apples on the palate with a very clean and very ripe finish. Lush and juicy.
£12.95 CVV

Wickham Limited Release Medium 2008, Hampshire
White

Ripe with hints of apples and honey. Off-dry on the palate with ripe red apple character, floral accents and lingering acidity. Long and fresh on the finish.
£6.80 EWC, GWW, WIK, WSK

Wickham Special Release Fumé 2008, Hampshire White

Candied nose with lively citrus and fresh lemon fruit. Well-balanced acidity with good weight and freshness. Ripe and lifted finish.
£9.29 EWC, GWW, WIK, WSK, WAIT

Camel Valley Pinot Noir Brut 2007, Cornwall Sparkling
Gently floral wine with oatmeal and stone fruits. Soft mousse. Pleasant dry, minimal length.
£29.95 CVV

Ridgeview Grosvenor Blanc De Blancs 2006, South East Sparkling
Fresh, bready notes. Beautiful sweetness and balance. Fresh, classy and long
£21.95 BB&R, ENO, EWC, RID

Ridgeview Knightsbridge Blanc De Noirs 2006, South East Sparkling
Good balance and complexity. Well textured bubbles. Good length. Nice baked apple character.
£24.95 BUT, EWC, HAR, HGT, HRY, RID

Chapel Down Pinot Reserve 2004, South East Sparkling Red
Tinned strawberries nose. Moderate intensity, attractive and mineral. Dry palate, fine bubble. No great intensity. Youthful.
£24.99 CDW, MWW

BRONZE

Chapel Down Lamberhurst Estate Bacchus Reserve 2009, South East White
Lightly aromatic on the nose with a touch of confected fruit. Juicy green apple on the palate with a brambly apple finish. Fresh and clean.
£9.99 M&S

Nutbourne Vineyard Sussex Reserve 2009, West Sussex White
Sweet on the nose with a ripe citrus character. A touch of vegetal flavours on the palate with a grapefruit, citrus finish.

Stanlake Park Regatta 2007, Berkshire White
Honeyed and soft on the nose. A touch of confected fruit on the palate with an appely finish. Fresh and smoky.
£7.99 EOR, WAIT

Three Choirs Cellar Door Release Bacchus 2009, Gloucestershire White
Intensely grassy with green leafy notes. Elderflower on the palate with a light palate tinged with green. Sweet and ripe with an off-dry finish.
£10.55

Sharpham Vineyard Rosé 2008, Devon Rosé
Rounded texture with a ripe fruit palate. Gentle and a bit savoury. Very attractive.
£12.50 SHV

Gusbourne Estate Blanc De Blancs 2006, Kent Sparkling
Nose fresh and lively. Light-bodied & crisp. Clean but slightly weak finish.
£24.99

Ridgeview Bloomsbury 2007, South East Sparkling
Creamy mousse, golden colour. Some autolytic notes: brioche, digestive biscuit. Rounded creamy flavours. Long soft finish.
£19.99 Widely Available

Throwley Reserve Brut 2003, Kent Sparkling
Beautiful floral character on the nose. Fresh, slightly creamy biscuit. Long finish. Classy with some complexity.
£16.00 BNK, HRW

**Warden Abbey Quality
Sparkling Wine Extra Dry
2007, East Anglia** Sparkling
Delicate citrus fruit. Light bodied,
refined acidity. Good refreshing
aperitif style.
£16.50 EPW

**Ridgeview Fitzrovia Rosé
2007, South East** Sparkling
Rosé
Light tinned fruit salad to nose.
Attractive fruity, dry palate. A
bit short.
£21.99 ENO, RID, SDC, WSO,
WAIT

GEORGIA

**Teliani Valley Tsinandali 2007,
Kakheti** White
Subdued, neutral nose. Moderate
acidity supports lemony bright
fruits. Pleasant almond flan,
broad creamy fruits.

**JSC Telavi Marani Kondoli
Vineyards Saperavi 2005,
Kakheti** Red
Tasty French oak nose, good fruit
beneath. Spicy, rich, coffeeish
lively palate. Elegant tannin and
long, dry but elegant finish.

**Teliani Valley Mukuzani 2006,
Kakheti** Red
Bitter cherry on the nose.
Chunky and firm at the start
of this palate, dry, red fruit.
Nice bittersweet character and
length.

**Badagoni Alaverdi Tradition
Red Dry 2007, Teliani Valley**
Red
Intense fruity aggression, red
berry style. Mid body balanced
and easy going. Very good with
food.

**JSC Telavi Marani Kondoli
Vineyards Saperavi Merlot
2007, Kakheti** Red
Merlot adds a softening edge to
the bold, black and dense fruit.
Quite juicy, rich, black, plum skin
tang. Big tannins.

**JSC Telavi Marani Mukuzani
2008, Kakheti** Red
Very clean, controlled, cherry and
black fruit nose. Tight, creamy,
rich black fruit. Dry tannin but
lively style.

**JSC Telavi Marani Napareuli
2008, Kakheti** Red
Some development, good fruit.
Mid body balanced, suave. Good
for food, lacks complexity but
enjoyable.

**JSC Telavi Marani Saperavi
Cabernet 2008, Kakheti** Red
Slightly more leathery
quality here, perhaps from
the Cabernet. Big chewy
tannins. Heaven!

GREECE

 **GREEK WHITE
TROPHY**

**Semeli Mantinia Nassiakos
2009, Mantinia** White
Vibrant and fresh. Green apple
fruit and bracing citrus
on the palate. Ripe and lush with
balanced acidity and good
structure. Refreshing finish with
long, lingering acidity.

**Estate Muses Vinum Gratum
2007, Central Greece** Red
Sweet, cedary, ripe nose. Tons
of eucalyptus. Ripe black fruit.
Full with supple, grainy tannins.
Developing some complexity.
Long. Textured.

GREEK RED TROPHY

Nemeion Estate Hgemon 2005, Peloponnese Red
Fragrant berry aromas. Slightly tannic, red berry fruits, potential for aging.
£60.00

SILVER

Kechris Kechribari Retsina 2009, Thessaloniki White
Minerally and green fruit aromas on the nose, practically leaping out of the glass. Citrus and stone fruits on the palate with a mineral backbone. Spice lingers on the finish.

Kechris The Pine's Tear Retsina 2009, Thessaloniki White
Fresh citrus fruit with a touch of spice. Pine and spice on the palate with zingy acidity and a ripe, lingering finish.

Robola Producers Of Kefalonia San Gerassimo 2009, Kefalonia White
Lots of grapefruit, floral and honeyed aromas. Leesy on the palate with a long, fresh finish.

A & G Papaioannou Ktima 2006, Nemea Red
Rich exuberant nose, very pure and well defined. Very well-integrated oak, modern style, very balanced and silky smooth on the finish.

Diamantakis Diamantopetra 2008, Crete Red
Expressive black cherry aromas. A touch of medicinal character with a drying yet flavoursome palate. Long and quite chewy.

Paris Sigalas Sigalas Vinsanto Santorini 2003, Santorini

Sweet
An oxidative character on the nose with very ripe and sweet aromas. Lush and sweet on the palate with burnt toffee and a touch of saltiness. Long and lush.

BRONZE

Avantis M' Malagousia 2009, Evia White
Greengage, lychee and mineral aromas. Guava and lychee on the palate with sweet honey, violets and confected fruit on the palate.
£4.00

Boutari Moschofilero 2009, Mantinia White
Clean, fresh fruit with ripe, floral aromas. The palate is fresh with ripe citrus fruit. Refreshing and long.
£9.99 WAIT

Domaine Costa Lazaridi Château Julia Assyrtiko 2009, Drama White
Fresh and clean with peach and pineapple fruit. Racy acidity with ripe tropical fruit on the palate. Delicious.

Gentilini Robola Of Cephalonia 2009, Ionian Islands White
Mineral apricot, stone fruit and citrus aromas. Balanced pineapple, blossoms and citrus freshness on the palate. Ripe with a balanced finish.
£12.65 YAM

Greek Wine Cellars D Kourtakis Assyrtiko 2009, Santorini White
Bracing acidity with bright peach and white stone fruit on the palate. Fresh.

Ktima Biblia Chora Areti White 2009, Pangeon White
Spicy and warm with a rich, peachy flavour. Ripe apricots and fresh acidity on the finish.

Michalakis Estate White Gold Cuvée 2009, Irakleion White
Lychee and honey on the nose with a very ripe fragrance. Ripe and lush on the palate with honeyed, lush fruit. Full and round on the finish.

Mylopotamos Mount Athos Lefkos 2009, Mount Athos Regional Wine White
Pale, with lifted banana and lychee on the nose. The palate is similar with ripe fruit and fresh citrus acidity. Fresh and long on the finish.

Oenoforos Asprolithi 2009, Peloponnese White
Citrus, mineral and stone fruit nose. Light, green with a fresh cut grass character. Grassy and citrusy on the finish.

Semeli Orinos Helios White 2009, Nemea White
Apple and citrus on the nose. Refined fruit with clean, ripe flavours. Lemon, green apple and ripe citrus on the palate. Fresh and easy to drink.

Stavros Koulocheris Evinos Sabbatino 2009, Attica White
Grassy, stone fruit nose with yeasty aromas. Stone fruit palate with a touch of honey. Ripe and fresh with a touch of asparagus on the finish.

A & G Papaioannou Cava Papaioannou 2004, Nemea Red
Cedary, pencilly, sweet currant nose. Palate is big, concentrated, quite extracted with chewy tannins, but a minty, mineral freshness to the black fruit. Needs time.

Biblia Chora Merlot 2006, Pangeon Red
Earthy, spicy but slightly leafy nose. Concentrated almost inky fruit. Lots of oak and tannin but some freshness. Needs time.

Biblia Chora Red 2008, Pangeon Red
Fresh, blackcurrant and black cherry nose. Tight, structured, a bit raisiny and tannic but tannins are ripe. Long.

Christoforos Pavlidis Thema Red 2007, Drama Red
Fresh, perfumed with hints of raspberries. Very fresh and lively on the palate. Good structure and delicious now, but will improve.

Ktima Karadimou Vissa 2007, Central Greece Red
Oaky, meaty and varnishy nose. Baked fruit with spicy, meaty, dried cherry flavours on the palate. Warming with chocolate richness. Dry, but with ripe tannins and fresh acidity.

Oinotechniki Zacharias Erythros Zacharias 2008, Corinth Red
Firmly structured, dark plum and berry fruits, good length, needs decanting.

Oinotechniki Zacharias Vineyards Black Cubed 2007, Peloponnese Red
Spicy savoury vanilla perfume. Basic palate, decent acidity and soft tannins.

Semeli Domaine Helios Grande Reserve 2004, Nemea Red
Savoury earthy aromas, dusty high acidity, good length, juicy rich raspberries, hints of morello cherry, sweet spice, lovely length.

Silva Daskalaki Enstikto 2008, Crete Red
Very scented and creamy with

toasty oak aromas. Class, lifted and fragrant. Very fresh with ripe, supple fruit on the finish.

Zacharias Vineyards Nemea 2008, Nemea Red
Ripe and fresh on the nose with good fruit concentration on the palate. Rounded, black fruit finish.

Greek Wine Cellars D Kourtakis Kourtaki Muscat Of Samos NV, Samos Island Sweet
Ripe fruit and honey flavours. Crème brulée.

Greek Wine Cellars D Kourtakis Mavrodaphne Of Patras NV, Peloponnese Sweet
Quince, honey and liquorice nose with a port-like palate. Long and honeyed with a ripe aftertaste.
£4.49 ADE, SAIN, MRN, TESC, WAIT, MRN

Mylopotamos Mount Athos Nama NV, Mount Athos Regional Wine Sweet
Herbaceous and ripe on the nose. Honeyed, sweetly stewed fruit on the palate with a long, fresh finish. Delicious.

Paris Sigalas Sigalas Apiliotis Regional Wine Of Cyclades 2004, Santorini Sweet
A touch of rancio with ripe aromas on the nose. Sweet and stewed fruit on the palate with a touch of spice on the finish.

HUNGARY

Patricius Borház Patricius Tokaji Aszú 6 Puttonyos 2003, Tokaj Botrytis
Clear and bright with a medium-pale gold colour. Ripe nose of tangerine, spice and dry hay. Rich, spicy and warm on the finish with medium weight and full finish.

Hilltop Neszmély Hárslevelu 2009, Neszmely White
Floral spice. Lovely fruit/acid balance. Light, crisp and fresh flavours. Good fine minerality.

Patricius Borház Tokaji Dry Furmint 2008, Tokaj White
Rich honey, mint subdued, nutty aromas - powerful. Firm acidity with nice fruit/honey, floral dryish finish.
£9.99 WAIT

Disznóko Tokaji Aszú 5 Puttonyos 2003, Tokaj Botrytis
Deep gold, tropical fruit on the nose with a rich palate. Elegant floral, honeyed notes. Quite sweet but well-balanced.
C@C

Dobogó Mylitta 2008, Tokaj Botrytis
Golden with honeyed orange marmalade on the nose and palate. Buttery finish with good complexity of fruit. Zingy acidity keeps the palate very fresh. Delightful.
£20.00 LIB

Dobogó Tokaji Aszú 6 Puttonyos 2005, Tokaj Botrytis
Dry, spicy and honeyed on the nose. Waxy with sweet, firm fruit. Apricot fresh with racy acidity on the palate. Deliciously seductive.
£50.00 LIB

Tokajicum Borház Tokaj Aszú 6 Puttonyos 2005, Tokaj Botrytis
Orange peel, figs and cinnamon,

ginger spice on the nose. The palate is sweet and rich with cinnamon and warm spice flavours. The finish is distinctly fresh with apple and citrus character.

BRONZE

Dobogó Tokaji Furmint 2008, Tokaj White
Rich, spicy Alsatian-style aromas. Dry and flavoursome with great depth and character. Lovely texture with a lingering spicy finish.
LIB

Hilltop Neszmély Tradition Cserszegi Fuszeres 2009, Neszmely White
Lightly scented with gentle notes of lime. Strong lime character on the palate, very refreshing with crisp, dry finish.
£3.99 MRN

Nyakas Pince Nyakas Budai Irsai Olivér 2009, Etyek-buda White
Fresh aromatics with citrusy character, very youthful. Fresh lime flavours, clean and refreshing with lively acidity on the finish.

Szent Korona Pincészet Viale Mandorlato Zenit 2009, Budapest White
Fresh pear-drop aromas, attractive fruit character on the palate. Clean and refreshing.

Törley Pezsgopincészet Gála NV, Magyarország Sparkling
Touch weedy but some ripe apple fruit comes through. Crisp mousse, short finish but some nice peachy, easy drinking style.

Róbert Koczuba Campanula Sparkling Pinot Noir Rosé Brut NV, Balatonboglár Sparkling Rosé
Delicate pink colour. Light strawberry fruit. Clean, rounded palate. Good finish.
LAI

Patricius Borház Tokaji Aszú 5 Puttonyos 2003, Tokaj Botrytis
Pale gold and elegant with nutty orange on the nose. Barley sugar and toasted nuts with ripe peach on the palate. Good depth.

Tokaj Disznóko Tokaji Aszú 5 Puttonyos 2001, Tokaj Botrytis
Pale gold with opulent orange peel nose. Molasses and peachy-almond flavours on the palate. Lingering and fresh on the finish.
£25.99 C@C, WAIT

Tokaji-Hétszolo Tokaji Aszú 5 Puttonyos 2001, Tokaj Botrytis
Deep yellow with fresh floral and nutty aromas on the nose. Apricot and marmalade layer the citrus finish.

Varga Pincészet Aranymetszés Badacsonyi Olaszrizling Késoi Szüretelésu 2007, Badacsony Botrytis
Rhubarb and apple on the nose. Good sweetness and balancing acidity.

ISRAEL

SILVER

Tzora Vineyards Neve Ilan Blanc 2008, Judean Hills White
Fresh, lemony vanilla cream. A well-balanced wine with mineral and white peach palate. Citrus notes on finish with delicious, lingering freshness.

BRONZE

Carmel Kayoumi Vineyard Shiraz 2006, Upper Galilee Red
Aromatic, fruity, balsamic and

spicy nose. Raspberries and cream fruit with firm, dry finish.

Tzora Vineyards Misty Hills 2007, Judean Hills Red
Lifted plum and liquorice spice aroma. Soft on the palate with medium length.

Tzora Vineyards Shoresh 2007, Judean Hills Red
Smoky, currant and pepper notes. Sweet, ripe berry fruits on the palate.

JAPAN

Suntory Liquors Ltd. Tomi No Oka Winery Koshu Barrel Fermented 2008, Yamanashi
Pale, yellow colour with citrus notes. Interestingly smoky, creamy palate. Good acidity and balance.
£25.00

Yamanashi Four Seasons 2008, Yamanashi
Quiet nose, oak edge good refreshing acidity. Pale green, golden colour apples and hints of green grapes.

Daisuke Motegi Koshu Verdinho 2009, Yamanashi
Water white, intensely aromatic with grapefruit and tangerine scents. Fresh, crisp acidity. Ripe sherbet finish.

LEBANON

Château Fakra Pinacle De Fakra 2009, Kfardebian Valley Red
Smoky tannins and a bit green and dry. Well rounded and complex finish. Easy drinking.

Château Ka Source De Rouge 2007, Bekaa Valley Red
Fragrant nose and notes of red cherries. Big tannins with spicy finish. Very nicely made.
£10.99 AAW, WAIT

MACEDONIA

Bovin Dooel Alexandar 2008, Tikves Red
Forward, complex, red fruits lengthy nose, ripe but not overripe, balanced. Plum and raisin notes, with supple tannins, lovely oak integration and length.

VV Tikves Ad Skopje Merlot 2008, Tikves Red
Rich spiciness, integrated oak, long finish.

Bovin Dooel Vranec 2008, Tikves Sweet
Caramel and sultana on the nose. Fruitcake, loaded with sultana richness and a touch of brandy flavour. Creamy and rich on the finish.

MEXICO

San Lorenzo Casa Madero Chardonnay 2008, Coahuila White
Peachy and pineapple fruit nose. Nice fruity palate. A fresh, pleasing drink.

Hugo D'Acosta Estapor Venir 2007, Baja California Red
Ripe, dark fruits on the nose. Tar and black plum and sweet damson fruit. Developed tannins. Vanilla and spice to the finish.
£10.99 BWL

San Lorenzo Casa Madero Shiraz 2008, Coahuila Red
Peppery, spicy blackberry and plum fruit aromas. Good acidity and supple texture with nice length and concentration.

ROMANIA

Budureasca Origini 2007, Dealu Mare White
Pale lemon with lychees and honey on the nose, aromatic, fruity with tropical notes, medium sweet, balanced.

Budureasca Origini 2009, Dealu Mare White
Very pale with lychees on the nose; medium dry, with peaches and exotic fruits on the palate. Great fruity finish with a touch of grapefruit.

Domenile Sahateni White Artisan 2009, Dealurile Munteniei White
Pale lemon, scented, grapey, grapefruit and icing sugar nose; off-dry, fruity palate with notes of pink grapefruit. Well-balanced.

Cramele Halewood Hyperion Feteasca Neagra 2008, Dealu Mare Red
Spicy savoury vanilla perfume. Palate is ripe and fleshy with clean, black fruit. Good freshness and acidity with soft tannins on the finish.

SLOVENIA

Marof Cru Chardonnay 2007, Podravje White
Mature, but still fresh. Ripe citrus fruit and a lovely sweetness

on the palate. Enjoyable and drinking now.

Marof Renski Rizling 2008, Podravje White
Pineapple and grapefruit on the nose. Lime with a hint of lemony herbaceousness. Ripe and round on the finish.
£9.00 RAE

Puklavec & Friends Rhine Riesling 2009, Podravje White
Floral, slightly cheese, pecan nose. High acid supports demure peach fruit. Simple.

Marof Breg Sauvignon Jagodni Izbor 2007, Podravje Botrytis
Waxy, honey nose with citrus notes. Sweet and spicy with a lime acidity to balance the wine.

Marof Cru Chardonnay Trockenbeerenauslese 2007, Podravje Botrytis
Yellow apricot and honey with candied peel on the nose. A touch of bitter orange on the palate with good depth and concentration.

SWITZERLAND

Domaine Du Daley Blanc De Noir Grand Cru 2007, Vaud White
White flowers on the nose. Tropical star fruit and guava on the palate. Nicely complex with ripe fruit intensity, well-balanced. Very long and weighty on the finish.
£24.00

Jean-Rene Germanier Amigne De Vétroz 2008, Valais White
Toffee notes on the nose, almost like botyrtis aromas. Tropical

peach and apricot flavours balanced with attractive citrus fruit. Very well-balanced with refreshing acidity and pleasing length.

Jean-Rene Germanier Cayas Syrah Du Valais 2007, Valais Red

Bright, violet, ripe berry fruit and spice. Well-balanced red fruit and chocolate. Pepper with a wild red fruit finish.

Jean-René Germanier Mitis Amigne De Vétroz 2007, Valais Botrytis

Spicy, with hard mineral palate. Sweet honey and ripe stone fruits, layered with warm spice. Delicious, unusual and intriguing.

TUNISIA

BRONZE

Les Vignerons De Carthage Magon Majus 2002, Morna Red

Good colour, lush palate. Ripe and juicy. Impeccably made.
£11.60 CDA, TOW

TURKEY

SILVER

Kavaklidere Ancyra Syrah 2009, Aegean Red

Smoky reduction. Bright, juicy fruit with a peppery edge. Fresh. Very good.
£5.17

Kavaklidere Prestige Bogazkere 2004, Eastern Anatolia Red

Red fruit on the nose. Opens with a vegetal note but evolves into cherries. Finishes long with pleasantly firm tannins.
£8.75

Kavaklidere Pendore Syrah 2008, Aegean Red

Wooded nose. Nicely lifted black fruit, smooth, elegant wine with long finish tinged with oak.

Ozkan Petrol Urunleri Likya Arykanda Cabernet Sauvignon 2008, Meditereanean Red

Purple with aromatic nose. Big tannins and slightly unbalanced. Simple finish.
£13.00

Kavaklidere Tatli Sert Beyaz 1999, Central Anatolia Fortified

Sweet, rich cut marmalade. Gingery, honied. Complex. Caramel, flan, nuts, cedar and spice box with a touch of amaretto on the nose and palate. A long lingering finish.

BRONZE

Kavaklidere Ancyra Narince 2009, Central Anatolia White

Clear and lightly aromatic orange zest nose with a soft attack; lively, juicy acidity with limes on the finish.
£5.17

Kavaklidere Prestige Narince 2007, Central Anatolia White

Honeyed, stone fruit nose and honeyed herbal palate showing green fruit and lingering finish. Fresh and lively.
£8.75

Kavaklidere Selection Narince-Emir 2006, Central Anatolia White

Fresh, fruity and elegant. Minerally and nicely balanced.
£5.52

Kavaklidere Ancyra Merlot 2009, Aegean Red

Solid, ripe, fleshy red. Generous

with soft acidity and ripe tannins.
Attractive and well-balanced.
£5.17

Kavaklidere Vin-art Carignan Alicante 2007, Aegean Red
Savoury, fleshy and ripe. The palate is layered with aniseed and liquorice. Ripe and savoury flavours on the finish.
£5.37

Kavaklidere Pendore Bogazkere 2008, Aegean Red
Floral, aromatic berry fruit. Simple, more primary palate. Lighter style, basic but pleasant.

Ozkan Petrol Urunleri Likya Kizilbel Cabernet Sauvignon Bogazkere 2007, Meditereanean Red
Slight reduction on the nose. Ripe blackberries and big tannins.

Complex wine with long finish.
£13.00

URUGUAY

BRONZE

Establecimiento Juanico Bodegones Del Sur Tannat Oak 2008, Canelones Red
Heavy, black fruit with a leafy-green aroma. Big and bold with a heavy mouthfeel. Drying tannins mingle with soft, black fruits and spice on the palate. Chewy tannins on the finish.
£12.00 WOU, WW

Filgueira Tannat 2008, Canelones Red
Deep coffee. Pretty floral and berry aromas. Intense dried fruit with a soft relaxed style.
£8.00 WOU

The International Wine Challenge

Presents

The Library Collection

The Library Collection

The **Octavian Vaults Library Collection**, in association with the International Wine Challenge, has established an international tasting to promote wines that have withstood the test of time through cellaring.

The purpose of this assessment of wines is to encourage the public to 'trade up', by investing money and time in wine for a greater return.

Focusing on 5 and 10 year old wines, the 2008 tasting reviewed the 1998 and 2003 vintages, while the 2009 tasting reviewed the 1999 and 2004 vintages.

Wines are judged blind by an international panel of experts on the 100-point scoring scheme. Tasting notes are provided and also information on how well the wine is expected to develop in future years.

The **Octavian Vaults Library Collection** encourages the knowledgable drinker to invest in current release wines for laying down. A score of 85 or more out of 100 is a significant endorsement of the quality of the wine tasted. Therefore, should the wine consumer be looking for a wine to lay down, such an endorsement helps to build trust in cellaring current vintages of the wine and assures quality for the future.

AUSTRALIA

Balgownie Balgownie Estate Cabernet 1999, Bendigo Red
Mature edges, fruit on nose, oak well in balance. On the palate the fruit is drying out. Drink now.
87

Balgownie Balgownie Estate Shiraz 1999, Bendigo Red
Good colour and fresh nose, sweet earthy, leathery fruit, well-balanced, good structure fading a little on the finish. Drink now to 2012.
92

D'Arenberg The Dead Arm Shiraz 1999, McLaren Vale Red
Mature colour, bright. Nose showing alcohol and drying a little. Fruit still firm on palate with ripe tannins but a little lacking in the mid-palate. Drink now.
87

Geoff Merrill Wines Henley 1999, South Australia Red
Fine mature brick red colour. Big firm fruit-driven aroma, but with some nice integrated oak. Similarly, the palate shows fruit with good ripe tannins, a nice easy structure and some bottle age. Drink now to 2012.
92

Moss Wood Cabernet Sauvignon 1999, Western Australia Red
Mid depth colour, nice intense bouquet with spice, soft attack, a rich palate. A lovely wine. Drink now to 2012.
86

Orlando Wyndham Group Jacob's Creek Centenary Hill 1999, South Australia Red
Good depth of colour. The palate shows good attack and lovely fruit which has developed well. The wine is ripe with soft easy generous tannins. Still bright and fresh. Drink from 2012 to 2015.
89

Orlando Wyndham Group Jacob's Creek St Hugo 1999, South Australia Red
Nose has classic, complex eucalyptus and mint nose. Sweet concentrated palate with elegance, flavour and vitality. Bright, alive on the finish, still evolving. Great food wine. Drink now to 2012.
91

Orlando Wyndham Group Jacob's Creek Steingarten 1999, South Australia White
Classic bruised apple aromas, also betraying some warmth. Very pure, expressive, off-dry, true to style, lovely balance, fresh and lively - still has time on its side. Drink now to 2020.
95

AUSTRIA

Erich Machherndl Jr Grüner Veltliner Smaragd Kollmitz 1999, Lower Austria White
Delicate pale strawberry colour. Fresh white flowers on nose. Palate starts rich and vibrant. Long resonating finish. Drink now to 2014.
90

Erich Machherndl Jr Weissburgunder Smaragd Hochrain 1999, Lower Austria White
Nice honey and white flower nose, melon, soft rich attack. Mineral palate, long aftertaste. Beautiful! Drink now to 2020.
95

CHILE

Viña Luis Felipe Edwards Doña Bernarda 1999, Colchagua Red
Youthful colour. Fresh, vibrant cherry

fruits, intense and pure. Cassis, mint and spice. Light elegant attack with pronounced acid and a drying finish. Drink now to 2013.
88

Viña Valdivieso Single Vineyard Cabernet Franc 1999, Central Red
Deep colour, young. Opulent aroma, spicy, earthy and well balanced wine with vibrant red fruit on medium palate. Lingering finish. Drink now to 2024.
91

J. Bouchon Assemblage 1999, Valle del Maule Red
Some evolution in terms of colour. Fresh acid, soft tannins, well balanced. Drink now to 2011.
91

FRANCE

Champagne G.H. Martel Victoire Fût de Chêne 1999 White
Rich complex ripe. Citrus/orange zest, super freshness on palate, wonderful weight and crisp finish. Clean, complex, elegant wine. Drink now to 2016.
93

Champagne Mailly Grand Cru Les Echansons 1999 White
Light, fresh, floral and red fruit nose. A little drying but holding up and still showing some youth. Drink now to 2014.
90

Champagnes P&C Heidsieck Charles Heidsieck Rosé 1999 Rosé
A well defined nose, rose petals, light strawberry. Well balanced palate, zesty entry. Great acidity, excellent. Drink now to 2011.
90

Champagnes P&C Heidsieck Piper-Heidsieck Rare 1999,

Champagne White
Superb nose. Intense, toasty, impressive. Palate less impressive but with a firm line of acid, lovely youth and lovely length. Superb! Drink from 2019.
95

Château Giscours 1999, Bordeaux Red
Deep garnet hue. Pencil box, cedar and some maturity on the nose. Good definition with dusty black fruit. Medium-bodied, blackberry and a touch of pepper. Lacks a little 'control' on the finish but nice austerity and weight. Drink now to 2012.
88

GERMANY

Weingut Balthasar Ress Hattenheimer Nussbrunnen Riesling Auslese 1999, Rheingau White
Bright gold, restrained aroma of honey and roasted almonds, with vibrant zippy citrus fruit on the palate. Elegant, with a long medium-sweet finish. Still very young, but a classic in the making. Drink now to 2029.
93

Weingut Schales Huxelrebe Trockenbeerenauslese 1999, Rheinhessen White
Deep golden colour. Honeyed, fat, marmaladey nose with spice. Palate: very sweet and concentrated with apricot and oily texture and citrus acidity. Intense, not subtle but characterful and balanced. Drink now to 2018.
92

ITALY

Fattoria le Sorgenti Scirus Rosso Toscana IGT 1999, Tuscany Red
Deep colour, earthy, lead pencil

aroma, animal notes, lively acidity. Drink now to 2014.
90

Fattoria Varramista SPA Varramista 1999, Tuscany Red

Savoury, nutty, earthy, plenty of personality. Palate well-balanced, tannins well-integrated. Plenty of complexity. Nice wine. Drink now to 2012.
87

I Balzini I Balzini White Label 1999, Tuscany Red

Mature, cedar. Fine sweetness and fruit on palate. Attractive savoury edge, good freshness, note of mint. Flavoursome. Drink now to 2014.
90

Poderi Colla Barolo Bussia 1999, Piemonte Red

Lovely complex wine. Earthy, spicy with cassis and pepper. Super attack and a lovely mid-palate. Tannins drying but super length and character. Drinking very well. Drink now.
92

San Felice Poggio Rosso Chianti Classico Reserva 1999, Tuscany Red

Expressive mix of chocolate, herbs and dried fruits. Good fruit cake flavours; good intensity of flavour. Balanced, with lovely lift on the finish. Drink now to 2016.
95

PORTUGAL

Adriano Ramos Pinto Vinhos SA Duas Quintas Reserva 1999, Douro Red

Fragant nose of wild strawberries and walnuts. Soft and velvety palate. Short and lacking substance. Drink now.
85

Adriano Ramos Pinto Vinhos SA Duas Quintas Reserva Especial 1999, Douro Red

Deep colour. Mature, tobacco, fruit cake and blackfruit. Concentrated palate with still-youthful blackberry fruit, fresh currant leaf and a lot of vanilla. Drink now to 2013.
86

Casa Agrícola Horácio Simões Moscatel de Setúbal 1999, Setúbal

Fine tawny colour, bright. Clean firm lovely toffee aroma. The palate shows fruit with a firmness of depth and weight. Rich, clean, good prominent but balanced acidity. Well made, lovely wine. Drink from 2020.
95

Casal de Valle Pradinhos Valle Pradinhos 1999, Trás-os-Montes Red

Dark, savoury aromas. Palate has firm but ripe tannins. Blackberry fruit with spicy, healthy length. Drink now.
92

Luís Pato Quinta do Ribeirinho Pé Franco 1999, Beiras Red

Spicy leathery nose. Liquoricey, but rather austere and tannic on the palate. Drink now to 2010.
88

SOUTH AFRICA

Jacobsdal Jacobsdal Pinotage 1999, Stellenbosch Red

Rather animally nose. Savoury fruit, mouldy orange. Sweet entry, meaty and savoury. Drink now to 2010.
90

Viña Concejo Reserva 1999, Rioja

Coconut, red fruits, some spice, liquorice combine with a nice texture in this well put together wine. Drink now to 2019.
93

2004

AUSTRALIA

Balgownie Balgownie Estate Cabernet 2004, Bendigo Red
Good deep colour. Quite a strong bouquet with a hint of mint. Strong flavour on the palate, juicy, although quite short on length. Drink from 2012.
88

Balgownie Balgownie Estate Shiraz 2004, Bendigo Red
Animal notes on the nose. Mineral, sulphides. Nice palate texture. Closed and needs air. Plenty of personality and not built on fruit. Tannins are soft. Nice Rhône style wine, still young. Drink from 2016.
90

D'Arenberg The Dead Arm Shiraz 2004, McLaren Vale Red
Serious wine. Bouquet fresh, vibrant, intense and very defined. Pepper, spice, ripe blue fruits. Tannins a little dry and alcohol a little hot. Nice wine. Drink now to 2016.
93

Ferngrove Vineyards Ltd The Stirlings 2004, Western Australia Red
Lovely ripe red fruits, wood spice. Liquorice. Impressive bouquet with elegance and complexity. Attack refined, palate weight balanced. Cool climate texture. Purity, complexity and length. Drink from 2011.
89

Geoff Merrill Wines Reserve Cabernet Sauvignon 2004, South Australia Red
Deep fresh black cherry colour, ripe blackcurrant and red pepper, hint of spice, good rich palate with long and still firm tannins. Very long and well balanced. Drink from 2015.
92

Geoff Merrill Wines Reserve Shiraz 2004, South Australia Red
Ripe jammy style. Plenty of oak. Lovely attack. Vibrant intense fat. Cedar, coconut notes still dominate. Needs time but this is a lovely well balanced, warm climate style. Drink from 2014.
91

McLaren Vale Associates Squid Ink Shiraz 2004, McLaren Vale
Good youthful cedar. Smooth and full with well-integrated oak and a good tannin balance. Long and peppery. Drink now to 2012.
90

Moss Wood Cabernet Sauvignon 2004, Western Australia Red
Good firm fruit aromas, a hint of oak and showing some depth. Nice structure. Ripe, generous tannins. Nicely made. Drink from 2012.
92

Orlando Wyndham Group Jacob's Creek Centenary Hill 2004, South Australia Red
Defined, fresh vibrant. Spice. Touch of greeness. Nice complexity. Balanced style for Barossa with supple tannins and freshness. Oak tends to dominate this nice wine. Drink from 2012.
87

Orlando Wyndham Group Jacob's Creek St Hugo 2004, South Australia Red
Cherry and brambly fruit on the nose. Palate dense and concentrated with great texture, depth and elegance. Drink from 2019 to 2024.
95

Punt Road Cabernet Sauvignon 2004, Yarra Valley Red
Harmonious medium ruby, nose sweet chocolate and cedarwood palate. Soft fruit with some racey acidity on the finish. Some length. Drink now to 2012.
88

AUSTRIA

Erich Machherndl Jr Pinot Blanc Hochrain 2004, Lower Austria White
Pale, bright. Aromatic, white peaches, sweet apples, flowers and herbs. Full-bodied, slightly oily textured with rich ripe citrus fruit. A hint of almond. Penetrating acidity. High alcohol. Drink now to 2013.
92

CHILE

Altaïr Vineyards & Winery Altaïr 2004, Cachapoal Valley Red
Rich, slightly smokey nose with red pepper aromas. Complex fruit, lovely tannins and good acidity. Alcoholic but with flavour and freshness to balance. Drink now to 2012.
91

Cono Sur Vineyards & Winery Cono Sur Ocio 2004, Casablanca Red
Lovely garnet. Cherries, spice and earthy notes with remains of dense ripe vibrant fruit. Palate sweet and dense, great elegance and texture Drink from 2010.
87

Emiliana Coyam 2004, Rapel Red
Dense purply red. Ripe, sweet, coffee and fruitcake nose. Soy sauce, coffee, chocolate and herbal notes. Carmenere makes its presence felt. Still very primary. Drink from 2012 to 2020.
90

Santa Rita Casa Real Cabernet Sauvignon 2004, Maipo Red
Deep purple colour. Attractive leafy nose, liquorice/black plum. Slightly bitter entry. Lacking a little backbone. Mushroomy, dry fruit. Drink now to 2011.
90

Viña Casa Silva SA Casa Silva Altura 2004, Colchagua Red
Deep green peppers and red fruits, touch gamey. Fresh, smells a bit like green tea. Sweet fruit, grainy tannins. Drink now to 2011.
92

Vina Concha y Toro SA Concha y Toro Don Melchor 2004, Maipo Red
Simple, wine-gum aromas, note of tobacco. Sweet, low acid. Drink now to 2012.
90

Viña Luis Felipe Edwards Doña Bernarda 2004, Colchagua Red
Nutty, roasted walnuts, creamy, vivid fruit, rich blackcurrant flavours. Balancing acidity. Drink now.
88

Viña Ninquen Ninquén Mountain Vineyard 2004, Colchagua Red
Rich notes of toasty oak. Richly flavoured, warming, impressive and harmonising well. Big and quite alcoholic. Drink now to 2011.
86

Viña Valdivieso Single Vineyard Cabernet Franc 2004, Central Red
Solid garnet. Nose: ripe spicy fruit with mint, eucalyptus and toasted coffee. Palate: baked, spicy fruit, chocolaty oak with fresh green herbal eucalyptus notes. Mouthfilling, slightly hot but fresh and savoury. Medium length. Drink now to 2016.
92

Viña Ventisquero Pangea 2004, Colchagua Valley Red
Deep colour. Nose: ripe cassis aromas. Palate: very ripe blackfruit. Big, full modern, mouthfilling with some freshness on the finish. Drink now to 2015.
88

FRANCE

Cave de Turckheim Grand Cru Brand Pinot Gris 2004, Alsace White
Deep gold, vinous barley sugar notes on the nose, ripe pineapple notes. Well-balanced, warm finish. Lingering tropical aftertaste. Drink now to 2014.
90

Champagne G.H. Martel Champagne Charles de Cazanove Vieille France 2004, Champagne White
Distinctive apple aroma. Attractive mousse but an austere high acid apple style. Drink now to 2011.
88

Champagne G.H. Martel Brut 2004, Champagne White
Limes, floral, autolytic character. Very pure, very focused. Lovely weight and balance and length. Very youthful, showing elegance and purity. Drink now to 2025.
94

Château Giscours 2004, Bordeaux Red
Deep garnet. Rich, ripe cedary smokey nose. On palate, good balance, complex. Medium length. Cedeary spice, delicate, minty finish Drink now to 2014.
87

Domaine Lafran Veyrolles Bandol Cuvée Spéciale 2004, Provence Red
Deep colour. Wild, herbal, exotic, slightly gamey nose. Concentrated with lots of peppery tannin. Not ready yet, but nicely textured and structured. Drink from 2012 to 2020.
89

La Cave de Die Jaillance Grande Réserve Jaillance 2004, Vallée du Rhône White
Lovely aromatic, fruit intense style. Floral elderflower, touch of chalky minerality. Fresh, with lovely attack and texture, well balanced with crisp acidity and well integrated. Perhaps a touch too much sugar but the finish is very clean. Drink now to 2012.
87

Maurice Velge Château Clauzet 2004, Bordeaux Red
Opaque, expressive aroma, cassis, liquorice, minty, curry notes. Lovely fruit and acidity on the palate. Austere finish. Drink now to 2019.
90

Ogier Clos de l'Oratoire des Papes 2004, Vallée du Rhône Red
Warm, ripe, stoney, sweet fruit nose. Full, ripe, mouthfilling palate with savoury, stoney notes and chocolaty, nutty, cheryish fruit. Developing well. Good solid Chateauneuf. Drink now to 2015.
86

Vivien de Nazelle L'Or de Cabidos 2004, South West White
Good full mature pineapple gold. Waxy ripe cherry tomatoes, quince and marrow jam. Perfect balance, a first time meeting of kindred spirits in unexpected harmony, mint and heather honey. Lovely lemon zest, a lovely bitter sweet kumquat marmelade. Drink now to 2024.
96

GERMANY

Weingut Balthasar Ress Hattenheimer Nussbrunnen Riesling Auslese 2004, Rheingau White

Straw, summer fields, apricot, fresh, pure. Great freshness, medium-sweet, still quite tight but good overall balance. A fine wine which needs time to develop. Drink from 2011 to 2020.
89

Weingut Schales Riesling Eiswein 2004, Rheinhessen White

Sweet, straightforward, pears and cream. Flavoursome, delicious and well balanced. Drink from 2011 to 2020.
95

Weingut Schales Spätburgunder Barrique Trocken 2004, Rheinhessen Red

Lovely fruit with still raw oak but lovely balance. Fruity nice rich palate, good length, very commercial wine with good life ahead. Drink from 2015.
90

ITALY

Agricola San Felice Poggio Rosso Chianti Classico Reserva 2004, Tuscany Red

Deep youthful ruby colour. Nose a little closed and oaky but showing some ripe black fruit. Dense, chewy palate, with ripe fruit, fine tannins and minty freshness. Compact. Long. Not ready yet, but this will be wonderful. Drink from 2011 to 2015.
95

Castiglion del Bosco Sarl Brunello di Montalcino 2004, Tuscany Red

Very evolved. Dried fruit and prune aromas. Tannins Are still firm but the fruit is drying. Savoury, firm, very traditional style and mature. Drink now to 2012.
89

Castiglion del Bosco Sarl Brunello di Montalcino 2004, Tuscany Red

Medium garnet red, sweet, cedary, mature but fresh nose. Touches of chesnut, medium bodied, dry, gently astringent with spicy fruit and dark chocolate. Fine tannins and a dry finish. Developed and ready now. Drink now to 2015.
88

Fattoria le Sorgenti Scirus Rosso Toscana IGT 2004, Tuscany Red

Deep damson. Good, red, sweet sour plum and touch of blackberry vinegar. Quite assertive tannin. Excellent version of sweet and sour richness. Drink from 2011 to 2019.
95

Fattoria Varramista SPA Varramista 2004, Tuscany Red

Nicely developed. Gamey, meaty nose. Palate: cedary sweet fruit, liquorice and black fruit with well integrated oak. Structured but not too powerful. Balanced, with medium length. Drink now to 2015.
92

Maci Angelo Brindisi Rosso Doc Riserva 2004, Puglia Red

Dark, opaque black purple. Intense baked cherry and prune nose with fresh plums and blueberries too. Big and alcoholic with plummy fruits and blueberries. Dark chocolate, fine-grainy tannins. Mouthfilling, long and fresh finish, slightly sweet. Drink now to 2017.
91

Negro Angelo e Figli Sudisfà Roero 2004, Piemonte Red

Lifted floral cherry and spice,

sweet fruit and good density on
the palate. Chunky but refined
tannins with bright acidity
on the finish. Drink from 5 to
15 years.
91

Poderi Colla Barolo Bussia 2004, Piemonte Red

Mid depth in colour, showing
some evolution. Lots of
spices and herbs on the nose.
Rich attack, full with lots of
concentration and well-balanced.
Drink from 2020.
95

Poderi Colla Barolo Bussia, Dardi le Rose 2004, Piedmonte Red

Lightish colour, lots of serious
toasted oak. Lovely attack, well
balanced, huge potential on the
palate, lots of tannins. Drink
from 2030.
92

Soc. Agr. Isole e Olena Srl Cepparello IGT Toscana 2004, Tuscany Red

A vibrant medium ruby garnet,
solid to the rim. Richness,
perfumed fruit and oak on the
nose. Sweet, quite concentrated,
red fruits on palate. Still
youthfull with acid and fine
tannins but texture already silky.
Good length and well-balanced.
Drink from 2010 to 2017.
89

NEW ZEALAND

Johanneshof Cellars Gewürztraminer 2004, Marlborough White

Excellent Gewürztraminer
aromatics - spice, roses, pure.
Sweet, juicy, ginger notes, really
flavoursome with great texture
and freshness. Hedonistic. Drink
now to 2014.
92

PORTUGAL

Adriano Ramos Pinto Vinhos SA Duas Quintas Reserva 2004, Douro Red

Opaque, elegant, crushed
strawberry, spicy aroma, firm
tannins, austere yet developing ripe
fruit on medium palate. Crisp fresh
finish. Drink from 2014 to 2019.
85

Adriano Ramos Pinto Vinhos SA Duas Quintas Reserva Especial 2004, Douro Red

Lively garnet colour. Complex
spicy nose. Rich, well balanced.
Drying finish. Drink now to 2019.
91

Adriano Ramos Pinto Vinhos SA Late Bottled Vintage 2004, Douro Red

Restrained, pencil-lead aromas.
Not too sweet, very classy, black
pepper. Sweet attack but not too
sweet on palate. Great freshness
and length. Very pure, thrilling,
needs plenty of time to evolve.
Drink from 2015 to 2040.
93

Adriano Ramos Pinto Vinhos SA Porto Vintage 2004, Douro Red

Dark intense colour, black cherry.
Very pleasant and balanced. Rich,
soft. Drink from 2015 to 2030.
93

Adriano Ramos Pinto Vinhos SA Vintage Ervamoira 2004, Douro Red

Intense, very chewy with preserved
fruit nose. Long, concentrated,
sweet liquorice palate. Well
executed and balanced. Lovely
wine! Drink from 2015 to 2040.
95

Casa Agrícola Horácio Simões Moscatel Roxo 2004, Setúbal

Nutty marmalade, mandarin

combined with an aroma of 'bitters'. Really compelling palate of honey, walnut, dried orange peel and fresh ginger. Great freshness and good weight. Very long, delicious and unusual. Drink now to 2039.

96

Hans Kristian Jorgensen Cortes de Cima Reserva 2004, Alentejo Red

Good youthful cedar with attractive spicy oak. Ripe fruit with a spicy dill finish. Drink now to 2011.

90

Herdade das Servas Tinta Reserva 2004, Alentejo

Ripe jammy, Christmas cake spice/cassis. Clean fresh vibrant. Chocolate, mint and tannins are a little dry but very nice. Drink from 2014.

90

Quinta de la Rosa Reserve 2004, Douro Red

Dull garnet colour. Oaky vanilla nose, good fruit but masked by too much oak. Long complex finish, savoury. Drink now to 2024.

95

Samuel Magalhães e Silva, Herdeiros Quinta da Prelada 2004, Douro Red

Deep colour and a very powerful palate of black fruit, black cherry, black liquorice, very rich, full, intense and long. Absolutely delicious! Drink from 2015 to 2040.

96

Sogrape Vinhos SA Callabriga Reserva Alentejo 2004, Alentejo Red

Good deep colour. Tight on the nose. A lean, traditional rustic style. Slightly lacks generosity and balance. Drink now to 2011.

86

SOUTH AFRICA

Jacobsdal Cabernet Sauvignon 2004, Stellenbosch Red

Opaque, restrained aroma, cassis, liquorice notes, fine framed tannin. Well balanced and elegant wine. Drink now to 2019.

87

Stellenzicht Vineyards Golden Triangle Pinotage 2004, Stellenbosch Red

Intense, medicinal, herbal nose. Tarry palate with black pepper and black fruits. Quite a fine texture but dominated by green herbal notes. Drink now to 2013.

88

SPAIN

Bodegas Olarra SA Añares Reserva 2004, La Rioja Red

An attractive, modern Rioja wine. Blackberry, touch of cedar, bilberry. Upfront, bold. Quite sharp acidity. Harmonius. Drink now to 2014.

88

Bodegas Ondarre SA Ondarre Reserva 2004, La Rioja Red

Creamy, gentle chocolate notes. Savoury red core of flavour. Black fruits, balanced oak, grainy tannins. Still young and fresh, this wine needs time and should last well. Drink from 2011 to 2020.

95

URUGUAY

Establecimiento Juanicó SA Familia Deicas 1er Cru d'Exception 2004, Canelones Red

Dark chocolate and dried herbs on the nose. Bilberry on the palate, simple, rather tart on the finish. Short, tea-leaf on aftertaste. Drink now to 2012.

88

Stockists

A

A&A	A & A Wines	01483 274 666
AAW	Alliance Wine	01505 506 060
ABS	ABS Wine Agencies	01780 755 810
ABW	Abbey Wines	01896 823 224
ABY	Anthony Byrne Wine Agencies	01487 811 008
ACG	AC Gallie Ltd	01534 734 596
ADE	Adel (UK) Ltd	020 8994 3960
ADN	Adnams Wine Merchants	01502 727 222
ADW	Andrew Darwin	01544 230 534
AKE	Akebono Unlimited Ab	www.akebono.se
ALD	Aldi Stores Ltd	01827 710 871
ALE	Alexander Wines	01418 820 039
ALI	Alivini Company Limited	020 8880 2526
AMA	Amathus Wines Ltd	0208 808 4181
AMP	Amps Fine Wines	01832 273 502
ANA	Annessa Imports	020 8804 3900
ANN	Ann Et Vin	01636 700 900
APW	Appellation Wines	07711 299 282
ARL	Auriol Wines	01252 843 190
ART	Artisan & Vine	020 7228 4997
ASDA	Asda Stores Ltd	0113 243 5435
AST	Astley Vineyards	01299 822 907
ASW	Andrew Stewart Wines	01179 620 956
ATC	Atlantico UK Ltd	020 8649 7444
ATM	Astrum Wine Cellars	020 8870 5252
AVB	Averys Wine Merchants	01275 811 100
AWC	Australianwinecentre.co.uk	0800 756 1141
AWO	Australian Wines OnLine	01772 422 996
AWS	Albion Wine Shippers	020 7242 0873

B

B&B	Bottle & Basket	0208 341 7018
B&N	Bertrand And Nicholas	01628 525 202
BAB	Bablake Wines Ltd	024 7622 8272
BAP	Bottle Apostle	020 8985 1549
BBL	Bat & Bottle Wine Merchants	0845 1084 407
BB&R	Berry Bros & Rudd	01256 323 566
BBV	Breaky Bottom Vineyard	01273 476 427
BCO	Bretby Wine Company	01283 225 029

BCR	Bon Coeur Fine Wines	01765 688 200
BCW	Blue Cove Wines Ltd	01923 261 197
BDG	Las Bodegas	01435 874 772
BDL	Bedales Ltd	020 7403 8853
BEC	Beaconsfield Wine Cellars	01494 675 545
BEE	Www.domaineofthebee.com	020 8274 9177
BEN	Bennetts Fine Wines Ltd	01386 840 392
BES	Bestway Cash & Carry Ltd	020 8453 8321
BHL	Bacchanalia (Cambridge)	01223 576 292
BKT	Bucktrout	01481 724 444
bky	Brinkley's	020 7351 1683
BLS	Balls Brothers of London	020 7739 1642
BLU	Belluna	81 48 7782 903
BLV	Bacchus Fine Wines	01234 711 140
BNK	The Bottleneck (broadstairs)	01843 861 095
BOC	Ballantynes Wine Merchants	02920 222 202
BOD	Bodegas Direct	01243 773 474
BOF	Bowland Forest Vintners	01200 448 688
BOO	Booker Cash & Carry	01933 371 238
BOQ	Bouquet Wines	020 7221 6081
BOV	Bookers Vineyard Ltd	01444 881 575
BOW	Bowes Wine Ltd	01380 827 291
BRG	Burgundy Wines	01273 870 055
BRI	Bordeaux Index	020 7269 0700
BSE	Beer Seller (Folio Wines)	01305 751 300
BTH	Booths Supermarkets	01772 693 800
BTN	Barton Vintners	01489 878 673
BTS	Batleys PLC	0113 387 7000
BTW	Bristol Wine Co	0117 373 0288
BUDG	Budgens Stores Limited	020 8422 9511
BUT	Butler's Wine Cellar	01273 698 724
BWC	Berkmann Wine Cellars	020 7609 4711
BWE	Boutique Wine Estates	+61 425 273 656
BWJ	HBJ Wines & Spirits	01473 232 322
BWL	Bibendum Wine Ltd	020 7449 4021
BZI	Banzai Beverage Corporation	1 31 0373 8504

C

C&B Corney And Barrow
020 7265 2400

C&D C&D Wines Ltd 020 8778 1711

C&F Catchpole &
Frogitt (UK) Ltd 01375 489 770

C@C Champagnes@chateaux
020 7326 9655

CAB Cork & Bottle Ltd 020 7534 5161

CAL Casa Leal 07957 572 957

CAM Cambridge Wine Merchants
01223 568 991

CAR CA Rookes Wine Merchants
& Shippers 01789 297 777

CAS Castang Wine Shippers
01503 220 359

CAV Les Caves de Pyrene
01483 538 820

CBC City Beverage Co Ltd
020 7729 2111

CBG Carlsberg UK Ltd
01442 206 800

CBK Cranbrook Wines 020 8554 8050

CBW Cornelius Beer & Wine
01316 522 405

CDA Www.cotes-d-afrique.co.uk
01394 410 319

CDL Classic Drinks Ltd
01744 831 400

CD-RDL Richmond Hill Wines
+1 403 686 1980

CDW Chapel Down Wines
01580 763 033

CEB Croque-en-bouche 01531 670 809

CEE Cheesewine 01767 348206

CEL The Cellar Door 01256 770 397

CEW Clark Estate Wines 01923 283 811

CFN Carringtons Fine Wines
0161 446 2546

CFW Clark Foyster Wines Ltd
020 8567 3731

CHA Chace Agencies +61 8836 37881

CHH Hennings Wine Merchants
01798 872 485

CHI Chai & Bar 32 02 4216080

CHN Charles Hawkins &
Partners Ltd 01572 823 030

CHO 1st Choice +61 1300 308 833

CHW Cornhill Wines 01460 55434

CJR C J Reid Of Eton 01753-863 819

CKY Corks Wines & Beers
01482 631 953

CLA Claribès Ltd 020 3239 9463

CLH Cockburns of Leith
0131 661 8400

CLN Collection Of Wines
7 495 5409124

CMI Charles Mitchell Wines
0161 775 1626

CMO Chamloss +32 3 252.77.63

CMR Cheers Wine Merchants
01366 382 213

CNL Connolly's 0121 236 9269

COC Corks of Cotham 0117 973 1620

COE Coe of Ilford
(Coe Vintners) 020 8551 4966

COL Corks Out 01925 267 700

COOP The Co-operative Society
01706 891 628

CORD Conwy Fine Wines
01492 573 050

COW Colina Wines 07810 551 706

CPB Campbell Moore 01624 611 793

CPE Champagne Par Excellence
0845 838 2860

CPW Christopher Piper Wines Ltd
01404 814 139

CRE Cressis.com 0845 652 9019

CRF Carrefour www.carrefour.com

CSM Château Saint Martin
+1-425-462-1717

CSS Charles Steevenson Wines
01822 616 272

CTL Continental Wine
& Food Ltd 01484 538 333

CUM Cumulus Wines +61 2639 07900

CVS Caviste 01256 770 397

CVV Camel Valley Ltd 0120 877 959

CWA Cheviot Wines 0141 649 3735

CWH Champagne Warehouse Ltd
07747 841 804

CWS Co-Operative Group
(CWS Ltd) 0161 827 5492

CWW Wine in Cornwall 01326 379 426

CYT Concha Y Toro UK Ltd
01865 338 013

CZF Czerwiks Food & Wine
01484 720 912

D

D&D D&D Wines International Ltd
01565 650 952

D&F D & F - Fine Wines 020 8838 4399

D&M Doudet & Major 01730 821 744

D2H Drinks2home.co.uk 01744 815 425

DBS Denbies Wine Estate
01306 876 616

DBW Den Boer Wines 01367 241 169

DBY D Byrne Ltd Clitheroe,
Lancashire 01200 423 152

DDK www.drinksdirect.co.uk

DEF deFINE Food & Wine
01606 882 101

DFW Delibo Fine Wines 01993 886 644

DGB DGB UK 020 8877 4960

DHF Dennhofer Wines Ltd.
01661 844 622

DLW Daniel Lambert Wines Ltd
01656 661 010

DMR Duncan Murray Wines
01858 464 935

DNL Dunell's Ltd 01534 736 418

DUV www.duvino.co.uk 01332 603 251

DVY Davy & Co Ltd 020 7407 9670

DWI Edward Fishlock Direct
Wine Imports 01208 814 222

DWM D'Arcy Wine Merchants Ltd
0845 270 1247

DWS Direct Wine Shipments
02890 508 000

DWS Dorset Wine Company
01305 266 734

E

EAL Elite Artisan Limited
07802 270 609

EAR Earle Wines Ltd 01765 677 296

EDV Eaux De Vie Ltd 207 724 5009

EGW Eagle's Wines 020 7223 7209

EHB EH Booth
www.booths-supermarkets.co.uk

EHL Ehrmanns Group PLC
020 7418 1800

EKO Ekont 420 225 340 223

ELV El Vino Company Ltd
020 7353 5384

EMP Empson (canada) Inc
(403) 503-9995

ENO Enotria Winecellars Ltd
020 8961 4411

EOR Ellis of Richmond Holdings Ltd
020 8744 5576

EPW Edward Parker Wines Limited
01263 860 938

ESL Edward Sheldon Ltd
01608 661 409

ETV Eton Vintners 01753 790 188

EUW Eurowines Ltd 0870 162 1420

EVI Evington's Wine Merchants
0116 254 2702

EVW www.everywine.co.uk
01772 799 023

EWC English Wine Centre
01323 870 164

EWG EWGA 0845 450 8983

F

F&F Food & Fine Wine 0114 266 8747

F&M Fortnum & Mason 020 7734 8040

F&P Flourish And Prosper
01430 430 006

F&W Fresh & Wild 020 7434 3179

FAL Fiandaca Limited 020 8752 1222

FAR Farr Vintners 020 7821 2000

FAS Fasano 551130743952

FAW Whole Foods Market /
Fresh & Wild 020 7434 3179

FEN Fenwick Ltd 0191 232 5100

FFT Field + Fawcett
Winemerchants 01904 489 073

FFW Field & Fawcet, York
01904 489 073

FLA Flagship Wines
shop - 01727 865 309
(office - 01727 841 968)

FLY Flying Corkscrew 01442 412 311

FMC F & M Cressi Ltd 0845 652 9019

FMV Field, Morris & Verdin
020 7589 5753

FNC Francis Fine Wines 0116 286 3521

FNW The Fine Wine Company
0131 669 7716

FPW Fulham Palace Wines
020 8748 1617

FRD France Domaines Ltd
020 7935 1551

FR-MLL Millesima 0800 917 0352

FRW Free Run Wines 01672 541 006

FSE Four Seasons Fine Wines
+61 81300853544

FSW Frank Stainton Wines
01539 731 886

FTD Fortitude Wines Ltd 0190 388 960

FTH Forth Wines 01577 866 001

FUL Fuller Smith & Turner
020 8996 2000

FWC Four Walls Wine Company
01243 535 360

FWD F. Wilman

FWL Fine and Rare Wines Ltd
20 89 60 1995

G

G&B Green & Blue Wines
020 7498 9648

GBL Gulf Brands International
97317729014

GGR Great Grog Company Ltd
0131 662 4777

GGW Great Gaddesden Wines
01442 412 312

GHL George Hill Of Loughborough
01509 212 717

GMP Gordon & Macphail
01343 545 111

GNO Great Northen Wine, Ripon
01765 606 767

GNS Genesis Wines 020 7963 9060

GOE Goedhuis & Co. 020 7793 7900

GOY Goyt Wines 01663 734 214

GPS Grape Sense 01359 270 318

GRO Grossi Wines Ltd 01629 733 969

GRP Grapevine (Fetcham)

GRW The General Wine Company
01428 722 201

GSH The Grape Shop/dp Wines Ltd
020 7924 3638

GSL Gerrard Seel Ltd 01925 819 695

GWC Guildford Wine Co Ltd
01483 560 647

GWI General Wine & Liquor Co
01428 722 201

GWS The Good Wine Shop Ltd
020 8892 7756

GWW Great Western Wine
Company Ltd 01225 322 800

H

H&H H&H Bancroft 08704 441 700

H&W Woodhouse Wines
01258 452 141

H2F Hard To Find Wines
0845 293 2925

HAC Hailsham Cellars 01323 441 212

HAP Happyland 7 495 728 5970

HAR Harrods 020 7225 5700

HAR	Harrods Wine Shop 020 7225 5925	**INT**	Interpartner HWG Weinimport GmbH & Co +49 40 524 10 11
HAV	Harrison Vintners 020 8579 5001	**INX**	Inxs Kicked 0131 556 9239
HAW	Harper Wells 01603 411 466	**IR-SPQ**	Superquinn 00353 1 651 5149
HAX	Halifax Wine Company 01422 256 333	**IRV**	Irvine Robertson Wines Ltd 0131 553 3521
HAY	Hayward Bros (Wines) Ltd 020 7237 0576	**IVV**	Inverarity Vaults 01899 308 000

HBC HB Clarke & Co 01484 341 220

J

HDS Hedley Wright Wine Merchants 01279 465 818

J&B Justerini & Brooks 020 7484 6407

JAK Aitken Wines 01382 641 111

HDW Hanging Ditch Wine Merchants 0161 832 8222

JAL Jalux Inc www.jalux.com

HFB Handford Wines Old Brompton Road 0207 589 6113

JAS Jascots Wine Merchants Ltd 020 8965 2000

HFW Handford Wines Holland Park 020 7221 9614

JAW John Armit Wines 020 7908 0655

HGT Harrogate Fine Wine Company 01423 522 270

JBF Julian Baker Fine Wines Ltd 01206 262 358

HIC Hic Cup Wines 01244 381 111

JCC Cooden Cellars 01323 649 663

HIG Highbury Vintners 020 7226 1347

JCP Palmers Brewery 01308 422 396

HKN Hammonds of Knutsford 01565 878 872

JFF Jfc France Sarl 33 1 40 86 42 00

JFI JFC (UK) Ltd 020 8963 7600

HLD Hallgarten Druitt 01582 722 538

JGW Just Great Wine 0845 230 8070

HMA Hatch Mansfield 01344 871 800

JKN Jackson Nugent Vintners 020 8947 9722

HOF House of Fraser 020 7963 2000

HOH Hallgarten Wines Ltd 01582 406 421

JNW James Nicholson Wine Merchant 02844 830091

HOP Hop Pocket Wine Co. 01531 640 592

JOB Jeroboams 020 7288 8865

JPC Japan Centre Online 020 3405 1151

HOT House of Townend 01482 326 891

HOU Hoults Wine Merchants 01484 510 700

JP-HAS Hasegawa Saketen Uk Ltd -

JP-OKA Okanaga Co Ltd 03 3663 0330

HPW The Holland Park Wine Company Ltd 0207 589 6113

JPS Japan Prestige Sake International Inc

JWL J W Lees & Co 0161 345 4433

HRC Hercules Wines 01795 530 050

HRO Harro Foods Limited 020 8543 3343

K

HRW Hercules Wine Warehouse 01304 617 100

K&L K & L Wines and Spirits UK Ltd 07919 445 816

HRY Harvey & Son Ltd 01273 480 209

KHE Kellermeister Holdings +61 (0)8 8524 4303

HSL Hanslope Wines 01908 510 262

KIN Kingsgate Wines 01962 785 4670

HSW Henderson Wines 0131 447 8580

KON John Konig

HTG Hermitage Wine Cellars 01243 431 002

KSW Ken Sheather Wines 01242 231 231

HTW HT White 01323 720 161

L

HUN Huntsworth Wine Company Ltd 020 7229 1602

L&C Lewis & Cooper, Northallerton 01609 772 880

HVN Harvey Nichols 020 7201 8537

L&C Lewis and Cooper 01609 772 880

HWG Heritage Wine 01454 294 099

L&W Lay & Wheeler Ltd 01795 892 073

HWM Hennings Wine Merchants 01798 872 485

LAI Laithwaites Wine 01189 030 903

HWW Hawkshead Wines 01604 497 928

LAR L'Art Du Vin 0131 555 6009

I

LAS Langdon Shiverick Imports 001 216 861 6800

ICE Ince Wines 07791 768 286

LAT Www.latourdechollet.com +33 557413966

ICL Italian Continental Stores Ltd. 01628 770 110

LAY Laytons Wine Merchant Ltd 020 7288 8853

IDO Indigo Wine 020 7733 8391

IDT Independant Wines & Spirits 01481 234 440

LBS Luvians Bottle Shop 01334 654 820

IFR Fingal-Rock 01600 712372

LBS Luvians Bottle Shop 01334 654 820

IMB Imbibros 01483 861 164

LBV Le Bon Vin 0114 256 0090

LCB	London City Bond Ltd	01375 853 700
LCD	Cochonnet Wines	01326 340 332
LDC	Ludlow Food Centre Ltd	01584 856 893
LDL	Lidl UK	0870 444 1234
LEA	Lea & Sandeman	020 7244 0522
LEW	John Lewis	020 7828 1000
LFW	Loch Fyne Whiskies	01499 302 219
LFW	Longford Wines	020 8676 5608
LIB	Liberty Wines	020 7720 5350
LIQ	Liquid Pleasure	01580 712 826
LKB	Lockett Brothers	01620 890 799
LLA	Louis Latour Agencies	020 7409 7276
LNC	Lanchester Wine Cellars Ltd	01207 521 234
LOH	Bakers and Larners of Holt	01263 712 323
LON	Londis	020 8941 0344
LOQ	Liquid Treasure	01773 825 754
LOS	Los Pasos S.a.	+54 1145553936
LOW	Lords Wines	01606 831 313
LPW	Laurence Philippe Wines Ltd	01245 475 454
LSF	Saki Bar & Food Emporium	020 7489 7033
LWC	The Local Wine Company	0161 343 5880
LWS	London Wine Shippers	020 7622 3000

M&S	Marks & Spencer	020 8718 6865
MAB	Mitchells and Butlers plc	0121 498 5045
MAC	Makro	0844 445 7445
MAG	Magnum's Wine Shop	01793 642 569
MAI	Maidenhead Wine Company	01628 411 273
MAN	Manor Wines	01227 833 888
MAP	Madeira Patisserie	020 7820 0314
MBS	Mumbles Fine Wines	01792 367 663
MBW	Molly Browns Wine List	0845 604 0100
MCC	McCabes Wines	353 1 288 2037
MCT	Matthew Clark	01275 890 427
MDV	Maison Du Vin	01580 753 487
MFS	Martinez Fine Wine	01943 816 515
MFW	Mallard Fine Wines	01328 700 602
MGM	Magnum Fine Wines Plc	020 7629 5607
MHW	Mill Hill Wines	020 8959 6754
MJF	Michael Jobling Fine Wines	01913 784 554
MKV	McKinley Vintners	020 7928 7300

MMD	Maison Marques & Domaine Ltd	020 8332 2223
MML	Mason & Mason Wines Ltd	01243 535 364
MOE	Moet Hennessy Australia	+61 0283449900
MOM	Momentum Wines	01691 654499
MON	Mondial Wine Ltd	020 8335 3455
MOR	Moreno Wine Importers	020 8960 7161
MRN	Morrison Supermarkets	0845 611 5261
MSW	Moor St Wines	+61 438 335 000
MVC	Merchant Vintners Company Ltd	01482 329 443
MWC	Milford Wine Centre	01483 421455
MWD	Merry Widows	07956 224 316
MWO	Michael Woolley Ltd	01435 865 520
MWW	Majestic Wine Warehouses Ltd	01923 298 200
MYL	Myliko Wines	0161 736 9500
MZC	Mentzendorff & Co Ltd	020 7840 3600

N&P	Nickolls & Perks	01384 394518
NDJ	ND John Wine Merchants	01792 363 284
NFW	Nidderdale Fine Wines	01423 711 703
NGR	Noble Green Wines Ltd	020 8979 1113
NIC	Nicolas UK	020 8944 7514
NKD	Naked Grape	01962 732 002
NKW	Naked Wines	01603 281 800
NOS	Nonsolovino	01246 276 760
NOV	Novum Wines	020 7820 6720
NRW	Noble Rot Wine Warehouses Ltd	01527 575 606
NSA	Nisaways	
NSH	Nishikidori Market.com	
NTD	Nisa Todays	01724 282 028
NWD	Northwest Distribution & Storage Inc	1-800-364-5745
NYW	Noel Young Wines	01223 566 744
NZD	New Zealand Wine Direct	0870 762 0093
NZH	New Zealand House Of Wine	01428 707 766

OAT	Oatley Vineyard	01278 671 340
OCO	Ocado.com	www.ocado.com
ODD	Oddbins	020 8944 4400
ODF	Oddbins Fine Wine	020 8944 4400
OMB	Ombersley Wines	01905 620580
OST	Costco	81 44 2812600
OST	Costco Wholesale Ltd	01923 213 113

OWA Oakley Wine Agencies
01787 220 070
OWC Oxford Wine Company
01865 301 144
OWL O W Loeb & Co Ltd
020 7234 0385
OZW Oz Wines 0845 450 1261

P

P&R Peckham & Rye Ltd
0141 445 4555
P&R Peckham's 0141 445 4555
P&S Philglas & Swiggot 020 7924 4494
P&S Philglas & Swiggot
020 7402 0002
PAL Palateur Imports +1 267 972 6190
PAR Partridges 020 7730 7102
PAT Patriarche Wine Agencies
020 7381 4016
PBA Boutinot Ltd +44 0 161 908 1338
PCC Penistone Court Wine Cellars
01226 766 037
PEA Peake Wine Associates
020 7733 5657
PFC Percy Fox & Co 01279 756 200
PGW Peter Graham Wines
01603 625 657
PHA Philip Alexander Wines
07875 109 158
PHM Palmer & Harvey McLane
01273 222 256
PIL Pacific International Liquor Inc
323 582 6605
PIM Pimlico Dozen 020 7834 3647
PLA Playford Ros 01845 526 777
PLB PLB Wines 01342 318 282
POG Planet of the Grapes
020 7405 4912
PON Peter Osborne Fine Wines Ltd
01491 612 311
POR Portland Wine Company
(Manchester) 0161 928 0357
PUR Purley Wines 020 8645 6976
PUS Octopus 01475 568 918
PVC Private Cellar Ltd 01353 721 999
PWA Phoenix Wine Agencies
07946 768 8438
PWC Premium Wine Collections
01603 427 554
PWI Portland Wine Cellar
(Southport) 01704 534 299
PWS Prince Wine Store 61396863033

Q

QDT Quinta Dos Termos, Lda
+351275471070
QFW Quaff Fine Wine Merchant Ltd.
01273 820 320
QSS Quintessentially Wine Ltd
020 7758 3300
QTK Quantock Abbey Wine Cellars
01963 440 404

R

R&B Ryhthm & Booze 01226 215 195
RAE Raeburn Fine Wines
0131 343 1159
RAR R&R Wines 0161 762 0022
RBC Richard Banks & Co
01225 310 125
REG Regency Wines 01392 444 123
REV Revelstoke 020 8879 1810
REY Raymond Reynolds
01663 742 230
RFC The Really Fine Wine Company
020 8426 1610
RIC Richard Granger Ltd
0191 281 5000
RID Ridgeview Wine Estate Ltd
0845 345 7292
RIW Ri Wine 01344 627 411
ROD Rodney Densem Wines Ltd
01270 212 200
RSO Robertsons 01796 472 011
RSV Reserve Wines 01614 380 101
RSW RS Wines 0117 963 1780
RVL The Revelstoke Wine
Company ltd 020 8879 1810
RWA Richmond Wine Agencies
01892 668 552
RWD Richards Walford & Co Ltd
01780 460 451
RWM Roberson Wine Merchants
020 7371 2121
RWW Red & White Wines
01548 854 473

S

SAB St Austell Brewery 01726 74444
SAIN Sainsbury's Supermarkets
020 7695 6000
SAIO Sainsbury Online 020 7695 6000
SAM The Sampler 020 7226 9500
SAO Sa Wines On-line
0845 456 2365
SAO www.sawinesonline.co.uk
020 8417 0038
SBB Susman Best Beef Biltong Co Ltd
01273 516 165
SCA Scatchard's Wine Merchants
0151 922 7346
SCK Seckford Agencies Ltd
01206 231 188
SCL Sheridan Coopers Limited
07767 887 540
SDC South Downs Cellars
01273 833 830
SEL Selfridges Ltd 020 7318 3730
SFW Shaftesbury Fine Wines
01747 850 059
SFW Stokes Fine Wines 01256 897 640
SGL Stevens Garnier 01865 263 308
SGL Stevens Garnier Ltd
01865 263 300
SHJ SH Jones & Company
01295 25 1179
SHJ SH Jones, Banbury 01295 251 177

SHN	Shepherd Neame Ltd 01795 532 206
SHV	Sharpham Vineyard 01803 732 203
SKE	Sake Europe www.sake.nl
SL	Slurp.co.uk 08445 445464
SMF	Somerfield Stores Ltd 0044 117 935
SMO	Smokehouse Wines 01625 548 499
SMP	The Sampler 020 8226 3500
SMV	Saint Martin's Vintners 01273 777 744
SOH	Soho Wine Supply 020 7636 8490
SOM	Sommelier Wine Company 01481 721 677
SPR	Spar (UK) Ltd 020 8426 3710
SPV	Specialist Vineyards 020 8969 9896
SSU	Stone, Vine & Sun 01962 712 351
STA	Stainton Wines 01539 731 886
STC	Sunday Times Wine Club 0118 903 1024
STE	Santé Wine Imports 01749 679 431
STE	Ste Kioko 331 4261 3366
SVG	Savage Selection 01451 860 896
SWB	Satchells 01328 738 272
SWE	Stony Wine Emporium 01908 267 373
SWG	SWIG 08000 272 272
SWM	Searsons Wine Merchants 35312800405
SWS	Stratford's Wine Agencies 01628 810 606

T

TAN	Tanners Wine Merchants 01743 234 455
TAN	Tanners Wines Ltd 01743 234 500
TAU	Taurus Wines 01483 548 484
TAW	Tay Au Wines 84 4 8730022
TBO	The Bottle Shop 01925 865 201
TCH	Touchstone Wines 01785 813 753
TESC	Tesco Stores Ltd 01992 632 222
TFW	Taylor's Fine Wine 020 8549 2984
TGW	The Global Winery 44-1531-660310
THC	Haslemere Cellar 01428 645 081
THI	Thierrys Wine Services 01794 507 104
THP	Greene King 01580 200 304
TKF	Tkf Ulana 38 0652522763
TKW	Talking Wines 01666 575 232
TMV	The Mount Vineyard 01959 524 008
TOP	Top Selection Ltd 020 8265 4995
TOW	Theatre Of Wine 020 8858 6363
TPE	Terry Platt Wine Merchant 01492 874 099
TPF	Thomas Peatling Fine Wines 01284 714 285

TPM	Topsham Wines 01392 874 501
TPW	The Perfect Wine 01508 486 000
TRO	Trout Wines 01264 781 472
TSC	The Secret Cellar 01895 537 981
TSS	Tate-Smith 01653 693 196
TTC	Taliana Trading Company 020 8664 6455
TVK	The Vineking 01737 248 833
TVS	The Vine Shop, Ware 019 2048 5522
TVY	The Vineyard 01306 876 828
TWH	The Winehouse +61 (8) 8323 8199
TWI	T Wright 01204 697 805
TWK	The Wine Keller 01628 620 143
TWL	TryWines Limited 01635 529 136
TZK	Tazaki Foods Ltd 020-8344-3000

U

UFW	Unique Fine Wines 88622702 9888
ULT	Ultracomida 01970 630 686
UNC	Uncorked 020 7638 5998
UPT	Upton Wines 01684 592 668
UWI	United Wineries International 020 7429 3230

V

V&C	Valvona & Crolla 0131 556 6066
VCR	Vintage Cellars +61 1300 366 084
VDI	Vineyards Direct
VDR	Vinardus +34600581296
VDV	Vin Du Van Wine Merchants 01233 758 727
VER	Vinceremos 0113 244 0002
VGN	Virgin Wines 0870 164 9593
VHS	Vintage House 020 7437 2592
VHW	Victor Hugo Wines 01534 507 977
VIC	Vine Connections 4153328466
VIN	Vinum 020 8847 4699
VIV	Vivaldi 0141 554 1177
VIW	Vintage Wines 0115 947 6565
VKY	Vicki's of Chobham 01276 858 374
VLW	Villeneuve Wines 01721 722 500
VNO	Ueno Gourmet Gmbh +49 6173976852
VOA	Vinoteca 020 7253 8786
VOL	Vinology 01789 2645 86
VPW	Victory Point Wines +61 417 954 655
VRT	Vintage Roots Ltd 01189 761 999
VSO	Vinissimo Ltd 01959 563770
VTL	Vine Trail 01179 211 770
VTS	Vinites Uk 020 7924 4974
VTW	Vino Wholesale +1 504.952.2832
VWS	Venus Wine And Spirits Merchants Plc 020 8801 0011

W

WAD Wadworth & Co.
01380 723 361
WAI Wai Shing 852 2476 3540
WAIT Waitrose 01344 825 847
WAM Winarium 48 22 831 1206
WAR Winearray 01423 323 337
WAV Waverley Vinters
01315 281 125
WAW Waterloo Wine Co 020 7403 7967
WBW William Baber Wines Ltd
0125 463 392
WCR Wine Circle 01344 843 562
WDI Wine Direct International
01323 441 941
WDR Wine Direct 0845 603 3717
WEA Weavers of Nottingham Ltd
01159 580 922
WET Wine Etcetera 01730 813 300
WHB Worth Brothers 01543 262 051
WHD Wine Hound Ltd 020 8744 5583
WHF Wholefoods Market
020 7368 4500
WI-AV Widely Available
WIB Wimbledon Wine Cellars
(Chiswick) 020 8994 7989
WIE Wine Importers Of Edinburgh
01506 468 900
WIK Wickham Vineyard 01329 834 042
WIL Wilks & Co Wine Merchants Ltd
01376 325 541
WIL Willoughby's Wine Warehouse
0161 643 4289
WIM Wimbledon Wine Cellars
020 8540 9979
WLY The Wine Library 020 7481 0415
WMA Addison Wines 01952 686 500
WMN Wineman 01635 203 050
WNS Winos 0161 652 9396
WNW Woody Nook Wines (UK) Limited
01491 68 0775

WOC Waters of Coventry Ltd
01926 888 889
WOI Wines of Interest 01473 215752
WOU Wines Of Uruguay UK
01983 530 241
WOW Wines of the World
020 8947 7725
WSI World Sake Imports - Honolulu
808 733 3332
WSK Wine Share Ltd 01329 836 201
WSM The Winesmith 01780 783 102
WSO The Wine Society Ltd
01438 741 177
WSR Wineservice 01342 837 333
WTA Winetraders (UK) Ltd
01993 848 777
WUO Wine Studio Ltd 0845 085 8855
WVM White Vin Man 01580 712 826
WW www.winesofuruguay.co.uk
01983 528 454
WWA World Wine Agencies
07764 372 229
WWC The Welsh Wine Company Ltd
WWD Waitrosewinedirect 0800 188 881
WWN Wood Winters 01786 469 624
WWT Whitebridge Wines
01785 817 229
WWW www.waitrosewine.com
0800 188 881

Y

YAM Yamas Wines
01684 578 786
YAP Yapp Brothers 01747 860 423
YNE YN Emporium, London
020 7262 1888
YOB Cockburn & Campbell
020 8875 7007

OTHER STOCKISTS

3DW 3D Wines 01205 820 745